TENAFLY PUBLIC LIBRARY, NJ
3 9119 09062839 0

EYEWITNESS TRAVEL
THAILAND'S
D0878502

EYEWITNESS TRAVEL

THAILAND'S BEACHES AND ISLANDS

LONDON, NEW YORK,
MELBOURNE, MUNICH AND DELHI
www.dk.com

MANAGING EDITOR Aruna Ghose
SENIOR EDITORIAL MANAGER Savitha Kumar
SENIOR DESIGN MANAGER Priyanka Thakur
PROJECT DESIGNER Amisha Gupta
EDITORS Smita Khanna Bajaj, Diya Kohli
DESIGNER Shruti Bahl
SENIOR CARTOGRAPHER Suresh Kumar
CARTOGRAPHER Jasneet Arora
DTP DESIGNERS Azeem Siddique, Rakesh Pal
SENIOR PICTURE RESEARCH COORDINATOR Taiyaba Khatoon
PICTURE RESEARCHER Sumita Khatwani

CONTRIBUTORS Andrew Forbes, David Henley, Peter Holmshaw

PHOTOGRAPHER David Henley

ILLUSTRATORS Surat Kumar Mantoo, Arun Pottirayil

Printed and bound by L. Rex Printing Company Limited, China

First American Edition, 2010
12 13 14 15 10 9 8 7 6 5 4 3 2 1

Published in the United States by Dorling Kindersley Limited, 80 Strand, London, WC2R 0RL, UK

Reprinted with revisions 2012

A CATALOG RECORD FOR THIS BOOK IS AVAILABLE FROM THE LIBRARY OF CONGRESS.

ISSN 1542-1554
ISBN 978-0-7566-8573-7

Front cover main image: Traditional boats, Andaman Coast

The information in this DK Eyewitness Travel Guide is checked regularly.

Every effort has been made to ensure that this book is as up-to-date as possible at the time of going to press. Some details, however, such as telephone numbers, opening hours, prices, gallery hanging arrangements and travel information are liable to change. The publishers cannot accept responsibility for any consequences arising from the use of this book, nor for any material on third party websites, and cannot guarantee that any website address in this book will be a suitable source of travel information. We value the views and suggestions of our readers very highly. Please write to: Publisher, DK Eyewitness Travel Guides, Dorling Kindersley, 80 Strand, London, WC2R 0RL, UK, or email: travelguides@dk.com.

Longtail tour boats at idyllic Hat Tham Phra Nang, Krabi

CONTENTS

An elephant sharing the road with cars in South Pattaya

◁ **View of islets rising from the calm lagoon surrounding Ao Maya, Ko Phi Phi Leh**

THAILAND'S BEACHES AND ISLANDS AREA BY AREA

Diver exploring coral reefs rich in marine life, Ko Chang

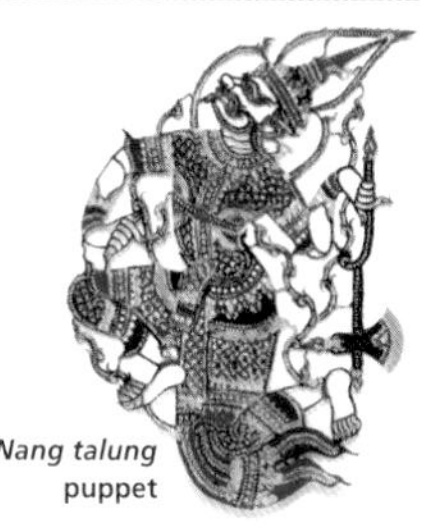

Nang talung puppet

TRAVELERS' NEEDS

Kayaking into limestone caves, Than Bok Koranee National Park

SURVIVAL GUIDE

Wat Phra Mahathat Woramahawihan, Nakhon Si Thammarat

HOW TO USE THIS GUIDE

This guide helps you get the most from your visit to Thailand's Beaches and Islands. It provides detailed practical information and expert recommendations. *Introducing Thailand's Beaches and Islands* maps the region and sets it in its historical and cultural context. The six regional chapters, plus *Bangkok*, describe important sights, using maps, pictures, and illustrations. Hotel and restaurant listings and information about watersports and other outdoor activities are found in *Travelers' Needs*. The *Survival Guide* has information on everything from transportation to personal safety.

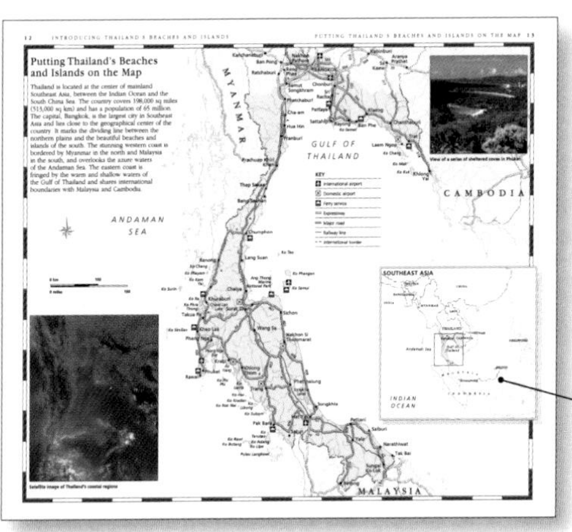

PUTTING THAILAND'S BEACHES AND ISLANDS ON THE MAP

The orientation map shows the location of coastal Thailand in relation to its neighboring countries. The guide specifically covers the beaches and islands of Thailand. These are divided into seven areas, including Bangkok which is covered as a separate section.

A locator map shows where you are in relation to other Southeast Asian countries.

THAILAND'S BEACHES AND ISLANDS AREA BY AREA

Each of the seven areas in the guide has its own chapter. The most interesting places to visit have been numbered on a *Regional Map*. The key to the map symbols is on the back flap.

A suggested route for a walk around the Street-by-Street area is shown in red.

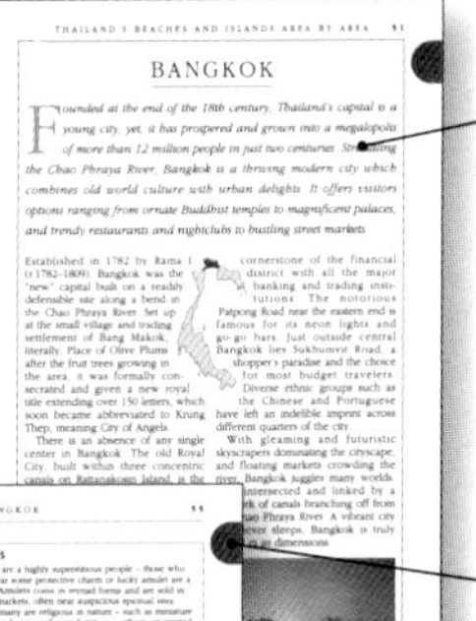

1 Introduction
The landscape and character of each area is outlined here, showing how the area has developed and what it has to offer the visitor today.

Each area of the book can be identified by its color coding, shown on the inside front cover.

Story boxes explore related topics.

Stars indicate the sights that no visitor should miss.

2 Street-by-Street Map
This gives a bird's-eye view of the key area in each chapter.

3 Regional Map

This shows the main road network and gives an illustrated overview of the whole region. All entries are numbered; there are also useful tips on getting around.

Sights at a Glance lists the chapter's sights by category: Towns, Cities, and Villages; National Parks and Historical Buildings; Beaches, Islands, and Bays.

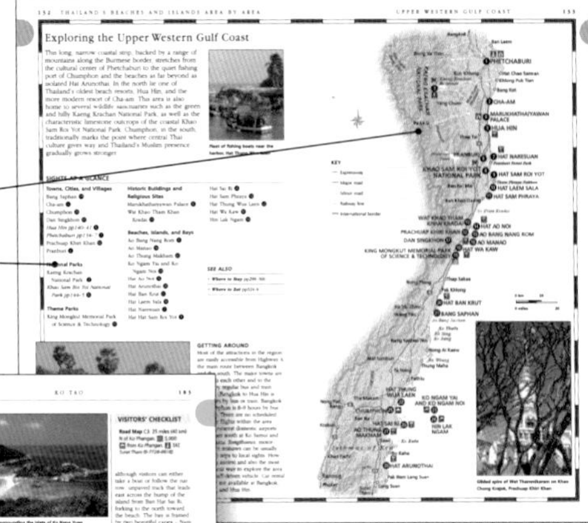

4 Information with Map

Some beaches and islands have illustrated maps with additional information. The map shows the main towns, beaches, and road networks.

5 Detailed Information

All important places are described individually. They follow the numbering on the Regional Map.

The information block provides details needed to visit each sight. Map references locate sights on the road map on the inside back cover.

A feature deals with a topic related to that region or place.

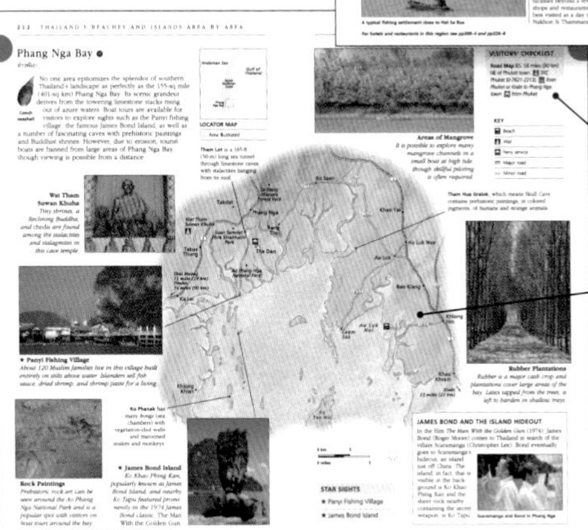

For all the top sights, a Visitors' Checklist provides the practical information needed to plan a visit.

6 Thailand's Beaches and Islands' Top Sights

These are given two or more full pages. An illustrated map shows the layout and landscape of the sight. Areas good for diving and watersports are marked along with other information.

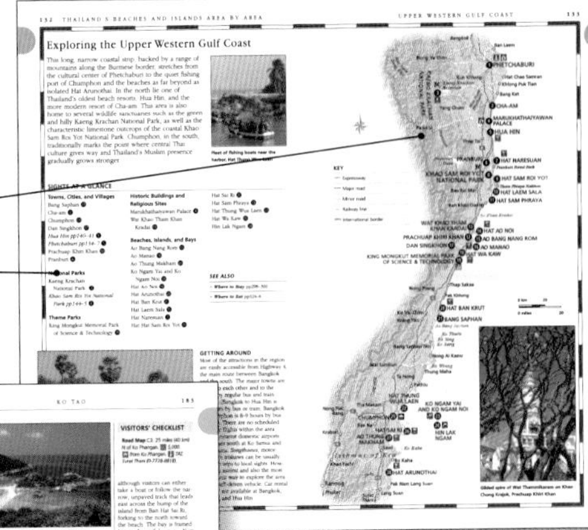

3 Regional Map
This shows the main road network and gives an illustrated overview of the whole region. All entries are numbered; there are also useful tips on getting around.

Sights at a Glance lists the chapter's sights by category: Towns, Cities, and Villages; National Parks and Historical Buildings; Beaches, Islands, and Bays.

4 Information with Map
Some beaches and islands have illustrated maps with additional information. The map shows the main towns, beaches, and road networks.

5 Detailed Information
All important places are described individually. They follow the numbering on the Regional Map.

The information block provides details needed to visit each sight. Map references locate sights on the road map on the inside back cover.

A feature deals with a topic related to that region or place.

For all the top sights, a Visitors' Checklist provides the practical information needed to plan a visit.

6 Thailand's Beaches and Islands' Top Sights
These are given two or more full pages. An illustrated map shows the layout and landscape of the sight. Areas good for diving and watersports are marked along with other information.

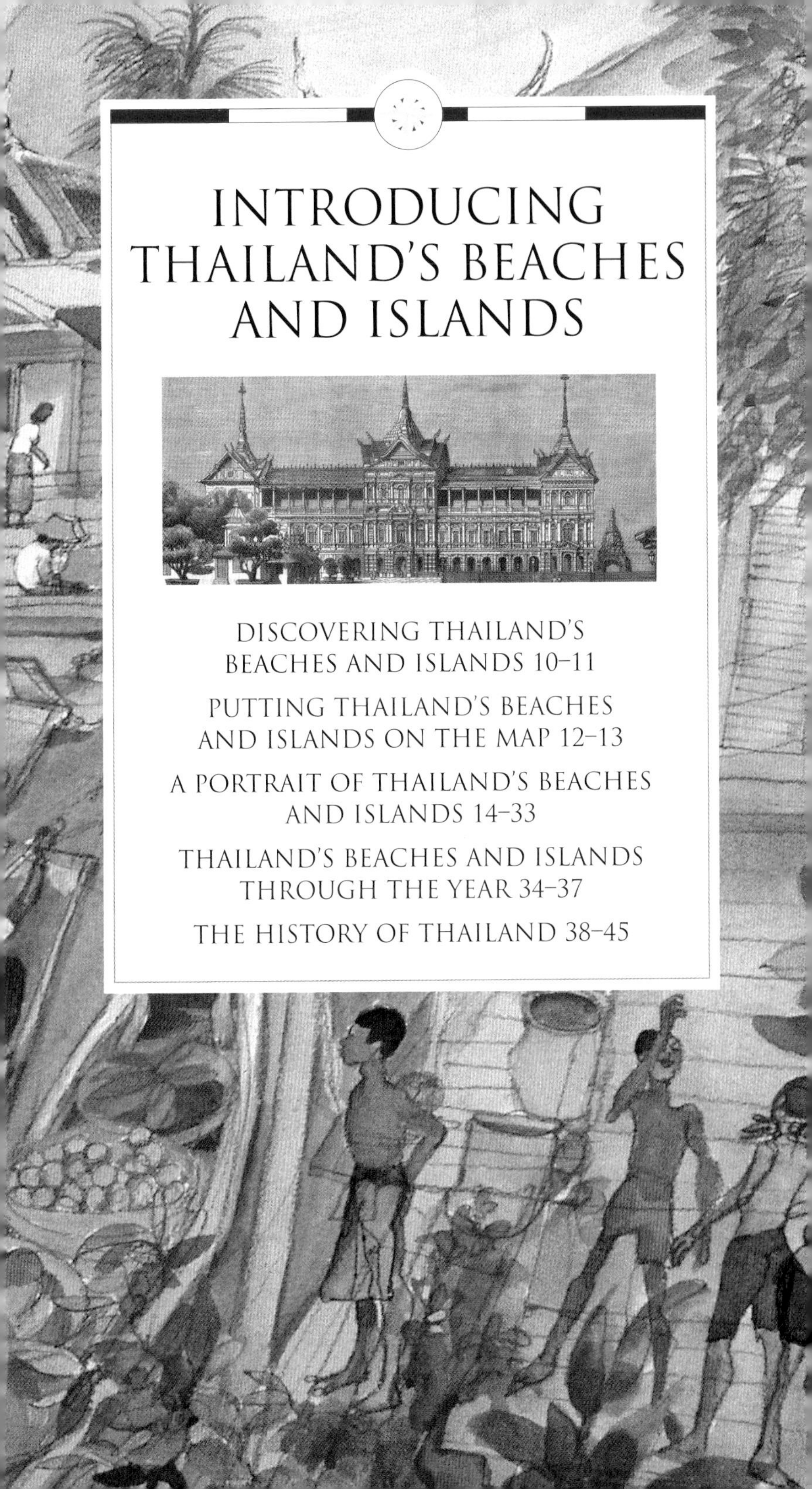

INTRODUCING THAILAND'S BEACHES AND ISLANDS

DISCOVERING THAILAND'S BEACHES AND ISLANDS

Thailand's long and diverse coastline has beautiful tropical islands ranging in size from Phuket, which is nearly as large as Singapore, to tiny palm-fringed outcrops. Even the most enthusiastic island hopper will be spoiled for choice. The coastline divides conveniently into six major regions – Eastern Seaboard, Upper Western Gulf Coast, Lower Western Gulf Coast, Lower Andaman Coast, Upper Andaman Coast, and the Deep South. The capital city of Bangkok is the gateway to the coast and Southeast Asia's largest and most vibrant city. Below is an overview of the highlights of the city and the sun-drenched beaches and islands.

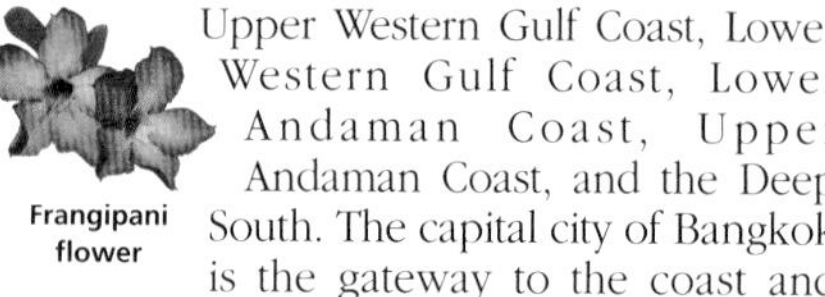

Frangipani flower

Majestic spires rising against the sky, Wat Phra Kaeo, Bangkok

BANGKOK

- **Glittering temples**
- **Canals and colorful floating markets**
- **Unparalleled shopping**
- **Sizzling nightlife**

Bangkok is truly a city of contrasts. Ultramodern glass-and-steel skyscrapers dominate the cityscape, towering over 19th-century Classical architecture. The ethnic diversity of **Chinatown** *(see p72)* is offset by the historic Rattanakosin Island, with its grand and traditional Thai architecture. This in turn opens up into the financial center at Silom Road, and the shopping malls and souvenir stalls of Phloen Chit and **Sukhumvit** *(see p78)* Roads. A truly memorable sight for visitors is the **Grand Palace** and **Wat Phra Kaeo** *(see pp56–61)*, housing a number of rare artifacts. A good way to get a feel of the city is to take a boat tour through its canals. From floating markets to trendy shopping malls, Bangkok is a shopper's haven. After dark, the city comes alive with entertainment options ranging from traditional theaters and chic nightclubs to gourmet restaurants.

EASTERN SEABOARD

- **Pattaya's dual identity**
- **Chanthaburi's gems**
- **Ko Samet's sandy beaches**
- **Diving off Ko Chang**

Pattaya *(see pp104–8)* is notorious for its buzzing and risqué nightlife, especially in the south. However, the north attracts a family crowd offering watersports, entertainment, and a fine selection of restaurants.

Chanthaburi *(see pp114–15)* is an old gem-mining town famous for its weekend gem markets. Within easy reach of the town are some less-visited reserves such as the **Khao Kitchakut National Park** *(see p116)* where visitors can enjoy the scenic beauty and wildlife along forest trails. The best-known islands in this region are **Ko Samet** *(see pp110–13)* and **Ko Chang** *(see pp118–26)*. The more developed Ko Samet, is a good weekend trip from Bangkok, while Ko Chang's serene beaches separate its hilly interior from some of the finest diving waters in the gulf.

UPPER WESTERN GULF COAST

- **Royal Phetchaburi**
- **Historic Hua Hin**
- **Cha-am's beaches**
- **Pristine national parks**

Ancient **Phetchaburi** *(see pp134–8)* has beautiful temples and boasts an ancient sweet-making tradition *(see p138)*. Further south lies the famous **Hua Hin** *(see pp140–41)*, the oldest beach resort and a favorite of the royal family. **Cha-am** *(see p139)*, just north of Hua Hin, is an ideal weekend getaway from

Lively street with neon signs in South Pattaya

Artist's impression of vendors hawking their wares at a colorful floating market in Bangkok

Bangkok. Also located in this region is the sprawling **Kaeng Krachan National Park** *(see p139)*, and the beautiful limestone studded **Khao Sam Roi Yot National Park** *(see pp144–5)*.

LOWER WESTERN GULF COAST

- **Beaches of Ko Samui and Ko Phangan**
- **Diving off Ko Tao**
- **Azure waters of Ang Thong Marine National Park**
- **Nakhon Si Thammarat's Wat Phra Mahathat**

The islands of **Ko Samui** *(see pp162–71)* and **Ko Phangan** *(see pp172–7)* are renowned for their palm-fringed beaches. The latter is also famous for its "full moon" parties. The neighboring island of **Ko Tao** *(see pp182–5)*, is very popular for its superb dive sites.

The beautiful **Ang Thong Marine National Park** *(see pp180–81)* is a verdant archipelago southwest of Ko Samui. Farther south lies the ancient cultural center of **Nakhon Si Thammarat** *(see pp192–5)*, home to the revered **Wat Phra Mahathat** *(see pp194–5)*.

UPPER ANDAMAN COAST

- **Phuket's luxurious resorts**
- **Diving among the corals off Surin and Similan Islands**
- **Trekking in national parks**
- **Exploring Phang Nga Bay**

The island of **Phuket** *(see pp220–39)* is a perfect holiday spot with its upscale resorts, gourmet restaurants, shopping malls, and fine white sand beaches. The nearby **Phang Nga Bay** *(see pp212–17)* is a stunning spot with imposing limestone stacks rising out of the sea.

Phuket is also a good base from which to visit the **Surin Islands Marine National Park** *(see pp204–5)* and **Similan Islands Marine National Park** *(see pp210–11)*, which have the country's best dive sites. Just a little inland lie the lush forests of **Khao Sok National Park** *(see pp206–7)* and the lesser known **Ao Phang Nga National Park** *(see p217)*.

Ko Khao Phing Kan or James Bond Island in Phang Nga Bay

LOWER ANDAMAN COAST

- **Sunbathing in Ko Phi Phi**
- **Rock climbing along the Krabi Coast**
- **Trang's offshore islands**
- **Ko Tarutao's idyllic and deserted beaches**

Ko Phi Phi *(see pp252–5)* is famous for its towering cliffs, horseshoe bays, and pristine beaches. The **Krabi Coast** *(see pp248–51)*, by contrast, is quiet and draws a young crowd who go rock climbing in the cliffs and caves around **Hat Rai Leh** *(see p248)*. The rapidly developing **Trang** *(see p264)* is a good base for exploring the offshore islands of **Ko Muk** and **Ko Kradan** *(see p266)*, where visitors can find secluded beaches. Farther offshore is the lovely **Ko Tarutao Marine National Park** *(see pp270–75)* which has some of the best diving sites in the world.

Sunbathers on the pristine beach at Ao Lo Dalam, Ko Phi Phi.

DEEP SOUTH

- **Quaint Songkhla**
- **Bird-watching at the Songkhla Lakes**
- **Languid Narathiwat**

The Deep South marks a transition between the Thai-Buddhist and Malay-Muslim worlds. The ancient fishing port of **Songkhla** *(see pp280–81)* retains its delightful period charm despite being transformed by oil wealth. Geographically, this region is dominated by the **Songkhla Lakes** *(see p282)* that is home to a spectacular variety of birds.

Islam dominates in the region south of Songkhla in the small fishing villages, casuarina-lined beaches, and main towns. **Pattani** *(see p284)*, is home to Malay-speaking Muslims, while **Narathiwat** *(see p285)* is characterized by ethnic diversity among its Muslims.

Putting Thailand's Beaches and Islands on the Map

Thailand is located at the center of mainland Southeast Asia, between the Indian Ocean and the South China Sea. The country covers 198,000 sq miles (513,000 sq km) and has a population of 65 million. The capital, Bangkok, is the largest city in Southeast Asia and lies close to the geographical center of the country. It marks the dividing line between the northern plains and the beautiful beaches and islands of the south. The stunning western coast is bordered by Myanmar in the north and Malaysia in the south, and overlooks the azure waters of the Andaman Sea. The eastern coast is fringed by the warm and shallow waters of the Gulf of Thailand and shares international boundaries with Malaysia and Cambodia.

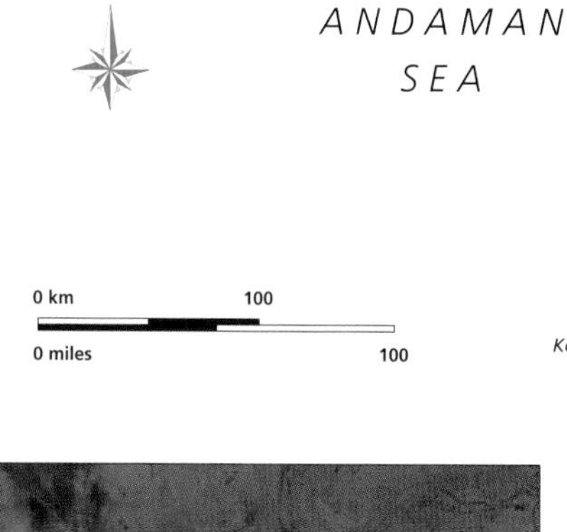

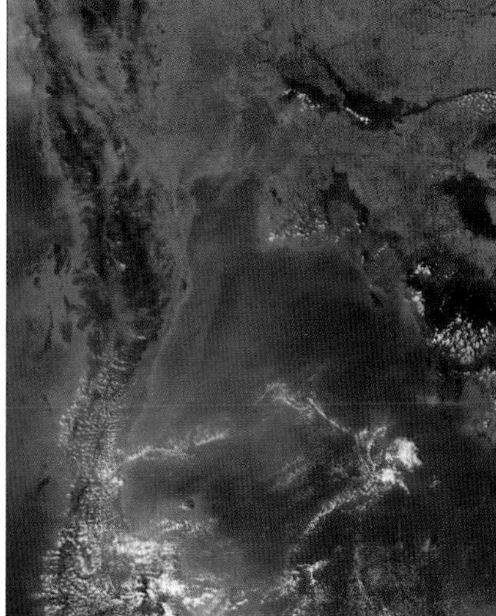

Satellite image of Thailand's coastal regions

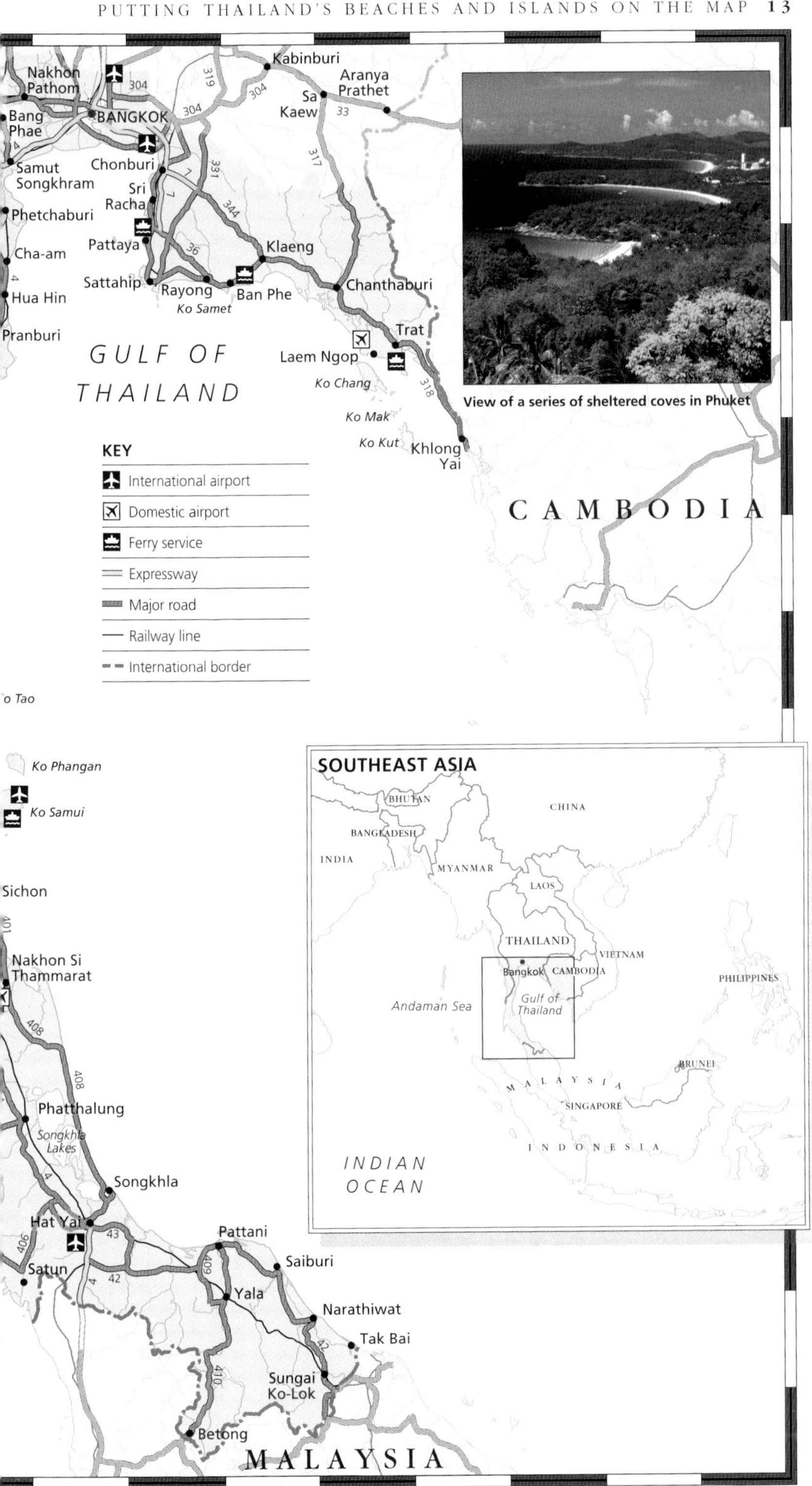

View of a series of sheltered coves in Phuket

A PORTRAIT OF THAILAND'S BEACHES AND ISLANDS

The outstanding natural beauty of Thailand's beaches and islands with miles of white sand lapped by azure waters, lush national parks, and teeming coral reefs, attract millions of visitors. The cultural heritage of the region reflected in the grand temples, palaces, and vibrant festivals further magnifies its appeal.

Thailand's coastline, located in a fertile monsoon zone, extends for more than 2,000 miles (3,200 km) and encompasses parts of the Indian and Pacific Oceans. It is set midway between India and China, the two great countries that have influenced Southeast Asia. Yet, this region has a distinct identity that derives from a number of factors. These include an uninterrupted history of independence while at some point all its neighbors were under Colonial rule, a rich Buddhist heritage, and a strong monarchical system. Coastal Thailand is politically linked to, but culturally distinct from the rest of the country. The population is a diverse ethnic mix, which although predominantly Thai, has a strong Chinese, Myanmar, Malay, Vietnamese, and Muslim influence. Bangkok, the nation's capital and gateway to the coast, is a pulsating megacity of more than 12 million people, celebrated for its palaces, temples, colorful street markets, glittering malls, and unrestrained nightlife. Tourism is the mainstay of the economy and Ko Samui, Phuket, as well as smaller islands such as the Surin archipelago are world-famous holiday retreats. Bangkok aside, there are no major cities along the coast and the region is overwhelmingly rural in aspect.

Guard at Wat Phra Kaeo

Bustling thoroughfare in the heart of colorful Pattaya

◁ Monks relaxing under a tree on a pristine beach, Surin Islands

Offices and shopping malls towering over the lake at Lumphini Park, Bangkok

ECONOMIC DEVELOPMENT

Rice, rubber, fishing, coconut farming, and tin mining have long been the mainstay of coastal Thailand's economy. Over the past 25 years, however, this traditional sector has been outstripped by light industrial and technologically advanced manufacturing, especially along the eastern coast. An offshore oil and natural gas industry is also being developed in the Gulf of Thailand. Regarded as one of Asia's "tiger" economies since the mid-1980s, it suffered greatly due to financial speculation in the late 1990s. The country has recovered since, and has weathered the 2008 global financial crisis quite well, suffering only a temporary slowdown. Tourism continues to be the region's largest foreign exchange earner, especially at internationally renowned beach resorts such as Phuket, Krabi, Ko Samui, Hua Hin, and Pattaya.

Rice-farming, a major occupation in the coastal region

The Indian Ocean tsunami of 2004 had a terrible but relatively brief impact on Thailand's Andaman Coast causing great loss of life and property and also severely hitting the tourism industry. However, Thailand was self-sufficient enough to rebuild and bounce back from this calamity. Today, with a tsunami warning system in place, the travel sector is well on its way to recovery.

ECOLOGY AND CONSERVATION

Unfortunately, the environment in this region has suffered from overdevelopment in the last 50 years and forest cover has been severely depleted. However, increasing awareness has led to the implementation of conservation measures by the government. Logging of forests is now illegal across Thailand, and emphasis is being placed on the preservation of rich and fragile ecosystems such as mangrove forests and coral reefs. Threatened marine animals such as turtles, dolphins, and dugongs are officially protected, as are endangered mammals such as tigers, gibbons, and tapirs.

SOCIETY AND POLITICS

In spite of the pressures of change, Thai society is quite cohesive. There is a growing and powerful middle class in Bangkok. Rural poverty is quite rare as the coastal regions, rich in natural resources, are among the most prosperous in the country, with a high standard of living. Thai women are estimated to control 62 percent of all small and medium businesses nationwide. The traditional family structures, however, have become increasingly fragmented owing to modernization and urbanization.

The Buddhist clergy and the King are the most venerated figures throughout the country. In contrast, politicians are less respected, and are in fact, criticized by the liberal Thai press. Prime Minister Thaksin Shinawatra was overthrown in a bloodless coup in 2006. A democratic coalition later took power, led by Abhisit Vejjajiva, although his leadership was plagued by protests and violence. After elections in 2011, Abhisit's party was unseated by a landslide victory for Thaksin's sister Yingluck Shinawatra's party.

Preparing for a bout at a Thai kickboxing match

CULTURE AND THE ARTS

Southern Thailand's traditional culture and arts are greatly influenced by Theravada Buddhism *(see pp24–5)*. The best showcase is the *wat* (temple), distinguished by sweeping, multitiered roofs, countless Buddha images, detailed murals, and varied architectural flourishes. The literary tradition is confined to the classics, the most important being the Ramakien *(see p59)*, an ancient moral epic. This tale provides the narrative content for many performing arts, including the stylized *khon* and *lakhon (see pp26–7)*. To this tradition, the south has added its own style of Islamic and Malay-influenced dance, music, and shadow puppetry *(see p191)*. Thailand's most notable literary figure, the 19th-century poet Sunthorn Phu, was inspired by the beauty of southern Thailand and based his poetry in this region. On the sports front, *muay thai* (Thai kickboxing) draws big crowds. Other traditional pastimes range from *takraw* (kick-volleyball) to kite flying. Many colorful festivals are also celebrated with fanfare. Whatever the activity, Thais believe that life should comprise *sanuk* (fun) and *sabai* (well-being) and visitors should embrace this spirit to get the most from their stay.

Ceremonial dragon steps leading to Big Buddha statue, Ko Samui

Landscape and Wildlife

Oriental White-eye

Thailand stretches from south of the Tropic of Cancer to 620 miles (1,000 km) north of the equator; its tropical climate is affected by two monsoons. Varied topography and a gentle climate have led to a rich diversity of flora and fauna. Limestone hills in the north are clad in dense tropical forest. Open forest is more usual in the northeast and central plains while the south and Gulf have superb coastlines and pockets of rain forest. Many habitats are threatened by industry and tourism; deforestation is rife, and some animal species face extinction. As a result, many national parks have been established. The largest among these is Kaeng Krachan National Park *(see p139)*.

Coconut palms on the island of Ko Samui in the Gulf of Thailand

MONTANE TROPICAL FOREST

This type of forest is made up mostly of broad-leaf evergreens and some deciduous trees such as laurel, oak, and chestnut. Mosses, ferns, and epiphytic orchids growing on other plants, are common.

Atlas moths *are the world's largest species. The female is larger than the male.*

Sun bear, *also known as honey bear or dog bear, is the smallest and most agile of all bear species.*

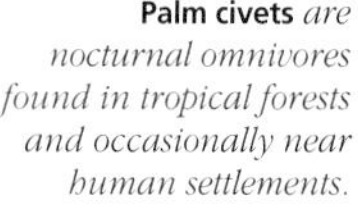

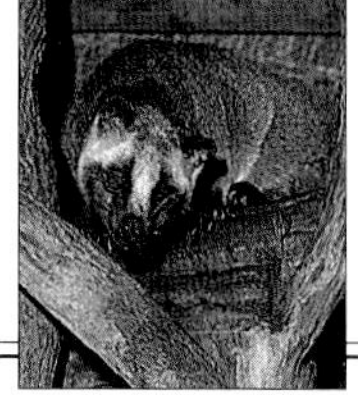

Palm civets *are nocturnal omnivores found in tropical forests and occasionally near human settlements.*

OPEN FOREST

The most common trees in the open forest, also called savanna forest, are dipterocarps, a family of trees native to Southeast Asia. The ground around them is often carpeted by coarse scrub.

Sambar, *Thailand's largest deer, can be seen in the central plains and in the northeast.*

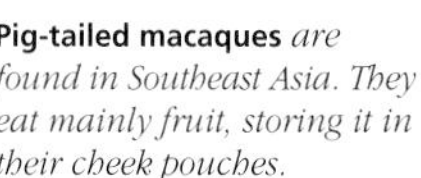

Pig-tailed macaques *are found in Southeast Asia. They eat mainly fruit, storing it in their cheek pouches.*

Wild boars *have been heavily hunted in the past. They feed mainly on grass.*

THAI FLOWERS

The diversity of Thailand's flowers reflects its range of natural habitats. Most famous are its orchids; there are some 1,300 different varieties. Unfortunately, illegal picking has made them rare in the wild. Other flowers are used as spices and for medicinal purposes.

The mallow flower, *a relative of the hibiscus, is common throughout Southeast Asia.*

Lotus lilies' *seed pods and stems are edible. Other lilies are grown for decoration.*

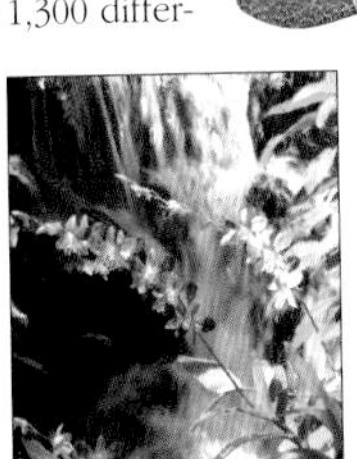

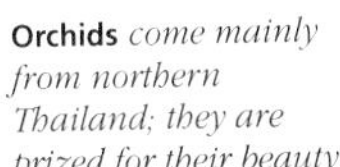

Mountain pitchers *are insectivorous plants. Their prey falls into the "pitcher" where the plant's juices slowly dissolve it.*

Orchids *come mainly from northern Thailand; they are prized for their beauty.*

WETLANDS

Freshwater swamp forests have been decimated by farming, although some survive in the south. River basins and man-made lakes and ponds can be found all over Thailand.

Dusky leaf monkeys *are found in the Thai-Malay peninsula. Three other species of leaf monkey also live in Thailand.*

Painted storks *migrate to Thailand's swamps to breed. During this time the pigment in their face turns pink.*

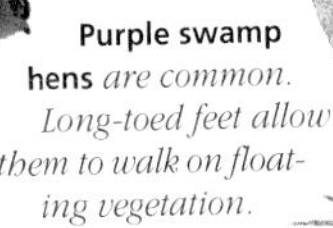

Purple swamp hens *are common. Long-toed feet allow them to walk on floating vegetation.*

COASTAL FOREST

The seeds of trees such as pines and Indian almond are transported by sea currents; thus ribbons of coastal forest are found all over Southeast Asia. Thailand's coastal forests are now threatened by farming and tourism.

Green turtles *are the only herbivorous sea turtles. They feed on sea grass and algae and are nocturnal.*

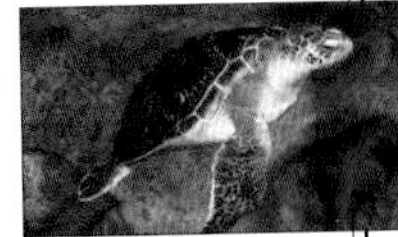

Lizards *are common in island forests. Most eat insects, although some species also eat mice and small birds.*

Crested wood partridges *are found in areas of coastal, lowland forest.*

Coral Reef Ecosystems

Thailand's many coral reefs support a complex biodiversity with more than 1,000 species of fish, 30 types of sea snake, crustaceans, invertebrates, millions of microscopic organisms, and birds. With enough warm water and sunlight, these flourishing and fragile ecosystems are made up of at least 300 different species of coral. Unfortunately, the reefs are under threat from industrial and human pollution, dynamite fishing, and irresponsible tourist activities. Several government and private initiatives are now attempting to protect and conserve this marine habitat.

Many types of sea birds *gather around coral reefs to feed on the abundant fish life. The great egret, a large wading bird, feeds by stabbing small fish with its razor-sharp bill.*

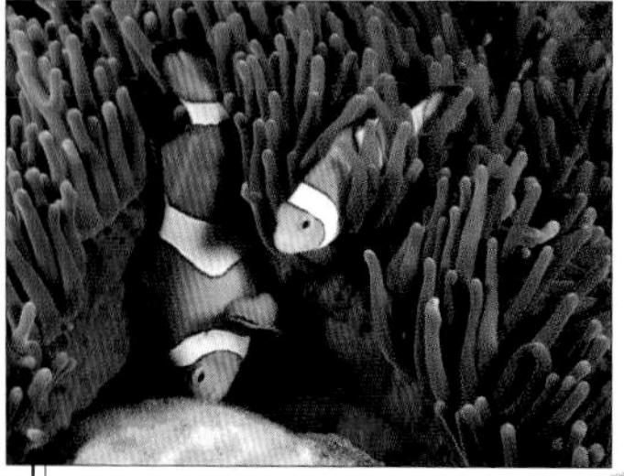

Colorful clown fish *come in over 20 varieties and live protected amid poisonous sea anemones. They stay in small groups and share a symbiotic relationship with their predatory host.*

A TYPICAL REEF

Thailand's coral reefs are found in a variety of formations. The fringing reef develops off the coastline and slopes into the sea. The reef flat curves away from the beach, rises to a crest, then drops to the seabed in a sharp incline or reef slope.

Shoals of colorful fish *swarm in and around the coral reefs. Smaller fish derive many benefits from this grouping, including some protection against predators and greater success in mating. Swimming in shoals also makes foraging more efficient.*

Leopard sharks, *also known as zebra sharks, are usually found around sandy bays. With cylindrical bodies and elongated tail fins, leopard sharks are fast swimmers who mostly stay at the bottom of the reef. These docile nocturnal creatures feed on mollusks and crustaceans.*

Five species of sea turtle *are found in Thai waters, including olive ridleys, green turtles, hawksbills, loggerheads, and leatherbacks. Unfortunately, all of these are listed as endangered species, and sightings even in the nesting season – between November and February – have become increasingly rare.*

Octopuses *are intelligent and skilled hunters who defend themselves against attack by hiding, changing their body color, and ejecting ink. They can also quickly squeeze into narrow gaps in the reef by means of their flexible structure, which lacks any skeleton.*

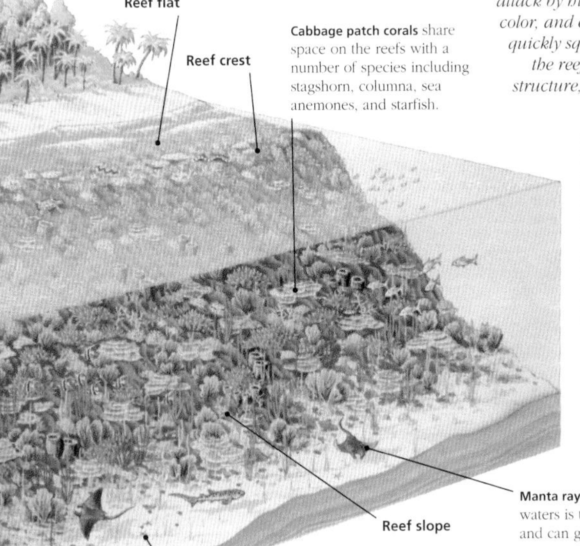

Cabbage patch corals share space on the reefs with a number of species including stagshorn, columna, sea anemones, and starfish.

Manta ray found in tropical waters is the largest of the rays and can grow up to 25 ft (8 m).

The squid *is an elusive decapod that hunts and hides in gaps within the coral. Like the octopus, it changes its color to blend with the surroundings.*

Giant hermit crabs *are soft-bodied crustaceans. They protect their bodies by living and moving around the seabed in the empty shells of mollusks such as whelks.*

CORAL: THE REEF'S BUILDING BLOCK

Coral is made of the skeletons of polyps, small animals related to sea anemones and jellyfish. Polyps are unusual in that they build their skeleton on the outside of their body. As they divide, the coral colony gradually builds up. There may be as many as 200 different species of coral in a reef, divided into hard corals such as brain coral, and colorful soft corals, which have no stony outer skeleton.

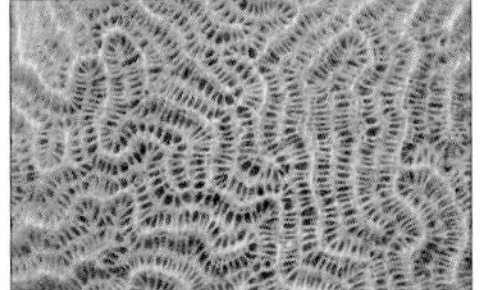

Hard, textured brain coral

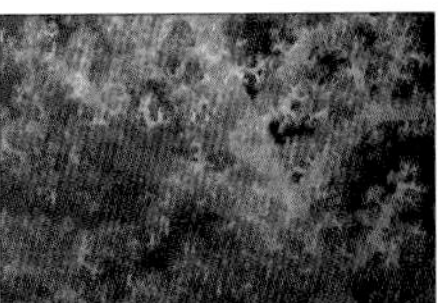

Soft coral

Diving and Snorkeling

Diving flippers

Thailand's clear waters and rich marine life draw diving enthusiasts from all over the world. All three of the country's major coastal regions – the Andaman Coast, the Western Gulf Coast, and the area around Ko Chang *(see pp118–26)* on the Eastern Seaboard – are popular diving and snorkeling destinations. The best and most advanced diving is available on the Andaman Coast, but this region is generally inaccessible during the southwest monsoon from June to September. Along the east coast, diving is a year-long activity. Over 50 dive schools operate around Thailand offering courses for all levels. Most offer PADI (Professional Association of Diving Instructors) certification to enrolled members.

Waterproof dive bags and other equipment on sale, Ko Chang

Boats *take divers back and forth from the jumping-off points or dive areas. It is possible to hire them locally at most dive-oriented beaches, but visitors must ensure that the operators are PADI licensed. These boats should be specially fitted for diving with enough space for diving gear.*

Wet suits are worn by divers to protect against the cold or other underwater hazards.

Coral reefs swarm with a wide variety of brightly colored tropical fish.

Scuba divers *must check the diving equipment carefully as any malfunction can be dangerous – even fatal. Divers should ensure that the oxygen tank is full and that the fins are in good condition. It is also useful to learn basic sign language to enable underwater communication.*

The dive instructor *is responsible for planning the dive and training groups according to the difficulty level. He usually explains the diving location, depth, currents, timing, and any hazards before setting off on the dive.*

The shallow waters *above coral reefs are generally clear and teeming with small fish and crustaceans. These stretches near the shore are great for snorkeling. Visitors uncomfortable with heavy equipment and deep dives can enjoy the underwater landscape with just a snorkeling mask.*

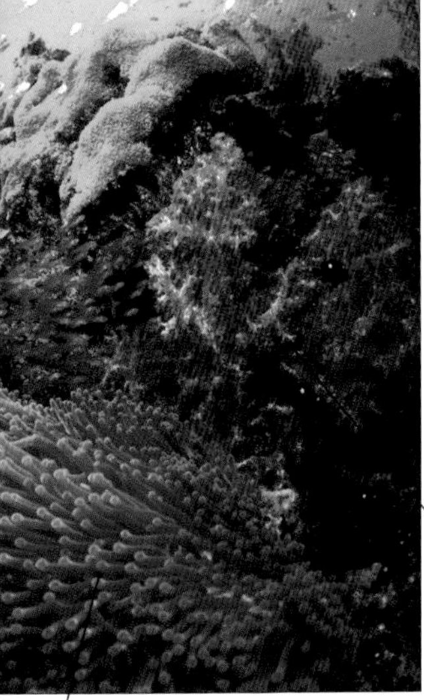

DIVING AT A CORAL REEF

Thailand's coral reefs offer unparalleled opportunities for snorkeling and scuba diving. It is essential to hire the best equipment available, as diving in the coral reefs can be hazardous for the unprepared. Divers should also be careful not to damage the corals in any way.

Coral heads shelter a host of tiny marine creatures that are important to the reef building process.

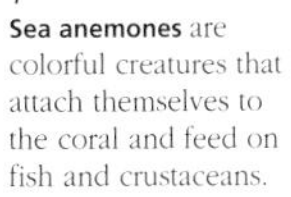

Sea anemones are colorful creatures that attach themselves to the coral and feed on fish and crustaceans.

Snorkeling for beginners *is safer and more enjoyable in groups where a guide can identify the marine life forms. It is also possible to undertake a PADI snorkeling course. First-timers should avoid going out alone unless accompanied by an experienced diver with proper qualifications and familiarity with the site.*

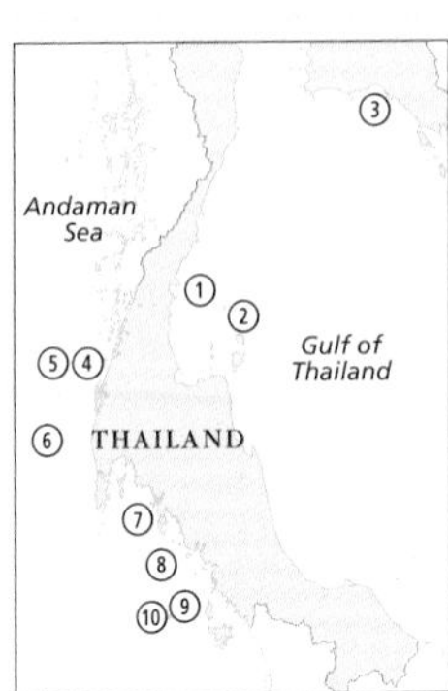

TOP TEN DIVE SITES

① Chumphon Pinnacle *(see p182)*
② Hin Bai *(see p174)*
③ Ko Chang *(see pp118–26)*
④ Richelieu Rock *(see p205)*
⑤ Surin Islands *(see pp204–5)*
⑥ Similan Islands *(see pp210–11)*
⑦ Ko Phi Phi *(see pp252–5)*
⑧ Ko Rok *(see p263)*
⑨ Hin Daeng *(see p263)*
⑩ Hin Muang *(see p263)*

DIVING TIPS

Never go diving if feeling sick or even a little under the weather.
Carry a safety balloon while ascending or diving in shallow waters. It is also a useful signaling device for divers in open waters.
Hire or buy equipment only from certified places.
Dive with a companion and also have back up and first aid on the boat at the surface.
Look for PADI-certified trainers and courses.
Beginners should head for the safer Gulf of Thailand, and leave the deeper Andaman Sea for experienced divers.

Instructor checking equipment prior to a dive, Ko Phi Phi

Thai Buddhism

Monk in deep meditation

At least 90 percent of Thais practice Theravada Buddhism. It was first brought to the region from India around the 3rd century BC and is based on the ancient Pali canon of Buddha's teachings, the Tripitaka. However, Thai practice incorporates many Hindu, Tantric, and Mahayana Buddhist influences. The worship of Buddha images, for example, is a Mahayana Buddhist practice. Thais are of the view that Buddhism is one of the three forces that gives their kingdom its strength; the other two being monarchy and nationhood. Religious rituals color daily life, especially in the form of merit-making, the performance of good deeds as mentioned in the Buddhist doctrine.

Rama IX (b.1927), *like other Thai rulers, spent time as a monk. For Thais, this act reinforces the notion that Buddhism and the monarchy are unified powers.*

Most Thai males *are ordained as monks in adolescence, a major rite of passage. They usually spend at least a few months as monks, earning merit for themselves and their families. Few Thai women become nuns.*

Siddhartha sets out to attain enlightenment.

STORY OF THE BUDDHA

The Buddha was born Prince Siddhartha Gautama in India in the 6th century BC. He gave up his riches to seek Enlightenment, and later taught the way to *nirvana* or perfect peace. Statues of the Buddha and murals depicting his previous lives, as told in the *jataka* stories, abound in Thailand.

Applying gold leaf *to Buddha images is a popular act of merit-making. Books of gold leaf can be readily purchased at temples, and the thin leaves are applied in profusion to Buddha statues,* wat *decoration, and murals.*

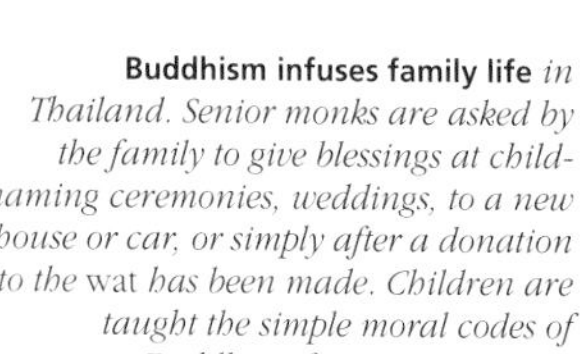

Buddhism infuses family life *in Thailand. Senior monks are asked by the family to give blessings at child-naming ceremonies, weddings, to a new house or car, or simply after a donation to the* wat *has been made. Children are taught the simple moral codes of Buddhism from an early age.*

Walking meditation *is practised by most monks. The most senior monk leads the line walking around the temple clockwise. Meditation on the nature of existence is a major way in which Buddhists progress toward enlightenment – Buddha literally means One who is Enlightened.*

Vishnu, with four arms, is part of the Hindu holy trinity.

Thai folding book painting, c.1900

A garland of jasmine *symbolizes the beauty of the Buddha's teachings and, as it perishes, the impermanence of all life. Vendors offer garlands of jasmine to be hung in cars and shrines.*

Devas (heavenly beings) bear Prince Siddhartha through air.

Ritualistic tattooing *is an ancient Hindu-Buddhist custom. Such tattoos are believed to act as powerful talismans against negative forces.*

Inscriptions in the ancient Pali script

Buddhist monks *collect alms from lay people every morning. Thais believe that this is a way to make merit and improve their* karma *(destiny) in this life as well as the next.*

ISLAM

Thailand's second religion is Islam. Thai-speaking Muslims are well integrated into Thai society, tracing their origins to a variety of ancestries – Arab, Persian, South Asian, and Chinese – all of whom are followers of the moderate Sunni Hanafi school. The only exception is in the far southern provinces of Satun *(see p268)*, Yala, Pattani *(see p284)*, and Narathiwat *(see p285)*, where most Muslims speak Malay and remain outside the mainstream. They are a rural people, generally working as farmers or by catching fish, studying their faith in *pondok* (religious schools), and traveling on *hajj* (pilgrimage) to Mecca. However, they are not overly rigorous or fundamentalist and although women cover their heads, they go unveiled.

Thai Muslim women covering their heads

Thai Theater and Music

The two principal forms of classical Thai drama are *khon* and *lakhon*. *Khon* was first performed in the royal court in the 15th century, with story lines taken from the Ramakien *(see p59)*. The more graceful *lakhon*, which also features elements from the *jataka* tales, is of two kinds – *lakhon nai* (inside *lakhon*) and *lakhon nok* (outside *lakhon*). *Khon* and *lakhon* involve slow, highly stylized, angular dance movements set to the music of a *piphat mon* ensemble.

Classical Thai dancer

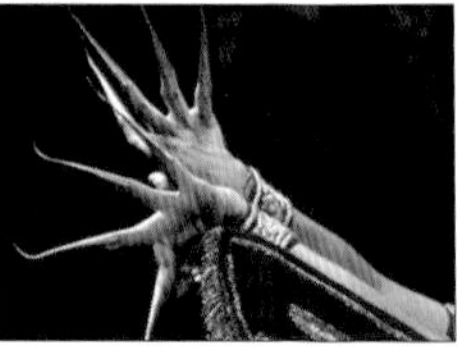

Finger extensions, *emphasizing the graceful curves of a dancer's hands, are seen in* lakhon *performances and "nail dances".*

Students learn *by imitating their teacher. Training begins at an early age (when limbs are still supple) and includes a sequence of moves known as* mae bot *(mastery of dancing).*

***Khon* and *lakhon* renditions** *are often staged at outdoor shrines. Dancers are hired to perform to the resident god by supplicants whose wishes have been granted.*

Natural-looking makeup enhances the features of characters who do not wear masks.

A *KHON* PERFORMANCE

In *khon* drama, demons and monkeys wear masks, while human heroes and celestial beings sport crowns. As the story is told mainly through gestures, *khon* can be enjoyed by non-Thais too. Visitors are most likely to see performances at restaurants catering to visitors.

INSTRUMENTS OF CLASSICAL THAI MUSIC

A *mahori* ensemble shown in a mural

Thailand's classical music originated in the Sukhothai era *(see p40)*. The basic melody is set by the composer, but, as no notation is used, each musician varies the tune and adopts the character of the instrument. A *piphat* (tuned percussion ensemble) accompanies theater performances and boxing matches *(see p283)*. A *mahori* ensemble includes stringed instruments.

***Ranat* (xylophone)**

The keys of a flat xylophone produce a different tone from those of a curved one.

***Likay**, by far the most popular type of dance-drama, is a satirical form of* khon *and* lakhon. *The actors wear gaudy costumes and the plot derives from ancient tales laced with improvized jokes and puns.*

***Khon* and *lakhon** troupes, employed by the royal palace until the early 20th century, are now based at the Fine Arts Department* (see p353).

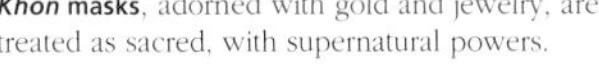

***Khon* masks**, adorned with gold and jewelry, are treated as sacred, with supernatural powers.

This mural *at Wat Benchamabophit* (see p68), *depicts a scene from a* khon *performance. In it, Erawan, the elephant mount of Indra, descends from heaven.*

Lavish costumes, made of heavy brocade and adorned with jewelry, are modeled on traditional court garments.

***Hun krabok**, are rodded marionettes, operated by hidden threads pulled from under the costumes.* Hun krabok *puppets are very rare today.*

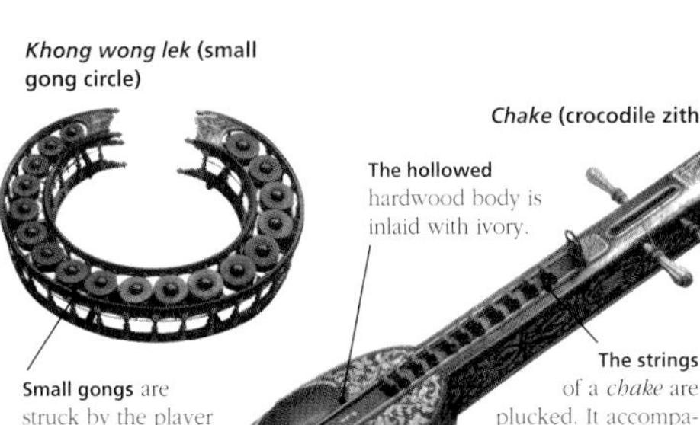

***Khong wong lek* (small gong circle)**

***Chake* (crocodile zither)**

The hollowed hardwood body is inlaid with ivory.

Small gongs are struck by the player to give the tune's basic melody.

The strings of a *chake* are plucked. It accompanies fiddles and flutes in a string ensemble.

A *piphat mon* ensemble, *including a vertical gong circle, is played at funerals because of its slow music.*

Vernacular Architecture

Coastal Thailand's architecture is very diverse. Traditionally, rural Thai, Cambodian, and Malay houses are built on stilts and their grandeur and size reflect the wealth and status of the occupying family. Thailand's location along important trade routes brought seafaring people such as Chinese and Portuguese merchants to this region. They built houses that differed from indigenous Thai and Malay styles and, over time, these evolved into Sino-Portuguese shophouses and mansions *(see pp226–7)*. The best examples of this type of architecture can be found in Phuket town.

Village on stilts, Chonburi province

TRADITIONAL THAI HOUSES

In the humid coastal regions, a large, centrally situated veranda, which also acts as an outdoor living area, is the dominant feature of many traditional houses. Some houses have covered verandas running alongside the main structure. In an extended family setup, a communal veranda will have several houses clustered around it. Traditionally, domestic animals were sheltered beneath the houses, and this practice still continues in some villages.

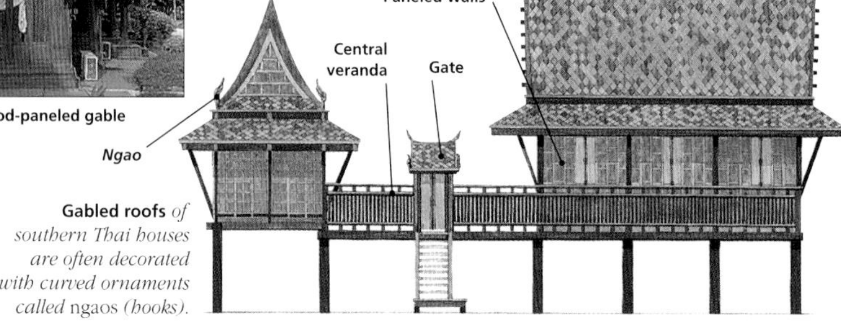

Wood-paneled gable

Gabled roofs *of southern Thai houses are often decorated with curved ornaments called* ngaos *(hooks).*

SINO-PORTUGUESE SHOPHOUSES

Known as *tiem chu* (row houses) in Cantonese, shophouses have a unique architectural style. The ground floor facing the street is a commercial space with living quarters and a courtyard further inside. A partially covered veranda or five-foot way connects the shophouses and protects pedestrians from the rain and sun.

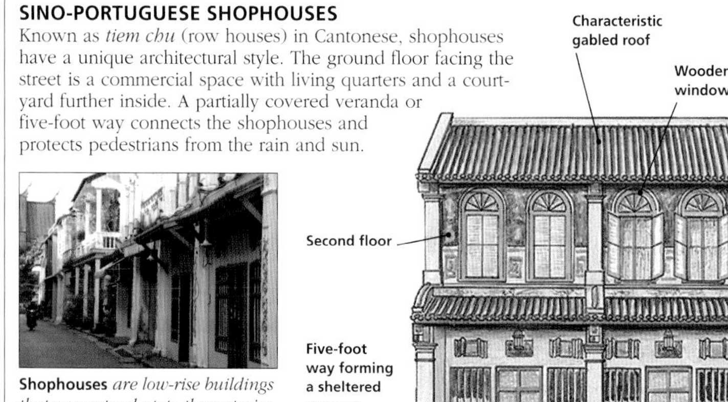

Shophouses *are low-rise buildings that can extend up to three stories in crowded areas. These quaint structures usually have tiled roofs and brightly colored façades.*

SINO-PORTUGUESE MANSIONS

These grand mansions, also known as *ang mor lau* (red hair buildings), were built in the early 20th century and were regarded as status symbols for nouveau riche merchants and traders. Greco-Roman pilasters and columns were added to embellish the existing structures. At the time these mansions must have seemed showy, but today, after restoration, they reflect a distinct old-world charm.

Grand exterior of a mansion

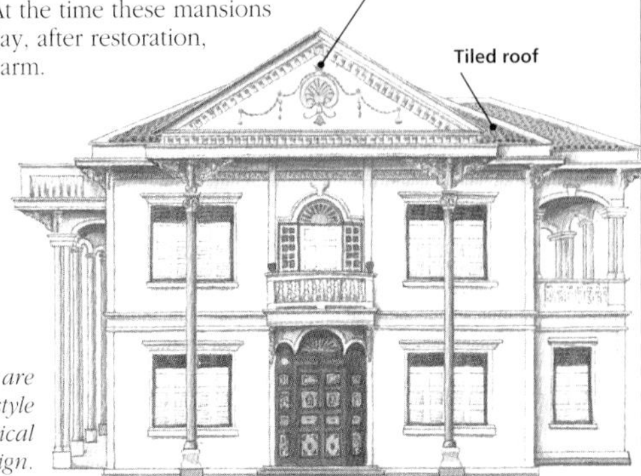

Elaborate pillars *and pediments are used to decorate Phuket's Western-style mansions blending aspects of Classical and Oriental architectural design.*

TRADITIONAL MALAY HOUSES

Found mainly in the Deep South, these houses are raised and centered around a main living room or covered by a pitched roof with gables to protect them from high winds. Shuttered windows, a suspended veranda in front, and an enclosed one at the back, enable ventilation and keep the house cool. The kitchen is usually built separately at the back of the house.

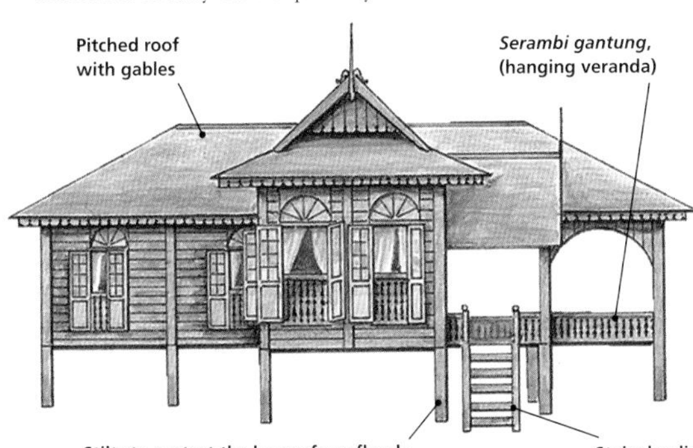

The interior *is carefully designed keeping the privacy of its inhabitants in mind, and there are many carved openings, slatted panels, and windows to keep it cool.*

Spirit house in the garden of Jim Thompson's House, Bangkok

SPIRIT HOUSES

Traditionally constructed within the grounds of many Thai homes, these houses shelter the guardian spirit of the property, and are usually elevated on a pole. Spirit houses come in a variety of styles that range from simple replicas of the homes to which they belong, to elaborate models of religious buildings. Erected to placate the spirits of the land, usually before the construction of the main building begins, they are worshiped daily with incense, flowers, and food. These miniature temples are placed in the grounds after consultation with a priest and the style depends upon the spirit that will inhabit it. Built out of wood or concrete, the spirit house can range in size from a small dollhouse to a big walk-in space.

Arts and Crafts

Wooden figurine

While the center of arts and handicrafts production in Thailand lies in and around Chiang Mai in the north, the coastal regions also have distinct art forms. Basket-making in Pattani, Benjarongware in Samut Songkhram, stoneware in Ang Sila, and woodcarving, are all part of the traditional arts and crafts of coastal Thailand. The gemstones of Chanthaburi *(see pp114–15)* and pewterware and cultured pearls of Phuket *(see p239)* are especially highly coveted. *Nang talung (see p191)* of Nakhon, among the most authentic of southern crafts, are a popular art form. The town is also the best producer of nielloware in the country.

Rattan vines being made into baskets and furniture

SHADOW PUPPETS

Among the most ancient art and theater forms in South Asia, shadow puppets date back to 400 BC, but are still very popular in the Nakhon province. Their most opulent version – *nang yai* – performed with the help of life-sized puppets, depicts stories from the Ramakien. These puppets are maneuvered by a puppet master, accompanied by a band of musicians.

***Nang talung* puppet**

***Nang talung* theater troupes** usually consist of five to 10 puppeteers and musicians.

Niello, *a black metallic alloy, is used as an inlay on engraved metal. Nielloware, which belongs to the Ayutthaya period* (see pp40–41), *usually features intricate patterns on items such as rings, bowls, knife handles, and trays.*

Benjarongware, *a five-colored ceramic ware, has long been popular at the royal court and celebrated throughout the kingdom. Although made in several southern localities, the best-known producer is Ban Benjarong (Benjarong Village) in Samut Songkhram province.*

Locally sourced granite *is used to make finely handcrafted kitchen tools such as pestles and mortars, as well as small figures of animals. The most renowned producer of stoneware is the fishing village of Ang Sila in Chonburi province.*

Batik *is a method of dyeing cloth in which portions are covered with wax and dipped in color to create patterns. Made into sarongs, tablecloths, mats, curtains, and picture frames, its patterns feature palms, fish, dolphins, and flowers. Batik sarongs are popular in the Deep South.*

Pearl culture *has emerged as a profitable business, making pearls an important export product. Fine, handmade silver and gold jewelry, featuring locally produced pearls, is sold in the many bazaars and malls of Phuket.*

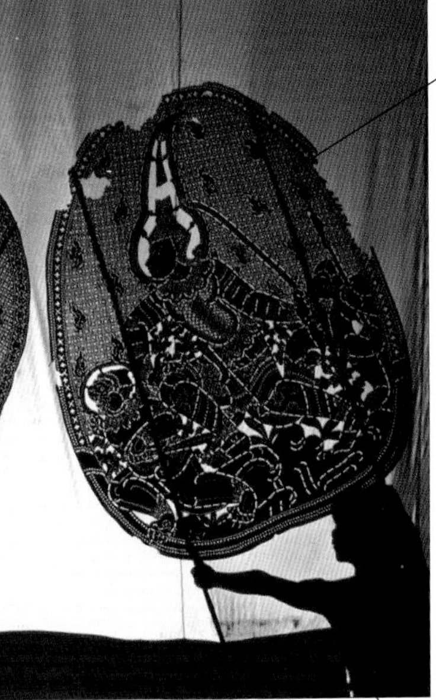

***Nang talung* puppets**, carved from buffalo skin.

***Nai nag* (puppet master)**

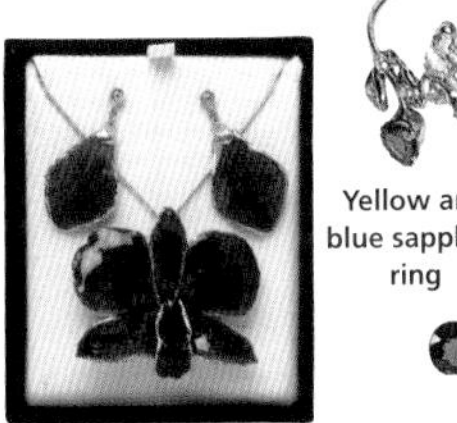

Orchid jewelry

Yellow and blue sapphire ring

A selection of sapphires

Gemstones *are usually bought and sold uncut and later fashioned into exquisite rings and pendants set in gold. Today, most gems come from across the Cambodian border in Pailin, but Si Chan Road in Chanthaburi remains the main gem market area in southern Thailand.*

Pewter *is an easily worked metal alloy of tin, with small quantities of copper and antimony that act as hardeners. Mostly manufactured in Phuket, it is used to make decorative objects such as statuettes and figurines, goblets, cups, plates, and pendants.*

Basketry and rattan work *products are mostly made in Pattani, which has a predominantly Malay-Muslim population. These materials are woven into geometric designs, typical of the non-representational art forms associated with Islam.*

Best Beaches

Blessed with clean, white sands and clear, blue waters, Thailand is home to some of the most stunning beaches in the world. These are also popular destinations for vacationers seeking active outdoor recreation and exciting watersports. Visitors expecting the luxuries of upscale resorts and spas will not be disappointed either. Thailand has holiday offers for every kind of traveler. Visitors can head to the secluded coves of Ko Phangan and Ko Chang, partake in the glittering nightlife at the lively, but crowded beaches of Phuket and Ko Samui, go diving and snorkeling in the waters surrounding Ko Tao, or spend some family time at the royals' favorite resort – Hat Hua Hin.

Sea surfing in Phuket

Visitors enjoying a game of volleyball on the beach at Ko Lipe

Ao Yai, or Big Bay *(see p200)*, Ko Chang, has a 2-mile (3-km) stretch of beach, with a selection of beach bungalows and restaurants.

Hat Kata Yai (see p228), *Phuket, may be quiet but it has the advantage of being close to Hat Patong, and its exciting nightlife. A great place for the young and adventurous, Hat Kata Yai is also excellent for windsurfing.*

Hat Tham Phra Nang (see p249), *Krabi, is perhaps the loveliest beach in Thailand with beautiful offshore coral reefs, coconut groves, and craggy limestone outcrops. Tham Phra Nang and Sa Phra Nang, popular sights located on the beach, are also worth a visit.*

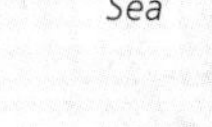

Ao Kantiang (see p262), *Ko Lanta, near the southwestern tip of the island, is backed by dense jungle-covered hills. Home to the exclusive Pimalai Resort and Spa* (see p309), *the beach here is also known for the beautiful coral reefs at its northern end. Ao Kantiang is a popular spot for snorkeling and swimming.*

Hat Khlong Phrao *(see p122),* Ko Chang, is isolated by the rocky cape of Laem Chaichet. There are some breathtaking views across the bay.

Hat Sai Kaew (see p112), *Ko Samet, also known as Diamond Beach, is among the busiest beaches on the island. A range of exciting watersports such as snorkeling and jet-skiing is on offer, along with a vibrant nightlife.*

Hat Hua Hin (see p140), *Hua Hin, was made popular by the Thai royal family in the early 20th century. The best stretch of beach is opposite the famous Sofitel Centara Grand Resort and Villas* (see p299). *Visitors can enjoy pony rides or a round of golf, as well as indulge in the usual watersports.*

Hat Sai Ri (see p182), *Ko Tao, is the longest stretch of beach on the island. This long curve of crisp, white sand is ideal for diving and snorkeling and popular throughout the year. There are some good restaurants as well as shops selling diving equipment lining the beach.*

Ao Thong Nai Pan (see p175), *Ko Phangan, is for those travelers who can brave the 8-mile (13-km) long dirt track to reach its beautiful beaches. Lack of facilities ensure the bay's continued isolation.*

THAILAND'S BEACHES AND ISLANDS THROUGH THE YEAR

The traditional Thai year revolves around the two monsoons – southwest and northeast – which dictate the year's farming activities and the religious calendar. Most festivals are Buddhist, and often observed on significant days of the lunar cycle, especially during full moon. Festivals may also mark a seasonal change, such as the end of the rains or a related agricultural event, such as the beginning of the rice-planting season. The three main seasons are rainy, cool, and hot. Farmers plant rice-seedlings at the start of the rainy season. The crop is dried during the cool, dry season and harvested before it gets too hot. During most weeks a festival is held somewhere in the country.

Harvesting the rice crop

HOT SEASON

High temperatures combined with high humidity make this an uncomfortable time inland, although cooling sea breezes help bring the temperature down nearer the shore. With fields fallow and rivers running low, the landscape appears dull. Considering the heat during this time, it is not surprising that Thailand's traditional New Year, Songkran, is celebrated with water.

MARCH

ASEAN Barred Ground Dove Fair *(1st week)*, Yala. Dove-singing contest that attracts bird lovers from as far away as Cambodia, Malaysia, Singapore, and Indonesia.
Thao Thep Kasatri and Thao Si Sunthorn Festival *(Mar 13)*, Phuket. This festival is held annually to commemorate the two courageous heroines of Phuket – Khun Chan and Khun Muk – who had rallied the people of the island to defeat the Burmese invaders in 1785 *(see p234)*.
Trang Food Festival *(Mar 30–Apr 3)*, Trang. Held at Somdet Phra Srinakharin Park to promote the local cuisine. A variety of delicious food, including southern Thai, Chinese, and seafood is available, along with local Trang specialities.

A religious procession during Songkran, the traditional Thai New Year

APRIL

Chakri Day *(Apr 6)*, Bangkok, nationwide. Commemorates founding of the ruling Chakri Dynasty by Rama I (r.1782–1809). The Royal Pantheon, at Wat Phra Kaeo, Bangkok, which displays statues of former kings, is open to the public on this day only.
Songkran *(Apr 13–15)*, nationwide. Traditional Thai New Year, celebrated with the pouring of fragrant water on revered Buddha images and a great deal of boisterous fun, which includes throwing water over all and sundry.
Wan Lai Festival *(mid-Apr)*, Pattaya. The Pattaya Wan Lai, or Water-Flowing Festival, is generally held a week after the Songkran celebrations. It features floral floats, colorful parades, and plenty of water-throwing.
Pak Lat Festival *(mid-Apr)*, Phra Pradaeng. The ethnic Mon people hold their New Year celebrations a week after Songkran. The emphasis is on entertainment, with a Miss Songkran procession, and traditional Mon games.

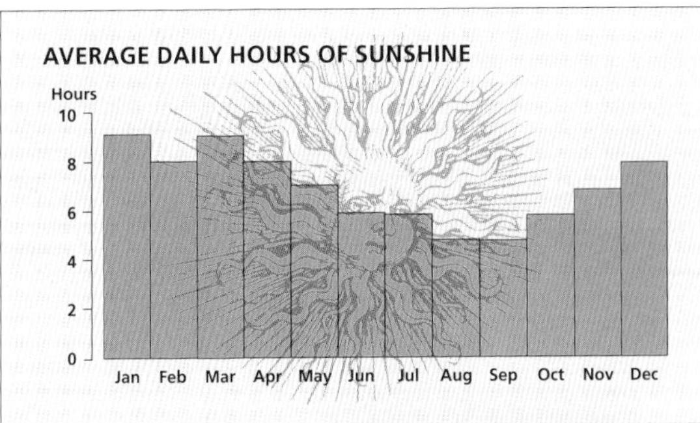

Sunshine Chart
Even during the rainy season, most days have some sunshine. The tropical sun can be very fierce, and adequate precautions against sunburn and sunstroke should be taken. Sunscreen, a sun hat, and sunglasses are highly recommended. Drinking plenty of water reduces the risk of dehydration.

MAY

Coronation Day *(May 5)*, Bangkok, nationwide. This ceremony marks the crowning of Rama IX (b.1927).
Visakha Bucha *(May full moon)*, nationwide. Most important date on the Buddhist calendar. Celebrates the birth, enlightenment, and passing of the Buddha. Sermons and candle-lit processions at temples.
World Durian Festival *(mid-May for 2 weeks)*, Chanthaburi. Highlights include fruit-decorated floats and beauty queens.

RAINY SEASON

The rural scene comes alive with the advent of the rains, which soften the soil, readying it for plowing. Once the rice has been planted, there is a lull in farming activity which coincides with the annual three-month Buddhist Rains Retreat (also referred to as Buddhist Lent). It is a period when young men traditionally enter monkhood for a brief period. It is a good time to observe the ordination ceremonies held throughout Thailand – a joyous blend of festivities accompanied by deep religious feelings.

JUNE

Hua Hin Jazz Festival *(variable)*, Hua Hin. Jazz festival featuring large numbers of Thai and international performers, generally held by the seaside at Hua Hin.

Monks chanting in front of golden Buddha on Asanha Bucha day

Sunthorn Phu Day *(Jun 26)*, Rayong. Festival in honor of Thailand's greatest poet, Sunthorn Phu *(see p111)*. Held at Sunthorn Phu Monument, Klaeng District.

JULY

Asanha Bucha *(Jul full moon)*, nationwide. Second of the year's three major Buddhist festivals. Commemorates the anniversary of the Buddha's first sermon.
Khao Pansa *(Jul full moon)*, nationwide. Marks the start of the Buddhist Rains Retreat. Monks remain in temples to devote themselves to study and meditation.

AUGUST

Rambutan and Thai Fruit Festival *(early Aug)*, Surat Thani. Annual rambutan fair held to celebrate the local fruit produce.
Her Majesty the Queen's Birthday *(Aug 12)*, nationwide. Buildings and streets are lavishly decorated in honor of Queen Sirikit's birthday. Bangkok is elaborately decorated, especially along Ratchadamnoen Avenue and the Grand Palace.
King's Cup and Princess' Cup Boat Races *(variable)*, Chumphon. Beautifully decorated boats from all over the south compete at Nong Yai, Tambon Na Cha-ang, and other places.

Lively performance by a jazz group during the Hua Hin Jazz Festival

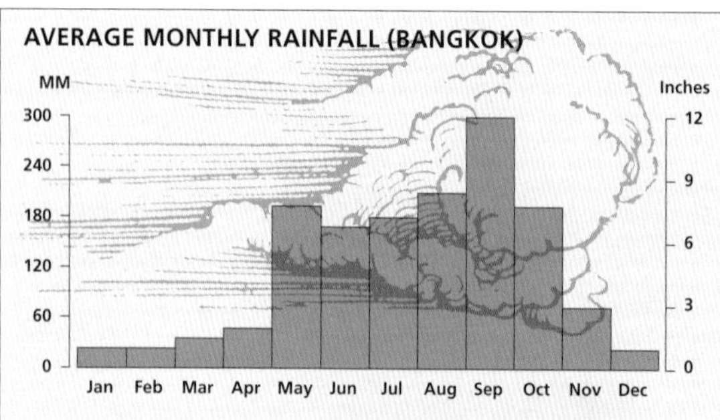

Rainfall Chart
Thailand's rainfall is not evenly distributed. The southern peninsula has the highest, some 95 inches (240 cm) annually; the north and central regions receive 51 inches (130 cm). In many places, torrential rain falls almost daily during the rainy season, from June to September.

SEPTEMBER

Festival of the 10th Lunar Month *(1st waning moon – 15th waning moon),* Nakhon Si Thammarat. Deceased sinners are permitted to rise and meet their relatives, but must return to the underworld before the 15th day. There is merrymaking at temples on the 15th day, accompanied by a magnificent procession along the central Ratchadamnoen Road.
Trang Pork Festival *(variable),* Trang. A celebration of Trang's special roast pork recipe featuring pork fermented with herbs and spit-roasted on a special grill.
Trang Moon Festival *(late Sep/early Oct full moon),* Trang. The ethnic Chinese of Thung Yao County, Palian District, commemorate the victory of the Chinese Ming Dynasty over the mighty Mongols in 1368.
Narathiwat Fair *(last week of Sep),* Narathiwat. A good opportunity to experience the mixed Thai-Malay culture of the Deep South.
Vegetarian Festival *(late Sep/ early Oct), (see p227)* Phuket, Trang. Self-mortification rituals accompanied by strict abstinence from meat. One of the most revered, spectacular, and unusual festivals in southern Thailand.

Dancers in Isaan dress perform during the festival of Ok Phansa

OCTOBER

Traditional Boat Procession and Races *(variable),* Chumphon. Elaborately decorated boats carrying Buddha images from local temples progress along the Lang Suan River in a local ceremony dating back to the reign of Rama III (r.1824–51).
Ok Phansa *(Oct full moon),* nationwide. Celebration of the Buddha's reappearance on earth after a season spent preaching in heaven. Marks the end of the Buddhist Rains Retreat.
Chak Phra Festival *(Oct full moon),* Surat Thani. Local southern festival celebrating the end of the Rains Retreat. Illuminated images of the Buddha are erected all over town, splendidly adorned floats are pulled by hand, and Buddha images are carried on a beautifully decorated barge across the river. Boat racing and traditional games.

COOL SEASON

After the rains, the skies are clear and the air cools to a comfortable warmth. The countryside looks its finest during this time – lush and green from the rains. It is the best time to visit Thailand, especially during the coolest months of December and January. Numerous festivals are held in December and January to celebrate the end of the rice harvest, which lasts from November to early December. This allows Thais a period of relaxation.

Spectacular street procession during the Vegetarian Festival, Phuket

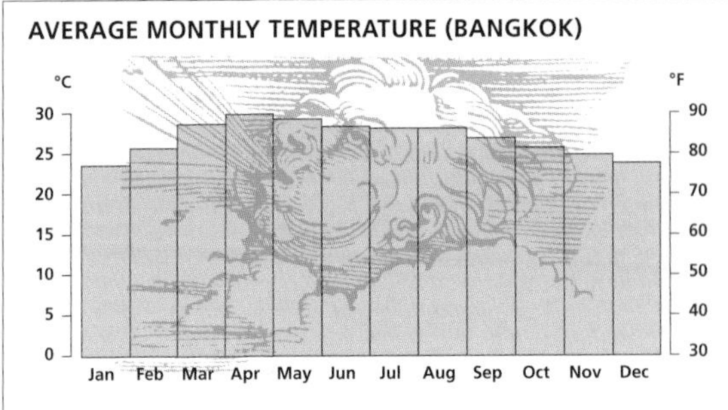

Temperature Chart
For visitors from temperate climes, Thailand is hot and humid throughout the year, especially in the south. It is uncomfortably so during April and May but pleasant in November and December. It can be chilly at night during the coolest months.

NOVEMBER

Golden Mount Fair *(1st week of Nov)*, Bangkok. Thailand's largest temple fair, held at the foot of the Golden Mount in Bangkok.

Loy Krathong *(Nov full moon)*, nationwide. Perhaps Thailand's loveliest national festival. Pays homage to Mae Khongkha, goddess of rivers and waterways. In the evenings, people gather at rivers, lakes, and ponds to float *krathongs*, or rafts, decorated with flowers, candles, and incense.

Thot Pah Pa Klang Nam *(Nov full moon)*, Rayong. Yellow robes offered to the monks on the occasion of Loy Krathong at the pier of the Prasae River in the middle of Rayong.

His Majesty the King's Birthday *(Dec 5)*, Bangkok, nationwide. Government and private buildings are elaborately decorated, and the area around the Grand Palace is illuminated. In the evening, excited crowds gather around Sanam Luang for the celebrations. This occasion shows the deep respect Thais have for their king.

King's Cup Regatta *(variable)*, Phuket. Phuket's Kata Beach Resort hosts international yachtsmen, who compete furiously in the neighboring Andaman Sea for trophies.

Photograph of the royal couple

Chanthaburi Gemstone Fair *(Dec 8–12)*, Chanthaburi. The largest gemstone fair in Thailand, held annually at Chanthaburi Gems Center on Tri Rat and Chanthanimit Roads.

DECEMBER

Trooping of the Colors *(Dec 3)*, Bangkok. A ceremony showcasing the regal pageantry, presided over by the king and queen.

JANUARY

King Taksin the Great's Commemoration Day *(Dec 28–Jan 4)*, Chanthaburi. Fairs and beauty pageants celebrating King Taksin the Great's expulsion of the Burmese invaders in 1767.

Chinese New Year *(Jan/Feb full moon)*, nationwide. This three-day festival is widely observed by Thais of Chinese ethnic origin with the lighting of fire crackers.

FEBRUARY

Phra Nakhon Khiri Fair *(late Feb)*, Phetchaburi. A five-day celebration of Phetchaburi's cultural heritage and royal rulers from the Dvaravati and Srivijaya periods.

Beautiful fireworks at Wat Mahathat during the Loy Krathong festival

PUBLIC HOLIDAYS

International New Year's Day (Jan 1)

Makha Bucha (Feb/Mar full moon)

Chakri Day (Apr 6)

Songkran/Thai New Year (Apr 13–15)

Labor Day (May 1)

Coronation Day (May 5)

Royal Plowing Ceremony (early May)

Visakha Bucha (May full moon)

Asanha Bucha and Khao Pansa (Jul full moon)

Queen's Birthday (Aug 12)

Chulalongkorn Day (Oct 23)

King's Birthday (Dec 5)

Constitution Day (Dec 10)

International New Year's Eve (Dec 31)

THE HISTORY OF THAILAND

The story of Thailand is that of an area of Southeast Asia, rather than of a single nation. From small regional kingdoms to a single unified nation, the country's past is a tumultuous history of conquests, rebellions, coups, as well as a resilient monarchy that has time and again steered the nation away from danger and anarchy, and continues to do so even today.

The earliest civilization in Thailand dates from around 3600 BC, when the people of Ban Chiang in the northeastern region developed bronze tools and pottery, and began rice cultivation. By 2000 BC, the Malay people were already settled in the peninsula along the Andaman and Gulf coasts. Inland, in the hills and jungles, lived small groups of Negrito hunter-gatherers, the ancestors of today's Mani people. Influenced by Indian and Chinese cultures, the first civilizations to develop along Thailand's coasts were Malay, Mon, and Khmer.

Ban Chiang pottery, 300 BC

THE INDIC KINGDOMS

As early as 250 BC, the Malay region, including peninsular Thailand, was strongly influenced by Indian traders, who called the region Suvarnabhumi, meaning Golden Land. At this time, three separate and powerful kingdoms were established – Dvaravati (6th–11th centuries AD) in what is now the heart of Thailand; the Sumatra-based Srivijaya Empire (7th–13th centuries) in the peninsula; and the Khmer Empire (9th–13th centuries) based at Angkor. All three were heavily influenced by Indian culture and religion. The Tai, from southern China, migrated to the area from the 11th century onward.

The Srivijaya Empire, ruled by Hindu maharajas, prospered through trade with India and China. However, its power began to decline from the 10th century onward due to a series of wars with Java, and the advent of Muslim traders and teachers who spread Islam in Sumatra and along the Malay coast. At the same time, the Dvaravati kingdom of the Mons played a significant role in the spread of Buddhism in Thailand.

The third powerful kingdom – that of the Khmers – was established by Jayavarman I. Although its capital was moved to Angkor between AD 889–915 by Yasovarman I (r.889–910), the empire reached its zenith under Suryavarman II (r.1113–50). The greatest Khmer ruler was Jayavarman VII (r.1181–1219), who unified the empire and constructed Angkor Thom, probably the greatest city in the world at that time. However, all three kingdoms eventually fell victim to the emerging power that was to become Siam.

TIMELINE

Srivijaya-style Buddha

250 BC Maritime trade established between India and Southeast Asia

500 Srivijaya Empire spreads to Sumatra and peninsular Thailand; Hindu-Buddhist culture dominates

790 Khmer kingdom of Cambodia established by Jayavarman I

1113 Suryavarman II orders the construction of Angkor Wat

4000 BC | AD 1 | AD 300 | AD 600 | AD 900

3600 BC Cultivation of rice in Ban Chiang

200 Chen La civilization established in lower Mekong region is influenced by Indo-Chinese cultures

550 Mon kingdom of Dvaravati flourishes; promotes Buddhism

Dvaravati coin

889 Yasovarman I founds new capital at Angkor

1289 City of Angkor Thom is completed

◁ **One of the oldest murals at Buddhaisawan Chapel, National Museum, Bangkok**

Stone engraving of the illustrious King Ramkhamhaeng

THE KINGDOM OF SUKHOTHAI

In 1238, two Tai chieftains seceded from the Khmer Empire establishing the first notable Tai kingdom – Sukhothai. It was the Khmers who referred to the Tai as Siam, a name that came to be used for this and subsequent Tai kingdoms. Sukhothai expanded by forming alliances with other Tai kingdoms and Theravada Buddhism was adopted as the state religion. Under King Ramkhamhaeng (r.1279–98), the kingdom enjoyed an era of prosperity. The Thai alphabet evolved during his reign, and the political and cultural foundations of Thailand were secured. Indeed, most Thai people today are descendants of the Tai. He conquered the Mon and Khmer territories in the south as far as the Andaman Sea and Nakhon Si Thammarat, as well as over the Chao Phraya Valley and along the south-eastern coast, to what is now Cambodia. In 1378, the capital was moved from Sukhothai to the city of Phitsanulok. Among the most prosperous of the ancient kingdoms, Sukhothai was peaceful and stable, lasting 200 years with only nine rulers.

Sukhothai-style Walking Buddha

THE KINGDOM OF AYUTTHAYA

As the power of Sukhothai waned, a rival Tai kingdom began to develop in the early 14th century, in the lower Chao Phraya Valley, centered on the ancient Khmer city of Lopburi, not far from present-day Bangkok. In 1350, the ambitious ruler U Thong moved his capital from Lopburi to Ayutthaya and proclaimed himself King Ramathibodi (r.1351–69). He propagated Theravada Buddhism as the state religion, inviting monks from nearby Sri Lanka to preach its doctrine. He even compiled a legal code based on the highly respected Indian text, *Dharmasastra*.

In AD 1369, the last year of his reign, Ramathibodi seized Angkor in the first of a series of successful attacks by the Tais, on the Khmer Empire. The weakened Khmer Empire eventually had to submit to Ayutthaya's overlordship, as did Sukhothai, which was finally conquered in 1438. The 15th century saw Ayutthaya become the strongest power in Southeast Asia.

Much of Ayutthaya's energies were also directed toward the Malay peninsula in the south, where Melaka, a great trading port, was opposing its claims to sovereignty. Melaka and other Malay states to the south of Nakhon Si Thammarat, had converted to Islam in the early 15th century and Islam served as a unifying symbol of Malay solidarity against the Tais. Although it failed to conquer Melaka, Ayutthaya gained control over much of the peninsular region extending Tai authority over Pattani, Kedah, and

TIMELINE

1238 First independent Tai state of Sukhothai founded

King Ramkhamhaeng

1350 Kingdom of Ayutthaya established. Theravada Buddhism becomes the state religion

Ayutthaya coin

1369 Ayutthaya conquers Angkor

Ayutthaya soldier

AD 1200 | AD 1280 | AD 1360 | AD 1440

1279 Beginning of King Ramkhamhaeng's reign

1300 Thai political control extends as far south as Nakhon Si Thammarat

1438 Sukhothai defeated; Ayutthaya most powerful state in the region

Kelantan. However, the kingdom met its nemesis in the rise of Burma during the 16th century. The first Burmese attack came in 1569. A vassal ruler, King Maha Thammaracha (r.1569–90), was appointed king, and his successor, King Naresuan the Great (r.1590–1605), later succeeded in regaining some of Ayutthaya's lost glory after defeating Burma in the Battle of Nong Sarai (1593). Meanwhile, Europeans found their way to the kingdom for trade. The Dutch arrived in 1604, followed by the French and the English. In 1767, Burmese armies invaded once again, destroying Ayutthaya, scattering Tai forces, and laying the capital to ruin.

Despite this disaster, Siam rapidly recovered under Taksin, a noble of Chinese descent. From Chanthaburi in the southeast, he defeated the Burmese and set up a new Siamese state with its capital at Thonburi, on the west bank of the Chao Phraya River, opposite modern-day Bangkok. Crowned King Taksin in 1768, he soon reunited the central Tai heartlands under his rule, and conquered Cambodia in 1769. He then marched south, establishing Siamese rule over all of the southern as well as the Malay States.

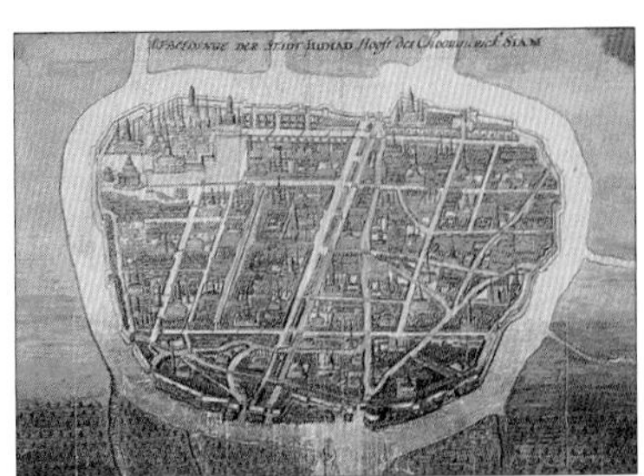

A 17th-century Dutch map of Ayutthaya

Yet, by 1779, Taksin was in trouble. He alienated the Buddhist establishment by claiming supernatural powers and attacking the powerful Chinese merchant class. In 1782, while his army was invading Cambodia, a rebellion broke out in Thonburi. The rebels, who enjoyed popular support, offered the throne to General Chakri, who accepted. King Taksin was later executed, although rumors persist that he eventually entered monkhood.

King Naresuan fighting the Burmese, a 19th century depiction of the Battle of Nong Sarai

1590 Death of King Maha Thammaracha; King Naresuan ascends the throne

Burmese harbor with ships

1767 Burmese forces sack Ayutthaya. General Taksin organizes stiff resistance at Chanthaburi

1782 Taksin is executed; General Chakri is made king

AD 1520 | **AD 1600** | **AD 1680** | **AD 1760**

1569 Burmese forces capture Ayutthaya and imprison the royal family

1604 Economic contact with Dutch, French, and English

1656–88 French influence reaches its highest point

King Taksin

1768 Taksin seizes throne with capital at Thonburi

The Chakri Dynasty

General Chakri replaced the vanquished Taksin as king in 1782, and took the title of Rama I. With him began the Chakri Dynasty, which continues to this day. Successive rulers, who also took the title of Rama, shaped present-day Thailand. The Chakri kings consolidated their power through treaties with the Europeans, expanded trade, built *wats* and canals, opened universities, patronized art and architecture, and modernized the country. Their policies and diplomacy kept colonial powers at bay. However, political turmoil and several coups forced the monarchy to become a constitutional entity in 1932.

Grand Palace and Wat Phra Kaeo, constructed by Rama I in 1782

EARLY CHAKRI DYNASTY

The early Chakri kings, Rama I, II, and III, reconstituted the Thai state and promoted Thai culture, following the model of the erstwhile kingdom of Ayutthaya. Patrons of art, literature, and poetry, they ushered in an era of stability in Thailand.

Rama I (r.1782–1809)
Rama I moved the capital from Thonburi to Bang Makok. Having defeated the Burmese, he expanded and strengthened the kingdom.

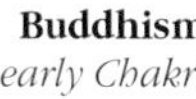

Court ceremonies until the reign of Rama V were formal affairs with courtiers prostrating before the king.

Early Bangkok
Known as Bang Makok (Place of Olive Plums), early Bangkok had waterways and canals, but hardly any paved roads.

Sunthorn Phu (1786–1855)
Court poet of Rama II, III, and IV, Sunthorn Phu is the most celebrated bard in Thailand.

Buddhism
The early Chakri kings were great proponents of Theravada Buddhism. They built beautiful wats *to house magnificent images of the Buddha.*

TIMELINE

1782 Rama I moves his capital to Bangkok and begins a massive building program on Rattanakosin Island

1785 Rama I defeats the Burmese near Kanchanaburi; Thai authority re-established

1809–24 Reign of Rama II; Wat Arun is built in Bangkok; ties strengthened with European powers, notably Great Britain

1824–51 Reign of Rama III; rivalry with Vietnam for control of Cambodia

Wat Arun

1851 Rama IV, the first great reformer, ascends the Chakri throne

1868 Reign of Rama V, Father of Modern Thailand, begins

1790 | 1805 | 1820 | 1835 | 1850 | 18

Rama IV (r.1851–68)
Also known as King Mongkut, he was the first reforming monarch of the Chakri Dynasty. Besides being a skilled linguist, Rama IV was also interested in science.

Modernization
Bangkok's first surfaced motor road, called Charoen Krung or New Road, was opened in 1861 during the reign of Rama IV.

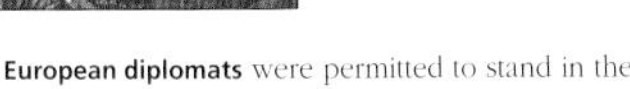

European diplomats were permitted to stand in the king's presence, but had to make a low bow.

REIGN OF RAMA IV AND RAMA V

Rama IV and Rama V were both far-sighted and wise rulers who chose to learn from the West and modernize Siam, thus avoiding colonization.

French Attacks (1893–1907)
The French attempted to assert their authority over Indochina and during the reign of Rama V, took over the Siam-controlled region of Laos.

Rama V (r.1868–1910)
Christened King Chulalongkorn, Rama V assiduously safeguarded the kingdom's independence from Colonial powers.

Rama IX (b.1927)
King Bhumibol Adulyadej, the reigning monarch, and Queen Sirikit are very popular with Thais.

CONSTITUTIONAL MONARCHS

A military coup in 1932 transformed Thailand from an absolute to a constitutional monarchy. As a result, the king today holds no formal political power.

Chulalongkorn University
The University, named after Rama V, was founded in 1917. It is the most prestigious institute of higher learning in Thailand.

1893 The French with their gunboats, become a huge threat for Bangkok, leading to a confrontation in Pak Nam

Thai flag

1917 Thailand's flag is officially adopted

1939 Siam is officially renamed Thailand

1942 Japanese invasion compels Thailand to enter World War II as Japanese ally

1880 | **1895** | **1910** | **1925** | **1940**

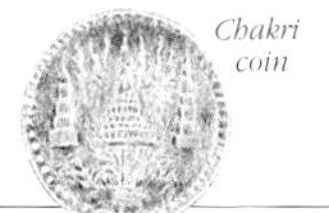

Chakri coin

1897 Rama V visits Europe for the first time

1932 Coup by Phibun Songkram establishes a constitutional monarchy

1945 Thailand on losing side in World War II

1946 Rama IX, the present king, ascends the throne

Student protest slogan, "You must return my people to me", 1973

AN ERA OF UNCERTAINTY

After World War II, the left-leaning Seni Pramoj became prime minister and re-established Thailand's fledgling democracy. He was succeeded in 1946 by the democratically elected Pridi Phanomyong. In 1947, the wartime leader, Phibun Songkram, staged another coup and set the country on a path of military dictatorships that would mark Thailand's politics for much of the remainder of the 20th century. Phibun's return to power coincided with the start of the Cold War, for the duration of which Thailand remained a loyal anti-communist ally of the United States, participating in the Vietnam War on behalf of Washington and the Saigon regime, and also fighting and eventually defeating a home-grown communist insurgency.

Military dictator Phibun Songkram

In 1973, a student uprising in Bangkok forced the retirement of military strongman Thanom Kittikachorn, and for a brief period, democratic government was reinstated. In 1976, however, the army once again seized power, with right-wing general Thanin Kraivixien (1976–7) being succeeded by Kriangsak Chomanand (1977–80) and then Prem Tinsulanond (1980–88). The latter, a firm royalist with a reputation for being incorruptible, stepped down voluntarily in 1988 paving the path for democracy. The army intervened in 1991, with Suchinda Kraprayoon seizing power in the 17th coup since 1932. However, on this occasion, the current king, Rama IX, used his unchallenged moral authority to bring a swift end to military rule. A series of more-or-less corrupt or incompetent civilian governments followed, leading to the election of Thaksin Shinawatra in 2001.

THE CRISIS DEEPENS

A devastating tsunami wreaked havoc in Phuket and the Andaman Coast in 2004. Thaksin was re-elected as Prime Minister in 2005. He adopted a carrot and stick policy in the Deep South in an attempt to end the insurgency, which began at the beginning of the 21st century, aimed at establishing an independent Pattani Republic. His rule was marked by corruption, nepotism, and brutality – more than 2,500 suspected drug dealers suffered extra-judicial execution at the hands of the police, and hundreds of local Muslims suffocated to death after being arrested and packed into trucks. While Thaksin managed to reinforce his power base in the rural north and northeast through a mixture of vote buying and populist policies, he made the mistake of alienating major elements of the army, and most disastrously of all, the royal court.

TIMELINE

SEATO military units in Bangkok

1947 Phibun Songkram stages coup to topple Pridi Phanomyong

1950

1954 The South East Asia Treaty Organization (SEATO) is formed

1960

1970

1973 Student uprising against military dictator Thanom Kittikachorn

1975 End of Vietnam War; US troops begin to leave Thailand

1976 Power seized by the army; Thanin Kraivixien, is succeeded by Chomanand

1979 Elections take place once again and parliamentary democracy is re-established

1980

Thousands of protesters demanding Prime Minister Thaksin Shinawatra's resignation in 2006

TROUBLED TIMES

Thaksin was overthrown in 2006 in another bloodless military coup. The military authorities appointed General Surayud Chulanont as Prime Minister. Thaksin was convicted for corruption and sentenced to two years imprisonment. Remaining in exile abroad, he formed the People's Power Party (PPP) to contest elections in December 2007. The PPP won a majority and assumed office.

For most of 2008, Thaksin effectively governed indirectly, infuriating not only the south, but also important elements of the Bangkok establishment and the middle classes, represented by the People's Alliance for Democracy (PAD), a political group better known as the Yellow Shirts. The PAD and its supporters used non-violent civic action to bring down the PPP, culminating in the illegal occupation of the Suvarnabhumi International Airport, in Bangkok, in November 2008.

The PPP was eventually dissolved for electoral fraud and Abhisit Vejjajiva, leader of the opposition Democratic Party, was sworn in as Prime Minister. In response to the PAD, a new movement, the Red Shirts United Front for Democracy against Dictatorship (UDD), took to the streets in support of Thaksin. Violence escalated between the Red Shirts and the police, culminating in a siege in Bangkok in 2010. Elections in July 2011 saw Thaksin's sister Yingluck Shinawatra's party elected to government, but it is King Rama IX who is holding Thai society together.

Abhisit Vejjajiva, with his cabinet to the right, prior to the swearing-in ceremony in December 2008

1990 | **2000** | **2010** | **2020**

1992 Coup by General Suchinda fails; period of increasing democracy and growth

1997 Thai economy suffers serious setback in Asian financial crisis

2001 Thaksin Shinawatra is elected as the Prime Minister

2004 Indian Ocean tsunami devastates Phuket and Thailand's Andaman Coast

2005 Thaksin re-elected; situation in Deep South deteriorates; rising communal violence

2006 Thaksin overthrown, while out of the country, in a bloodless coup

2007 New constitution announced; PPP is established

2008 PAD supporters illegally occupy Suvarnabhumi International Airport

2011 Elections held – Thaksin's sister elected

Former Prime Minister Thaksin

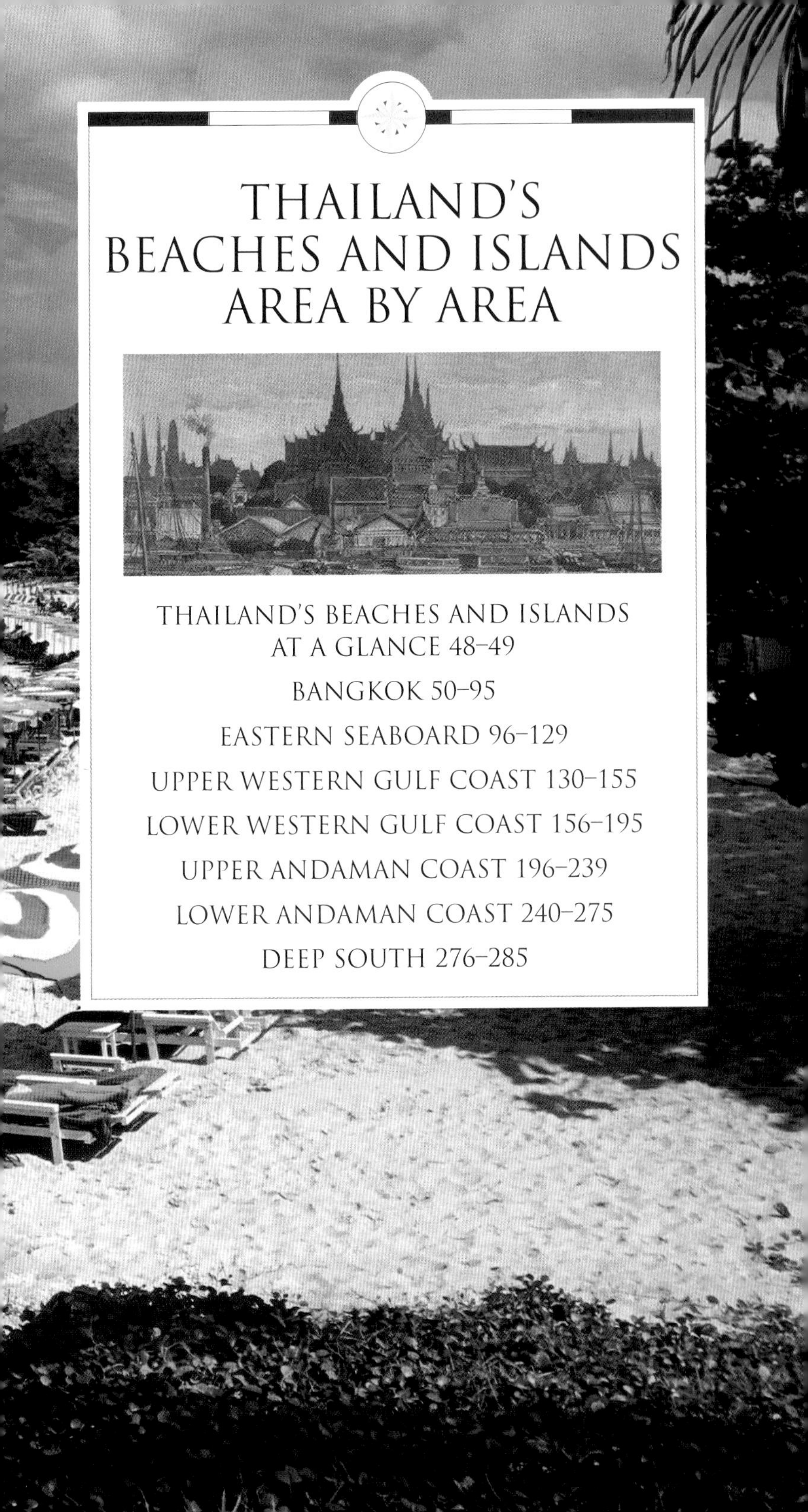

THAILAND'S BEACHES AND ISLANDS AREA BY AREA

Thailand's Beaches and Islands at a Glance

The southern peninsula of Thailand is dominated by the Andaman Sea to the west and the Gulf of Thailand to the east. A central spine of jungle-covered mountains to the north marks the frontier with Myanmar. While the capital, Bangkok, influences the whole country, the old Buddhist city of Nakhon Si Thammarat is the political and cultural capital of the south. Hat Yai, newer and vibrant, is the south's economic stronghold. Major resorts include Phuket, Krabi, and Ko Samui, while the seaside resort of Pattaya offers an eclectic mix of family entertainment alongside its risqué go-go bars. The region is also well known for the astounding beauty of its national parks and wildlife sanctuaries.

White *prangs* of Wat Mahathat Worawihan in Phetchaburi

Ang Thong Marine National Park (see pp180–81) *is among the most pristine areas in Thailand, offering a variety of activities ranging from snorkeling, trekking, and caving to simply enjoying breathtaking views of sunsets.*

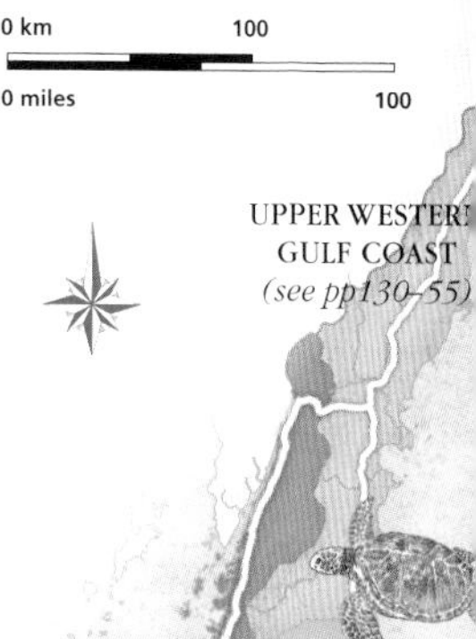

Similan Islands (see pp210–11), *is an isolated archipelago of tiny granitic islands set in the midst of the Andaman Sea. They offer some of the best diving and snorkeling sites in southern Thailand.*

Hat Rai Leh (see p248) *is perhaps one of southern Thailand's most popular beaches, with the best swimming and rock climbing opportunities. The large number of resorts and restaurants here cater to varied tastes and budgets.*

◁ **Long winding shoreline of picturesque Hat Karon in Phuket, lined with colorful beach umbrellas**

BANGKOK
(see pp50–95)

EASTERN SEABOARD
(see pp96–129)

Pak Khlong Market (see p72), *located in the heart of Bangkok, is the kingdom's single largest flower market. On sale are local orchids, fragrant imported roses, hyacinths, and tulips from Europe, as well as several other varieties of lovely tropical blooms.*

Khao Sam Roi Yot National Park (see pp144–5) *was the country's first coastal national park. Its varied landscape is home to hundreds of species of migratory birds.*

Pattaya (see pp104–8) *is one of the most popular destinations in Thailand. It is known for its decadent but vibrant nightlife, discos, and go-go bars.*

LOWER WESTERN GULF COAST
(see pp156–95)

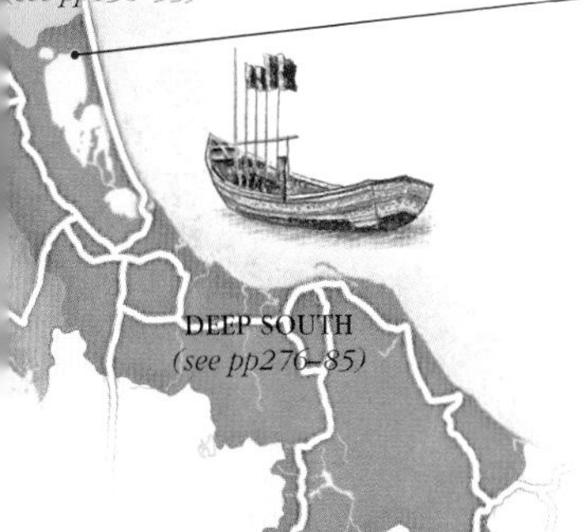

Songkhla Lakes (see p282) *form the largest natural lake system in Thailand. Divided into three distinct parts, it is home to the Thale Noi Waterfowl Park, a haven for native fowls and migratory birds from Siberia and China.*

BANGKOK

Founded at the end of the 18th century, Thailand's capital is a young city, yet, it has prospered and grown into a megalopolis of more than 12 million people in just two centuries. Straddling the Chao Phraya River, Bangkok is a thriving modern city which combines old world culture with urban delights. It offers visitors options ranging from ornate Buddhist temples to magnificent palaces, and trendy restaurants and nightclubs to bustling street markets.

Established in 1782 by Rama I (r.1782–1809), Bangkok was the "new" capital built on a readily defensible site along a bend in the Chao Phraya River. Set up at the small village and trading settlement of Bang Makok, literally, Place of Olive Plums after the fruit trees growing in the area, it was formally consecrated and given a new royal title extending over 150 letters, which soon became abbreviated to Krung Thep, meaning City of Angels.

There is an absence of any single center in Bangkok. The old Royal City, built within three concentric canals on Rattanakosin Island, is the cultural and historical heart of the city, home to the Grand Palace and the much-revered Wat Phra Kaeo. Downtown Bangkok's Silom Road and the surrounding area is the cornerstone of the financial district with all the major banking and trading institutions. The notorious Patpong Road near the eastern end is famous for its neon lights and go-go bars. Just outside central Bangkok lies Sukhumvit Road, a shopper's paradise and the choice for most budget travelers. Diverse ethnic groups such as the Chinese and Portuguese have left an indelible imprint across different quarters of the city.

With gleaming and futuristic skyscrapers dominating the cityscape, and floating markets crowding the river, Bangkok juggles many worlds. It is intersected and linked by a network of canals branching off from the Chao Phraya River. A vibrant city that never sleeps, Bangkok is truly global in its dimensions.

The Bangkok skyline at night dominated by bright lights and soaring skyscrapers

◁ **Vendors selling their produce from boats at the colorful Damnoen Saduak floating market**

Exploring Bangkok

The country's capital, Bangkok is an exhilarating metropolis. It is also the center of most Thai commercial and cultural activity. Dotted with some of the most magnificent palaces and *wats* (temples) in Asia, and laced by the mighty Chao Phraya River, it boasts such glorious sights as the Grand Palace and Wat Phra Kaeo in the heart of royal Bangkok. Southeast of the center lies Chinatown, a bustling commercial quarter. Dusit area is the bureaucratic stronghold dominated by government offices, broad avenues, and Wat Benchamabophit, where the ashes of Rama V (r.1868–1910) lie. Silom Road houses the city's financial center, while the main shopping hub is along Sukhumvit Road.

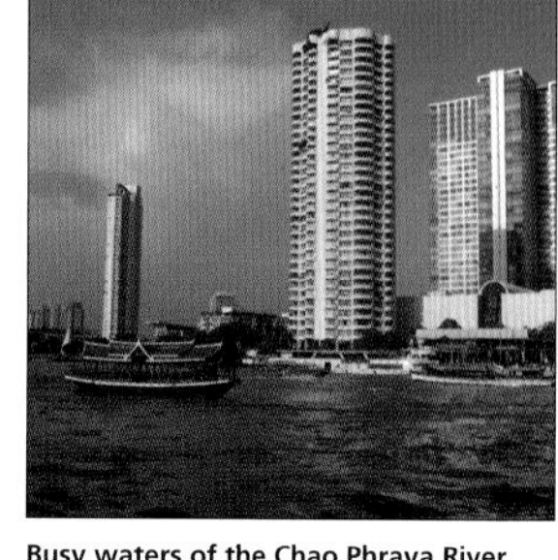

Busy waters of the Chao Phraya River

SIGHTS AT A GLANCE

Temples and Shrines

Erawan Shrine 27
Grand Palace and Wat Phra Kaeo pp56–61 1
Wat Arun 9
Wat Benchamabophit 14
Wat Bowonniwet 13
Wat Kalayanimit 10
Wat Mahathat 5
Wat Pho pp64–5 2
Wat Rakhang 8
Wat Ratchabophit 11
Wat Ratchapradit 4
Wat Saket and the Golden Mount 17
Wat Suthat and the Giant Swing 12
Wat Traimit 22

Museums and Palaces

Jim Thompson's House pp76–7 28
Museum of Siam 3
National Museum 6
Royal Barge Museum 7
Suan Pakkad Palace 29

Neighborhoods and Markets

Chinatown 21
Hua Lampong Station 23
Monk's Bowl Village 18
Pak Khlong Market 20
Patpong 25
Phahurat Market 19

Parks and Gardens

Dusit Park pp70–71 15
Dusit Zoo 16
Lumphini Park 26

Hotels

Mandarin Oriental 24

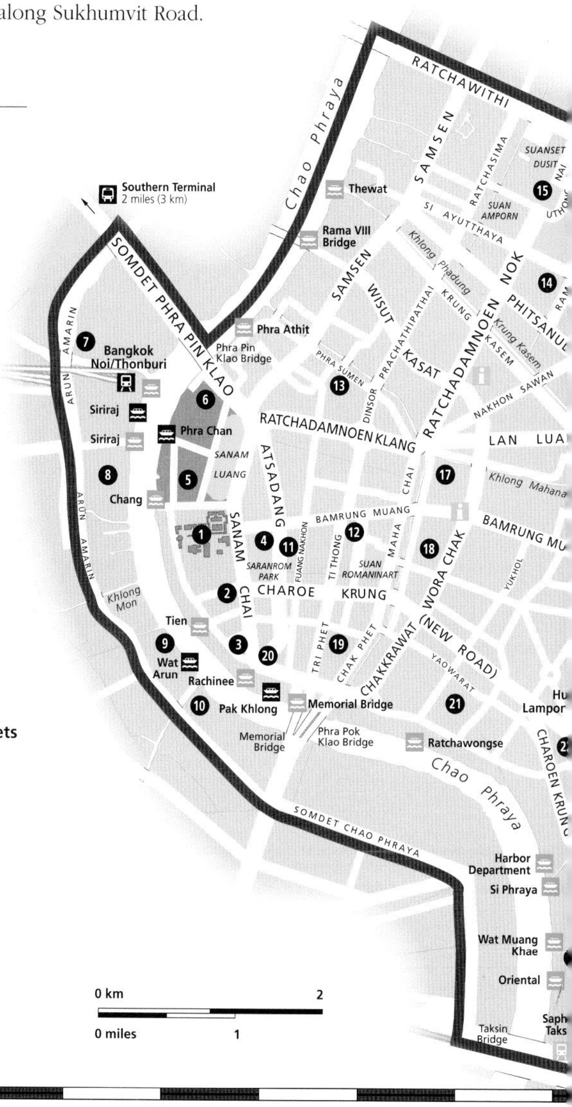

Southern Terminal
2 miles (3 km)
RATCHAWITHI
Chao Phraya
SAMSEN
Thewat
Rama VIII Bridge
SUANSET DUSIT
SI AYUTTHAYA
SUAN AMPORN
RATCHASIMA
NOK
PHITSANULOK
SOMDET PHRA PIN KLAO
WISUT KASAT
Phra Athit
Phra Pin Klao Bridge
Bangkok Noi/Thonburi
AMARIN
ARUN
Siriraj
Phra Chan
SANAM LUANG
RATCHADAMNOEN KLANG
RATCHADAMNOEN
PRACHATHIPATHAI
DINSOR
PHRA SUMEN
KRUNG KASEM
NAKHON SAWAN
LAN LUANG
Khlong Mahanak
Chang
ATSADANG
BAMRUNG MUANG
SANAM CHAI
SARANROM PARK
TI THONG
MAHA CHAI
SUAN ROMANINART
WORA CHAK
YUKHOL
Khlong Mon
CHAROEN KRUNG
Tien
Wat Arun
Rachinee
TRI PHET
CHAK PHET
CHAKKRAWAT
(NEW ROAD)
YAOWARAT
Pak Khlong
Memorial Bridge
Phra Pok Klao Bridge
Ratchawongse
SOMDET CHAO PHRAYA
Harbor Department
Si Phraya
Wat Muang Khae
Oriental
Taksin Bridge
0 km
2
0 miles
1

GETTING AROUND

Bangkok is a large city which is consistently hot and humid for most of the year – not the best place for those who prefer exploring a city on foot. Fortunately, Bangkok has an excellent local transport system comprising taxis, buses, ferries, the metro, and Skytrain. Getting around by taxi is simple and relatively cheap. Buses are even cheaper, but require some knowledge of the city's routes. The Skytrain and metro offer easy, fast, and reliable access to most downtown areas. Finally, the ferries and other crafts operating on the Chao Phraya River as well as on several major *khlongs* (canals), are reasonably priced and a remarkably picturesque way of exploring the city.

Serene grounds of Wat Phra Kaeo, Thailand's holiest shrine

SEE ALSO

• ***Street Finder*** pp84–95

• ***Where to Stay*** pp290–94

• ***Where to Eat*** pp318–22

KEY

Street-by-Street map *see pp54–5*

Major sight

International airport

Train station

Long-distance bus station

Skytrain station

Riverboat pier

Chao Phraya Express pier

Metro Station

Visitor information

Skytrain route

Railway line

Expressway

Street-by-Street: Around Sanam Luang

สนามหลวง

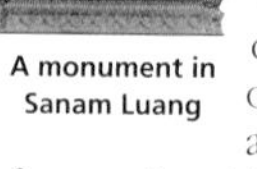

A monument in Sanam Luang

One of the few large open spaces in Bangkok, Sanam Luang, meaning Field of Kings, is the traditional site for royal cremations. The annual Kite Flying Festival and the Royal Plowing Ceremony, an ancient festival marking the beginning of the rice-growing season, are also held here. Bordered by the Grand Palace, the Lak Muang shrine, and the Amulet Market, this is regarded as one of the holiest areas in the city. The streets overflow with salesmen hawking potions and amulets for luck, love, or protection from evil spirits, and astrologers who read palms. Notable sights include Wat Mahathat, Thailand's revered center of Buddhist studies and the National Museum, which traces the country's fascinating history.

Colorful and intricately designed gable at Lak Muang

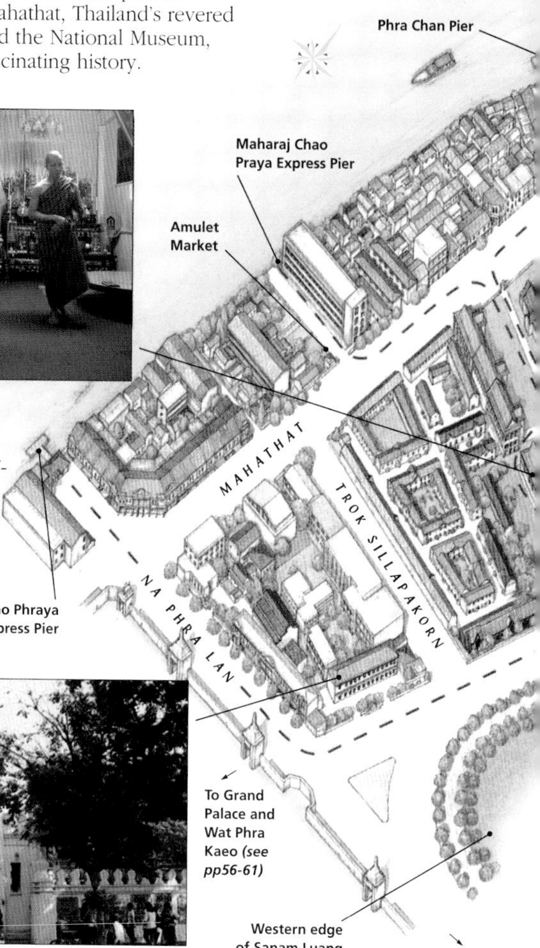

Phra Chan Pier

Maharaj Chao Praya Express Pier

Amulet Market

MAHATHAT

TROK SILLAPAKORN

NA PHRA LAN

Wat Mahathat

Dating from the 18th century, this wat is known more for its bustling ambience than its architecture. Meditation classes are held at the Buddhist university within the temple compound. ❹

0 meters 500

0 yards 500

Chang Chao Phraya Express Pier

Silpakorn University of Fine Arts

Thailand's most famous art school, the Silpakorn University of Fine Arts, regularly hosts excellent art shows in its exhibition hall. The signs outside the entrance have more details and opening times.

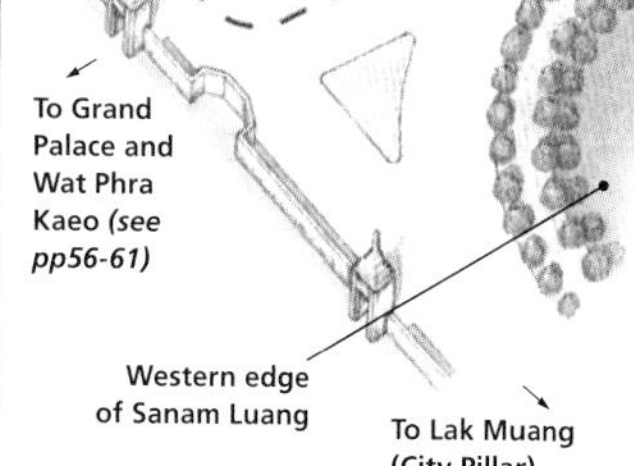

To Grand Palace and Wat Phra Kaeo *(see pp56-61)*

Western edge of Sanam Luang

To Lak Muang (City Pillar)

KEY

— — — Suggested route

AMULETS

The Thais are a highly superstitious people – those who do not wear some protective charm or lucky amulet are a minority. Amulets come in myriad forms and are sold in specialty markets, often near auspicious spiritual sites. Although many are religious in nature – such as miniature Buddhas and copies of sacred statues – others are created for more worldly purposes, such as model phalluses to ensure sexual potency. Amulets are such a big business that they even have magazines dedicated to them.

A selection of charms sold at stalls around Sanam Luang

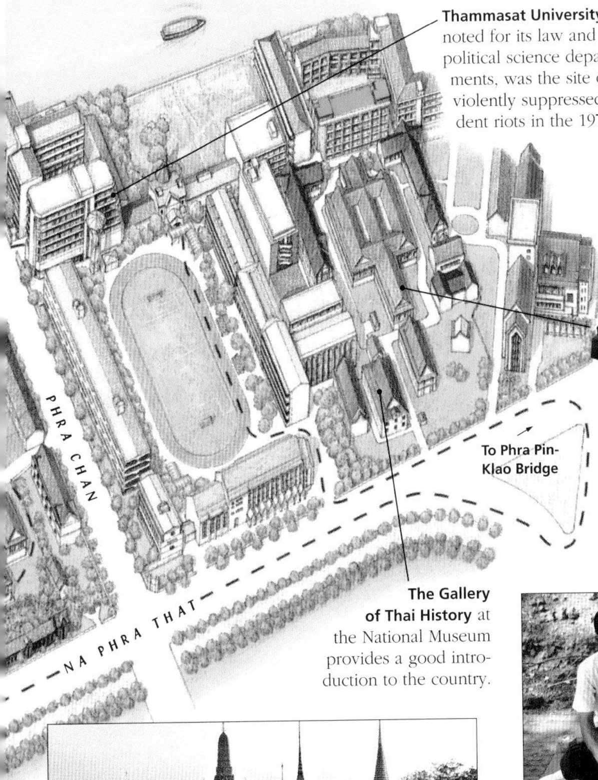

Thammasat University, noted for its law and political science departments, was the site of violently suppressed student riots in the 1970s.

PHRA CHAN

NA PHRA THAT

To Phra Pin-Klao Bridge

★ National Museum
A magnificent range of arts and crafts from every period of Thai history are displayed in this huge museum ❺

The Gallery of Thai History at the National Museum provides a good introduction to the country.

Fortune Teller at Sanam Luang
Thai people set great store by the predictions of fortune tellers, many of whom are found at Sanam Luang near Wat Phra Kaeo.

★ Kite Flying at Sanam Luang
Rama V was an avid kite flyer and allowed Sanam Luang to be used for the sport. Even today, fiercely contested kite-flying matches are regularly held between February and April.

STAR SIGHTS

★ National Museum

★ Kite Flying at Sanam Luang

Grand Palace and Wat Phra Kaeo ❶

พระบรมมหาราชวังและวัดพระแก้ว

Detail on Phra Mondop Library

Construction of this site began in Rattanakosin island in 1782, to mark the founding of the new capital and provide a resting place for the sacred Phra Kaeo, or the Emerald Buddha, and a residence for the king. Surrounded by walls stretching for 6,234 ft (1,900 m), the complex was once a self-sufficient city within a city. Visitors must cover their knees and heels before entering. Note that the complex is always open; if you are told otherwise it's an attempted scam.

Wat Phra Kaeo's skyline, as seen from Sanam Luang

★ Bot of the Emerald Buddha
Devotees make offerings to the Emerald Buddha at the entrance to the bot, *the most important building in the* wat.

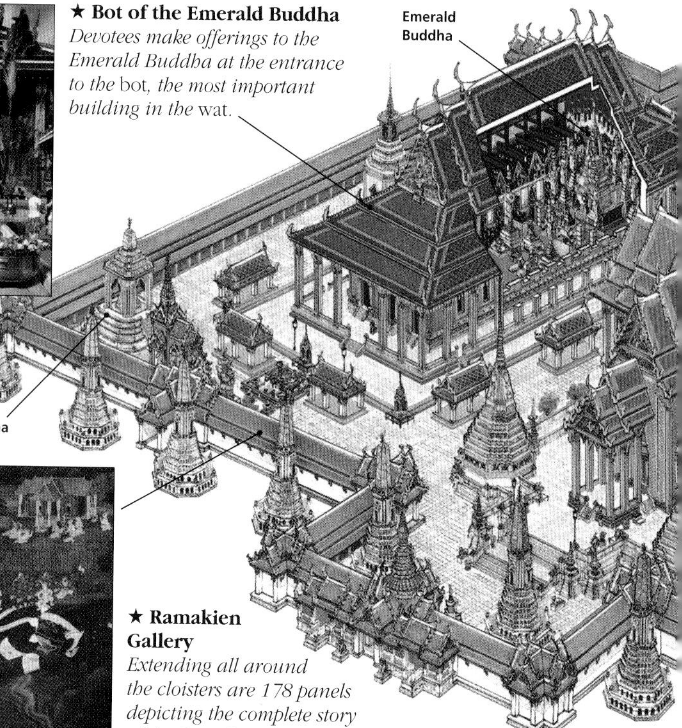

Emerald Buddha

Chapel of the Gandharara Buddha

★ Ramakien Gallery
Extending all around the cloisters are 178 panels depicting the complete story of the Ramakien (see p59).

TIMELINE

1782 Official founding of new capital

1783 Work begins on Wat Phra Kaeo, Dusit Throne Hall, and Phra Maha Monthien

1809 Rama II (r.1809–24) introduces Chinese details

1840s Women's quarter laid out as a city within a city

1855 New buildings epitomize fusion of Eastern and Western styles

1880 Rama V (r.1868–1910), the last king to make major additions, involves 26 of his half-brothers in the renovation of the *wat*

1925 Rama VII (r.1925–35) chooses to live in the Chitrlada Palace at Dusit. Grand Palace reserved for special occasions

1932 Chakri Dynasty's 150th year celebrated at palace

1982 Renovation of the complex

1750 | 1800 | 1850 | 1900 | 1950

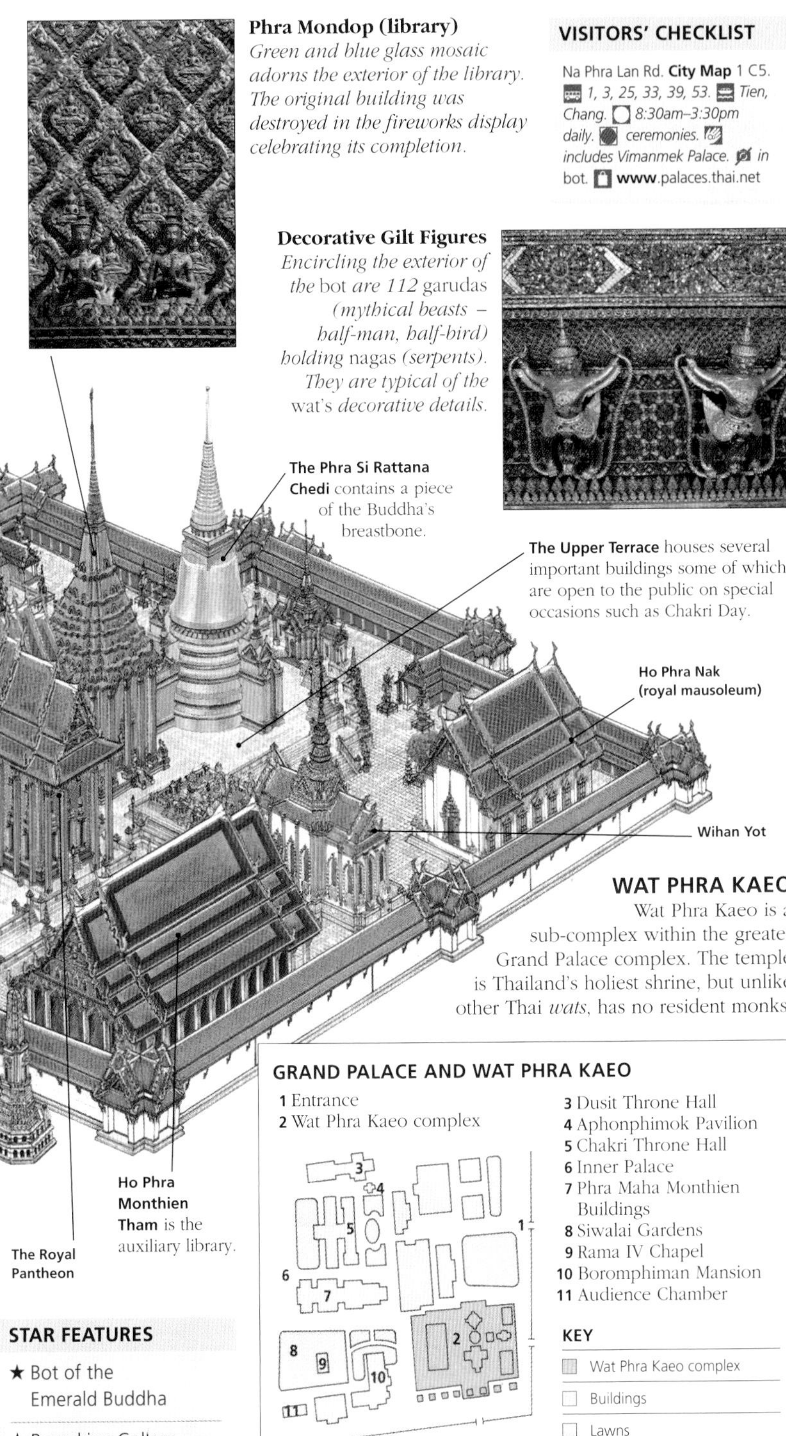

Phra Mondop (library)
Green and blue glass mosaic adorns the exterior of the library. The original building was destroyed in the fireworks display celebrating its completion.

Decorative Gilt Figures
Encircling the exterior of the bot *are 112* garudas *(mythical beasts – half-man, half-bird) holding* nagas *(serpents). They are typical of the* wat's *decorative details.*

The Phra Si Rattana Chedi contains a piece of the Buddha's breastbone.

The Upper Terrace houses several important buildings some of which are open to the public on special occasions such as Chakri Day.

Ho Phra Nak (royal mausoleum)

Wihan Yot

Ho Phra Monthien Tham is the auxiliary library.

The Royal Pantheon

VISITORS' CHECKLIST

Na Phra Lan Rd. **City Map** 1 C5. *1, 3, 25, 33, 39, 53.* *Tien, Chang.* *8:30am–3:30pm daily.* *ceremonies.* *includes Vimanmek Palace.* *in bot.* **www**.palaces.thai.net

WAT PHRA KAEO

Wat Phra Kaeo is a sub-complex within the greater Grand Palace complex. The temple is Thailand's holiest shrine, but unlike other Thai *wats*, has no resident monks.

GRAND PALACE AND WAT PHRA KAEO

1 Entrance
2 Wat Phra Kaeo complex
3 Dusit Throne Hall
4 Aphonphimok Pavilion
5 Chakri Throne Hall
6 Inner Palace
7 Phra Maha Monthien Buildings
8 Siwalai Gardens
9 Rama IV Chapel
10 Boromphiman Mansion
11 Audience Chamber

KEY

Wat Phra Kaeo complex
Buildings
Lawns

STAR FEATURES

★ Bot of the Emerald Buddha

★ Ramakien Gallery

Exploring Wat Phra Kaeo

Celestial figure

When Rama I established the new capital of Bangkok in 1782, his ambition was to construct a royal temple along the lines of the grand *wats* in previous Thai capitals. Symbolizing the simultaneous founding of the Chakri Dynasty, this temple would surpass its Sukhothai and Ayutthaya predecessors in both design and decor. The result of his vision was Wat Phra Kaeo, or Temple of the Emerald Buddha, officially known as Wat Phra Si Rattana Sasadaram. It is so called because the *bot* (ordination hall) houses the Emerald Buddha, brought from Wat Arun *(see p66)* in 1785.

Fine decorations adorning the façade at Chapel of the Gandharara Buddha

THE BOT AND PERIPHERAL BUILDINGS

The most sacred building within the palace complex, the *bot* or *ubosot* of Wat Phra Kaeo was erected to house the most revered image of the Buddha in Thailand – the Emerald Buddha.

The doors and windows in the exterior of the *bot* are inlaid with delicate mother-of-pearl. There are a series of gilded *garudas* along the marble base supporting the structure. The staircase leading to the main entrance are guarded by Cambodian-style *singhas* or lions.

Inside, the surprisingly small image of the Emerald Buddha sits in a glass case high above a golden altar. Carved from a single piece of jade (not emerald), it is 26-in (66-cm) tall and has a lap span of 19 in (48 cm). The Buddha has been attributed to the late Lanna style of the 15th century. It is dressed in one of three costumes – a crown and jewelry for the summer season, a golden shawl in winter, and a gilded monastic robe and headdress in the rainy season. The reigning monarch or a prince appointed by him presides over each changing of the Buddha's attire in a deeply symbolic ceremony.

Inside the *bot* are murals from the reign of Rama III (r.1824–51). They depict themes from the Traiphum, texts based on Buddhist cosmology; the Buddha's victory over Mara, the god of death; and scenes from the *jatakas* (tales from the previous lives of the Buddha). Around the temple are 12 open-sided *salas* (small pavilions) built as contemplative shelters.

To the southeast of the *bot* is the 19th-century **Chapel of the Gandharara Buddha** with a bronze Buddha image. The figure is depicted calling the rains and is used in the Royal Plowing Ceremony *(see p54)*. The bell in the nearby belfry is rung only on special occasions such as New Year's Day.

THE UPPER TERRACE

Of the four structures on this elevated terrace, the **Phra Si Rattana Chedi** is the most striking. Located at the western end, this was built by Rama IV (r.1851–68) as a shrine for a portion of the Buddha's breastbone. The golden tiles that decorate the exterior were later added by Rama V.

The adjacent **Phra Mondop**, used as a library, was built by Rama I as a hall to house Buddhist scriptures. Although the library is closed to the public, the exterior is splendid in itself. The Javanese Buddha images on the four outer corners are copies of early 9th-century originals, which are preserved in the

Entrance to the Phra Mondop guarded by a pair of gold *yakshas*

Mural depicting a scene from the Ramakien in the Ramakien Gallery

museum near the entrance to the palace complex. Outside the building are memorials to the kings of the Chakri Dynasty, as well as bronze elephant statues that represent the royal white elephants *(see p69)* from the first five reigns of the dynasty.

To the north of the *mondop* is a model of Angkor Wat in Cambodia which was commissioned by Rama IV to show his people the scale and splendor of 12th-century Khmer architecture.

The **Royal Pantheon** which houses statues of the Chakri kings was built to commemorate the founding of the Chakri Dynasty. Rama IV built the hall to house the Emerald Buddha but later decided it was too small. The pantheon is open to the public only on Chakri Day *(see p34)*.

THE NORTHERN TERRACE

Ho Phra Nak was originally constructed by Rama I in the late 18th century to enshrine a *nak* (alloy of gold, silver, and copper) Buddha image that had been rescued from Ayutthaya. Rama III, however, demolished the original hall, preferring to build the present brick and mortar structure to house the ashes of minor members of the royal family. The Nak Buddha was moved into the neighboring **Wihan Yot**, which is shaped like a Greek cross and decorated with Chinese porcelain.

The Northern Terrace housing the **Ho Phra Monthien Tham**, or Auxiliary Library, was built by Rama I's brother. The door panels inlaid with mother-of-pearl, were salvaged from Ayutthaya's Wat Borom Buddharam. Inside, Buddhist scriptures are stored in fine cabinets.

Ramakien figure outside *chedi*

THE PRANGS, YAKSHAS, AND RAMAKIEN GALLERY

Surrounding the temple complex is the cloister-like Ramakien Gallery, decorated with lavishly painted and meticulously restored murals. This is Thailand's most extensive depiction of the ancient legend of the Ramakien, the Thai version of the Indian epic Ramayana. This is a tale of the triumph of good over evil with the virtuous hero, Rama, as the central character. The 178 panels were painted in the late 18th century, but damage from humidity means that frequent renovation is necessary. The murals are divided by marble pillars inscribed with verses relating the story, that begin opposite the Wihan Yot and proceed in a clockwise direction.

Guarding each gateway to the gallery is a pair of *yakshas* (nature spirits). Placed here during the reign of Rama II, they are said to protect the Emerald Buddha from evil spirits. Each *yaksha* represents a different character from the Ramakien myth.

The eight *prangs* (conical towers) at the edge of the temple complex, representing the eight elements of Buddhism are painted in different colors and decorated with delicate Chinese porcelain.

THE LEGEND OF THE EMERALD BUDDHA

The most sacred image in Thailand, the Emerald Buddha is revered by kings and commoners alike. In 1434, lightning struck the *chedi* of Wat Phra Kaeo in Chiang Rai in northern Thailand, revealing a stucco image. The abbot of the temple kept it in his residence until the flaking plaster exposed a jade statue beneath. Learning about the discovery, the king of Chiang Mai sent an army of elephants to bring the image to him. The elephant bearing the Emerald Buddha, however, refused to take the road to Chiang Mai, and, treating this as an auspicious sign, the entourage rerouted to Lampang. The image was moved over the next century and taken to Laos in 1552. It was not until Rama I captured Vientiane in 1778, that the Emerald Buddha was returned to Thailand. It was kept in Wat Arun for 15 years, before a grand river procession brought it to its current resting place on March 5, 1785.

The small Emerald Buddha inside the *bot*

Exploring the Grand Palace

Built at the same time as Wat Phra Kaeo, the Grand Palace was the king's official residence from 1782 to 1946, although Rama V was the last monarch to live here. Today, the royal family resides at Chitrlada Palace, Dusit. Throughout the palace's history, many structures have been altered. Within the complex there are a few functioning government buildings, such as the Ministry of Finance, but most others are unused. Important ceremonies are still held in the Dusit Throne Hall and the Amarin Winichai Hall.

Decorative *yaksha* statue

DUSIT THRONE HALL

This cross-shaped throne hall was originally built in 1784 as a reproduction of one of Ayutthaya's grandest buildings, the Sanphet Maha Prasat. Five years later, the hall was struck by lightning and rebuilt on a smaller scale. Crowned with a sumptuously decorated, tiered spire, it is one of the finest examples of early Rattanakosin architecture. Inside is a masterpiece of Thai art – the original Rama I teak throne, inlaid with beautiful mother-of-pearl. In the south wing is a window in the form of a throne. The hall is used for the annual Coronation Day celebrations *(see p35)*.

APHONPHIMOK PAVILION

Rama IV built this small wooden structure as a royal changing room for when he was giving audience at the Dusit Throne Hall. The king would be carried on a palanquin to the pavilion's shoulder-high first step. Inside the building he would change into the appropriate apparel for the occasion. The pavilion's simple structure, complemented by its elaborate decoration, makes it a building of perfect proportions – a glory of Thai architecture. It inspired Rama V so much so that he had a replica built at Bang Pa-in, in northern Thailand.

Exterior of the Dusit Throne Hall, with its elegant multitiered roof

CHAKRI THRONE HALL

Also known as the Grand Palace Throne Hall, the Chakri Throne Hall was built in Neo-Classical style by the British architect John Chinitz. Rama V commissioned the building in 1882 to mark the centenary of the Chakri Dynasty, a fact reflected in the theme of its elaborate decoration. The structure was originally intended to have a domed roof, but the royal court decided that in the interest of maintaining aesthetic harmony with surrounding buildings, a Thai-style roof would be more appropriate.

Housed on the top floor of the Central Hall are the ashes of royal monarchs. The first floor functions as the main audience hall where the King receives ambassadors and entertains foreign monarchs.

Behind the Niello Throne in the Chakri Throne Room is the emblem of the dynasty – a discus and trident. The paintings in the room depict diplomatic missions, including Queen Victoria welcoming Rama IV's ambassador in London. The East Wing is used as a reception room for royal guests. Although most of the Chakri Throne Hall is restricted for use by the royal family and VIPs, an impressive exhibit of ancient arms and armor is open to the public. Entering this exhibit also gives visitors a close-up look at this unique and impressive 19th-century building.

Elephant statue by Chakri Throne Hall

PHRA MAHA MONTHIEN BUILDINGS

This cluster of connected buildings, located to the east of the Chakri Throne Hall, is the Grand Residence of the palace complex.

The focal point of the 18th-century **Amarin Winichai Hall**, the northernmost building of the group, is Rama I's boat-shaped Busabok Mala Throne. When an audience was present, two curtains hid the throne as the king ascended, and the curtains were drawn back with elaborate fanfare, to reveal the king wearing a loose, golden gown and seeming to float on the prow-like part of the throne.

In the 19th century, two British ambassadors were received in such manner here,

Visitors taking a tour of the exquisite Phaisan Thaksin Hall

John Crawfurd by Rama II and Sir John Bowring by Rama IV. The hall is now used for some important state ceremonies.

Connected to the hall by a gateway through which only the king, queen, and royal children may walk is the **Phaisan Thaksin Hall**. This was used by Rama I as a private hall when dining with family, friends, and members of the royal court. In 1809, a Borom Rachaphisek Ceremony was performed in this hall to mark the coronation of Rama II. On the high altar is the Phra Siam Thewathirat, a highly venerated guardian figure, placed here by Rama IV.

The third building is the **Chakraphat Phiman Hall**. It served as a residence for the first three Chakri kings. It is still the custom for a newly crowned king to spend a night here as part of his coronation ceremony.

INNER PALACE

Behind a gateway to the left of the Chakri Throne Hall is the entrance to the Inner Palace, which is closed to the public. Until the time of Rama VII, the palace was inhabited solely by wives and daughters of the royal family. Apart from sons, who had to leave the palace on reaching puberty, the king was the only male allowed to live within its walls. The palace functioned as a small city, with its own government and laws, complete with prison cells. Under the strict eye of a Directress of the Inside, a small army of uniformed officers policed the area.

Rama III renovated the overcrowded and precarious wooden structures, and, in the late 19th century, Rama V built small, fantastical Victorian-style palaces here for his favorite consorts. Since his successor, Rama VI, had only one wife, the complex was left virtually empty, and it eventually fell into disrepair.

One of the palace buildings continues to function as a finishing school for daughters of high-society Thai families. They are taught a variety of grooming skills such as flower weaving, Thai royal cuisine, and social etiquette.

SIWALAI GARDENS

These beautiful gardens, closed to the public, lie east of the Inner Palace and contain the **Phra Buddha Ratana Sathan**, a personal chapel built by Rama IV. The pavilion is covered in gray marble and decorated with white and blue glass mosaics. The marble *bai sema* (boundary stones) are inlaid with the insignia of Rama V, who placed the stones here, Rama II, who had the gardens laid out, and Rama IV.

A Neo-Classical palace, **Boromphiman Mansion** in the gardens was built by Rama V, in 1903, as a residence for the Crown Prince (later Rama VI). The building served as a temporary residence for several kings including the present monarch Rama IX. Today, it is used as a guesthouse for visiting dignitaries.

AUDIENCE CHAMBER

Visible from outside the palace walls, this chamber – Phra Thinang Sutthaisawan Prasat – is located between Thewaphithak and Sakchaisit gates. It was built by Rama I to grant audience during royal ceremonies and to watch the training of his elephants. Rama III strengthened the wooden structure with brick, and decorative features were added later. These include the crowning spire and ornamental cast-iron motifs.

The grand Boromphiman Mansion, designed by Hercules Manfredi

Wat Pho 2

วัดโพธิ์

See pp64–5.

Museum of Siam 3

พิพิธภัณฑ์สยาม

Sanam Chai Rd. **City Map** 5 C1. ***Tel*** *0-2225-2777.* *12, 47; AC: 3, 82.* *Thien.* *10am–6pm Tue–Sun.* *Songkram Holiday, 31 Dec, 1 Jan.*

This museum is housed in a handsome Italianate building designed by the Milanese architect Mario Tamagno, and completed in 1922. Permanent interactive exhibits are spread over three floors and explore what it means to be Thai throughout ancient and contemporary history. Buddhism, village life, politics, and communication are some of the themes that are examined.

Wat Ratchapradit 4

วัดราชประดิษฐ์

Saran Rom Rd. **City Map** 2 D5. ***Tel*** *0-2223-8215.* *AC: 501, 502, 512.* *Tien.* *5am–10pm daily.*

This small temple was built in the mid-19th century by Rama IV and the Western flourish in his architecture is apparent in the choice of building materials. The main *wihan* (assembly hall), for instance, is in forbidding gray marble. The murals in its interior were painted in the late 19th century and depict festivals from the Thai lunar calendar.

The grounds contain graceful pavilions, Khmer-style *prangs*, and a marble *chedi* (stupa).

Entrance to the Buddhist University within Wat Mahathat

Wat Mahathat 5

วัดมหาธาตุ

Na Phra That Rd. **City Map** 1 C5. ***Tel*** *0-2972-9473.* *AC: 203, 506.* *Chang, Maharaj.* *daily.*

This is a large, busy temple complex, which is interesting because of its atmosphere rather than its architecture. Dating back to the 1700s, the *wihan* and *bot* were both rebuilt between 1844 and 1851. The *mondop* gives the temple its name – Temple of the Great Relic – and has a cruciform roof, a rare feature in Bangkok.

The *wat* is the national center for the Mahanikai monastic sect, and it has one of Bangkok's two Buddhist universities (meditation classes are offered at 7am, 1pm, and 6pm, near the monks' quarters). A traditional herbal medicine market and a weekend market with stalls are also found here.

Mural depicting a festival in the main *wihan* at Wat Ratchapradit

National Museum 6

พิพิธภัณฑสถานแห่งชาติ

1 Na Phra That Rd. **City Map** 1 C4. ***Tel*** *0-2224-1333.* *15, 19, 32, 39, 53, 59, 70; AC: 506, 507, 508.* *Phra Athit.* *9am–4pm Wed–Sun.*

The National Museum has one of the most comprehensive collections in Southeast Asia and provides an excellent introduction to the art and history of Thailand. This building was originally the residence of the King's viceroy, which was then turned into a museum by Rama V in 1887 in order to showcase the country's rich past and cultural heritage.

Two of the buildings in the museum – the 18th-century Wang Na Palace, and the Buddhaisawan Chapel – are works of art in themselves. The chapel, constructed in 1787, is decorated with some of the best murals of the Rattanakosin period. It also houses the sacred Phra Sihing Buddha image, which is one of Thailand's holiest images after the Emerald Buddha. It claims to be the original of the three extant pieces and is crafted in the Sukhothai style. The Wang Na Palace has an eclectic selection of artifacts from ancient weaponry to shadow puppets.

Sukhothai Buddha Image, National Museum

Two wings of the museum, set around Wang Na Palace, are devoted to art and sculpture. This section includes several important exhibits such as the Dvaravati Wheel of Law, an 8th-century stone wheel set above a deer representing the Buddha's first sermon at Sarnath. There is also a handcrafted 14th-century Sukhothai Buddha image in bronze with a red lacquer and gold finish. The works of art in this museum are historically significant as they represent the styles of the Rattanakosin, Sukhothai, Lanna, and Ayutthaya periods. Other interesting places

Interior of Buddhaisawan Chapel at National Museum

include the Gallery of Thai History which takes visitors right through the annals of Thai history, from the ancient period to the modern era.

The Royal Funeral Chariots Gallery with its display of ornate carriages is also worth a visit. The collection is not very well labeled and taking one of the free guided tours is highly recommended.

Royal Barge Museum 7

พิพิธภัณฑ์เรือพระที่นั่ง

Khlong Bangkok Noi. **City Map** 1 B3. ***Tel*** *0-2424-0004.* *7, 9, 19.* *longtail boat from Chang.* *9am–5pm daily.*

This is a huge warehouse-like structure that houses a collection of Thailand's royal barges which had once comprised the naval fleet. The museum also contains paintings of Ayutthaya barges engaged in battles and stately processions, as well as photographs of royal barge ceremonies in Bangkok over the past 150 years. These have often provided representative images for Thailand in postcards and brochures. The vessels are rarely used and have been kept in this museum since 1967. They are reproductions of Ayutthaya-style barges built over 200 years ago by Rama I (r.1782–1809).

In 1981, most of the royal barges underwent a face-lift and have ever since appeared in all their glory for auspicious occasions such as the 1982 Bangkok Bicentennial celebrations and the present king Rama IX's 60th birthday among others. On such occasions, more than 50 barges sail down the Chao Phraya River with a crew of about 2,000 sea cadets dressed in traditional uniforms.

The central vessel in the museum, Supphanahongsa, meaning Golden Swan, is the most important royal barge. Made from a single piece of teak, it is 165-ft (50-m) long, weighs 15 tons and requires a trained crew of 64. The prow is fashioned as the mythical bird Hongsa. Anantanagaraj, another barge, bearing a multiheaded *naga* (snake) and a Buddha image on its prow, is used for conveying monks' robes. Narai Song Suban Rama IX is the first new barge built during Rama IX's reign.

Wat Rakhang 8

วัดระฆัง

Soi Wat Rakhang. **City Map** 1 B5. *57, 83.* *Chang to Wat Rakhang.* *daily.*

Wat Rakhang was among the last major temples to be constructed by Rama I in the early 19th century. The fine murals in the main *wihan* were painted between 1922 and 1923 by a monk, Phra Wanawatwichit, and depict recognizable scenes of life in Bangkok. Although the capital has changed much, the Grand Palace, which stands just across the river, is easy to identify. One mural shows the Grand Palace in the middle of an imaginary attack while another one is a portrayal of an elaborate procession of royal barges.

Rama I used to live in the *ho trai* (wooden library) of Wat Rakhang, in the west of the compound, before he became king. The building's eaves support delicately carved bookcases, and the gold and black doors are period masterpieces. Inside the library are murals depicting scenes from the Ramakien *(see p59)* as well as a portrait of Rama I.

Facade of the raised wooden library at Wat Rakhang

Wat Pho ❷

วัดโพธิ์

Farang guard

Officially known as Wat Phra Chetuphon, Wat Pho is not only Bangkok's oldest and largest temple, but also Thailand's foremost center for public education. Unlike the Grand Palace *(see pp56–61)*, it has a lived-in, dilapidated grandeur. In the 1780s, Rama I rebuilt the original 16th-century temple on this site and enlarged the complex. In 1832, Rama III built the Chapel of the Reclining Buddha, and turned the temple into a place of learning. Today, Wat Pho is a traditional medicine center which includes the famous Institute of Massage. Nearby, on Chetuphon Road, is the temple monastery, home to some 300 monks.

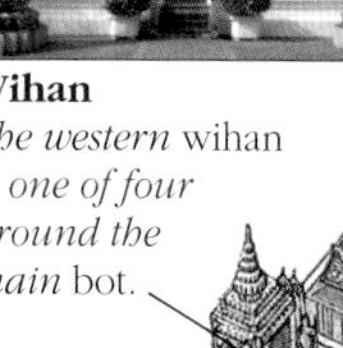
Wihan
The western wihan *is one of four around the main* bot.

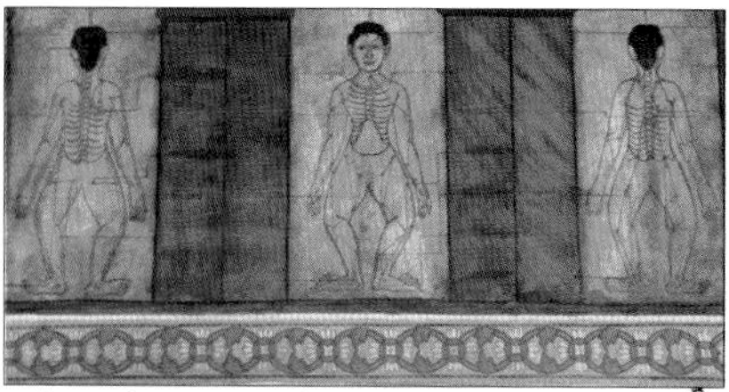

★ Medicine Pavilion
Embedded in the inner walls of this pavilion are stone plaques showing massage points. The pavilion is now a souvenir shop.

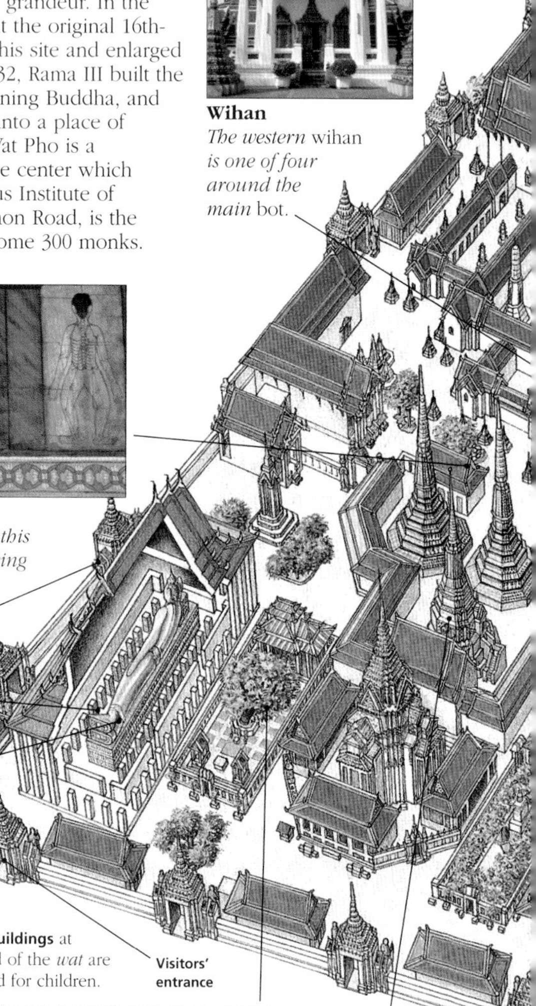

Visitors' entrance

The feet of the Reclining Buddha have images representing the 108 *lakshanas*, signs of the true Buddha.

★ Reclining Buddha
The 150-ft (46-m) long, gilded plaster-and-brick image fills the whole wihan.

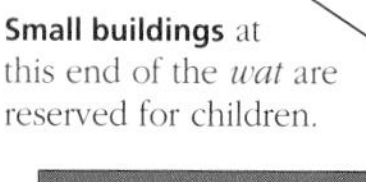

Small buildings at this end of the *wat* are reserved for children.

Visitors' entrance

The Phra Si Sanphet Chedi encases the remains of a sacred Buddha image.

Bodhi Tree
It is said that this tree grew from a cutting of the one under which Buddha meditated in India.

Ceramic Decoration
This porcelain design is on the Phra Si Sanphet Chedi.

Main Bot
The bot *houses a bronze image of a meditating Buddha salvaged from Ayutthaya by Rama I's brother. Scenes from the Ramakien* (see p59) *are carved into the outer base and inner doors.*

Miniature Mountains
This stone mountain by the southern wihan *is one of several within the complex. It has statues of naked hermits in different positions of healing massage.*

***Farang* guards** stand at the compound's inner gates. These huge stone statues with big noses, beards, and top hats are caricatures of Europeans.

VISITORS' CHECKLIST

Sanam Chai Rd. **City Map** 5 C1. ***Tel*** *0-2226-0335. AC: 25, 32, 44, 60, 508. Tien, Chang, Rachinee. 9am–5pm daily.* **Institute of Massage** ***Tel*** *0-2622-3550-1. 8:30am–6pm daily.*

STAR FEATURES

★ Medicine Pavilion

★ Reclining Buddha

TRADITIONAL MASSAGE

Since the 1960s, Wat Pho has run the most respected massage school in the city. *Nuat paen boran*, or traditional Thai massage, supposedly dates from the time of the Buddha and is related to Chinese acupuncture and Indian yoga. The highly trained masseurs at the *wat* specialize in pulling and stretching the limbs and torso to relieve various ailments ranging from general tension to viruses. Visitors can experience a massage or learn the art through a 10- or 15-day course in Thai or English.

A traditional Thai massage at the Institute of Massage

Staircase on the central *prang* at Wat Arun, Bangkok

Wat Arun ❾

วัดอรุณราชวราราม

Arun Amarin Rd. **City Map** 5 B1. *19, 57, 83.* *Tien to Wat Arun.* *7am–5pm daily.*

Named after Aruna, the god of dawn, Wat Arun is a striking landmark in Bangkok, which looks best when viewed from across the river at sunset. Its name is derived from a legend which says that King Taksin (r.1779–82) arrived here at sunrise in October 1767, from the sacked capital of Ayutthaya. He soon enlarged the tiny temple that stood on the site into a Royal Chapel which housed the Emerald Buddha for a while.

Also known as the Olive Temple or Temple of Dawn, the structure was developed and decorated over the years by Rama I (r.1782–1809) and Rama II (r.1809–24) who are also responsible for the size of the current temple – the main *prang* is 260 ft (79 m) high and the circumference of its base is 768 ft (234 m). The colorful ceramics which cover the *prang* in enticing details of gods and demons are actually recycled pieces of porcelain that formed the ballast of merchant ships from China. Unfortunately, these ran out and the king had to ask his people to donate broken pieces of crockery to complete the edifice; Rama III (r.1824–51) introduced this form of ornamentation. The monument's style, deriving mainly from Khmer architecture, is unique in Thailand.

The central *prang*, reached by a series of steep steps, is seen by Buddhists as a symbol of the path to enlightenment. Atop the *prang* is a thunderbolt which symbolizes the attainment of enlightenment. Four smaller *prangs* are located one on each side of the *wat*; they contain statues of Phra Phai or Nayu, the wind god. Between the smaller *prangs* are painstakingly detailed *mondop* (altars), each containing a statue of the Buddha at various important stages of his life – birth, meditation, preaching his first sermon, and *nirvana*. The *bot* (ordination hall), located next to the *prangs*, houses an imposing image of the Buddha, which is supposed to have been molded by Rama II himself. Two guardians, figures from the Ramakien, guard the *wat* from the front, while the entire complex is guarded by eight *yakshas* (nature spirits).

Thailand's biggest bronze bell, in the tower of Wat Kalayanimit

Wat Kalayanimit ❿

วัดกัลยาณมิตร

Soi Wat Kanlaya. **City Map** 5 B2. *2, 8; AC: 2 to Pak Khlong Talad, then cross the river by ferry at the pier.* *8:30am–4:30pm daily.*

This temple complex is among the five built in Bangkok by Rama III, who liked Chinese designs, as can be seen from the Chinese-style polygonal *chedi* and the detailed statuary around the courtyard. The statues were brought to Thailand as ballast on empty rice barges returning from China.

The complex's immense *wihan* contains a large image of the Sitting Buddha. In the temple grounds is the biggest bronze bell in Thailand.

Near the *wat*, on the other side of Khlong Bangkok Yai, is **Wichai Prasit Fortress**, built to guard the river approach to Thonburi when Ayutthaya *(see pp40–41)* was the dominant city in Thailand.

Wat Ratchabophit ⓫

วัดราชบพิธ

Fuang Nakhon Rd. **City Map** 2 D5. ***Tel*** *0-2222-3930.* *2, 60; AC: 501, 502, 512.* *Tien.* *5am–8pm daily.*

The circular structure of Wat Ratchabophit is a successful blend of Eastern and Western

Detail of porcelain tiles in the temple complex at Wat Ratchabophit

styles. The construction of this temple began under Rama V (r.1868–1910) in 1869 and continued for over 20 years. The whole complex is splendidly decorated with porcelain tiles, which were made to order in China. The focal point of the *wat* is the central, Sri Lankan-style, gilded *chedi*, whose full height from the terrace is a good 140 ft (43 m).

Inside the *wat* are four Buddha images, each facing one of the cardinal points. Leading off from the circular gallery are the *bot* to the north, the *wihan* to the south, and two lesser *wihans* to the east and west – an unusual layout for a Thai *wat*.

East-West flourishes permeate the entire complex. The 10 door panels and 28 window panels of the *bot* are decorated with typically Thai mother-of-pearl inlay that illustrates the insignia of five royal orders, while the moldings over the door depict Rama V's seal. The carved, painted guards on the doors are distinctively *farang* (European), and the interior is decorated in an incongruous Italian-Renaissance style.

Accessible through the temple grounds (parallel to Khlong Lot) is a fascinating royal cemetery rarely explored by visitors. The monuments to members of Rama V's family are an eccentric yet admirable mix of Khmer, Thai, and European styles.

Wat Suthat and the Giant Swing ⓬

วัดสุทัศน์และเสาชิงช้า

Bamrung Muang Rd. **City Map** 2 E5. ***Tel*** *0-2224-9845.* *10, 12, 19, 35, 42, 56, 96.* *8:30am–4pm daily (*wihan *Sat & Sun only).*

There are several unrivaled features in the famous Wat Suthat, a temple that was begun by Rama I in 1807 and completed by Rama III. Its *wihan* is the largest in Bangkok and its art and architecture beautifully exemplify the Rattanakosin style. Its central Buddha, at 26 ft (8 m), is one of the largest surviving Sukhothai bronzes. The murals in the immense *wihan* are some of the most celebrated in Thailand. Amazingly intricate, they depict the Traiphum or Buddhist cosmology and were restored in the 1980s. The beautiful teak doors to the *wihan* are carved in five delicate layers and stand 18 ft (6 m) high. (The ones carved by Rama II are in the National Museum). The cloister around the outside of the *wihan* is lined with 156 golden Buddha images.

The Giant Swing, in the square in front of the *wat*, stood in that same spot for 224 years. It was finally moved in 2007 to the Devasathan Brahmin temple and replaced by a new swing which was made from six 100-year-old teak trees.

Golden Buddha statue, Wat Suthat

Wat Bowonniwet ⓭

วัดบวรนิเวศ

248 Phra Sumen Rd. **City Map** 2 D4. ***Tel*** *0-2281-5052.* *12, 15, 56; AC: 511 (express).* *8am–5pm daily.*

Hidden in quiet, tree-filled grounds, this mid-19th-century temple was constructed by Rama III. The style bears his trademark Chinese influence. A central gilded *chedi* within the *wat* is flanked by two symmetrical chapels. The interior murals in the *wat* are attributed to monk-painter Khrua In Khong, who is famous for the introduction of a Western perspective into Thai temple murals. As court painter to Rama IV (r.1851–68), he was exposed to Western ideas and adapted these to a Thai setting. The result was a series of murals that on first glance look wholly European, but which portray the same Buddhist allegories found in traditional Thai murals. For instance, a mural of a physician healing a blind man can be interpreted as symbolic of the illuminating power of Buddhism. The images are all the more remarkable for the fact that Khrua In Khong never traveled to the West. The main Buddha image, Phra Buddha Chinasara, is one of the best examples from the Sukhothai *(see p40)* period.

Rama IV served as abbot here during his 27 years in monkhood and founded the strict Tammayut sect of Buddhism, for which the temple is now the headquarters. Several successors of Rama IV, including the current monarch Rama IX, also served their monkhood here. The temple also houses Thailand's second Buddhist university. Across the road from the temple is a Buddhist bookstore that also sells English-language publications.

Grounds of Wat Bowonniwet, away from the main city

Singhas guarding the entrance to Wat Benchamabophit

Wat Benchamabophit ⓮

วัดเบญจมบพิตร

69 Rama V Rd. **City Map** 3 A3. ***Tel*** *0-2282-7413.* *3, 16, 23, 505.* *8:30am–5:30pm daily.*

The European influence on Thai architecture is exemplified by Wat Benchamabophit, the last major temple to be built in central Bangkok. In 1899, Rama V commissioned his brother Prince Naris and Italian architect Hercules Manfredi to design a new *bot* and cloister for the original Ayutthaya-period temple which stood on the site. The nickname for the new *wat* – Marble Temple – is derived from the gray Carrara marble used to clad the walls.

Laid out in cruciform with cascading roof levels, the *bot* is elegantly proportioned. Victorian-style stained-glass windows depict scenes from Thai mythology and represent a fusion of traditions. The *bot* stores the ashes of Rama V. It also houses a copy of the revered Phitsanulok Phra Phuttha Chinnarat, a 14th-century Buddha image. This venerated bronze statue is a prime example of late Sukhothai art. The cloister has 53 different images of the Buddha from Thailand and other Buddhist countries, assembled by Rama V.

Inside the *wat* is one of the three sets of doors inlaid with mother-of-pearl that were salvaged from Wat Borom Buddharam in Ayutthaya. The building in which Rama V lived as a monk features murals depicting events that occurred during his reign.

Wat Benchamabophit is a popular place for witnessing monastic rituals, including Buddhist holiday processions and the daily alms round, in which merit-makers donate food to the monks lined up outside the *wat* along Nakhon Pathom Road. This is a reversal of the usual practice where the monks go out in search of alms.

Dusit Park ⓯

สวนดุสิต

See pp70–71.

Dusit Zoo ⓰

สวนสัตว์ดุสิต (เขาดิน)

Rama V & Ratchawithi Rds. **City Map** 3 A2. ***Tel*** *0-2281-2000.* *AC: 510, 515.* *8am–6pm daily.* **www**.zoothailand.org

The Dusit Zoo forms a green wedge in between Dusit Park and Chitrlada Palace. One of Asia's better zoos, it has reasonable space for birds and mammals such as tigers, bears, elephants, and hippos, although some of the other enclosures are more confined. The grounds were originally the private gardens of Rama V, and some varieties of tropical flora are still grown here. It is a pleasant walk through the lawns, lakes, and wooded glades of this zoo. There are also elephant rides and several animal-feeding shows which make it an entertaining day out for locals as well as visitors.

Visitors enjoying a ride around Dusit Zoo

The Golden Mount, a distinctive Bangkok landmark

Wat Saket and the Golden Mount ⓱

วัดสระเกศและภูเขาทอง

Chakkaphatdi Phong Rd. **City Map** 2 F5. 🚌 *8, 15, 37, 47, 49; AC: 38, 543.* ◯ *7:30am–5:30pm daily.* *Golden Mount Fair (Nov).*

Built by Rama I in the late 18th century, Wat Saket is one of the oldest temples in Bangkok. During the 19th century, it served a rather macabre function as a crematorium where the bodies of the poor were often left as carrion for vultures and dogs.

Rama III built the first Golden Mount, but the soft soil around the structure led to its collapse. It was Rama V who provided the necessary technology to create the 250-ft (76-m) high representation of the mythical Mount Meru – an artificial hill with a golden tower on its crest. It is believed to house relics of the Buddha presented to Rama V by the Viceroy of India. A circular staircase lined with monuments and tombs leads to the top, where there is a small sanctuary. The view from the gallery takes in the Grand Palace *(see p56–61)*, Wat Pho *(see p64–5)*, Wat Arun *(see p66)*, and the octagonal Mahakan Fort – among the 14 pivotal watchtowers of the old city.

Until the 1960s, the Golden Mount was one of the highest points in Bangkok. Although it has since been dwarfed by modern skyscrapers, the golden spire is a prominent landmark even today.

Visitors come to Wat Saket to climb the Golden Mount and to attend the fair and candle-lit procession that is held here every November.

Monk's Bowl Village (Ban Bat) ⓲

บ้านบาตร

Bamrung Muang Rd, Soi Ban Bat. **City Map** 2 F5. 🚌 *AC: 508.*

Monks' bowls were first seen 2,500 years ago and are still widely used in many Buddhist countries. Such bowls have been made at Monk's Bowl Village in Bangkok since the late 18th century as part of an age-old tradition. The bowls are mostly used for early morning alms gathering.

It is quite hard to find the village amid the maze of *sois* especially since it once stretched as far as Wat Saket, and is now reduced to just four homes and a few small workshops. These monks' bowls are available at Wat Suthat *(see p67)* as well. The process of making bowls is quite time-consuming and requires eight pieces of metal, representing the eight spokes of the wheel of Dharma. The first strip is beaten into a circular form to make the rim. Three pieces are then beaten to create a cross-shaped frame. Four triangular pieces complete the sides. After being welded in a kiln, the bowl is shaped, filed smooth, and fired again to produce an enamel-like surface. Just about 20 bowls are produced daily in the village.

At the center of this maze of alleys is also an unusual shrine, constructed from old Chinese cylinder bellows.

An artisan shaping pottery at Monk's Bowl Village

ROYAL WHITE ELEPHANTS

Manuscript depicting a white elephant

The importance of the *chang samkhan* (white elephant) in Thailand derives from a 2,500-year-old tale. Queen Maya, once barren, became pregnant with the future Buddha after dreaming of a white elephant entering her womb. Ever since the 13th century, when King Ramkhamhaeng (r.1279–1298) gave the animal great prestige, the reigning monarch's importance has been judged in part according to the number of white elephants he owns. Indeed, the white elephant's status as a national icon was symbolized by its presence on the Siamese flag until 1917. The origin of the phrase "white elephant", meaning a large and useless investment, lies in the Thai tradition according to which all white elephants must belong to the king. They cannot be used for work and, therefore, have to be cared for at a huge expense. Often, the white elephants are not fully albino. But tradition states that seven parts of their body – the eyes, palate, nails, tail hair, skin, hairs, and testicles – must be near white.

Dusit Park ⓯

สวนดุสิต

Topiary at Vimanmek

This magnificent park is the major attraction of the Dusit area. Rama V, the first Thai sovereign to visit Europe, was determined to develop Bangkok after the style of the West, and the manicured gardens, elegant architecture and teak mansions in Dusit Park all bear testimony to his efforts. The highlights include Vimanmek Mansion – the world's largest golden teak building and the graceful Abhisek Dusit Throne Hall, which houses the SUPPORT Museum of traditional arts and crafts. A visit to the park and the neighboring zoo *(see p68)* can take a whole day.

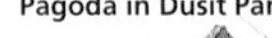
Pagoda in Dusit Park

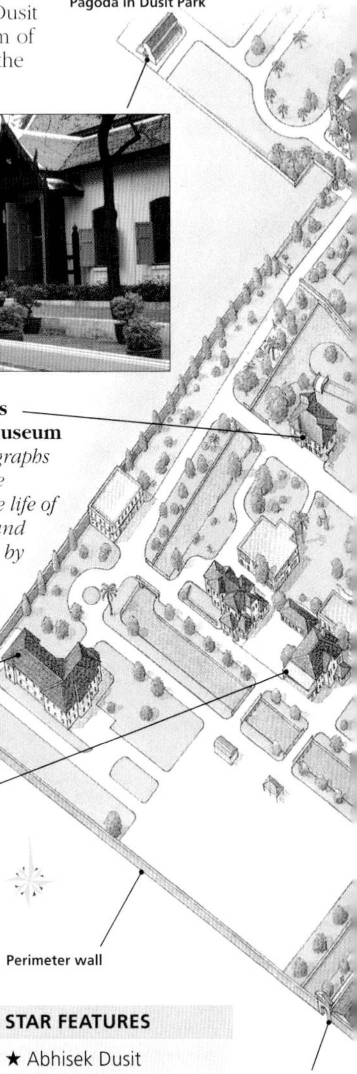

Royal Elephant Museum
Originally a stable for the royal elephants, this museum contains all kinds of paraphernalia including mahouts' amulets, tusks, photos, and a model of the present king's favorite elephant.

King Bhumibol's Photographic Museum
Most of the photographs on display feature moments from the life of the royal family and many were taken by the current King Rama IX, an avid photographer.

Royal Paraphernalia Museum

Antique Textile Exhibition Hall
This collection includes the luxurious robes of the Kings Rama IV and Rama V. There are also displays of different types of Thai silk from all over the country.

Perimeter wall

Entrance

STAR FEATURES

★ Abhisek Dusit Throne Hall

★ Vimanmek Mansion

★ Abhisek Dusit Throne Hall
This hall is a beautifully ornamented white edifice. The major attraction inside is the SUPPORT Museum, with its large collection of traditional artifacts, such as works using the exquisitely colored wings of jewel beetles.

VISITORS' CHECKLIST

City Map 2 F2. ***Tel*** *0-2628-6300-9.* 56, 70; AC: 70, 510, 515. *9am–4pm daily.* *for royal ceremonies.* *Royal Mansion ticket (valid for 30 days) includes admission to Dusit Park and all buildings.* **Vimanmek Mansion** *9:30am–3:15pm Tue–Sun (tickets sold till 3pm).* **SUPPORT Museum** *9:30am–3:15pm daily.* **www**.palaces.thai.net

Canal

Bridge

Lakeside Pavilion
An elegant pavilion behind Vimanmek Mansion offers a great view across the lake to some particularly fine traditional Thai houses. The further bank is, however, closed to visitors.

★ Vimanmek Mansion
Built more in the style of a Colonial mansion rather than a Thai palace, this three-storied, golden teak structure was built using wooden pegs instead of nails. The palace is full of intriguing artifacts.

Ticket office

Old Clock Museum
This museum houses the collection of clocks acquired by Kings Rama V and Rama IX on their trips to Europe. It includes timepieces of European, American and Japanese origin.

0 meters 50

0 yards 50

Phahurat Market ⓳

ตลาดพาหุรัด

Phahurat-Chak Phet Rd. **City Map** 6 D1. *6, 37, 82, 88; AC: 3, 82.*

This predominantly Indian market offers all the sights and smells of India. The main bazaar, around Phahurat and Chak Phet roads, specializes in fabrics. Along these roads, cloth merchants sell everything from tablecloths to wedding saris. This is an ideal place to look out for traditional Indian accessories such as sandals, jewelry, and an eclectic selection of spices and incense. In the surrounding streets are delicious hole-in-the-wall Indian restaurants and samosa stalls. Off Chak Phet road is Shri Guru Singh Sabha, a Sikh temple.

Pak Khlong Market ⓴

ปากคลองตลาด

Maharaj Rd. **City Map** 5 C2. *AC: 501, 512. Rachinee, Pak Khlong. daily.*

Open 24 hours a day, Pak Khlong Market provides the city with fresh flowers and vegetables. Known for offering the best array of flowers in Thailand, it is a florist's one-stop shop. Blooms arrive from 1am onward and by dawn roses, orchids, lotus, jasmine, and Dutch tulips are on display. The widest variety can be seen at 9am. Visitors can buy bouquets or floral basket arrangements from here.

Chinatown ㉑

ตลาดเยาวราช

Yaowarat Rd. **City Map** 6 E1. *AC: 501, 512. Rachinee, Pak Khlong. daily.*

Generally called Yaowarat by the Thais, this historic area is centered on and around Yaowarat Road, Ratchawong Road, and Sampeng Lane. The area is evocative of Bangkok's past and the dominant commercial role played by the city's ethnic Chinese population over the last 200 years. A plethora of gold stores, traditional Chinese medicine shops, bustling street markets, and beautiful temples dedicated to any or all of the *san jiao* (three religions) of Mahayana Buddhism, Taoism, and Confucianism, make the area well worth a visit.

Vendor selling a wide range of chilies, Pak Khlong Market

The bustling Yaowarat Road with Chinese signage, Chinatown

Wat Traimit ㉒

วัดไตรมิตร

Tri Mit Rd. **City Map** 6 F2. *1, 4, 11, 25, 53, 73; AC: 501, 507. 9am–5pm daily.*

Also called the Temple of the Golden Buddha, Wat Traimit houses the world's largest solid gold Buddha. This 13-ft (4-m) high, 13th-century Sukhothai image, is made of 18 carat gold and weighs five tons. It was discovered by accident, in 1955, by workers of the East Asiatic Company.

Local Chinese residents come here to worship the Golden Buddha and to make merit by rubbing a gold leaf on the temple's smaller Buddha images.

Hua Lampong Station ㉓

สถานีหัวลำโพง

Rama IV Rd. **City Map** 7 A2. ***Tel*** *0-2223-3786. 4, 21, 25, 29, 34, 40, 48, 109; AC: 501, 507, 529. M Hua Lampong.*

Rama V, a great champion of modernization, was the propagator of rail travel in Thailand. The first railroad line, begun in 1891, was a private line from Pak Nam to Hua Lampong. Today, this historic station is Bangkok's main rail junction. From here, trains leave for the north, northeast, the central plains, and the south. The city's other station, Bangkok Noi, was rebuilt in 2003.

The Chinese in Bangkok

The first of the Chinese immigrants arrived in Thailand as merchants in the 12th century. During the late 18th and early 19th centuries, following years of war in Thailand *(see p41)*, Chinese immigration was encouraged in order to help rebuild the economy. The subsequent integration of the Chinese into Thai society was so successful that by the mid-19th century, half of Bangkok's population was of pure or mixed Chinese blood. There have been periods of anti-Chinese feeling and immigration restrictions, but the Chinese still dominate Thailand's commercial sector. At the same time, Chinese traditions and beliefs remain strong in their communities.

Dual-language shop sign in Chinatown

CHINESE SHOPHOUSES

Shophouses are a common feature in Chinatown. The family lives on the first floor, which usually has a large living room and a ceramic-tiled floor. The ground floor is devoted to the family business, whether it is a small workshop or a store selling food or other household goods.

The front veranda joins to form a sheltered walkway called the five-foot way.

Sign painting *is not just a decorative art form. These good luck messages, written in gold, are said to ward off evil and sickness. They are displayed in great numbers during the Chinese New Year.*

Dim sum, *which means touch the heart, can be sampled in many of the area's Chinese restaurants. These bite-size snacks include shrimp toast and pork dumplings.*

Leng Noi Yee Temple *in Bangkok is an important Mahayana Buddhist shrine that also incorporates elements of Taoism and Confucianism. The temple, with its glazed ceramic gables topped by Chinese dragons, is the focal point of the Vegetarian Festival* (see p227).

Chinese opera, *performed by traveling troupes, features martial arts, acrobatics, singing, and dance.*

"Hell's banknotes", *are a form of* kong tek – *paper replicas of real objects, burned to provide for the dead during their next life.*

Neo-Classical façade of the Authors' Wing of the Mandarin Oriental

Mandarin Oriental ㉔

โรงแรมโอเรียนเต็ล

48 Oriental Ave, off Charoen Krung Rd. **City Map** 6 F4. ***Tel*** *0-2659-9000.* 🚌 *35, 75.* ⛴ *Oriental.* **www**.mandarinoriental.com

Repeatedly voted the world's best hotel for its service and attention to detail, Mandarin Oriental was Thailand's first large hotel. It was established in 1876 and completely rebuilt in 1887. More wings have since been added. The hotel owes much of its charm to the Armenian Sarkies brothers, creators of the luxurious Raffles Hotel in Singapore. Mandarin Oriental's status, lavish decor, and spectacular setting on the banks of the Chao Phraya River account for its elevated prices.

The hotel's original white-shuttered wing contains the renowned Authors' Suites. Somerset Maugham, the acclaimed author, stayed here in the 1920s. Recovering from a bout of malaria, he wrote of the "dust and heat and noise and whiteness and more dust" of Bangkok, although his perception of the city changed once he was able to explore the *wats* and *khlongs*. Classic, English-style high tea is served in the Authors' Lounge, a riot of potted plants and fan-backed wicker chairs. A teak barge shuttles back and forth to the Sala Rim Naam *(see p321)* on the opposite bank, one of the hotel's highly acclaimed restaurants. Here, guests can enjoy *khon* performances *(see pp26–7)* as they dine. The hotel also runs a respected school of Thai cookery.

Patpong ㉕

พัฒน์พงษ์

Silom Rd, Patpong 1 and 2. **City Map** 7 C3. 🚌 *AC: 76, 177, 504, 514.* 🚆 *Sala Daeng (skytrain).* Ⓜ *Silom.*

The streets of Patpong 1 and 2, named after Chinese millionaire Khun Patpongpanit, owner of the properties in the area, comprise what is probably the world's most notorious red-light district. In the 1960s, the area was the home of Bangkok's entertainment scene – the go-go bars sprang up to satisfy airline crews and US GIs on leave during the Vietnam War. Since the 1970s, the sex shows have been sustained mainly through tourist patronage. A less visible homosexual scene exists in adjacent Silom Soi 4, while Soi Taniya's hostess bars are frequented mainly by Japanese clients.

Poster inside a go-go bar

The Department of Tourist Police monitors Patpong, and the area is surprisingly safe. A night market, with stalls selling souvenirs, and original and fake fashions, gives the area a thin veneer of respectability. A bookstore in the center of Patpong is one of Southeast Asia's major outlets for all kinds of books. Many visitors come to Patpong out of curiosity rather than to indulge in the flesh trade.

Lumphini Park ㉖

สวนลุมพินี

City Map 8 D3. 🚌 *14; AC: 50, 507.* 🚆 *Sala Daeng (skytrain).* Ⓜ *Silom, Lumphini.* 🕔 *5:30am–9pm daily.*

Named after the Buddha's birthplace, Bangkok's main greenbelt sprawls around two boating lakes. The best time to visit the park is usually early morning, when it is used by Thais for jogging and by Chinese for practising *tai chi chuan*. The superstitious can be seen consuming fresh snake blood and bile, purchased from stalls placed along the park's northern edge, to keep ill health at bay.

Lumphini Park is a relaxing place to take a stroll, observe elderly Chinese people play chess, and impromptu games of *takraw,* a type of volleyball that does not allow the use of hands. Dominating the Silom Roadside of the park is an imposing statue of Rama VI (r.1910–25), who ordered the creation of the park.

Early morning visitors relaxing by a lake, Lumphini Park

For hotels and restaurants in this region see pp290–94 and pp318–22

Dancers in traditional Thai costume performing at Erawan Shrine

Erawan Shrine ㉗

ศาลพระพรหมเอราวัณ

Ratchadamri Rd. **City Map** 8 D1. *AC: 501, 504, 505. Ratchadamri or Siam (skytrain).*

Drivers take their hands off the steering wheel to *wai* (a gesture of respect) as they pass the Erawan Shrine; such is the widespread faith in the luck that this landmark brings. The construction of the original Erawan Hotel in the 1950s, on the site now occupied by the Grand Hyatt Erawan Hotel, was plagued by a series of mishaps. In order to counteract the bad spirits believed to be causing the problems, this shrine dedicated to Indra, the god of rain and thunder, and his elephant mount, Erawan, was erected in front of the hotel. Ever since, the somewhat gaudy monument has been decked with garlands, carved wooden elephants, and other offerings in the hope of, or thanks for, good fortune. Women dancers in beautiful, traditional costumes can occasionally be paid by devotees to dance for the deity. This is a way of expressing gratitude for some recent good fortune or even a fulfilled wish.

Near the shrine, and along Phloen Chit and Rama I roads toward the north and east, are several of Bangkok's most well-known and upscale shopping complexes *(see pp80–81)*, including Siam Central, CentralWorld, Erawan, Gaysorn Plaza, Amarin Plaza, Emporium, and the swankiest of them all, the Siam Paragon.

Jim Thompson's House ㉘

บ้านจิมทอมป์สัน

See pp76–7.

Suan Pakkad Palace ㉙

วังสวนผักกาด

352 Si Ayutthaya Rd. **City Map** 4 D4. ***Tel** 0-2245-4934. Phaya Thai (skytrain). AC: 201, 513. 9am–4pm daily.* **www**.suanpakkad.com

This palace, a group of five traditional teak houses, was originally the home of Prince and Princess Chumbhot. The houses were assembled in the 1950s, within a lush garden landscaped out of a *suan pakkad*, or cabbage patch, that gives the palace its name. Each building has been converted into a museum, and together they house an impressive collection of art and artifacts belonging to the royal couple.

The eclectic assortment ranges from Khmer sculpture, betel nut sets, and pieces of antique lacquered furniture, to Thai musical instruments and exquisite shells and crystals. Most important, perhaps, is the first-class collection of whorl-patterned red and white Bronze Age pottery, excavated from tombs at Ban Chiang in northeast Thailand. The highlight is the Lacquer Pavilion, which was built from two exquisite temple buildings retrieved by Prince Chumbhot from the Ayutthaya province.

Immaculately crafted, black and gold lacquered murals inside each edifice depict scenes from the Buddha's life and the Ramakien *(see p59)*. They also portray ordinary Thai life from just before the fall of Ayutthaya, in 1767. These are some of the only murals to survive that period. Scenes include foreign traders exchanging goods, battles, and gruesome depictions of hell.

The elegant facade of the Lacquer Pavilion, Suan Pakkad Palace

Jim Thompson's House ㉘

บ้านจิมทอมป์สัน

Spirit House in the garden

One of the best preserved Thai houses in Bangkok and finest museums in the country is the former home of Jim Thompson (b.1906). An enterprising American, Thompson revived the art of Thai silk weaving, which had waned before World War II. His house is in a flower garden across the ancient silk weavers' quarter of Ban Khrua. In 1959, Thompson dismantled six teak houses in Ban Khrua and Ayutthaya and reassembled them here in an unconventional layout. An avid collector of antiques and art from all over Southeast Asia, his extensive array, which spans 14 centuries, is well displayed, and left as it was when he mysteriously disappeared in 1967. Unlike many other home museums, this one feels lived in.

Master Bedroom
Fine 19th-century paintings of the jataka *tales line the walls of the master bedroom.*

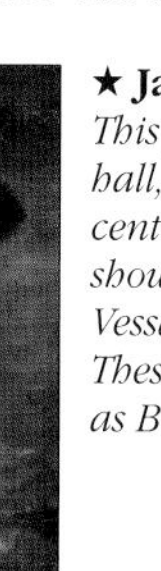

★ Jataka Paintings
This panel, in the entrance hall, is one of eight early 19th-century paintings in the house showing scenes from the Vessantara jataka (see p24). *These show Prince Vessantara as Buddha's incarnation.*

★ Burmese Carvings
Wooden figures of animist Nat *spirits are part of an extensive collection of Burmese images. Buddhism in Burma incorporated pre-existing worship of* Nat *spirits.*

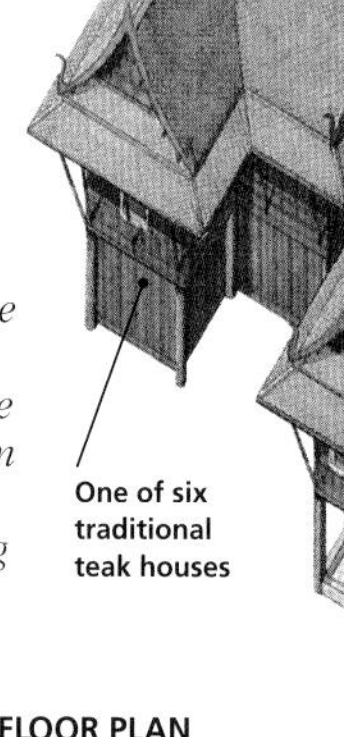

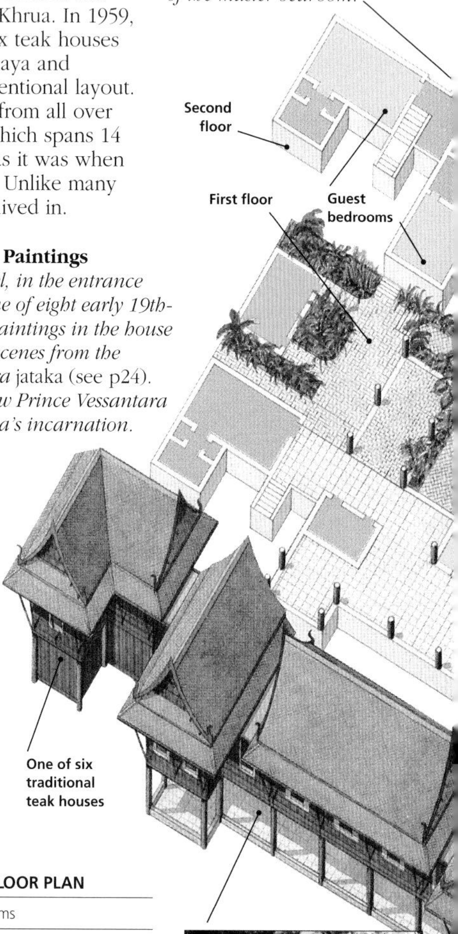

KEY TO FLOOR PLAN

- Bedrooms
- Study
- Entrance hall
- Drawing room
- Dining room
- Secure room
- Bencharong room
- Silk Pavilion
- Other exhibition space

View from the Terrace
The terrace offers great views of Khlong Saen Sap, the garden surrounding the house.

STAR EXHIBITS

- ★ Jataka Paintings
- ★ Burmese Carvings
- ★ Dvaravati Torso of the Buddha

Drawing Room
Carved wooden figures of Burmese spirits from the 18th-century adorn the alcoves in the drawing room. Soft silk cushions in various hues give the place a colorful appeal.

VISITORS' CHECKLIST

6 Soi Kasemsan 2, Rama I Rd. **City Map** 3 C5. **Tel** *0-2216-7368.* *National Stadium (skytrain).* *15, 48, 204; AC: 508.* *9am–5pm daily.*

The *khlong* (canal) was once used by silk weavers, who dried threads of silk on poles along the banks.

Dining Room
Precious blue and white porcelain fills the cabinets along the walls in the dining room.

★ Dvaravati Torso of the Buddha
A torso of the Buddha, made of limestone, stands in the garden. Dating from the early Dvaravati period (7th century), it is said to be one of the oldest surviving Buddha statues in Southeast Asia.

Spirit house with offerings

Entrance

The steep roofs of traditional teak houses are ideal for ventilation, and the inward leaning walls create a greater sense of height.

WHO WAS JIM THOMPSON?

An architect by profession, Thailand's most famous American came here in 1945 as the Bangkok head of the Office of Strategic Services (OSS), a forerunner of the CIA. In 1948, he founded the Thai Silk Company Ltd, turning the ailing industry into a thriving business once again. Thompson became a social celebrity in Bangkok and finally achieved mythical status following his disappearance on Easter Sunday in 1967 while walking in the Cameron Highlands in Malaysia. Explanations for his vanishing include falling from a path or having a heart attack to more sinister suggestions of CIA involvement.

Jim Thompson inspecting Thai silk in 1964

Farther Afield

Many interesting sights lie outside central Bangkok. Extending eastward is Sukhumvit Road, with a plethora of shops, restaurants, small galleries, and museums. Shopaholics will certainly not want to miss the bustling Chatuchak Market, perhaps the largest open-air market in the world, selling everything from handicrafts to live animals. The Damnoen Saduak Floating Market, southwest of the center, is a market for fresh products, sold mostly by women, on small, flat boats. The Crocodile Farm displays various species of crocodiles from across the world and reptile wrestling is a major attraction.

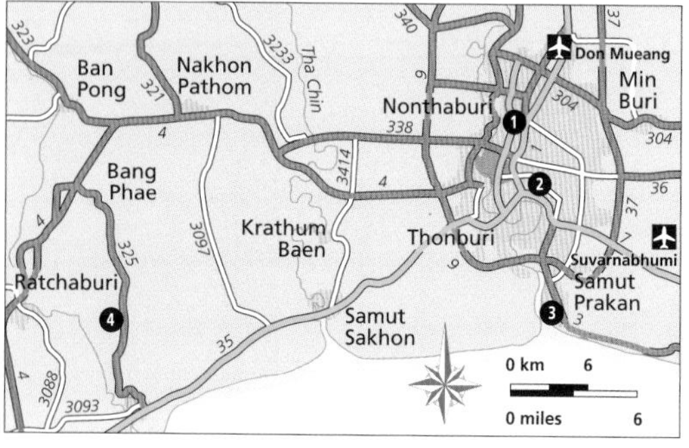

KEY

- Central Bangkok
- Built-up area
- International airport
- Expressway
- Major road
- Minor road

SIGHTS AT A GLANCE

Chatuchak Market 1

ตลาดจตุจักร

Road Map C1. Chatuchak district. *Mo Chit (Skytrain). AC: 38, 502, 503, 509, 510, 512, 517, 518, 521, 523. Kampangphet. TAT, Bangkok (1672). 7am–6pm Sat & Sun.* **http**://chatuckak.org

Thailand's biggest market is held each weekend in a northern suburb of Bangkok, between the Northern Bus Terminal and Bang Sue Railroad Station. The market moved to this location in 1982 because it had outgrown its original site on Sanam Luang *(see pp54–5)*. Now, it is a chaotic collection of over 6,000 stalls, which together occupy the space of over five football fields. It is always filled with eager shoppers, many of whom spend a whole day browsing among the large variety of products on display. Goods range from seafood to antiques, and from Siamese fighting fish to secondhand jeans. The plant section provides a good introduction to Thai flora, while the food stalls display every conceivable ingredient of Thai food. The antiques and hill-tribe handicrafts sections sell a good selection of artifacts and textiles, both fake and genuine, from all over Thailand as well as neighboring countries.

Buddha images for sale at the Chatuchak market, Bangkok

The market is also referred to as the "wildlife supermarket of the world," owing to some endangered species, such as leaf monkeys, being illegally sold here. Fortunately, such trade is now on the decline.

Sukhumvit Road 2

ถนนสุขุมวิท

Road Map C1. Phra Khanong district. *AC: 38, 501, 508, 511, 513.*

This road begins at the eastern end of Bangkok's downtown and continues all the way to the Cambodian border in Trat province *(see p117)*. In Bangkok, it is the main thoroughfare of an expanding business quarter popular with foreigners.

Although a long way from Bangkok's best-known sights, the area has numerous good quality, moderately priced hotels and restaurants, and a few attractions of its own.

Foremost of these is the **Siam Society**, which was founded in the early 1900s by a group of Thais and foreign residents under the patronage of Rama VI, to research, rediscover, and preserve Thai culture. Within the grounds are two traditional teakwood northern Thai houses that comprise the country's only genuine ethnological museum. The Kamthieng House, a farm dwelling, was transported piece by piece in the 1960s to Bangkok from the bank of the Ping River, near Chiang Mai, in northern Thailand. The Sangaroon House is a later addition donated by the architect Sangaroon Ratagasikorn who – inspired by the utilitarian beauty of rural utensils – amassed a sizable collection.

Also on the grounds is a reference library on Thai culture, open to visitors. The *Journal of the Siam Society*, available in the library, is one of Asia's most respected publications on art history, culture, and society.

Located next to the Eastern Bus Terminal, the **Bangkok Planetarium**, traces the history of space travel. It also includes an aquarium as well as a computer world.

The sprawling **King's Royal Park**, inaugurated on the 60th birthday of Rama IX, the reigning monarch, is farther out toward Samut Prakan province. With its botanical gardens and area for watersports, this park is one of Bangkok's most pleasant oases. The park also has an exhibition on the king's life.

Siam Society
131 Soi Asoke, Sukhumvit Rd, Soi 21. ***Tel*** *0-2661-6470.* *Tue–Sat.* **www**.siam-society.org

Bangkok Planetarium
928 Sukhumvit Rd. ***Tel*** *0-2392-5951.* *Tue–Sun.* *public hols.*

King's Royal Park
Soi Udomsuk, Sukhumvit Rd, Soi 103. ***Tel*** *0-2328-1385.* *daily.*

Crocodile Farm ❸

ฟาร์มจระเข้

Road Map C1. Old Sukhumvit Highway, Samut Prakan province. ***Tel*** *0-2703-4891.* *AC: 511 to Samut Prakan, then* songthaew*, or join tour from Bangkok.* *8am–5pm daily.*

The largest among Thailand's (and, supposedly, the world's) crocodile farms, this breeding park, or zoo, is home to some 30,000 reptiles. Fresh and salt-water species, from South American caimans to fierce crocodiles from the Nile, can all be seen here. The farm also has the biggest crocodile ever kept in captivity – a 20-ft (6-m) long reptile weighing over 2,200 lb (1,000 kg).

The highlight of the farm is the hourly show during which visitors can see handlers wrestle with crocodiles, even putting their heads in the creatures' mouths. A souvenir shop nearby sells a variety of crocodile skin products such bags and key rings.

Reconstructed traditional living area in Kamthieng House, Sukhumvit Road

Damnoen Saduak Floating Market ❹

ตลาดน้ำดำเนินสะดวก

Road Map C1. 1 mile (2 km) W of Damnoen Saduak, Ratchaburi province. *or join tour from Bangkok.* *4am–11am daily.* *TAT, Phetchaburi (0-3247-1005).*

In contrast to the numerous floating markets in Bangkok that are now organized solely for the benefit of tourists, this is a more authentic example.

Located 62 miles (100 km) southwest of Bangkok, the market is a labyrinth of narrow *khlongs* (canals) and actually comprises three separate markets. The largest, **Ton Khem**, is on Khlong Damnoen Saduak. On the parallel *khlong*, a short way south, is **Hia Kui**, where structures anchored to the banks function as warehouses selling souvenirs to large tour groups. Further south, on a smaller *khlong*, is **Khun Phitak**, the least crowded of the three markets.

Most vendors, mainly women, paddle around in *sampan* (rowing boats) wearing *mo homs* (traditional farmers' shirts) and a *ngop* (traditional hat). They sell farm-fresh produce, including fruit, vegetables, and spices. Some vendors also sell souvenir straw hats as well as refreshments.

The best way of getting around the three markets is by boat – trips can be taken along the *khlongs* and to the nearby coconut plantations. The best time to arrive is between 7am and 9am, when the market is in full swing.

Crocodile wrestling show at the Crocodile Farm

SHOPPING IN BANGKOK

Bangkok is regarded as a shoppers' paradise with its many retail outlets, high quality products, and surprisingly good bargains. Staff in department stores are attentive, and whether it is designer clothes, traditional crafts, or electronic equipment, there are some great deals to be had. Visitors enjoy bargaining in the open-air markets, where vendors often drop their prices by 50 percent or more. However, it is better to avoid the heat and humidity of mid-afternoon, and limit the buying spree to one or two locations per day.

Shopping center sign

Shoppers visiting the huge Siam Paragon mall

PRACTICAL INFORMATION

Opening hours are usually early morning to mid-afternoon in fresh markets, 10am–10pm in shopping malls, and 24 hours in convenience stores. Credit cards are accepted in shopping malls and modern boutiques, but market vendors expect cash payment. VAT refunds are possible, but the shop where the item is bought must fill out a form for customs, which can be time consuming, so it is only worth while for significant savings. Bargaining is expected at street stalls and markets, but prices are fixed in department stores and boutiques. For more information, see pages 334–7.

SHOPPING DISTRICTS

Boutiques and markets are scattered all over the city, but there is a high concentration of shopping outlets around Siam Square, Silom, Phloen Chit, and Sukhumvit Roads.

SHOPPING MALLS

Leading the way in the race to be Bangkok's best and biggest mall, **CentralWorld Plaza** is Southeast Asia's largest shopping complex. Another favorite shopping destination is **Siam Paragon**, where anything from a sports car to a bowl of noodles is available for a price. **Mahboonkrong** (or MBK) is more like a street market spread over eight floors. Other centrally located malls are **Siam Center and Siam Discovery**, **Emporium**, **Silom Complex**, **Amarin Plaza**, **Gaysorn Plaza**, and **Erawan**.

MARKETS

No self-respecting shopaholic can claim to know Bangkok without going to the city's vast **Chatuchak Market**, said to be the world's largest open-air market. Impossible to cover in a day, prudent visitors are selective about the places they see.

Bangkok's night markets in the Khao San, Patpong, and Sukhumvit Sois 3–15 regions consist of stalls set up each evening on the sidewalk. They make it possible to combine souvenir shopping with dining and clubbing, for visitors who are short on time.

Brightly lit stalls selling various goods, night market at Patpong

Colorful display of authentic silk products at the Jim Thompson

SILK AND COTTON

Thai silk is renowned for its high quality, unique designs, and reasonable price. In the night markets, some items that claim to be silk are, in fact, made of synthetic fabric.

It pays to visit a reputable shop, such as **Jim Thompson**, which has outlets in many top hotels, to ensure the authenticity of products. Those who have an eye for the real thing can head for the crowded **Phahurat Market**, where prices are much lower.

Thai cotton is also a good deal. The eye-catching designs on items such as bedspreads and cushion covers make distinctive souvenirs.

CLOTHES

With prices only a fraction of what they are in the West, it makes sense to stock up on clothes, either off-the-peg in shopping malls or tailor-made. Tailors abound in all tourist areas, but workmanship varies, so it is better to visit a reputable tailor such as **Raja's Fashions** or **Marzotto**, and allow several days for preparation and fittings.

ANTIQUES

So-called ancient craft items are available in many shops, but few of these are genuine antiques, for which a permit from the Fine Arts Department is required for export. A couple of reliable outlets are the **River City Complex**, which has four floors of antique furniture, carvings, and old maps, and **Oriental Plaza**, with rare collectibles such as beautiful sculptures and prints.

Lacquerware items and wooden carvings at Chatuchak Market

THAI CRAFTS

From silverware to celadon, lacquerware to woodcarvings, and basketry to hand-woven textiles, Thailand has a rich variety of crafts. Good places to see a wide range of crafts include Chatuchak Market, **Narayana Phand**, **Silom Village**, and **Nandakwang**.

GEMS AND JEWELRY

As with antiques, extreme caution should be exercised when buying gems or jewelry, since potential customers are often exposed to sophisticated scams. Serious shoppers may want to browse through the glittering displays of jewelry at **Peninsula Plaza** or the gem boutiques at reliable hotels.

ELECTRONIC GOODS

Computer equipment, video games, cameras, and mobile phones are on sale in shopping malls throughout the city, but one place that specializes in such goods is **Pantip Plaza**. Customers should be aware that some items on sale, such as software, are pirated and offer no money-back guarantee.

BOOKS

Book addicts should explore the massive selection at any one of the outlets of **Asia Books** and **Kinokuniya Books**. Other bookstore chains with outlets in central Bangkok are **B2S** and **Bookazine**.

DIRECTORY

SHOPPING MALLS

Amarin Plaza
Phloen Chit Rd.
City Map 8 E1.
Tel *0-2256-9111.*

CentralWorld Plaza
Ratchadamri Rd.
City Map 8 D1.
Tel *0-2635-1111.*
www.centralworld.co.th

Emporium
Sukhumvit Sois 24–26.
Tel *0-2669-1000.*
www.emporium thailand.com

Erawan
Phloen Chit Rd.
City Map 8 E1.
Tel *0-2250-7777.*

Gaysorn Plaza
Phloen Chit Rd.
City Map 8 E1.
Tel *0-2656-1149.*

Mahboonkrong
Phaya Thai Rd.
City Map 7 B1.
Tel *0-2217-9111.*

Siam Center and Siam Discovery
Rama I Rd. **City Map** 7 C1. **Tel** *0-2658-1000.*

Siam Paragon
Rama I Rd.
City Map 7 C1.
Tel *0-2690-1000.*

Silom Complex
Silom Rd.
City Map 8 D4.
Tel *0-2632-1199.*

MARKETS

Chatuchak Market
Kamphaeng Phet 2 Rd.

SILK AND COTTON

Jim Thompson
9 Surawong Rd. **City Map** 7 C3. **Tel** *0-2632-8100.*

Phahurat Market
Phahurat. **City Map** 6 D1.

CLOTHES

Marzotto
3 Soi Shangri-La Hotel, Charoen Krung Rd.
City Map 6 F5.
Tel *0-2233-2880.*

Raja's Fashions
1/6 Soi 4. **City Map** 8 B2.
Tel *0-2253-8379.*
www.rajasfashions.com

ANTIQUES

Oriental Plaza
Charoen Krung Rd.
City Map 6 F4.

River City Complex
23 Trok Rongnamkaeng Yotha Rd.
City Map 6 F3.
Tel *0-2237-0077.*

THAI CRAFTS

Nandakwang
Sukhumvit Soi 23.
Tel *0-2259-9607.*

Narayana Phand
Ratchadamri Rd.
City Map 8 D1.
Tel *0-2252-4670.*

Silom Village
Silom Rd.
City Map 7 A4.
Tel *0-2235-8760.*

GEMS AND JEWELRY

Peninsula Plaza
Ratchadamri Rd.
City Map 8 D1.
Tel *0-2253-9762.*

ELECTRONIC GOODS

Pantip Plaza
Phetchaburi Rd. **City Map** 4 D5. **Tel** *0-2250-1555.*

BOOKS

Asia Books
Sukhumvit Soi 15–19.
One of several branches.

B2S
CentralWorld Plaza, Ratchadamri Rd.
City Map 8 D1.
One of several branches.

Bookazine
Silom Complex, Silom Rd.
City Map 8 D4.
One of several branches.

Kinokuniya Books
Siam Paragon.
City Map 7 C1.
One of several branches.

ENTERTAINMENT IN BANGKOK

Bangkok provides a fantastic range of entertainment, from classical puppet theater to nightclubs. One of the most popular choices for short-stay visitors is a cultural show accompanied by a Thai meal, but there are plenty of alternatives, such as transvestite cabaret shows or an unusual drink at one of the city's trendy cocktail bars. Many of the pubs and restaurants offer live music, ranging from traditional Thai ballads to rock classics, while the city's clubs are a musical melting pot where locals and foreigners find common ground. It is best to plan out journeys in order to beat Bangkok's notorious traffic snarls.

A traditional Thai puppet show

GENERAL INFORMATION

For information about daily events, visitors can consult English-language newspapers such as the *Bangkok Post* and *The Nation*, or pick up one of the free magazines, such as *BKK*, that are distributed at tourist spots. Tickets for events are usually easy to come by. Visitors can ask at the hotel desk or a travel agent, or go online and take a look at the websites designed to help travelers. For more information, *see pp338–41*.

CULTURAL SHOWS AND THEATER

The nightly show at **Siam Niramit** is quite a cultural extravaganza, which features spectacular sets and more than 500 elaborately dressed dancers. More intimate performances take place at the riverside **Patravadi Theater**, where traditional and modern dance techniques are fused to great effect. Classical dance shows with buffet or à la carte dinners can be enjoyed at **Sala Rim Nam** and **Silom Village**, while the city's top cabaret location is **Calypso Cabaret**. For performances of *khon*, or classical masked drama, the **Sala Chalermkrung Theater** and the **National Theater** are good options.

Puppet shows may seem like children's entertainment, but the puppeteers at the **Aksra Theatre** are so accomplished that most adults will be as enthralled as their kids.

MUAY THAI

To enjoy a more visceral kind of entertainment, visitors can head to the local Thai boxing ring. *muay thai* (Thai kickboxing) is the national sport, which draws in a large crowd. Spectators usually bet on the outcome of *muay thai* matches, and cheer excitedly for their chosen fighter.

At **Ratchadamnoen Stadium** and **Lumphini Stadium**, spectators can watch the boxers prepare for their matches with slow, concentrated movements to the accompaniment of wailing instruments.

CINEMAS

It may seem strange to travel all the way to Thailand and end up going to the cinema, but with the air-conditioned interiors, comfortable seats, and cheap prices, cinema halls can be the antidote to a tiring shopping spree or a day spent sightseeing. Most modern cinemas are located in shopping malls, such as the **Paragon Cineplex** in Siam Paragon and **Major Cineplex** in CentralWorld Plaza, although a few independent theaters still exist, such as the **Scala** and **Lido** in Siam Square, which occasionally show arthouse cinema or independent films. The Thai national anthem is played before the screening of every film, and everyone is expected to stand, including foreigners. Travelers can also log on to websites to get more information and film listings.

The brightly lit exterior of Major Cineplex at CentralWorld Plaza

Lively dance floor at the popular Bed Supperclub

BARS AND NIGHTCLUBS

Bangkok has an astonishing range of bars to cater to different tastes. There is the hole-in-the-wall **Ad Here the 13th**, with an in-house band that plays soulful blues music and despite being a cramped space, the crowds keep pouring in and even spill on to the sidewalk. The super-chic **Sky Bar** is where the city's glitterati sip cocktails and admire the view from the 63rd floor. Many bars feature live bands in an effort to draw in the crowds – for example, **Saxophone** offers a heady mix of jazz, blues, and reggae, while **Hard Rock Café** has bands playing covers of rock classics. Visitors can dance till late at a number of clubs such as **Bed Supperclub**, **Q Bar**, **DJ Station**, and **Café Democ**. Those looking for a more sophisticated and elegant environment should make their way to **Diplomat Bar**, **Moon Bar**, or **Syn Bar**.

Bangkok has long been known for its liberal attitude toward alternative sexual preferences, and Silom has a number of gay bars, such as the **Telephone Pub**. The main areas in Bangkok famous for their hostess and go-go bars are the infamous Patpong, Nana Plaza, and Soi Cowboy. This is the other side of the nightlife in Bangkok and many people visit these spots out of curiosity. However, it is best to avoid the seamier bars in Patpong, where scams have often left many foreign visitors with empty wallets.

Posh environs for live rock music and cocktails, Hard Rock Cafe

DIRECTORY

CULTURAL SHOWS AND THEATER

Aksra Theatre
8/1 Rangnam Rd.
City Map 4 D4/E4.
Tel 0-2677-8888.

Calypso Cabaret
Asia Hotel, Phaya Thai Rd.
City Map 3 C5.
Tel 0-2216-8973.

National Theater
Rachinee Rd.
City Map 2 D5.
Tel 0-2224-1342.

Patravadi Theater
69/1 Soi Wat Rakhang.
City Map 1 B5.
Tel 0-2412-7287.

Sala Chalermkrung Theater
Charoen Krung Rd.
City Map 6 D1.
Tel 0-2222-0434.

Sala Rim Nam
The Mandarin Oriental, 48 Oriental Avenue.
City Map 6 F4.
Tel 0-2659-9000.

Siam Niramit
Ratchada Theater, 19 Tiam Ruammit Rd.
Tel 0-2649-9222.

Silom Village
Silom Rd.
City Map 7 A4.
Tel 0-2235-8760.

MUAY THAI

Lumphini Stadium
Rama IV Rd.
City Map 8 E4.
Tel 0-2251-4303.

Ratchadamnoen Stadium
Ratchadamnoen Nok Rd.
City Map 2 F3.
Tel 0-2281-4205.

CINEMAS

Lido
Siam Square.
City Map 7 C1.
Tel 0-2252-6498.

Major Cineplex
CentralWorld Plaza, Ratchadamri Rd.
City Map 8 D1.
Tel 0-2635-1111.

Paragon Cineplex
Siam Paragon, Rama I Rd.
City Map 7 C1.
Tel 0-2515-5555.

Scala
Siam Square.
City Map 7 C1.
Tel 0-2251-2861.

BARS AND NIGHTCLUBS

Ad Here the 13th
13 Samsen Rd.
City Map 2 D3.
Tel 08-9769-4613

Bed Supperclub
Sukhumvit Soi 11.
Tel 0-2651-3537.

Café Democ
Ratchadamnoen Klang Rd.
City Map 2 E4.
Tel 0-2622-2571.

Diplomat Bar
Conrad Hotel, Wireless Rd.
City Map 8 E2.
Tel 0-2690-9999.

DJ Station
Silom Soi 2.
City Map 7 C4.
Tel 0-2266-4029.

Hard Rock Café
Siam Square.
City Map 7 C1.
Tel 0-2251-0797.

Moon Bar
Banyan Tree Hotel, South Sathorn Rd.
City Map 8 D4.
Tel 0-2679-1200.

Q Bar
Sukhumvit Soi 11.
Tel 0-2252-3274.

Saxophone
3/8 Victory Monument.
City Map 4 E3.
Tel 0-2246-5472.

Sky Bar
63rd Floor, lebua at State Tower, Silom Rd.
City Map 7 B4.
Tel 0-2624-9555.

Syn Bar
Swissotel Nai Lert Park, Wireless Rd.
City Map 8 E1.
Tel 0-2253-0123.

Telephone Pub
Silom Soi 4.
City Map 7 C4.
Tel 0-2234-3279.

BANGKOK STREET FINDER

Map references for *wats*, entertainment venues and other attractions in Bangkok refer to the Street Finder maps on the following pages. Map references are also provided for hotels *(see pp290–94)* and restaurants *(see pp318–22)* in Bangkok. The first figure in the map reference indicates which Street Finder map to turn to, and the letter and number which follow give the grid reference on that map. The lack of standard transliterations for Thai words means that street names listed here will not always match those seen on street signs. Most *thanons* (major roads) have many numbered (and sometimes named) *sois* and *troks* (minor roads and lanes) leading from them. Symbols used for sights and useful information are displayed in the key below.

The quickest way to get around Bangkok

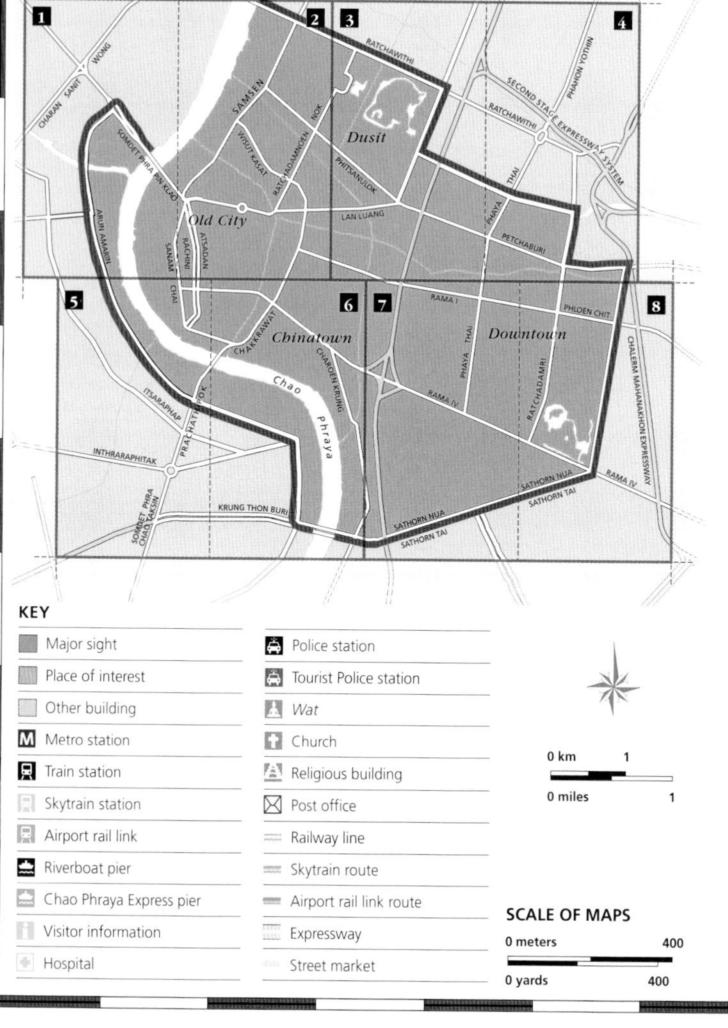

T

U

V

W

Y

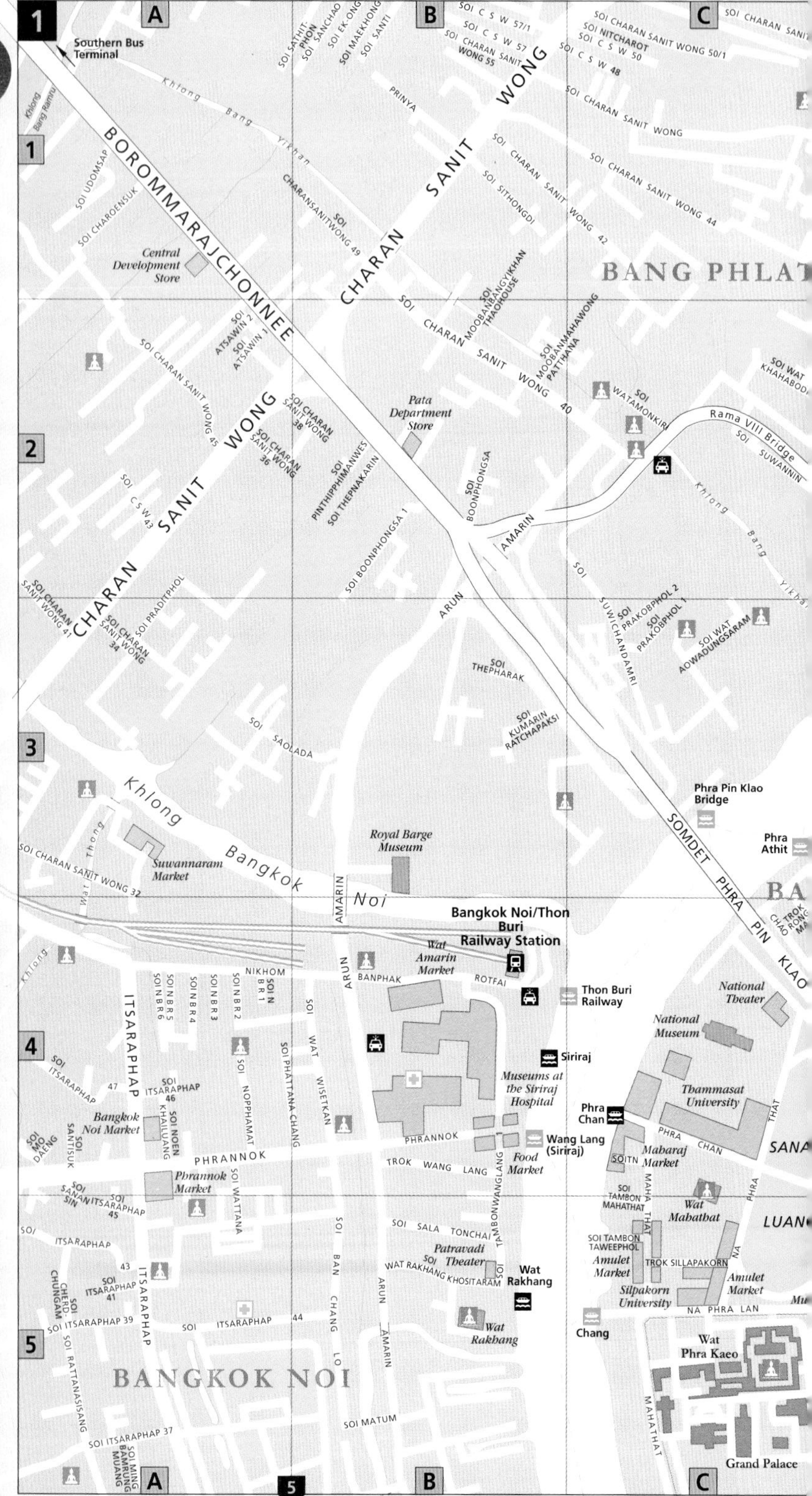

1
A
B
C
Southern Bus Terminal
Khlong Bang Ramru
Khlong Bang Yikhan
BOROMMARAJCHONNEE
CHARAN SANIT WONG
SOI UDOMSAP
SOI CHAROENSUK
Central Development Store
SOI SATHIT-PHON
SOI SANCHAO
SOI EK-ONG
SOI MAEKHONG
SOI SANTI
SOI C S W 57/1
SOI C S W 57
SOI CHARAN SANIT WONG 55
SOI CHARAN SANIT WONG 50/1
SOI NITCHAROT
SOI C S W 50
SOI C S W 48
SOI CHARAN SANIT WONG
SOI CHARAN SANIT WONG 44
SOI CHARAN SANIT WONG 42
SOI SITHONGDI
PRINYA
CHARANSANITWONG 49 SOI
BANG PHLAT
SOI MOOBANBANGYIKHAN THAOROUSE
SOI MOOBANMAHAWONG PATTHANA
SOI CHARAN SANIT WONG 40
SOI WAT KHAHABODI
SOI WATAMONKIRI
Rama VIII Bridge
SOI SUWANNIN
SOI ATSAWIN 2
SOI ATSAWIN 1
SOI CHARAN SANIT WONG 45
SOI CHARAN SANIT WONG 38
SOI CHARAN SANIT WONG 36
Pata Department Store
SOI PINTHIPPHIMANWES
SOI THEPNAKARIN
SOI BOONPHONGSA
SOI BOONPHONGSA 1
AMARIN
2
SOI C S W 43
SOI CHARAN SANIT WONG 41
SOI CHARAN SANIT WONG 34
SOI PRADITPHOL
ARUN
SOI SUWICHANDAMRI
SOI PRAKOBPHOL 2
SOI PRAKOBPHOL 1
SOI WAT AOWADUNGSARAM
SOI THEPHARAK
SOI KUMARIN RATCHAPAKSI
SOI SAOLADA
3
Khlong Bangkok Noi
Wat Thong
Suwannaram Market
SOI CHARAN SANIT WONG 32
Royal Barge Museum
Phra Pin Klao Bridge
Phra Athit
SOMDET PHRA PIN KLAO
Bangkok Noi/Thon Buri Railway Station
Wat Amarin Market
BANPHAK
ROTFAI
Thon Buri Railway
NIKHOM
SOI N BR 1
SOI NBR 5
SOI NBR 6
SOI NBR 4
SOI NBR 3
SOI NBR 2
ITSARAPHAP
SOI WAT WISETKAN
SOI PHATTANA CHANG
SOI NOPPHAMAT
National Theater
National Museum
4
Siriraj
Museums at the Siriraj Hospital
Thammasat University
Phra Chan
PHRA CHAN
SOI ITSARAPHAP 47
SOI ITSARAPHAP 46
SOI NOEN KHAILUANG
Bangkok Noi Market
SOI MO DAENG
SOI SANTISUK
PHRANNOK
Wang Lang (Siriraj)
TROK WANG LANG
Food Market
SOI TAMBONWANGLANG
Mabaraj Market
SOITN
SOI TAMBON MAHATHAT
MAHA THAT
Wat Mahathat
PHRA
SANAM
LUANG
Phrannok Market
SOI WATTANA
SOI SANANSIN
SOI ITSARAPHAP 45
SOI SALA TONCHAI
SOI BAN CHANG LO
SOI TAMBON TAWEEPHOL
Amulet Market
TROK SILLAPAKORN
NA PHRA LAN
Silpakorn University
Patravadi Theater
SOI WAT RAKHANG KHOSITARAM
Wat Rakhang
Wat Rakhang
Chang
SOI ITSARAPHAP 43
SOI ITSARAPHAP 41
SOI CHERD-CHUNGAM
SOI ITSARAPHAP 39
SOI ITSARAPHAP 44
SOI RATTANASISANG
Wat Phra Kaeo
5
BANGKOK NOI
MAHATHAT
SOI MATUM
SOI ITSARAPHAP 37
SOI MING BAMRUNG MUANG
Grand Palace
5

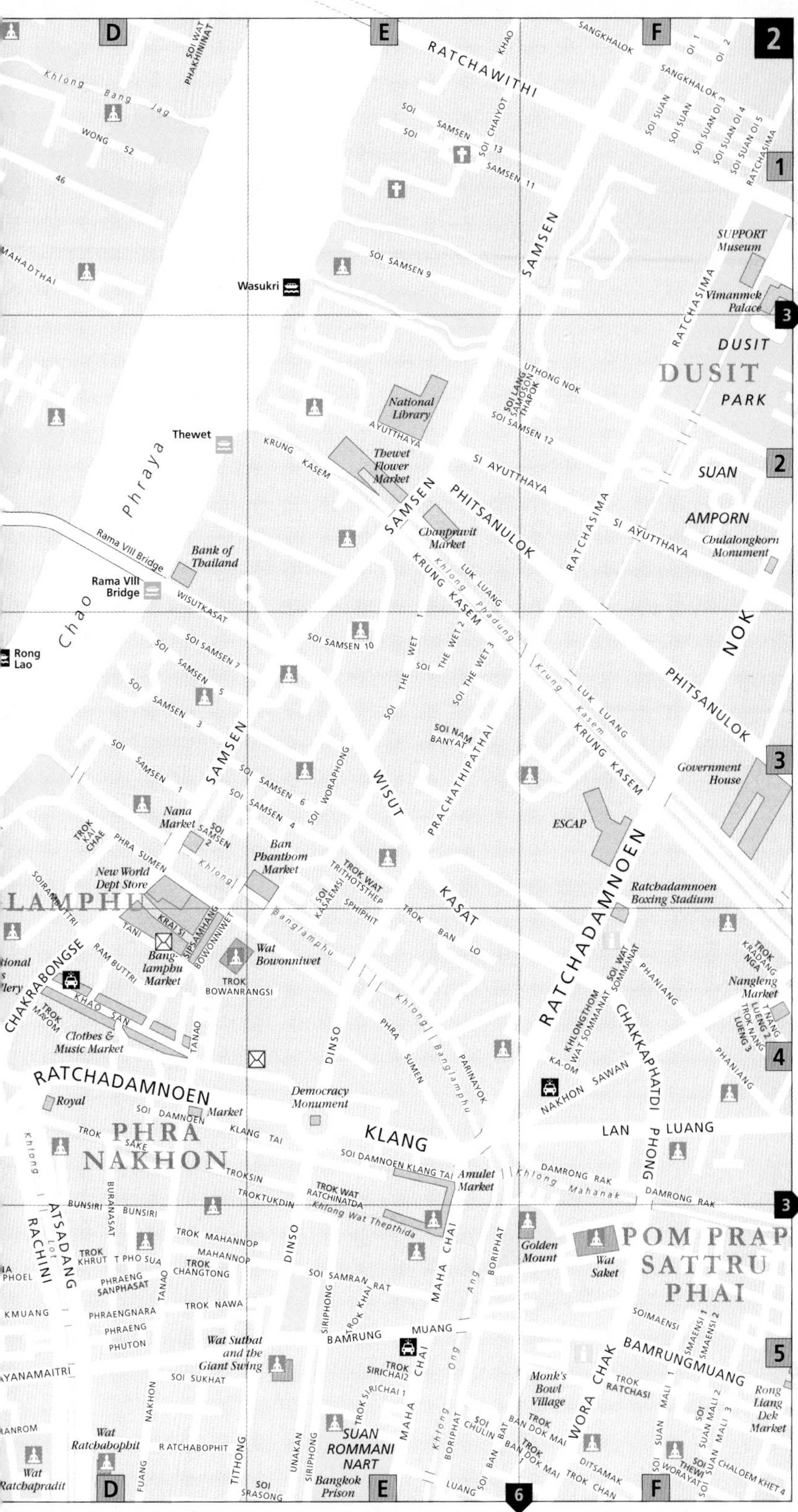

D
E
F
2
1
2
3
4
5
RATCHAWITHI
SAMSEN
Wasukri
Thewet
Chao Phraya
Rama VIII Bridge
Bank of Thailand
National Library
Thewet Flower Market
Chanpravit Market
PHITSANULOK
KRUNG KASEM
SUPPORT Museum
Vimanmek Palace
DUSIT
DUSIT PARK
SUAN AMPORN
Chulalongkorn Monument
RATCHASIMA
SI AYUTTHAYA
NOK
Government House
ESCAP
Ratchadamnoen Boxing Stadium
RATCHADAMNOEN
WISUT KASAT
PRACHATHIPATHAI
Nana Market
New World Dept Store
Ban Phanthom Market
Banglamphu Market
Wat Bowonniwet
CHAKRABONGSE
KHAO SAN
Clothes & Music Market
RATCHADAMNOEN KLANG
Democracy Monument
Royal
PHRA NAKHON
Amulet Market
Golden Mount
Wat Saket
POM PRAP SATTRU PHAI
Nangleng Market
Wat Suthat and the Giant Swing
Wat Ratchabophit
Wat Ratchapradit
SUAN ROMMANI NART
Bangkok Prison
Monk's Bowl Village
Rong Liang Dek Market
BAMRUNGMUANG
Rong Lao
LAMPHU
6

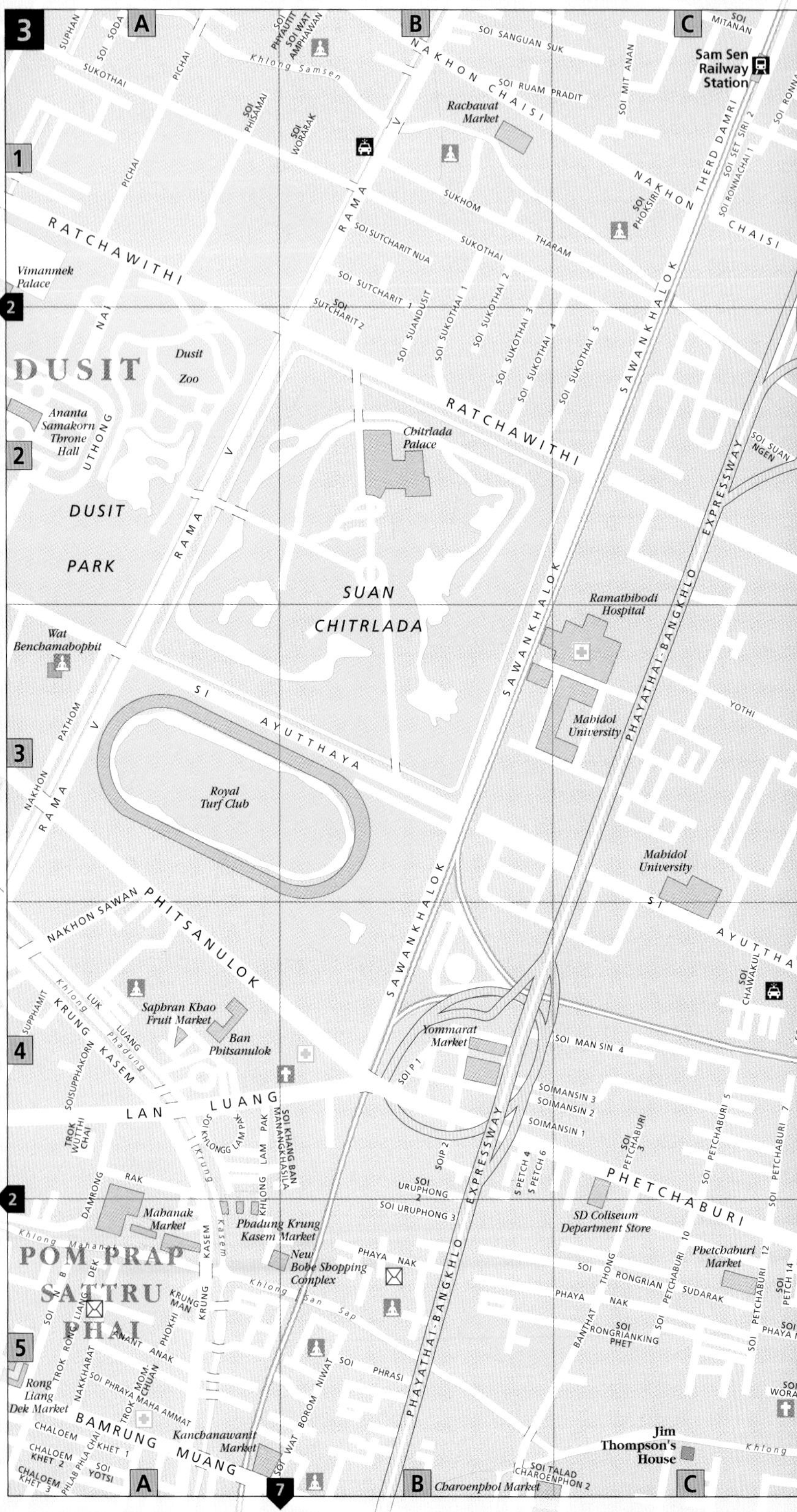

3
A
B
C
1
2
3
4
5
Sam Sen Railway Station
Rachawat Market
Vimanmek Palace
DUSIT
Dusit Zoo
Ananta Samakorn Throne Hall
DUSIT PARK
Chitrlada Palace
SUAN CHITRLADA
Ramathibodi Hospital
Mahidol University
Wat Benchamabophit
Royal Turf Club
Mahidol University
Saphran Khao Fruit Market
Ban Phitsanulok
Yommarat Market
SD Coliseum Department Store
Phetchaburi Market
Mahanak Market
Phadung Krung Kasem Market
New Bobe Shopping Complex
POM PRAP SATTRU PHAI
Rong Liang Dek Market
Kanchanawanit Market
Jim Thompson's House
Charoenphol Market
RATCHAWITHI
NAKHON CHAISI
SUKHOTHAI
SUKHOM
THARAM
RAMA V
SAWANKHALOK
PHAYATHAI-BANGKHLO EXPRESSWAY
THERD DAMRI
SI AYUTTHAYA
NAKHON PATHOM
NAKHON SAWAN
PHITSANULOK
KRUNG KASEM
LAN LUANG
PHETCHABURI
BAMRUNG MUANG
UTHONG NAI
PICHAI
SUPHAN
SOI SODA
YOTHI
DAMRONG RAK
PHAYA NAK
PHRASI
Khlong Samsen
Khlong Phadung Krung Kasem
Khlong Mahanak
Khlong San Sap
2
7

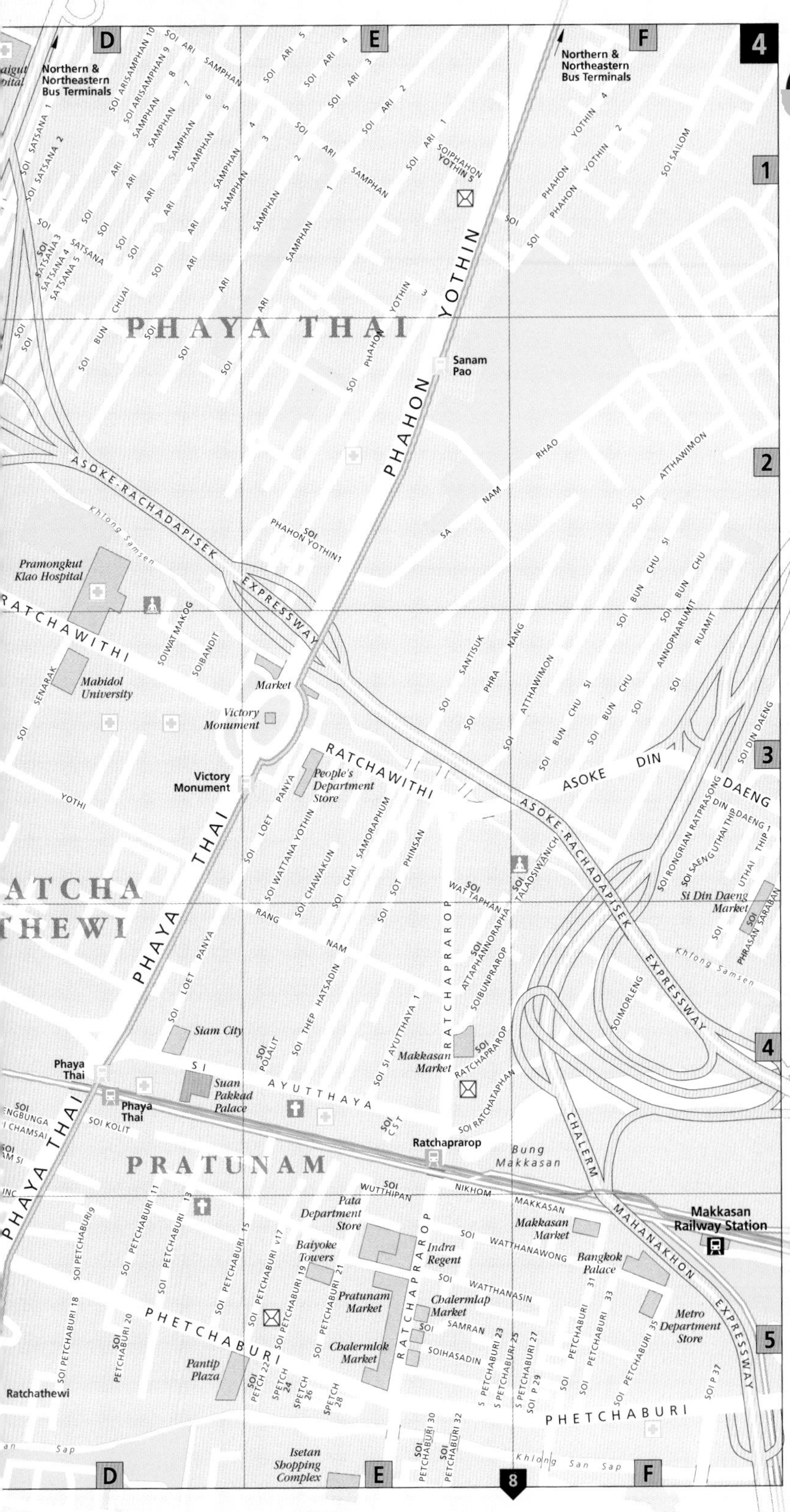

D
E
F
4
1
2
3
4
5
Northern & Northeastern Bus Terminals
Northern & Northeastern Bus Terminals
PHAYA THAI
PHAHON YOTHIN
Sanam Pao
ASOKE-RACHADAPISEK EXPRESSWAY
Khlong Samsen
Pramongkut Klao Hospital
RATCHAWITHI
Mahidol University
Market
Victory Monument
Victory Monument
People's Department Store
RATCHAWITHI
ASOKE DIN DAENG
ATCHA THEWI
PHAYA THAI
Si Din Daeng Market
Siam City
Makkasan Market
Phaya Thai
Phaya Thai
Suan Pakkad Palace
SI AYUTTHAYA
Ratchaprarop
Bung Makkasan
CHALERM MAHANAKHON EXPRESSWAY
PRATUNAM
NIKHOM MAKKASAN
Pata Department Store
Baiyoke Towers
Indra Regent
Makkasan Market
Makkasan Railway Station
Bangkok Palace
Pratunam Market
Chalermlap Market
Metro Department Store
Chalermlok Market
PHETCHABURI
Pantip Plaza
Ratchathewi
RATCHAPRAROP
PHETCHABURI
Khlong San Sap
Isetan Shopping Complex
D
E
F
8

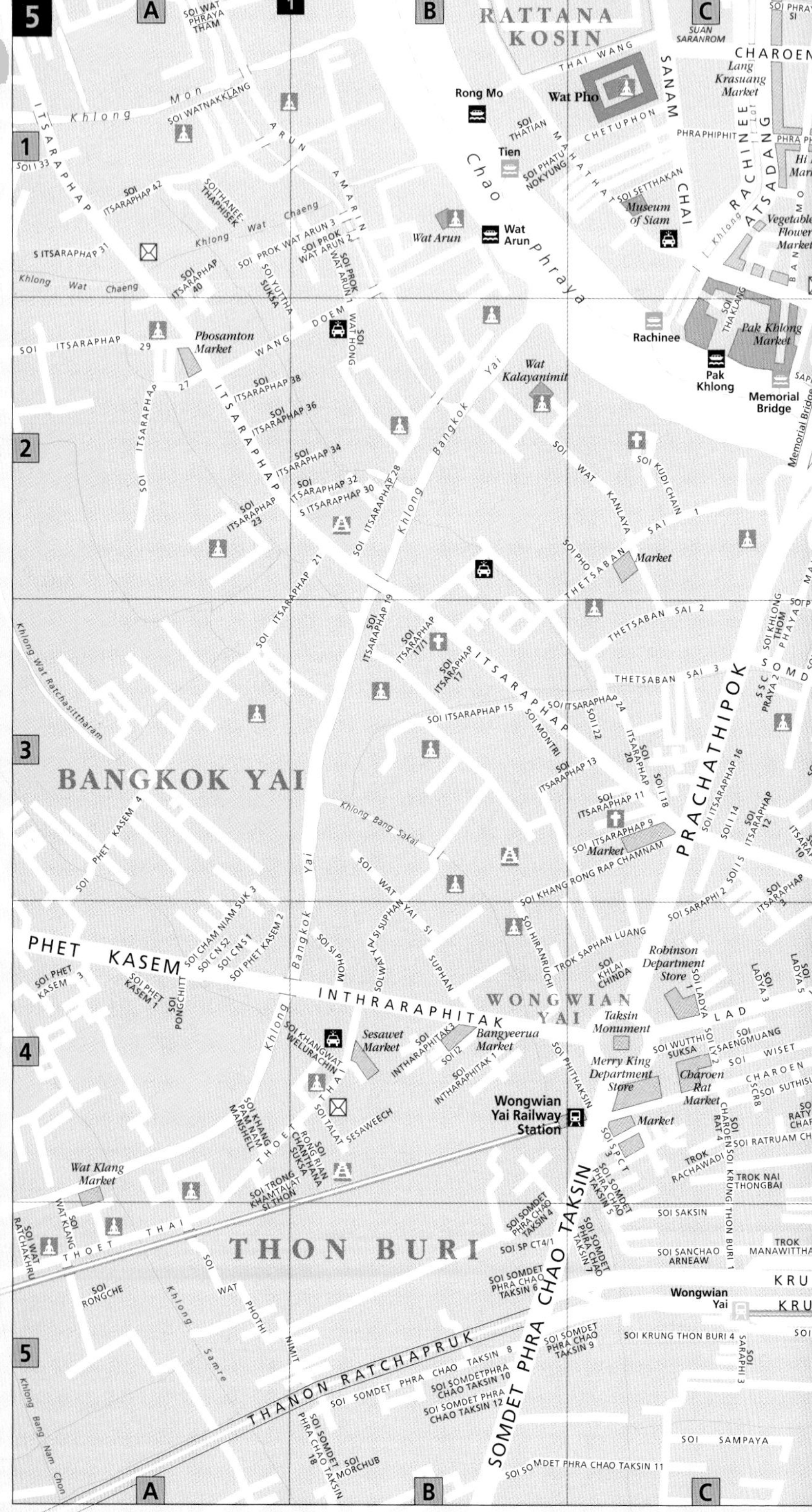

5
A
B
C
1
2
3
4
5
RATTANA KOSIN
BANGKOK YAI
THON BURI
WONGWIAN YAI
Wat Pho
Rong Mo
Tien
Wat Arun
Museum of Siam
Rachinee
Pak Khlong
Pak Khlong Market
Memorial Bridge
Lang Krasuang Market
Vegetable Flower Market
Wat Kalayanimit
Phosamton Market
Market
Robinson Department Store
Taksin Monument
Merry King Department Store
Charoen Rat Market
Wongwian Yai Railway Station
Sesawet Market
Bangyeerua Market
Wat Klang Market
Wongwian Yai
Chao Phraya
PHET KASEM
INTHRARAPHITAK
PRACHATHIPOK
SOMDET PHRA CHAO TAKSIN
THANON RATCHAPRUK
ITSARAPHAP
Khlong Bangkok Yai
Khlong Mon
Khlong Wat Chaeng
Khlong Wat Ratchasittharam
Khlong Bang Sakai
Khlong Samre
Khlong Bang Nam Chon
THETSABAN SAI 1
THETSABAN SAI 2
THETSABAN SAI 3

D
E
F
2
6
1
2
3
4
5
7
CHINATOWN
HAHURAT
SAMPHAN
THAWONG
KHLONG SAN
CHAROEN KRUNG (NEW ROAD)
CHAKKRAWAT
YAOWARAT
RAMA IV
SOMDET CHAO PRAYA
LAD YA
ITSARAPHAP
CHAROEN NAKHON
KRUNG THONBURI
Chao Phraya
Sala Chalermkrung Theater
Central Super-market
Merry Kings Dept Store
Central Market
Central Dept Store
Phahurat Market
Nakorn Kasem
Sampeng Market
Khlong Thom Market
Central Hospital
Cathay Department Store
Mai Market
Kao Market
Wat Traimit
Ratchawongse
Din Daeng
Wongwian Lek Market
Song Sawat
Wat Thong
Chakkawat Market
Market
Swat Market
Harbor Department
River City Complex
Khlong San
River City
Millenium Hilton Hotel
Royal Orchid Sheraton
Si Phraya
Krom Prisanee
Central Post Office
Wat Muang Kae
Mandarin Oriental
Oriental Plaza
Oriental
Peninsula Hotel
Shangri-La
Dumake
Bangkok Shopping Complex
Bangrak Market
Taksin Bridge
Saphan Taksin
Sathorn (Central)
Supphakan Shopping Complex
Krung Thonburi
Khlong Phadung Krung Kasem

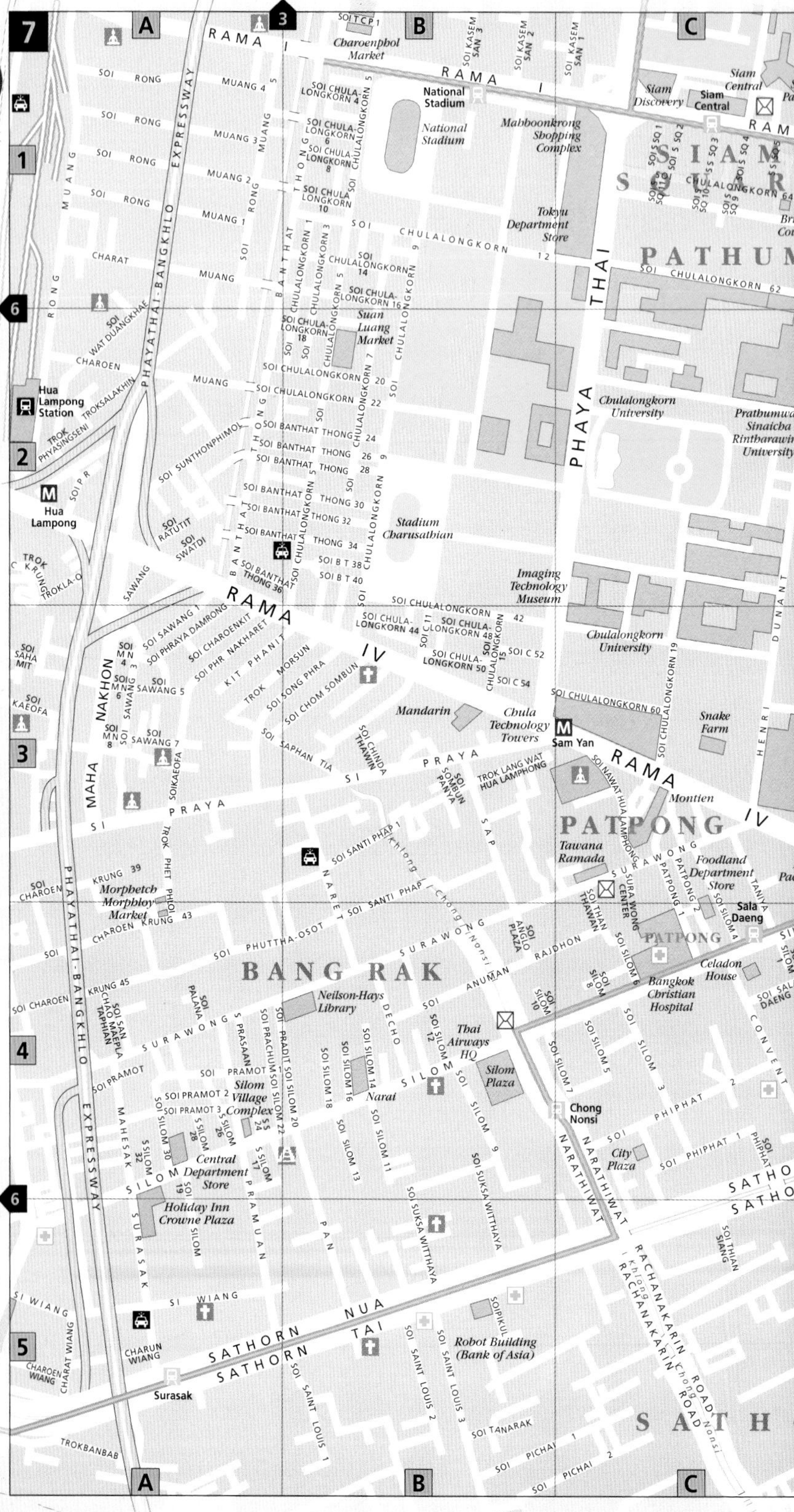

7
A
B
C
1
2
3
4
5
6
RAMA I
Charoenphol Market
National Stadium
Mahboonkrong Shopping Complex
Siam Discovery
Siam Central
SIAM SQUARE
Tokyu Department Store
PATHUM
SOI CHULALONGKORN 62
PHAYA THAI
EXPRESSWAY
PHAYATHAI-BANGKHLO
Suan Luang Market
Hua Lampong Station
Hua Lampong
Chulalongkorn University
Prathumwan Sinaicha Rinthbarawin University
Stadium Charusathian
Imaging Technology Museum
RAMA IV
DUNANT
HENRI
Mandarin
Chula Technology Towers
Sam Yan
Snake Farm
Montien
PATPONG
Tawana Ramada
Foodland Department Store
Sala Daeng
SI PRAYA
MAHA NAKHON
Morphetch Morphloy Market
BANG RAK
SURAWONG
Neilson-Hays Library
Thai Airways HQ
Silom Plaza
Silom Village Complex
Narai
Central Department Store
Holiday Inn Crowne Plaza
Bangkok Christian Hospital
Celadon House
CONVENT
Chong Nonsi
City Plaza
NARATHIWAT
RACHANAKARIN ROAD
SATHORN
SATHORN NUA
SATHORN TAI
Robot Building (Bank of Asia)
Surasak
SOI SAINT LOUIS 1
SOI SAINT LOUIS 2
SOI SAINT LOUIS 3
SOI TANARAK
SOI PICHAI 1
SOI PICHAI 2
TROKBANBAB
SAPHAN TIA
CHAROEN KRUNG
SOI PRAMOT
SURASAK
PRAMUAN
SI WIANG
SOI SUKSA WITTHAYA

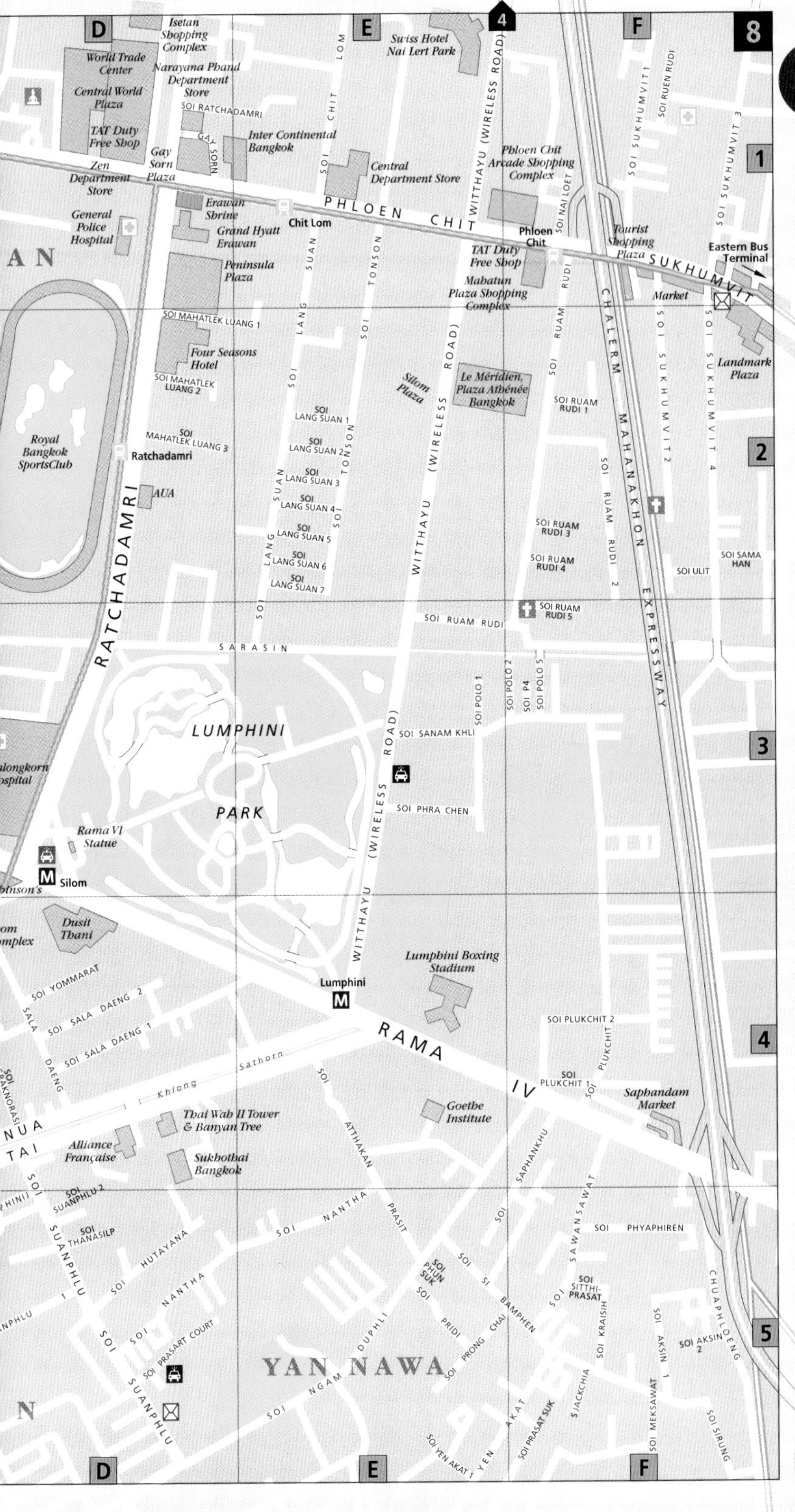

8
D
E
F
4
1
2
3
4
5
Isetan Shopping Complex
World Trade Center
Central World Plaza
TAT Duty Free Shop
Narayana Phand Department Store
Swiss Hotel Nai Lert Park
Inter Continental Bangkok
Gay Sorn Plaza
Zen Department Store
Central Department Store
Phloen Chit Arcade Shopping Complex
General Police Hospital
Erawan Shrine
Grand Hyatt Erawan
Chit Lom
Phloen Chit
Tourist Shopping Plaza
Eastern Bus Terminal
TAT Duty Free Shop
Mahatun Plaza Shopping Complex
Market
Peninsula Plaza
Four Seasons Hotel
Silom Plaza
Le Méridien, Plaza Athénée Bangkok
Landmark Plaza
Royal Bangkok SportsClub
Ratchadamri
AUA
LUMPHINI PARK
Rama VI Statue
Silom
Dusit Thani
Lumphini
Lumphini Boxing Stadium
Saphandam Market
Goethe Institute
Thai Wah II Tower & Banyan Tree
Alliance Française
Sukhothai Bangkok
YAN NAWA
PHLOEN CHIT
SUKHUMVIT
RATCHADAMRI
WITTHAYU (WIRELESS ROAD)
CHALERM MAHANAKHON EXPRESSWAY
RAMA IV
SARASIN
Khlong Sathorn
SOI RATCHADAMRI
SOI CHIT LOM
SOI LANG SUAN
SOI TONSON
SOI NAI LOET
SOI RUAM RUDI
SOI MAHATLEK LUANG 1
SOI MAHATLEK LUANG 2
SOI MAHATLEK LUANG 3
SOI LANG SUAN 1
SOI LANG SUAN 2
SOI LANG SUAN 3
SOI LANG SUAN 4
SOI LANG SUAN 5
SOI LANG SUAN 6
SOI LANG SUAN 7
SOI RUAM RUDI 1
SOI RUAM RUDI 2
SOI RUAM RUDI 3
SOI RUAM RUDI 4
SOI RUAM RUDI 5
SOI SUKHUMVIT 1
SOI SUKHUMVIT 2
SOI SUKHUMVIT 3
SOI SUKHUMVIT 4
SOI RUEN RUDI
SOI SAMA HAN
SOI ULIT
SOI POLO 1
SOI POLO 2
SOI P4
SOI POLO 5
SOI SANAM KHLI
SOI PHRA CHEN
SOI YOMMARAT
SALA DAENG
SOI SALA DAENG 2
SOI SALA DAENG 1
SOI PLUKCHIT 1
SOI PLUKCHIT 2
SOI ATTHAKAN PRASIT
SOI SAPHANKHU
SOI SAWANSAWAT
SOI PHYAPHIREN
SOI NANTHA
SOI HUTAYANA
SOI SUANPHLU 2
SOI THANASILP
SUANPHLU
SOI PRASART COURT
SOI PHUN SUK
SOI SI BAMPHEN
SOI PRIDI
SOI PRONG CHAI
SOI SITTHI-PRASAT
SOI KRAISIH
SOI AKSIN 1
SOI AKSIN 2
CHUAPHLOENG
SOI NGAM DUPHLI
SOI YEN AKAT
SOI YEN AKAT 1
SOI PRASAT SUK
SJACKCHIA
SOI MEKSAWAT
SOI SIRUNG

EASTERN SEABOARD

Thailand's Eastern Seaboard is a region of contrasts. While it is the nation's most developed region with ports, oil refineries, and industrial complexes, it is also home to picturesque and untouched islands. Travelers can explore the varied dimensions of this region, which include commercial resorts, verdant archipelagos with pristine beaches of white sand, and little-visited national parks, all of which lie within easy reach of Bangkok.

Stretching from Bangkok to the Cambodian border, the Eastern Seaboard was originally a frontier between the Khmer and Sukhothai empires in the 15th century. As the Khmer empire declined, ethnic Tais settled here attracted by the region's natural resources. They were joined by Vietnamese refugees fleeing persecution in Cambodia in the 19th century.

Industrial development in this area is aided by its proximity to Bangkok. The older occupations of gem-mining and fishing coexist with the newer oil and tourism industries. Good road links have helped in economic growth as well as tourism. However, this also has a downside, as many of the beaches have become too crowded. Visitors can head south farther away from Bangkok, to the less popular resorts such as Sri Racha, famous for its seafood, or to the stunning Nam Tok Phliw or Khao Kitchakut national parks whose interiors shelter a wealth of flora and fauna. Pattaya continues to attract crowds of visitors to its go-go bars, restaurants, and raucous nightclubs. However, more intrepid travelers can go diving among Ko Chang's reefs or relax on its pristine beaches. Ko Samet is a popular weekend destination from Bangkok, while those interested in traditional Thai crafts can head to Chanthaburi's historical gem market to see the spectacular collection of gemstones.

With its vibrant nightlife, neon-lit streets, luxury resorts, virgin beaches, and traditional fishing villages, the Eastern Seaboard holds a wealth of attractions for a first-time visitor.

Gaudy neon signs hanging overhead, along the famous Walking Street in South Pattaya

◁ Holiday-makers relaxing in a thatched beachside restaurant-bar in Ko Chang

Exploring the Eastern Seaboard

Blessed with miles of idyllic beaches and warm temperatures, the Eastern Seaboard is a sun lover's paradise. Visitors can choose to just unwind and enjoy the local food or try some of the many available watersports. Beach resorts range from busy Pattaya, with its lively nightlife, to lesser-known islands such as Ko Chang, part of a stunning national marine park. Other national parks such as Khao Kitchakut and Nam Tok Phliw are characterized by tropical forests, mountains, and waterfalls, and are home to a wealth of wildlife. The main town in the area is Chanthaburi, center of the thriving gem-mining industry.

Thai-style pavilion with landscaping at Nong Nooch Tropical Garden

SIGHTS AT A GLANCE

Towns and Villages

Ban Hat Lek 20
Bang Saen 2
Chanthaburi pp114–15 9
Chonburi 1
Laem Ngop 13
Pattaya pp104–8 7
Sri Racha 4
Trat 12

National Parks and Zoos

Khao Khieo Zoo 3
Khao Kitchakut National Park 10
Nam Tok Phliw National Park 11
Sri Racha Tiger Zoo 5

Beaches and Islands

Hat Ban Chuen 19
Hat Sai Kaew 16
Hat Sai Ngam 15
Hat Samran 18
Hat Thap Thim 17
Ko Chang pp118–26 14
Ko Samet pp110–13 8
Ko Si Chang pp102–3 6

SEE ALSO

• ***Where to Stay*** pp294–8

• ***Where to Eat*** pp322–4

Sunbathing on the beaches of South Pattaya

GETTING AROUND

The Eastern Seaboard has a comprehensive transport system with the bigger islands well connected not only to each other, but also to the mainland. A twice daily train service runs from Hua Lampong Station in Bangkok to Sri Racha and Pattaya, while Trat is served by a domestic airport. Buses are the easiest way to get around the region – there is a regular service from Bangkok's Eastern Bus Terminal to the main towns. For places not on bus routes, *songthaews* are available. On the mainland, transportation is provided by *songthaews*, and tuk-tuks. Several ferries leave Ban Phe each day for Ko Samet. On the island, *songthaews* serve the main beaches, and longtail boats can be hired to reach surrounding islands. Ko Chang and Ko Mak are reached by ferry from Laem Ngop, but infrastructure on these islands is poor.

Locals fishing on the pier at Sattahip

KEY

- Expressway
- Major road
- Minor road
- Railway
- International border
- Peak

Tamun
Laem
Khao Soi Dao Nua 5,138 ft
Non Kha
Khao Soi Dao Nua Wildlife Sanctuary
Khao Chamao Khao Wong National Park
Khao Chamao 3,360 ft
Pong Nam Ron
Nam Khun
Nong Samet
10 KHAO KITCHAKUT NATIONAL PARK
Nong Chek Soi
Klaeng
3
317
Klong Krabi
Pak Nam Prasae
Wat Khao Sukim
Nong Khala
Makham
Ko Man Klang
Tha Mai
9 CHANTHABURI
Chang Thun
Bo Rai
Ko Man Nok
11 NAM TOK PHLIW NATIONAL PARK
Dan Chumpon
Khlung
Tha Chot
3
Khao Saming
Bang Kradan
Bang Noen Sung
TRAT 12
318
LAEM NGOP 13
15 HAT SAI NGAM
14
KO CHANG
Laem Sok
16 HAT SAI KAEW
HAT THAP THIM 17
18 HAT SAMRAN
Ban Mai Rut
Ko Wai
HAT BAN CHUEN 19
Ko Kham
Ko Mak
Ko Rang
318
0 km 15
0 miles 15
Ko Kut
Khlong Yai
BAN HAT LEK 20

Beautiful white flamingoes, one of the many bird species found at the Khao Khieo Zoo

Chonburi ❶

ชลบุรี

Road Map D1. 50 miles (80 km) SE of Bangkok. 250,000. *Chonburi Water Buffalo Racing (Oct).*

Capital of the Chonburi province and hub of the Eastern Seaboard's industrial zone, Chonburi has earned itself the epithet "Thailand's Detroit". The town's **Nacha Sa Thai Chue Shrine**, a four-story building located near the river pier, draws large crowds. This brightly colored Chinese temple houses several deities. The **Wat Yai Inthraram**, located near the old market, belongs to the Ayutthaya period *(see pp40–41)* as is evident from the architecture of its *bot* and *wihan*. The *wat's* hightlight is a series of beautiful murals adorning the walls of the *bot*. Another temple, **Wat Dhamma Nimitr**, which houses a 121-ft (37-m) high image of the Buddha covered in gold mosaic tiles, is also well worth a visit.

Bang Saen ❷

บางแสน

Road Map D1. 9 miles (14 km) SW of Chonburi. *25,000.*

This pleasant beachfront town makes for an ideal day trip, and is a favorite destination for Thais seeking an escape from the big cities and their endless suburbs. It is not unusual to find entire families from Bangkok vacationing here; weekends are especially busy. Kids play fully clothed in the warm waters of Hat Bang Saen (Thais prize pale skin and usually avoid sunbathing), while adults, especially women, can be found huddling under parasols on the sand, enjoying their picnics. The beach is an ideal place for a walk, particularly at dusk. This is the time when vendors start grilling seafood along the boardwalk. Deck chairs, inflatable tyres, and bicycles are available for hire.

Nong Mon market, near the center of the town, has stalls offering produce from every corner of Thailand. Highly recommended is the delectable *khao larm* – a traditional dessert made of sweet sticky rice, coconut milk, taro, bananas, and peanuts – served in a bamboo cylinder.

Bang Saen does not have much of a nightlife and is quiet in the evenings – an ideal alternative to nearby Pattaya *(see p104–8).*

Vacationers relaxing under colorful umbrellas on pleasant Hat Bang Saen

Khao Khieo Zoo ❸

สวนสัตว์เขาเขียว

Road Map D1. Off Route 344, 10 miles (16 km) SE of Chonburi. ***Tel*** *0-3829-8195.* *8am–6pm daily; night safari till 9pm.*

This open zoo has over 50 species of birds and animals, including flamingoes, deer, gibbons, zebras, snakes, and tigers. The animals inhabit spacious enclosures, while birds are kept in a large aviary. There is a separate section from where visitors, including children, can buy food to feed the sheep, deer, turtles, and other animals. The night safari, which goes on till 9pm, is an added attraction.

Covering an area of 3 sq miles (8 sq km), a day at the zoo can mean a lot of walking. It is advisable to hire a bicycle or make use of the trams that chug through the park.

The wild marshland of **Bang Phra Reservoir**, 12 miles (19 km) south of Khao Khieo, is an ornithologist's haven, where the brown-spotted whimbrel, among other species, can be seen during the cool season *(see p36)*.

Fierce competition during the Water Buffalo Racing, Chonburi

CHONBURI WATER BUFFALO RACING

Thailand's version of the Kentucky Derby comes in the form of the three-day-long, bareback water buffalo racing competition, which takes place in October every year. Riding for trophies and prizes, the jockeys and cheering crowds take the event quite seriously, with a lot of illegal betting happening on the side. The buffaloes are whipped to get them to start sprinting, and the furious animals often throw the jockeys right off their backs. The event takes place in front of the Chonburi Town Hall and features buffalo strength competitions, a Miss Farmer beauty contest, and an outrageous, yet unique, buffalo "fashion show".

Local delicacies on display at a seafood stall, Sri Racha

Sri Racha ❹

ศรีราชา

Road Map D1. 12 miles (19 km) S of Chonburi. 20,000. *Songkran Si Maha Racha Festival (Apr 19–21). (Rice offerings to spirits).*

Famous for its seafood and the spicy *nam prik si racha* (Sri Racha pepper sauce) – Thailand's answer to Tabasco sauce – this sleepy seaside town is the jumping-off point for trips to Ko Si Chang *(see pp102–3)*. Several piers run off Jermjompol Road, Sri Racha's main waterfront street. At the end of each pier are breezy open-air restaurants, ideal for sampling delicious local delicacies such as *hoi nang rom* (oysters) and *hoi thot* (fried mussels) dipped in the famous fiery sauce.

Sri Racha Tiger Zoo ❺

สวนเสือศรีราชา

Road Map D1. 6 miles (10 km) SE of Sri Racha. ***Tel*** *0-3829-6556-8.* *8am–6pm daily.* **www**.tigerzoo.com

With probably the largest collection of tigers in the world, the Sri Racha Tiger Zoo is worth a visit, especially for families with children. Apart from the 400 beautifully groomed Royal Bengal tigers, the zoo also houses Indian elephants, birds and animals such as ostriches and wallabies, and over 10,000 crocodiles. Its accompanying circus features crocodile wrestling; the record-breaking Scorpion Queen, who poses for photographs covered in deadly scorpions; and some hilarious dancing hogs.

The zoo's restaurant serves a variety of dishes made from crocodile, scorpion, and other exotic curiosities, designed chiefly to appeal to the palates of visitors from countries such as China and Korea.

There is also a shop selling memorabilia such as T-shirts, mugs, and wall-hangings. The zoo can be reached by tuk-tuk from Sri Racha.

A fully grown Royal Bengal tiger at the Sri Racha Tiger Zoo

Ko Si Chang ❻

เกาะสีชัง

Laughing Buddha statue

A small and lovely island getaway, Ko Si Chang's rugged coastline has few coves or beaches, but is surrounded by clear waters that attract divers. The island has royal associations as it was the summer retreat of several kings of the Chakri Dynasty as well as an erstwhile French colony for a brief period in 1893 and still retains traces of this heritage. Several ruins stand testament to the history of the island which was once a customs check-point for Bangkok-bound ships. Ko Si Chang, today, is a quiet holiday spot resplendent in its natural beauty, home to a variety of nesting seabirds and the yellow squirrel which is endemic here.

Visitors sunbathing at Ko Si Chang's bustling beach, Hat Tham Pang

Saan Chao Paw Khao Yai

ศาลเจ้าพ่อเขาใหญ่

dawn to dusk daily.

An aura of mystery surrounds this colorful, multitiered Chinese temple, which dates back to the Chinese Ming dynasty (1368–1644). It is commonly believed that a shrine was built at this site by Chinese seafarers after they spotted a light shining from a cave, which they used as a makeshift lighthouse for navigation and which kept them safe. The temple was built some time later, mainly for Chinese pilgrims. A steep flight of stairs leads up to the temple and offers picturesque views of the sea and the harbor. Visitors can also explore other caves in the area, many of which have been turned into shrines. The Chinese New Year *(see p37)* is the biggest festival here, drawing large crowds.

A trail from the temple leads to a small shrine housing what locals claim is the Buddha's footprint.

Wat Tham Yai Prik

วัดถ้ำยายปริก

Tel *0-3821-6104.* *8am–6pm daily.* **www**.watthamyaiprik.com

Also known as the Tham Yai Prik Vipassana Meditation Center, this monastery is built into a series of limestone caves. The monastery was discovered by the highly revered Buddhist monk, Prasit Thavaro, in 1970. He added to its existing spartan form, nearly rebuilding the entire structure along with his monks. His teachings revolved around a self sufficient existence and inner peace that are still practised at the monastery. The monks tend to a vegetable garden set up by Thavaro that provides for the whole monastery. He died in 2007 and his body was embalmed and kept for a year before it was cremated. A relic has been preserved for devotees to pay their respects.

Devotee offering prayers at the temple of Saan Chao Paw Khao Yai

Hat Tham Pang

หาดถ้ำพัง

A backpackers' hangout, Hat Tham Pang is a thin and long crescent of white sand on the west coast of the island. This is Ko Si Chang's only real beach, with a few guesthouses and beachfront restaurants serving local delicacies as well as Western food. Visitors can also avail of camping facilities. This beach can be reached by motorized *samlors* (bicycle rickshaws) from the pier. These take 30 minutes and cost around 80 baht. Deck-chairs, umbrellas, kayaks, and snorkeling gear can be easily hired on this beach. The clear waters are good for snorkeling but enthusiasts usually head south for a more dazzling array of corals.

For hotels and restaurants in this region see pp294–8 and pp322–4

Palace of Rama V

วังรัชกาลที่ห้า

9am–5pm daily.

The overgrown ruins of this 19th-century palace, also known as Phra Chutathut Ratchasathan, are currently under renovation. This golden teak palace was designed by Rama V (1868–1910) who used it as a sanctuary for members of the royal family in summer. The ruins are of particular interest to visitors who have seen the grand Vimanmek Mansion *(see p71)* in Bangkok. The structure was originally located at this site until it was moved, in 1901, to Dusit Park.

Surrounded by lotus ponds and frangipani trees, a visit to these ruins can take up to half a day. One of the restored villas has a display of Rama V's memorabilia and a new site under construction aims to symbolize the king's association with Ko Si Chang. Rama V's birthday is celebrated here in a grand manner with a *son et lumière* show and a beauty pageant showcasing period fashions.

Wat Atsadang

วัดอัษฎางค์

dawn to dusk daily.

Located on top of a hill, close to the ruins of the Palace of Rama V, is Wat Atsadang with its distinctive white *chedi*. The temple is best explored on foot while exploring the palace ruins. The *wat*, the only part of the palace complex that remains intact, is quite unusual in its architecture. It has a Sri Lankan-style round *chedi* while the *bot* and the pagoda are constructed in European style with stained-glass windows.

The ornate gateway of the Palace of Rama V at Ko Si Chang

Tourist speedboat anchored in the waters off Hat Sai Kaew

Hat Sai Kaew

หาดทรายแก้ว

Also known as Crystal Beach, Hat Sai Kaew is a remote beach on the island's east coast. Best reached by *samlors* from the pier, the beach is an ideal picnic spot. A handful of restaurants and shops have sprung up in recent times along with a few other facilities. These include Thai massages as well as fresh seafood barbecued right on the beach. Hat Sai Kaew is an ideal snorkeling base for the tiny islands near the southern tip of the island. On a calm day, snorkelers can follow the rocky coastline southward to view the rich coral reefs teeming with a variety of marine animals.

VISITORS' CHECKLIST

Road Map D1. 8 miles (13 km) W of Sri Racha. *6,000.* *TAT, Pattaya (0-3842-7667).* *from Sri Racha.* *Chinese New Year (Jan–Feb); Rama V Festival (Sep).*

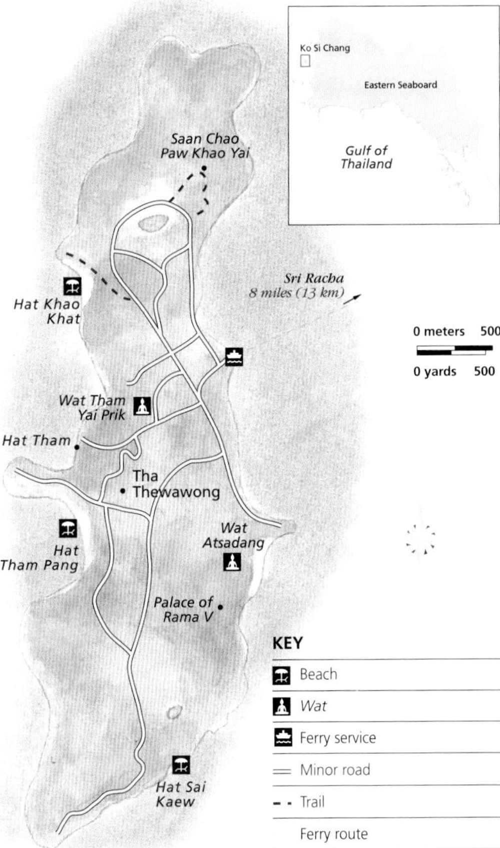

Pattaya 7

พัทยา

Originally a quiet fishing village, Pattaya, was transformed in the 1960s and 1970s by the arrival of US servicemen on R&R (Rest and Recreation) during the Vietnam War. Its subsequent reputation was built on the sex trade, and the industry continues to thrive; but today, Pattaya has much more to offer. With more than 5 million visitors a year, it has emerged as Thailand's premier resort. Upscale hotels, restaurants, theme parks, adventure sports, numerous golf courses, and cabaret shows are just a few of its many attractions. A watersport enthusiast's haven, windsurfing and kiteboarding are especially popular in Pattaya.

Entrance to Crocodile Farm

Jet skis parked along Hat Pattaya as their riders take a break

Hat Pattaya

หาดพัทยา

A perfect tropical paradise at one time, Hat Pattaya is barely recognizable today. This 2-mile (3-km) long beach is usually packed with sunbathers, especially on the weekends. Having earned a seedy reputation and the nickname "Patpong by the Sea," it is more frequented by youngsters, who spend time in go-go clubs, bars, and massage parlors, than vacationing families. Among Hat Pattaya's most prominent features, the ever popular transvestite shows, have venues mainly at the northern end of the beach.

The Beach Road, which runs along the length of Hat Pattaya, overflows with food joints, bars, and shopping malls. Visitors can try a variety of watersports such as parasailing, kayaking, and scuba diving, besides other activities such as golf and tennis.

Sanctuary of Truth

ปราสาทสัจธรรม

206/2 Moo 5, Naklua Soi 12, Pattaya-Naklua Rd. ***Tel*** *0-3836-7229.* *8am–6pm daily.* **www**.sanctuaryoftruth.com

This magnificent teakwood temple stands 345-ft (105-m) high on the shoreline between Hat Pattaya and Ao Naklua. Every square inch of its architecture is carved with intricate figures reminiscent of Cambodian, Hindu, Buddhist, Chinese, and Thai religion and mythology.

Carved figure, Sanctuary of Truth

The temple complex hosts a variety of other activities such as dolphin training, horseback riding, and speedboat excursions. Visitors can also watch classical Thai dance performances while dining.

Ao Naklua

อ่าวนาเกลือ

2 miles (3 km) N of Hat Pattaya.

With fishermen setting out from the pier every morning and returning at sundown with the day's catch, Ao Naklua, or Naklua Bay, has still managed to preserve the erstwhile charm of Pattaya.

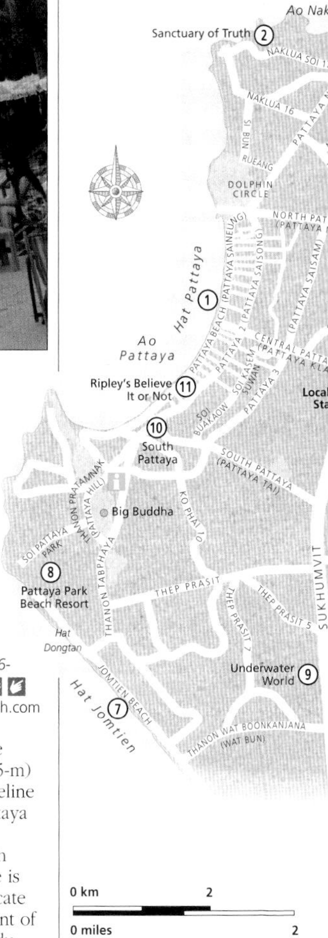

Key to Symbols *see back flap*

For hotels and restaurants in this region see pp294–8 and pp322–4

Many of the town's local workers live by Ao Naklua, and their accomodations lend the area an authentic rural atmosphere, although several hotels and condominiums are beginning to crowd the beach. Fishing tackle is available on Soi Photisan for those who want to spend a day on the pier. Fresh seafood can also be bought daily at the Naklua market, next to Lan Pho Park. Devoid of the raunchiness of Hat Pattaya, it is a better option for families, with little traffic on the sea, and less noise and pollution.

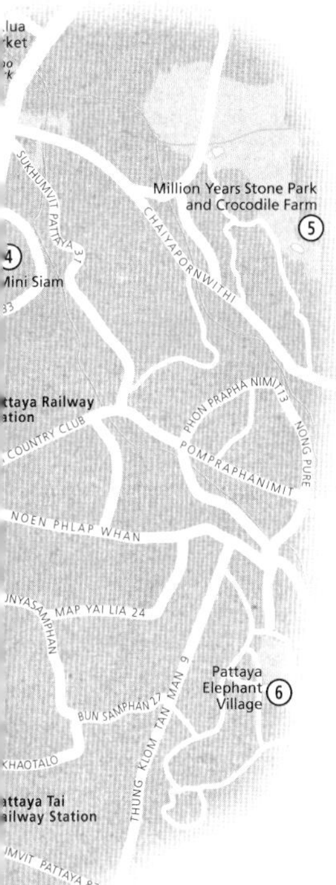

PATTAYA TOWN CENTER

Ao Naklua ③
Hat Jomtien ⑦
Hat Pattaya ①
Million Years Stone Park and Crocodile Farm ⑤
Mini Siam ④
Pattaya Elephant Village ⑥
Pattaya Park Beach Resort ⑧
Ripley's Believe It or Not ⑪
Sanctuary of Truth ②
South Pattaya ⑩
Underwater World ⑨

Miniature replica of Bangkok's famous Wat Arun at Mini Siam

Mini Siam

มินิสยาม

387 Moo 6, Sukhumvit Rd. ***Tel*** *0-3872-7333.* *7am–10pm daily.* **www**.minisiam.com

First opened in 1986 as a research project and continually growing, this interesting theme park is divided into Mini Siam and Mini Europe. The park displays miniature models of renowned monuments and structures such as Bangkok's Grand Palace, the Sydney Opera House, Paris's Eiffel Tower, the Colosseum, and Cambodia's Angkor Wat. Each of these models has been built on a scale of 1:25 with the Democracy Monument in Bangkok being the first edifice to be replicated. Along with the other activities, including weddings, that take place in Mini Siam, there are daily traditional Thai dance shows. Quite popular with visitors to Pattaya, this theme park also has several souvenirs shops nearby.

VISITORS' CHECKLIST

Road Map D1. 37 miles (60 km) S of Chonburi. *150,000.* *TAT, 609 Moo 10, Pratamnak Road, Pattaya (0-3842-7667).* *Pattaya Music Festival (Mar 20–22); Pattaya Festival (mid-Apr, during Songkran).* **www**.pattayacity.com

Million Years Stone Park and Crocodile Farm

อุทยานหินล้านปีและฟาร์มจระเข้

22/1 Moo 1, Nongplalai, Banglamung. ***Tel*** *0-3824-9347–9.* *8am–6:30pm daily.* **www**.thaistonepark.org

Also known as Uttayan Hin Laan Pee, the Million Years Stone Park and Crocodile Farm features an eclectic mix of curiosities. Among the major attractions are petrified trees over a million years old, bonsai, rocks shaped like animals, gigantic catfish, and hundreds of crocodiles. It also boasts of having the largest artificial waterfall in Thailand.

Pattaya Elephant Village

หมู่บ้านช้างพัทยา

48/120 Moo 7, Tambon Nong Prue. ***Tel*** *0-3824-9818.* *9am–5pm daily.* **www**.elephant-village-pattaya.com

Locally known as Mooban Chang, Pattaya Elephant Village is more of a theme park than a zoo. Visitors get a chance to go on elephant rides, as well as see them paint, play sports, and bathe. The admission fee includes lunch and rafting on the river, along with an hour-long elephant show.

Curiously shaped stones at the Million Years Stone Park

Keen anglers taking a speedboat to catch game fish, Hat Jomtien

Hat Jomtien

หาดจอมเทียน

1 mile (2 km) S of Hat Pattaya.

Thailand's premier spot for windsurfing and kiteboarding, this 9-mile (14-km) long beach is generally abuzz with visitors. At its northern end lies Hat Dongtan, dominated by high-rise apartments and popular with gay and lesbian travelers. An ideal place for watersport enthusiasts, water-skiing and paragliding are among the leading activities on the beach.

Scuba diving and snorkeling trips set out from the shore, as do jet skis and kayaks. Speedboats are available for game-fishing trips too. Other activities include target shooting, horseback riding, tennis, and golf. Hat Jomtien also has several banana boats that can be hired to take children to and from the shore.

The southern end of the beach, however, is devoid of a lot of this activity and is a preferred spot for those who want to keep away from the crowds, noise, and excitement at the northern end.

Hat Jomtien is vibrant at night and a number of beer and go-go bars attract crowds in large numbers. A host of international restaurants, seafood shacks, Irish pubs, and German beer bars also vie for visitors' attention.

Pattaya Park Beach Resort

พัทยาปาร์คบีชรีสอร์ท

345, Hat Jomtien. **Tel** *0-3825-1201–8.* **www**.pattayapark.com **Pattaya Park Funny Land**. *11am–10pm daily.*

Located at the northern end of Hat Jomtien, Pattaya Park Beach Resort is the perfect destination for children. While it has a private shopping arcade and various dining facilities, its main appeal is the host of varied indoor activities. Kids delight in the whirlpools and waterslides, while adults busy themselves in swimming pools, a fitness center, sauna, jogging track or cable-pulled water ski. A center within the resort has scuba diving classes for beginners. Those less interested in strenuous physical activities can head for the snooker club.

Pattaya Tower, the highest point not only of the resort but in the whole of Pattaya, offers splendid views – across Pattaya to the north and Ao Jomtien to the south – from the Apex Observation Point on the 55th floor. Visitors can also use the tower for bungee jumping or taking a ride in the sky shuttle or speed shuttle. It has three different revolving restaurants on the 52nd, 53rd, and 54th floors.

Pattaya Park Funny Land, also designed to entertain children, boasts a fantastic range of roller coaster rides, monorail, a musical carousel, and a bumper car ride.

Underwater World

อันเดอร์วอเตอร์เวิลด์

22/22 Moo 11, Sukhumvit Road, Banglamung. **Tel** *0-3875-6879.* *9am–6pm daily.* **www**.underwaterworldpattaya.com

An excellent showcase for the rich and varied marine life in the region with over 200 species of marine animals, Underwater World is an impressive aquarium. Adults and children alike will love this place. Visitors begin the tour from the beach on the edge of the sea and are gradually taken underground passing a variety of corals and other marine life on the way.

Visitors admiring the marine life visible from the large fiberglass tunnels, Underwater World

Neon signs drawing crowds to seafood restaurants and go-go bars, Walking Street, South Pattaya

Farther below is a 328-ft (100-m) long tunnel made of fiberglass through which various kinds of colorful fish, sea horses, turtles, sharks, corals, rays, and crustaceans can be viewed. Visitors can also go scuba diving in the coral reef tank or with the rays and sharks, for an additional fee.

Gold painted Big Buddha, 300 ft (91 m) above Pattaya's coastline

South Pattaya

พัทยาใต้

www.pattaya-bars.net

The area between Pattaya Beach Road and South Pattaya Road is crowded with hundreds of bars, nightclubs, and massage parlors. It is located about half a mile (1 km) from Hat Pattaya, in the *sois* (lanes) south of Soi 13 – between Soi 13/1 and Soi 13/5 – an area better known as Pattayaland. This zone is all about the sex trade. Hundreds of men, women, and *kathoey* or transvestites can be found crowding the bars and nightclubs, making the atmosphere in this part of Pattaya like the world's largest bachelor party. Soi 3 is also known as Boyztown and is the center of the Pattaya gay scene with several nightclubs and beer bars.

A half mile (1 km) stretch of road to the south of Pattaya Beach Road is known as **Walking Street**. Vehicles are prohibited from entering this stretch from 7pm onward. Thronged by sex workers, it has open-air bars, fast food joints, private massage parlors, go-go bars, nightclubs, and cabaret shows along the street.

For those looking for a more spiritual experience, to the south, on Buddha Hill, lies Pattaya Fitness Park with a large golden statue of the Buddha, called the **Big Buddha**. Visitors come to the park to admire this magnificent image as well as several other smaller images of the Buddha dotting the park.

Ripley's Believe It or Not

พิพิธภัณฑ์ริปลีส์

3rd floor, Royal Garden Plaza, 218 Moo 10, Beach Rd. ***Tel*** *0-3871-0294. 11am–11pm daily. in Cinema and Haunted House.* www.ripleysthailand.com

One of Pattaya's most popular attractions, Ripley's Believe It or Not features 10 theme galleries and over 300 extraordinary exhibits. These include a real shrunken head, a mask made from human skin, and an astonishing model of the *Titanic* made from 1 million matchsticks. The exterior of the building appears to be the site of a plane crash, with a giant plane nose-diving into its roof. Apart from the weird and wacky collection of trivia in the museum, there is a haunted house, a 4-D simulator cinema, an infinity maze, and various other activities for children.

Building exterior with "crashed" fighter plane, Ripley's Believe It or Not

Around Pattaya

Statue at Rayong

There is a lot to see and do around Pattaya, especially on the coastal road south toward Sattahip and among the numerous offshore islands. Getting around independently is very easy as jeeps, motorcycles, and bicycles are readily available for hire. Most activities are aimed squarely at vacationers on package tours and families, with novelties and attractions – such as elephant rides and hill-tribe villages – imported from across Thailand. There are also plenty of sporting opportunities ranging from watersports to golfing.

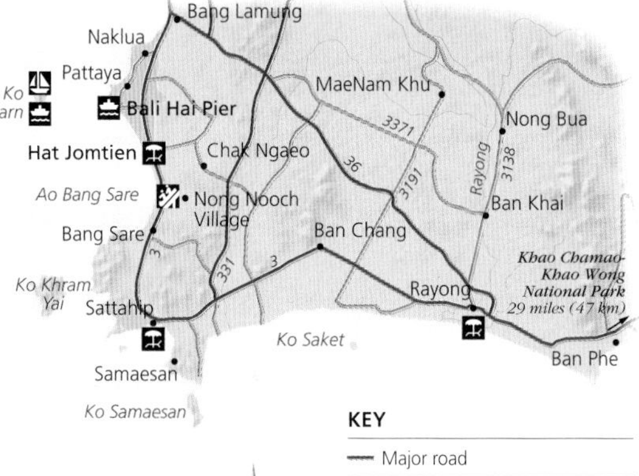

Ko Larn

เกาะล้าน

5 miles (8 km) W of Pattaya. *from Bali Hai Pier, Pattaya.* **www**.kohlarn.com

A tiny island about 2 miles (3 km) long and 1 mile (2 km) wide, Ko Larn is ringed by six picturesque little coves and fantastic offshore coral reefs. For its size, the island offers an amazing variety of activities; from tours in a semi-submerged glass-bottomed boat from which passengers can view coral and fish, to jet-skiing, parasailing, banana boat rides, scuba diving, snorkeling, fishing, and target shooting.

Visitors can get around Ko Larn on pickup truck taxis, motorcycle taxis, or rented motorcycles. Each beach has guesthouses, restaurants, shops, and tourist facilities. If traveling in a small group, visitors can also hire a speedboat for a few hundred baht from Pattaya.

Nong Nooch Village

สวนนงนุช

9 miles (15 km) S of Pattaya. ***Tel*** *0-3870-9358-61.* *8am–6pm daily.* **www**.nongnooch-tropicalgarden.com

Essentially a theme park, Nong Nooch Village (pronounced "Nong Noot" in Thai), offers examples of Thai agriculture, Thai-style houses, a small zoo, a butterfly farm, and a beautiful botanical garden with a variety of orchids. A great place for an educational trip, there are also several options for entertainment such as Thai boxing bouts, an elephant show, and a Thai cultural show featuring traditional dance and music. Visitors can also make use of the swimming pool and picnic area. Pickups, directly from visitors' hotels in Pattaya, are available.

Sattahip

สัตหีบ

21 miles (33 km) S of Pattaya.

Once a Thai naval base which housed US servicemen during the Vietnam War, Sattahip today is best known for a small sea turtle conservation center located here. Visitors usually pass through Sattahip en route to Ko Samet, Rayong, or Ko Chang from Pattaya. A stopover at the sprawling floating market on Highway 3 is worthwhile. With around 80 boats selling various kinds of goods, it is a great place to pick up souvenirs.

Rayong

ระยอง

108 miles (174 km) SE of Pattaya.

Popular for weekend trips from Bangkok, Rayong is well-known for its cool breezes and great seafood. The beaches along the coast – Ban Phe, Suan Son, and Suan Wang Kaew – have plenty of hotels overlooking the sea. There are good camping and diving facilities at Ko Talu, located across from Suan Wang Kaew. Located 29 miles (47 km) east of Rayong, **Khao Chamao-Khao Wong National Park** is a scenic spot with waterfalls, caves, cliffs, and ponds.

French-style garden with beautiful landscaping at Nong Nooch Village

Elephants in Thailand

The largest land animal currently living in Asia, the elephant was first mentioned centuries ago in Hindu and Buddhist texts. They have long played a significant spiritual role in Thailand, enjoying a higher status than any other animal. Unfortunately, the elephant has become increasingly threatened by human encroachment on its habitat, and to a lesser extent, by poaching. The introduction of bulldozers and other heavy equipment has tended to make the legendary power of the elephant redundant, and a ban on most commercial logging in 1989 led to a sharp decline in the number of captive elephants. Today, their numbers in the wild are estimated to be just 40,000 to 50,000. It is increasingly common to see elephants being led around resorts and big cities by their *mahouts* (elephant keepers). A surer way to see them is at elephant camps and shows in places such as Pattaya.

Ceramic elephant figure

Popular as a means of transport, *elephants were used to carry both heavy loads such as teak logs as well as people, with the* mahout *sitting astride the elephant's neck.*

ELEPHANTS IN HISTORY

Elephants were used in the construction of *wats*, clearing of forests, and logging. Throughout Thai history, they were also a symbol of prestige for Thai kings – the more elephants a king had, the more powerful he was.

White elephants, *in fact albinos, have traditionally been attributed semi-divine status and are considered to be the property of the king. From 1855–1916, the Thai national flag depicted a white elephant on a red background.*

Elephants were used in war *with Thai and Burmese rulers, in particular, choosing to enter the battlefield on elephant back.*

ELEPHANTS TODAY

Increasingly endangered in Thailand today, elephants are more likely to be seen in sanctuaries, camps, and shows. No longer used for logging, they have little employment outside the tourism industry.

Wild elephants, today, are under the protection of only a few national parks.

Elephant shows *are hugely popular and are staged at several destinations, most notably at Nong Nooch Village in Pattaya.*

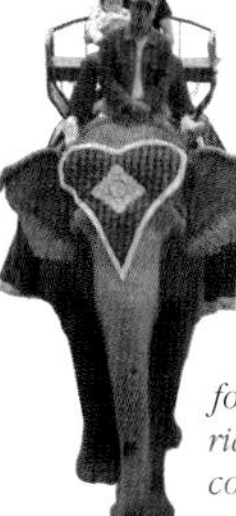

Elephant rides *are especially popular with children. Visitors also use them for trekking. These rides are quite common in southern Thailand.*

Elephant motifs *are often engraved by Thai silversmiths on decorative objects.*

Ko Samet 8

เกาะเสม็ด

Located off the Rayong Coast, Ko Samet is blessed with clear blue waters and crystalline sands and is popular with foreign visitors and Thais alike. The island derives its name from the evergreen, flower-bearing Cajeput trees – Samet is the Thai word for Cajeput – found throughout the island. Despite attaining national park status in 1981, Ko Samet has faced quite a bit of development. Its 5-mile (8-km) long eastern shore is a string of beautiful, white sand beaches populated with restaurants and bars. The western side of the island is less crowded, while the narrow interior is wild, undeveloped, and riddled with trails, making it ideal for exploring the flora and fauna.

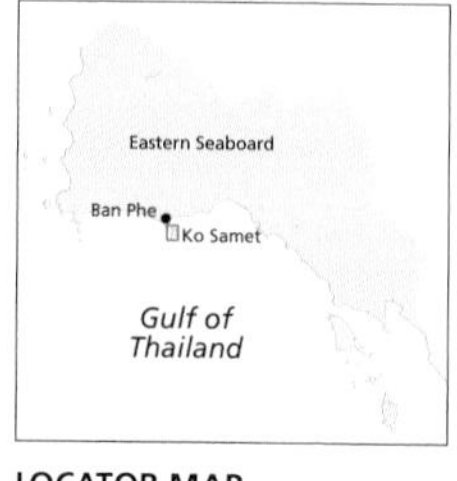

LOCATOR MAP

Area illustrated

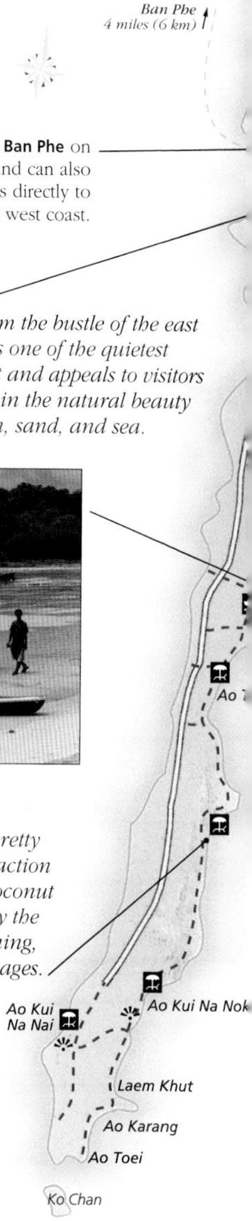

Ban Phe 4 miles (6 km)

Ferries from Ban Phe on the mainland can also bring visitors directly to island's west coast.

★ Ao Phrao

Located away from the bustle of the east coast, Ao Phrao is one of the quietest bays on Ko Samet and appeals to visitors who wish to soak in the natural beauty and enjoy the sun, sand, and sea.

Ao Wong Deuan

Home to the second longest beach on the island, Ao Wong Deuan is enduringly popular with both Thais and foreigners. It offers a wide range of facilities including exotic seafood restaurants, bars, and a lively nightlife.

Ao Wai

This bay shelters a quiet and pretty beach located south of all the action at Hat Sai Kaew. Shaded by coconut palms, Ao Wai is dominated by the Samet Ville Resort, offering dining, entertainment, and Thai massages.

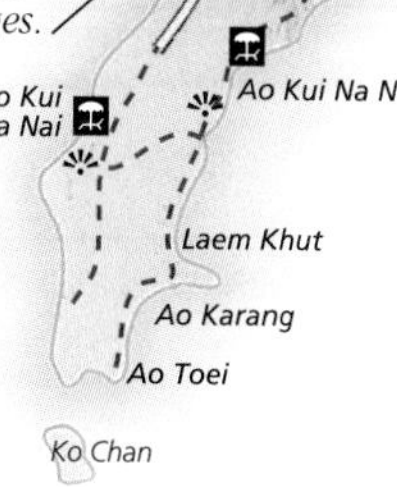

Ko Chan

STAR SIGHTS

- ★ Ao Phrao
- ★ Hat Sai Kaew
- ★ Ao Phai

Na Dan
The small fishing town of Na Dan is the island's main ferry port. As its largest settlement, the town also functions as the de facto capital.

VISITORS' CHECKLIST

Road Map D2. 52 miles (84 km) SE of Pattaya. *1,500.* *from Ban Phe to Na Dan, Ao Wong Deuan, and Ao Phrao.* *TAT, Rayong (0-3865-5420).*

★ Hat Sai Kaew
A gorgeous stretch of white sand, Hat Sai Kaew is the longest and most developed beach on the island, offering watersports such as water-skiing, windsurfing, and parasailing.

Chao

★ Ao Phai
A small and lovely bay, Ao Phai's beach is rather busy with many restaurants and cafés. Popular with backpackers and sunbathers, the beach serves as a starting point for exploring trails across the island.

KEY

- Beach
- Watersports
- Viewpoint
- Ferry service
- Minor road
- Trail
- Ferry route

THE POETRY OF SUNTHORN PHU

Sunthorn Phu (1786–1855) is Thailand's most respected poet. His long, lyrical verses made him a favorite of the Thai kings. The epic *Phra Aphaimani*, Sunthorn Phu's first poem, was inspired by beautiful Ko Samet which he adopted as his home. The poem tells the story of a prince, Aphaimani, who is banished to an underwater kingdom ruled by a giantess. Helped by a mermaid, Phra Aphaimani escapes and then defeats the giantess by playing his magic flute which puts her to sleep. The prince is subsequently betrothed to a beautiful princess.

Statue on Ko Samet depicting characters from *Phra Aphaimani*

Exploring Ko Samet

Beach vendor, Hat Sai Kaew

A low-lying sliver of land, Ko Samet is easily accessible on a weekend trip from Bangkok. Its location has led to steady development over the years and despite being a protected area, the island risks becoming overcrowded during peak season. Also known as Ko Kaew Phitsadan, or Magic Crystal Island, this place was immortalized in Sunthorn Phu's romantic epic *Phra Aphaimani*. Ko Samet offers visitors an idyllic tropical setting along with a lively nightlife as well as secluded beaches. Prices at restaurants and hotels, however, increase on busy weekends. Foreign visitors are required to pay an admission fee at the ferry port of Na Dan before venturing farther into the island.

Sailing, kayaking, and other watersports at Hat Sai Kaew

Shrine with offerings dedicated to Sage Pu Dam, Na Dan

Na Dan

หน้าด่าน

4 miles (6 km) S of Ban Phe.

A small but fairly busy pier in the northeastern part of the island, Na Dan is the entry point into Ko Samet and is used by commercial as well as privately owned speedboats and ferries.

Na Dan is a nondescript fishing settlement with a clinic, a few Internet cafés, two ATMs, and a market. It offers basic accommodations, but very few travelers actually stay here. Close to the pier is a shrine dedicated to Pu Dam, a venerated holy man – also known as Grandfather Black – who lived on this idyllic island. Communal taxis leave from Na Dan's pier to Ko Samet's many beaches.

Ao Phrao

อ่าวพร้าว

1 mile (2 km) SW of Na Dan.

The narrow white beach at Ao Phrao, or Paradise Bay, is interspersed with trees and a lush mountainous background. The rugged coastline is not very accessible, but there are several trekking trails and spectacular sunset views.

This is the only developed beach on the rocky west coast of Ko Samet. Apart from a few guesthouses, Ao Phrao also has two luxury resorts with swimming pools and spas. There is a PADI center for those interested in diving. However, this is the extent of facilities on this rather peaceful beach. Visitors can hire taxis at Na Dan or take a boat from the mainland.

Hat Sai Kaew

หาดทรายแก้ว

One of the most popular beaches in Thailand which is especially busy with weekend visitors from Bangkok, Hat Sai Kaew is a beautiful crescent of crisp, white sand located just half a mile (1 km) southeast of Na Dan.

The 2-mile (3-km) stretch is lined with bungalows, guesthouses, bars, restaurants, and shops. Although the sea still looks pristine, the beach has lost some of its charm due to overcrowding. The large number of beach activities often make it difficult to find a quiet spot.

Hat Sai Kaew is a revelers' beach with many nightclubs and bars that stay open till

Quiet beach at Ao Phrao backed by a thickly forested hillside

For hotels and restaurants in this region see pp294–8 and pp322–4

dawn. Visitors can sign up for PADI authorised diving courses as well as induge in a plethora of watersports such as jet-skiing, banana boat rides, water-skiing, snorkeling, and scuba trips.

Ao Hin Khok

อ่าวหินกก

A short distance from Hat Sai Kaew and separated by a rocky hill, the beach at Ao Hin Khok is dominated by the statue of a prince and a mermaid – the central characters in *Phra Aphaimani* written by Sunthorn Phu. A backpackers' haven, the beach is lined with rows of small huts, basic restaurants, and loud neon-lit bars. There is also a gymnasium, and a Thai boxing ring. Typical evening entertainment includes fire juggling.

Ao Phai

อ่าวไผ่

Located just half a mile (1 km) southwest of Hat Sai Kaew, Ao Phai is a famous party zone attracting party-goers from all over the island. The beach hosts parties for just about any reason, but full moon celebrations tend to go over the top. It is a popular rendezvous for young backpackers. Visitors can also mingle with the local Thais during these celebrations.

Ao Phai has some small shops and mid-range hotels, but it is the nightly revelry that draws crowds.

Ao Nuan

อ่าวนวล

2 miles (3 km) SW of Hat Sai Kaew.

Just south of the commercial beaches of Hat Sai Kaew and Ao Phai are a couple of small secluded coves for those who want to get away from the maddening crowds.

Ao Nuan is a little rocky for swimming, but the stretch of sand is set amid unspoiled nature. The beach hut accommodations are very basic and without electricity, but visitors can enjoy the excellent restaurant or spend evenings under a beautiful canopy of

Visitors enjoying beers at an open-air beach restaurant, Ao Hin Khok

stars unhindered by other lights. Just north of Ao Nuan is the even quieter **Ao Phutsa**, also known as Ao Tubtim. Devoid of vendors and loud music, it is very peaceful.

Five minutes south of Ao Nuan is **Ao Cho** which draws weekend crowds. It has basic and upscale accommodations as well as a small pier ideal for fishing and snorkeling.

Ao Wong Deuan

อ่าววงเดือน

2 miles (3 km) SW of Hat Sai Kaew.

A horseshoe-shaped cove in the middle of the east coast, Ao Wong Deuan is serviced by ferries from the mainland. It is popular with holidaymakers on package tours and Thai families, and is more upscale than Hat Sai Kaew.

A designated lunch stop for day-trippers, the beach at Ao Wong Deuan is lined with restaurants and bars and has a lively nightlife. It also offers a wide range of watersports. The central part of the beach is often covered at high tide and visitors should be careful.

Ao Wai

อ่าวหวาย

3 miles (5 km) SW of Hat Sai Kaew.

Heading farther south along the east coast, the beaches become quieter and less commercial. Ao Wai is a good option for mid-range accommodations, intimate dining, and a less raucous nightlife. The soft sandy beach is partially shaded and has a couple of shops with Internet access.

The beach is also close to the southern coves of Ao Kui Na Nai, and Ao Khut. Located offshore, the secluded mini island of Ko Chan has an interesting underwater landscape, ideal for snorkeling.

Colorful kayaks for hire at Ao Phai

Chanthaburi 9

จันทบุรี

Mangosteen, a local fruit

Surrounded by acres of chili and rubber plantations, Chanthaburi, which means City of the Moon, is one of Thailand's most charming towns and the capital of the Chanthaburi province. King Taksin, (r.1767–82), is the most revered monarch here with several shrines and monuments, commemorating his famous victory over the Burmese in 1767. The town has a diverse ethnic population and strong historical and cultural links with both France and Vietnam due to its proximity to the former French Indochina. A gem-trading center since the 15th century, Chanthaburi is a prosperous city and a significant part of the present-day economy.

Vietnamese-style houses on stilts along Chanthaburi River

Gem Market

ตลาดพลอย

Thanon Sri Chan-Trok Kachang.

Famous as a gem center for more than five centuries, Chanthaburi has drawn prospectors, dealers, traders, and adventurers to its gem markets throughout history. The gem market, locally known as *talat phloi*, is located on the banks of the Chanthaburi River. Known for its natural wealth of sapphires and rubies, Chanthaburi continues to be an important center of this trade despite the exhaustion of its natural resources. Today, most stones are brought from areas along the Cambodian frontier, yet the market continues to be famous for the workmanship of its gem cutters. All kinds of precious and semi-precious stones are bought and sold for jewelry production. There are a range of rare gems and beads from all over Southeast Asia and even as far as Madagascar. Visitors can go to the market to see dealers and prospectors doing business. The best gem stores are along Trok Kachang and Thanon Sri Chan. This market is at its busiest on weekends.

Chanthaburi Cathedral

โบสถ์จันทบุรี

Chanthanimit Rd.

Located just across the river, east of the Gem Market, is Chanthaburi Cathedral, Thailand's largest Christian

Gem dealer examining some precious stones at the Gem Market

Ornate golden shrine inside the Chanthaburi Cathedral

edifice. Also known as the Church of the Immaculate Conception, this structure is designed in the French Provincial style and was built by Christian missionaries in the 18th century. Since then it has been renovated a number of times, especially due to the influx of many Vietnamese Christians. Some of the stained-glass windows in the church date from before its 19th century restoration.

Vietnamese Quarter

ตลาดเวียดนาม

Thanon Rim Nam.

Extending along the west bank of Chanthaburi River, and a short distance from the Gem Market, the Vietnamese Quarter is the most interesting part of Chanthaburi. The Vietnamese have migrated to Thailand over a century, initially to avoid persecution and later as political refugees.

This quarter has a distinct flavor, evident in its architecture and cuisine. The houses along Thanon Rim Nam are lovely old structures made out of bamboo or wood and standing on stilts. They follow the style of Vietnamese tube architecture and are usually narrow in width with the living quarters extending along the building's depth.

The nearby market offers a whole array of delicious Vietnamese snacks. Great stacks of Vietnamese spring roll wrappers and local desserts offer appetizing alternatives to traditional Thai fare. Today, there are

For hotels and restaurants in this region see pp294–8 and pp322–4

THAILAND'S VIETNAMESE

Vietnamese farmer in rice fields

The Vietnamese came to Thailand in a three-part exodus – refugees escaping French colonial rule in the 19th century, Vietnamese Catholics fleeing the communist regime in the 1950s, and migrants who left after the collapse of the Southern regime in 1975. The Thais mistrusted them because of an age-old rivalry and the Vietnamese were constantly displaced because of wars. However, over time, this community has been assimilated into the country's diverse ethnic fabric bringing with them distinct elements of their own culture.

few immigrants who speak the Vietnamese language, and the process of integration into Thai society is well advanced.

King Taksin Park

สวนพระเจ้าตากสิน

Thanon Leap Noen.

A lush, open space located half a mile (1 km) west of the Gem Market, King Taksin Park is a popular spot with the citizens of Chanthaburi for walks or early morning exercises. The main park area is divided by two lakes filled with a variety of fish. The park is dominated by a great bronze statue of King Taksin in a heroic pose on the battlefield. This iconic image also figures on the 20 baht note. Tall trees providing shade make this an excellent place for a picnic or a stroll. Visitors can also sample some of the tropical fruits for which Chanthaburi is famous.

VISITORS' CHECKLIST

Road Map E2. 113 miles (182 km) SE of Pattaya.
50,000. *TAT Rayong (0-3865-5420).* *daily.* *Fruit Festival (May/Jun).*

King Taksin Shrine

ศาลพระเจ้าตากสิน

Tha Luang Road.

A nonagonal structure with a helmet-shaped roof, King Taksin Shrine is a curious structure. Constructed in 1920, the shrine houses the king's statue that is revered by the locals. Every year on December 28, a ceremony is held commemorating Taksin's accession to the throne.

Helmets and weaponry placed as offerings at King Taksin's Shrine

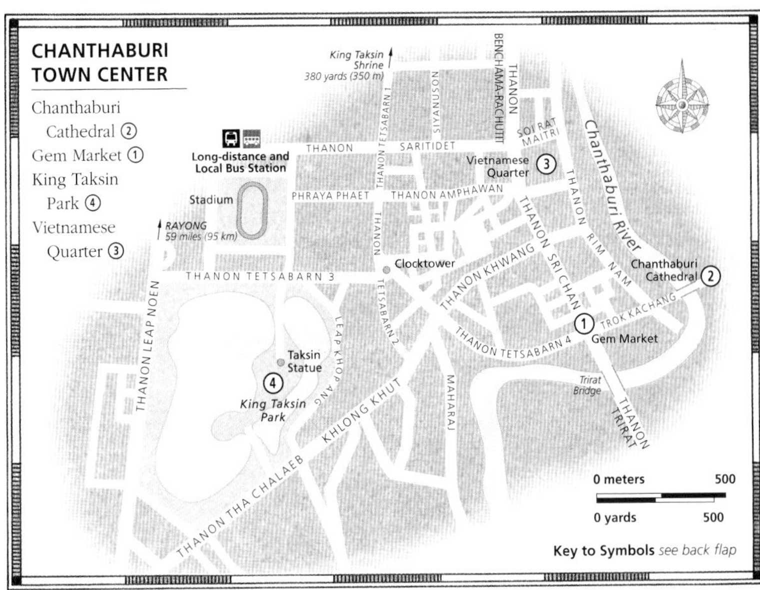

Khao Kitchakut National Park ⑩

อุทยานแห่งชาติเขาคิชฌกูฏ

Road Map E1. Park HQ off Hwy 3249, 15 miles (24 km) NE of Chanthaburi. *Chanthaburi, then* songthaew. *Park HQ (0-3945-2074).*

Covering an area of about 23 sq miles (60 sq km), Khao Kitchakut National Park is one of Thailand's smallest national parks and encompasses Khao Kitchakut, a granite mountain, just over 3,300-ft (1,006-m) high. The park's best-known site, the 13-tier **Krathing Waterfall**, is located near the park headquarters. From here, visitors can follow an easy trail to the mountain's peak.

More ambitious hikers and a large number of pilgrims make the arduous 4-hour climb to the summit of the impressive Phrabat mountain, 10 miles (16 km) from the park headquarters. This mountain is famous not only for an impression of the Buddha's footprint etched in granite, but also for its strange collection of natural rock formations shaped like an elephant, a large turtle, a pagoda, and a monk's bowl.

Khao Kitchakut is near the much larger, but less visited, **Khao Soi Dao Wildlife Sanctuary** which covers 290 sq miles (751 sq km). Both protected areas enclose some of the last surviving tracts of a once-great lowland forest. They are vital to the economy of the region as important water reservoirs and provide protection to many endangered species. These include sun bears, spot-bellied eagle owls, spiny-breasted giant frogs, and binturongs. The upland forests of Khao Soi Dao provide a habitat for the tree-dwelling pileated gibbon.

Phliw Waterfall, sourced from an underground stream

Khao Soi Dao Wildlife Sanctuary
Park HQ off Hwy 317, 16 miles (26 km) N of Chanthaburi. *Chanthaburi, then* songthaew.

One of the 13 tiers of the Krathing Waterfall, crossed by a bridge

Nam Tok Phliw National Park ⑪

อุทยานแห่งชาติน้ำตกพลิ้ว

Road Map E2. Park HQ off Hwy 3, 9 miles (14 km) SE of Chanthaburi. *Chanthaburi, then* songthaew. *Park HQ (0-3943-4528); Forestry Dept (0-2562-0760) for bungalow bookings.* **www**.dnp.go.th

Immensely popular with Thais, this 52-sq mile (135-sq km) park contains some of Thailand's richest rain forest. It is also a haven for wildlife, with over 156 species of birds and 32 species of mammals including the Asiatic black bear, tiger, leopard, barking deer, and macaque. The park's other attractions are its pretty waterfalls – the most impressive being **Phliw Waterfall**. Nearby are two *chedis* – the Alongkon *chedi* and the 10-ft (3-m) high pyramid-shaped *chedi*, Phra Nang Reua Lom, built by Rama V (r.1868–1910) in honor of Queen Sunantha, who died by drowning in the Chao Phraya River at Bang Pa-in in 1876.

A tough hike leads to the 66 ft (20 m) roaring Trok Nong Falls and the forest-encircled Klang Waterfall.

Trat ⓬

ตราด

Road Map E2. 36 miles (58 km) SE of Chanthaburi. *72,000.* *TAT, Trat (0-3959-7259-60).* *daily.* *Rakham Fruit Fair (May–Jun).*

This provincial capital is a small but busy commercial town. Currently, most travelers pass through Trat en route to Ko Chang *(see pp118–26)*. However, it is likely that the town will draw larger crowds as more and more travelers visit the archipelago. Trat has several attractions, including its markets, most of which are centered around Tat Mai and Sukhumvit roads. The busy market on Sukhumvit Road has a fine selection of food and drink stalls.

Also of interest are the gem-mining villages, such as Bo Rai, around Trat, where rubies are mined. Local guest-houses can arrange trips for visitors. Located about 1 mile (2 km) southwest of Trat, **Wat Bupharam**, or Flower Temple, is set in pleasant grounds with large, shady trees. Some of the original buildings within the temple complex, including the *wihan*, the bell tower, and the *kutis* (monks' quarters), are quite old and date from the late Ayutthaya period *(see pp40–41)*.

Wat Bupharam, the oldest temple in Trat

Laem Ngop ⓭

แหลมงอบ

Road Map E2. 12 miles (19 km) SW of Trat. *18,000.* *TAT, Trat (0-3959-7259-60).* *Ko Chang Naval Battle Commemoration (Jan 17–21).*

A small, sleepy, fishing port, Laem Ngop serves as the ferry point for nearby Ko Chang and the islands that lie beyond. In January 1941, the Thai Navy engaged French forces at this point, losing three vessels, but claiming a moral victory which is still celebrated today. Traditional merit-making ceremonies are performed for the deceased, and there is an exhibition by the Royal Thai Navy. The town also has a monument and museum dedicated to the martyrs of the battle.

Laem Ngop has little to offer the visitor beyond a wooden pier where rows of boats and ferries are tied. Although very much a one-horse town, it has a number of privately operated tourism information centers, several hotels for those who miss the ferry to Ko Chang and decide to stay overnight, as well as some excellent restaurants.

Visitors traveling by ferry from Laem Ngop to Ko Chang

THE CAMBODIAN CONNECTION

Visitors waiting to cross the border to Cambodia, Hat Lek

Thailand's long, narrow, eastern-most tip stretches far down the coast of the Gulf of Thailand, all but severing Cambodia's Cardamom region from the sea. In times past, this has led to tensions between the two countries, but today, both Bangkok and Phnom Penh seem happy to cooperate in profiting from the region's development as a tourist destination. The small but picturesque port of Khlong Yai is the last settlement in Thailand before the riverine border crossing to Cambodia at Hat Lek. Thai visitors generally cross to the somewhat notorious town of Koh Kong to indulge in gambling at local casinos. A vibrant trekking industry around the Cardamom Mountains is also beginning to develop in the region.

Ko Chang ⓮

เกาะช้าง

Named after the largest island in an archipelago of 52, Ko Chang is one of the best-known national marine parks in Thailand. Its appeal lies in its ruggedness – stunning beaches, a thick, jungled interior teeming with a wide variety of flora and fauna, and beautiful coral reefs. The prominent beaches on the island are scattered along its western and southern coasts, while the eastern coast is more suited for trekking and bird-watching. Marine life enthusiasts will find the waters south and west of Ko Chang endowed with fascinating coral formations. The northern coast of Ko Chang is the most developed part of the island, with several upscale restaurants and a variety of accommodation options.

LOCATOR MAP

☐ Area illustrated

Ban Khlong Son is the main settlement on the island.

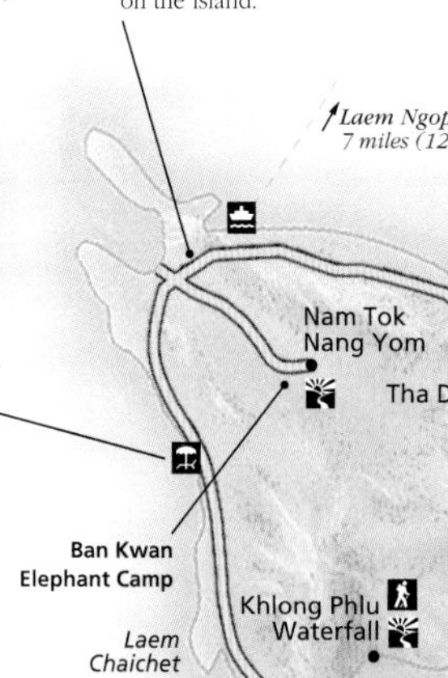

Hat Sai Khao

The largest and most developed beach on Ko Chang, Hat Sai Khao is also the most crowded, with plenty of bars and restaurants, and the liveliest nightlife.

Hat Khlong Phrao

A great spot for a family vacation, Hat Khlong Phrao is lined with restaurants that produce some of the freshest and most delicious seafood on the island.

Hat Kai Bae is an ideal spot for sea-kayaking, with kayaks easily available for hire.

STAR SIGHTS

- ★ Bang Bao Fishing Village
- ★ Ban Kwan Elephant Camp
- ★ Than Mayom Waterfall

★ Bang Bao Fishing Village

A pretty village along the southern coast, Bang Bao is easily identified by its simple, wooden houses on stilts built near or over the water.

★ Ban Kwan Elephant Camp
One of the most popular elephant camps on the island, Ban Kwan offers exciting rides on elephant back into the wild interiors of Ko Chang, or Elephant Island, accompanied by an experienced mahout, *or guide.*

VISITORS' CHECKLIST

Road Map E2. Park HQ near Than Mayom, Ko Chang, 31 miles (50 km) SW of Trat. *from Laem Ngop. Park HQ (0-3955-5080). for Ko Chang National Park.* **www**.dnp.go.th

★ Than Mayom Waterfall
The most popular waterfall on the island, Than Mayom was visited by Rama V, VI, and VII. Evidence of their visits can be seen on the rocks near the falls which bear the kings' insignia.

Hat Wai Chek
Among the quieter and more serene beaches on Ko Chang, Hat Wai Chek is popular with campers. The beach is inaccessible by road and can only be reached by trekking across the island's forested interior.

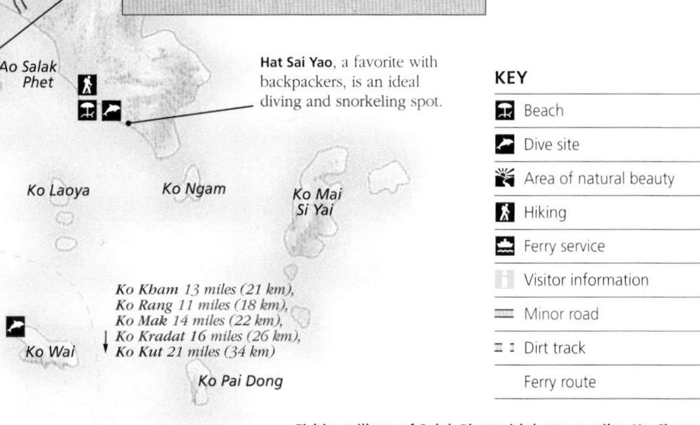

Hat Sai Yao, a favorite with backpackers, is an ideal diving and snorkeling spot.

Fishing village of Salak Phet with huts on stilts, Ko Chang ▷

Exploring Ko Chang

A spirit house

The serenity and outstanding beauty of Ko Chang, the second largest island in Thailand, have combined to place it prominently on the visitors' map. Easy accessibility from Bangkok, combined with the island's scenic beauty, which includes mangrove forests, cliffs, and clear waters, make this an ideal place for a varied holiday experience. While the best beaches on Ko Chang are on its west coast, the coastal road, which was begun in the early 1990s, has helped to increase accessibility to other remote beaches on the island as well. Increased development also means that Ko Chang now has no shortage of upscale hotels, resorts, and spas catering to an ever-increasing influx of visitors.

Hat Sai Khao

หาดทรายขาว

7 miles (11 km) W of Tha Dan Kao.

The longest, most popular beach on the island, Hat Sai Khao, or White Sands Beach, is easily accessible from Tha Dan Kao, one of the many piers where ferries heading to Ko Chang arrive.

The narrow 1-mile (2-km) stretch of beach is crowded with hotels, resorts, and beach bars, all competing for a glimpse of the sea. The road running parallel to the beach is lined with shops, travel agents, seafood shacks, bars, and a few small shopping malls. While the available accommodations are inadequate as well as overpriced, there are some less expensive places for the budget traveler at the northern end of the beach, which is also quieter. Swimming in the waters is not recommended here as the current can get very strong and dangerous.

Visitors enjoying refreshments outdoors at Hat Khlong Phrao

Hat Khlong Phrao

หาดคลองพร้าว

3 miles (5 km) S of Hat Sai Khao.

A small fishing port with one of the most popular family beaches on Ko Chang, Hat Khlong Phrao is best suited for visitors seeking mid-range accommodations. The beach is divided into two, the northern and southern parts, each with its own peaceful stretch of sand. The southern end has the added advantage of being screened off from the main road by a thick cluster of coconut trees. Visitors can experience exciting elephant rides through rubber plantations, starting from nearby Ban Khlong Phrao. These are operated by the Chang Chutiman Tours and Ban Kwan Elephant Camp, 1 mile (2 km) inland from Ban Khlong Son. Other activities include kayaking and hiking.

Khlong Phlu Waterfall

น้ำตกคลองพลู

1 mile (2 km) NE of Hat Khlong Phrao.

Ko Chang's highest waterfall, the three-tiered Khlong Phlu, locally known as Nam Tok Khlong Phlu, cascades down 65 ft (20 m) into a small pond of clear water surrounded by smooth rocks. Located almost in the middle of the island, the fall flows down to Hat Khlong Phrao on the west coast, forming an estuary. Visitors usually follow the 2-mile (3-km) walk upstream by taking the road inland between Ko Chang Plaza in Laem Chaichet and Chang Chutiman Tours to reach this beautiful site.

The waterfall is very popular with visitors and quite crowded at all times, except in the early morning.

The picturesque Khlong Phlu Waterfall, best viewed in the rainy season

For hotels and restaurants in this region see pp294–8 and pp322–4

A great spot for picnics, visitors can jump off the rocks into the cool waters below, swim, and trek in the dense rain forest surrounding the waterfall. Sharp-eyed visitors may be lucky enough to spot a civet cat, macaque or mongoose – all part of the fauna at the national park.

Foreign visitors have to pay an entry fee (which varies for children and adults) at the ranger station, located at the car park a short distance from the waterfall, as the cascade is part of the Ko Chang Marine National Park.

Basic beach accommodations, Ao Bai Lan

Kayaks available to residents to explore nearby islands, Hat Kai Bae

Hat Kai Bae

หาดไก่แบ้

7 miles (11 km) S of Hat Sai Khao. Songthaew *from Tha Dan Kao or Hat Sai Khao.*

A narrow beach overgrown with shrubs, Hat Kai Bae all but disappears at high tide. Despite its size, the beach has been undergoing considerable development, and Hat Kai Bae has a few upscale resorts with private swimming pools, a handful of modest restaurants and bars, as well as supermarkets. Visitors can hire kayaks to explore the tiny islands just off the west coast. Motorcycles and boats are also available for hire at the dive shops.

Hat Tha Nam

หาดท่าน้ำ

6 miles (10 km) S of Hat Sai Khao. Songthaew *from Tha Dan Kao.*

Better known as Lonely Beach, Hat Tha Nam was discovered by backpackers years ago as an ideal location for swimming and scuba diving. Despite the name, visitors continue to flock here in droves. Several resorts with concrete, air-conditioned bungalows have opened shop in recent times, but cheap wooden huts also dot the landscape.

Hat Tha Nam is probably the best area for swimming on the island, with a shallow seabed, although the northern end of the beach has a steep shelf and swimmers need to be careful. Scuba diving equipment is easily available for hire from a dive shop on the beach, as are kayaks and motorcycles at most of the bungalow accommodations.

Youngsters frequent Hat Tha Nam playing frisbee, juggling balls, and drinking beer. The nights are often busy with noisy parties.

Ao Bai Lan

อ่าวใบลาน

8 miles (13 km) S of Hat Sai Khao.

Quieter and more private than Lonely Beach, Ao Bai Lan is the perfect destination for backpackers. Built around a pier, where a few fishing vessels moor and locals cast lines, Ao Bai Lan has no beach, just rocks, clear pristine water, and a chance to snorkel around the reef.

A few resorts have been springing up, including the luxurious Mercure Koh Chang Hideaway *(see p295)*, which nestles among the more traditional picturesque huts set on stilts.

Vacationers partying late into the night at the many lively bars on Ao Bai Lan can also head for a relaxing sauna treatment at the popular Herbal Sauna Bailan.

Sunbathing along the poolside, Sea View Resort and Spa, Hat Kai Bae

Water gushing down tiers of the spectacular Than Mayom Waterfall

Bang Bao

บางเบา

12 miles (19 km) S of Hat Sai Khao.

A unique experience awaits visitors to Bang Bao – it is a village built entirely on stilts, overlooking the bay. The wooden houses as well as shops, guesthouses, and restaurants are connected by narrow bridges, creating a miniature colony over the sea. Several shacks have been converted into seafood restaurants, famed locally for their giant crabs and prawns.

Keen anglers can go fishing, perhaps directly from their balcony; snorkeling, diving, and swimming are other options. Dolphins and sea turtles often swim off the southern coast, and tracking them can prove to be a rewarding experience, as long as visitors hire the services of an experienced tour guide. Boats and other equipment are also easily available.

Bang Bao usually witnesses a steady flow of camera-happy visitors, but the evenings are blissfully peaceful, especially after the crowds have dispersed and the souvenir shops have closed. A hilly trail, which is marked out between Bang Bao and Ao Bai Lan, 3 miles (5 km) to the north, is excellent for hiking. A short distance south from the village is the small, albeit picturesque, beach called Hat Sai Noi. Some 330-feet (101-m) long, the beach has a small restaurant, a few fresh fruit bars, and some scattered chairs, with women offering traditional Thai massages.

Hat Wai Chek

หาดไวเชค

3 miles (5 km) E of Bang Bao.

from Bang Bao.

One of Thailand's last untouched slices of paradise, the isolated cove of Hat Wai Chek is almost completely off the tourist map. There are currently no road signs leading to it. Those keen to visit the picturesque and isolated beach can take the Salak Phet-Bang Bao route, which passes first through a rubber plantation, then to the coconut plantation and the beach, a short distance away. There is little development on the beach, and there are no guesthouses, restaurants, or shops. However, it is gradually becoming more accessible because of the construction of a road between Bang Bao and Ban Salak Phet which completes the long, winding, loop around the island.

Visitors are allowed to camp overnight on the beach, but must remember to carry their own supplies. Those keen to undertake some physical activity can go hiking along the narrow wooded trails or hire a motorcycle or 4WD jeep from Ban Bang Bao.

Than Mayom Port and Waterfall

น้ำตกธารมะยม

4 miles (6 km) S of Tha Dan Kao.

The east coast of Ko Chang is lined with mangroves and has few facilities for visitors or beaches and scant accommodations. The Than Mayom Port has a pier where various varieties of fruit are loaded for the mainland, but there is little other activity. A 1-mile (2-km) walk south of the port leads to the Than Mayom Waterfall on a steep hill toward the interior. This natural cascade is surrounded by lush vegetation and offers spectacular views over the coastline. Camping around

Wooded hills and trails ideal for trekking, Hat Wai Chek

Panoramic view of calm waters and outlying islands off Ko Chang

the waterfall is usually permitted, but visitors need to bring their own supplies. Successive kings of Thailand have visited the falls as the inscriptions on the rocks indicate. Foreign visitors have to pay an entry fee, which covers all of the sites within the marine national park.

Squid drying at the fishing village of Ban Salak Phet

Ban Salak Phet

บ้านสลักเพชร

10 miles (16 km) S of Tha Dan Kao.

A traditional fishing village with houses on stilts, Ban Salak Phet has found a place for itself on the tourist map, especially after the construction of the long, winding road around the island.

Visitors can take diving or snorkeling tours from the bay to the wreckage of two Thai naval ships which were sunk by the French Navy during World War II. For a more leisurely activity, a visit to the fish and shrimp farms and the lighthouse is recommended. There are a couple of beautiful waterfalls within 2–3 miles (3–5 km) of Salak Phet called Ke Rephet and Khlong Nung. Two Buddhist temples – Wat Salak Phet, built during the reign of Rama V (r.1868–1910), and another about 6 miles (10 km) from it – are also worth a visit.

Hat Sai Yao

หาดทรายยาว

14 miles (22 km) S of Tha Dan Kao.

Located on the southeastern tip of Ko Chang, Hat Sai Yao, or Long Beach, had so far been one of the least developed areas on the island. Endowed with breathtaking views, it is an ideal sanctuary for backpackers searching for solitude. However, Hat Sai Yao is now changing slowly – the winding bumpy road to the beach has improved, and taxis are more willing to negotiate a pretty reasonable fare from either Salak Phet or Salak Kok.

Hat Sai Yao is the closest point for swimming, snorkeling, and fishing trips to a handful of tiny, yet picturesque islands nearby, including Ko Wai *(see p126)*, Ko Mai Si Yai, Ko Mai Si Lek, and Ko Mai Daeng, some of which still remain uninhabited. Hat Sai Yao is not without its bit of intriguing history; close to the coastline is a memorial dedicated to Thai soldiers who lost their lives in a battle against the French in 1941. Visitors can trek to this site.

Keen photographers might want to climb the 1,500-ft (457-m) high mountain behind the Treehouse Lodge to capture the panoramic views of the islands and coastline below.

Thatched accommodations at the beachfront, Hat Sai Yao

Exploring Ko Chang's Outlying Islands

The stunning islands of Ko Kham, Ko Wai, Ko Mak, and Ko Kut, with their beautiful, deserted beaches, are perfect for swimming and sunbathing. Located south of Ko Chang, these islands are accessible by ferry or speedboats and offer some of the best snorkeling and diving experiences in the Gulf of Thailand. Underwater explorers can see a wealth of marine life among the reefs as well as the wrecks of two naval warships – the *Songkhla* and the *Chonburi* – which sank in these waters. These have since become notable dive sites.

Traditional fishing village backed by mangroves at Ko Kut

Diver exploring the rich and unspoiled coral reefs off Ko Chang

Ko Kham

เกาะขาม

13 miles (21 km) SE of Ko Chang.

from Bang Bao.

Isolated Ko Kham, also known as Emerald Island, is so small that visitors can swim or snorkel around it in just 40 minutes. This is one of the few islands where black volcanic rocks are found on the beaches. The west coast has a profusion of mangroves and wild orchids, while the east coast has two small beaches.

Since this island lacks its own resources, it imports water and runs its own generators. There is only one resort on the island offering basic accommodations.

Ko Wai

เกาะหวาย

6 miles (10 km) SE of Ko Chang.

from Bang Bao or Laem Ngop.

Bounded by white sands, palm trees, and coral reefs, Ko Wai provides the perfect tropical setting with gorgeous views of the neighboring islands. The surrounding waters are so clear that the ocean floor can be viewed even without snorkeling gear. This L-shaped island is hilly and connected in the middle by shallow lagoons, which are safe even for young children. The locals are very friendly and there are a couple of resorts offering simple accommodations. These can be accessed on foot via a jungle path along the northern coast. Ko Wai does not have many facilities, but its pristine beauty makes it ideal for a family holiday.

Ko Mak

เกาะหมาก

14 miles (22 km) S of Ko Chang.

from Bang Bao or Laem Ngop.

Covered with coconut and rubber plantations, Ko Mak is named after the areca nut – Mak is the Thai word for areca nut – found all over the island. Most of Ko Mak is privately owned by the powerful Prompakdii family – civil servants who later turned landowners. Almost deserted until the late 1990s, Ko Mak is now home to about 30 resorts. There is electricity, Internet, boats for hire, and a good choice of restaurants and shops. Most of the action is on Ao Suan Yai and Ao Kao. Scuba diving is a popular activity on Ko Mak and the surrounding cluster of tiny islands – Ko Rayang, Ko Kra, Ko Rang, and Ko Kradat.

Ko Kut

เกาะกูด

21 miles (34 km) S of Ko Chang.

from Bang Bao.

The second largest island of the Ko Chang archipelago, Ko Kut is also the farthest from the mainland. The original inhabitants of this island were both Cambodian and Thais who fled to this remote spot during the French occupation of Trat *(see p117)* in 1904.

Agriculture is the mainstay of the locals – coconut and rubber are the most important crops. Most beaches are on the west coast and Khlong Chao and Hat Tapao are the most popular spots. The pristine, untouched interior of this island is home to the beautiful Khlong Chao Waterfall. Visitors can also stop by the fishing village of Ao Salad and sample the fresh seafood on offer.

Thick coconut plantations along the coast of Ko Mak

Beach Life

The sunny, tropical beaches of the Eastern Seaboard are a hedonistic escape from the daily grind. Popular with both foreign visitors and locals due to their proximity to Bangkok, they are both a hub of activity and a place to lie back and relax, with all the concomitant pleasures of the sun, sand, and watersports. Visitors can choose between basic backpacker haunts and luxurious, romantic getaways; deserted beaches or bustling commercial spots with a vibrant nightlife. The clear aquamarine waters provide good diving and snorkeling oppurtunities offering a wealth of marine life. Other attractions such as seafood, beach parties, traditional massages, and souvenir shops complete the perfect holiday.

Decorated rubber swimming tubes

Sunbathing *is a favorite occupation with travelers and most of the popular beaches have deck chairs and umbrellas to lounge under. However, it is easy to get serious sunburn and a good sunscreen is a must.*

Beach games *such as soccer, netball, and volleyball are extremely popular. Nets strung up on the beach with youngsters playing impromptu matches are a common sight.*

Thai foot massages *use traditional techniques to relieve tension. Many beaches have expert masseurs who charge very reasonable rates.*

Thai beach vendors *tend to be friendly rather than pushy or impolite and sell everything from fresh seafood snacks to trinkets.*

The beach nightlife *includes cabarets, full moon parties, fire shows, and live bands. Apart from this, groups of revelers are often seen singing around a bonfire.*

Beach shacks *are simple thatched structures serving iced drinks and delicious local snacks. They provide shade from the sun as well as the perfect vantage point to enjoy the sea.*

Watersports *of all kinds are available at Pattaya and other developed beaches. These range from kayaking – available on even the smaller beaches – to more extreme sports such as parasailing, windsurfing, and kiteboarding.*

Poolside bungalows at a beach resort, Hat Thap Thim

Hat Sai Ngam ⓯

หาดทรายงาม

Road Map E2. 24 miles (39 km) SE of Trat.

On the mainland east of Ko Chang, is a sliver of land along the shore that connects the provincial town of Trat *(see p117)* with the border crossing to Cambodia at Ban Hat Lek. This stretch is home to a string of small fishing villages, as well as some of the loveliest and as yet undeveloped beaches in Thailand. Hat Sai Ngam, or Beautiful Sands Beach, is a small and lovely stretch of pure white sand running parallel to a grove of pine trees. Facilities are fairly simple – although it should always be possible to get something to eat and drink. This is an ideal place to try out shrimp paste and dried fish which are famous local products. This beach is visited by relatively few people, Thai or foreign travelers, and it is still possible to unwind by the sea without being assailed by commercial development. To get to the beach visitors need to cross a 144-ft (44-m) long wooden bridge.

Hat Sai Kaew ⓰

หาดทรายแก้ว

Road Map E2. 25 miles (40 km) SE of Trat.

A quiet beach, Hat Sai Kaew, or Crystal Sands Beach, is yet to be discovered by travelers. Crisp white sands shaded by a narrow fringe of casuarinas and coconut palms along the shore makes this beach attractive to those who are looking for peace and tranquility. The area is best explored on motorcycles or longtail boats. It is possible to reach Hat Sai Kaew by minibus from Trat.

Colorful boats anchored at the fishing village, Hat Samran

Hat Thap Thim ⓱

หาดทับทิม

Road Map E2. 30 miles (48 km) SE of Trat.

Located near the village of Ban Mai Rut, Hat Thap Thim, or Ruby Beach, is close to the narrowest strip of Thai territory dividing the Cambodian mountains from the Gulf of Thailand. This 1,500-ft (450-m) narrow sliver of sand is a pretty spot ideal for picnics or a day trip en route to Cambodia.

Basic accommodations are available here and the beach with its seafood shacks is often filled with Thai locals from Trat who come to Hat Thap Thim on weekends. The ambience here is laid-back and decidedly different from the international vibe of nearby Ko Chang.

Hat Samran ⓲

หาดสำราญ

Road Map E2. 36 miles (58 km) SE of Trat.

Located between Trat and the Thai-Cambodian frontier at Hat Lek, Hat Samran, better known as Hat Mai Rut, is an almost deserted beach. Despite limited facilities, its relative quiet and stunning beauty adds to its charm and appeal. While some of the regular watersports such as windsurfing or diving might not be available due to lack of infrastructure, this beach is an excellent spot for swimming. Visitors can also enjoy the authentic experience of a fishing village at Ban Mai Rut with plenty of seafood and an insight into the lives of the local fishermen.

Hat Ban Chuen ⓳

หาดบานชื่น

Road Map E2. 39 miles (63 km) SE of Trat.

Located between Ban Mai Rut and Khlong Yai, Hat Ban Chuen is the longest beach in Trat. This stretch of powdery sand crosses the foundation structure of a non-functional Cambodian refugee camp. Simple bungalow accommodations offer lodging to overnight visitors and a small restaurant sells fresh seafood dishes. This beach attracts a lively local crowd from Trat.

Thatched beachside seafood shacks at Hat Ban Chuen

Ban Hat Lek ⓴

บ้านหาดเล็ก

Road Map E2. 57 miles (92 km) SE of Trat. *4,500.* *daily.*

The tiny settlement of Ban Hat Lek marks the actual border crossing between Thailand and Cambodia. It is an outpost from where travelers can take a boat out of the country to Cambodia. Visas and other immigration formalities can be completed at Khlong Yai – the last town before the border crossing.

However, this region has had a troubled past due to incessant political instability and geographical proximity to Cambodia. During the time of Pol Pot and the Khmer Rouge, and the subsequent disputes over control of the country from 1975 to 1986, this area was referred to as "bandit country" and was quite unsafe. Things have changed now, but there is still a palpable "Wild East" feel to the place, with touts seeking to speed up the visa application process to get travelers to the Cambodian side of the border. On the other side is a similar, if slightly more debauched, remote frontier post. Although officials are beginning to crack down, it is better to be careful here, especially after dark.

The border is currently open from 7am–8pm daily. Travelers crossing over to Cambodia can stay overnight at Koh Kong, the first town on the other side.

Cambodian houses along the border at Ban Hat Lek

UPPER WESTERN GULF COAST

The alluring Upper Western Gulf Coast extends from Phetchaburi to Chumphon covering a distance of almost 292 miles (470 km). Close to Bangkok, notably around the old, historic town of Phetchaburi and the royal getaway Hua Hin, the beach resorts are well developed and extremely popular. Further south, however, there are fewer people, and miles of long, white, sandy beaches stretch gloriously into the distance.

Steeped in history and culture, Thailand's Upper Western Gulf Coast is characterized by historically relevant towns such as Phetchaburi, with its crumbling architectural remnants of the Khmer, Mon, Ayutthaya, and Rattanakosin epochs.

The Tenasserim Mountains, rising to 4,350 ft (1,326 m), form a long spine down the peninsula, dividing Thai territory from that of neighboring Myanmar. This range absorbs much of the rain that falls during the southwest monsoon, keeping the region relatively dry, even when there is heavy rain on the nearby Andaman Coast to the west. However, this coastal region is still fertile, famed for its juicy, tropical fruits such as pineapples, coconuts, sugarcane, "lady finger" bananas, sugar palms, and mangosteens. The Upper Western Gulf Coast's heavily forested interior and spectacular beaches, which are sheltered by mountains, attract vacationers more than its historic buildings and museums. The beautiful, casuarina-lined fronts of Cha-am and Hua Hin are enduringly popular, particularly with weekenders from Bangkok, as are gorgeous and unspoiled strands such as Hat Ao Noi and Ao Manao at Prachuap Khiri Khan. The many golf courses within easy reach of Cha-am and Hua Hin make this area arguably the country's premier golf destination. Trekkers and bird-watchers will also be drawn to the natural beauty of Khao Sam Roi Yot and Kaeng Krachan national parks, where migratory birds rest and feed in the salt marshes between the months of August and April.

Fishing boat sailing in calm waters off Bang Saphan Yai at sunset

◁ Magnificent images of the Buddha inside Wat Mahathat Worawihan, Phetchaburi

Exploring the Upper Western Gulf Coast

This long, narrow coastal strip, backed by a range of mountains along the Burmese border, stretches from the cultural center of Phetchaburi to the quiet fishing port of Chumphon and the beaches as far beyond as isolated Hat Arunothai. In the north lie one of Thailand's oldest beach resorts, Hua Hin, and the more modern resort of Cha-am. This area is also home to several wildlife sanctuaries such as the green and hilly Kaeng Krachan National Park, as well as the characteristic limestone outcrops of the coastal Khao Sam Roi Yot National Park. Chumphon, in the south, traditionally marks the point where central Thai culture gives way and Thailand's Muslim presence gradually grows stronger.

Fleet of fishing boats near the harbor, Hat Thung Wua Laen

SIGHTS AT A GLANCE

Towns, Cities, and Villages
Bang Saphan 21
Cha-am 2
Chumphon 25
Dan Singkhon 17
Hua Hin pp140–41 5
Phetchaburi pp134–7 1
Prachuap Khiri Khan 12
Pranburi 6

National Parks
Kaeng Krachan National Park 3
Khao Sam Roi Yot National Park pp144–5 8

Theme Parks
King Mongkut Memorial Park of Science & Technology 19

Historic Buildings and Religious Sites
Marukhathaiyawan Palace 4
Wat Khao Tham Khan Kradai 13

Beaches, Islands, and Bays
Ao Bang Nang Rom 15
Ao Manao 16
Ao Thung Makham 27
Ko Ngam Yai and Ko Ngam Noi 23
Hat Ao Noi 14
Hat Arunothai 28
Hat Ban Krut 20
Hat Laem Sala 10
Hat Naresuan 7
Hat Hat Sam Roi Yot 9
Hat Sai Ri 26
Hat Sam Phraya 11
Hat Thung Wua Laen 22
Hat Wa Kaw 18
Hin Lak Ngam 24

SEE ALSO

• ***Where to Stay*** pp298–300

• ***Where to Eat*** pp324–6

Farmers harvesting rice in a field, Prachuap Khiri Khan

GETTING AROUND

Most of the attractions in the region are easily accessible from Highway 4, the main route between Bangkok and the south. The major towns are linked to each other and to the capital by regular bus and train services (Bangkok to Hua Hin is 3–4 hours by bus or train; Bangkok to Chumphon is 8–9 hours by bus or train). There are no scheduled domestic flights within the area and the nearest domestic airports are further south at Ko Samui and Surat Thani. *Songthaews*, motorcycles, or trishaws can be usually hired for trips to local sights. However, the easiest and also the most convenient way to explore the area is by a self-driven vehicle. Car rental facilities are available at Bangkok, Cha-am, and Hua Hin.

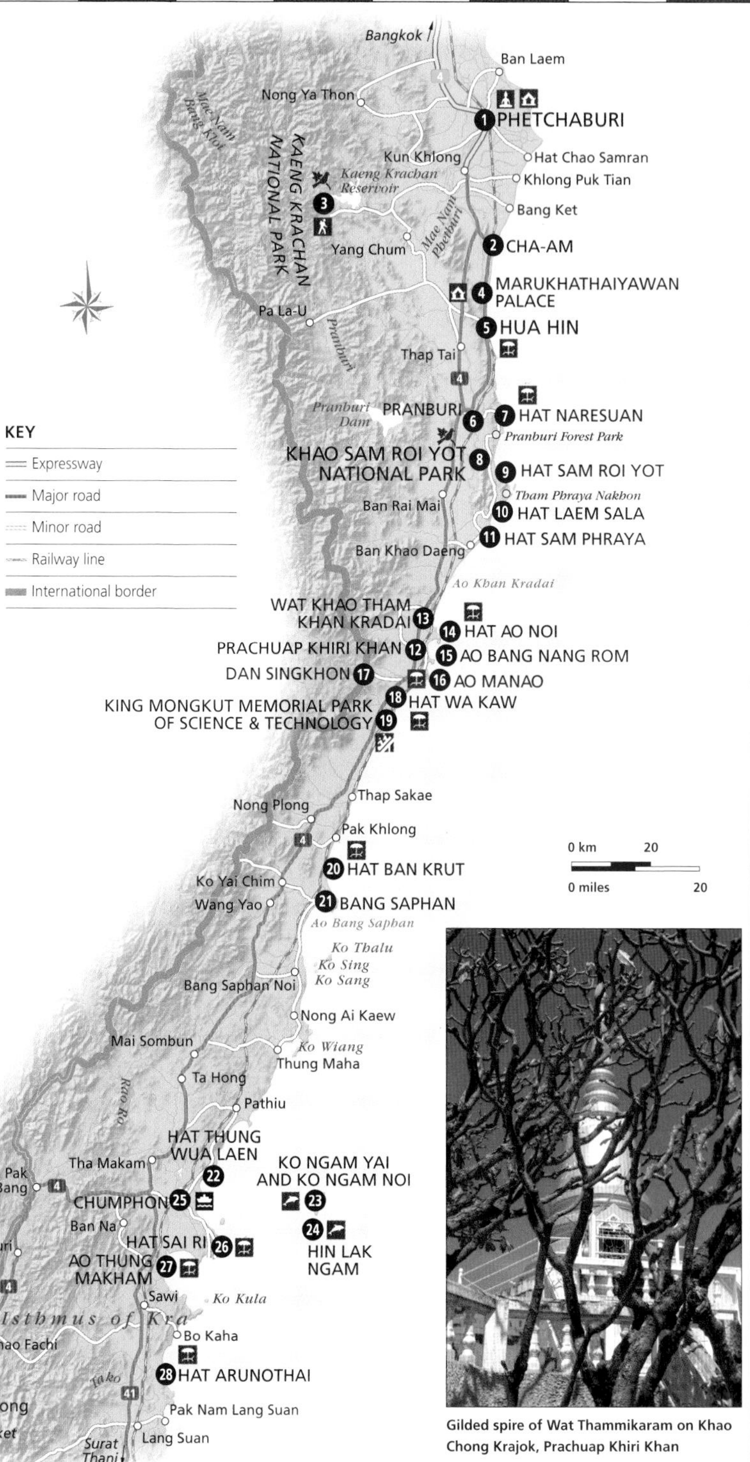

Gilded spire of Wat Thammikaram on Khao Chong Krajok, Prachuap Khiri Khan

Street-by-Street: Phetchaburi ❶

เพชรบุรี

Settled since at least the 11th century, Phetchaburi (often spelled Phetburi) is one of Thailand's oldest towns. Capital of the Phetchaburi province, it has long been an important trading and cultural center, and Mon, Khmer, and Ayutthayan influences can be seen in its 30 temples. During the 19th century it became a favorite royal retreat, and Rama IV *(see p151)* built a summer house here on a hill, Khao Wang, west of the center. This is now part of the Phra Nakhon Khiri Historical Park *(see p136)*. Other major sights are the 17th-century Wat Yai Suwannaram, the five Khmer *prangs* of Wat Kamphaeng Laeng, and an old quarter that has retained much of its original charm. However, accommodations are scant and most visitors come only on day trips from Bangkok.

Fountain, Phra Nakhon Khiri

Phra Song Road
A crowded road in the heart of Phetchaburi.

To Phra Nakhon Khiri Historical Park

BANDAI-IT

Wat Mahathat Worawihan
The five white Khmer-style prangs *of this much-restored 14th-century temple dominate the town's central skyline. Figures of angels and gods decorate the roofs of the main* wihan *and* bot.

STAR SIGHTS

★ Phra Nakhon Khiri Historical Park

★ Wat Yai Suwannaram

★ Wat Kamphaeng Laeng

To Wat Tho

Wooden Shophouses
Concrete may have replaced wood in most Thai towns, but attractive wooden buildings, many lining the river bank, are still a feature in Phetchaburi.

★ Phra Nakhon Khiri Historical Park

As an avid astronomer, Rama IV had this observatory conveniently built next to his hilltop summer palace; this is now a museum. The surrounding park is magnificently landscaped and forested, offering extensive views of Phetchaburi.

VISITORS' CHECKLIST

Road Map C1. 75 miles (120 km) SW of Bangkok. *80,000. TAT, Cha-am (0-3247-1005). daily. Phra Nakhon Khiri Fair (8 daysin early Feb).*

★ Wat Yai Suwannaram

Built during the Ayutthaya period (see pp40–41), *the temple is notable for the lovely original murals of Hindu gods in the* bot. *A scripture library stands on stilts in the middle of a large pond on the grounds.*

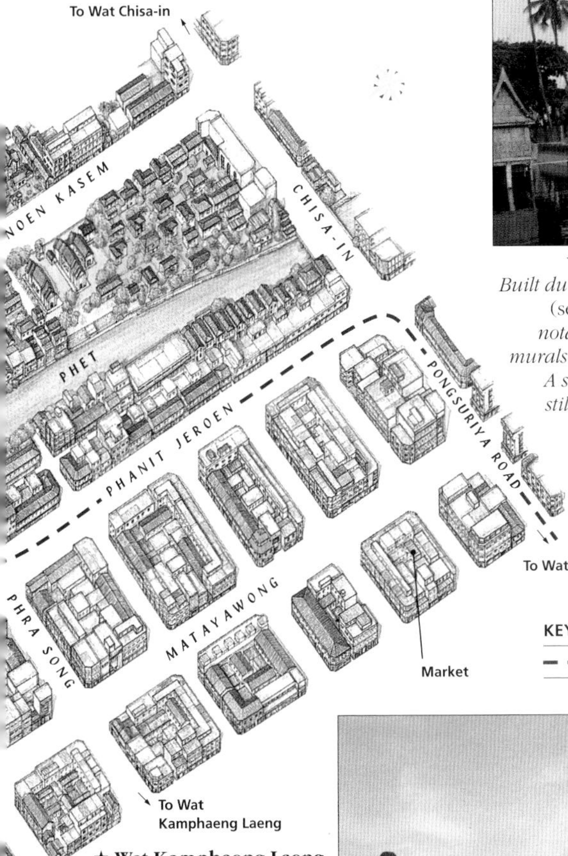

To Wat Chisa-in

NOEN KASEM

CHISA-IN

PHET

PHANIT JEROEN

PONGSURIYA ROAD

PHRA SONG

MATAYAWONG

Market

0 meters 75

0 yards 75

To Wat Yai Suwannaram

KEY

Suggested route

★ Wat Kamphaeng Laeng

This is one of the few surviving Khmer shrines in Thailand outside the northeast. The five laterite prangs *of the temple, in varying states of disrepair, are typically Khmer in design and may date from the 12th century. Originally a Hindu temple, it was later adapted for Buddhist use.*

Exploring Phetchaburi

Statue of Rama V

An old city replete with historical buildings and temples, Phetchaburi, which means Diamond Town, is a royal city of frangipani flowers and exotic sweets. It is divided by the Phet River, which winds its way through this provincial capital. Many of Phetchaburi's *wats* and temples, especially from the Ayutthaya period, are well preserved and others have been expertly restored. The city skyline is dominated by the pinnacles of the *wats* and three large hills over its western side. Phetchaburi's architecture is influenced by Buddhist iconography and is a combination of Oriental, Indian, European, and Khmer styles.

Three-tiered gilded Buddha images at Wat Mahathat Worawihan

Sunlight illuminating the main chamber at Khao Luang Cave

Khao Luang Cave

ถ้ำเขาหลวง

3 miles (5 km) NW of town center.

8am–6pm daily. voluntary donation.

The large and spectacular Khao Luang Cave has three linked chambers filled with stalactites and a number of Buddha images, including a *phra non* (Reclining Buddha). The main bronze image was cast on the orders of Rama V (r.1868–1910) and dedicated to his illustrious predecessors, Rama III (r.1824–51) and Rama IV (r.1851–68). There is a natural opening in the roof of the second chamber and sunlight streams through, especially on clear days, illuminating the images inside. To the right of the cave entrance at the foot of the hill, is **Wat Tham Klaep**. Also known as Wat Bun Thawi, the monastery's distinctive *wihan* and *bot* have beautifully carved wooden doors.

Khao Wang and Phra Nakhon Khiri Historical Park

เขาวังและอุทยานประวัติศาสตร์พระนครคีรี

Off Phet Kasem Road. ***Tel*** *0-3242-5600. 9am–5pm daily.*

Perched on the summit of the 302-ft (92-m) high Khao Khiri hill, Phra Nakhon Khiri, literally, Celestial City of the Mountain, is now a historical park dominating the northwestern skyline of Phetchaburi. This palace complex was built as the summer residence of Rama IV in the 1850s and the hill is now locally known as Khao Wang or Palace Hill. The king ordered the building of this complex as a getaway from Bangkok. Chinese, European, and Japanese architectural flourishes are blended with local Thai designs. Set among forests, rocks, and caverns, it offers a fine view of the town as well as a panoramic vista of the province. The entire complex extends over three peaks and includes royal halls, temples, palaces, and other buildings. The Royal Palace and Ho Chatchawan Wiangchai, an observatory tower built for Rama IV who was an accomplished astronomer, are both perched on the western rise. The Phra That Chomphet, a white *chedi* erected by Rama V, stands on the central rise while Wat Maha Samanaram, containing some fine murals, dominates the eastern rise. In 1988, the complex was converted into a historical park. Access to the summit is either by way of winding cobblestone paths, or by funicular railway to the west of the hill, for visitors who do not want an energetic uphill trek. This park merits at least a half-day excursion.

Wat Mahathat Worawihan

วัดมหาธาตุวรวิหาร

Thanon Damnoen Kasem.

8:30am–4pm daily.

Located in the center of town, the five unmissable white *prangs* of the Wat Mahathat Worawihan rise

View of Phra Nakhon Khiri Historical Park

against the skyline forming the spiritual heart of Phetchaburi. It is thought to have been built in the 14th century, but attained *mahathat* status – the rank of a monastery with a *chedi* containing a relic of the Buddha – only in 1954. The relic at Worawihan was donated by the present king, Rama IX. The temple, distinguished by its *prangs* – the central one 180-ft (55-m) high – and its Khmer-style *chedi*, is influenced by the Mahayana school of Buddhism. The sacred *sema* stones that mark the temple precincts may be relics of an even older version of the *wat*. Some of these stones date back to the late Dvaravati period *(see p39)*. There is a large *wihan* in front of the temple, housing a splendid multitiered Buddha statue. The walls of the *wihan* are decorated with more than 100 murals. Many of these depict Thai people dressed in European-style clothing from the Victorian era.

Ancient murals depicting Buddhist mythology, Wat Yai Suwannaram

Wat Yai Suwannaram

วัดใหญ่สุวรรณาราม

Thanon Phongsuriya. *8:30am–4pm daily.*

Perhaps the most appealing of Phetchaburi's many temples, Wat Yai Suwannaram is a 17th-century temple noted for its series of 300-year-old murals of *thevada* (Buddhist angels) on the interior walls of the main *wihan*. Nearby lies a teak *sala* with finely carved doors, one of them bearing a cut reportedly made by an invading Burmese soldier's sword during the war of 1767 *(see p41)*. The

Buddha statue among Khmer ruins, Wat Kamphaeng Laeng

main *bot* constructed in the Ayutthaya style, is without any windows. The complex also has an unusual *hor trai* (scripture repository) in the middle of a lotus-filled pond. It is raised on stilts above the water to protect the palm leaf manuscripts from white ants and other destructive insects.

Wat Kamphaeng Laeng

วัดกำแพงแลง

Thanon Phongsuriya. *8:30am–4pm daily.*

Located in the eastern part of Phetchaburi, Wat Kamphaeng Laeng is undoubtedly the town's oldest surviving structure. This semi-ruined Khmer building indicates that the city was probably the southernmost part of the Khmer Empire (9th–13th century) that stretched east as far as the Mekong delta and the South China Sea, and north to central Laos. Originally believed to be a Hindu place of worship, it was converted into a Buddhist temple. Five rather ramshackle Khmer *prangs* survive, each of which was probably dedicated to a particular Hindu deity. They are set in a cruciform arrangement facing east. Made of sandstone and laterite, with Dvaravati stucco work on the walls, the complex dates back to the 11th or 12th century.

Phra Ratchawang Ban Puen

พระราชวังบ้านปืน

1 mile (2 km) S of town center.

Tel *0-3242-8506–9.* *8am–4pm daily.*

Located in the middle of the Phetchaburi military barracks, Phra Ratchawang Ban Puen is an early 20th-century palace. Constructed by Rama V, the building is more a grand European-style villa than a palace. The work began shortly before his death in 1910, but was not completed until 1916. The palace designed by German architects is in the modernist European style patronized by Thai monarchs and has beautiful glazed tiles adorning its interiors.

Glazed tiles and marble figurines inside Phra Ratchawang Ban Puen

Thailand's Sweet and Dessert Capital

Phetchaburi is well known throughout Thailand for the variety and excellence of its sweets, which are based on natural local products such as palm sugar, palm seeds, coconut, banana, rose apple, pineapple, and many other fresh seasonal fruits. Phetchaburi *tanot* (palm sugar) is believed to be particularly sweet and refreshing, and is combined with other ingredients such as flour, eggs, and rice. These *Thai khanom* (Thai sweets) differ in textures and cooking styles from their Western counterparts and are often served with ice, wrapped in banana leaves, or as small cakes. Two of Phetchaburi province's most important festivals – the Phra Nakhon Khiri Fair and Thai Song Dam Festival – showcase these local sweets. Villagers dressed in traditional costumes demonstrate traditional sweet-making and also sell them at the festival fairs.

Ripe bananas, used in sweets

Thai khanom, unlike Western sweets, are rarely stored or wrapped. They are usually made for swift consumption and taste better fresh.

SWEET AND DESSERTS MARKET
Almost all markets in Thailand have a sweet and dessert section offering everything from national favorites to local specialties. Most vendors are happy to let visitors sample the merchandise before purchase.

Coconut *is one of the most versatile ingredients in Thai sweets. It is used in various forms to make a wide array of desserts.*

Khao tom mat sai kluay *is made using another typical Thai base – sweetened sticky rice. Flavored with coconut milk and steamed in a banana leaf, this dessert is eaten with fresh fruits such as ripe bananas and durians.*

The golden three – thong yip, thong yawt, *and* foy thong – *are famous Phetchaburi desserts made by boiling duck egg yolks in a palm sugar syrup. Different textures emerge due to the cooking process.*

Wun maphrao *is a colorful jelly made with coconut, agar-agar, and sugar. It is often found in open-air markets.*

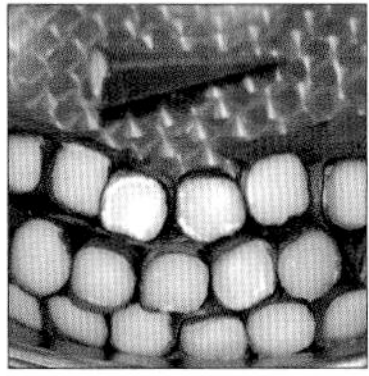

Tako *is a delicious custard made out of green pea flour, water chestnuts, sugar, and coconut cream. It is cooked in pandanus leaves and served chilled.*

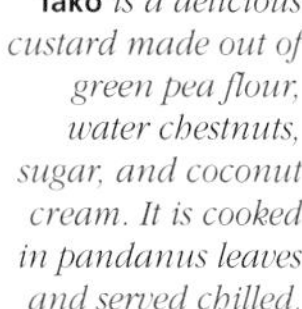

Kalamae *is a local toffee made out of coconut cream, sugar, and flour that is thickened into a sticky solid and then cut into bite-sized pieces.*

Long verandas connecting different halls and chambers in Marukhathaiyawan Palace

Cha-am ❷

ชะอำ

Road map C1. 21 miles (34 km) S of Phetchaburi. 20,000. *TAT, 500/51 Phet Kasem Rd, Cha-am (0-3247-1005).* *daily.*

Famous for its 3-mile (5-km) long sandy beach, Cha-am has experienced a dramatic surge in popularity since the mid-1980s. From a quiet fishing village and local market town, it has developed into a lively weekend getaway for visitors from Bangkok.

Other attractions in the town include the large market for fresh produce, the fishing pier lined with seafood restaurants, and Wat Cha-am, a small cave temple dating back to the Ayutthaya period *(see pp40–41)*. The town caters chiefly to Thais who are fond of their food and drink and there are plenty of options in and around the beach. Stalls and vendors sell delicious grilled fish and other fresh seafood alongside local specialties of roast chicken and roast pork. Large resorts have sprung up alongside the beach. Apart from this, there are also some formal dining options along the northern end of the beach.

Kaeng Krachan National Park ❸

อุทยานแห่งชาติแก่งกระจาน

Road map C1. Park HQ off Hwy 3175, 30 miles (48 km) W of Cha-am. *Park HQ (0-3245-9293); Forestry Dept (0-2562-0760)* for bungalow bookings. **www**.dnp.go.th

Containing pristine tracts of tropical evergreen forest, Kaeng Krachan National Park attracts few visitors despite being the largest national park in Thailand. Established in 1981, it spans an area of 1,150 sq miles (2,920 sq km) covering nearly half of the Phetchaburi province. It is home to at least 40 species of mammals including tigers, leopards, elephants, gibbons, and Asiatic bears. Thousands of migratory birds come here from as far as China and Siberia to breed and feed in the salt marshes.

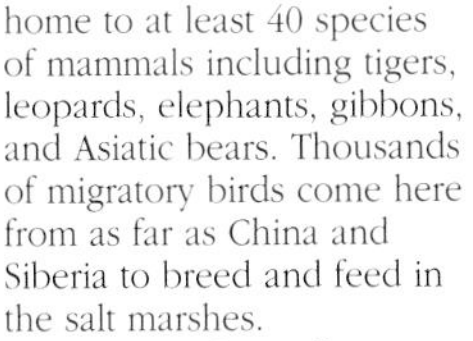

Kaeng Krachan offers visitors some excellent hiking as well as boat rides through the 45-sq km (17-sq mile) **Kaeng Krachan Reservoir**, fed by forest streams and rivers.

Marukhathaiyawan Palace ❹

พระราชวังมฤคทายวัน

Road map C1. Off Hwy 4, 5 miles (9 km) S of Cha-am. *TAT, Cha-am (0-3247-1005).* *from Cha-am.* *8:30am–4:30pm daily.* *donation.* *in bedroom.*

The erstwhile summer home of Rama VI (r.1910–25), Marukhathaiyawan Palace, meaning the Palace of Love and Hope, is a grand teak building. Designed by an Italian architect, this palace was constructed in just 16 days in 1923. However, it was abandoned when Rama VI died two years later and stood neglected for decades. It has since been restored to its original glory. Yet, despite its accessibility, the palace is rarely visited.

The airy building with its simply decorated halls, verandas, and royal chambers is painted in pastel shades. The walkways have lovely views of the beach and the sea.

Horses for hire along the long stretch of beach at Cha-am

Hua Hin 5

หัวหิน

Royal waiting room

Hua Hin was Thailand's first beach resort. The key to its success was its rail connection to Bangkok, completed in 1911. Following the international trend for recuperative spa resorts at the time, Hua Hin became a popular retreat for minor Thai royalty, Bangkok high society, and affluent foreign visitors. A nine-hole golf course was built in 1922 and Prince Chulachakrabongse (1908–63) built a summer palace here in 1926, which he called Klai Klangwon, literally, Far from Worries. Despite a decline in fortunes post World War II, this seaside town has grown into an international resort, with beer bars sharing the seafront with several upscale resorts.

Red- and white-tiled platform at Hua Hin Railway Station

Hua Hin Railway Station

สถานีรถไฟหัวหิน

Thanon Liap Thang Rot Fai.

Billed as Thailand's "most beautiful train station", this is also one of the oldest, dating back to the late 19th century. The most striking feature is the main wooden building, which today serves as the passenger reception and waiting room. It was originally a royal pavilion at the Sanam Chan Palace in Nakhon Pathom. Constructed in the late Rattanakosin style of Rama VI (r.1910–25), it features temple-like multitiered roofs with typically Thai uptilted eaves, as well as elongated, lozenge-shaped vertical windows painted in rust red and creamy yellow. A gleaming, retired steam locomotive is on display opposite the platform. The building exudes a seductive, period charm and is a favorite with most camera-happy visitors to Hua Hin.

Railway Hotel

โรงแรมรถไฟ

1, Thanon Damnoen Kasem. *Tel 0-3251-2021.*

www.sofitel.com

Built in 1923, the splendid Colonial-style Railway Hotel provides an insight into the Hua Hin of the 1920s. A luxurious upscale spa and resort in its modern guise, the hotel, now known as the Sofitel Centara Grand Resort and Villas *(see p299)*, retains its period charm with winding teak staircases and high-ceilinged rooms. It is almost obligatory to stop by for a drink, just to soak in the atmosphere. The hotel fell into disrepair in the 1960s, but sensitive restoration won it the Outstanding Conservation Award in 1993. It was used in the film *The Killing Fields*, as a stand-in for the Renakse Hotel in Phnom Penh, Cambodia.

Hat Hua Hin

หาดหัวหิน

Thanon Damnoen Kasem.

Named for the large, smooth, boulders that litter its northern end, Hat Hua Hin, or Hua Hin Beach, is a surprisingly good beach with clean, soft, white sand. Extending for about 3 miles (5 km), it is lined with small souvenir shops, bars, and restaurants. The best stretch, however, is in front of the Railway Hotel. Set back from Hat Hua Hin for much of its length is a long line of condominiums and luxury homes. Relatively quiet on weekdays, the beach is usually bustling with activity on weekends. Good for swimming, Hat Hua Hin also offers pony rides for children and a variety of thrilling watersports such as waterskiing and kiteboarding.

Night Market

ตลาดโต้รุ่ง

Thanon Dechanuchit West. *5pm to midnight daily.*

Bustling with people and activity, the Hua Hin night market extends for a short

Beachside restaurant with great sea views, Railway Hotel

Picturesque park with walking track atop Khao Hin Lek Fai

distance along both sides of Thanon Dechanuchit, and especially at the Thanon Sasong crossroad. The market is open from 5pm to midnight. The area is usually teeming with locals intent on commerce and visitors who flock to the various reasonably priced stalls, bargaining for souvenirs and other purchases. The roadside eateries, usually quite clean and hygienic, are wonderful for a delicious fresh seafood dinner, made to order. This is also the place to buy souvenir T-shirts and other cheap clothing, DVDs, as well as secondhand books in English and other Western languages.

Khao Hin Lek Fai

เขาหินเหล็กไฟ

2 miles (3 km) W of town center.

A 518-ft (158-m) high hill, Khao Hin Lek Fai, or Flintstone Hill, has a quiet park at the summit offering scenic views across town. There are six separate viewpoints identified by signs. The park's entrance is by Suksamran Temple and can be reached on foot, car, or bicycle. It is frequented by early birds who come here to exercise or relax and enjoy the beauty of the area. By the side of the road leading up the hill, bustling Chatchai Market sells a wide variety of snacks and souvenirs.

VISITORS' CHECKLIST

Road Map C2. 17 miles (27 km) S of Cha-am. *85,000.* *TAT Cha-am, (0-3247-1005).* *daily.* *Hua Hin Jazz Festival, Jun* **www**.tourismhuahin.com

Khao Takiab

เขาตะเกียบ

4 miles (6 km) S of town center.

Rising just 250 ft (76 m) above sea level, Khao Takiab, or Chopstick Hill, is covered with several small shrines and images of Guan Yin, Goddess of Mercy. Near the foot of the hill is a 66-ft (20-m) tall statue of a Standing Buddha. Nearby stands Wat Khao Lad, an impressive Buddhist temple with a distinctive pagoda.

Southern end of Hat Hua Hin, with Khao Takiab in the background

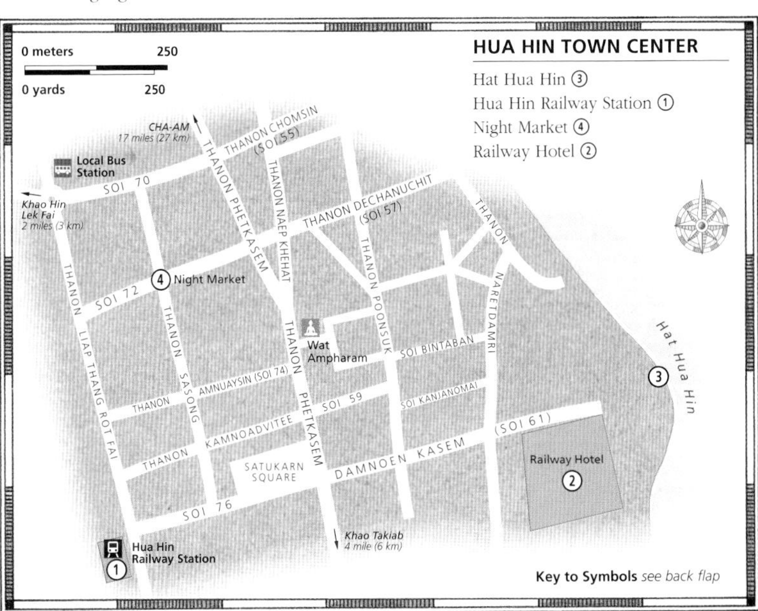

Coastal road linking Hat Naresuan to Pranburi

Pranburi ❻

ปราณบุรี

Road Map C2. 22 miles (35 km) S of Hua Hin. *70,000.* *daily.*

A small town which is now becoming a preferred destination for visitors to Thailand, Pranburi is blessed with pristine beaches and a handful of good resorts. A popular attraction here is the **Pranburi Forest Park**, an area of mangrove forests located by the Pranburi River. Declared a forest park in 1982, it covers an area of 2 sq miles (5 sq km). The reserve lies close to the sea and boasts a 1-mile (2-km) long beach, lined with palm trees. An elevated wooden platform runs above part of the mangrove swamp making it easy to trek through the forest. River trips by boat can be arranged from the park office open throughout the day. Pranburi is also well located for visitors to Hat Naresuan and Khao Sam Roi Yot National Park nearby.

Pranburi Forest Park
dawn to dusk daily.

Hat Naresuan ❼

หาดนเรศวร – ปากน้ำปราณ

Road Map C2. 6 miles (10 km) E of Pranburi. *TAT, Cha-am (0-3247-1005).*

Perhaps the first quiet beach south of Bangkok, Hat Naresuan is a long stretch of almost deserted golden sand, lined with tall palm and casuarina trees. The beach is known by several names. A small hill at its southern end which resembles a *kalok* (skull) gives it the popular name of Hat Khao Kalok, or Skull Hill Beach. Another name for the beach is Pak Nam Pran after the town located 5 miles (8 km) to its north, at the mouth of the Pranburi River. Its official name, Hat Naresuan, however, honors King Naresuan *(see p41)* who re-established Siamese independence and drove out the Burmese in the late 16th century. Originally frequented by rich Thai families, it is now developing into a busy resort with several upscale as well as inexpensive boutique hotels and restaurants, a few small markets, and a variety of utility stores. Although not a spectacular beach, Hat Naresuan is popular for its attractive and reasonably priced accommodations. Dolphins playing in the sea are a common sight here and can usually be seen directly from the shore. There are several seafood restaurants in Pak Nam Pran town, as well as along the beachfront, which serve fresh food.

Popular beachfront restaurant on Hat Naresuan

Khao Sam Roi Yot National Park ❽

อุทยานแห่งชาติเขาสามร้อยยอด

See pp144–5.

Hat Sam Roi Yot 9

หาดนมสาว

Road Map C2. Khao Sam Roi Yot National Park. *TAT, Cha-am (0-3247-1005).*

A clean beach with crisp, golden sand and shaded by palm trees, Hat Sam Roi Yot, also called Hat Nom Sao, runs through the eastern part of the Khao Sam Roi Yot National Park. This beautiful beach is considered safe and good for swimming. Basic, yet comfortable beachside accommodations are available and there are also a number of small and friendly restaurants and bars. Hat Sam Roi Yot also serves as the jumping-off point for several small, offshore islands including Ko Nom Sao, Ko Kho Ram, Ko Rawing, and Ko Rawang, all excellent for snorkeling and private sunbathing. These islands are easily accessible by speedboat.

Beautiful Hat Sam Phraya, an ideal beach for campers

Hat Laem Sala 10

หาดแหลมศาลา

Road Map C2. Khao Sam Roi Yot National Park. *TAT, Cha-am (0-3247-1005).*

An attractive beach surrounded by steep limestone hills and fringed by casuarina trees, Hat Laem Sala is an isolated stretch of sand. Located at the eastern edge of the Khao Sam Roi Yot National Park, the beach is equipped with a visitor center, restaurants, and basic bungalow accommodations. Beachfront restaurants serve a variety of fried seafood. The water here is safe for swimming; other outdoor activities include camping, trekking, and cave diving. Hat Laem Sala also marks the approach to **Tham Phraya Nakhon**. Built for Rama V (r.1868–1910), it is among the most popular caves in Thailand.

Rocky outcrop with thick vegetation, Hat Sam Roi Yot

Hat Sam Phraya 11

หาดสามพระยา

Road Map C2. Khao Sam Roi Yot National Park. *TAT, Cha-am (0-3247-1005).*

A relatively untouristed white sand beach Hat Sam Phraya is well-equipped for campers visiting the Khao Sam Roi Yot National Park, with washing facilities as well as toilets on either end of the beach. There are also adequate, if not luxurious, bungalow accommodations, and small seafood restaurants and shops. Fine views across Hat Sam Phraya can be had from the summit of nearby Khao Daeng, or Red Hill, especially at sunset. Visitors can also embark on a cruise to explore **Khlong Khao Daeng**, or Khao Daeng canal. Located only about 1 mile (2 km) from the park, the canal is fringed by mangroves. This relaxing trip, lasting over an hour, covers a distance of 3 miles (5 km), and is best taken at sundown.

Khao Sam Roi Yot National Park 8

อุทยานแห่งชาติเขาสามร้อยยอด

"Beware of monkeys" sign

A small coastal park, Khao Sam Roi Yot, which means Mountain of Three Hundred Peaks, covers an area of 38 sq miles (98 sq km). It is a region of contrasts – sea, sand, and marsh, backed by mountains and caves. The park is best known for its distinctive limestone pinnacles, the highest of which, Khao Krachom, rises to a height of 1,985 ft (605 m). The park's fine beaches, freshwater marshes, and mangrove forests provide sanctuary to millions of migratory birds flying from Siberia to Sumatra and Australia; these birds rest, feed, and breed here. It is also home to the dusky langur, the slow loris, and crab-eating macaques.

Villagers fishing in the rich waters off Khao Sam Roi Yot National Park

★ Spectacular Birdlife

Located on the East Asian-Australian Flyway, the marshland areas of the park are home to some 300 species of birds – migratory species account for almost half of these. They can be seen between the months of September and November and from March to May.

Thung Sam Roi Yot

Ban Rong Jai is the location of one of the three park headquarters at Khao Sam Roi Yot. It has an attached nature study center.

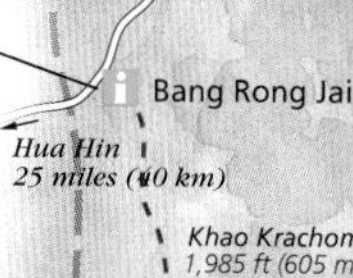

Khao Krachom dominates the limestone crags of the park. At 1,985 ft (605 m), it is not an easy climb.

Mangroves

Mangrove swamps and forests form an important coastal defence against high waves and storms; they also provide an impenetrable sanctuary for all kinds of wildlife, notably macaques and crabs.

Ban Don Yai Nu

1026

Prachuap Khiri Khan
30 miles (48 km)

STAR SIGHTS

- ★ Spectacular Birdlife
- ★ View of the Three Hundred Peaks
- ★ Tham Phraya Nakhon

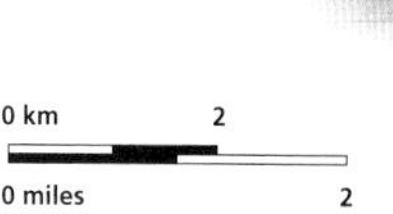

The southern marshlands have been little affected by encroaching shrimp farms. These pristine areas remain the best bird-watching spots.

For hotels and restaurants in this region see pp298–300 and pp324–6

VISITORS' CHECKLIST

Road Map C2. Park HQ off Hwy 4, 27 miles (43 km) S of Pranburi. *Park HQ (0-3282-1568); Forestry Dept (0-2562-0760).* *Pranburi, then* songthaew. **www**.dnp.go.th *(for bungalow bookings).*

★ View of the Three Hundred Peaks
The park's many limestone peaks are clad in evergreen and deciduous bushes and trees. These peaks do not make easy walking or climbing, but offer a wonderful spectacle, particularly at sunrise and sunset.

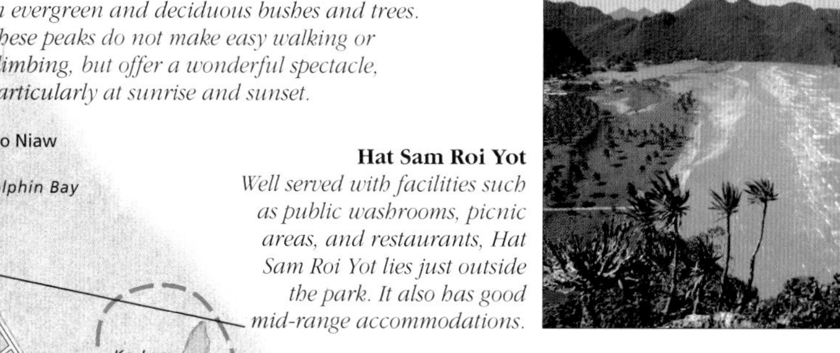

Hat Sam Roi Yot
Well served with facilities such as public washrooms, picnic areas, and restaurants, Hat Sam Roi Yot lies just outside the park. It also has good mid-range accommodations.

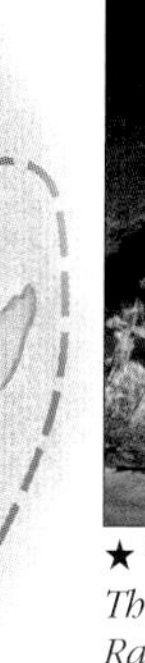

★ Tham Phraya Nakhon
This mesmerizing cave was made famous after Rama V ordered the building of an attractive sala *(pavilion) for himself here. Its attractions include the curiously shaped "crocodile rock" and "pagoda rock."*

Tham Sai, a small cavern, provides sanctuary for numerous bats and swiftlets.

Hiking trails
Marked hiking trails are scattered throughout the park. The Khao Daeng Viewpoint Trail, however, remains the most popular. The panoramic views from its summit, of the park and surrounding sea, are breathtaking.

KEY

- Beach
- Viewpoint
- Peak
- Visitor information
- Minor road
- Trail
- Park boundary

Monk ringing a bell for an early morning prayer call, Prachuap Khiri Khan ▷

Wat Thammikaram atop Khao Chong Krajok at Prachuap Khiri Khan

Prachuap Khiri Khan ⓬

ประจวบคีรีขันธ์

Road Map C2. 47 miles (75 km) S of Pranburi. TAT Cha-am (0-3247-1005). daily.

Located along the thinnest stretch of Thailand, between Myanmar on the west and the Gulf of Thailand on the east, Prachuap Khiri Khan is a fairly significant fishing port. A prominent provincial capital in southern Thailand, the town was prosperous during the Ayutthaya period *(see pp40–41)*, but skips most tourist itineraries nowadays.

Historically, Prachuap is significant as one of the seven landing points from where Imperial Japanese troops stormed ashore in 1941, on their way to occupy Malaysia and Singapore. Today, the town is rather pleasant and laid-back. Fishing is the primary occupation of the locals and their colorful, painted fishing vessels are usually anchored in the local harbor. Pineapple farms and coconut plantations occupy many acres of land and contribute to the economy of the area. The inland edge of the town is ringed with limestone mountains. A famous landmark – **Khao Chong Krajok**, or Mirror Tunnel Mountain – derives its name from a natural opening that resembles a giant mirror. **Wat Thammikaram** perched on its peak is Prachuap's most revered site, and offers visitors fine panoramic views right across the town and bay. Hundreds of macaques live in the area and visitors often come here to watch them. Every evening, the monkeys climb to the top to feed on the many beautiful frangipani trees.

The town makes up for its lack of entertainment by its fantastic cuisine. Freshly caught seafood is available at quality restaurants and stalls along the promenade near the pier. Prachuap Khiri Khan is also a good base to explore the surrounding areas. The common mode of transport here is the *saaleng* (an improvised motorcycle with a side car).

Wat Khao Tham Khan Kradai ⓭

วัดถ้ำเขาคั่นกระได

Road Map C2. 5 miles (8 km) N of Prachuap Khiri Khan. 8:30am–4pm daily.

Monk's residence, Wat Khao Tham Khan Kradai

A Buddhist cave temple set above the beautiful Ao Khan Kradai, also known as Ao Khan Bandai, Wat Khao Tham Khan Kradai is slightly off the beaten track. The road to the temple winds its way up a limestone hill overlooking the bay. There is a trail paved with shells and signposts marking the route. From the cave entrance, there are stunning views across the broad

Buddha images lining the inner chamber at Wat Khao Tham Khan Kradai

Handcrafted fishing boats anchored along the shore at Ao Bang Nang Rom

sweep of Ao Khan Kradai. The *wat* complex comprises two caves; entrance is through the smaller cave. This opens into a larger cave with a *phra non* (Reclining Buddha). A chamber near the entrance is filled with Buddha images brought by devotees as part of merit-making acts. Carrying a flashlight is useful as the interior is quite dark.

Visitors from Prachuap Khiri Khan will need to arrange a *songthaew* or *saaleng* from town. Those with vehicles can combine a visit to the *wat* with a picnic at Hat Ao Noi.

Hat Ao Noi ⓮

หาดอ่าวน้อย

Road Map C2. 3 miles (5 km) N of Prachuap Khiri Khan.

A quiet, laid-back bathing spot, Hat Ao Noi, or Little Bay Beach, is a casuarina-lined beach popular with joggers and day-trippers from nearby Prachuap Khiri Khan. To the northern end of the bay lies the small fishing village of Ao Ban Noi. The southern end is connected to the busier Ao Prachuap by a bridge. The beach is quite deserted but offers good accommodations along with a few restaurants that serve appetizing seafood. The northern end of the bay is protected by a limestone massif.

Ao Bang Nang Rom ⓯

อ่าวบางนางรม

Road Map C2. 3 miles (5 km) E of Prachuap Khiri Khan.

Located close to Prachuap Khiri Khan and its satellite beach, Hat Ao Noi, Ao Bang Nang Rom is home to a prosperous fishing village reputed for its excellent handmade wooden fishing vessels. These colorful boats are used either by the local fishermen themselves or sold to neighboring communities. Fishermen go out in these vessels to catch the *ching chang* – a prized local fish and an important source of livelihood. These small saltwater fish, part of the anchovy family, are cleaned, dried, and then preserved with condiments. These fish are popular among South Asian buyers. Although there is not much to do here, the friendly locals and the beautiful, well-located beach make it worth a stopover.

Ao Manao ⓰

อ่าวมะนาว

Road Map C2. 4 miles (6 km) S of Prachuap Khiri Khan.

Prachuap's loveliest bay, Ao Manao, or Lemon Bay, is lined by a fine beach. Originally an R&R (Rest and Recreation) site for officers from the nearby Royal Thai Air Force base, the beach is well maintained thanks to the military presence. A fair is held every December in the air force compound commemorating the soldiers who died during the Japanese landing in 1941. Facilities at the beach include loungers, umbrellas, cold drink stands, and a few restaurants. The locals are friendly, but visitors may be asked to show their passports.

Scenic view of the wide sweeping bay at Ao Manao

Burmese products from across the border on sale in shops at Dan Singkhon

Dan Singkhon ⓱

ด่านสิงขร

Road Map C2. 12 miles (19 km) S of Prachuap Khiri Khan.

A small border post of considerable historical interest, Dan Singkhon is perched high on a watershed in the Tenasserim Mountains that divide Thailand from neighboring Myanmar. This crossing used to mark the Mawdaung Pass, which was the most important road link between the Tenasserim province and old Thailand, with a regular movement of people and commodities between the two countries till the British conquest of Burmese Tenasserim in 1826. Since then, this trade route has been closed and is now only used by local Burmese and Thai merchants. Dan Singkhon is at Thailand's narrowest point – the distance from the village to the Gulf of Thailand is a mere 8 miles (13 km). The mountain road allows visitors to look across the hills into southern Myanmar. This outpost is positioned to become a gateway to the Tenasserim archipelago.

The real attraction of Dan Singkhon, however, is the weekend flower market with a variety of rare flora, in particular orchids, imported from neighboring Myanmar. Unfortunately, many of the species are endangered, but the illegal trade continues to flourish. One of the unusual specimens on sale at Dan Singkhon is the Rafflesia, the world's largest flower whose buds are sold here. However, as the plant is parasitic and cannot be cultivated artificially, its life span is limited. The drive to Dan Singkhon is an interesting day trip from nearby Prachuap Khiri Khan, and unusual migratory birds can be seen en route. It is best to avoid purchasing plants protected under the Convention on International Trade in Endangered Species of Wild Flora and Fauna (CITES).

Rafflesia in full bloom

Hat Wa Kaw ⓲

หาดหว้ากอ

Road Map C2. 10 miles (16 km) S of Prachuap Khiri Khan.

A beautiful casuarina-lined beach encircling a small bay, Hat Wa Kaw is a quiet and clean beach. It is an ideal place for a day trip especially for visitors based in Prachuap Khiri Khan nearby. Facilities here include simple bungalow accommodations as well as a number of small restaurants serving local food. Although there are relatively few overseas travelers to be found at Hat Wa Kaw, the beach is a popular picnic spot for Thai families, especially school children visiting the King Mongkut Memorial Park.

King Mongkut Memorial Park of Science and Technology ⓳

พิพิธภัณฑ์วิทยาศาสตร์รัชกาลที่สี่

Road Map C2. 10 miles (16 km) S of Prachuap Khiri Khan. *Tel 0-3266-1098.* *8.30am–4.30pm daily.*

The largest open-air park in Thailand, King Mongkut Memorial Park of Science and Technology is both a memorial and an educational facility. Established in 1989, this park is dedicated to the memory of King Mongkut, or Rama IV (r.1851–68), one of Thailand's most revered monarchs. This park commemorates his contribution to modern Thai science. More specifically, it celebrates his visit to the area in 1868 to view an eclipse that he had predicted. Attractions include an exhibition on outer space and astronomy, a butterfly garden, and a good aquarium with a walk-through glass tunnel with many local species of fish and other marine life. Other exhibits include a statue of King Mongkut and an American steam locomotive dating back to 1925. Located close to Prachuap, the park is ideal for a day trip and is frequented by Thai families and students, who usually combine a trip to the park with a picnic at Hat Wa Kaw.

Feeding fish in the aquarium at King Mongkut Memorial Park

For hotels and restaurants in this region see pp298–300 and pp324–6

Mongkut, Thailand's Scholar King

Mongkut and his wife Debsirindra

King Mongkut, or Rama IV, was the fourth in the line of the present ruling Chakri Dynasty, and father of the illustrious Rama V (r.1868–1910). He ruled the country from 1851 until his death in 1868. A serious, scholarly man and an able ruler, Mongkut was interested in matters of religion and brought important changes in Buddhism. His government also formed new alliances with the Western world and began a series of far-sighted reforms which contributed to Thailand's uninterrupted independence right through the period of Colonial rule elsewhere. A liberal and educated man, he traveled extensively, learning about different aspects of his country and its people. Mongkut continues to be venerated as one of Thailand's most important monarchs and bears the posthumous title of *maharat* (Great King).

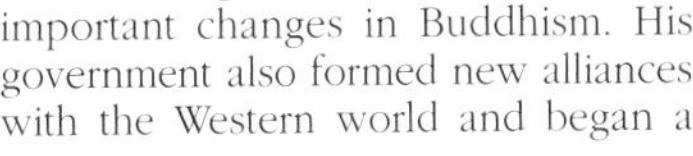

Mongkut's envoys *at the court of Queen Victoria were part of his policy to gain the backing of European powers. He turned away from his traditional allies and corresponded with foreign rulers to develop new ties with the West.*

Mongkut *took on the title of Rex Siamensis (King of Siam) after the style of Western kings. His ideas on monarchy were very progressive, influenced by international governments. Mongkut's foresight contributed much to the development of the nation.*

Wat Bowonniwet, *is where Mongkut served as a monk and later became abbot, devoting the first half of his life to religion. It still continues to be patronized by the royal family.*

Mural at Wat Ratchapradit, *Bangkok, depicts Mongkut observing a solar eclipse. He took a great interest in astronomy and was regarded as the father of modern Thai science.*

Mongkut's son Chulalongkorn, *or Rama V, was given a liberal education by his father and exposed to Western ideas. He grew up to become Thailand's greatest king who took Mongkut's legacy forward in modernizing the country.*

View of a popular resort and spa at beautiful Hat Ban Krut

Hat Ban Krut ⑳

หาดบ้านกรูด

Road Map C2. 44 miles (71 km) S of Prachuap Khiri Khan. *TAT, Hua Hin (0-3251-3885).*

With the beautiful Thong Chai Mountains forming a backdrop, Hat Ban Krut is a lovely, 4-mile (6-km) stretch of beach facing the clear, aquamarine waters of the Gulf of Thailand. The beach is used mainly as a weekend destination by Thais and remains deserted during the week. This quiet stretch of coast between Prachuap Khiri Khan and Chumphon *(see p154)* is still developing. Hat Ban Krut, however, is easily accessible, with its own bus station 8 miles (13 km) from the long shoreline, and train station, 3 miles (5 km) from the beach. There are comfortable, mid-range bungalow accommodations available here, as well as numerous restaurants, cafés, and bars set back from the shore along the palm-fringed coastal road. The area is also well known for batik production. These products are available at local shops and make excellent souvenirs.

The northern end of the beach is dominated by a Buddhist temple, Wat Phra Mahathat Phraphat, easily identified by its nine golden stupas and a 49-ft (15-m) high golden statue of the Buddha, locally known as the Big Buddha.

The picturesque offshore island of Ko Lamla is a great spot for snorkeling enthusiasts and easily accessible by boat. The clear waters surrounding the island are a haven for exotic marine life.

Buddha at Wat Phra Mahathat Phraphat

Bang Saphan ㉑

บางสะพาน

Road Map C3. 56 miles (90 km) S of Prachuap Khiri Khan. *TAT, Hua Hin (0-3251-3885).*

A quiet fishing harbor with good rail and road links to the cities of Bangkok and Chumphon, Bang Saphan dominates an attractive bay, Ao Bang Saphan, that faces south and east across the Gulf of Thailand. Bang Saphan's two beaches, **Bang Saphan Yai** and **Bang Saphan Noi**, 10 miles (16 km) to the south, are usually frequented by Thais from Bangkok and locals from the nearby areas, who visit these spots on weekends and vacations. The town also offers plenty of other attractions in the form of several stunning waterfalls, caves, as well as a driving range for golfers.

Three small islands in the vicinity of Bang Saphan Yai, **Ko Thalu**, Ko Sang, and Ko Sing, are located about 20 minutes away by boat, and are ideal for swimming and sunbathing. Ko Thalu, in particular, is an excellent snorkeling destination with schools of moon wrasse, parrot fish, as well as corals inhabiting the clear, warm waters. Snorkeling tours can be arranged for visitors between the months of January and May.

Bang Saphan Yai provides plenty of mid-range accommodations, reasonably priced seafood restaurants, beachside bars, and motorcycle rentals. The beaches are particularly crowded around holidays such as Songkran *(see p34)* and it is advisable to make hotel bookings in advance.

Houses on stilts and anchored boats belonging to the fishing community at Bang Saphan

For hotels and restaurants in this region see pp298–300 and pp324–6

Kiteboarding along the beach at Hat Thung Wua Laen

Hat Thung Wua Laen ㉒

หาดทุ่งวัวแล่น

Road Map C3. 10 miles (16 km) N of Chumphon. *TAT, Surat Thani (0-7728-8818).*

An extremely popular beach, Hat Thung Wua Laen's name, which means Running Bull Field, derives from a local legend about a magical bull that came alive while being skinned by hunters and ran into the forest. The beach is a long, lovely stretch of white sand that slopes gently into the warm waters of the Gulf of Thailand. Popular with local Thais, Hat Thung Wua Laen now draws growing numbers of vacationers who come here for the relative solitude, reasonable prices, and excellent authentic Thai seafood. The picturesque beachfront is lined with a few resorts offering bungalow accommodations. A number of good seafood restaurants have also opened shop.

Hat Thung Wua Laen is a perfect spot for swimming and also offers great snorkeling opportunities. The surrounding waters are home to some fine coral reefs supporting sea fans, marine sponges, sea flowers, and shoals of tropical fish. Visitors can hire canoes, bicycles, and motorcycles from shops along the beach to explore the area or take a ferry to the popular dive sites nearby.

Ko Ngam Yai and Ko Ngam Noi ㉓

เกาะงามใหญ่และเกาะงามน้อย

Road Map C3. 11 miles (18 km) E of Hat Thung Wua Laen. *from Hat Thung Wua Laen.* *TAT, Surat Thani (0-7728-8818).*

Located within easy reach of Hat Thung Wua Laen, the twin islands of Ko Ngam Yai, or Big Beautiful Island, and Ko Ngam Noi, or Small Beautiful Island, are especially popular among vacationers and day-trippers for their excellent dive sites. The islands are best known locally, however, for their tens of thousands of swiftlets, tiny inhabitants that ensure a rich harvest of nests for Thailand's famous bird's nest soup. The surrounding clear waters are home to coral reefs, unusual underwater rock formations, and caves. Snorkelers will find a rich variety of marine creatures including humpback snappers, clams, oysters, and sea anemones. These islands make for an ideal day trip by a chartered boat from Hat Thung Wua Laen.

Hin Lak Ngam ㉔

หินหลักงาม

Road Map C3. 5 miles (8 km) S of Ko Ngam Yai. *from Hat Thung Wua Laen.* *TAT, Surat Thani (0-7728-8818).*

A rocky outcrop, offshore from Hat Thung Wua Laen, Hin Lak Ngam, along with nearby Hin Pae, is one of the most rewarding dive spots off Chumphon's coast. The outcrop, just a few feet wide, is devoid of any vegetation or even a landing spot. The appeal of Hin Lak Ngam however, lies not above water, but beneath it. The surrounding waters offer fantastic underwater views of coral reefs, gardens, and narrow swim through caves, as well as an amazing variety of brightly colored shoals of fish and other marine life. On a good day, visibility is around 64 ft (20 m), although at low tide or in choppy weather it is much less. The rock is sometimes visited by sea turtles, as well as flights of migratory sea birds. Although an excellent diving spot, divers must be aware that there are poisonous fish which frequent the underwater reefs including lionfish, devilfish, and trigger fish.

A colony of the white-bellied swiftlets on a cliffside in Ko Ngam

HMS *Chumphon* commemorating the province's naval history, Hat Sai Ri

Chumphon ㉕

ชุมพร

Road Map C3. 105 miles (169 km) S of Prachuap Khiri Khan. *35,000.* *daily.*

An important provincial capital, Chumphon is located on the Isthmus of Kra with the jagged mountain range of the Ranong province to the west and the Gulf of Thailand to the east. The town is a cultural border between the Thai-Buddhist north and the Thai-Muslim south. In ancient times, Chumphon used to be a military post of strategic importance. It was used by the army and navy as a place to rally their forces before any major war engagements. The town supposedly derives its name from the Thai word *chumnumphon*, which means accumulation of forces.

One of its main attractions is the **National Museum** showcasing the province's history. The **Military Youth Monument**, located a few miles from the town, commemorates the bravery of the Thai soldiers who fought against the Japanese during World War II. The town was also the residence of Admiral Phra Borommawong Thoe Kromluang Chumphon, one of the sons of Rama V (r.1868–1910). Also known as Prince Chumphon, the admiral was regarded as the father of the Royal Thai Navy.

The town is also a transit point for boats to nearby Ko Samui *(see pp162–71)*, as well as to Ko Phangan *(see pp172–7)*, and Ko Tao *(see pp182–5)*. However, there are several attractive beaches at Hat Thung Wua Laen *(see p153)* to the north, and at Hat Sai Ri and Ao Thung Makham to the south. There are about 47 offshore islands and the town is a good base to explore the surrounding reefs. Visitors can also head to the nearby beach of Hat Paradonpap which is famous for its seafood.

THE KRA CANAL

For almost 400 years an idea has been mooted for building a canal across the Thai-Malaysian peninsula, approximately between Ranong on the Andaman Coast and Lang Suan on the Gulf of Thailand. The Kra Canal was proposed to cut across the peninsula at its narrowest point, the Isthmus of Kra where the distance is just 28 miles (45 km). This would shorten shipping routes by creating a direct passage between the Andaman Sea and the Gulf of Thailand. Actual plans were first floated under Narai the Great (r.1656–88) as early as 1677 when he asked French engineers at his court to evaluate the possibility of a trans-peninsular canal. A century later, Ferdinand de Lessops, the designer of the Suez Canal, visited the area but his plans were foiled by the British who wished to maintain the prominence of the port of Singapore. Proposals have resurfaced regularly without any effect as the consequent politico-economic advantages would tilt the axis of power in Southeast Asia. Thus, although the Kra Canal exists only on paper, its projected strategic benefits refuse to let the concept disappear altogether.

King Narai the Great

Thatched seafood shacks lining the beach at Hat Sai Ri

Hat Sai Ri ㉖

หาดทรายรี

Road Map C3. 8 miles (13 km) S of Chumphon.

The main beach in this area, Hat Sai Ri (not to be confused with Hat Sai Ri Sawi further south) and the small village of Ban Hat Sai Ri, are easily accessible by bus or motorcycle from Chumphon. The beach is a long curving stretch of white sands backed by coconut palms. It doubles as an idyllic spot for holidaymakers as well as a ground for local fishermen.

This beach hosts the annual **Chumphon Sea World Fair**, in March to promote tourism, preserve the natural beauty of the region, and raise awareness about the local ecology. The nearby **Prince Chumphon Monument** includes a much revered shrine as well as the 225-ft (68-m) long decommissioned torpedo boat HMS *Chumphon*.

Most people prefer to visit Hat Sai Ri as a day trip from Chumphon. However, the beach has several resorts, restaurants, and bars to cater to visitors who might decide to stay the night.

Ao Thung Makham pier, a jumping-off point to nearby islands

Ao Thung Makham ㉗

อ่าวทุ่งมะขาม

Road Map C3. 15 miles (24 km) S of Chumphon.

The next stop down the coast from Hat Sai Ri is neighboring Ao Thung Makham, a twin bay with two shallow semi-circles fringed by a long white sand beach backed by pretty casuarinas and coconut palms. Right in the middle of the twin bay is a small rocky peninsula which acts as a dividing spit of land between Ao Thung Makham Nai to the north, and Ao Thung Makham Nok to the south. Toward the southern end of the latter is **Wat Suwan Khuha Wari Wong**. Known locally as Wat Pong Pang, this venerated temple set in front of a 256-ft (78-m) high cliff and shaded by coconut trees. The beach is visited by locals from Chumphon, and the seafood restaurants and bars primarily cater to them. However, Ao Thung Makham is becoming increasingly popular with foreign visitors en route to more popular destinations such as Ko Samui *(see pp162–71)*. It is a good place to stay and recuperate from traveling as well as escape the crowds on the commercial beaches for a few days.

Hat Arunothai ㉘

หาดอรุโณทัย

Road Map C3. 38 miles (60 km) S of Chumphon.

A lovely beach close to the Tako River estuary south of Chumphon, Hat Arunothai is at the very edge of the Chumphon province. Located 6 miles (10 km) off Highway 41, the long palm-lined stretch of white sand curves gently away to the south. The beach has a memorial shrine to Admiral Chumphon, revered by sailors and fishermen alike throughout the province. This beach also has a series of small seafood restaurants, food stalls, bars and mid-range accommodations. Longtail boats are available for hire to visit the many offshore islands.

Hat Arunothai, is in fact, a good place to experience the local flavor of the Chumphon province. The picturesque fishing village of Ban Ao Mamuang is just about 9 miles (14 km) north of the beach. Visitors can also stop at the nearby estuary of **Pak Nam Thung Tako** to take in the colorful sight of fishermen departing for their daily catch.

Panoramic view of the Gulf of Thailand at sunset from Hat Arunothai

LOWER WESTERN GULF COAST

The Lower Western Gulf Coast extends south from the Isthmus of Kra to Nakhon Si Thammarat, the ancient cultural center of southern Thailand. This region is home to the beautiful palm-clad islands of Ko Samui and Ko Phangan, the diving hub of Ko Tao, and the unmatched splendor of the Ang Thong Marine National Park, collectively offering visitors a choice of destinations including gorgeous tropical beaches, lush forests, and historical temples.

For over 2,000 years, the Lower Western Gulf Coast has been a major cultural crossroads with Hindu, Buddhist, and Islamic influences. It has also been an important part of the ancient trade routes through the Straits of Malacca. Finds from historic trading centers around the Isthmus of Kra testify to strong links with China, India, the Middle East, and the Roman Empire before AD 1000. From the 16th century onward, development of trade ties with the Spanish and Portuguese, followed a century later by trade with the Dutch and British, introduced greater diversity to this region. The Srivijaya Empire held sway over these parts between the 7th and 13th centuries and upon its decline both Myanmar and Thailand fought to control this territory. This coastal area also acts as a bridge between the Buddhist-north and the Malay-Muslim influenced Deep South.

The forested Tenasserim Mountains continue south into the Lower Western Gulf Coast tapering away after Ranong. The mountains give way to rich and wide agricultural lands. Palm trees stud the coast while sharp limestone peaks characterize the interiors. Both the mainland and the offshore islands offer a wide choice of beaches from the bustling Hat Lamai and Hat Chaweng at Ko Samui, to the more isolated stretches at Ko Phangan. The rich waters of the Gulf of Thailand can best be explored at Ang Thong Marine National Park and Ko Tao, while historic Nakhon Si Thammarat, and the ancient port of Chaiya offer an insight into the area's past.

Holiday-makers enjoying a sundowner at a beachfront café, Ko Tao

◁ **Visitors taking elephant treks through the forested interiors of Ko Samui**

Exploring the Lower Western Gulf Coast

This part of the coast overlooking the Gulf of Thailand has miles of beautiful white sand beaches. It is home to the gorgeous Samui archipelago with its luxurious hotels, as well as the lesser developed Ko Phangan favored by young backpackers. Ko Tao, to the north, is a diver's paradise while Ang Thong Marine National Park is a tiny archipelago whose natural beauty is unmatched in all of Thailand. Apart from the surrounding islands, the Lower Western Gulf Coast has attractive beaches, some of which are quieter than their busy offshore counterparts. Historic towns such as Chaiya, an ancient Srivijaya settlement, and Nakhon Si Thammarat, the cultural capital of southern Thailand, are also located here. Farther inland, the Khao Luang National Park shelters some of this area's extraordinary wildlife.

Palm trees on beautiful cliffs overlooking Hat Tong Yi

SIGHTS AT A GLANCE

Towns and Villages
Chaiya 1
Nakhon Si Thammarat pp192–5 21
Surat Thani 3

Areas of Natural Beauty
Laem Talumphuk 20

National Parks
Ang Thong Marine National Park pp180–81 6
Khao Luang National Park 19

Historical and Religious Sites
Khao Kha Archaeological Site 16
Wat Suan Mokkhaphalaram 2

Beaches and Islands
Hat Hin Ngam 14
Hat Khanom 8
Hat Na Dan 9
Hat Nai Phlao 11
Hat Nai Phraet 10
Hat Piti 15
Hat Sa Bua 18
Hat Saophao 17
Hat Sichon 13
Hat Tong Yi 12
Ko Phangan pp172–7 5
Ko Samui pp162–71 4
Ko Tao pp182–5 7

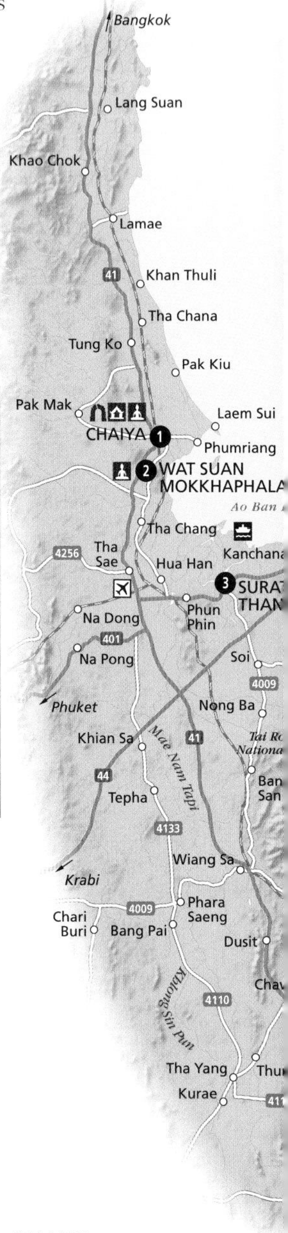

Bangkok
Lang Suan
Khao Chok
Lamae
41
Khan Thuli
Tha Chana
Tung Ko
Pak Kiu
Pak Mak
Laem Sui
CHAIYA 1
Phumriang
2 WAT SUAN MOKKHAPHALA
Ao Ban
Tha Chang
4256
Tha Sae
Hua Han
Kanchana
3 SURAT THAN
Na Dong
Phun Phin
401
Na Pong
Soi
4009
Phuket
Nong Ba
Khian Sa
Mae Nam Tapi
41
44
Tepha
4133
Wiang Sa
Krabi
Phara Saeng
4009
Chari Buri
Bang Pai
Dusit
Khlong Sin Pun
4110
Tha Yang
Kurae

SEE ALSO

• ***Where to Stay*** pp300–4
• ***Where to Eat*** pp326–8

For additional map symbols *see back flap*

Snorkeling in the clear waters around Ang Thong

GETTING AROUND

The main domestic airports in the region are at Surat Thani and Nakhon Si Thammarat on the mainland, and the international airport is at Ko Samui. There are also regular flights between Ko Samui and Phuket. Most of the mainland attractions are linked via Highway 41 and Highway 401 leading to Surat Thani and Nakhon Si Thammarat. The major towns are linked to each other and to Bangkok by regular bus and train services. Taxis, *songthaews*, and tuk-tuks can be hired for short trips and motorbike and bicycle rentals are easily arranged. The most convenient way to explore the area is by self-driven car. Car rental facilities are easily available at Surat Thani, Nakhon Si Thammarat, and Ko Samui. Ferry services are frequent and fairly fast, linking Ko Tao, Ko Phangan, and Ko Samui.

Chaiya ❶

ไชยา

Road Map C4. 367 miles (591 km) S of Bangkok. *48,000.* *TAT, Surat Thani (0-7728-8818).* *daily.* *Chak Phra Festival (Oct–Nov).*

Once an important center of Srivijaya culture in southern Thailand, modern Chaiya still contains a number of significant archaeological sites that have survived from the Srivijaya period *(see p39).* Situated on the main railway line between the well-known towns of Chumphon *(see p154)* and Surat Thani, Chaiya was the regional capital of the mighty Srivijaya kingdom in the 5th–13th centuries. Its name is probably a derivative of Srivijaya, which means radiant victory. Chaiya boasts such intriguing sights as rare statues of Bengali-style Buddha images and deities such as Vishnu, part of the Hindu holy trinity. These fascinating statues, proud survivors of a bygone era, are evidence of the Mon-Dvaravati and Indic-Srivijaya influences on the art of the time. These, together with a variety of votive tablets, are preserved and displayed at the **Chaiya National Museum**, located a 10-minute walk from the railway station. Also on display at the museum are several other examples of art from the later Ayutthaya period *(see pp40–41).* The most important surviving relic is **Wat Phra Boromathat Chaiya**, an important Srivijaya temple. Within the compound of the *wat* stands a central *chedi* that has been painstakingly restored. This square-shaped structure has four porches which ascend in tiers and are topped with small towers. Dating from the 8th century, the *chedi* is built of brick covered with stucco. Other less well preserved, but still beautiful, relics of Chaiya's luminous past include three ancient and crumbling *chedis* at Wat Hua Wiang, Wat Lhong, and Wat Kaew, all of which are located on a north-south axis within the precincts of the town.

Stone relief on the side of the meditation hall, Wat Suan Mokkhaphalaram

Chaiya National Museum
Phra Boromathat Chaiya, 1 mile (2 km) W of town center.
Tel *0-7743-1066.* *9am–4pm Wed–Sun.* *public holidays.*
www.thailandmuseum.com

Wat Suan Mokkhaphalaram ❷

วัดสวนโมกข์

Road Map C4. Off Hwy 41, 4 miles (6 km) S of Chaiya. **Tel** *0-7743-1552.* *from Chaiya.* *TAT, Surat Thani (0-7728-8818).* *daily.*
www.suanmokkh.org

Perhaps the best known and most popular meditation temple in Thailand, Wat Suan Mokkhaphalaram (often shortened to Wat Suan Mokkh), meaning Temple of the Garden of Liberation, is associated with the well-known International Dhamma Heritage movement. Run by the World Fellowship of Buddhists, it is an organization that seeks to promote *dhamma* (teachings of the Buddha) through meditation.

The inspiration behind the *wat's* meditation techniques is the back-to-basics Buddhist

Buddha images at Wat Phra Boromathat Chaiya, one of the few remaining temples from the Srivijaya period

philosophy of the temple's founder, Buddhadhasa Bhikku, who died in 1993. Within the temple a strict regimen of physical labor, cleaning, and gardening underpins a simple monastic life devoid of elaborate religious ceremonies, superstition, and spirit worship, usually associated with Buddhism in Thailand.

The *wat* complex includes the monks' quarters, a spiritual theater, a meditation hall, and a sculpture workshop, as well as a library. A clearing on the top of a hill, which is reached by walking past the monks' quarters and the cremation site of Buddhadasa Bhikku, marks the most holy spot in the complex. It is decorated with statues of the Buddha and the Buddhist Wheel of Law. Ten-day meditation retreats are held here, beginning from the first of each month.

Monk's living quarters in the midst of the jungle, Wat Suan Mokkhaphalaram

Surat Thani ❸

สุราษฎร์ธานี

Road Map C4. 38 miles (60 km) S of Chaiya. *126,000. 19 miles (31 km) SW of Surat Thani. TAT, 5 Talat Mai Rd, Surat Thani (0-7728-8818). Rambutan Fair (Aug), Chak Phra Festival (Oct–Nov).*

Strategically located at the mouth of the Tapi and Phum Duang rivers, Surat Thani was a prominent commercial center as far back as the Srivijaya period. Today, it is significant as the capital of the Surat Thani province, the largest province in southern Thailand. The town, whose name literally means City of the Good People, is an important center with an economy that is heavily dependent on its fishing harbor, commercial seaport, and cultivation of rambutan, rubber, rice, and coconut. It features on visitors' itineraries, however, as an airport and ferry port as well as an important stop on the railway line between Bangkok and Hat Yai *(see p280)*. Despite having little to offer, except its links to the past, Surat Thani's prominence as a jumping-off point to the islands in its vicinity is well established. Visitors usually stop overnight on their way to Ko Samui *(see pp162–71)*, Ko Phangan *(see pp172–7)*, or even Ko Tao *(see pp182–5)*.

Boat anchored on the Phum Duang riverfront, Surat Thani

The riverside is also an appealing area with small boats ferrying people back and forth to the busy markets on the waterfront. These bustling markets sell fresh produce such as coconut and flowers.

CHAIYA'S ROLE IN THE SRIVIJAYA EMPIRE

Srivijaya votive tablet

The Mahayana Buddhist Empire of Srivijaya dominated the whole Malaysian peninsula and parts of Indonesia between the 7th and 13th centuries AD. Although the majority of scholars now believe that Palembang in Sumatra was the Srivijaya capital, discoveries of temple remains and some exquisite stone and bronze statues (many now in the National Museum in Bangkok) in Chaiya, provide evidence of Chaiya's importance. Its strategic geographical position as a coastal port, meant that the town played an important role in the trade between India, the Thai peninsula, and China. In fact, Chaiya was mentioned in the writings of the Chinese monk I Ching, who, while visiting the area in the late 7th century, testified to its religious and cultural sophistication. It is known that some of Chaiya's rulers were connected by marriage to those of central Java. Furthermore, it is possible that the name "Chaiya" originated as a contraction of "Siwichaiya" (a different transliteration of Srivijaya), which follows the local tendency to emphasize the final syllable of a word.

An 8th-century bronze statue, Chaiya

Ko Samui ❹

เกาะสมุย

Coconuts, a key crop in Samui

Located in the Gulf of Thailand south of Bangkok, Ko Samui is Thailand's third-largest island after Phuket and Ko Chang. It was originally settled by mariners from China who began cultivating coconut on the island. Even today, its inhabitants refer to themselves as *chao samui*, or people of Samui. A backpackers' haven in the 1970s, tourism has now become its main income generator. Rapid development, the arrival of major hotel and spa chains, persistent promotion by tourism authorities, and its beautiful beaches have led to a huge influx of visitors. Despite this, Ko Samui retains its position as a tropical paradise.

Getting ready for a dip at the cooling Na Muang Waterfalls

Elephant Treks

Elephant treks to the central Samui Highlands are not only enjoyable, but also a convenient way to explore the relatively inaccessible interior of the island.

Secret Buddha Garden

Also known as Uncle Nim's Garden after its founder Nim Thongsuk, the Secret Buddha Garden features statues of various figures from Buddhist mythology. The garden is surrounded by lush tropical forests.

Ko Taen is a gorgeous offshore island with isolated beaches of white sand and some beautiful coral reefs.

STAR SIGHTS

★ Big Buddha Statue

★ Hat Chaweng

★ Hat Lamai

For hotels and restaurants in this region see pp300–4 and pp326–8

★ **Big Buddha Statue**
The 39-ft (12-m) high statue of Phra Yai, also known as Big Buddha, dominates Hat Bangrak. It draws a regular stream of local pilgrims and other visitors.

VISITORS' CHECKLIST

Road Map C4. 68 miles (110 km) NE of Surat Thani. *42,000.* *14 miles (22 km) E of Na Thon.* *Surat Thani, Tha Thong, and Don Sak.* *TAT, Samui (0-7742-0504).* *daily.* **www.**samui.sawadee.com

★ **Hat Chaweng**
The most popular spot in Ko Samui, Hat Chaweng is best known for its lively nightlife, noisy beer bars, and exotic dining options. Local DJs play Western hits alongside Thai and other music.

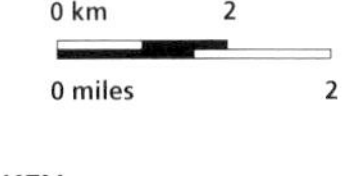

★ **Hat Lamai**
Ko Samui's second-longest beach, Hat Lamai is great for watersports. Swimming is possible year round; visitors can also go water-skiing or windsurfing.

KEY

- Beach
- Dive site
- Watersports
- *Wat*
- Peak
- International Airport
- Ferry service
- Visitor information
- Major road
- Minor road
- Ferry route

Exploring Ko Samui

Hotel sign, Hat Bophut

Exploring Samui is both easy and enjoyable. The mountainous interior is ringed by a narrow two-lane, well-maintained road. Public transport is by *songthaew*, tuk-tuk, or taxi. Those who prefer driving can hire a vehicle from the mainland – there are plenty of shops renting motorbikes and bicycles. Car rental facilities are also available at the airport. But drivers must be careful while venturing on their own at night, particularly around Hat Lamai and Hat Chaweng, where drunk driving is common; flash floods in the rainy season are another hazard. It is also possible to hire longtail boats as taxis between any two points on the coast.

Surf breaking on the gorgeous beach at Hat Maenam

Delicious tropical fruits for sale at the local market in Na Thon

Na Thon

หน้าทอน

Founded in 1905 as the administrative center of Ko Samui, Na Thon is the island's capital and main ferry port. A sleepy town with a distinct charm of its own, Na Thon is home to a majority of the local populace and also well-equipped with a supermarket, post office, police station, immigration office, as well as foreign exchange facilities. Although the beach here is not spectacular, the local market which sells fresh produce such as fruits, vegetables, and seafood, is certainly worth a visit, also for a taste of the delicious local cuisine. A haven for shoppers, visitors can strike some great deals at the various batik and souvenir shops in the area.

Few visitors stay here, using the town only as a transit point from where to catch the early morning boat to Surat Thani *(see p161)*. The town is also well connected to other places on the island through the main 31-mile (50-km) long circular road. Local *songthaews* departing from Na Thon's ferry port travel either toward Hat Chaweng and the airport in the north, or popular Hat Lamai in the south.

Ao Bang Pho

อ่าวบางปอ

4 miles (6 km) NE of Na Thon.

Located close to the northwestern tip of Ko Samui, Ao Bang Pho receives relatively few visitors. The bay is backed by a beautiful stretch of beach, fringed with palm trees and offers stunning views across the Gulf of Thailand as far as Ko Phangan *(see pp172–7)*. The clear waters off the beach present good snorkeling opportunities. During the northeast monsoon, from November to March, when the winds are particularly strong, visitors can also go windsurfing and kiteboarding.

Hat Maenam

หาดแม่น้ำ

7 miles (11 km) NE of Na Thon.

A 2-mile (3-km) long beach with gorgeous views across the waters to Ko Phangan, Hat Maenam is a fairly quiet

Fishermen setting out to sea in longtail fishing boats from the pier at Na Thon

beach and a great place to unwind. The main road behind the beach is lined with several go-go and beer bars, cafés, and Thai restaurants, as well as shops selling local handicrafts such as handbags, coconut bowls, Buddha statues, and beautiful ceramic products.

Visitors flock to Hat Maenam for the excellent windsurfing opportunities, aided by the strong breeze that blows onshore during the northeast monsoon. Swimming is another relaxing option. Hat Maenam is easily accessible by *songthaew* or a hired motorcycle from the nearby town of Na Thon.

Quiet road in Fisherman's Village, Hat Bophut

Hat Bophut

หาดบ่อผุด

11 miles (18 km) NE of Na Thon.

Popular with families and backpackers alike, Hat Bophut is a 1-mile (2-km) long beach with facilities better than those at Hat Maenam. Fisherman's Village, located to the east of the beach, is the center of Bophut. Bungalow accommodations, a bank, bars, and restaurants, are some of the utilities available in the village, Ban Bophut. There is also a range of watersports and several dive shops.

Hat Bangrak

หาดบางรัก

13 miles (21 km) NE of Na Thon.

An ideal getaway for a family vacation, Hat Bangrak, also known as Big Buddha Beach, stretches for nearly 3 miles (5 km) and its eastern end is a great spot for snorkeling. A narrow causeway links this end of the beach to **Ko Faan**, a tiny islet also on the eastern end, dominated by a 39-ft (12-m) high Buddha statue, which lends the beach its name. This statue is popular with locals as well as foreign visitors. A bazaar of souvenir stalls and cafés has sprung up at the foot of the staircase, decorated with *nagas* (serpents), leading to the statue. There are plenty of accommodation options ranging from bungalows to upscale resorts. Visitors can enjoy watersports, swimming, and Thai massages.

Staircase leading to the towering Big Buddha, Ko Faan, Hat Bangrak

Ao Thong Son and Hat Choeng Mon

ท้องสนและเชิงมน

15 miles (24 km) NE of Na Thon.

A peaceful inlet with great views across Hat Choeng Mon, Ao Thong Son is dominated by a rocky cove on one side and a beach on the other. The bay is ideal for swimming, diving, and snorkeling, while the beach is lined with restaurants and bars – great for spending a quiet evening. This area is dominated by several upscale resorts and spas offering state-of-the-art facilities, but inexpensive accommodations are hard to come by.

Sandy headland jutting into the sea at Hat Choeng Mon

Busy Hat Chaweng, the longest and most attractive beach on Ko Samui

Hat Chaweng

หาดเฉวง

14 miles (22 km) E of Na Thon.

The longest, busiest, and most beautiful beach on Ko Samui, Hat Chaweng stretches for 3 miles (5 km) down the east coast of the island. Its warm waters, white sands, and back-to-nature beach bungalows have attracted budget travelers for many years.

At the northern end of Hat Chaweng is a tranquil 3-ft (1-m) deep lagoon, ideal for children and novice windsurfers. The southernmost end, Chaweng Noi, is bordered by coconut palms and separated from the main beach by a small headland and a narrow stream. This part of the beach is not only quieter than the long northern strand, but also more beautiful – large boulders alternating with discreet sandy coves. The beach offers a wide range of sporting activities including windsurfing, canoeing, paragliding, scuba diving, tennis, and beach volleyball. The fine coral reefs offshore make the beach an ideal spot for some easy diving and snorkeling.

Hat Chaweng also boasts the most developed tourist infrastructure on Ko Samui. Upscale resorts, luxury hotels, and spas dominate the area, while travel agencies, banks, supermarkets, and car and bike rentals can be easily located. Although a great place for a family vacation, Hat Chaweng is predominantly visited by young travelers, who come here particularly for the exciting nightlife centered in the area known as Soi Green Mango. This part of the beach is cluttered with an increasing number of bars, restaurants, and clubs. Visitors spend the nights partying, drinking, and dancing till the early hours.

Hat Lamai

หาดละไม

12 miles (19 km) SE of Na Thon.

The second-largest and second most popular beach on Ko Samui, Hat Lamai caters primarily to European budget travelers. Initially a quiet fishing village, tourism has slowly taken over, becoming the mainstay of tiny Ban Lamai, at the northern end of the beach. The main focus is at the center of the 2-mile (3-km) long beach. The long road behind the beach here is lined with all kinds of bars, nightclubs, and restaurants serving delicious Thai and Western food. This is also the spot where most of the beach's nightlife is centered.

Picturesque Hat Lamai with drooping palms skirting the sea

Although Ban Lamai still has many old teak houses, most buildings have tiled roofs – a sign of the growing prosperity of the area. The village's main cultural sight is **Wat Lamai Cultural Hall**, built in 1826, with a small folk museum dedicated to local arts and crafts. Just south of Hat Lamai, almost as an extension, is another long stretch of sandy beach known as **Hat Hua Thanon**. This pretty beach has a predominantly Muslim fishing village at its center. A fresh market sells a large variety of fruits, vegetables, and seafood.

Secret Buddha Garden

สวนพระ

7 miles (11 km) SE of Na Thon.

Tucked away in the heavily forested interior of Ko Samui, the Secret Buddha Garden, also known as Magic Garden, was founded by a 76-year-old fruit farmer, Nim Thongsuk, in 1977. Surrounded by lush tropical forest and rocky hillsides, the garden is studded with beautiful statuary. Made of concrete, the stunning statues represent various deities, mythical beasts, and human beings in different postures, including a statue of a seated Nim Thongsuk. A beautiful waterfall continues as a stream through the length of the garden. Set in the highest part of the island, the garden also offers spectacular views across the tall

For hotels and restaurants in this region see pp300–4 and pp326–8

coconut palm-covered lowlands and the Gulf of Thailand. Getting to the garden however, can prove to be quite challenging as it is only sometimes accessible via a dirt track using a 4WD from Hat Lamai. The easiest way to do this is to take a jungle tour from Hat Lamai.

Na Muang Waterfalls

น้ำตกหน้าเมือง

7 miles (11 km) SE of Na Thon.

Along Route 4169, near Ban Thurian, a steep side track beside a rushing stream leads off into the central mountains of Ko Samui. About 1 mile (2 km) along this track is a stunning cascade known as Nam Tok Na Muang, or Na Muang Waterfall. A 2-mile (3-km) trek farther into the interior leads to another waterfall, also called Na Muang by the locals. Tour operators generally refer to the two as Na Muang 1 and Na Muang 2. The larger of two the falls, Na Muang 2, is a popular local picnic spot. About 98 ft (30 m) in height, the falls form a deep basin at the foot creating a cool and pleasant pool which is great for swimming and bathing. Both the falls are at their spectacular best in the months of December and January when the monsoon has ended and they swell with fresh rainwater from Ko Samui's hilly interior. An elephant trekking company operates in the area and will take visitors to the foot of Na Muang 2 by arrangement.

Popular picnic spot for locals, the spectacular Na Muang Waterfalls

Hin Ta and Hin Yai

หินตาหินยาย

11 miles (18 km) SE of Na Thon.

Located on a tiny headland immediately between Hat Lamai and Hat Hua Thanon, Hin Ta and Hin Yai, or Grandfather Stone and Grandmother Stone, are natural rock formations bearing an uncanny resemblance to the human male and female sexual organs. According to local lore, in times past a fisherman and woman fell in love, but were caught in a storm off this small headland and drowned. Through supernatural forces, the rocks on the headland took on their present shape, celebrating and commemorating the love of the two fisherfolk for eternity. These rock formations are perhaps the most visited site on Ko Samui after the Big Buddha statue. Small souvenir stalls selling T-shirts, snacks such as *galamae* (a Thai sweet dish), and other knick-knacks have sprung up in the area.

View of the curiously shaped Hin Ta, or Grandfather Stone

Wat Khunaram

วัดคุณาราม

8 miles (13 km) SE of Na Thon.

Located near Ban Thurian just south of Route 4169, Wat Khunaram is one of Ko Samui's more unusual spiritual attractions. While the *wat* is architecturally appealing, it has no historical significance. What draws visitors to it are the mummified remains of a famous Buddhist monk, Phra Khru Sammathakittikhun who died here in 1973. The preserved mummy of the monk, sitting in an upright position in a glass casing, is on display in a separate building within the complex. The place is highly venerated by the locals who come here to place flowers and incense on the remains of this former abbot of the *wat*. In surprisingly good condition and still quite undecomposed, the remains are said to be here in accordance with the wishes of Phra Khru himself.

One of the many varieties of butterflies at the Samui Butterfly Garden

Hat Laem Set

หาดแหลมเสร็จ

10 miles (16 km) S of Na Thon.

A tiny but lovely beach at the southern end of Hat Hua Thanon, Hat Laem Set's soft sand is strewn with huge smooth boulders. The main attraction on this beach is the Ko Samui Kiteboarding Center at the well-known Samui Orchid Resort. Kiteboarding is a relatively new but exhilarating addition to the busy watersports scene on the island and is at its best off Hat Laem Set during the cool season from November to February. The Kiteboarding Center offers courses for all abilities and hires out kiteboards for rental. In addition to kiteboarding, visitors can snorkel out to a beautiful offshore coral reef nearby. The sea is shallow at this point, and the sandy bottom clearly visible. Beyond the reef, however, the waters are deep and can get treacherous, especially during choppy seas and high winds. Snorkelers and swimmers must be careful before venturing any further. There are a few upscale resorts and spas on the beach, as well as a handful of good restaurants serving local food.

Samui Aquarium and Tiger Zoo

สมุยอควาเรียม และสวนเสือ

33/2 Moo 2, Maret, 10 miles (16 km) SE of Na Thon. ***Tel*** *0-7742-4017-8.* *9am–6pm daily.* **www**.samuiaquarium-andtigerzoo.com

An ideal stop for marine and wildlife enthusiasts, the Samui Aquarium and Tiger Zoo is a fascinating place to experience the fauna of the region. Perfect for a day trip, especially with children, the aquarium has a variety of marine creatures, such as tropical fish, sharks, sea turtles, corals, mollusks, starfish, and sea horses, housed in large, clear, acrylic aquariums. Visitors can also take a look at an amazing variety of birds kept here while enjoying a fascinating bird show. Getting photographed with birds is permitted.

The affiliated Tiger Zoo nearby houses large numbers of big cats, including Royal Bengal tigers, leopards, clouded leopards, and lions, enabling visitors to get a closer look at these predators and their way of life. Those willing, can get themselves photographed with these splendid creatures for a few hundred baht. The souvenir shop in the complex sells T-shirts and stuffed toys.

Samui Butterfly Garden

สวนผีเสื้อสมุย

10 miles (16 km) S of Na Thon. ***Tel*** *0-7742-4020.* *8:30am–5pm daily; observatory opens 10am–4pm.*

Situated on the side of a small hill at Laem Na Tien, the Samui Butterfly Garden is set in lush tropical gardens. It features hundreds of species of protected butterflies and moths which are kept from escaping by a series of high nets. The butterflies, of which there are more than a 100 Thai and Malaysian varieties, are truly beautiful. Honey beehives and a selection of less appealing insects such as scorpions, tarantulas, and spiders are kept safely behind glass casings to avoid unpleasant accidents. The fee to the Butterfly Garden

Large smooth boulders strewn across the sand and water at pretty Hat Laem Set

Enthusiastic divers among coral reefs in the clear waters off Ko Taen

includes a welcome drink as well as a visit to a hillside observatory with a number of observation platforms. These platforms offer sweeping views across the coast and the Gulf of Thailand. Marine life enthusiasts can take a trip in a glass-bottomed boat to observe corals in the surrounding sea.

Ko Taen

เกาะเตียน

10 miles (16 km) S of Na Thon.

from Ban Thongkrut.

A picturesque island located just off Samui's southwest shore, tiny Ko Taen is easily reached by boat from the small settlement of Ban Thongkrut. Formerly home to an isolated fishing community, it has now been transformed into a marine nature reserve. The island is an ideal spot for diving, snorkeling, or for land-based activities such as trekking. There are just three resorts on the island, which has a population of less than 30 permanent residents. The two most popular attractions here are Ao Ok, a bay with fine coral reefs, which are great for diving or snorkeling, and Ao Tok, a small bay with perfect white sands backed by a mangrove forest, home to a variety of birds and animals. A wooden walkway runs through this forest, making it easy for visitors to explore the area. Several dark caves in the interior are the bastion of thousands of bats. The waters offshore are deep, clear, and perfect for diving and snorkeling.

Laem Hin Khom

แหลมหินคม

9 miles (14 km) S of Na Thon.

Located at the southern end of Samui's undeveloped west coast, Laem Hin Khom is a rocky headland that cuts off Ban Thongkrut from Ao Phangkha. Thong Tanote, a long, narrow and sandy beach, backed by tall, slender coconut palms and a tropical jungle, runs along the southern shore of the cape and is the setting for one of Ko Samui's most isolated getaways, the beautiful Coconut Villa Resort and Spa *(see p302)*. This is an intimate and luxurious development with beachfront and sea view villas. The quiet beach at Laem Hin Khom is ideally suited for long walks and swimming, although the latter should be avoided at high tide.

Ao Phangkha

อ่าวพังกา

8 miles (13 km) S of Na Thon.

Located just north of Laem Hin Khom is the perfectly gorgeous bay, Ao Phangkha, also known as Emerald Cove. Isolated from the rest of Ko Samui by the 1,312-ft (400-m) Khao Kwang, a jungle-covered massif to the northeast, this is certainly one of the most remote escapes on the island. Once the almost exclusive preserve of the backpacker crowd, Ao Phangkha is now becoming increasingly upscale. Phangkha Paradise Resort, among the popular resorts in the area, is prominently set back from the center of the crescent beach, along with a couple of smaller bungalow-type accommodations. There is not much to do here, but visitors can take a boat to some of the offshore islands, such as Ko Thalu, Ko Din, Ko Maleng Po, and Ko Mae Ko, for snorkeling over the colorful coral reefs. Alternatively, the soft white sands of the beach at Ao Phangkha provide an ideal resting place for die-hard sunbathers.

Swimming pool at Coconut Villa Resort and Spa, Laem Hin Khom

Longtail fishing boats anchored at the small pier at Ao Phangkha

Long, curving stretch of coast at Ao Taling Ngam

Ao Taling Ngam

อ่าวตลิ่งงาม

5 miles (8 km) S of Na Thon.

The main west coast bay to the south of Na Thon, Ao Taling Ngam stretches for almost 2 miles (3 km). The beach along the bay is a long, narrow curve of sand, with the small settlement of Ban Thong Yang – the port for ferries from Don Sak – to its south. Relatively undeveloped, Ao Taling Ngam is divided into Five Islands Beach to the south and Dhevatara Cove to the north by a tiny stream and low headland, now home to the Am Samui Resort *(see p302)*. Visitors will find inexpensive accommodations here. Looming above the bay and with its own section of private beach lies what many consider to be Samui's classiest hotel – Baan Taling Ngam Resort and Spa *(see p302)*.

Ao Thong Yang

อ่าวท้องยาง

4 miles (6 km) S of Na Thon.

A quiet spot, much like the other places on the west coast of Ko Samui, Ao Thong Yang is conveniently located a 20-minute stroll from the Ko Samui Immigration Office, which lies to its north. The headland to the south of the bay belongs to the Royal Thai Navy and is a prohibited area. The area offers a variety of options for fine dining including restaurants that serve delectable local Thai food.

Samui Highlands

สมุยไฮแลนด์

3 miles (5 km) E of Na Thon.

Wat Hin Lat *Tel 0-7742-3146.*

A short drive inland from Na Thon along Route 4172 due east leads to the forested highlands of Ko Samui. An easy getaway far from the sun and sand, the highlands are an excellent point to start jungle treks and visit Samui's famous waterfalls. Visitors who want to trek the hard way will need sturdy boots. Those who want to do it in more style can do so on an elephant courtesy of Camp Chang Elephant Trekking. The camp arranges treks up into the highlands around the 2,016-ft (614-m) high Khao Pom, in the very center of the island. These mountains are accessed using a network of steep, rough tracks. Other sights worth visiting include **Wat Hin Lat**, a meditation temple offering daily courses in Vipassana meditation, and the beautiful **Hin Lat Waterfall**. This is a steep 2-mile (3-km) hike from Wat Hin Lat, but the journey follows a beautiful jungle path and can be rounded off with a swim in the clear pool at the foot of the falls. Unlike most other waterfalls on Ko Samui, Hin Lat is quite off the beaten track, and rarely visited by island tour package groups. It is a great place for swimming and picnics, but hikers must remember to keep their legs covered and wear good walking shoes, especially during the rains when leeches can be a problem. Those looking for some more adventure can press on further for 2 miles (3 km) to the Wang Sao Tong Falls. Experienced bikers can also explore the area on a dirt bike, but should avoid doing so during the rainy season.

Statue of Seated Buddha at Wat Hin Lat, Samui Highlands

Coconut Monkeys

Monkey helping himself to a coconut

Coconut harvesting was once the main source of income for the people of Ko Samui. Much of the island's interior is covered with coconut palms and, even today, coconuts remain a significant economic crop. Palm trees can grow up to 130–160 ft (40–50 m) high and harvesting coconuts is a difficult, dangerous, and time-consuming process. To make it easier, locals train macaques to pluck the rich harvest for them. These monkeys are usually trained at the Monkey Training School on the island. Another place to see monkeys being trained is the Samui Monkey Center, which also holds demonstrations three times a day. Visitors can see these monkeys at work on coconut plantations all over Ko Samui, especially along the north-west coast around Ban Maenam, Ban Tai, and Ban Bang Pho.

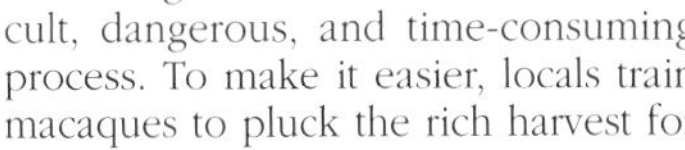

COCONUT HARVESTING BY MONKEYS

A male macaque is capable of picking between 1,000 to 1,500 coconuts a day while a female macaque can pick 600 to 700. This makes excellent economic sense, especially when compared to a human male who can pick only about 80 coconuts a day.

Trainers in Ko Samui treat their monkeys almost like members of the family.

Somporn Saekow, *who died in 2002, began his monkey training school in 1957. He applied the Buddhist principles of tolerance and insisted on humane treatment of his "students".*

Ropes tied to the monkey are used to guide its movements and not meant to restrain it.

Coconut palms *are extremely difficult to climb because their tall, thin trunks have no branches. Besides, strong winds add to the risk.*

Monkey training schools *are fairly common on Ko Samui. Here monkeys learn to harvest the coconut – turn the coconuts with their hands and legs, place the plucked nut in a bag, and bring the bag back to the owner. The entire learning process takes about six months.*

Coconut harvesting, *together with fishing, were the mainstays of Ko Samui's economy before the onset of tourism. Even today, they remain a vital part of its economy.*

Ko Phangan ❺

เกาะพะงัน

Beach totem

About two thirds the size of Ko Samui, Ko Phangan is the original backpacker's destination. The cheap accommodations, full moon parties, and bohemian atmosphere make the island attractive to young people and budget travelers, while its powdery beaches, calm bays, accessible corals, excellent dive sites, and a rugged forested interior make it a perfect destination for nature enthusiasts. Large parts of the island are undeveloped due to its difficult terrain. Much of it is accessible only by sea or along rutted roads by pickup trucks. Yet, it is Ko Phangan's virgin beauty that makes it more attractive than commercial tourist spots.

Thong Sala

ท้องศาลา

The largest settlement and de facto capital of Ko Phangan, Thong Sala is the most important town on the island. Although it is not very big, Thong Sala is the main port from where boats and ferries depart to other parts of the island as well as to nearby Ko Samui and Ko Tao. The town provides useful facilities for visitors including banks, a post office, supermarkets, and travel agencies. This is also the only place on Ko Phangan with an international hospital, pharmacies, and a police station. There are a fair number of restaurants, budget hotels, and bars. It is also famous for its Thai massage which locals claim is the best on the island. Visitors to the island can explore it by renting motorcycles or jeeps. Alternatively they can get around by hiring a *songthaew* from next to the pier.

Longtail fishing boats anchored at the pier, Ao Wok Tum

Ao Wok Tum

อ่าววกตุ่ม

3 miles (5 km) N of Thong Sala.

Immediately around a small headland from Thong Sala is the long, undeveloped beach at Ao Wok Tum. Although its sandy stretches are good for sunbathing or strolls, the main attraction here are the coral reefs. Located 320 ft (300 m) offshore, these reefs are perfect for novices as the shallow bay offers safe and easy snorkeling. Small cafés, bars and restaurants, a fishing village, and a local temple – Wat Amphawan – are located nearby. There are bungalow accommodations as well as a 24-hour convenience store.

Ao Hin Kong

อ่าวหินกอง

4 miles (6 km) N of Thong Sala.

Ao Wok Tum blends almost imperceptibly into Ao Hin Kong. A narrow coastal road runs along the bay all the way to Hat Yao. An undeveloped beach that offers a 2-mile (3-km) stretch of clean, white sand running down to the water's edge. The coral reefs skirting Ao Wok Tum continue here and the palm-fringed beach is backed by mangroves. Serviced by a few low-scale bungalow operations, and reasonably priced cafés and restaurants, Ao Hin Kong appeals to backpackers intending a long stay on Ko Phangan. Although it offers little by way of entertainment, it is within cycling distance of Thong Sala from where visitors can make their way to the more bustling nightspots. Swimming in this shallow bay is only possible during high tide.

Ao Si Thanu

อ่าวศรีธนู

5 miles (8 km) N of Thong Sala.

Located just a short distance beyond the Laem Si Thanu headland, Ao Si Thanu has a small beach considered to be among the most beautiful in Ko Phangan. There are adequate bungalow accommodations here as well as two small and attractive hotels, Loy Fa and Chai Country, near the top of the cape, which offer excellent views of the nearby offshore islands and beyond. A small fishing village located at the western end of Ao Si Thanu offers basic facilities including Internet access, noodle stalls, fruit and vegetable shops, and a few bars. The main appeal of this bay, apart from the gorgeous sunset views, is the accessible offshore coral reef.

Mangroves growing along the water's edge at Ao Hin Kong

For hotels and restaurants in this region see pp300–4 and pp326–8

Beach bungalows along the water's edge at Ao Chaophao

Ao Chaophao

อ่าวเจ้าพ่อ

6 miles (10 km) N of Thong Sala.

The coastal route north from Ao Si Thanu cuts inland for a short distance before coming out into the palm-fringed bay of Ao Chaophao. Its long beach used to be quite undeveloped and only visited by those seeking to get away from the crowded beaches of the south coast. However, in recent times, Ao Chaophao has become busier and facilities have sprung up to keep pace with the increased footfall. These include a few bungalow operations, restaurants, and bars. The Pirate Bar, set in a hidden cove at the end of the beach, is definitely worth a visit.

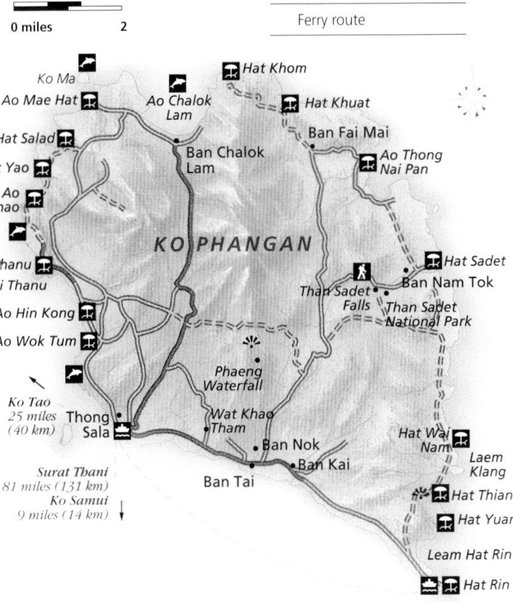

VISITORS' CHECKLIST

Road Map C4. 9 miles (14 km) NE of Surat Thani. *12,000.* *from Ko Samui and Ko Tao.* *TAT, Surat Thani (0-7728-8818).* *daily.*

Hat Yao

หาดยาว

7 miles (11 km) N of Thong Sala.

The main beach resort on Ko Phangan, Hat Yao is a lovely curved stretch of white sand. Although, it is getting busier by the year, the beach is wide enough to accommodate the upcoming resorts, restaurants, and bars, along with other facilities without seeming crowded. Visitors can explore the surrounding waters on sea kayaks or travel inland on motorcycles and jeeps, which are available for hire. The surrounding waters are good for diving and snorkeling.

Hat Salad

หาดสลัด

8 miles (13 km) N of Thong Sala.

The beautiful, small and deeply recessed bay around Hat Salad is fairly off the beaten track even by Ko Phangan standards. Despite this, it has a few guesthouses, small shops, a bike rental, as well as Internet access. According to local legend, this beach used to be a loading point for pirate ships of yore and this adds to the appeal of the beach. Visitors can read, laze, or enjoy a nap in the hammocks strung up between palm trees.

Long swings suspended from coconut palms at Hat Salad

Ao Mae Hat

อ่าวแม่หาด

9 miles (14 km) N of Thong Sala.

An isolated and beautiful cove with crisp white sand, Ao Mae Hat is located on the coast just beyond Mae Hat village in the northeastern part of the island. The eastern end of the beach is mostly used by the fishermen who go out looking for the crabs that populate this area and their longtail boats often lie anchored here. The western end is far more beautiful and has long been a favorite with travelers; however, Mae Hat's stunning natural beauty has led to the development of upscale resort-style accommodations to keep pace with the tourist influx. Apart from being a good spot for swimming and snorkeling, the beach is also linked to the tiny island of Ko Ma by a beautiful sandy causeway that gets exposed at low tide and is shallow enough to cross by wading through the water. The reefs off Ko Ma are among the best snorkeling spots in all of Ko Phangan. A short walk from Mae Hat is the Wang Sai Waterfall with a clear rocky pool that is perfect for swimming.

Ao Chalok Lam

อ่าวโฉลกหลำ

6 miles (10 km) NE of Thong Sala.

The pretty bay of Ao Chalok Lam is home to Ko Phangan's most authentic, and consequently also the smelliest fishing village. Ban Chalok Lam offers an insight into the typical rural life on the island. Piles of squid drying on the beach is a common sight, and the smell of the freshly caught fish is part of the overall experience. Fishing-related activities such as mending nets and gutting fish coexist with shophouses selling pizzas and other snacks. Visitors often stop here to buy fish after a trip to the revered Chinese shrine dedicated to the goddess Chao Mae Koan Im just outside the village. There is also a Buddhist temple near Ban Chalok Lam.

Fisherwomen drying squid in the sun at Ban Chalok Lam

Fishing rig at Ao Chalok Lam

Located offshore from Ao Chalok Lam, **Hin Bai**, or Sail Rock, is one of Thailand's premier dive sites. Diving and snorkeling are popular activities here and the bay has a number of well-equipped bungalows and resorts to cater to the diving crowd. Yet, Ao Chalok Lam is usually treated as a stopover between Thong Sala and **Hat Khom**, a small and attractive beach near the northernmost point of Ko Phangan.

Hat Khuat

หาดขวด

10 miles (16 km) NE of Thong Sala.

from Ban Chalok Lam.

An idyllic spot, Hat Khuat, or Bottle Beach, is one of those glorious unspoiled beaches that draw millions of visitors to Thailand's coast. It is accessible by a dirt track from Hat Khom, but this entails a tough trek through heavy undergrowth. More easily reached by longtail boats, this beach has now become a mid-range destination that is popular with the younger crowd. A delightful expanse of sand, looking out over pristine waters in different shades of aquamarine, Hat Khuat is sheltered inland by the wooded flanks of the 1,408-ft (429-m) high Khao Kin Non. Those seeking affordable bungalow accommodations in a beautiful setting away from the noisy parties will find this beach appealing. However, visitors must avoid this beach during bad weather as they can be stranded without a way back. A short stroll along a dirt track leads to Ban Fai Mai village with a few small grocery stores and snack bars.

Holiday-makers relaxing on the picturesque beach at Ao Mae Hat

Cafés and bungalows along a rocky outcrop, Ao Thong Nai Pan

Ao Thong Nai Pan

อ่าวธงนายพรานน้อยใหญ่

11 miles (18 km) NE of Thong Sala. *from Thong Sala.*

Beyond Hat Khuat, Ko Phangan's coastline curves to the southeast and opens into Ao Thong Nai Pan, a lovely and deeply indented bay backed by forested hills and facing east across the Gulf of Thailand. A tall rocky outcrop divides the bay into two coves – **Ao Thong Nai Pan Noi** to the north and **Ao Thong Nai Pan Yai** to the south. This is perhaps the least accessible bay on the island, and as a result Ao Thong Nai Pan is relatively less crowded. However, the bay offers some of the most attractive scenery on Ko Phangan. Only one rough dirt road links it to Ban Tai on the southern coast, which is 9 miles (14 km) to the south and is a bumpy and bone-jarring ride. Alternatively, it can be reached by boat from Ko Samui between September and January which is a more comfortable option.

Despite being isolated, Ao Thong Nai Pan has developed a fair bit offering restaurants, bars, Internet cafés, travel agents, and banking facilities. Both sides of the beach are equally appealing, with shallow, warm waters that are ideal for swimming or snorkeling. The eastern end of Ao Thong Nai Pan Yai has some rock formations which are good for climbing. Visitors should note that the road to Ban Tai can become impassable during heavy rains, posing a serious hazard to motorcyclists and drivers.

Hat Sadet

หาดเสด็จ

10 miles (16 km) NE of Thong Sala. *from Thong Sala.*

An untouched and fairly inaccessible spot, Hat Sadet is a replica of the romantic and deserted beaches shown in films. Access by land is along the difficult dirt track that runs north from Ban Tai. It is far easier to reach this cove by boat from Thong Sala. Neighboring the island's only national park, the beach has basic seaside bungalows. Despite lacking restaurants, bars, or entertainment options, Hat Sadet is a delightful spot. The beach is narrow as it is flanked by steep rocky outcrops which come straight down to the sea and this further contributes to its isolated charm.

Rama V's seal on a rock

Than Sadet National Park

อุทยานแห่งชาติธารเสด็จ

10 miles (16 km) NE of Thong Sala. *from Thong Sala.*

Established in 1983, Than Sadet National Park was originally much smaller before being enlarged to its present size of 25 sq miles (65 sq km) in 1999. The park is named after the Sadet River. The word *sadet* in Thai means a stream visited by royalty; the name was given after Rama V's (r.1868–1910) visit to the spot in 1889. The largest waterfall on the island – **Than Sadet Falls** – is at the end of a popular hiking trail and has become a favored destination among visitors interested in an alternative to beach activities. The highest point in the park is Khao Ra, which rises to a height of 1,984 ft (605 m). Much of Than Sadet is covered with dense forest, although there are a few trails. The most accessible point is at Hat Sadet, where the Sadet River meets the sea. In the past, this area was popular with Thai monarchs, and Rama V even left his royal monogram inscribed on a large boulder as did his successors Rama VII (r.1925–35) and the present king, Rama IX. In fact, it is said that Rama V liked this place so much that he visited it on as many as ten occasions between 1888 and 1909.

Sadet River cascading down in rocky pools, Than Sadet National Park

Secluded palm-lined cove with aquamarine waters, Hat Thian

Hat Thian

หาดเทียน

8 miles (13 km) E of Thong Sala.

from Hat Rin.

South of Hat Sadet, the east coast of Ko Phangan is almost inaccessible and well off the beaten path. There are hardly any roads along the coast that are better than dirt tracks and one of them extends southward right through the small settlement of Ban Nam Tok to join up with the main southern coastal road near Hat Rin. It is probably wiser and easier to visit the island's east coast by boat from Hat Rin, especially during the rainy season, from June to September. There is a small ferry that makes the daily run between Hat Rin and Ao Thong Nai Pan and stops at Hat Thian on the way, but it is easier to take a water taxi.

Hat Thian is the best among the cluster of three beaches around the headland at Laem Klang. The main reason for staying in this out-of-the-way place is its isolated beauty, although it has undergone some development. There is a decent selection of restaurants serving Thai and Western food, and a few bars with live music and parties on weekends. There are about four resorts around this cove with bungalow-style accommodations and a spa and even a wellness center offering alternative treatments. There are some good dive sites nearby that are famous for sightings of whale sharks.

Hat Yuan

หาดญวน

8 miles (13 km) E of Thong Sala.

Just south of Hat Thian, and within easy walking or even swimming distance, is the even smaller beach at Hat Yuan. This beach, strewn with rocks at either end, has a family atmosphere and there are cafés offering oven-fresh food and fruity yogurts alongside more traditional Thai dishes. This is a good and safe spot for swimming and snorkeling although visitors should be careful during stormy weather. Although Hat Yuan is just a short distance away from noisy Hat Rin, it is laid-back, quiet, and far removed from the party scene. Visitors to this beach can indulge in regular beach activities such as swimming, sunbathing, and snorkeling.

Hat Rin

หาดริน

7 miles (11 km) SE of Thong Sala.

Located on the southeastern tip of Ko Phangan, the bustling beach of Hat Rin and the adjoining village of Ban Hat Rin are the most developed places on the island as well as its party paradise. Set

Bungalows along the palm-fringed beach at Hat Yuan

astride a narrow, sandy peninsula, Hat Rin is divided into two beaches – the lively **Hat Rin Nok**, or Sunrise Beach, to the east and the quieter **Hat Rin Nai**, or Sunset Beach, to the west. Hat Rin is popular with young people who enjoy loud music and definitely for those travelers who come to Ko Phangan for its full moon parties. These famous parties, held on the beach each month, start after dark and go on beyond sunrise the next day. Although the parties are concentrated around the southern end of Hat Rin, especially at Hat Rin Nok, the crowds often overflow to other parts of the beach. A festive ambience is created with lamps, makeshift bars, fire shows, and food and drink stalls.

During these parties, visitors should take care of their belongings and be wary of strangers.

Hat Rin has a constantly expanding group of hotels, guesthouses, restaurants, bars, and Internet cafés. Accommodations are often fully booked for a week on either side of the full moon parties.

Statue at a bar, Hat Rin

In the past, most visitors to Hat Rin were drawn to the clean, wide expanse of sand. Unfortunately, the tourist influx has reduced some of this charm. Today, the beach is often noisy and littered with flotsam, and should certainly be avoided by those seeking isolation.

Wat Khao Tham

วัดเขาถ้ำ

3 miles (5 km) E of Thong Sala.

www.watkowtahm.org

Ko Phangan is known for its lovely beaches and unspoiled vistas. Old temples or Buddhist architecture are not what a visitor would expect to see here. However, Wat Khao Tham, located to the northwest of Ban Tai on the island's southern coast, draws both Asian and Western visitors keen to participate in its meditation retreats. More a meditation center than a monastery, Wat Khao Tham is an interesting place for the spiritually inclined. Sessions on healing the body and mind are held on a monthly basis over several days. The entry costs are quite reasonable and include food and accommodations. Billed as a Theravadin Buddhist Monastery and Retreat Center, the monastery is run by two resident foreigners, Rosemary and Steve Weissman, who are also the teachers. The objective of the retreat is to gain insight into human nature through a mental development practice. The monastery is a perfect contrast to the crowds and the wild, over-the-top full moon parties at Hat Rin just around the corner.

Serene backdrop for meditation retreats at Wat Khao Tham

FULL MOON PARTY

These famous parties are held at Hat Rin every month during full moon. From its small origins some 25 years ago, these full moon parties now attract thousands of partygoers from all over. Many enthusiasts flock to this beach and the numbers can reach anything between 10,000 and 20,000 a month. The event features a mix of international and Thai DJs playing every kind of music from techno to commercial pop. Visitors paint themselves with ultraviolet colors and also carry lights and props which glow. Alcohol – which is legal – flows freely and is usually sold as cocktail buckets. Unfortunately, a lot of illegal psychotropic drugs are also easily available. These are best avoided as they can cause severe illness or even death by overdosing. Possession of these drugs can lead to fines or even imprisonment.

Revelers crowding the beach at a full moon party, Hat Rin

Visitors swimming in the shallow waters of a rock-strewn beach, Ko Samui ▷

Ang Thong Marine National Park ❻

อุทยานแห่งชาติทางทะเลอ่างทอง

Ferry to Ang Thong Marine National Park

The Ang Thong, or Golden Basin, archipelago includes nearly 42 stunning and virtually uninhabited islands covering an area of 39 sq miles (101 sq km). A former naval base, it became accessible to the public only in 1980, when it was declared a marine national park. The islands are the submerged peaks of a flooded range of limestone mountains some of which soar above sea level to 1400 ft (427 m). Ang Thong's beauty attracts visitors who come to relax on the mica white sands, explore the lush forests and caves, and snorkel among excellent corals. Another attraction is the abundant wildlife, both on land and in the sea.

LOCATOR MAP

Area illustrated

★ Thale Nai Crater Lake

A stunning green seawater lake in the middle of Ko Mae Ko, Thale Nai Crater Lake is the golden basin that gives Ang Thong its name. Encircled by limestone cliffs, and linked to the open sea by an underground passage, the lake offers spectacular views which more than compensate for the strenuous hike.

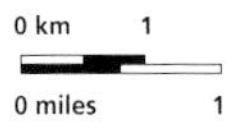

Ko Phaluai, the largest island in the archipelago, is inhabited by a community of fishermen.

Kayaking

Professionally guided sea-kayaking tours in and around Ang Thong can be easily arranged from Hat Chaweng or Hat Lamai in nearby Ko Samui (see pp162–71).

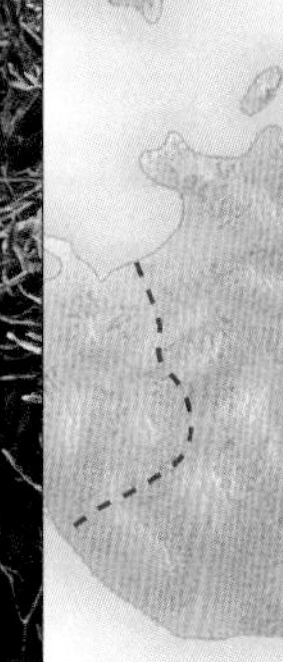

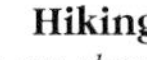

Hiking

Distances are short in Ang Thong, but some climbs are steep, and it can get very hot in the day. Visitors are advised to carry hats, sunscreen, and lots of water.

STAR SIGHTS

- ★ Thale Nai Crater Lake
- ★ Tham Bua Bok Cave
- ★ Ko Wua Talab Viewpoint

For hotels and restaurants in this region see pp300–4 and pp326–8

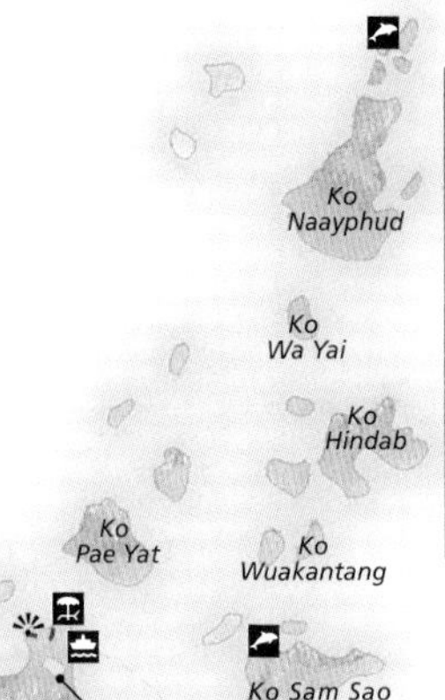

VISITORS' CHECKLIST

Road Map C4. Park HQ on Ko Wua Talab, 16 miles (26 km) N of Ko Samui. ***Tel*** *0-2562-0760 (bookings).* *from Ko Samui.* *Park HQ (0-7728-6025).* *Nov–Dec.*

KEY

- Beach
- Dive site
- Watersports
- Viewpoint
- Ferry service
- Visitor information
- Trail
- Ferry route

Ko Sam Sao
This tiny island is a favorite with divers and snorkelers, offering the best coral reefs in the whole park.

The Stone Bridge at Ko Sam Sao is a natural formation popular with sea-kayakers.

Thale Nai Crater Lake

★ Tham Bua Bok Cave
A strenuous hike leads to this cave near the summit of Ko Wua Talab. Its interior is filled with stalactites and stalagmites which resemble lotus flowers giving the cave its name – Bua Bok, meaning Waving Lotus.

★ Ko Wua Talab Viewpoint
Located at the summit of this island, this viewpoint is at the end of a fairly difficult trek. However, it offers stunning views of the green islands rising out of the waters of the Ang Thong archipelago. Ko Wua Talab also has basic bungalow accommodations for visitors to the park.

Boat trips
These operate in good weather between Ko Samui, Ko Phangan (see pp172–7), *and Ang Thong. Some tours are specifically for divers and snorkelers while other more expensive options offer overnight accommodations.*

Ko Tao ❼

เกาะเต่า

Visitor on motorcycle

Picturesquely located in the midst of the Gulf of Thailand, north of Ko Phangan *(see pp172–7)*, Ko Tao is the smallest of the three main islands in the Samui archipelago. While the island itself is rugged, with dense forest inland, quiet coves along the east coast, and a fine sweep of sandy beach on the western side, the surrounding sea offers excellent underwater visibility, a wide range of dive sites, and a variety of coral and marine life. The Chumphon Pinnacle *(see p23)*, 7 miles (11 km) northwest of Ko Tao, is among the best dive sites in the area with known sightings of the gray reef shark. Ko Tao is also a significant breeding ground for hawksbill and green turtles.

Longtail and speedboats anchored along Hat Ao Mae

Ban Mae Hat

บ้านแม่หาด

The unofficial capital of Ko Tao, Ban Mae Hat is one of the few large settlements on the island. A small, pleasant fishing village that is now being rapidly transformed into a small tourist town, Ban Mae Hat houses various facilities and services – banks, clinics, and pharmacies, Internet cafés, a post office, police station, and supermarkets. It becomes all the more important because of the main ferry pier from which a surfaced road leads inland to Ao Chalok Ban Kao on the southern coast. The town is large enough to offer a reasonable selection of accommodations, the best dining facilities on the island, as well as a few Irish pubs, pool tables, and video and sports bars with wide-screen televisions. Motorcycles are available for hire for those who wish to explore the island for a day or two before making a choice of resort or beach bungalow.

Hat Ao Mae

หาดอ่าวแม่

Located in a shallow bay, a short distance north of the Ban Mae Hat ferry pier, and perhaps too close to the village for visitors seeking a tranquil holiday, Hat Ao Mae is a small beach. Nevertheless, it is well equipped with a comfortable resort, the Montra, offering convenient access to Ban Mae Hat to the south and the beautiful Hat Sai Ri to the north – both within easy walking distance of the beach. The area is also famous locally for Laem Jor Por Ror, or the Rama V Cape, a historically relevant site – on June 18, 1899, Rama V (r.1868–1910) visited Ko Tao and left his monogram carved on a large rock here, called the Rama V boulder. This site has since been venerated, especially by locals.

Hat Sai Ri

หาดทรายรี

1 mile (2 km) N of Ban Mae Hat.

An idyllic beach, perfect for admiring spectacular sunsets over the Gulf of Thailand, Hat Sai Ri is the longest stretch of sandy beach on Ko Tao. It is framed to the east by swaying coconut palms, an increasing number of small restaurants, bars, and simple bungalow accommodations. The beach is paralleled by a narrow surfaced path and, slightly further inland, by a small paved road leading to the settlement of Ban Hat Sai Ri. Once a tiny fishing village, it now serves as a service center for the fast growing local tourism industry with dive centers, travel agents, and small supermarkets; there are even ATMs and Internet cafés. Beyond the beach, the surfaced road continues to the upscale Dusit Buncha Resort *(see p304)* and Nangyuan Terrace. Beyond this point, the road ends in steep cliffs and jungle.

Ko Nang Yuan

เกาะนางยวน

2 miles (3 km) N of Ban Mae Hat.

from Ban Mae Hat.

Perhaps the most beautiful natural formation off Ko Tao, Ko Nang Yuan is a group of three islets linked by a narrow causeway of white sand. The smallest among them is also known as **Japanese Garden**. This spectacular location is easily reached by ferry and

Utility market offering ATMs and other facilities, Hat Sai Ri

Sparkling, azure waters surrounding the islets of Ko Nang Yuan

makes a popular sunbathing and swimming day trip. Strict regulations are in force to protect the environment and no cans, plastic bags, or bottles are permitted. Visitors have to pay a nominal fee to land, although full-day all-inclusive tours, complete with a picnic lunch, snorkeling, or diving can be arranged at one of the many travel agencies in Ban Mae Hat. The islands are administered by the Nangyuan Island Dive Resort *(see p303)*, and visitors staying here receive free transfers to and from the mainland.

Ao Mamuang

อ่าวมะม่วง

3 miles (5 km) NE of Ban Mae Hat.

Located on the northernmost shore of Ko Tao, Ao Mamuang, or Mango Bay, is a long, lovely, cove backed with lush greenery. It has a shallow offshore reef which usually draws snorkelers on day trips from Ban Mae Hat and elsewhere on the island. There is a small beach here, as well as comfortable bungalow accommodations, restaurants, and bars. Getting to Ao Mamuang, however, is not so easy although visitors can either take a boat or follow the narrow, unpaved track that leads east across the hump of the island from Ban Hat Sai Ri, forking to the north toward the beach. The bay is framed by two beautiful capes – Nam Dok to the west and Grachom Fai (equipped with a lighthouse) to the east. Although quite isolated, it is comfortably appointed, and a great place to relax.

VISITORS' CHECKLIST

Road Map C3. 25 miles (40 km) N of Ko Phangan. *5,000.* *from Ko Phangan.* *TAT, Surat Thani (0-7728-8818).*

Ao Hinwong

อ่าวหินวง

4 miles (6 km) NE of Ban Mae Hat.

Located on the northeastern shore of Ko Tao, well away from the bustle of Ban Mae Hat, Ao Hinwong is a delightful, isolated cove, surrounded by charming coconut groves and large boulders. Best reached by boat, Ao Hinwong can also be approached by a narrow track across the island from Ban Hat Sai Ri. The track, however, is only suitable for motorcycles, rugged pickups, or vehicles with 4WD. Despite its isolation, it is becoming popular with visitors to Ko Tao, as it offers two comfortable resorts and a bungalow complex. Its appeal lies in its overwhelming peace, and the clear, and sheltered waters of the beautiful bay, with dark shoals of sardines clearly visible from above. A hill to the north offers great ocean views. Ao Hinwong is an ideal spot for snorkeling and diving enthusiasts.

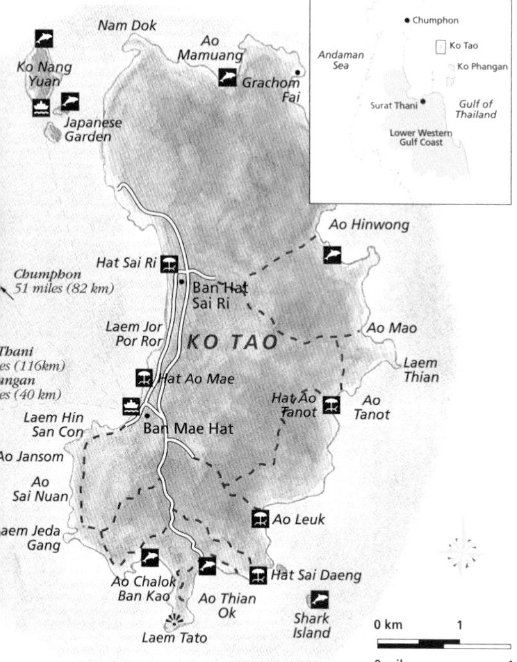

KEY

- Beach
- Dive site
- Viewpoint
- Ferry service
- Minor road
- Trail
- Ferry route

Sandy cove at Ao Tanot dotted with roofs of resort buildings

Laem Thian

แหลมเทียน

4 miles (6 km) E of Ban Mae Hat.

An isolated cape located almost midway down the deserted east coast of Ko Tao, Laem Thian is a tiny water-body with a white, sandy beach. Sheltered in the southern lee of a rocky headland, it is best reached by boat, although there is a treacherous dirt track that crosses the center of the island. The northern branch of this track leads to Ao Mamuang and Ao Hinwong, and the southern branch to Laem Thian. Among the more popular sites for snorkeling enthusiasts on Ko Tao, Laem Thian is well known for its underwater tunnels and swim-through passages. Made of limestone, they are easy to navigate. The area is also known for frequent sightings of the exotic unicorn fish. Comfortable bungalows and other basic facilities are available on the beach here.

Ao Tanot

อ่าวโตนด

4 miles (6 km) E of Ban Mae Hat.

A small, horsehoe-shaped bay facing east across the Gulf of Thailand, Ao Tanot is a beautiful setting, well known for its vistas of fine sunrises. Just south of Laem Thian, and clearly visible across Ao Tanot is the isolated and beautiful beach, Hat Ao Tanot. As with the other beaches on the east coast of Ko Tao, its appeal lies in its relative inaccessibility. Large boulders lie scattered across Hat Ao Tanot, as do a large variety of seashells. The primary activity here is snorkeling and snorkeling enthusiasts can hire equipment from the dive shops nearby. There are several good resorts and simple bungalow accommodations, as well as a dive school, and small, attractive terrace bars set against colorful groves of bougainvillea. Ao Tanot can also be reached by a southern track leading inland and over the mountainous spine of Ko Tao from the Ban Mae Hat-Ao Chalok surfaced road.

Bougainvillea, a common shrub

Ao Leuk

อ่าวลึก

3 miles (5 km) SE of Ban Mae Hat.

Located close to Ko Tao's south-easternmost point, Ao Luek has among the most beautiful beaches on Ko Tao and offers a variety of outdoor activities. Visitors can go sea-kayaking, water-skiing, and windsurfing, all of which can be easily arranged through any one of the several resorts on the beach. Sunbathing and swimming are other options. There are beautiful coral reefs offshore, and snorkeling in the clear waters is another delightful pastime. Despite its reputation, the waters off the bay are quite safe, with the only shark sighted being the inoffensive blacktip. Both accommodation options and dining facilities are good, as are the few inviting bars.

Hat Sai Daeng

หาดทรายแดง

3 miles (5 km) SE of Ban Mae Hat.

An attractive and unspoiled white sands beach, backed by a narrow peninsula jutting into the warm waters of the Gulf of Thailand, Hat Sai Daeng is located along the busier and more accessible southern coast of Ko Tao. The beach, also known as Red

Kayakers rowing across the waters off Shark Island, Hat Sai Daeng

For hotels and restaurants in this region see pp300–4 and pp326–8

Sands Beach, points directly at the popular diving and snorkeling site around tiny, unpopulated Shark Island, which is also known as Ko Chalam. Hat Sai Daeng offers good views across the sea, lying in the shelter of a mangrove-covered headland. The beach has adequate bungalow accommodations, restaurants, and bars. It is easily approached by a narrow, seldom-used track running east from the main Mae Hat-Ao Chalok road, which is usable the year round. However, visitors should be careful to avoid using the smaller tracks which are quite dangerous, and even impassable, during heavy rains.

Beautiful, rocky beachfront backed by thick foliage, Hat Sai Daeng

Ao Thian Ok

อ่าวเทียนออก

2 miles (3 km) SE of Ban Mae Hat.

The southernmost bay on the island, Ao Thian Ok has one of the prettiest beaches in Ko Tao. It is sheltered on the east by the Hat Sai Daeng headland and Shark Island, and to the west by the much larger headland of Laem Tato. Despite being frequented by reef sharks, the waters off Ao Thian Ok are very popular with divers. The beach offers luxurious spa accommodations as well as a few reasonably priced bungalows, a series of bars with spectacular ocean views, and some of the best restaurants on the island. Visitors can also take courses in Thai massage, yoga, and *chi gong* (a component of Chinese martial arts) as well as enjoy the usual maritime activities – swimming, snorkeling, and diving in the surrounding waters.

Enjoying a relaxed evening at a beachside shack, Ao Chalok Ban Kao

Ao Chalok Ban Kao

อ่าวโฉลกบ้านเก่า

1 miles (2 km) S of Ban Mae Hat.

The largest, most developed, and best-appointed beach resort on Ko Tao, Ao Chalok Ban Kao is sheltered by Laem Tato on the east and Laem Jeda Gang on the west. Easily accessible by a good, if narrow, road from Ban Mae Hat, this beautiful bay is protected by forest-clad hills during both the northeast and southwest monsoons. The bay is home to three separate, but closely-linked beaches – Freedom Beach, to the southeast, Hat Chalok in the center, and smaller Hat San Jao to the west. Ao Chalok Ban Kao is among the biggest dive centers on Ko Tao with a large number of divers, snorkelers, and keen anglers frequenting the beach. As a result, the beach is equipped with several dive shops, travel agents, guesthouses, decent restaurants, and bars. In the center of Laem Tato, **Jon Suwan Mountain Viewpoint** offers fine views across the deeply indented bay and the surrounding wooded hills.

Sunbathing on the white, sandy beach, Ao Thian Ok

Ao Sai Nuan

อ่าวสายนวล

A group of sandy coves fringed by tall palms and warm, azure waters, come together to form this attractive spot. Ao Sai Nuan, a short distance southwest of Ban Mae Hat, is really a southern extension of the village and is characterized by a string of bungalows and several upscale resorts. Backed and sheltered by a densely-wooded 620-ft (189-m) high mountain, the bay offers mesmerizing vistas of picture-perfect sunsets across the Gulf of Thailand. Good for diving and snorkeling, there are several spots from which enthusiasts can plunge into the waters around Laem Jeda Gang and Laem Hin San Con. The ease of accessibility makes Ao Sai Nuan a popular spot with visitors to Ko Tao. It can be approached on foot or motorcycle from Ban Mae Hat, although it is advisable to avoid four-wheeled vehicles. Various facilities including dive shops, restaurants, and bars combine to make any visit to Ao Sai Nuan a pleasant experience.

Open-air restaurant at a beach resort, Hat Na Dan

Hat Khanom ❽

หาดขนอม

Road Map C4. 56 miles (90 km) E of Surat Thani. *TAT, Nakhon Si Thammarat (0-7534-6515).*

A long and attractive beach, Hat Khanom is a part of the largest bay in the region. However, despite being easily accessible by road, it does not feature on most itineraries. The beach is also the center for the **Hat Khanom-Mu Ko Thale Tai National Park** which covers mainland areas in the districts of Khanom and Sichon, as well as the offshore islands of Ko Noi, Ko Wang Nai, Ko Wang Nok, Ko Tan, Ko Rap, Ko Tha Rai, and Ko Phi. Hat Khanom is to the north of Khanom town, a small coastal settlement dating back to the Ayutthaya period *(see pp40–41)*. Originally a major trading and cultural center, Khanom is today a tranquil and sleepy fishing town. Coconut and rubber plantations provide the main source of livelihood apart from fishing. It has a few restaurants, cottages, and a single hotel. However, most visitors prefer the beaches, especially as they also offer a wider range of accommodations right by the sea, ranging from luxurious resorts to homely bungalows. The area is rich in natural beauty as it is located near a string of lovely beaches sheltered by limestone mountains. These outcrops are riddled with several caves; **Khao Wang Thong Cave** is the most significant among them. Located about 9 miles (14 km) from Khanom town, it has unusual stalagmite and stalactite formations. With the Samui archipelago *(see pp162–71)* becoming more congested, Ao Khanom is being developed as the next big holiday destination.

There is also a growing diving and snorkeling industry in this area, and tour operators can organize overnight stays or day trips to the nearby islands. They also arrange fishing trips to the Gulf of Thailand. This bay is a popular spot for sea golf which takes place between April and July. During this time locals organize golf tournaments on the exposed flat sands of the seabed as the water drains out almost completely during low tide.

PINK DOLPHINS OF SICHON AND KHANOM

One of the unusual attractions of the Sichon-Khanom coast is the pod of rare pink dolphins that lives in the shallow waters of the Gulf of Thailand just offshore. It is usually possible to see these friendly and intelligent creatures by boat. The best time to view these mammals is between October and April. Formally known as Chinese White Dolphins, the adults of the species are usually grey or white in color. The much rarer pink variety is found here and on the South China coast. Unfortunately, this dolphin is threatened by over-fishing in both areas and is now officially protected by the government.

A pink dolphin and its calf swimming along the water's surface

Limestone mountains forming a scenic backdrop to Khanom town

Hat Na Dan ❾

หาดหน้าด่าน

Road Map C4. 6 miles (10 km) S of Hat Khanom. *TAT, Nakhon Si Thammarat (0-7534-6515).*

Moving southward along the coastline from Hat Khanom, is the pristine Hat Na Dan. This is a long, curving, white sand beach fringed by coconut palms and washed by the warm aquamarine waters of the Gulf of Thailand. Although this beach is only half an hour away by boat from Ko Samui, it is not very popular with foreign visitors. There is little by way of facilities, although there are a few beach vendors who sell local specialties such as dried squid. However, the pristine nature of the beach is changing with the arrival of sprawling resorts. The calm bay is good for swimming but there are no coral reefs. It is as yet undisturbed by the noise or pollution of jet skis and watersports. However, it is only a matter of time before it becomes a commercial spot.

Rustic beach bungalows with tiled roofs at Hat Nai Phraet

Hat Nai Phraet ⑩

หาดในแพรด

Road Map C4. 2 miles (3 km) S of Hat Na Dan. *TAT Nakhon Si Thammarat (0-7534-6515).*

Lying immediately to the south of Hat Na Dan, Hat Nai Phraet is a gorgeous, long, and curving beach that is almost deserted, especially on weekdays. This peaceful spot has been drawing locals for years, but remains relatively unknown to foreign visitors. The beach is composed of crisp, golden sand backed by coconut palms and casuarina trees. There are some large boulders strewn about the beach that add to the ambience and natural beauty, as well as provide some shade from the midday sun. Facilities are minimal, although there are a few simple beachside restaurants serving local food and cold drinks. There are also some basic bungalows right by the beach for an overnight stay. However, most travelers make their way to the busier town of Khanom, for more options.

Hat Nai Phlao ⑪

หาดในเพรา

Road Map C4. 3 miles (5 km) S of Hat Na Dan. *TAT Nakhon Si Thammarat (0-7534-6515).*

Located south of Hat Nai Phraet, Hat Nai Phlao is the longest beach in the Khanom district and its most popular attraction – although most visitors are local Thais on a weekend break. The beach is bordered by the Gulf of Thailand to the east, and the forest-clad hills of the Khao Luang range to the west, creating an idyllic setting. This beach offers basic and affordable bungalow accommodations and campsites. There are also a couple of simple restaurants and bars offering local seafood delicacies along with beer or iced drinks. A few upscale resorts have also come up in recent years. Travel agencies are also developing watersports facilities such as snorkeling and fishing. Visitors can take longtail boats to the nearby islands, or hike to pretty Nam Tok Hin Lat along a 2-mile (3-km) long trail that winds its way through a scene of rural tranquility, surrounded by lush vegetation.

Waves washing over the expansive sandy shore, Hat Nai Phlao

Breathtaking Hat Tong Yi in an idyllic tropical setting

Hat Tong Yi ⓬

หาดท้องหยี

Road Map C4. 25 miles (40 km) S of Hat Nai Phlao. *TAT, Nakhon Si Thammarat (0-7534-6515).*

A slender stretch of sand, beautiful Hat Tong Yi is a little known beach, completely cut off from other beaches to its north and south by thick, wooded headlands. This picture-perfect beach is accessed by following a rough laterite road from Hat Nai Phlao's *(see p187)* Rachakiri Resort for about 2 miles (3 km). However, the journey is worth the trouble, especially when welcomed by the sheer isolation of the beach. Simple accommodations are available at Hat Tong Yi, but most visitors choose to stay at better-appointed Hat Nai Phlao to the north, visiting the beach only as a day trip. There are very few facilities available at the beach, so bringing along a picnic basket is advisable. Those keen to experiment with local flavors can find simple yet exotic seafood specialties, such as fried rice or grilled squid, nearby.

Hat Sichon ⓭

หาดสิชล

Road Map C4. 1 miles (2 km) S of Hat Tong Yi. *TAT, Nakhon Si Thammarat (0-7534-6515).*

Little more than a fishing village, Sichon is still a small settlement and port. However, it has seen some development and basic accommodations and restaurants have set up shop here. Beautiful Hat Sichon, also known as Hat Hua Hin Sichon, is distinguished by large numbers of rocky boulders strewn along the white sand, and is popular with locals, just like its namesake Hat Hua Hin *(see p140)*. Tall palms fringe the beach, while the small pier is lined with colorful longtail fishing boats. Hat Sichon is also a regular swimming spot, but those looking for somewhere even quieter could move southward to pretty Hat Piti.

Visitors wishing to get away from regular beach activities can also head to the scenic Nam Tok Si Khit, or Si Khit Falls, some 10 miles (16 km) inland from Hat Sichon, along Highway 4105. The Si Khit River originates in the Khao Luang Mountains to the west and flows through gorgeous natural surroundings before reaching these falls. Securing the area as a protected national park site is currently under consideration.

Hat Hin Ngam ⓮

หาดหินงาม

Road Map C4. 2 miles (3 km) S of Hat Sichon. *TAT, Nakhon Si Thammarat (0-7534-6515).*

Covered with small rocks and boulders of various colors which give the beach its name, Hat Hin Ngam, or Beach of Beautiful Stones, is best visited as a day trip from nearby Hat Sichon. A good place for diving and

Busy pier at Hat Sichon, lined with fishing boats

Unspoiled sweeping bay of Hat Hin Ngam

snorkeling, Hat Hin Ngam is pretty quiet with no accommodation options or restaurants so bringing along food and water is advisable.

Thatched shelter providing shade from the tropical sun at Hat Piti

Hat Piti ⓯

หาดปิติ

Road Map C4. 1 mile (2 km) S of Hat Hin Ngam. *TAT, Nakhon Si Thammarat (0-7534-6515).*

A favorite with locals who frequent the beach for its beauty and relative anonymity, Hat Piti is now witnessing a rise in the number of foreign visitors to its shores. Blessed with a white sandy beach and rows of coconut palms that provide adequate shade, the beach is a great place to sunbathe. Swimming and watersports such as windsurfing, albeit limited, are other options. However, there are no facilities available and visitors should head to nearby Sichon in the north for accommodations and restaurants serving local Thai as well as other cuisine.

Khao Kha Archaeological Site ⓰

แหล่งโบราณคดีเขาคา

Road Map C4. Tambon Sao Phao, 6 miles (10 km) S of Hat Piti. *TAT, Nakhon Si Thammarat (0-7534-6515).* *9am–4pm.* *Mondays.*

Located on a mountain in the Tambon Sao Phao district, the Khao Kha Archaeological Site dates back almost 1,500 years. An ancient city with a laterite shrine, the site was restored in 1997 by the Thai Fine Arts Department before it was opened for public viewing. Khao Kha appears to be a predominantly Hindu site, formerly sacred to the Saiwinikai sect which was known to worship Shiva as the supreme deity of the Hindu pantheon. The site has revealed several monuments with the most important of them being located at its northern end. Many interesting artifacts from Saivite rituals including *lingas* (symbolic phalluses), a sacred tank, holy water pipes, and other related ruins, have also been excavated. These relics have now been preserved in a bungalow-like building, located near the site, and are also maintained by the Fine Arts Department. Even today, archaeologists continue to study the numerous artifacts unearthed here in relation to the once-popular Hindu Saivite sect.

Building housing relics from the Khao Kha Archaeological Site

Local fisherwoman drying shrimps near the waterfront, Hat Saophao

Hat Saophao ⓱

หาดเสาเภา

Road Map C4. Tha Sala, Hwy 401, 36 miles (60 km) N of Nakhon Si Thammarat. *TAT, Nakhon Si Thammarat (0-7534-6515).*

Perfect for a pleasant day trip from nearby Nakhon Si Thammarat *(see pp192–5)*, Hat Saophao is a long, often deserted strip of sand. Devoid of the regular tourist influx, this beautiful beach continues to be a safe haven for holiday-makers looking for some peace and quiet. The beach is equipped with small restaurants and cafés aimed chiefly at the locals. Further inland are vast shrimp farms and tiny, predominantly Thai Muslim villages. Visitors will find Muslim kitemakers selling their wares – beautiful, colored kites – on the road between Nakhon and Hat Saophao. The beach is best reached by local bus from Nakhon Si Thammarat or by motorcycle taxi, and draws mainly young backpackers.

Hat Sa Bua ⓲

หาดสระบัว

Road Map C4. 24 miles (39 km) N of Nakhon Si Thammarat. *TAT, Nakhon Si Thammarat (0-7534-6515).*

A picturesque beach, about 3 miles (5 km) long and dotted with lovely coconut groves, Hat Sa Bua is a favorite weekend resort for locals. Just north of Nakhon, the road to the beach winds through pleasant rural scenery, past small fishing villages and rustic kilns used for firing bricks and pottery. Tamarisks and palm trees shade stretches of sandy shoreline, while thatched umbrellas provide cool, shaded sanctuaries. There are simple bungalow accommodations available, along with numerous small bars and seafood restaurants, which are quite reasonably priced.

Khao Luang National Park ⓳

อุทยานแห่งชาติเขาหลวง

Road Map C4. Park HQ off Hwy 4015, 28 miles (45 km) NW of Nakhon Si Thammarat. *Park HQ (0-7530-0494).*

One of the largest and least developed national parks in southern Thailand, Khao Luang covers an area of 230 sq miles (596 sq km). Declared a national park in 1974, Khao Luang surrounds the region's main peak, Khao Luang, which is 6,020 ft (1,835 m) high. The park is home to a wide variety of tropical flora and fauna, and provides sanctuary to several endangered species.

Animals inhabiting the park include musk deer, Malaysian tapir, binturong, and serow. Park authorities have also identified more than 200 species of birds, including both permanent residents and migratory species. The flora in the park is tropical, dense, and magnificent with colorful orchids and rhododendrons.

The most popular attraction of the park is the nine-tiered **Krung Ching Waterfall**, accessible by a steep 3-mile (5-km) trek from the park entrance. Overnight accommodations are available in the park, as are camping facilities.

Cascading waters of the nine-tier Krung Ching Waterfall

Laem Talumphuk ⓴

แหลมตะลุมพุก

Road Map C4. 14 miles (22 km) E of Nakhon Si Thammarat. *TAT, Nakhon Si Thammarat (0-7534-6515).*

A long and narrow cape facing Nakhon Si Thammarat to the east, Laem Talumphuk is a popular haven for local fishing vessels. The coast at this point is divided into two sections where the Phanang River runs down to Ao Nakhon from the mountains nearby. The eastern shore is inhabited in places with small fishing villages and shrimp farms, as well as a long, beautiful beach, fringed with towering palm trees. Although an area of great natural beauty, the beach here has limited facilities beyond a few small shops and restaurants, and is best visited as a day trip from Nakhon Si Thammarat.

A typical fishing settlement close to Hat Sa Bua

Shadow Puppets

An art form said to have originated as early as 400 BC in Southeast Asia, *nang talung* is a popular southern Thai version of puppetry that originated in Phatthalung. Light is shone behind the puppets, creating shadows on a cloth screen, giving it the name "shadow puppets." Often compared with *wayang kulit*, shadow puppetry in neighboring Malaysia, *nang talung* performances generally begin after dark and last well into the night.

A *nang talung* puppet

They remain an essential, although diminishing, part of village life in southern Thailand. It is the task of a single skilled person, the *nai nag* (puppet master) to conceptualize the whole show. While the more formal *nang yai* is based on traditional stories from the Ramakien *(see p59)*, *nang talung* often takes its inspiration from daily life. Each story is created by the *nai nag* and includes easily recognizable characters.

Illuminated cloth screens are used to reflect the shadow of the puppets

The *nai nag*, maneuvers up to six puppets per screen

Musicians accompany the *nai nag* in *nang talung* performances

NANG TALUNG THEATER

Theater performances of *nang talung* are held in large open spaces. The changing tone of voice of the puppet master, who manipulates the puppets through complex movements from behind the screen, differentiates between the characters. A traditional orchestra adds tension to the plot.

Nang *(water buffalo leather) is cut, colored, and rendered movable by joints to make the 20-inch (50-cm) high shadow puppets. This is highly skilled work and done only by master craftsmen.*

Ramakien stories, *depicted through* nang yai *or large shadow puppets, are adapted from the original epic. Here, Hanuman, the monkey god, is usually given a prominent role.*

Nang talung, *smaller shadow puppets, portray comic figures with exaggerated features. From demons and heroes to farmers, these characters play a central role in performances.*

Nakhon Si Thammarat 21

นครศรีธรรมราช

Silver figurine

Although the historic town of Nakhon Si Thammarat features on few tourist itineraries, the cultural capital of southern Thailand is a lively center with several attractions. Under the name of Ligor, it is said to have been the capital of Tambralinga prior to the 7th century. From the 7th–13th centuries, it was an important city of the Srivijaya Empire *(see p39)* when it became a religious center with the Sanskrit name Nagara Sri Dhammaraja, meaning City of the Sacred Dharma King. Many Indian traders settled here and Hindu shrines are common, as are *nang talung (see p191)* plays and intricately etched nielloware *(see p30)*.

Relaxing way of taking in the sights, Nakhon Si Thammarat

Delicately carved southern Thai wooden house, Wat Sao Thong Tong

Wat Sao Thong Tong

วัดเสาธงทอง

Ratchadamnoen Rd. ◯ *daily.*

The main attraction of Wat Sao Thong Tong is the southern Thai wooden house, started in 1888 and finished in 1901. The *wat* now occupies the area which had earlier housed the first primary school in the district. It is actually three houses joined together by a common pointed roof and features delicately carved wooden door panels, gables, and window surrounds. The Architects' Association of Thailand gave a conservation award to the building in 1993.

Ancient City Wall and North Gate

กำแพงเมืองเก่า

E of Ratchadamnoen Rd.

The ancient city wall, built as a fortification, originally contained an area which was 1,320 ft by 7,350 ft (402 m by 2,240 m). It was restored in the 14th and again in the 17th century. The red brick North Gate is a reconstruction of the original gate.

Ho Phra I-suan

หอพระอิศวร

Ratchadamnoen Rd. ◯ *daily.*

In the hall of this shrine is a 3-ft (1-m) *linga*, a phallic image of the Hindu god Shiva, which may date back to the 6th century AD. The worship of Shiva was a potent force in the early peninsular city-states of the first millennium AD.

Ho Phra Narai

หอพระนารายณ์

Ratchadamnoen Rd. ◯ *daily.*

Five *lingas* (phallic symbols) discovered on the site of this shrine may date from before AD 1000. They are now in the Wihan Kien Museum *(see p195)*.

Ho Phra Buddha Sihing

หอพระพุทธสิหิงค์

Ratchadamnoen Rd. ◯ *Wed–Sun.*

The Phra Buddha Sihing is one of Thailand's most revered images. The replica kept in this shrine is of an original cast in Sri Lanka in AD 157 and brought to Nakhon at the end of the 13th century. Local artisans put their characteristic stamp on the Buddha by giving it a half

Reconstructed Ancient City Wall and North Gate

smile, a rounder face, and a full chest. This style has a special name – *khanom tom*, or banana and rice pudding. It is similar to Buddha images in Wat Phra Sing in Chiang Mai in northern Thailand.

Shadow Puppet Theater
บ้านหนังตะลุงสุชาติ
10/18 Si Thammasok Soi 3.
Tel *0-7534-6394.* *daily.*
The *nang talung* workshop of puppeteer Suchart Subsin keeps alive a uniquely Southeast Asian form of entertainment in danger of dying out. Visitors can watch the puppets being cut from leather and buy the finished product. Sometimes impromptu shows are also staged.

Wat Phra Mahathat Woramahawihan
วัดพระมหาธาตุ
See pp194–5.

National Museum Nakhon Si Thammarat
พิพิธภัณฑสถานแห่งชาตินครศรีธรรมราช
Ratchadamnoen Rd, 1 mile (2 km) S of town center. **Tel** *0-7534-1075.*
Wed–Sun.
The centerpiece of this branch of the National Museum *(see p62)* is the 9th-century statue of Vishnu, part of the Hindu holy trinity, in the Pala style of South India. It was found in the base of a tree in Kapong district near Takua Pa in Phang Nga province, then a major transit point for Indians colonizing the south. Two rare bronze drums made by the Dong Son people of northern Vietnam are another highlight. The Thai gallery displays religious art from the Dvaravati and Srivijaya periods to the Rattanakosin era. The Buddha images in the distinctive local Sing style, characterized by stumpy features and animated faces, are also worth a visit.

Buddha image in characteristic local style, Ho Phra Buddha Sihing

VISITORS' CHECKLIST

Road Map C4. 89 miles (144 km) SE of Surat Thani. *147,000.* *9 miles (14 km) N of Nakhon Si Thammarat.* *TAT, Sanam Na Muang, Ratchadamnoen Rd, Nakhon Si Thammarat (0-7534-6516).* *daily.* *Tenth Lunar Month Festival (Sep/Oct).*

Imposing façade and grounds, National Museum, Nakhon Si Thammarat

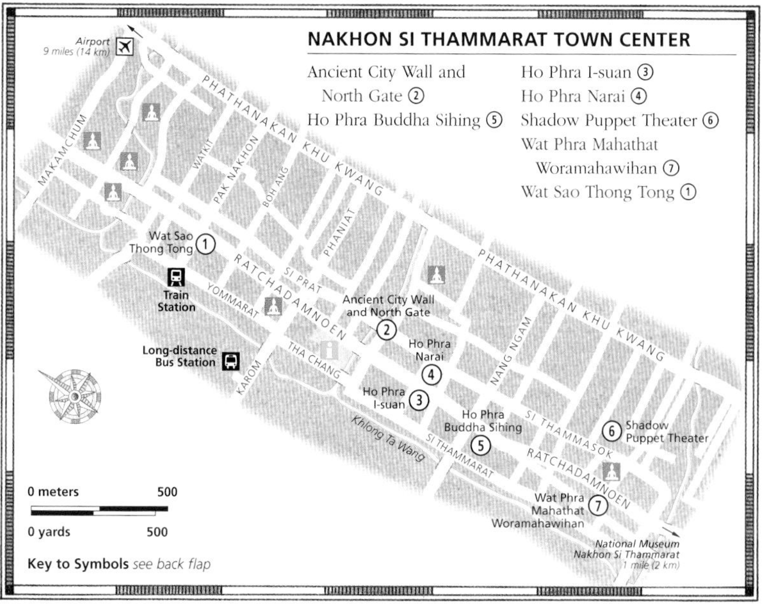

Wat Phra Mahathat Woramahawihan

วัดพระมหาธาตุ

Wat Phra Mahathat Woramahawihan, or Temple of the Great Chedi, is one of the most revered temples in southern Thailand. It is believed to contain a sacred tooth relic of the Buddha. Legend says that Prince Thanakuman and Queen Hemchala brought this relic to Hat Sai Kaew and built a pagoda to mark its location. Later, in the 13th century when King Si Thammasokarat founded Nakhon Si Thammarat, he constructed a new temple and shifted the relic there. The buildings inside the *wat* are an amalgam of different Thai styles. The present *wat* has a Sri Lankan design and its *chedi* is an important Thai symbol, featuring on the provincial seal as well as the current 25 satang coin.

Offerings in front of Taksin's statue outside the *wat* complex

★ Phra Chedi Boromathat
The 247-ft (77-m) high Sri Lankan-style chedi *houses the tooth relic. This structure is supposedly built over an older Srivijaya* chedi, *and its spire is covered in pure gold.*

Royal Wihan

Dharma Sala Wihan, in the temple's east wall, is dedicated to the study of Dhamma, or teachings of the Buddha.

Visitors' entrance

173 smaller chedis surround the Phra Chedi Boromathat and are replicas of the central spire.

Wihan Tap Kaset
Surrounding the main chedi *is the Wihan Tap Kaset, a gallery with lines of golden Buddha images in varied styles. The* wihan *is also decorated with statues of elephant heads.*

STAR FEATURES

- ★ Phra Chedi Boromathat
- ★ Royal Wihan
- ★ Wihan Phra Song Ma

For hotels and restaurants in this region see pp300–4 and pp326–8

★ Royal Wihan
South of the main chedi, *and outside the cloister walls is a large* ubosot, *or ordination hall, called the Royal Wihan. It houses several Buddha images as well as a beautiful elephant figurine.*

VISITORS' CHECKLIST

Ratchadamnoen Rd, Nakhon Si Thammarat. *dawn to dusk daily. Chak Phra Pak Tai (Oct); Hae Pha Khuen That (Feb/ May).* **Wihan Kien Museum** *8am–4:30pm daily.*

★ Wihan Phra Song Ma
An ornamental stairway located inside the Wihan Phra Song Ma leads to the most important part of the complex – the walkway around the chedi. *It is decorated with figures from both Hindu and Buddhist mythology.*

The Phra Rabieng Wihan is an elongated, cloistered gallery that surrounds the temple on all sides, forming an outer wall or boundary. It shelters many precious gilt Buddha images.

A roof of glazed red and emerald green tiles protects the gallery.

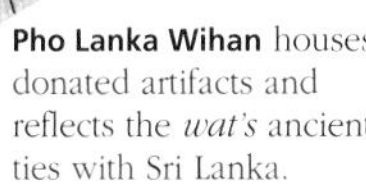

Pho Lanka Wihan houses donated artifacts and reflects the *wat's* ancient ties with Sri Lanka.

Statue of Ram and Sita
A three-tier gilt umbrella shelters this statue of Ram and Sita and represents Nakhon's ancient links with Hinduism.

Wihan Kien Museum
This is a small temple-museum housing images, amulets, and other artifacts. It is located next to Wihan Phra Song Ma.

UPPER ANDAMAN COAST

The abiding image of Thailand's Upper Andaman Coast is of sandy beaches backed by swaying palms, a lush forested interior, and hundreds of limestone outcrops rising dramatically out of azure waters. This region provides a multitude of options for travelers: from the pristine coral reefs of the Surin and Similan archipelagos to the luxurious comforts of Phuket, Thailand's largest island and premier beach resort.

From the earliest times, both Thais and foreigners have been attracted to the Andaman Coast. Merchants and traders were drawn by its strategic position on the spice route, prospectors came for the rich tin deposits, and visitors were attracted by the outstanding natural beauty of the region. The ancient Srivijaya port at Takua Pa, and the distinctive architecture of the Chinese shophouses and the Sino-Portuguese mansions of Phuket town reflect these historical connections.

The Upper Andaman Coast is a prosperous and fertile region with rubber, cashew, banana, durian, and coffee plantations making it a prime agricultural zone. Yet it also offers urban facilities including designer resorts, chic bars, and gourmet restaurants on the island of Phuket.

The entire coastline is lined by lovely beaches while the hinterland is covered with virgin rain forests preserved in national parks such as Khao Sok. The limestone stacks of Phang Nga Bay are home to a variety of wildlife while the waters of the Andaman Sea teem with rich marine life. This underwater landscape is best visible at the Surin and Similan Islands which offer unparalleled diving opportunities.

This region is a melting pot of towns populated by Thais of Tai and ethnic Chinese descent, fishing villages inhabited by Thai Muslims and a few communities of sea gypsies, all of whom have enriched the cultural traditions of this region. Although the Upper Andaman Coast was badly affected by the tsunami in 2004, it has recovered well.

Towering karst formations dominating the landscape at Khao Sok National Park

◁ **Scuba diver exploring marine life around a colorful fan coral, Similan Islands**

Exploring the Upper Andaman Coast

Extending along the Andaman Sea, the Upper Andaman Coast is home to some of the most inviting beaches in Southeast Asia. The internationally renowned resort of Phuket serves as a good base for visitors to explore this region with its wide range of shopping, dining, entertainment, and watersports options. The stunning limestone stacks of Phang Nga are definitely worth a day trip, while the thickly forested hills of Khao Sok National Park and the mangroves of Laem Son national Park shelter a variety of birds and animals and are perfectly suited for nature lovers. The extensive sandy stretches along the Khao Lak coast form an idyllic retreat, and the Similan and Surin archipelagos are famous for their spectacular underwater landscape and rich marine life, making them a haven for divers and snorkelers.

Devotees thronging outside San Chao Chui Tui temple in Phuket

SIGHTS AT A GLANCE

SEE ALSO

• ***Where to Stay*** pp304–8

• ***Where to Eat*** pp328–31

0 km 25

0 miles 25

Visitors relaxing on one of the six beaches along Khao Lak coast

GETTING AROUND

Most visitors make use of Phuket's airport, and this island is the best base from which to explore the Upper Andaman Coast. Reliable air-conditioned bus services link Phuket, Phang Nga, and Ranong, although renting a car in Phuket or Ranong is more convenient. There is no railroad in the region. The Similan Islands are accessible from Phuket, while the Surin archipelago can be reached by boat from Ranong, Khao Lak, and Khuraburi. Longtail boats are the easiest mode of transportation for exploring the smaller bays and islands such as Phang Nga Bay and Ko Chang.

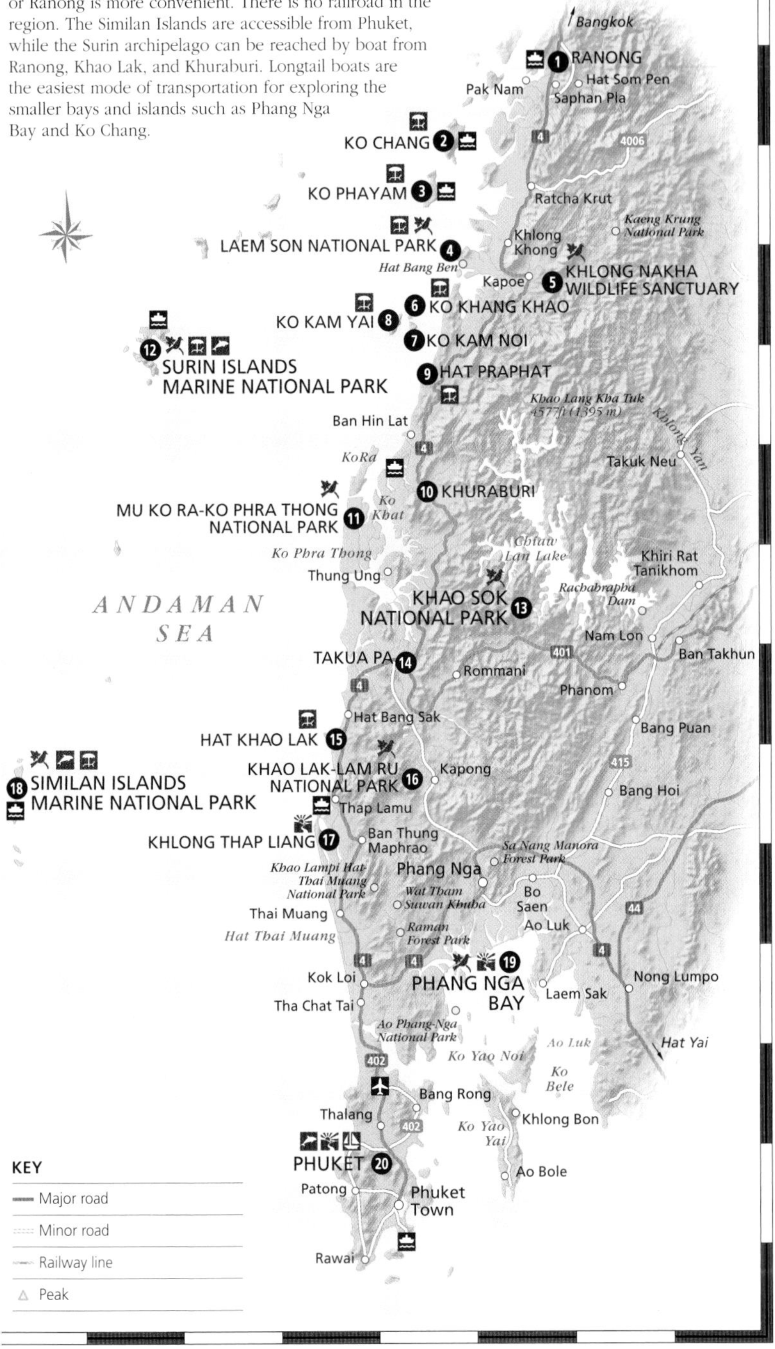

Ranong ❶

ระนอง

Road Map B3. 351 miles (565 km) SW of Bangkok. *175,000.* *TAT, Surat Thani (0-7728-8818-9).*

The town was originally settled in the late 18th century by Hokkien Chinese, who were hired to work as laborers in the region's tin mines. The area grew rich, and Ranong became a major border town. From here Thai nationals can travel to **Victoria Point** in Myanmar on half- or full-day boat trips. Foreign nationals, however, are not allowed to go to Victoria Point without a visa. Referred to as Kawthaung by the Burmese, Ranong is well known for duty-free goods and handicrafts available at bargain prices.

Ranong's main attractions are the Bo Nam Ron (Ranong Mineral Hot Springs) that rise by the Khlong Hat Sompen River at **Wat Tapotaram**, just east of the town center. These are channeled into three concrete tubs called Mother, Father, and Child. At an average temperature of 65°C (150° F), the water is too hot for bathing. However, a short walk down the river, the Jansom Thara Spa Resort Hotel has tapped and cooled the water; visitors not staying at the hotel can also take a spa bath for a nominal fee.

Fishing boats, ideal for rowing around rustic Ko Chang

Ko Chang ❷

เกาะช้าง

Road Map B3. 15 miles (24 km) SW of Ranong. *from Saphan Pla, Ranong.*

Located in the warm waters of the Andaman Sea, this idyllic little island is much less developed than its more famous namesake on the Eastern Seaboard (*see p118–19*). There is little to do on Ko Chang but lie back and relax in a beach bungalow, the basic accommodations available, or make trips to the island's tiny fishing village capital for supplies. Visitors could, however, head for **Hat Ao Yai**, a white, sandy beach on the west coast of the island, which is a great place to watch sunsets. Among the prettiest beaches in the area, it offers guesthouses for those who prefer to stay the night.

Ko Phayam ❸

เกาะพยาม

Road Map B4. 21 miles (34 km) S of Ko Chang. *from Saphan Pla.* *from Ko Chang.*

A picturesque island with a population of only 500 inhabitants, Ko Phayam offers reasonably priced bungalow accommodations, charming beachside restaurants, and the occasional sleepy bar. Locals earn their livelihood through prawn, crab, and squid fishing, or farming sator beans and cashewnuts. However, there is an abundance of flora and fauna with a wide variety of snakes, monkeys, and hornbills. Motorcycle taxis provide service on the island's popular routes. The island offers few facilities – even electricity is switched off by 11pm.

Visitors washing around a hot spring tub, Wat Tapotaram

Laem Son National Park ❹

อุทยานแห่งชาติแหลมสน

Road Map B4. Park HQ off Hwy 4, 37 miles (60 km) S of Ranong. *Park HQ (0-7786-1431 or 0-2562-0760).* **www**.dnp.go.th

Extending south from Kapoe district in Ranong province to Khuraburi district in Phang Nga province, Laem Son National Park, the sixth largest national park in Thailand, covers 122 sq miles (316 sq km) of mangrove swamps and forests, and around 63 miles (101 km) of the Andaman shoreline – the longest protected shoreline in Thailand. Established in 1983, much of the park is undeveloped and does not feature on most tourist itineraries.

Laem Son, which is home to 138 different species of birds, has its headquarters at **Hat Bang Ben**, the most attractive and accessible beach in the park. This casuarina-lined beach has a few unpretentious bungalows, but visitors can hire tents and camp beneath the shady trees. Swimming is good and safe all year round – although it is a good idea to approach the Andaman Coast with caution, especially during the height of the wet and stormy southwest monsoon from June to September. Several other islands in the area including Ko Kam Yai, Ko Kam Noi and Ko Khang Khao *(see p202)*, are accessible by longtail boat, which can easily be arranged through the park office.

It is also possible to explore the fascinating mangrove forests, home to crab-eating macaques, sea turtles, fishing eagles, wild boars, white-bellied sea eagles, hawk-eagles, hornbills, and sandpipers.

Statues at the entrance to Khlong Nakha

Khlong Nakha Wildlife Sanctuary ❺

เขตรักษาพันธุ์สัตว์ป่าคลองนาคา

Road Map B4. Park HQ off Hwy 4, 48 miles (77 km) S of Ranong.

Malayan sun bear

Established in 1972 and covering an area of 205 sq miles (531 sq km), Khlong Nakha Wildlife Sanctuary is one of Thailand's older and larger national reserves. However, it is relatively less frequented. Wildlife here includes some large mammals such as the Asiatic elephant, serow, Malaysian tapir, gaur, ox, Malayan sun bear, sambar deer, and the common barking deer. Wild tigers and leopards are reported to roam the jungle interiors, but most visitors will be lucky to hear more than a nighttime roar.

As with most national parks in southern Thailand, it is best visited during the cool season from November to February and avoided during the steamy southwest monsoon, when leeches can become unwelcome companions for trekkers. A popular trekking destination within the sanctuary is the **Nam Tok Phan Met**, or One-thousand-meter Waterfall, set amid verdant rain forest. However, it is advisable to make reservations at least a month in advance before visiting the park.

Longtail boat waiting to carry passangers to the nearby islands, Laem Son National Park

Navigating a motorized longtail boat off Ko Khang Khao

Ko Khang Khao ❻

เกาะค้างคาว

Road Map B4. 6 miles (10 km) S of Hat Bang Ben. *from Hat Bang Ben.*

This remote island off the Andaman Coast, south of Hat Bang Ben (*see p201*), was earlier uninhabited and home to bats, resulting in its name – Ko Khang Khao, meaning Bat Island. Located on its northern coast is the beautiful Hat Hin Ngam, a white sand beach strewn with colorful circular pebbles. Ko Khang Khao is a verdant, untouched tropical island where visitors can relax on the warm sands or go snorkeling in the shallow waters surrounding the island. Although there are some colorful corals just offshore, the underwater visibility is not very good due to proximity to inland rivers flowing into the sea. Ko Khang Khao is a perfect day trip from Hat Bang Ben. The island is accessible through the year, except during the rainy season from June to September.

Ko Kam Noi ❼

เกาะกำนุ้ย

Road Map B4. 11 miles (18 km) SW of Hat Bang Ben. *from Hat Bang Ben.*

Located offshore from Hat Bang Ben, Ko Kam Noi is a popular spot among campers. Uncluttered by commercial infrastructure, this island is undisturbed in its serenity. The western coast is rocky, while the northeastern side has the sandy stretches. Grassy patches on the island can be used to pitch tents and fresh water is available. Visitors can also go snorkeling in the surrounding waters.

Ko Kam Yai ❽

เกาะกำใหญ่

Road Map B4. 10 miles (16 km) SW of Hat Bang Ben. *from Hat Bang Ben.*

Despite being fairly large and busy, Ko Kam Yai is quite laid-back. The island is almost completely encircled by white sand beaches. Lush, forested hills provide plenty of bird-watching opportunities as a variety of migrating birds make their way here especially during the cool season from November to February. There are also camping facilities and bungalow accommodations. Just 660 ft (201 m) away lies the tiny island of **Ko Tam Tok** which is connected to Ko Kam Yai by a sandy strip that gets exposed at low tide. It can be easily reached by swimming or taking a boat.

Hat Praphat ❾

หาดประพาส

Road Map B4. 31 miles (50 km) S of Hat Bang Ben.

Located on the Andaman Coast, Hat Praphat has a long sandy frontage backed by graceful casuarinas and pines.

Scrub-covered rocks lining a stretch of pristine white sand at Ko Kam Yai

Fishing boat against the backdrop of the setting sun, Hat Praphat

There are simple bungalow accommodations as well as a few beach shacks serving fresh seafood. This area suffered some damage during the 2004 tsunami, but has recovered well. Laem Son National Park *(see p201)* has a second park office on Hat Praphat, which is a nesting ground for sea turtles.

Khuraburi ⑩

คุระบุรี

Road Map B4. 88 miles (142 km) S of Ranong.

Well on the road to recovery after the 2004 tsunami, Khuraburi is a jumping-off point for the Surin archipelago *(see pp204–5)* located 38 miles (60 km) offshore. It is also the main ferry port for the nearby Mu Ko Ra-Ko Phra Thong National Park.

Set amid rubber, palm oil, and coconut plantations, this one-horse town is kept busy by coaches traveling along Highway 4 between Phuket, Ranong, and all points north of Bangkok. The town has adequate accommodations, a good selection of restaurants, and a few shops.

Khuraburi also has some community-based tourism programs run by NGOs that allow visitors to experience and understand the culture and ecosystem of the area. The funds raised from these initiatives are pumped back into the local economy.

Mu Ko Ra-Ko Phra Thong National Park ⑪

อุทยานแห่งชาติหมู่เกาะระ เกาะพระทอง

Road Map B4. 6 miles (10 km) W of Khuraburi. *from Khuraburi pier.* *Park HQ (0-7649-1378).* **www**.dnp.go.th

Covering an area of 248 sq miles (642 sq km) on both land and water, the Mu Ko Ra-Ko Phra Thong National Park was declared a protected area in September 2000 amid much controversy and protest from the locals, especially, fishermen who would lose their rights to fish in the surrounding rich waters. The main islands within the park are **Ko Phra Thong** and **Ko Ra**. Of the two, tiny Ko Ra is a lovely and uninhabited island running about 6 miles (10 km) from north to south, and about 2 miles (3 km) from east to west. It is covered in dense rain forest which shelters many birds including several species of hornbill. There are some fine beaches along its western coast facing the Andaman Sea. This end of the island is usually deserted and can be reached either by longtail boats or sea kayaks.

Visitors coming to Ko Ra on a rented boat should ensure that it is available for the return journey as well. Sea-kayaking is another alternative, but novices should beware of potentially strong currents, particularly along the west coast. There are no permanent facilities here, so visitors are advised to carry food and water. The hilly terrain is ideal for trekking and the whole island can be covered on foot.

Unlike Ko Ra, Ko Phra Thong has a handful of inhabitants. The eastern part of the island is covered with mangrove forests while beaches line the western part. Ko Phra Thong is being developed as an eco-resort with several resorts offering accommodations. This island is also home to the luxurious Golden Buddha Beach Resort *(see p305)*. A temporary park office is also located on this island and its beaches are a nesting site for the giant leatherback turtle. Other wildlife includes flying foxes and the occasional dugong.

Visitors waiting for boats to the offshore islands, Khuraburi pier

Snorkeling in the clear waters off Ko Surin Nua

Surin Islands Marine National Park ⓬

อุทยานแห่งชาติหมู่เกาะสุรินทร์

Road Map B4. 38 miles (60 km) NW of Khuraburi. *from Ranong, Khao Lak, and Khuraburi.* *Park HQ (0-7647-2145) or Forestry Dept (0-2562-0760).* *mid-Nov–mid-May.* **www**.dnp.go.th

Comprising a group of five enchanting islands set in the heart of the Andaman Sea, the Surin Islands were declared a national park in 1981 and remain one of the most pristine and beautiful maritime destinations in Thailand. The archipelago offers unparalleled diving and snorkeling opportunities, especially around Richelieu Rock and Burma Banks, with underwater visibility of up to 81 ft (25 m). Ko Surin Nua and Ko Surin Tai, the two larger islands, are separated by a narrow strait about 656 ft (200 m) wide. This strait contains some of the most spectacular coral reefs in the Andaman Sea. The three smaller islands – Ko Ri, Ko Kai, and Ko Klang – are mere rocky islets with sparse vegetation and remain uninhabited even today. The islands boast rich marine life, as well as sandy beaches, mangroves, and stretches of verdant rain forest, that provide ample opportunities for hiking and bird-watching. Vacationers should look out for crab-eating macaques, Bengal monitors, and over 57 species of birds. The Surin Islands are also home to the flying fox, a rare species of bat, which lives in trees.

Shoals of brightly colored fish on the reefs off Surin Islands

Ko Surin Nua

เกาะสุรินทร์เหนือ

Ko Surin Nua, or Surin North Island, is the largest island of the Surin archipelago, and is heavily forested with tall hardwood trees. The island has several bays, the largest being Ao Mae Yai. The surrounding sea offers an outstanding array of soft corals and frequent sightings of shovel-nose rays, bow-mouthed guitar fish, and whale sharks. Some of the best and most accessible dive sites are to be found off the park headquarters in the so-called HQ Channel between the two main islands. The clear water makes diving or snorkeling quite redundant as the corals can easily be observed from above. Although excessive fishing and the 2004 tsunami have caused some damage in the area, disturbing its natural ecological balance and leading to a slight depletion in marine life, the damage has been minimal. There are some excellent hiking trails on the island, especially around Ao Mae Yai, as well as some good campsites. The site of the park headquarters, Ko Surin Nua also has a restaurant that provides Thai food and simple but adequate overnight accommodation in bungalows.

SEA GYPSIES

Probably the earliest inhabitants of the region, the *chao lae*, or sea gypsies, are thought to be descendants of Malaysia's *orang laut*, or sea people. Numbering around 5,000, they continue to lead a nomadic life, living on the Andaman Coast in houseboats called *kabang*. Their largest group, the Urak Lawoi, numbering around 3,000, live in simple shacks making a living by fishing and are well integrated into Thai society. The smaller groups comprise the Moklen and Moken, the latter being the least sophisticated of the group. They make their living by harvesting the bounty of the seas – sea cucumbers, oysters, and shellfish – and selling handicrafts to visitors. They believe in propitiating tutelary spirits, especially those associated with nature and the sea. Their annual rites include a spiritual cleansing ceremony to rid themselves of evil spirits.

Moken children playing outside their huts, Ko Surin Tai

For hotels and restaurants in this region see pp304–8 and pp328–31

Ko Surin Tai

เกาะสุรินทร์ใต้

Ko Surin Tai, or Surin South Island, is the second largest island in the Surin archipelago and similar to Ko Surin Nua as far as the flora and fauna is concerned, but without the park facilities. The simple village of Chao Thalae, populated by the Moken sea gypsies, is also located on this island. Ao Tao, a beautiful bay situated to the southeast of the island, is home to sea turtles. Snorkeling in the waters off the bay is the perfect way to admire not just the turtles, but also the gorgeous coral reefs in the area.

Huts on stilts and fishing boats at Chao Thalae, Ko Surin Tai

Richelieu Rock

ไรเชเลีย รอค

9 miles (14 km) SE of Surin Islands.

An isolated, limestone seamount shaped like a horseshoe and almost completely submerged in the sea, Richelieu Rock is considered to be among the best dive sites in Thailand. The rocky summit of the seamount just about manages to break the surface at low tide and is a navigational hazard for boats in the area, as it rises perpendicularly from the sea floor 100 ft (30 m) below.

Fortunately, Richelieu Rock did not suffer during the 2004 tsunami and the marine ecology of the area remains intact. It provides feeding grounds and shelter to a wide variety of fish including barracuda, jacks, batfish, manta rays, and whale sharks although their numbers have declined over the years. The coral reefs are also home to a great variety of marine life including the tigertail seahorse, harlequin shrimps, frog fish, lion fish, as well as the yellow and spiny pineapple fish. Visitors wishing to dive here should only do so if accompanied by an experienced dive operator who knows the area well.

Burma Banks

ชายแดนพม่า

38 miles (60 km) NW of Surin Islands.

More remote and probably more exotic than Richelieu Rock, Burma Banks is a succession of submerged seamounts. The three main seamounts – Silvertip, Rainbow, and Roe – offer an unparalleled diving experience over pristine coral reefs, home to an amazing variety of large fish and other exotic marine creatures such as the great barracuda and moray eels. Day trips for visitors can be organized from either Khuraburi *(see p203)* or from Khao Lak *(see p208)*.

Diving here is recommended only for the experienced since divers must go into the open ocean. The main attraction is the almost guaranteed sighting of sharks such as the nurse shark, which can grow up to 10 ft (3 m) in length; silvertip; as well as the exotic leopard shark.

Thick rain forest backed by dramatic limestone peaks at Khao Sok National Park

Khao Sok National Park ⓭

อุทยานแห่งชาติเขาสก

Road Map B4. Park HQ off Hwy 401, 53 miles (85 km) S of Khuraburi. *Park HQ (0-7739-5139).* **www**.dnp.go.th

Together with the neighboring reserves of Mu Ko Ra-Ko Phra Thong National Park *(see p203)* and Khao Lak-Lam Ru National Park *(see p208)*, the Khao Sok National Park forms the largest tract of virgin rain forest in southern Thailand. Khao Sok is a part of the oldest forest system that has remained unchanged through the Ice Ages of the past and dates back a 160 million years. The 285-sq mile (738-sq km) park rises to a height of 3,150 ft (960 m) and includes more than 100 spectacular islands formed as a result of the construction of the Rachabrapha Dam in 1982.

Elephants, tigers, bears, tapirs, gibbons, and monkeys are found in the park, along with over 300 species of birds, including hornbills and argus pheasants. Sightings of the larger animals are usually at night, and animal tracks are regularly seen along the marked trails. Sadly, poaching of the animals persists despite the efforts of park officers.

There is also a wide range of interesting flora, including the rare *Rafflesia kerri*; Khao Sok is one of the few places in the world where it grows. This foul-smelling plant is wholly parasitic and lies dormant inside the roots of the host tree. Once a year it breaks the surface of the bark and over a few months grows into the world's largest flower measuring up to 31 inches (79 cm) in width. The flower's fetid smell attracts pollinating insects. However, it has a short life span and shrivels into a putrescent mass in a few days.

Great Asian hornbill

Khao Sok receives the brunt of both the southwest and northeast monsoons which results in an extended rainy season from May to November. Thus the best time to visit the park is between January and April.

The park is famous for its beautiful karst limestone peaks, numerous waterfalls, and caves. Along with the limestone outcrops, the Chiaw Lan Lake forms the most distinctive geographical feature of Khao Sok.

Longtail boats, a convenient mode of transportation at Khao Sok

This park is a popular spot and offers activities such as kayaking, elephant trekking, as well as the extreme sport of spelunking, where participants go diving into a series of subterranean caves. Khao Sok also has a number of hiking trails; most are suitable for all levels. A few demanding trails might suit experienced trekkers. Basic accommodations and food are available inside the park. There are also a few mini-markets just outside the entrance to Khao Sok and at the park headquarters.

Nam Tok Than Sawan

น้ำตกธารสวรรค์

4 miles (7 km) W of Park HQ.

A spectacular waterfall, the Nam Tok Than Sawan, or Heavenly Waterfall, is at the end of a picturesque trekking trail which can get quite inaccessible at the height of the rainy season. The waterfall bursts from the edge of a steep cliff, and creates a stunning rainbow effect due to the reflection of the sunlight in the water.

Nam Tok Sip-Et Chan

น้ำตกสิบเอ็ดชั้น

3 miles (5 Km) N of Park HQ.

A large waterfall that descends over eleven tiers of rock stairs, Nam Tok Sip-Et Chan is not too far from the park headquarters, but takes up to three hours to reach because of the difficult terrain and the number of river crossings.

Trekkers should watch out for wildlife such as gibbons and hornbills along the way.

Chiaw Lan Lake

ทะเลสาบเชี่ยวหลาน

41 miles (66 km) E of Park HQ.

A star attraction of the park, Chiaw Lan Lake is approximately an hour's drive from the park headquarters. This large freshwater reservoir created by the construction of the Rachabrapha Dam in 1982, is also known as Rachabrapha Lake. Spectacular karst outcrops, isolated from the mainland by the flooding waters, rise from the lake to almost 3,000 feet (914 m) in height – about three times the height of similar karst outcrops at Phang Nga Bay *(see pp212-17)*. Gibbons and eagles can be seen on these peaks which are a haven for rare wildlife but are inaccessible to all but the most intrepid climbers. Accommodations are in the form of floating chalets or eco-friendly huts built on the lake which offer spectacular views of the surroundings.

View of distant karst outcrops across Chiaw Lan Lake

Tham Nam Thalu

ถ้ำน้ำทะลุ

One of the most rewarding spots in the park, Tham Nam Thalu is a 2,625-ft (800-m) long horseshoe-shaped cave which is located near the southwestern shore of Chiaw Lan Lake. A visit to the cave is an exciting trek through dark and slippery terrain and is not really recommended for those who are frightened of bats, or suffer from claustrophobia. A marked trail follows a small river into the cave system and visitors have to wade through water for a part of the journey. Anyone entering Nam Thalu must wear suitable footwear and carry a flashlight. It is not advisable to visit the cave during the the rainy season, despite whatever guides may say, as there have been several casualties. Hazards aside, a visit to this cave is a highlight of the Khao Sok experience offering visitors an unparalleled oppurtunity to see rare cave creatures.

Tham Si Ru

ถ้ำสี่รู

Another well-known cave system, Tham Si Ru, or Four Holes Cave, has four converging cave passages that were used as a secret base by communist insurgents in southern Thailand during the 1970s. The caves can be reached on foot from the southern shore of the lake.

KEY

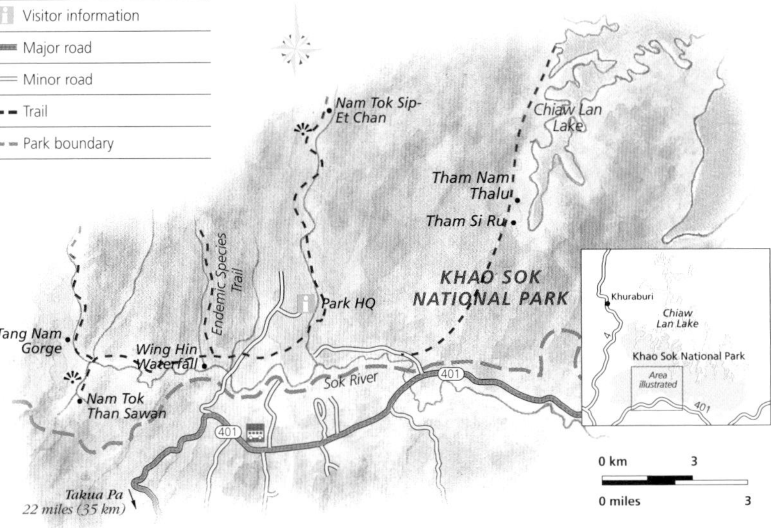

Takua Pa 14

ตะกั่วป่า

Road Map B4. 33 miles (53 km) S of Khuraburi. *35,000.*

Known to have been one of the finest harbors in peninsular Thailand, Takua Pa, also known as Takkolam or Takola, was once a busy port handling mercantile traffic between the ancient kingdoms of Srivijaya *(see p39)* and the Tamil kingdoms of South India. The town is divided into two distinct areas, better known as the old and the new quarters. While the former is reminiscent of Takua Pa's historic past with several charming Sino-Portuguese-style houses, the latter is situated along the Takua Pa River. Vacationers can roam the streets of this little-visited friendly town, dotted with Buddhist and Chinese temples, or head for the exotic **Hat Bang Sak**, or Teak Tree Beach, Takua Pa's best-known spot. A lovely, stretch of white sand, Hat Bang Sak is shaded by casuarinas and best reached by following Route 4 between Thai Muang and Takua Pa. It currently offers simple accommodations, but plans for more upscale hotels and resorts are already on the table.

Sunbathers taking a stroll along pretty Hat Khao Lak

Hat Khao Lak 15

เขาหลัก

Road Map B4. 21 miles (34 km) SW of Takua Pa. *from Takua Pa or Phuket.* *TAT, Phuket (0-7621-1036).*

The coastline south of Takua Pa consists of long stretches of rocky and sandy beaches. Hat Khao Lak, halfway between Takua Pa and Thai Muang, is the southernmost of six beaches separated by rocky outcrops. It has so far been relatively quiet but, is now beginning to attract more visitors. Commercial development is also on the rise and a variety of accommodations are now available.

Hat Khao Lak is a fine beach and a good base from which to explore the pristine Surin *(see pp204–5)* and Similan Islands *(see pp210–11)* located 4 hours away by boat. Many visitors come here to book their dive trips. Between November and April, the fishing ports of Thap Lamu and Hat Khao Lak operate as ferry points for trips to these islands.

Sights such as the 199-ft (61-m) high Nam Tok Sai Rung, or Sai Rung Waterfall, vie for visitors' attention. This lovely waterfall, situated close to the beach off Highway 4, is good for swimming, although caution is advised.

Open-air restaurant with thatched pavilions along the coast, Hat Bang Sak

Observation deck at Khao Lak-Lam Ru National Park

Khao Lak-Lam Ru National Park 16

อุทยานแห่งชาติแหลมรู

Road Map B4. Park HQ off Hwy 4, Laem Hin Chang, 21 miles (34 Km) S of Takua Pa. *from Takua Pa or Phuket.* *Park HQ (0-7648-5243).* *8am–4:30pm daily.* **www**.dnp.go.th

Established as a land-based park in 1991, Khao Lak-Lam Ru National Park was made into a marine national park in 1995 due to the inclusion of several offshore areas. The park covers an area of 49 sq miles (127 sq km) and is justly famous for its outstanding natural beauty, encompassing islands, sea cliffs, forested hills, and beaches, in addition to karst and granite outcrops dating

Colorful flags adorning the entrance to Khao Lak-Lam Ru

from the Cretaceous period. The park is home to a variety of flora and fauna. The tropical evergreen forests on the hills near Khao Lak have a three-tier canopy with some gigantic trees towering over them. The lower level is rich in epiphytes such as orchids and ferns, as well as the useful rattan vines.

Species of fauna in the park include macaques, langurs, black drongos, Asiatic black bears, gold-whiskered barbets, reticulated pythons, giant black squirrels, wild boar, and several types of hornbill. There are a number of treks leading to several waterfalls, the most popular of which is the spectacular **Nam Tok Lam Ru** or Lam Ru Waterfall, located about 19 miles (31 km) from the park headquaters at Laem Hin Chang. Others include Nam Tok Saeng Thong and Nam Tok Chong Fa. Thai visitors also like to trek to a popular jungle shrine dedicated to Chao Po Khao Lak, said to be the tutelary guardian spirit of the national park.

Khlong Thap Liang ⓱

คลองทับเหลียง

Road Map B4. 6 miles (10 km) SW of Khao Lak-Lam Ru.

An interesting and exciting addition to any visit to Khao Lak is a longtail boat trip to the nearby Khlong Thap Liang estuary, and the contiguous Khlong Thung Maphrao and Khlong Hin Lad waterways. The mangrove forests here are worth a visit and are inhabited by troops of crab-eating macaques, who generally venture from the mangroves to the mudflats in search of food at low tide. These estuaries – styled *khlongs* (canals) – lie immediately to the south of Thap Lamu between the southern limits of the verdant Khao Lak-Lam Ru National Park and the northern limits of the nearby Hat Thai Muang National Park.

Longtail boats stranded in an estuary at low tide, Khlong Thap Liang

TAKUA PA, THE ANCIENT SRIVIJAYA PORT OF TAKOLA

Originally named Takola, Takua Pa is one of the oldest human settlements in southern Thailand, dating as far back as the Srivijaya era *(see pp38–9)*, when it was an important port. The name Takola is thought to have been derived from the Tamil word *takkolam* (pepper), and is indicative of the area's strong historic links with South India. Takola was probably the main harbor on the Andaman Coast for trade between the Thai-Malay kingdom of Srivijaya and the southern Indian Tamil kingdoms of the Pallavas (4th–9th centuries) and the Cholas (9th–13th centuries). It is believed to have played an important role in the spread of South Asian, Hindu, and Buddhist culture and beliefs throughout southern Thailand and the Malay Peninsula. Little physical evidence survives from this period. However, the single most important artifact of this era is a tall statue, nearly 8 ft (2 m) high, of Lord Vishnu, god of the Hindu holy trinity, found at Takua Pa. It is now on display at Thalang National Museum *(see p234)* in Phuket.

Statue of Lord Vishnu displayed at Thalang National Museum, Phuket

Extraordinary rock shapes and pristine waters off Ko Similan

Similan Islands Marine National Park 18

อุทยานแห่งชาติหมู่เกาะสิมิลัน

Road Map A4. 38 miles (60 km) W of Thap Lamu. *from Thap Lamu, Kha Lak, and Phuket.* *Park HQ (0-7659-5045); Forestry Dept (0-2562-0760) for bungalow bookings.* *Nov–May.* **www**.dnp.go.th

Established in 1982, the enchanting Similan Islands Marine National Park covers an area of 54 sq miles (140 sq km). The name Similan is derived from the Malay word *sembilan* (nine), for the number of islands in the archipelago. These granitic islands, rising from the Andaman Sea, are stunning – verdant rain forest surrounded by a ring of white sand beaches, coral reefs, and azure sea. The seabed is decorated with staghorn, star, and branching corals. In these seemingly perfect waters there are also some potentially threatening species of fish such as giant groupers, poisonous stone fish, and lion fish; as well as a variety of sharks including leopard sharks, hammerheads, bull sharks, and whale sharks, which can be found swimming off these islands.

Ko Similan, the largest island in the archipelago, covers an area of 2 sq miles (5 sq km) and is home to a variety of marine animals, land mammals, and reptiles such as crabs, snakes, and bats and 40 species of birds.

Young leopard shark

The main attraction however, are the 20 or so recognized dive sites offering all levels of diving experience. The underwater grottoes and swim-through tunnels appeal to divers and snorkelers.

However, it is necessary to book a dive tour at Thap Lamu or through an agency in Phuket, since there are no diving agencies in the park. Half-day park-run snorkeling tours depart for Ko Miang on a daily basis. It is also possible to arrange day trips from Ko Miang to the more remote islands such as Ko Bon further north.

Ko Bangu

เกาะบันกู

The northernmost island in the Similan archipelago, Ko Bangu, also known as Hua Kalok, or Skull Island, has a couple of excellent dive spots just off the shore. Christmas Point is particularly good with some exciting fish such as jacks and bluefin trevally. Another great snorkeling site lies in the sheltered eastern lee of the island, which is also home to a park ranger station.

Ko Similan

เกาะสิมิลัน

The largest island, Ko Similan is located near the northernmost point of the archipelago. Although it has no accommodations, there are two favored dive spots – Fantasy Reef to the west of the island, and a scuba spot to the south of Ao Nang Chan, the longest beach, on the island's eastern shore. Fantasy Reef has been closed indefinitely to allow recovery from the 2004 tsunami.

Snorkeling, one of the main outdoor activities on Ko Similan

Hin Pusa

หินภูษา

Set in the Andaman Sea, just south of Ko Similan and to the north of Ko Payu, Hin Pusa, or Elephant Head, is

Ko Bangu, an idyllic swimming spot where the forest comes down to the beach

For hotels and restaurants in this region see pp304–8 and pp328–31

really just a rocky outcrop. The various boulders that make up Elephant Head form a series of tunnels, arches, and swim-through channels which can be quite challenging, even for accomplished swimmers. A very popular dive spot, it has a host of spectacular marine creatures clearly visible even without snorkeling gear. These include a colony of spider crabs, a range of soft corals, cuttlefish, mantis shrimps, the twin-colored parrot fish, an occasional olive ridley turtle, and even the gentle whale sharks.

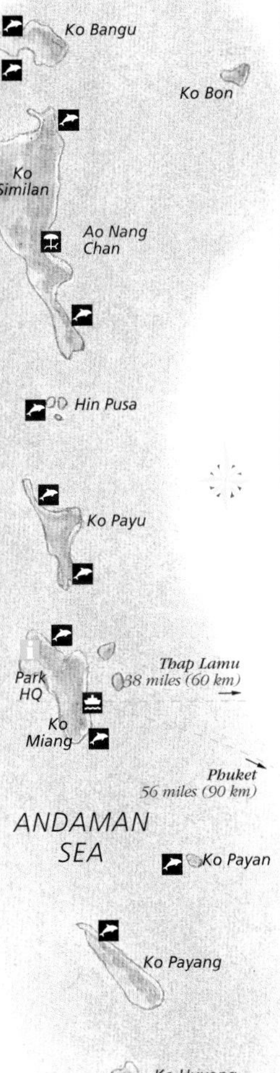

Vacationers disembarking from the boat at Ko Miang

Ko Payu

เกาะพายุ

A tiny forest-capped marble outcrop, Ko Payu is surrounded by a reef of staghorn corals. It has two excellent dive sites – one to the east of the island, and the other, just west of the narrow headland that marks the island's northern extremity. Divers can see large numbers of big and small fish such as lion fish, triggerfish, box fish, wrasse, and eels.

Ko Miang

เกาะเมี่ยง

The most important and well developed island in the archipelago, Ko Miang is where visitors will find the information center, restaurant, bungalow and dormitory accommodations, as well as a campsite. Just to the east of the island, beyond a narrow headland, lie the tiny seamounts of Hin Muan Diao. There are recommended dive sites in the shallow waters to the north and south.

In addition to diving and swimming opportunities, Ko Miang offers a few short but sometimes steep inland trails, combined with the possibility of sighting the rare Nicobar pigeon, which thrives here. The two most popular trails are Viewpoint Trail, leading to the island summit, and Sunset Point, leading – as the name suggests – to an idyllic spot from where truly glorious sunsets over the Andaman Sea can be enjoyed.

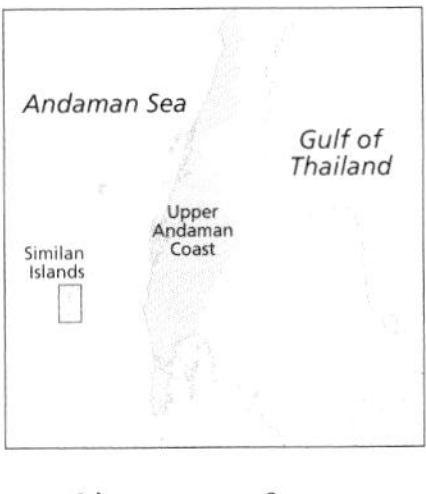

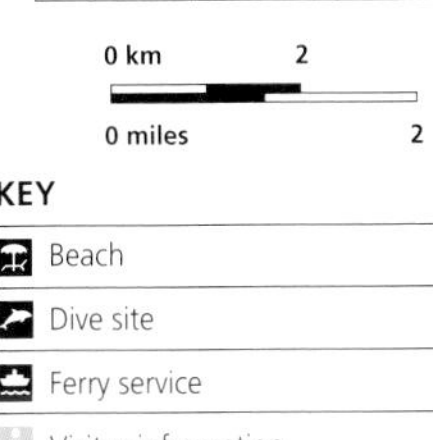

KEY

- Beach
- Dive site
- Ferry service
- Visitor information
- Ferry route

Ko Payang

เกาะพยาง

Verdant, pristine, and quite uninhabited, tiny Ko Payang is yet another haven for enthusiastic divers. There are dive sites just off the northern shore, and farther to the east, off Ko Payang, as well as at a nearby seamount called Hin Phae or Shark Fin Point.

Ko Huyong

เกาะหูยง

The southernmost island in the Similan archipelago, Ko Huyong has a long, white beach where sea turtles lay eggs. It also has a turtle breeding station. The island is not open to visitors, nor are there any offshore diving sites here. However, it is a beautiful place to sail around. The shallow waters allow plenty of sunlight to penetrate through, making the seabed around the island a real haven for its teeming diversity of marine creatures and numerous corals.

Phang Nga Bay ⓳

อ่าวพังงา

Conch seashell

No one area epitomizes the splendor of southern Thailand's landscape as perfectly as the 155-sq mile (401-sq km) Phang Nga Bay. Its scenic grandeur derives from the towering limestone stacks rising out of azure waters. Boat tours are available for visitors to explore sights such as the Panyi fishing village, the famous James Bond Island, as well as a number of fascinating caves with prehistoric paintings and Buddhist shrines. However, due to erosion, tourist boats are banned from large areas of Phang Nga Bay, though viewing is possible from a distance.

LOCATOR MAP

Area illustrated

Tham Lot is a 165-ft (50-m) long sea tunnel through limestone caves with stalactites hanging from its roof.

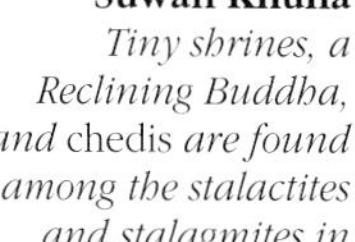

Wat Tham Suwan Khuha
Tiny shrines, a Reclining Buddha, and chedis *are found among the stalactites and stalagmites in this cave temple.*

★ Panyi Fishing Village
About 120 Muslim families live in this village built entirely on stilts above water. Islanders sell fish sauce, dried shrimp, and shrimp paste for a living.

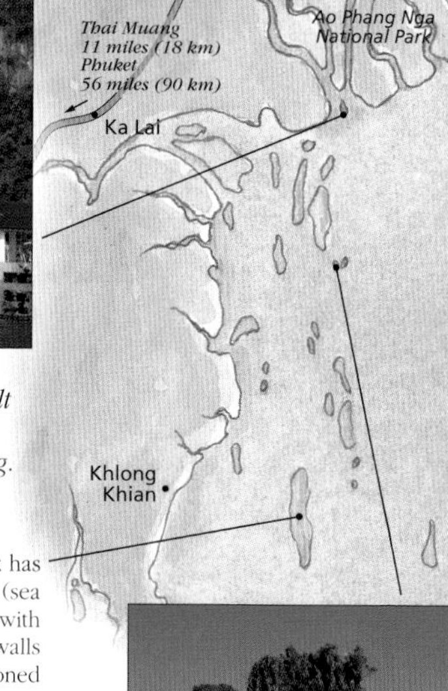

Ko Phanak has many *hongs* (sea chambers) with vegetation-clad walls and marooned snakes and monkeys.

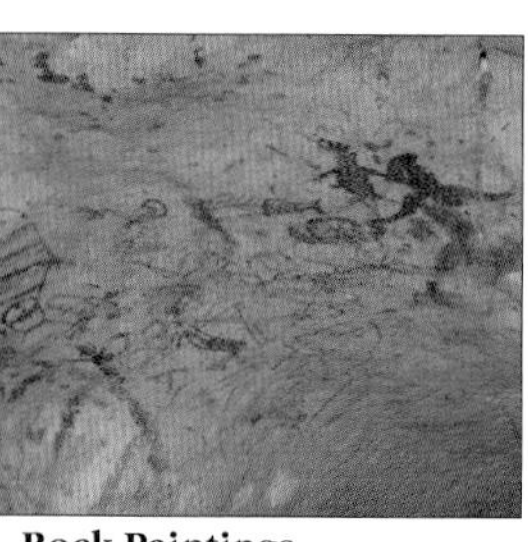

Rock Paintings
Prehistoric rock art can be seen around the Ao Phang Nga National Park and is a popular spot with visitors on boat tours around the bay.

★ James Bond Island
Ko Khao Phing Kan, popularly known as James Bond Island, and nearby Ko Tapu featured prominently in the 1974 James Bond classic, The Man With the Golden Gun.

For hotels and restaurants in this region see pp304–8 and pp328–31

Areas of Mangrove

It is possible to explore many mangrove channels in a small boat at high tide, although skillful piloting is often required.

VISITORS' CHECKLIST

Road Map B5. 56 miles (90 km) NE of Phuket town. *TAT, Phuket (0-7621-2213).* *from Phuket or Krabi to Phang Nga town.* *from Phuket.*

KEY

- Beach
- *Wat*
- Ferry service
- Major road
- Minor road

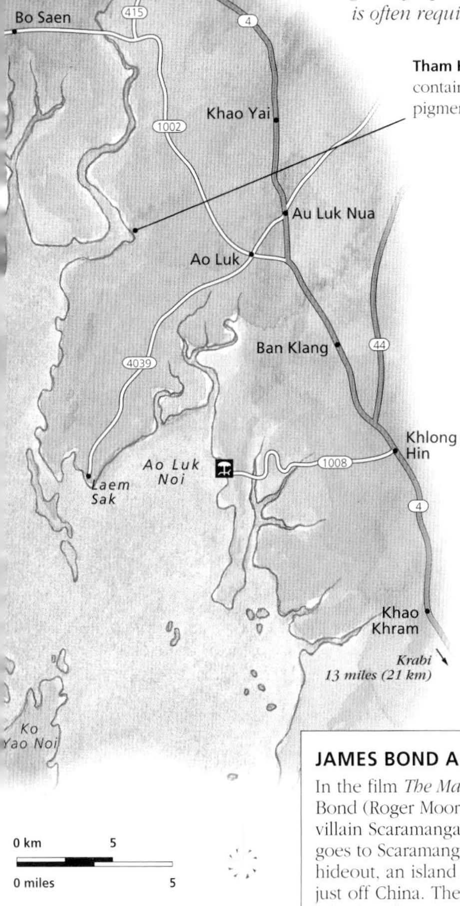

Bo Saen
415
4
Khao Yai
1002
Au Luk Nua
Ao Luk
Ban Klang
44
4039
Khlong Hin
1008
Ao Luk Noi
Laem Sak
4
Khao Khram
Krabi 13 miles (21 km)
Ko Yao Noi

Tham Hua Gralok, which means Skull Cave, contains prehistoric paintings, in colored pigments, of humans and strange animals.

Rubber Plantations

Rubber is a major cash crop and plantations cover large areas of the bay. Latex tapped from the trees, is left to harden in shallow trays.

0 km 5

0 miles 5

STAR SIGHTS

★ Panyi Fishing Village

★ James Bond Island

JAMES BOND AND THE ISLAND HIDEOUT

In the film *The Man With the Golden Gun* (1974), James Bond (Roger Moore) comes to Thailand in search of the villain Scaramanga (Christopher Lee). Bond eventually goes to Scaramanga's hideout, an island just off China. The island, in fact, that is visible in the background is Ko Khao Phing Kan and the sheer rock nearby containing the secret weapon, is Ko Tapu.

Scaramanga and Bond In Phang Nga

Phang Nga Bay Limestone Stacks

Phang Nga Bay is, in fact, the most spectacular remnant of the once mighty Tenasserim Mountains which still form a spine through Thailand to China. Its lime stacks rise sheer from calm, shallow waters up to 1,150 ft (350 m). There are about 40 stacks and inside many of them are narrow tunnels and sea caves. The karst scenery with its majestic pinnacles continues inland to the east, where cliffs soar above the hidden valleys with cascading rivers. A protected site, the bay is home to diverse ecosystems and a variety of wildlife.

Sea eagle, Phang Nga

Mangroves *at the bay's silted northern end are Thailand's largest and best preserved mangrove area.*

Isolated stacks *are a number of sheer, thin projections in the bay. These columns of rock are splinters of limestone that are shaped through heavy erosion by the sea.*

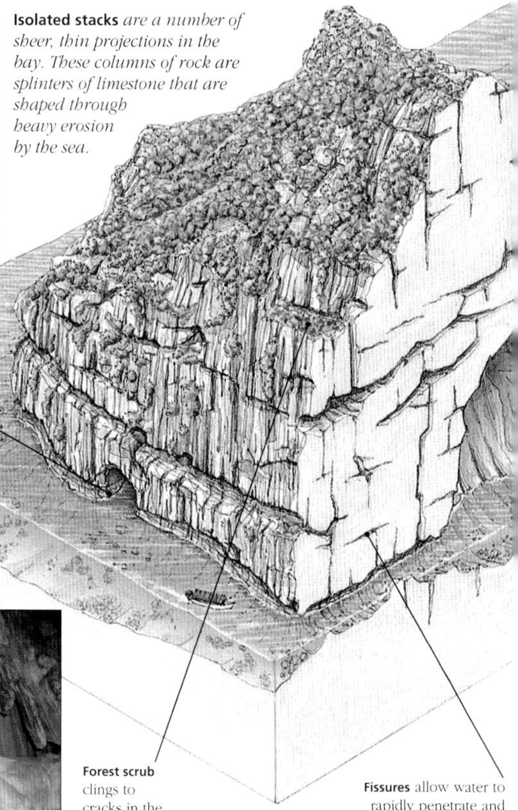

Caves form quickly at sea level. Some are exposed only at low tide.

Forest scrub clings to cracks in the limestone.

Fissures allow water to rapidly penetrate and erode the limestone.

Calcite deposits *result in speleothems, or cave formations, such as stalagmites and stalactites due to the combination of chemicals, air, water, and bacteria.*

CROSS SECTION OF TYPICAL STACKS IN PHANG NGA BAY

The limestone landscape at Phang Nga Bay is known by geologists as drowned karstland. Karst is characterized by its internal drainage system, whereby water finds its way into the interior of the limestone through fissures, then erodes the rock from within riddling it with tunnels, chasms, and vast *hongs*.

Undercut cliffs *form when wave action erodes the base of the stacks at the rate of about 3 ft (1 m) every 5,000 years.*

The aerial view of Phang Nga Bay *is a striking sight, with vertical formations jutting straight out of the surrounding azure waters.*

Ko Hong *has a vast network of lagoons, chasms, and tunnels running underneath it. As a conservation measure, access to the area is forbidden at present.*

HOW PHANG NGA BAY WAS FORMED

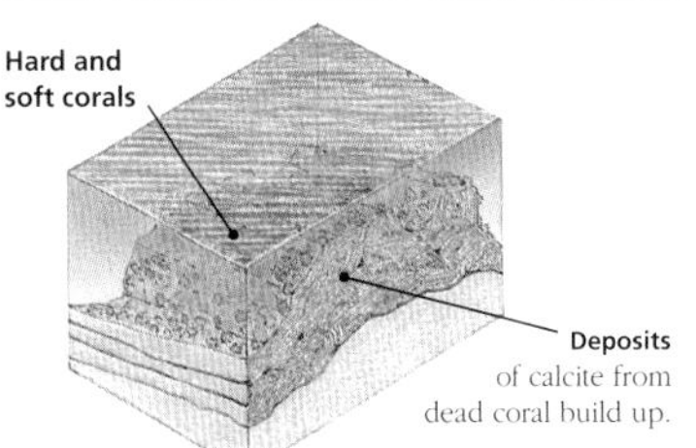

130 million years ago, *the area was part of a vast underwater coral reef. Calcite deposits from dead coral built up in thick layers.*

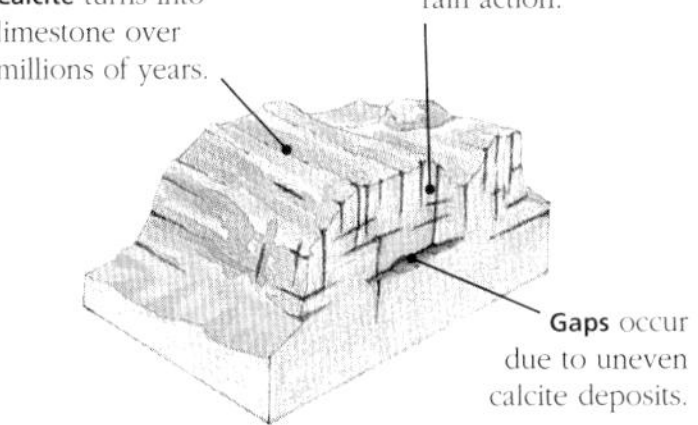

75 million years ago, *plate movements pushed these deposits, which had turned to limestone, out of the ocean. The rigid rock ruptured.*

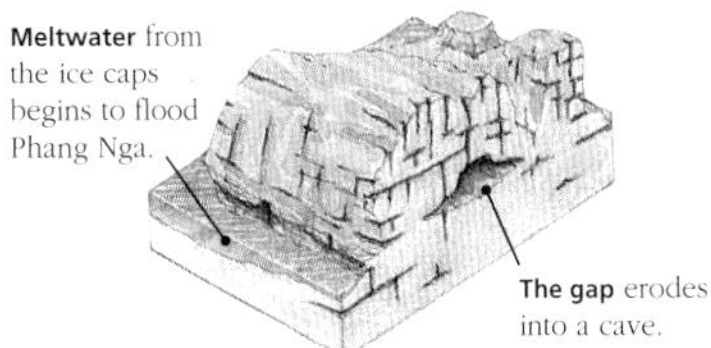

20,000 years ago, *at the end of the last Ice Age, the sea level rose, flooding Phang Nga. Waves and tides accelerated the process of erosion.*

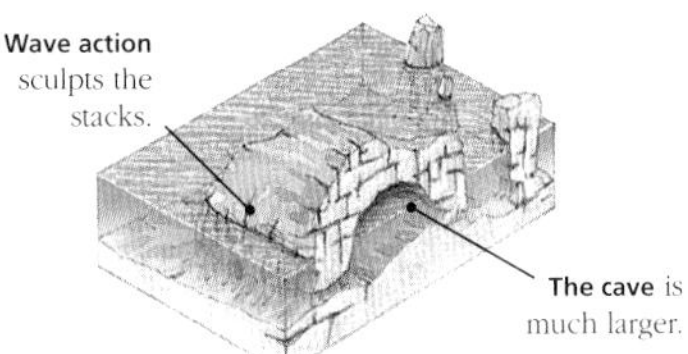

8,000 years ago, *the sea reached its highest level, about 13 ft (4 m) above its present height, sculpting a shelf, visible on most of the stacks.*

Exploring Phang Nga Bay

Phang Nga Bay can be easily reached either from Phuket *(see pp220–38)* or Krabi *(see p244)*. Distances are not great and most places on the mainland are accessible by bus, taxi, cars, or motorcycles. Visitors should keep in mind that the natural beauty of the area attracts a large number of people, so those who want to avoid the crowds should hire a longtail boat as an alternative to packed tour boats. An even better option is to join a daylong sea-kayaking tour and explore the collapsed cave systems that make the offshore islands fascinating. Phang Nga is a good base for those who want to spend some time exploring the bay.

Limestone cliffs forming a backdrop against charming Phang Nga

Phang Nga

พังงา

56 miles (90 m) NE of Phuket town.

As the capital of Phang Nga province, Phang Nga is perhaps destined to be overshadowed by the livelier island of Phuket, but it more than makes up for this, owing to its spectacular location. There is a great deal to do and see in the vicinity, most notably in and around the beautiful Phang Nga Bay. Very few visitors choose to stay in the town given the variety of accommodations available at the luxurious beach resorts on neighboring Phuket. Yet, Phang Nga is laid-back, friendly, and provides an authentic Thai experience for those who want to escape the bustle of a commercial tourist spot. It is an ideal place for an overnight stay.

Thai Muang

ไทยเมือง

32 miles (51 km) W of Phang Nga. *Turtle Releasing Festival (Mar).*

A small Sino-Thai market town on the Andaman Sea coast, Thai Muang is best known for the **Thai Muang Beach Golf Course and Resort**. This 18-hole golf course is one of the most popular seaside golf clubs in Thailand. The town is a jumping-off point for the **Khao Lampi Hat Thai Muang National Park**. Hat Thai Muang is a nesting ground for sea turtles. Other animals in the park include the oriental honey-buzzard and Malayan pit viper. The town is also famous for its celebration of the Turtle Releasing Festival at the end of the nesting season in March. During this festival, participants release turtles bred by the fishery department into the sea.

Sa Nang Manora Forest Park

วนอุทยานสระนางมโนราห์

Off Hwy 4, 5 miles (8 km) NE of Phang Nga. *Park HQ (0-7535-6134).*

www.dnp.go.th

This beautiful but little-visited park features simple dirt trails running through dense rain forests with many streams, waterfalls, and pools for swimming. The park is named after the mythical Princess Manora. According to legend, she supposedly bathes in the pools of this forest when no one is around – a tale which undoubtedly adds to the forest's charm. The various waterfalls are linked by a series of trails which are good for hiking. Picnic tables laid out at intervals can be used for rest or grabbing a bite. Visitors should carry enough drinking water as the park has very high humidity levels.

Waterfalls dotting the interior of the Sa Nang Manora Forest Park

For hotels and restaurants in this region see pp304–8 and p328–31

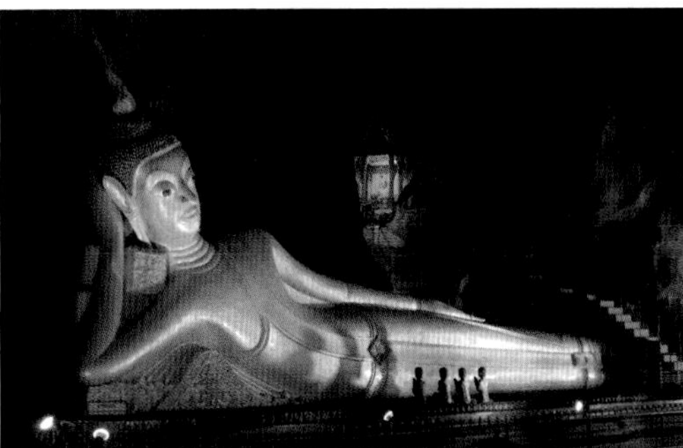

Reclining Buddha statue within the larger cave at Wat Tham Suwan Khuha

Wat Tham Suwan Khuha

วัดถ้ำสุวรรณคูหา

6 miles (10 km) SW of Phang Nga. *dawn to dusk daily.*

Venerated by locals, Wat Tham Suwan Khuha is one of Phang Nga province's chief attractions, and is almost as popular as Phang Nga Bay.

This temple fascinates most visitors with its two conjoined caves filled with images of the Buddha in all shapes and sizes. The larger cave has a 50-ft (15-m) Reclining Buddha and is tiled with Laikhraam and Benjarong (different styles of ceramics). Various spirit flags as well as the statue of a seated hermit adorn the caves. In the past, the cave-temple has attracted royal visitors, and the seals of several Chakri *(see pp42–3)* kings including Rama V (r.1868–1910), Rama VII (r.1925–1935), and the current king, Rama IX, are etched in the wall of the smaller cave. Visitors should watch out for the large number of monkeys in the vicinity.

Suan Somdet Phra Sinakharin Park

อุทยานสวนสมเด็จพระศรีนครินทร์ - สวนสมเด็จย่า

Off Nonthaburi Pathum Thani Rd, 2 miles (3 km) SW of Phang Nga. *dawn to dusk daily.*

An attractive botanical park, the Suan Somdet Phra Sinakharin Park, is surrounded by karst peaks limestone pinnacles, and beautiful gardens. The park has two entrances and is replete with caves, tunnels, and limestone formations, as well as a large lake with a fountain and a sundial. Paddle boats are available for hire and can be used to explore the lake. Wooden walkways have been built to link the main caverns both for ease of access and to keep visitors' feet dry, as many of the caves and tunnels are often flooded. One of the caves, **Tham Reusi Sawan**, shelters the golden statue of a hermit wearing a tiger skin, who is regarded as a symbol of good fortune. Another well-known cave is the **Tham Luk Seua**, which means Tiger Cub Cave, although the word *luk seua* also means Boy Scout in Thai. The park can be easily reached on motorcycles.

Ao Phang Nga National Park

อุทยานแห่งชาติอ่าวพังงา

Off Hwy 402, 7 miles (11 km) S of Phang Nga. *Park HQ (0-7641-2188). dawn to dusk daily.* **www**.dnp.go.th

Inaugurated in 1981, Ao Phang Nga National Park covers an area of around 155 sq miles (401 sq km) and is made up of a number of small and large islands, karst outcrops, inaccessible and tall cliff faces – some as high as 980 ft (299 m) – overlooking the azure waters of the Andaman Sea. The coastal areas of the park are lined with mangrove forests, the largest remaining area of the original primary mangrove forest in Thailand. The park is home to a wide variety of land and marine creatures, including Malayan dolphins, hammerhead sharks, manta rays, finless porpoises, and the 7-ft (2-m) long water monitor. Most people, however, visit the park for the fantastic vistas of the surreal limestone towers rising from the surrounding waters, teeming with sea eagles and macaques – a complete haven for nature enthusiasts.

Dramatic cliffside entrance to Suan Somdet Phra Sinakharin Park

Aerial view of the limestone stacks and mangrove forests, Phang Nga Bay ▷

Phuket 20

ภูเก็ต

A blue glassy tiger butterfly

Thailand's largest island, Phuket first became prosperous as a result of tin production, but now tourism is the major earner. This is one of Southeast Asia's most popular holiday destinations with its stunning beaches, clear waters, and vibrant nightlife. In recent years, there has been a huge growth in chic resorts and spas on Phuket. Phuket town is the island's administrative capital and cultural center. The northern tip of Phuket is separated from the mainland just by a narrow channel, over which runs the 2,295-ft (700-m) long Sarasin Bridge.

Game fishing
The rich waters off Phuket attract keen anglers.

Half-Buried Buddha
Wat Phra Thong is built around an unusual Buddha image, half-buried in the ground. Legend says that whoever tries to remove it will die.

★ West Coast Beaches
The clearest waters, best sands, and the most luxurious hotels are on the west coast. Patong is the most developed resort; Karon and Kata are quieter.

Laem Promthep is the southernmost accessible point on Phuket. The sunset views from this rugged headland, are among the most stunning sights on the island.

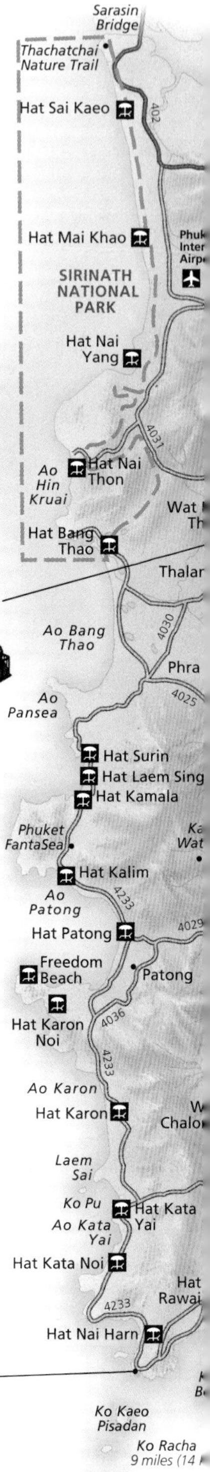

Sarasin Bridge
Thachatchai Nature Trail
Hat Sai Kaeo
402
Hat Mai Khao
SIRINATH NATIONAL PARK
Hat Nai Yang
4031
Ao Hin Kruai
Hat Nai Thon
Hat Bang Thao
Ao Bang Thao
4030
Phra
4025
Ao Pansea
Hat Surin
Hat Laem Sing
Hat Kamala
Phuket FantaSea
Hat Kalim
Ao Patong
4233
Hat Patong
4029
Patong
Freedom Beach
Hat Karon Noi
4036
4233
Ao Karon
Hat Karon
Laem Sai
Ko Pu
Ao Kata Yai
Hat Kata Yai
Hat Kata Noi
4233
Hat Rawai
Hat Nai Harn
Ko Kaeo Pisadan
Ko Racha

KEY

Beach
Aquarium
Wat
International airport
Ferry service
Visitor information
Main road
Minor road
Ferry route
Park boundary

STAR SIGHTS

- ★ West Coast Beaches
- ★ Phuket Orchid Garden and Thai Village
- ★ Phuket Aquarium

Sirinath National Park
Spreading over land and water, this park supports a variety of flora and fauna. It is especially famous as a nesting ground for endangered sea turtles.

VISITORS' CHECKLIST

Road Map B5. 56 miles (90 km) S of Phang Nga. *18 miles (29 km) N of Phuket town center.* *TAT, 73–75 Phuket Rd, Phuket town (0-7621-1036).* *Vegetarian Festival (late Sep/early Oct, for nine days), King's Cup Regatta (Dec).* **www**.phuket.com

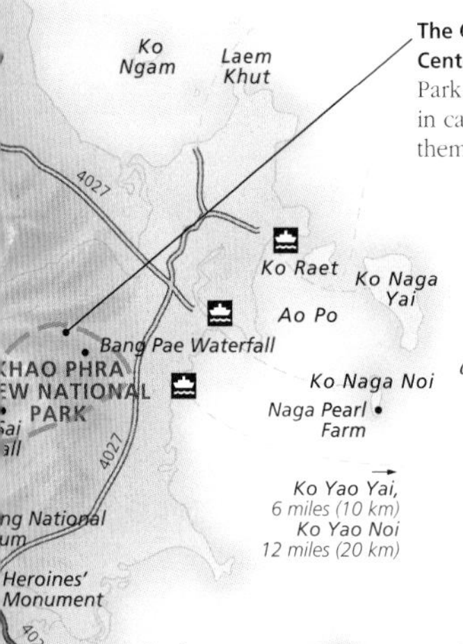

The Gibbon Rehabilitation Center in Khao Phra Taew Park teaches gibbons reared in captivity to fend for themselves in the wild.

Heroines' Monument
This monument is dedicated to two sisters who rallied the local women to successfully defend Phuket against Burmese invaders during the Battle of Thalang in 1785.

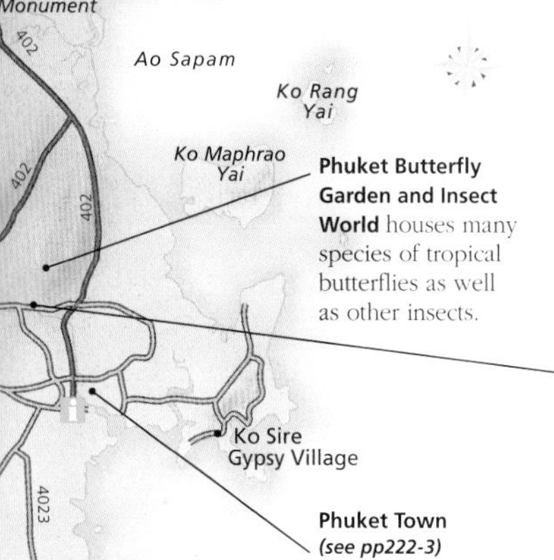

Phuket Butterfly Garden and Insect World houses many species of tropical butterflies as well as other insects.

★ Phuket Orchid Garden and Thai Village
This village has an exotic orchid garden and cultural performances with elephant shows, Thai kickboxing, and folk dances.

Phuket Town
(see pp222-3)

★ Phuket Aquarium
This well-designed aquarium is a part of the the Phuket Marine Biological Center. It houses sea and freshwater fish, turtles, and mollusks.

Phuket Town

Pillar at San Chao Chui Tui

Around the beginning of the 19th century, Phuket town grew to prominence with the island's tin resources attracting thousands of Chinese migrants. Many merchants made fortunes from tin, built splendid residences, and sent their children to British Penang in Malaysia for education. Hokkien-speaking tin-mining families soon intermarried with the indigenous Thai population. Today, the busy downtown area retains some of its earlier charm, although, unlike most of Phuket, it is geared toward residents rather than visitors. The Chinese influence remains intact in the Sino-Portuguese shophouses, temples, and the local cuisine.

Devotee placing incense sticks in a canister at San Chao Chui Tui

Rang Hill

เขารัง

Located to the northwest of the town center, Rang Hill is a beautiful spot, shaded by a thick canopy of tropical trees and covered with soft grass. Extremely popular with couples, students, and visitors, the hill provides breathtaking views of the town. There is also a fitness park and a jogging track here. On the top of the hill stands a bronze statue of Khaw Sim Bee Na-Ranong (1857–1913), governor of Phuket for 12 years from 1901 onward. He enjoyed considerable autonomy from Bangkok, but is credited with bringing the island firmly under central rule. An enterprising visionary, he also imported the first rubber tree into Thailand. Vachira Road, which leads to the hill, has a Buddhist temple with a statue of a golden, Seated Buddha. There are also some excellent restaurants in the area.

Bronze statue of Khaw Sim Bee Na-Ranong, Rang Hill

San Chao Chui Tui

ศาลเจ้าจุ้ยตุ่ย

Ranong Rd. *dawn to dusk daily.*

Elaborately decorated and painted bright red and gold, this Chinese temple receives a steady flow of devotees. Visitors come here, in particular, to shuffle numbered sticks kept in a canister dedicated to the vegetarian god Kiu Wong In. Each number corresponds to a preprinted fate that, according to belief, the person will inherit. Most popular with Chinese residents in the area, the temple is particularly crowded during the Vegetarian Festival *(see p225)*.

San Chao Put Jaw

ศาลเจ้าปุดจ้า

Ranong Rd. *dawn to dusk daily.*

The cultural and economic influence of Phuket's urban Chinese business-class is apparent at San Chao Put Jaw, the island's most celebrated shrine. A temple dedicated to the three teachings of northern Buddhism practiced in Vietnam and China, the temple has little to associate it with Theravada Buddhism. Founded by settlers from southern China, it was originally located on Soi Ang Ah Lai until it was severely damaged by fire and moved to its present location. Rebuilt in characteristic Chinese style with guardian lions at the gates and a traditional roof, it is a riot of color and clouds of incense smoke, especially during festivals.

Chinese Mansions

ตึกจีน

Thalang, Yaowarat, Dibuk, Krabi, and Phang Nga Rds.

The heart of Phuket town is the old Sino-Portuguese quarter with its spacious, if now rather run-down, Colonial-style residences set in large grounds. Most of them date from the reigns of Rama IV and Rama V. Among the best examples are those used today as offices by the Standard Chartered Bank and Thai Airways International on Ranong Road as well as the restored residential estates on

Exterior façade of typical Chinese mansion, set in lush grounds

Typical Rattanakosin-style architecture at Wat Mongkol Nimit

Dibuk and Thalang roads. However, none of them have been converted into museums and are not open to visitors.

Wat Mongkol Nimit

วัดมงคลนิมิต

Yaowarat Rd. *dawn to dusk daily.*

A large, Rattanakosin-style temple, Wat Mongkol Nimit exudes an air of austerity. The *wat*, a fitting example of classic Thai architecture, has a soaring multitiered roof, finely carved doors, glass tiling, and beautiful mosaic work, all of which combine to give it an extremely bright and colorful effect. Highly revered by the local Chinese population, the *wat's* compound acts as a community center where monks play *takraw* (kick-volleyball) with the laity.

VISITORS' CHECKLIST

Road Map B5. 56 miles (90 km) SW of Phang Nga. *100,000.* *18 miles (29 km) N of town center.* *TAT, 73–75 Phuket Rd. (0-7621-1036).* *daily.* *Chinese New Year (Jan/Feb full moon); Phuket Vegetarian Festival (early Oct, for nine days).*

Phuket Philatelic Museum

พิพิธภัณฑ์ไปรษณียากร

Phuket Post and Telegraph Office, Montri Rd. ***Tel*** *0-7621-1020.* *9:30am–5:30pm Tue–Sat.*

This charming little museum, set in the restored old Phuket Post Office, is a delight for visitors. The building, with typical Sino-Portuguese-style architecture, is a historical site in its own right, reminiscent of how the town looked almost 40 years ago, before the advent of commercial tourism in Thailand. Although more of a curiosity for its old world charm than as a center for any major stamp collection, the Phuket Philatelic Museum nevertheless has a collection which includes many series of fascinating stamps from early Thai postal history; the service dates back to the early years of the 20th century.

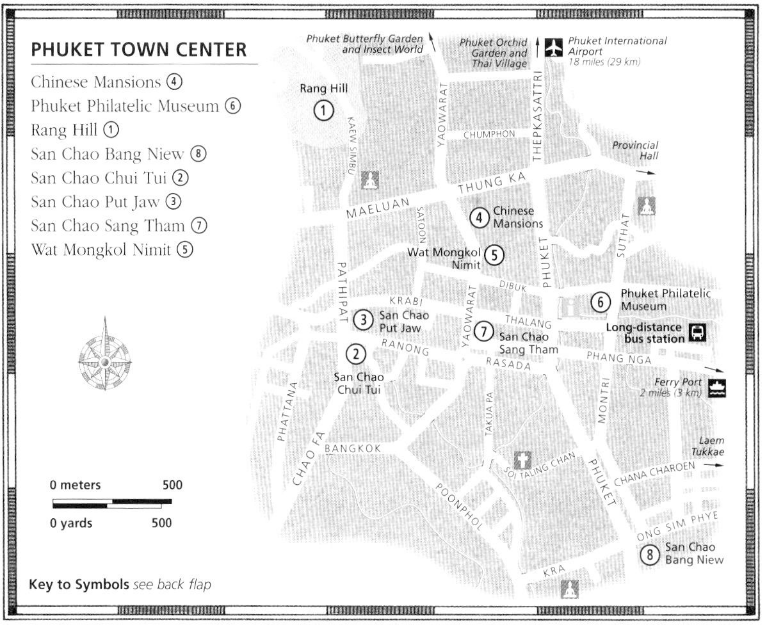

PHUKET TOWN CENTER

Chinese Mansions ④
Phuket Philatelic Museum ⑥
Rang Hill ①
San Chao Bang Niew ⑧
San Chao Chui Tui ②
San Chao Put Jaw ③
San Chao Sang Tham ⑦
Wat Mongkol Nimit ⑤

0 meters 500
0 yards 500

Key to Symbols *see back flap*

San Chao Sang Tham, a Chinese temple in Phuket's old town

San Chao Sang Tham

ศาลเจ้าแสงธรรม

Yaowarat Rd. *dawn to dusk daily.*

Another significant link in the string of shrines that serve Phuket's Vegetarian Festival, San Chao Sang Tham is said to be almost 200 years old. The shrine, a beautiful symbol of Chinese architecture, is decorated in a dazzling array of colors. Inside is a plethora of Buddhist and Taoist divinities, ancestor tablets, and clouds of incense smoke. Although visitors do not need to take off their shoes here, they must be modestly dressed. They should avoid standing on the threshold when entering the holy building, as this is traditionally considered to bring bad luck.

San Chao Bang Niew

ศาลเจ้าบางเหนียว

Phuket Rd. *dawn to dusk daily.*

One of Phuket's oldest and most revered Chinese temples, San Chao Bang Niew is thought to have been founded by migrants from Fujian in the 19th century. The temple is dedicated to Giu Ong and Yok Ong, spirits who must be invited from *bang niew* (the sea) at the beginning of the Vegetarian Festival to bless the community and to banish evil spirits said to disrupt proceedings.

The inner compound of the temple is devoted to several Chinese mythological gods. The most prominent are Siew, Hok, and Lok representing longevity, power, and happiness. San Chao Bang Niew is known for the spectacle created by *naga* devotees while climbing knife ladders during the festival.

Provincial Hall

ศาลากลาง

Narison Rd.

This fine building, inaugurated by Rama VI in 1917, still functions as an administrative office for the governor and his staff, but is not open to visitors. Originally built with 99 doors but no windows, it may be recognized as a setting from Roland Joffe's movie *The Killing Fields* (1984). The outer corridor is adorned with a number of framed photographs which pictorially narrate the history of Phuket.

The elaborately detailed fretwork on the exterior is a fine example of the original architecture of the town. Each piece is said to have taken almost six years to complete.

Laem Tukkae

แหลมตุ๊กแก

2 miles (3 km) SE of town center.

Chao Le Boat Floating Festival, 6th and 11th lunar months.

With around 1,500 sea gyspies, Laem Tukkae is home to Phuket's second-largest community of *chao thalae* after Hat Rawai. These *chao thalae* make a living from traditional pursuits such as fishing.

They organize the Chao Le Boat Floating Festival, a ceremony similar to Loy Krathong *(see p37)* in which small boats are released into the sea during evening hours to drive away evil spirits and bring good luck.

Phuket Butterfly Garden and Insect World

สวนผีเสื้อและโลกแมลงภูเก็ต

2 miles (3 km) N of town.

9am–5pm daily.

A haven for tropical butterflies, the Phuket Butterfly Garden breeds 40 species of butterflies from across Thailand each year. The accompanying Insect World is home to a variety of arachnids, giant millipedes, and scorpions.

Phuket Orchid Garden and Thai Village

ภูเก็ตออร์คิดการ์เด้นแอนด์ไทยวิลเลจ

3 miles (5 km) N of town.

9am–9pm daily.

A popular cultural center, the Thai Village hosts cultural performances and animal shows from different regions of Thailand. The village is a great place to buy *yan lipao* (reed grass bags) and ornaments. The nearby Phuket Orchid Garden grows and sells more than 40,000 orchids each year.

Façade of the grand Phuket Provincial Hall

Phuket's Vegetarian Festival

Phuket hosts a nine-day Vegetarian Festival each year, at the start of the ninth lunar month of the Chinese calendar. This tradition, accompanied by gruesome rites, began over 150 years ago when a troupe of Chinese entertainers in Phuket recovered from the plague by adhering to austere rituals practised in China. Today, believers use the festival to purge the body and soul of impure thoughts and deeds. Devotees follow a 10-rule regimen during the festival which includes dressing in white, following a vegetarian diet, and abstaining from alcohol and sex. While events are held at various temples, the highlight of the festival is the parade of *nagas* (spirit mediums) whose flesh is pierced by metal rods. Other *nagas* climb ladders of knives, plunge their hands into hot oil, or walk on burning coals. The worse the suffering, the greater the reward is said to be for the *naga* and his temple.

Pineapples, used as an offering

STREET PARADES

The main shrines organize street parades on different days during the festival. Devotees burn firecrackers and beat drums in order to drive away evil spirits, making these parades quite noisy and even dangerous at times.

Carriage bearers are young men of ethnic Chinese origin, who compete for the honour of carrying the festival divinities around town on their shoulders.

Deity carriages are elaborately decorated in bright red and gold – symbolic of good luck in Chinese communities.

Commercial and privately owned shops *are set up as stalls or altars outside houses or at nearby temples. They offer cups of tea and fresh fruits to passersby and* nagas.

Chui Tui temple *and neighboring San Chao Put Jaw* (see p222) *are two of Phuket's most celebrated shrines. Offering tables are set up in front of the temple gates and the inner shrines.*

Self mutilation *involves piercing various parts of the body with sharp instruments such as knives, yet bloodshed is minimal. This gruesome ritual is a highlight of the Vegetarian Festival.*

Walking on hot coals *is another form of self mortification in which devotees walk barefoot on a bed of red-hot glowing embers. Like other forms of self torture, devotees endure it to invoke the gods.*

Firework displays *are popular during the Vegetarian Festival. Loud crackers are burst by devotees in the belief that the din will keep evil spirits at bay.*

Mansions of Phuket

The traditional architecture of Phuket is an amalgam of Sino-Thai and Portuguese styles and is similar to the 19th-century architecture found in Singapore, and Penang and Malacca in Malaysia. Shophouses began to spring up to serve Phuket's affluent Chinese migrants and by the turn of the 20th century, these wealthy settlers started building elaborate mansions that can be seen to this day. The construction blended Chinese architecture with Western styles, ranging from Classical Greek to Art Deco and was distinguished from the local houses by its sheer size and grandeur. Opulently decorated with imported furniture and marble, these mansions reflected the status of their owners. Many have been restored and they add a distinct character to present-day Phuket.

Brightly colored façades of Sino-Portuguese houses in Phuket

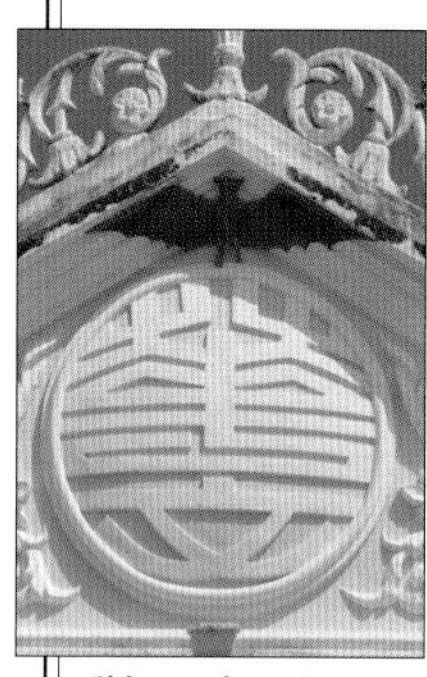

Chinese characters *on buildings are often stylized, indicating the wealth and influence of Phuket's sizeable migrant, ethnic Chinese community.*

MANSION FAÇADES

Phuket's Sino-Portuguese mansions are called *ang mor lau*, or red head buildings, based on a common epithet for Europeans. Constructed with large windows and plenty of shaded spaces, these buildings were designed to ensure that the interiors stayed well ventilated and cool.

Windows often feature louvered shutters to permit easy circulation of air.

Elaborate stucco designs decorate many eaves and arches adding ornate touches as well as grandeur to these mansions.

Chinese-style buildings *are decorated with pilasters or false pillars. These elaborate mansions have a triple-arched façade common to other buildings of the time. The increasingly prosperous Chinese migrants who climbed the social ladder usually demonstrated their status through the grand houses they built.*

Greco-Roman motifs *were widely used. The upper classes blended Classical and Chinese designs creating a hybrid style that is reflected in public buildings such as the* Thai Hua Museum.

Large arches and pillars *support shaded terraces and verandas, provide access to its inhabitants and visitors, as well as shelter them from the piercing tropical sun and the frequent monsoon downpours.*

Birds and animals *feature in elaborate and fanciful stucco designs. Swooping cranes, dragons, phoenixes, bats, stylized peacocks, and various mythological creatures are considered to be symbols of good luck.*

Tiled roofs were regarded as a status symbol in Thai society where thatch or corrugated iron were the common roofing materials.

Elaborate doors and lintels *characterized* ang mor lau *mansions, with Chinese characters prominently displayed over the door and intricate gingerbread fretwork suspended from the eaves.*

Art Deco style *became popular among Phuket's Chinese businessmen from about 1918 onward, and was incorporated into designs used for doors and windows. Largely adopted as an imitation of European sophistication, this was part of the style statement of the nouveau riche.*

PHRA PITAK CHINPRACHA MANSION

Built between 1937 and 1940 for the wealthy Tantawanitj family, this large and well-preserved mansion is set in sprawling gardens. Although not open to the public, it is among the grandest red-roofed mansion in the city, reflecting the luxurious lifestyle of the erstwhile tin barons and their families.

Chinpracha Mansion nestled in its wooded estate

Exploring Phuket's West Coast

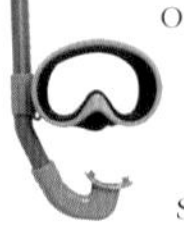

Mask and snorkel

Phuket owes its fame to the beauty, warmth, and safety of its beaches, nearly all of which are situated on the island's western, Andaman Coast, which runs from Hat Nai Harn in the south to Hat Sai Kaeo in the north. Hat Patong is among the best-known beaches and boasts a glitzy, sybaritic nightlife, unlike the risque indulgence of Pattaya (*see pp104–8*), and the more sedate Karon and Kata beaches. Hat Mai Khao, in northwest Phuket, remains the island's quietest beach with rare sea turtles – which are being encouraged by local ecologists to return to the beaches – nesting there from time to time. All of Phuket's west coast offers a fine choice of accommodations, dining, and watersports, as well as mesmerizing views especially toward dusk when the sun sets across the idyllic waters of the Andaman Sea.

Pristine waters with the Royal Phuket Yatch Club in background, Hat Nai Harn

Hat Nai Harn

หาดในหาน

11 miles (18 km) SW of Phuket town. www.tourismthailand.org

Crisp white sands and clear offshore waters make Hat Nai Harn one of Phuket's most attractive beaches. Its relative tranquility, when compared to the bustle and development of nearby Hat Patong in particular, comes at a price – Hat Nai Harn is not aimed at the budget traveler. Restaurants and cafés at Hat Nai Harn are also exclusive and expensive, with uniformly high standards. The beach is dominated by the exclusive Royal Phuket Yacht Club (*see p308*). Much of Hat Nai Harn is owned by the Buddhist foundation Samnak Song Nai Harn, which has helped to keep all major commercial activity away. Set back from the beach are two beautiful lagoons surrounded by coconut palms, rubber trees, and brightly colored bougainvillea. This spot is frequented by visitors looking for cheaper accommodations.

Hat Nai Harn is not suitable for offshore swimming during the southwest monsoon from June to September when waves can be high and completely unpredictable. Bright red flags warn swimmers of dangerous swimming conditions. However, the beach is excellent for sunbathing and swimming in shallow waters.

The prestigious Phuket's King's Cup Regatta, an exciting yachting event with international participants, is held on the beach each year in December (*see p37*).

Hat Kata Noi

หาดกะตะน้อย

10 miles (16 km) SW of Phuket town.

The beach at Ao Kata, or Kata Bay, is divided into Kata Noi, or Little Kata, to the south and Kata Yai, or Big Kata, to the north. Hat Kata Noi is undoubtedly one of the livelier beaches on Phuket. A great place for young travelers who will enjoy the vibrant atmosphere and delectable local food the beach has to offer, Hat Kata Noi also attracts the bohemian vacationer who prefers to stay away from the crowds. The beach at Kata Noi is more deserted than the one at Kata Yai, but is well equipped with comfortable accommodations, a fine selection of some of the best restaurants and cafés on the island, as well as facilities for watersports and other outdoor activities.

Hat Kata Yai

หาดกะตะใหญ่

10 miles (16 km) SW of Phuket town.

Like Hat Kata Noi, Hat Kata Yai is also popular for its snorkeling, diving, shopping, and exquisite food. Sheltered by rocky promontories, the sea here is quite shallow for nearly 100 ft (30 m) offshore, making access to coral reefs, and their colorful accompanying marine life, easier and safer than anywhere else on the island. Ko Pu, or Crab Island, lies a short distance off Laem Sai, which separates the two beaches. A tiny island, Ko Pu has its own coral reef which can be easily reached by boat or by swimming.

Visitors sunbathing on beach chairs, Hat Kata Yai

Vacationers sunbathing and jet-skiing on the pretty beach at Hat Karon

Hat Karon

หาดกะรน

12 miles (19 km) SW of Phuket town.

A long, gently curving beach with almost 3 miles (5 km) of pristine white sand, Hat Karon usually does not witness too much commercial activity, except during the peak season, when it gets slightly crowded.

Although the northern part of the beach is not worth a visit, the southern end, where most restaurants, cafés, and hotels line the beachfront, is quite pleasant. The beach is backed by a heady mix of small sand dunes, coconut palms, and casuarina trees. This is also the section where some of the most upscale accommodations on the beach are located, although reasonably priced bungalows are also available. Visitors can partake of some of the most deliciously fresh seafood on the beach and while their prices are not the lowest on the west coast, there is usually something available to suit most budgets.

During the rainswept months of the southwest monsoon, swimming off the beach can be affected by sharp currents and dangerous undertows, sometimes necessitating the flying of warning flags. Most of the time, however, the high waves that sweep across the bay are good for surfing, particularly at the southern end where boards can be hired. Just to the north of Karon, sheltered between two headlands, is a shallow bay backed by the small and picturesque Hat Karon Noi. To the south of this beach lies a fine coral reef, great for snorkeling. Completely dominated by the exclusive upscale Le Meridien Phuket *(see p307)*, an expensive place by any standards, Hat Karon Noi can be reached by road from either Hat Karon to the south, or busy Hat Patong to the north.

Sign at a restaurant

Hat Patong

หาดป่าตอง

10 miles (16 km) W of Phuket town.

Heavily developed and with an active nightlife, Hat Patong is one of the most popular beach destinations on Phuket and is always bustling with visitors. A 2-mile (3-km) long, crescent-shaped expanse of white sand, Hat Patong is set magically between low, palm-covered hills and the clear blue waters of the Andaman Sea. Dotted with a confusingly large choice of guesthouses, hotels, restaurants, cafés, banks, shops, and bars – including go-go bars – it is more reminiscent of Pattaya and Patpong *(see p74)* than Phuket. The beach offers a wide range of watersports including water-skiing, jet-skiing, parasailing, windsurfing, fishing, and sailing.

Breathtaking view of the beachfront and skyline, Hat Patong

Here visitors will find enough to keep themselves entertained. It also has its fair share of restaurants offering a variety of cuisines. Authentic Thai food, however, may be hard to come by; so those keen to experience the local flavors must head for Phuket town *(see pp222–5)*. By night, Hat Patong is the busy nerve center of Phuket's increasingly risqué nightlife, especially in the central area around Soi Bangla.

Visitors who might want to escape from the overwhelming activities on Hat Patong for a while, can head for the quieter Freedom Beach just round the southern tip of Hat Patong. This beach is only accessible by boat from Patong. A short distance to the north, Hat Kalim, an extension of Hat Patong, is another quiet retreat with clear waters and corals – home to a variety of marine life.

Entrance to Phuket Fantasea, amid lush mountains

Phuket FantaSea

ภูเก็ตแฟนตาซี

16 miles (26 km) W of Phuket town.
Tel 0-7638-5000. *6pm–11:30pm Fri–Wed.* www.phuket-fantasea.com

Phuket FantaSea is billed as a cultural theme park which, at a fairly steep price, offers displays of traditional Thai dances on an elaborate, Angkor-inspired stage with sophisticated sound systems and state-of-the-art lighting. There are plenty of souvenir shops and places to eat and drink, such as a 4,000-seater buffet restaurant, which serves royal Thai cuisine, in an enchanting forest setting. Phuket FantaSea is all about showtime extravaganza – a good place for children.

Hat Kamala

หาดกมลา

16 miles (26 km) W of Phuket town.

A relaxed beach, in marked contrast to nearby Patong, Hat Kamala is a popular destination for those seeking a quiet time sunbathing on the white sands or swimming in the clear waters with little else for distraction. Ao Kamala, arguably Phuket's prettiest bay, can be easily reached by a 10-minute drive from the beach. On the way, visitors can pause at Khao Phanturat, a hill, from which they can enjoy magnificent vistas of Hat Kamala's 2-mile (3-km) sweep of dazzling white sands, azure ocean, and tall, casuarina trees. The sea, especially near the northern end of the beach, is well known for its clear waters, with the colorful coral reefs lying not far offshore. This makes Hat Kamala an excellent place for snorkeling and diving enthusiasts.

To the center of Hat Kamala lies an authentic Muslim fishing village, with a couple of mosques and a few restaurants serving excellent Thai, Muslim, and southern Thai cuisine. The locals are very warm and friendly, but visitors should remember to dress respectably in the village – no bikinis or thongs, and certainly no topless displays – particularly in the vicinity of the mosques.

Hat Laem Singh

แหลมสิงห์

15 miles (24 km) W of Phuket town.

Just a stone's throw north of Hat Kamala, beyond a small, rocky headland, is tiny Hat Laem Singh, concealed from both Hat Kamala and the coastal road by palm-covered hills. The approach is by way of a narrow footpath, leading to about 640 ft (195 m) of pristine, white sand and some of the best snorkeling and scuba diving sites off Phuket island. Facilities on this beach are limited, especially compared to Hat Patong, but so are the number of hawkers, and masseurs.

Sweeping white sands, ideal for sunbathing, Hat Kamala

For hotels and restaurants in this region see pp304–8 and pp328–31

Pontoon used for swimming and diving, Hat Surin

Hat Surin

หาดสุรินทร์

14 miles (22 km) W of Phuket town.

Like Hat Kamala nearby, Hat Surin is much quieter and less developed than Hat Patong. With the beach running down to the warm waters of the Andaman Sea, it is a great place to sunbathe and relax. However, it is not recommended for swimming and diving because the beach slopes quite steeply, making for treacherous currents and a palpable undertow during the wet southwest monsoon from June to September.

Hat Surin is also a good place to drink and dine, especially in the evenings after the sun goes down. There are dozens of inexpensive food joints lining the beach which dish out some of the best seafood in Phuket. The beach is also home to the most attractive mosque on the west coast, the tiny but pleasing **Matsayit Mukaram**, which is open for visitors at all times except during prayers. Visitors however, must remember to dress appropriately before visiting the mosque. A golf course overlooking the beach is located nearby.

Ao Pansea

อ่าวแพนซี

About 14 miles (22 km) W of Phuket town.

Separated from Hat Surin by a small headland, Ao Pansea and the accompanying beach of the same name are among the best locations on Phuket. The beach is also one of the most exclusive spots and the accommodations are similarly pricey. Ao Pansea is more or less the private preserve of two world-class establishments – The Chedi and the **Amanpuri** *(see p307)* – which jointly control access to the beach. Amanpuri Resort, in particular, draws a lot of celebrities who find it a glamorous retreat. Ao Pansea, blessed with a beautiful coral reef, provides quiet getaways in the form of upscale, and relatively private access to some of the best diving and snorkeling on the island.

Hat Bang Thao

หาดบางเทา

13 miles (21 km) W of Phuket town.

Immediately to the north of Ao Pansea, Hat Bang Thao is as broad and wide a sweep of white coral sand as the former is small. Fringed with casuarina and palm trees, this crescent-shaped beach is breathtakingly beautiful and stretches for 5 miles (8 km), and is hugely popular with visitors. The central part of the bay is dominated by a luxurious resort, the Laguna Beach Resort *(see p307)*, which is actually a group of several interdependent hotels set on the banks of a placid lagoon. It has several attractive gardens complete with artificial waterfalls, and every convenience and luxury conceivable.

Hat Bang Thao is the site of the Phuket Laguna Triatholon, held here every December. In addition to the usual watersports facilities, the bay is also home to the exclusive Phuket Laguna Riding Club, a good place for horseback riding. A constant sea breeze makes the bay ideal for windsurfing.

The vibrant Hibiscus flower

View of the exclusive Laguna Beach Resort, Hat Bang Thao

Beach restaurant overlooking the gorgeous bay at Hat Nai Yang

Sirinath National Park

อุทยานแห่งชาติสิรินาถ

19 miles (31 km) NW of Phuket town. *Park HQ (0-7632-7152).* *dawn to dusk daily.*

Covering an area of 29 sq miles (75 sq km) on water, and 9 sq miles (23 sq km) on land, this small national park was inaugurated in 1981, with the primary objective of conserving the offshore coral reefs. The sandy beaches near the northern boundary of the park are protected territory as they are a nesting ground for various species of marine turtles. On land, the park is little more than a narrow strip of sand running between Hat Sai Kaeo in the north and Hat Nai Yang to the south. There are numerous species of trees lining the coast including ironwood and screwpine. There are also large tracts of mangrove forest near the northern end of the park which support a diverse ecosystem. The area is known for birds such as mynahs and the Asian fairy bluebird.

Thachatchai Nature Trail

ทางเดินเท้าท่าฉัตรไชย

Sirinath National Park. *8:30am–2:30 pm daily.*

Named after the tiny fishing village on the northwestern shores of Phuket, Thachatchai Nature Trail is part of the island's Sirinath National Park. The trail is located 2,250 ft (686 m) south of the Sarasin Bridge which connects Phuket to the mainland. It winds through the mangroves giving visitors an insight into its complex ecosystem. There are a handful of simple guesthouses and restaurants in the village of Ban Thatchatchai. The trail itself is just 640 yards (600 m) long, and follows a raised wooden walkway through the mangrove swamp. Signs written in Thai and English explain the ecology of the region. The surroundings swarm with all kinds of wildlife that include fiddler crabs, shrimps, small fish and the occasional crab-eating macaque monkey.

Hat Nai Yang

หาดในยาง

Sirinath National Park.

A gorgeous bay with a beach shaded by pine trees, Hat Nai Yang is pristine and quiet. The park headquarters for Sirinath National Park are also located on this beach. This is

Stream running through the mangrove forest at Sirinath National Park

a great place for a picnic with a long coral reef, located less than a mile offshore that is ideal for snorkeling. However, it is recommended for good swimmers as the currents can get quite strong. Enthusiastic visitors can hire a boat to experience the beauty of the surroundings in comfort and safety. This beach is still untouched by commercial development although there are some chic beach cafés, bars, as well as a few upscale spas. Travelers can also camp here without a permit.

Tall trees lining the walking trails at Sirinath National Park.

Hat Mai Khao

หาดไม้ขาว

Sirinath National Park.

Situated within the precincts of Sirinath National Park, Hat Mai Khao stretches for over 6 miles (10 km), and is the longest sandy beach on Phuket. It is also known as Hat Sanambin, or Airport Beach, due to its proximity to the Phuket airport. Hat Mai Khao is still off the tourist map, and is quite tranquil and untouched, especially when compared to the more developed and commercial southern beaches. Although construction is controlled in this protected area, camping is permitted at several locations and is a popular option for many travelers especially backpackers.

This is a famous nesting site for sea turtles who come onshore in hordes to lay their eggs during the cool season from November to February. During this period visitors can see them on the beach at night and also in the surrounding waters. Although the authorities are maintaining a careful watch over the area, the efforts are slightly belated and the number of turtles visiting Hat Mai Khao has started to diminish. Every year from the beginning of the Songkran festival (*see p34*), baby turtles bred in tanks are released into the sea.

Hat Mai Khao is also home to sea cicadas, a kind of crustacean which is prepared as a delicious snack around this area. The beach is great for sunbathing, but it shelves steeply into the sea, and only strong swimmers should venture in, especially during the rainy season from June to September. Visitors can try the seafood at the beach shacks or splurge on any of the restaurants at the upscale Marriot Resort and Spa.

Hat Nai Thon

หาดในทอน

Sirinath National Park.

One of the more secluded beaches on Phuket, Hat Nai Thon is set along a picturesque bay. This half-mile (1-km) long beach served by the Nai Thon fishing village is gradually adapting to Phuket's tourism industry. Improved roads to this beach have brought in some development. However, Hat Nai Thon retains its untouched charm with small, inexpensive bungalows as well as a handful of restaurants, cafés, bars, and shops at the northern end. Both the northern and southern extremities of the bay are protected by large granite outcrops. These rocks shield the bay providing a home to many species of marine flora and fauna and are ideal spots for fishing. A few hundred meters south, beyond a low headland lies Ao Hin Kruai, a quiet and deserted bay for travelers seeking solitude.

Azure waters surround the long sandy beach, Hat Mai Khao

Exploring Phuket's East Coast

Chinese pond heron

Overlooking the calm waters of the Andaman Sea, Phuket's east coast is divided into the southeast; facing Ao Chalong and lying to the south of Phuket town, and the northeast; stretching north of Phuket town right up to the mainland. The island's good roads and availability of different modes of transportation such as buses, cars, and boats make traveling easy. Visitors can choose among options ranging from watersports to exotic cuisine, national parks to deserted beaches, and ancient temples to museums. The northeastern coast is undeveloped; yet, the main road between Phuket town and the mainland passes through it, making the region crucial to the island. Ao Chalong and Thalang are other well-developed areas.

Showcasing Phuket's history and artifacts, Thalang National Museum

Thalang

ถลาง

11 miles (18 km) N of Phuket town.

Located in the center of the island, Thalang was once the capital of Phuket; in fact the island itself was called Thalang till the late 19th century. With the emergence of Phuket town further to the south, Thalang was soon eclipsed and, today, serves more or less as a junction town. However, it still is one of the larger settlements on the island astride the central north-south Highway 402, leading from Phuket town to the mainland. The town has quite a few cultural attractions which draw visitors here. Notable sights include two highly revered temples – Wat Phra Nang Sang and Wat Phra Thong – both of which house very old Buddha images. Apart from this, there are a few simple restaurants serving local cuisine, and a busy and interesting market for fresh produce. The town is a good base to explore the nearby beaches and islands.

Thalang National Museum

พิพิธภัณฑ์สถานแห่งชาติถลาง

Route 4027, 5 miles (8 km) SE of Thalang. ***Tel*** *0-7631-1426.*

8:30am–4pm daily.

Phuket's main museum, the Thalang National Museum, is worth a visit for a fairly comprehensive insight into the island's history. There are five exhibition halls that cover various aspects of the history, ethnic diversity, economy, and the ecology of Phuket. The museum also has displays on the island's tin mining history as well as on ancient art. A 9th-century image of Vishnu, part of the Hindu holy trinity, discovered at Takua Pa *(see p208)* in the early 20th century, is an impressive exhibit. However, the original head has long been lost and has since been replaced by a substitute in gray sandstone. The exhibits showcasing the famous Battle of Thalang where Burmese invaders were repulsed by Khun Chan and Khun Muk are also noteworthy.

Heroines' Monument

อนุสาวรีย์วีรสตรี

5 miles (8 km) SE of Thalang.

This life-sized monument, built by the locals, is dedicated to the sisters – Khun Muk and Khun Chan – for driving Burmese invaders out of Phuket in 1785. They rallied the women of Phuket together and convinced them to dress in men's clothes and carry fake weapons to drive the Burmese army out. As a reward for their bravery, they were given titles by Rama I (r.1782–1809).

Wat Phra Nang Sang

วัดพระนางสร้าง

3 miles (5 km) S of Thalang.

dawn to dusk daily.

This temple was supposedly founded in the 19th century by a charitable local lady and is also known as Phra Nang Sang, literally, Built by the

Mural representing myths from Buddhist cosmology, Wat Phra Nang Sang

Main *wihan* containing Budhha image at Wat Phra Thong

Revered Lady. Legend says that after a pilgrimage to Sri Lanka, she wanted to express her gratitude for her safe return. Thus, she sponsored the construction of this temple. Later, however, she somehow came into conflict with a local ruler who condemned her to death. At the beheading her blood apparently flowed white reflecting her purity. Today, the temple is famous for its collection of religious statuary as well as the murals in the main *wihan*.

Wat Phra Thong

วัดพระทอง

Route 402, 3 miles (5 km) N of Thalang. *dawn to dusk daily.*

Thalang's other well-known Buddhist temple is Wat Phra Thong, or the Temple of the Golden Buddha. This unusual temple is named after the gilded Buddha image that is buried within the temple precincts so that only its head and shoulders are visible above ground. According to an ancient legend, a local cowherd attempted to tether one of his charges to an outcrop he mistook for a tree stump. This actually was the *ushnisha* (topknot) of a buried Buddha image. Both boy and buffalo unfortunately died for the unintentional heresy. Later, the boy's father had a dream in which he saw that his son had achieved nirvana instead of being punished for his deed. Upon hearing this story, a local landowner ordered the image to be excavated and installed in a temple. However, despite the villagers' best efforts, the image could not be fully dug out, and remained buried from the shoulders down. Thereafter, a roof was erected to shelter the exposed head and shoulders, and since then the temple has become an important site of worship for both local Thais as well as Chinese migrants. The latter believe that the image was brought from Tibet and installed on the island of Phuket after a shipwreck.

Today, the *wat* is among the most venerated Buddhist sites not just in Phuket, but in all of southern Thailand and attracts devotees from as far afield as Trang (*see p264*) and Krabi (*see p244*).

Gilded Buddha figure at Wat Phra Thong

Khao Phra Taew National Park

อุทยานแห่งชาติเขาพระแทว

3 miles (5 km) E of Thalang town. *Park HQ (0-7631-1998).* *dawn to dusk.*

Gibbon Rehabilitation Center

Tel *0-7626-0491.* *9am–4pm daily.* *donations.*

www.gibbonproject.org

The last of Phuket's once ubiquitous rain forest is preserved at the Khao Phra Taew National Park. Within the park lies the island's largest and grandest waterfall, **Bang Pae**, which is best seen in its full glory during the southwest monsoon from June to September.

The 1-mile (2-km) long hiking trail winds its way right through the forest which is home to *Kerriodoxa elegans* – a species of palm which is unique to this forest. Visitors should dress appropriately to avoid being bitten by insects. The **Gibbon Rehabilitation Center**, a project set up in 1992 by Phuket's Royal Forest Department, is also located within Khao Phra Taew. The main initiative teaches gibbons reared in captivity to survive in the wild. The center also aims to stop the illegal use of these animals as tourist attractions. Visitors are encouraged to donate money and "adopt a gibbon" to help the cause.

Gibbon learning to survive in the wild, Gibbon Rehabilitation Center

Boats lined up in front of a popular bar, Ao Chalong

Ao Chalong
อ่าวฉลอง

6 miles (10 km) SE of Phuket town.

A dominant geographical feature of this region, Ao Chalong is located between Laem Promthep and Laem Phanwa. Sheltered from the Andaman Sea by the hilly Ko Lon, the bay has clusters of bungalows, hotels, and restaurants stretching from Ao Chalong pier to Hat Rawai along Phuket's western shore. The nearby Chalong Yacht Club organizes weekly races and yachting events. The shoreline along the bay is quite muddy and unsuitable for swimming. However, Ao Chalong is an ideal base for fishing, diving, and swimming to the offshore islands.

Wat Chalong
วัดฉลอง

6 miles (10 km) SE of Phuket town.

Temple fair (Dec)

The best-known temple in Phuket, Wat Chalong dates back to the early 19th century. Also known as Wat Chaiyataramit, the temple was granted royal status in 1846. Luang Pho Saem, the celebrated abbot of the temple, was a noted local healer who died in 1908. His successors have maintained his reputation for healing. The most striking structure in the temple is its tall gilded *chedi*, constructed in 2001, and built in the style of the Tat Phanom *chedi* – northeast Thailand's famous temple which houses relics of the Buddha. The extensive temple grounds and buildings include a cruciform *mondop* containing images of former abbots, photographs, local historical and religious paraphernalia; an *ubosot*, a cremation hall, as well as a funeral *sala* (open pavilion). A lifelike waxen image of Luang Pho Saem in saffron robes is on display in the *kuti* (monks' quarters).

Wat Chalong attracts many pilgrims and is busiest during the annual temple fair held in mid-December.

Phuket Aquarium
ภูเก็ตอะควาเรียม

51, Moo 8, Sakdidet Rd, Cape Panwa. ***Tel*** *0-76 39-1126.*

8:30am–4:30pm (last entry 4pm) daily.

www.phuketaquarium.org

Located on Laem Panwa and part of the Phuket Marine Biological Center, the Phuket Aquarium houses over 150 different species of marine life. The interactive display covers endangered coral reefs, mangrove swamps, tidal estuaries, rivers, and lakes. The most popular attraction, however, is the long walk-through glass tunnel tank which houses electric eels, sting rays, cuttlefish, and a host of other marine life. The idea is to provide visitors with a fun experience as well as create awareness about the coastal environment.

Ko Hai
เกาะไห

13 miles (21 km) S of Phuket town.

from Hat Rawai.

A picturesque and deserted island, Ko Hai, also known as Coral Island, is an idyllic spot. Visitors can enjoy modern amenites at the upscale Coral Island Resort *(see p307)* with a swimming pool and a dive center or try out the cafés and restaurants in the vicinity. Swimming, snorkeling, windsurfing, and parasailing are other attractions on this island. Day trips to Ko Hai can be organized by any travel agent or dive center in Phuket town or Ao Chalong. This is a good dive spot with high visibility. The small fishing village at Ko Lon is an interesting stopover en route.

Ko Kaeo Pisadan
เกาะแก้วพิสดาร

12 miles (19 km) S of Phuket town. *from Hat Rawai.*

An idyllic little island, Ko Kaeo Pisadan, also known as Ko Kaeo Yai, is

Ornate gilded *chedi* housing the Buddha relic at Wat Chalong

Palm trees cover the headland overlooking a wide expanse of sea at Laem Promthep

located off Phuket's southern headland, in the clear blue waters of the Andaman Sea. Day trips to this island are possible from Hat Rawai on the east coast, and Hat Nai Harn (*see p228*) on the west coast. Boat rides from both spots offer fine views of Laem Promthep on the way.

Ko Kaeo Pisadan is a tiny island with a single fine 642-ft (196-m) long beach. The whole island can be traversed on foot and its shallow waters and offshore coral reefs make it an ideal snorkeling spot. Visitors can also kayak right around the island. There is a small resort offering simple and comfortable accommodations with a restaurant specializing in seafood and Thai specialties. Smoking is banned at the resort, and elsewhere on the island. The resort also offers camping facilities.

The island also has an isolated monastery – Wat Ko Kaeo Pisadan – which attracts Thai Buddhist pilgrims. The *wat* sustains a small number of monks who are permanent inhabitants of this island. Visitors should dress appropriately at this sacred spot.

Hat Rawai

หาดราไว

10 miles (16 km) from Phuket town. **Phuket Seashell Museum** 12/2, Moo 2, Wiset Road, Hat Rawai. ***Tel*** *0-7638-1266.* *8am–6pm daily.*

One of the main beaches of southeastern Phuket, Hat Rawai was once a major attraction of Phuket, but has since been replaced by the more appealing west coast beaches. Today, it is better known as an out-of-town dinner destination for those staying in Phuket town, and is justly celebrated for its seafood restaurants and upscale bars. Visitors can experience a little of the bustling excitement and entertainment of Hat Patong here. One of the local attractions here is the **Phuket Seashell Museum** with a large collection of seashells from Thailand and around the world. Those eager to explore nearby islands rather than look for entertainment in restaurants and bars, tend to skip Hat Rawai and go directly to Laem Promthep.

A small community of *chao lae*, or sea gypsies (*see p204*), also live here, but they are rather shy and keep to themselves. Visitors often travel to Laem Promthep to see the spectacular sunset, before stopping at Hat Rawai for a rather appropriately named "sundowner" and dinner and then head back into town.

Laem Promthep

แหลมพรหมเทพ

11 miles (18 km) S of Phuket town.

An imposing rocky headland, Laem Promthep projects southwest into the Andaman Sea. Locally known as Laem Jao, or Cape of the Gods, this place offers the island's most famous sunset view and is popular with Thais and foreigners alike. There are food and drink stalls, shops, and a car park. A lighthouse marks the southwestern extremity of the island and visitors can get a 360 degree view across the sea. A rocky path leads down to the water, and offers good views of Ko Kaeo Pisadan. However, the surrounding waters are not good for swimming, as the currents get quite fierce.

Fishing boats belonging to the *chao lae* community, Hat Rawai

Exploring Phuket's Outlying Islands

Fresh, green coconuts

There are about 39 islands scattered across the Andaman Sea, mainly on Phuket's east coast. These are either uninhabited or home to small communities of Thai fishermen and coconut farmers. Despite relative isolation and tranquility, change is slowly approaching these islands. Some, such as Ko Racha Yai, have already attracted exclusive and luxurious resorts while others, such as Ko Yao Yai, remain off the tourist track, catering mainly to backpackers. These islands can be visited on a day trip or on weekend trips by taking fishing boats, ferries, or longtailed speedboats from various harbors and piers on and around Phuket. However, Ao Chalong still remains the most popular jumping-off point to reach these islands.

Thai Muslim fisherman perched on his boat, Hat Yao Noi

Ko Yao Yai

เกาะยาวใหญ่

9 miles (14 km) E of Phuket.

from Bang Rong.

Located within the boundaries of Phang Nga province, Ko Yao Yai is the larger, albeit less crowded, of the two Ko Yao islands. The island is characterized by a long and irregular coastline, small fishing villages, coconut and rubber plantations, and small areas of rice paddy. Ensconced in a rural setting, it is a far cry from the bustling beaches on Phuket's west coast and an excellent place to sit back, relax, and enjoy a bit of authentic Thai rural life.

There are, as yet, no major resorts on Ko Yao Yai, so its infrastructure remains quite basic with poor and undeveloped roads. It is possible to hire a motorcycle on the island, but many visitors prefer to bring one across with them on the boat from Phuket. Guesthouses and bungalows are simple and laid-back, as are the few restaurants and cafés. Most of the population – and most activities – are centered in the south of the island, especially around Lohjak pier, which is served by boat from the Phuket town pier. Small boats also ply on a regular basis between Chonglad pier on the island's northeast coast and Manok pier near the southern tip of neighboring Ko Yao Noi.

Ko Yao Noi

เกาะยาวน้อย

12 miles (19 km) E of Phuket.

from Bang Rong.

Located in the Andaman Sea almost equidistant from the beach resorts of Phuket, Phang Nga *(see p216)* and Krabi *(see p244)*, Ko Yao Noi is about 8 miles (13 km) long. This island is a quiet getaway with an indigenous population of over 3,000, many of them Thai Muslims, who make a living by fishing and coconut farming. Its main beach, Hat Yao, or Long Beach, is located on the eastern shore facing the mainland.

The interior of the island provides plenty of opportunities for short treks between the small villages, past patches of forest, shrimp farms, green rice fields, and unfrequented coves. Another popular pastime is sea-kayaking, along the island's irregular and indented coast as well as to other offshore islets.

Accommodations are plentiful and cheap. There are several restaurants and bars along the east coast, as well as at Tha Kai, the island's tiny capital.

Ko Racha Yai

เกาะราชาใหญ่

9 miles (14 km) S of Phuket.

from Ao Chalong.

Also known as Ko Raya Yai, Ko Racha Yai's chief attractions are the two beaches at Ao Patok and Ao Siam as well as the good offshore diving. The island also has several resorts offering comfortable bungalow accommodations. The largest and most luxurious of these, The Racha, dominates Ao Patok.

Just 5 miles (8 km) farther south is **Ko Racha Noi**, also a fine diving spot. The island is under the aegis of the Royal Thai Navy, which sometimes restricts access, but permits offshore diving among the unspoiled coral reefs.

In fact, both islands have fine, hard coral reefs which are suitable for all grades of divers.

Breathtaking expanse of sand and sea at Ko Racha Yai

For hotels and restaurants in this region see pp304–8 and pp328–31

Pearls of the Andaman Sea

Chanthaburi may have its rare gems, and Bangkok's Yaowarat District *(see p72)* may be dotted with gold shops, but Phuket is justly famous for its spectacular *mook andaman* (Andaman Sea pearls). Originally, they were a natural product, harvested from the shallow waters around the island on a purely ad hoc basis, but this is not the case anymore. Over the past three decades, Phuket has emerged as a major player in the cultured pearl business, growing to compete internationally with other established major sources such as Japan and the Persian Gulf. Cultured pearls now play a very important role in the island's economy, and the island has several pearl companies. Some of these companies allow visitors to tour their pearl farms and also give demonstrations of pearl culture and harvesting. The 2004 tsunami, however, adversely affected the industry by causing large numbers of oysters to be washed away.

Fine pair of pearl earrings

CULTIVATING PEARLS

Pearl cultivation involves raising oysters in a tank until they are large enough to be placed in the sea. These oysters are then injected with an artificial irritant. After 3–4 years, sometimes longer, a cultured pearl is produced. However, this is not an error-free process since only five percent of the nucleated pearls ever become jewelry.

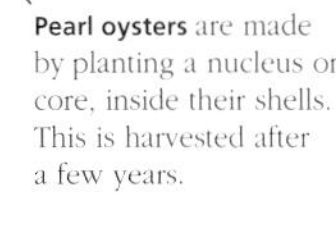

Pearl oysters are made by planting a nucleus or core, inside their shells. This is harvested after a few years.

Pearl farms *are generally located in shallow waters, making the Andaman Sea, off the east coast of Phuket, an ideal place for the process.*

Pearl extraction *is carried out with the help of chemicals and machines which remove the pearl by tearing open the pearl sac. Harvested pearls are then washed, polished, and graded for sale purposes.*

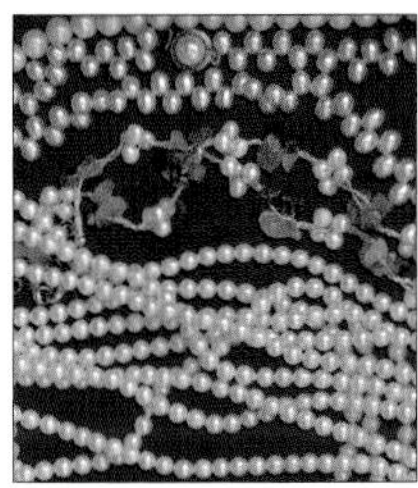

Jewelry stores *in Phuket sell pearls that are locally produced, cultured, and polished. Visitors can choose from a wide and sparkling range of products, including necklaces.*

Visitors to pearl farms *can ask for guided tours. Such trips include seafood, dining, and visiting showrooms selling locally produced pearls.*

LOWER ANDAMAN COAST

Long regarded as the lesser developed counterpart of the Upper Andaman Coast, the Lower Andaman Coast is now a region of limitless possibilities. From the verdant islands of Ko Phi Phi and Ko Lanta to the idyllic beaches around Krabi and Trang, it has become popular for its diving, snorkeling, and rock climbing. Further south, however, both the Malay-Muslim fishing port of Satun, and the pristine Ko Tarutao are still off the beaten track and relatively quiet.

The long, serrated coastline of the Lower Andaman Coast, extending from Krabi to the Malaysian frontier is a lush, fertile region. Blessed with stunning natural beauty, it is a heady mix of white or golden sand beaches and towering limestone outcrops. The vegetation comprises tall, swaying casuarinas and coconut palms, dense rain forests and rubber plantations, as well as green paddy fields.

Gorgeous and unspoiled, the region is frequented by travelers who head for towns such as Krabi and Trang, popular destinations for watersports and rock climbing. Home to a substantial Chinese ethnic population, both towns offer visitors – in addition to the Sino-Thai architecture – an exciting variety of eating options including *dim sum* which is a specialty in many restaurants in Trang. Ko Phi Phi, with its romantic environs and truly outstanding scenic beauty, offers some of the best diving in the area, and is now firmly on the tourist trail. Visitors wanting sand and sun without the crowds head for relatively undeveloped islands such as Ko Lanta.

Few venture as far south as Satun, a peaceful and laid-back town with the highest number of Thai Muslims in the country. Satun also serves as the gateway to the spectacular Ko Tarutao Marine National Park and its outlying islands, within easy sight of Pulau Langkawi and the west coast of Malaysia.

The southwest monsoon, which lasts from June to September, however, makes outlying islands such as Ko Lipe and Ko Rawi inaccessible.

Macaques grooming each other on the grounds of Wat Tham Seua, near Krabi

◁ Holiday-makers relaxing on the stunning beach at Hat Tham Phra Nang, Krabi

Exploring the Lower Andaman Coast

Breathtaking natural beauty, verdant rain forests and stunning beaches beckon visitors to the Lower Andaman Coast. The tropical mangrove forests, home to a variety of land and water animals, are one of the region's best kept secrets. Quiet Krabi combines fine beaches with spectacular cliff landscapes. The idyllic island scenery of Ko Phi Phi and Ko Lanta is also accessible from Krabi. The Trang coast and Tarutao archipelago, with sandy beaches and fine corals, still remain relatively untouristed due to undeveloped facilities. National parks such as Hat Chao Mai, Thale Ban, and Ko Phetra are a haven for all kinds of marine animals and wildlife, besides providing ideal trails for trekking and nature walks. Visitors will also find plenty of opportunity for sea-kayaking, diving, and snorkeling from the islands of Ko Hai, Ko Kradan, and Ko Muk.

Longtail boats anchored in the waters off Ko Muk

GETTING AROUND

Most visitors to the Lower Andaman Coast make use of the airports at Trang and Krabi. Reliable air-conditioned buses link these towns with Bangkok and farther south with Satun. Both Krabi and Trang make suitable bases for exploring the region by hired car in the absence of a railway network. Ko Phi Phi, Ko Lanta, Ko Tarutao, and Ko Bulon Leh are all on ferry routes. Longtail boats are the best way to explore the smaller bays and waterways. Satun's port can also be used to reach Malaysia's Langkawi archipelago by boat.

SIGHTS AT A GLANCE

Towns and Villages
Krabi 1
Pak Bara 29
Satun 31
Trang 17

Areas of Natural beauty
Mangroves 6
Tha Pom 5

National Parks
Hat Chao Mai National Park 20
Khao Nor Chuchi Wildlife Sanctuary 11
Khao Phanom Bencha National Park 4
Ko Lanta Marine National Park 16
Ko Phetra Marine National Park 28
Ko Tarutao Marine National Park pp270–75 33
Thale Ban National Park 32
Than Bok Koranee National Park 3

Beaches and Islands
Hat Chang Lang 19
Hat Pak Meng 18
Hat Yao 22
Hat Yong Ling 21
Ko Bubu 14
Ko Bulon Leh 30
Ko Hai 23
Ko Jum 13
Ko Klang 7
Ko Kradan 25
Ko Lanta pp260–63 15
Ko Libong 26
Ko Muk 24
Ko Phi Phi pp252–5 9
Ko Si Boya 12
Ko Sukorn 27
Krabi Coast pp248–51 8

Museums and Religious Sites
Wat Khlong Thom Nua Museum 10
Wat Tham Seua 2

For additional map symbols *see back flap*

SEE ALSO

- ***Where to Stay*** pp308–11
- ***Where to Eat*** pp331–3

Rock climbing on precipitous cliffs at Hat Rai Leh

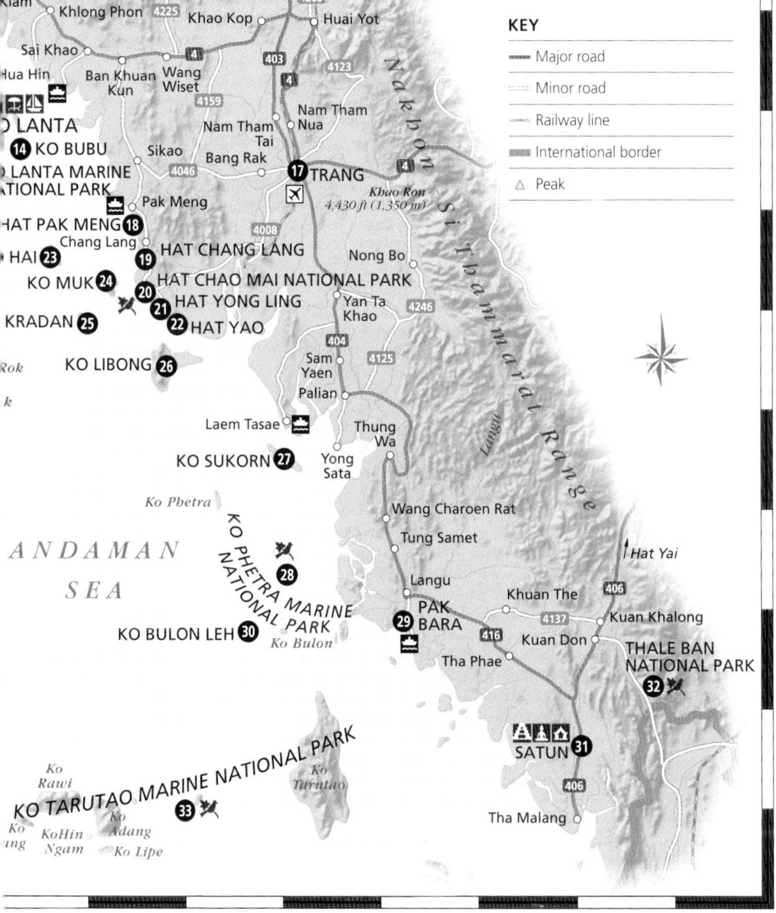

KEY

- Major road
- Minor road
- Railway line
- International border
- △ Peak

Twin peaks of Khao Khanap Nam forming a picturesque backdrop for Krabi

Krabi ❶

กระบี่

Road Map B5. 478 miles (770 km) SW of Bangkok. *68,000.* *10 miles (16 km) NE of Krabi.* *TAT, Krabi (0-7562-2163).* *daily.*

A small town and provincial capital, Krabi is an important embarkation point for ferries to Ko Lanta, Ko Phi Phi, and Ao Nang. Set on the banks of the Krabi estuary, the town takes its name from a *krabi*, or sword, allegedly discovered here. This quaint and bustling market town is the administrative center of the province with banks and other facilities. Surrounded by tall limestone outcrops, similar to those in Phang Nga Bay *(see pp212–17)*, it is a scenic spot in its own right. The twin limestone peaks of **Khao Khanap Nam** are among the most notable outcrops which stand like sentinels on each side of the river. The eastern side is flanked by mangroves. Both the limestone karsts and the mangroves can be visited by renting a longtail boat from the Khong Kha pier in the center of town. Although Krabi itself is generally used as a departure point for the nearby islands, it is fast developing with several bars, restaurants serving eclectic cuisine, and a burgeoning nightlife. There is also a busy market at Thanon Sukhon, a tourist center, and a good foreign-language bookshop on Thanon Utarakit.

Devotees kneeling in front of the Buddha statue in Wat Tham Seua

Wat Tham Seua ❷

วัดถ้ำเสือ

Road Map B5. 5 miles (8 km) N of Krabi. *TAT, Krabi, (0-7562-2163).* *dawn to dusk daily.*

Built into a limestone cave, Wat Tham Seua, which means Tiger Cave Temple, is regarded as one of southern Thailand's most renowned forest temples. It is named after a rock formation that resembles a tiger's paw. The *wat*'s main *wihan* (assembly hall) is built inside a deep limestone cave which contains various *memento mori* (grim symbols depicting the forsaking of worldly desires). At the rear of the *wihan*, a flight of stairs leads up to the main cave of the *wat* where visitors can see a much-venerated Buddha footprint on a gilded rock platform. The *wat* complex also has a large statue of the highly revered *bodhisattva* Avalokitesvara, in its Chinese manifestation as Guan Yin, the Mahayana goddess of mercy. It is sheltered by a newly built Chinese-style pagoda nearby. A circular path in the nearby forest hollow offers a pleasant walk among towering trees and

For hotels and restaurants in this region see pp308–11 and pp331–3

kutis (monks' quarters). The landscaped grounds have a 1,272-step pathway which leads to a Seated Buddha image. Although a strenuous climb, the view from the top is worth the effort. Wat Tham Seua is also famous for its Vipassana Meditation courses.

Than Bok Koranee National Park ❸

อุทยานแห่งชาติธารโบกขรณี

Road Map B5. Park HQ off Rte 4039, 28 miles (45 km) NW of Krabi. *Park HQ (0-7568-1071).* *dawn to dusk daily.* **www**.dnp.go.th

Covering an area of 47 sq miles (122 sq km), Than Bok Koranee National Park is characterized by a series of limestone outcrops, evergreen rain forest, mangroves, peat swamps, and several islands. A part of the national park is being developed as a botanical garden. The park headquarters set amid a series of small streams and dark green pools is a popular picnic spot. It is possible to camp here by arrangement with park authorities.

Than Bok Koranee is also famous for its cave systems. **Tham Lot** is a cave complex full of winding passages and stalactites and stalagmites and can be reached by boat from the Bho Tho pier in Ao Luk. The nearby **Tham Hua Kalok**, is well known for its 70 odd ancient cave paintings

Huay To Waterfall at Khao Phanom Bencha National Park

depicting humans and animals and dating back to over two millennia. Other well-known caves in the area include **Tham Sa Yuan Thong**, which has a natural spring; **Tham Phet**, or Diamond Cave, which derives its name from its shimmering rock walls; and **Tham Song Phi Nong**, where skeletal remains of humans, ancient pottery, bronze tools, and earrings were discovered.

Than Bok Koranee can be easily reached by bus or car. The best way to explore the park's mangrove swamps is by longtail boat as they are virtually impassable by foot apart from some places where a boardwalk is constructed. Visitors can also hike along marked trekking trails.

A clouded leopard cub

Khao Phanom Bencha National Park ❹

อุทยานแห่งชาติเขาพนมเบญจา

Road Map B5. Park HQ off Hwy 4, 12 miles (19 km) N of Krabi. *Park HQ (0-7566-0716).* *dawn to dusk daily.* **www**.dnp.go.th

This 20 sq mile (52 sq km) national park comprising tropical rain forest is named after the five-shouldered peak of Khao Phanom Bencha, which rises to a height of 4,470 ft (1,397 m).

Despite illegal logging and poaching, the park's rain forest still holds at least 156 species of birds, including the white-crowned hornbill and the striped wren-babbler. Other wildlife includes the Asiatic black bear, wild boar, clouded leopard, and smaller mammals such as the binturong, and serow. The thundering Nam Tok Huay To, or Huay To Waterfall and Nam Tok Huay Sadeh, or Huay Sadeh Waterfall are located less than 2 miles (3 km) from the park headquarters. Park authorities can arrange treks to the Khao Phanom Bencha peak. The difficult climb is compensated by the lovely view.

Visitors admiring limestone formations inside the extensive cave system in Than Bok Koranee National Park

Tha Pom ❺

ท่าปอม

Road Map B5. 21 miles (34 km) NW of Krabi. *TAT, Krabi (0-7562-2163).* *dawn to dusk daily.*

A peat swamp and forest, Tha Pom runs from various sources which originate from a pool called Chong Phra Kaew, along a natural waterway. This waterway is locally referred to as Khlong Song Nam, meaning two types of water canals. Here, freshwater meets seawater at high tide, and Lumphi palms *(Eleiodoxa conferta)* grow alongside thick mangroves. The area is best explored by hired riverboat, although a raised wooden walkway has also been built through parts of the forest, running a circular course for some 2,250 ft (686 m). Signs along the way, in English and Thai, explain the natural ecology of the region. Wooden chairs are placed at intervals for visitors to sit back and take in the pristine beauty of the area. Another way to explore the area is in a hired canoe.

Longtail boats frequenting the waterway along the mangroves of Tha Pom

Mangroves ❻

สวนรุกขชาติกระบี่

Road Map B5. 3 miles (5 km) W of Krabi. *TAT, Krabi (0-7562-2163).*

Home to several types of birds, fish, crabs, shrimps, and mollusks, the mangroves of Krabi are easily accessible and among the most beautiful tracts of forest in Thailand. These mangroves have remained remarkably intact and are important nesting grounds for hundreds of species of bird and are among the most frequently visited areas by enthusiastic bird-watchers. They also provide shelter for a variety of land and marine animals, especially birds such as the mangrove blue flycatcher. A visit to the Krabi mangrove swamps is easily organized; half-day boat tours to nearby estuaries are also widely available. Boats frequent the area almost every hour from Krabi and are available for hire.

Fortunately, the ecological significance of the Krabi mangrove forests has been recognized by the Thai people and plans for further development of Krabi as a deep-water port are currently under regular review. These reviews are aimed at protecting this unique environment.

Fishing farm owned by local fishermen in Ko Klang

Ko Klang ❼

เกาะกลาง

Road Map B5. 2 miles (3 km) S of Krabi. *from Krabi.* *TAT, Krabi (0-7562-2163).*

Among the few remaining non-commercialized islands in Thailand, Ko Klang, or Central Island, is situated across the Krabi River estuary a short distance from Krabi. Clearly visible from the town, the island is a pristine tropical paradise ringed by thick mangrove swamps and can be easily reached by a hired riverboat or longtail boat from Krabi. There are a few beautiful coral reefs off the shore, although they have been damaged by traffic in the water. Offshore swimming is another good option for visitors. Quite a few of the local mangrove swamp tours stop by at the island for an hour or so, but those interested in learning more about Krabi fishermen, boatmen, and their families, can arrange a homestay visit through one of the many travel agencies in Krabi. There are three small fishing villages on this predominantly Thai Muslim island and locals offer homestays including accommodations, food, and hired bicycles or motorcycles.

For hotels and restaurants in this region see pp308–11 and pp331–3

Mangrove Ecosystems

The coastal estuaries of southern Thailand are home to dense mangrove forests – a natural haven for all kinds of wildlife. These ecosystems once covered much of the coast, but over the past five decades, many have been destroyed. Those that survive are now being brought under conservation programs. Mangrove species are the only trees to have adapted to the inhospitable conditions of these muddy intertidal zones. However, this vital ecosystem is home to many fish, crabs, mollusks, shrimps, as well as wild birds such as the ruddy kingfisher, mangrove pitta, the white-bellied sea eagle, and the masked fin-foot. Larger animals living in the swamps include the dugong or sea cow, macaque monkeys, lizards, and endangered sea turtles.

White-bellied sea eagle

CROSS SECTION OF A MANGROVE LEVEE

This is a typical gradation of trees in a mangrove forest. At high tide, small fish and invertebrates feed in the nutrient-rich waters around the roots. At low tide, when the roots are exposed, crabs and wading birds scour the mudflats for trapped fish and decaying matter.

The soil in this region is rich in nutrients and away from direct wave action.

Pneumatophores or finger-like projections are used for "breathing".

Excess salt is excreted via the shedding of leaves.

Stilt roots grow down from the trunk and absorb oxygen.

Yellow-ringed cat snakes *are adept swimmers and tree climbers. They rest by day and hunt for fish, frogs, and other small game by night.*

Small-clawed otters *are common to this area. They eat crustaceans such as mollusks and crabs.*

Crab-eating macaques *inhabit mangroves and are good swimmers. They forage for crabs at low tide and also subsist on seeds.*

Male fiddler crabs *use their one enlarged claw to select tiny organic particles to eat. Their colorful claws are also used in courtship displays.*

DESTRUCTION OF MANGROVE FORESTS

Despite the provision of a national mangrove management program (set up in 1946), some 60 percent of Thailand's mangroves have been cleared since the 1960s. This loss of habitat has not only decimated marine life, but is also contributing to coastal erosion. Tiger shrimp farming, charcoal production, and road and harbor construction in former mangrove areas have further exacerbated this destruction and are responsible for the loss of biodiversity in this region.

Fish farm in a mangrove area

Krabi Coast 8

ชายฝั่งกระบี่

Located on the peninsular mainland to the east and south of Phuket, Krabi province comprises more than 1,800 sq miles (4,662 sq km) of forested hills along with more than 62 miles (100 km) of coastline and an estimated 200 islands, all facing the aquamarine waters of the Andaman Sea. Much of the coastline is studded with steep, impenetrable and uniquely-shaped karst outcrops which offer caving, trekking, and some of the finest rock-climbing in the world. The area is also known for its fantastic snorkeling, scuba diving, and sea-kayaking opportunities. Despite rapid development, the Krabi Coast is still largely off the beaten track.

Display of fossilized seashells in limestone slabs, Susaan Hoi

Susaan Hoi

สุสานหอย

13 miles (21 km) SW of Krabi.

Located on the southeastern extremity of the Krabi Coast, Susaan Hoi is easily accessible by longtail boat from Krabi. Also known as the Shell Cemetery, this spot is a fantastic agglomeration of thousands of seashells that date back at least 75 million years. It was originally a large freshwater swamp, home to a variety of mollusks. These have petrified over the passage of time accompanied due to changes on the earth's surface and fused into large limestone slabs that now project into the sea. A small museum by the site explains the history of these fossils. There are also some souvenir shops selling shells and other local handicrafts. Visitors to this spot can enjoy the secluded stretches, offering good views of islands.

Hat Rai Leh East

หาดไร่เลย์ตะวันออก

7 miles (11 km) SW of Krabi.

Hat Rai Leh comprises two separate beaches – Hat Rai Leh East and Hat Rai Leh West. Both can be easily accessed by longtail boat from Krabi. The eastern stretch is attractive at high tide, but less appealing at low tide when wide muddy flats are exposed. The more developed of the two beaches, Hat Rai Leh East offers a wide range of accommodations, including beach bungalows. Visitors can explore the mangroves or practice rock climbing on the limestone outcrops on the beach. Many travelers prefer to stay at this beach and walk over to Hat Rai Leh West and Hat Tham Phra Nang during the day.

Climbers scale the bolted outcrops along Hat Rai Leh East

Visitors sunbathing on the pristine sands at Hat Rai Leh West

Hat Rai Leh West

หาดไร่เลย์ตะวันตก

10 miles (16 km) SW of Krabi.

A gently curving stretch of white sand, Hat Rai Leh West faces west across the Andaman Sea offering spectacular sunset views. More attractive but somewhat more expensive than the eastern flank, the beach has little by way of budget accommodation and although it attracts visitors from all over the coast, most choose not to stay here. For those willing to splurge, there are plenty of mid-range and upscale places, as well as some excellent seafood restaurants and bars. It is also the main landing point for longtail water taxis from Ao Nang. The rocky limestone outcrops particular to this region extend into Hat Rai Leh West offering opportunities for climbers of all levels. There are plenty of local companies that rent out guides and equipment. Sea-kayaking around the limestone cliffs is another very popular sport.

For hotels and restaurants in this region see pp308–11 and pp331–3

Hat Tham Phra Nang

หาดพระนาง

9 miles (14 km) SW of Krabi.

Located at the southern end of the small peninsula that divides Hat Rai Leh East from Hat Rai Leh West, Hat Tham Phra Nang is considered one of the loveliest spots in southern Thailand. The white sand beach is sheltered by a variety of karst outcrops.

The limestone cliffs that surround this area have made it a world-famous rock climbing destination. The forbiddingly sheer **Taiwand Wall** and its extensions dominate Hat Tham Phra Nang and have hundreds of routes – from the simple to truly demanding. They are marked by bolts fixed in the rock where climbers can attach their ropes. However, corrosive weather conditions may threaten the integrity of the bolts, thus visitors should take suitable safety precautions. These spectacular outcrops are the highlight of the Krabi experience offering unparalleled climbing opportunities as well as stunning views.

Fertility shrine dedicated to Phra Nang, Tham Phra Nang

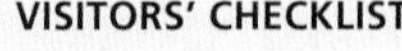

Road Map B5. 2 miles (3 km) W of Krabi. *10 miles (16 km) NE of Krabi.* *from Krabi.* *TAT, Krabi (0-7562-2163).*

Tham Phra Nang

ถ้ำพระนาง

9 miles (14 km) SW of Krabi.

Located along the eastern end of Hat Tham Phra Nang is Tham Phra Nang, which means Cave of the Revered Lady. This cave is dedicated to the memory of an Indian princess who supposedly drowned offshore centuries ago. A fertility cult has developed around her and locals have set up a small shrine within Tham Phra Nang. Packed with red-tipped phalluses placed here by fishermen praying for a good catch, the shrine is also revered by women, especially expectant mothers and those who want to be blessed with a child. Near the cave is a marked path leading to the small lagoon of Sa Phra Nang, which means Lady's Bathing Place, and offers a good view across Hat Rai Leh East.

Longtail boats functioning as makeshift restaurants, Hat Tham Phra Nang

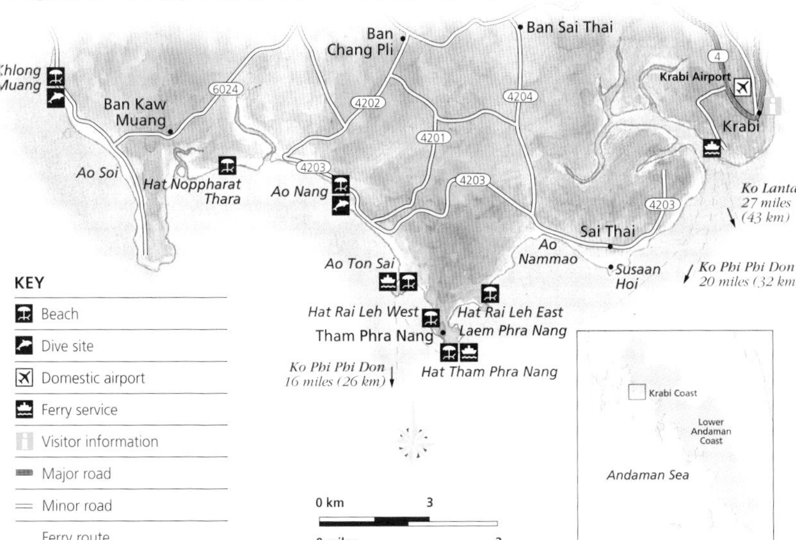

Limestone karsts and thick scrub dominating the isolated beach at Ao Ton Sai

Ao Ton Sai
อ่าวต้นไทร
11 miles (18 km) SW of Krabi.

The least developed of the beaches around Ao Nang, Ao Ton Sai is also the least expensive. It is possible to reach Ao Ton Sai from the western end of the coast on foot, but visitors should be prepared to walk through sticky mudflats. There is also access from Hat Rai Leh West to the south, but this is made uncomfortable and potentially dangerous by jagged rocks studded with sharp-shelled clams. Like the nearby beaches of Hat Rai Leh East, Hat Rai Leh West, and Hat Tham Phra Nang, Ao Ton Sai can be best reached by boat. Hat Ton Sai is not a standout beach like Hat Rai Leh West or Hat Tham Phra Nang; it is often littered with flotsam and the bay is backed by mangroves rather than the more common coconut palms. However, the view from the bay is quite magnificent and includes sheer, karst outcrops. Accommodation options, as well as drinking and dining facilities on this beach are appreciably cheaper than at the more upscale Hat Rai Leh West. Many travelers often stay here, heading out to the nearby beaches, such as Hat Tham Phra Nang, during the day and returning to eat and enjoy the fine sunset views across the Andaman Sea.

Massage huts and restaurants along the beach road at Ao Nang

Ao Nang
อ่าวนาง
13 miles (21 km) W of Krabi.

A beautiful and busy bay, Ao Nang is just west of Hat Tham Phra Nang, and is separated from Ao Ton Sai by a rocky headland. Originally a small fishing hamlet popular with the backpacking crowd, the bay has grown into prominence in recent times. Easily accessible by road from Krabi, Ao Nang is extremely popular during peak season with many overseas visitors, especially Europeans. This beach is one of the liveliest spots on the Krabi Coast.

The huge tourist influx has led to the development of all kinds of facilities including a variety of accommodations ranging from upscale resorts to budget guesthouses, as well as many restaurants, bars, travel agents, and dive operators. Highway 4203, the main road from Krabi, is lined with hotels, mini-markets, and dive shops as it enters Ao Nang from the east. The nightlife here is vibrant without being sleazy. There are bars with live music, pool tables, and even a McDonalds outlet making this beach lively and full of activity. Visitors looking for a quieter beach, can make their way to nearby Hat Rai Leh West, a 10-minute boat ride from Ao Nang.

Hat Noppharat Thara

หาดนพรัตน์ ธารา

11 miles (18 km) W of Krabi.

A popular picnic spot that is just around the corner from Ao Nang, Hat Noppharat Thara is a less-developed extension of the beach at Ao Nang and can be easily accessed on foot from the bay. This quiet 2-mile (3-km) long casuarina-lined beach offers magnificent views of the area's massive karst outcrops. Formerly called Hat Khlong Haeng, meaning Dried Canal Beach, Hat Noppharat Thara derives its name from a canal which divides the beach into two and dries up at low tide.

The beach is similar to that at Ao Nang without its resorts, bars, or crowds. However, Hat Noppharat Thara's proximity to the latter beach means that it is a matter of time before this area develops as a commercial spot. At low tide the waters are too shallow for swimming, but ideal for walking across to the tiny offshore island of Ko Kao Pak Klong for a good view of the bay. This area is famous for its seafood especially *hoi chak teen* (wing shells), a local delicacy whose shells are also sold as souvenirs.

Colorful longtail boats anchored off Hat Noppharat Thara

Coconut palms along the sheltered beach at Hat Khlong Muang

Hat Khlong Muang

หาดคลองม่วง

14 miles (22 km) W of Krabi.

Shielded from Ao Nang and Laem Phra Nang by a long, rocky headland, Hat Khlong Muang presents the luxurious side of the Krabi Coast. This beach can be easily reached by longtail boats from Ao Nang or *songthaews* or hired cars from Krabi. Once a backpackers' destination, the development of the luxurious Krabi Sheraton *(see p310)* has transformed this pristine stretch on the Andaman Sea into an upscale resort offering all kinds of facilities. The palm-lined beach is interspersed with rocky boulders and a portion of the reef is exposed at low tide; the offshore islands only add to the visual appeal of staying here. Dive schools and travel agents abound in Hat Khlong Muang and can arrange scuba diving, snorkeling, and sea-kayaking trips to the offshore islands. Places to eat include sundowner bars, beach cafés, and noodle bars. In sharp contrast, the resorts offer luxurious restaurants serving international cuisine as well as gourmet Thai food.

THE LEGEND OF PHRA NANG

According to legend, Phra Nang was an Indian princess who drowned in the Andaman Sea many centuries ago. Her spirit supposedly inhabited the cave that is now known as Tham Phra Nang *(see p249)*. In the past, locals created a simple shrine here and left offerings in the form of carved *lingas* (phallic symbols). Over time, the status of this shrine rose, becoming associated with fertility and good fortune, and the cave itself became a symbol of the female sexual organ. Residents of this area believe that any carved wooden *linga* cast into the sea off the Krabi Coast will eventually find its way to Tham Phra Nang. A minor deity in this region, Phra Nang is the patron saint of women who want to conceive as well as of fishermen out for a good day's haul. She is believed to be capable of great anger and, according to popular belief, insults to her shrine cause damage to those involved. Thus, locals and outsiders generally seek her blessings before undertaking any project in the area.

Phallic symbols as offerings at the shrine of Phra Nang

Ko Phi Phi 9

เกาะพีพี

Cashew fruit

This archipelago comprises six islands set like scattered jewels amid the azure waters of the Andaman Sea. Ko Phi Phi Don is the main island, comprising two land masses joined by a narrow palm-fringed isthmus lined with restaurants, bars, and guesthouses. The beautiful and uninhabited Ko Phi Phi Leh lies to its south while the other islands are just tiny limestone outcrops. Nature lovers will find a haven in the surrounding coral beds teeming with marine life. Tall cliffs and underwater reefs protect the islands from the rough seas. Ko Phi Phi is renowned for its beauty, drawing visitors from all over the world.

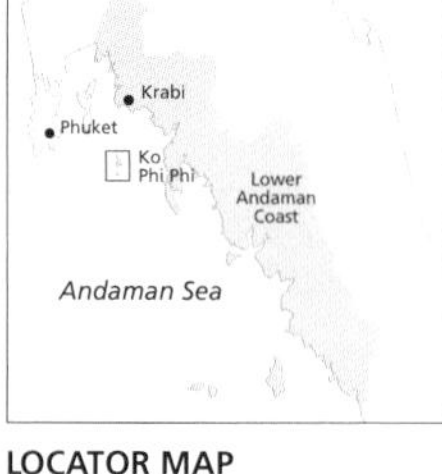

LOCATOR MAP

Area illustrated

★ **View of Twin Bays**

These are spectacular view of Ko Phi Phi Don and the twin bays of Ao Lo Dalum and Ao Ton Sai from the famous viewpoint at the eastern end of the island. The best views are during sunrise and sunset.

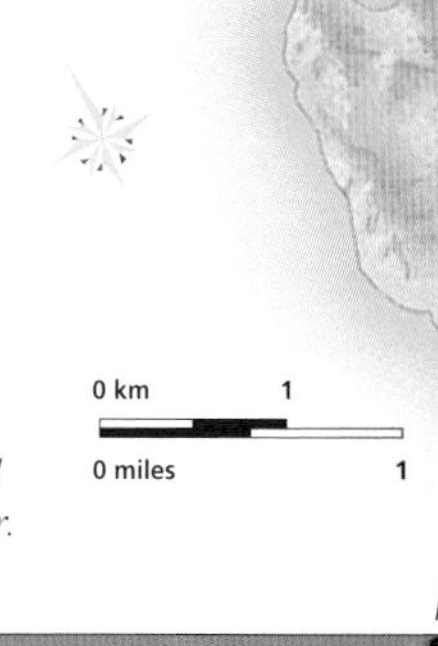

Beach Activities

Ko Phi Phi is renowned for diving and snorkeling among its superb corals and vibrant marine life. Sea-kayaking and rock climbing are also popular.

★ **Ban Ton Sai**

The largest settlement on Ko Phi Phi, Ban Ton Sai also serves as a ferry port. Once a small Muslim fishing village, today it is a hive of restaurants, bars, and hotels.

STAR SIGHTS

★ View of Twin Bays

★ Ban Ton Sai

★ Ao Maya

For hotels and restaurants in this region see pp308–11 and pp331–3

DANNY BOYLE'S *THE BEACH*

Hollywood director Danny Boyle decided upon Ao Maya in Ko Phi Phi Leh as the perfect location for filming Alex Garland's *The Beach* (2000). The movie, about a commune of young people living on a secret island, shows them partying and living a hedonistic life. The film, however, ran into trouble with accusations of environmental damage and profiteering during its making. 20th Century Fox and their local agents were sued by Thai courts for alleged damage to the bay. Nonetheless, the movie was instrumental in bringing Ao Maya into the limelight, and has led to a substantial increase in the number of visitors.

Taking a shot of Ao Maya during the filming of Danny Boyle's *The Beach*

VISITORS' CHECKLIST

Road Map B5. 25 miles (40 km) S of Krabi. *7,700.* *from Phuket or Krabi.* *TAT, Phuket (0-7621-2213).* *Chinese New Year (Feb), Songkran (Apr).* **www**.phi-phi.com

Colorful Coral Reefs
Ko Phi Phi's surrounding waters have several renowned dive sites with a variety of soft corals, anemones, and even sharks.

Hiking trails cut through the eastern half of Ko Phi Phi Don.

KEY

- Beach
- Dive site
- Watersports
- Viewpoint
- Ferry service
- Trail
- Ferry route

Viking Cave
This cave has ancient carvings of Chinese junks resembling Viking-style vessels. These petroglyphs, dating back a few centuries, confirm the legends of Viking boats visiting the Andaman coast.

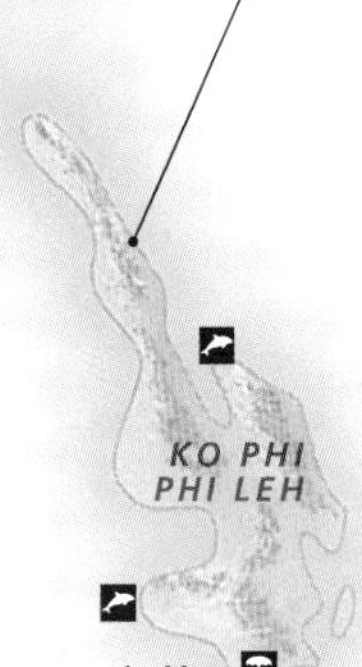

★ Ao Maya
Popularized by the movie The Beach, *Ao Maya is one of the most beautiful bays in Ko Phi Phi sheltered by cliffs on three sides, with excellent snorkeling in the surrounding coral reefs.*

Exploring Ko Phi Phi

Sign at dive shop

Although Ko Phi Phi consists of six islands, most of them, including Ko Phi Phi Leh, are uninhabited and undeveloped limestone outcrops. Ko Phi Phi Don, the main island with some settlements is small enough to be explored on foot. There are no motorized vehicles or proper roads, and visitors have to hike to get to the remote parts. However, it is possible to access most of the coast by longtail boats or ferries from the Ban Ton Sai pier. Ko Phi Phi Leh on the other hand has no walking paths or marked trails and the only means of accessing this island is by boat from Ban Ton Sai.

Ban Ton Sai

บ้านต้นไทร

As the only settlement of any size on the archipelago, Ban Ton Sai is the de facto capital of Ko Phi Phi as well as the commercial hub of the island. Having developed out of a small Muslim fishing village, this is the only ferry port with links to the mainland. Located along Ao Ton Sai, the village covers the narrow isthmus connecting the two parts of Ko Phi Phi Don. Ban Ton Sai is a crowded hive of small streets packed with foreign visitors as well as Thais from the mainland. Although, it was badly damaged by the 2004 tsunami, the village has bounced back, busier than ever. Despite promises from the authorities to control unrestricted building, new resorts keep springing up on this island, which is part of an ecologically sensitive zone.

Everyone visiting Ko Phi Phi passes through Ban Ton Sai, and many choose to stay here for its facilities including hotels, restaurants, and bars. The village is also home to a bank, a police station, a post office, and a clinic. This is an ideal place for visitors to set up base to explore the rest of Ko Phi Phi.

A narrow street lined with shops and restaurants, Ban Ton Sai

Ao Lo Dalum

อ่าวโละดาลัม

Immediately north of Ban Ton Sai, Ao Lo Dalum is a gorgeous bay fringed by a fine beach with lush green coconut palms. Within a stone's throw of bustling Ban Ton Sai, this beach is busy, attracting day-trippers and visitors on a tight schedule. Holiday-makers on long stays usually have more time to explore the less accessible beaches on the other islands. Ao Lo Dalum is picturesque at high tide but somewhat less appealing at low tide, when the mudflats stretch out endlessly. A steep trail at the eastern end of the bay follows a path across the island's spine and leads up to the island's famous viewpoint. Located at a height of 610 ft (186 m) above sea level, the viewpoint offers a vista spanning the narrow isthmus and its twin bays.

Limestone cliffs rising from the calm waters of Ao Lo Dalum

Hat Yao

หาดยาว

Located on the southeastern shore of Ko Phi Phi, Hat Yao is sheltered by a small, rocky promontory to the east. A world-class destination, this beach is a place of exquisite beauty – the sand is fine, white, and powdery, and the surrounding waters are shallow and warm, swarming with all kinds of colorful fish, which live in the rich coral reef. Hat Yao attracts many travelers and the beach is generally quite crowded. Also present are numerous vendors selling everything from cold drinks to a Thai massage. It is easily reached by boat from Ban Ton Sai or on foot via a narrow track leading east from the village.

Hat Ranti

หาดรันตี

Tucked away from the busy Ban Ton Sai, Hat Ranti is one of three linked beaches on the east coast of Ko Phi Phi Don. It offers basic accommodations, affordable restaurants, and is well suited for budget travelers. Hat Ranti is slightly off the beaten track, and can be reached by a 45-minute walk on the trail across the spine of the main island, or by longtail boats from Ban Ton Sai. This beach with its rocky outcrops and calm waters is a peaceful getaway which is perfect for a picnic or a day trip. However, visitors should bring their own diving gear and other supplies as this beach has minimal facilities.

Ao Lo Bakao

อ่าวโละบาเกา

Located on the eastern coast of Ko Phi Phi Don, Ao Lo Bakao is a long, curved bay facing the mainland. This bay which is about half a mile (1 km) north of Hat Ranti, is separated from Ban Ton Sai and the rest of the island by a rocky spine. Ao Lo Bakao can be reached on foot via a single narrow trail. Yet, its beach has developed as an upscale spot, characterized by expensive, well-appointed resort accommodations. The lovely 2,880-ft (878-m) white sand beach is well-served by restaurants and bars without being overcrowded. This rather exclusive bay attracts upper-class Thais, and is a popular honeymoon spot.

Snorkeling among the corals off Hat Laem Thong

Hat Laem Thong

หาดแหลมทอง

A lovely strip of sand on Ko Phi Phi Don's northern-most tip, Hat Laem Thong is a jumping-off point for nearby offshore islands. This area is also among the best diving spots in the archipelago. Thus, despite being quite far from Ban Ton Sai, Hat Laem Thong is busy with a constant flow of divers who come to explore the rich coral reefs. The beach is easily accessed by boat from Ban Ton Sai. Hat Laem Thong has quite a few upscale resorts including the Zeavola *(see p309)*, as well as shops, restaurants, and diving agencies. Visitors can go deep-sea fishing or even take cookery courses.

Cave paintings depicting ancient ships at Ko Phi Phi Leh

PIRATES OF THE ANDAMAN COAST

Rock paintings of Arab, Chinese, and European vessels in Ko Phi Phi Leh's caves may be evidence of the existence of pirates on the Andaman Coast. Studies suggest that these paintings were made by the pirates while hiding in these remote spots to escape bad weather, transfer cargo, or avoid authorities. The drawings are believed to date back at least a few centuries. The Andaman Coast with its many islands, coves, and inlets is a perfect vantage point and hideout. The theory is further proven as the nearby Straits of Malacca continues to be plagued by piracy even today.

Ko Phi Phi Leh

เกาะพีพีเล

Only a quarter of the size of Ko Phi Phi Don and much less accessible, Ko Phi Phi Leh is a 25-minute boat ride from Ban Ton Sai. Completely uninhabited with pristine coves and bays, and rich offshore coral reefs, the island's main attraction is its startling beauty and isolation. However, this has changed since Danny Boyle put the island on the world map with his movie *The Beach* (2000) starring Leonardo Di Caprio. Since then a number of visitors have come here to experience this tropical paradise as captured on celluloid. The island's greatest attraction is Ao Maya, located along the southwestern coast. This exquisite bay offers fine swimming and snorkeling. Apart from tourists, Ko Phi Phi Leh also has regular local visitors. These are the daring climbers who engage in the swiftlet nest trade. This is a coveted ingredient used to make bird's nest soup, an exotic delicacy and among the most expensive animal products. Intrepid climbers scale sheer rock faces and caves on the island to gather these rare products.

In ancient times, Ko Phi Phi Leh was a mooring spot for fishermen and possibly, pirates. The Viking Cave on the northern coast has petroglyphs of Chinese-style junks on its walls, which visiting Europeans likened to Viking ships.

Visitors enjoying a boat ride in the pristine waters off Ko Phi Phi Leh

Vast expanse of coral reef in the shallow waters off Ko Phi Phi Don ▷

Excavated pottery displayed at Wat Khlong Thom Nua Museum

Wat Khlong Thom Nua Museum ⑩

พิพิธภัณฑ์คลองท่อมเหนือ

Road Map C5. 26 miles (42 km) SE of Krabi. *TAT, Krabi (0-7562-2163).*

Southeast of Krabi along Highway 4, the small town of Khlong Thom is the site of one of the earliest human civilizations in Thailand yet discovered. Excavations in this town, set amid fertile rice paddies and fruit orchards, have revealed stone tools, bronze implements, metal coins, shards of pottery, and colored beads dating back almost five millennia. These exhibits are now on display in the Wat Khlong Thom Nua Museum in Tambon Khlong Thom Tai, about half a mile from the Khlong Thom district office. Ideal for history lovers, the museum is popular with visitors to the area.

Khao Nor Chuchi Wildlife Sanctuary ⑪

เขตรักษาพันธุ์สัตว์ป่านอจู้จี้

Road Map C5. 38 miles (60 km) SE of Krabi. *TAT, Krabi (0-7562-2163). 8am–5pm daily.*

One of the largest and most important wildlife sanctuaries in the Krabi province, Khao Nor Chuchi Wildlife Sanctuary lies to the southeast of Krabi town in a small area of lowland tropical forest. This area, which extends to nearly 71 sq miles (184 sq km), is surrounded by lush green rice paddies, palm oil and rubber plantations, and other arable crops. Popular with birdwatchers, the Khao Nor Chuchi Wildlife Sanctuary is home to the Gurney's pitta, an endangered species once thought to be extinct, but rediscovered in very small numbers both here and across the border in remote parts of southern Myanmar. Other resident birds include the vernal hanging parrot and the Chinese pond heron. There are several wooded walking trails within the forest, the most popular being the 2-mile (3-km) long **Tung Tieo Forest Trail**. This trail winds through the thick woods, leading to two freshwater pools, one of which is called Sra Morakot, or Emerald Pool. These pools are ideal for swimming and make great picnic spots.

Wooded Tung Tieo Forest Trail, Khao Nor Chuchi Wildlife Sanctuary

Ko Si Boya ⑫

เกาะสีบอยา

Road Map B5. 19 miles (31 km) S of Krabi. *1,000. from Ban Laem Kruat. TAT, Krabi (0-7562-2163).*

Located just off the Krabi coast and accessible by boat from Ban Laem Kruat, Ko Si Boya is an escape-from-it-all retreat. Of the 1,000 people living on the island, most are local Muslims working as fishermen or on rubber plantations. There are about five small settlements on the island, all connected by narrow, unpaved tracks, ideal for bicycling or walking. The main attractions, however, are

Taking a refreshing dip in the freshwater pool, Sra Morakot, Khao Nor Chuchi Wildlife Sanctuary

For hotels and restaurants in this region see pp308–11 and pp331–3

the isolated, undeveloped beaches and mangrove forests. The island offers a few simple and reasonably priced bungalows, and some restaurants, and shops. Ko Si Boya has little to offer by way of nightlife, but visitors have plenty of quieter options to choose from – swimming, sunbathing, reading, or relaxing. There is limited electricity on the island and almost every bungalow establishment has its own generator-powered electricity supply. Snorkeling enthusiasts can kayak to a small island called Ko Kah just offshore from Ko Si Boya, where the clear waters make snorkeling an exciting and rewarding experience.

Expansive green cover on isolated Ko Si Boya

Brightly colored longtail boat, docked in the waters off Ko Jum

Ko Jum ⓭

เกาะจำ

Road Map B5. 24 miles (39 km) S of Krabi. *3,000.* *from Ban Laem Kruat.* *TAT, Krabi (0-7562-2163).* **www.** kohjumonline.com

Yet another quiet retreat, the beautiful island of Ko Jum is divided into two, with the mountainous and rugged northern part being referred to as Ko Pu, or Crab Island, by the locals. Ko Jum, with its small population of 3,000, has an overwhelming majority of Thai Muslims, although there are also some small and isolated sea gypsy settlements. The main settlement is at Ban Ko Jum on the island's southern tip, while the best beaches are on its western shore. Visitors to Ko Jum must remember to dress appropriately on the beach, keeping in mind the sentiments of the resident Muslims.

More developed than Ko Si Boya, Ko Jum has better accommodation facilities, although electricity supply on this island too is limited. Most bungalows manage their own supply through generators. An island getaway without the touts and go-go bars, Ko Jum's low-key attractions include swimming, reading, and sunbathing during the day and enjoying a quiet meal and drinks at one of the few beachside bars at night. Transport around the island is by foot, bicycle, or on hired motorcycle taxis.

Ko Bubu ⓮

เกาะบูบู

Road Map C5. 44 miles (70 km) SE of Krabi. *from Ko Lanta.* *TAT, Krabi (0-7562-2163).*

A privately owned islet covered by thick woods and little more than half a mile (1 km) across, Ko Bubu can be easily traversed in about half-an-hour on foot. This pretty island, however, is closed during the height of the rainy season from June to September. Ko Bubu's only resort, Bubu Island Resort, offers basic albeit comfortable accommodations in its bungalows, as well as simple food. Longtail boats are available from Ko Lanta *(see pp260–3)*, but reservations must be made in advance.

Bubu Island Resort, set in thick woods on the private islet of Ko Bubu

Ko Lanta ⓯

เกาะลันตา

A group of 50 islets dominated by two main islands – Ko Lanta Yai, or Big Ko Lanta and Ko Lanta Noi, or Small Ko Lanta – Ko Lanta has only recently developed as a holiday spot. An erstwhile destination for hippies and backpackers, the island is now rapidly becoming an upscale resort. On offer are miles of sandy beaches, sapphire waters, reasonably priced accommodations, good restaurants, and watering holes. While Ko Lanta Noi remains largely deserted for the present, by comparison, the more developed island of Ko Lanta Yai has a good surfaced road which runs down most of the island's western coast. Although the eastern coast, with thick forests and mangrove swamps, is less accessible, it is a great place for bird-watching and kayaking.

Main street in Ban Sala Dan, packed with tour agents and utility stores

Ban Saḷa Dan

บ้านศาลาด่าน

Located near the northern tip of Ko Lanta Yai, Ban Sala Dan is the main town in the Ko Lanta archipelago. The ferry arrival and departure point for destinations such as Ko Phi Phi, Phuket, Krabi, and Trang, it is also the main tourist center for the entire district. Despite the amenities, however, Ban Sala Dan is a fairly laid-back fishing village which is now increasingly dedicated to tourism. Visitors will find a number of tour agencies, vehicle rentals, banks, ATMs, medical clinics and pharmacies, Internet cafés, and shops here, along with a post office, reasonable accommodations, and restaurants. Even so, few people opt to stay in Ban Sala Dan, preferring to relax on the long row of beaches further south, and coming to the village only for necessities.

Hat Khlong Dao

หาดคลองดาว

1 mile (2 km) S of Ban Sala Dan.

The longest and most popular beach on Ko Lanta, Hat Khlong Dao is blessed with golden sands that rise into low, vegetation-covered dunes. The beach itself is wide and a perfect place for sunbathing and swimming, which is quite safe here. Hat Khlong Dao, relatively uncrowded and friendly, draws vacationing families seeking a relaxing stay within walking distance from town. There are plenty of mid-range as well as some budget accommodations available, and the beach strip is home to numerous restaurants, cafés, and small bars. While there are no diving or snorkeling opportunities in the immediate vicinity of the beach, dive shops at Hat Khlong Dao arrange diving trips offshore, as well as visits to the area's many mangrove forests and local *chao lae* or sea gypsy communities.

Ao Phra-Ae

อ่าวพระแอะ

2 miles (3 km) S of Ban Sala Dan.

Located just south of Hat Khlong Dao, beyond a small headland, the beach at Ao Phra-Ae is 3 miles (5 km) long. Blessed with crisp white sand and backed by casuarina trees, it was once a backpackers' retreat. Today, however, Ao Phra-Ae is well developed and quite similar to Hat Khlong Dao, although a longer walk from Ban Sala Dan. The beach offers inexpensive accommodations, guesthouses, restaurants, and cafés for the budget traveler. However, more upscale resorts are presently under construction here. Ao Phra-Ae can be easily reached on hired *songthaews* that ply the route on the island's west coast road, running behind the row of casuarina trees marking the end of the beach. Motorcycles and bicycles are also available at rental shops near the beach.

Chang beer

Hat Khlong Khong

หาดคลองโขง

4 miles (6 km) S of Ban Sala Dan.

A fine stretch of crisp white sand, Hat Khlong Khong is nearly 3 miles (5 km) long. Located close to two small fishing villages, Ban Phu Klom and Ban Khlong Khong, the beach is ideal for budget

Beautiful beach at Ao Phra-Ae, fringed by swaying casuarina trees

For hotels and restaurants in this region see pp308–11 and pp331–3

One of the Viewpoint Hill restaurants, offering lovely views of the area

VISITORS' CHECKLIST

Road Map B5. 42 miles (68 km) S of Krabi. *28,000.* *from Krabi, Phuket, and Ko Phi Phi.* *TAT, Krabi (0-7562-2163).* *Laanta Lanta Festival (Mar).*

travelers, as it offers cheap bungalow accommodations and simple, friendly bars and restaurants. At the same time, its distance from Ban Sala Dan ensures the beach's tranquility. While Hat Khlong Khong is perfect for sunbathing, the offshore waters are rather shallow and rocky, and only suitable for swimming during high tide. There are also good snorkeling opportunities when the tide is in.

Viewpoint Hill

จุดชมวิว

6 miles (10 km) SE of Ban Sala Dan.

Set in the middle of Ko Lanta Yai, close to its geographical center, Viewpoint Hill marks the highest point on the island. It is reached by the road running between Hat Khlong Nin on the west coast and Ban Si Raya on the east coast. The views from this vantage point are stunning; they encompass the mangrove fringed east coast of Ko Lanta Yai as well as the many smaller islets scattered across Ko Lanta Marine National Park *(see p263)* and the Trang *(see p264)* coastline in the distance. Viewpoint Hill is a popular spot to watch mesmerizing sunrises and sunsets over the Andaman Sea. Visitors can enjoy a meal while taking in panoramic views across the sea at any of the two picturesquely located Viewpoint Hill restaurants nearby.

Hat Khlong Nin

หาดคลองนิน

6 miles (10 km) S of Ban Sala Dan.

A delightful stretch of beach with soft white sand, Hat Khlong Nin has a distinct appeal for youngsters. The beach is lined with palm trees, casuarinas, and the occasional frangipani. Although lesser developed than the beaches to the north of Ko Lanta, Hat Khlong Hin offers reasonably priced accommodations and food. The nightlife, focused on a number of small and unpretentious bars playing music till late, draws revelers to the beach. Swimming is safe here and visitors often stay at Hat Khlong Nin for days at a time, alternating between regular beach activities and attending one of several Thai cooking schools operating in the area.

Sunbathing on quiet, but well-equipped Hat Khlong Nin

Krabi 42 miles (68 km)
Ban Sala Dan
KO LANTA NOI
Ko Klang
Krabi
Ko Lanta
Lower Andaman Coast
Andaman Sea
Ban Phra-Ae
Ban Thung Yee Pheng
Ban Phu Klom
Ban Khlong Khong
Viewpoint Hill
Ban Khlong Nin
Tham Khao Mai Kaew
Hat Khlong Nin
Tham Seua
Ban Si Raya
Hat Khlong Nam Jud
KO LANTA YAI
Ban Khlong Hin
Hat Nui
Ao Kantiang
Ban Sang-Ga-U
Ko Kluang
Ao Khlong Jaak
Ao Mai Pai
Park HQ
Laem Tanod
0 km 2
0 miles 2

KEY

- Beach
- Dive site
- Viewpoint
- Ferry service
- Visitor information
- Major road
- Minor road
- Ferry route

Exploring the jungle trail to Tham Khao Mai Kaew

Tham Khao Mai Kaew

ถ้ำเขาไม้แก้ว

7 miles (11 km) SE of Ban Sala Dan.

Located in the wooded interior of Ko Lanta Yai, Tham Khao Mai Kaew is a complex of caverns and tunnels. The caves are reached by a 1-mile (2-km) long narrow track leading east through a rubber plantation on the road between Hat Khlong Nin and Ban Si Raya. The cave complex is extensive and potentially confusing, and can only be explored with the help of a guide. There are chambers filled with stalactites and stalagmites; small cavities which can be reached only by crawling on all fours, and a cave pool that offers a cool dip. Visitors have a choice of 1- or 2-hour tours. The tour operator in charge of the caves also offers half-day and full-day jungle treks in the vicinity.

Tham Seua

ถ้ำเสือ

7 miles (11 km) SE of Ban Sala Dan.

A smaller and less visited cave complex, Tham Seua, or Tiger Cave, is located about 1 mile (2 km) east of the coastal road between Hat Khlong Nin and Laem Tanod. The caves can be reached by a narrow trail that also leads to the headquarters of the Ko Lanta Marine National Park. Since Tham Seua is not as well organized as nearby Tham Khao Mai Kaew, visitors are free to wander through the passages at will, where several caves with stalactites, stalagmites, and still pools wait to be explored. The interior of the caves is quite cool, making them an excellent place to visit during the heat of the day.

Hat Nui

หาดนุ้ย

10 miles (16 km) S of Ban Sala Dan.

An attractive and fairly isolated beach, Hat Nui, also known as Hat Khlong Nui, is located along Ko Lanta Yai's west coast, south of Hat Khlong Nin and the junction east leading to Viewpoint Hill and Ban Si Raya. The beach is distinguished by the ecologically conscious Narima Bungalow Resort *(see p308)*. The buildings in the resort are all constructed from local, natural materials and have a quaint, rustic feel. Lush tropical jungle sweeps down to the beach from the hills behind, providing the idyllic setting for a quiet holiday. Tour operators at Hat Nui organize elephant rides up to nearby Tham Seua as well as to the surrounding jungle-covered hills.

A restaurant perched on a cliff overlooking the sea at Hat Nui

View of an upscale resort nestled among the trees at Ao Kantiang

Ao Kantiang

อ่าวกันเตียง

11 miles (18 km) S of Ban Sala Dan.

A lovely bay with a perfect white sand beach, Ao Kantiang is home to a number of upscale resorts which fight for space with other more reasonably priced budget accommodations. Although some distance away from Ban Sala Dan, Ao Kantiang is well equipped with facilities varying from travel agencies and Internet access to motorcycle and jeep rentals. The casuarina-lined beach, also has a good selection of restaurants as well as a few bars. While the beach and the bay are ideal for sunbathing and swimming, there is also a small coral reef near the northern end of the bay, considered quite good for snorkeling, especially when the tide is in. These are the only activities to indulge in, other than relaxing on the beach, observing the sunset, and enjoying a chilled drink.

Ao Khlong Jaak

อ่าวคลองจาก

12 miles (19 km) S of Ban Sala Dan.

South of Ao Kantiang the surfaced road that runs down the island's west flank deteriorates rapidly, becoming a rutted track that is difficult to negotiate even on a two-wheeler, especially during the rainy season when the unpaved roads can get very slippery. The bay south of Ao Kantiang, known as Ao Khlong Jaak, offers a varied selection of accommodations – from upscale resorts to simple places suited for those on a modest budget. It is rather off the beaten track, but readily accessible by boat from Ban Sala Dan and other points north along the coast. Ao Khlong Jaak is a good place for getting away from it all. A stay here is usually a rejuvenating and relaxing experience with little activity. The days largely involve going for a drink in a sundowner bar, followed by star gazing from the white, sandy beach.

Getting ready for kayaking on the beach at Ao Khlong Jaak

Ao Mai Pai

อ่าวไม้ไผ่

13 miles (21 km) S of Ban Sala Dan.

The southernmost beach on Ko Lanta Yai, Ao Mai Pai marks the end of the unsurfaced and rutted track leading toward the southern part of the island. A little distance inland are the headquarters for the Ko Lanta Marine National Park. The beach here is beautiful, more so because it is not too busy. An offshore coral reef, great for snorkeling especially during high tide, makes up for the lack of other activity on the beach. Ao Mai Pai offers good mid-range resort accommodations and some more reasonably priced bungalows. The shady beach lined with palms, casuarinas, and screwpine is ideal for sunbathing and taking in views across the Andaman Sea.

Ban Si Raya

บ้านศรีรายา

12 miles (19 km) SE of Ban Sala Dan.

A surprisingly attractive village, Ban Si Raya, or Old Lanta Town, is the oldest settlement in Ko Lanta, predating Ban Sala Dan by many decades. Once a marine staging post for British flagged ships sailing between Phuket, Penang, and Singapore, the town has hardly kept up with the rapid development elsewhere on the island. It retains a period charm and not much has changed here since the mid-1990s. Nevertheless, a steady trickle of visitors has necessitated the renovation and restoration of its Chinese-style shophouses. There is a small Chinese shrine facing the sea half-way down the main street, and the mosques nearby stand testimony to the presence of a thriving Thai-Muslim community. A few guesthouses cater to visitors staying overnight, but the real appeal lies in the restaurants and bars that have begun to spring up.

Tranquil beach lined with shady casuarinas and screwpine trees at Ao Mai Pai

Snorkeling in the clear waters off pretty Ko Rok Nok

Ko Lanta Marine National Park 16

พิพิธภัณฑ์ทางทะเลเกาะลันตา

Road Map B5. Park HQ 5 miles (8 km) S of Hat Nui, 44 miles (70 km) S of Krabi.
Park HQ (0-7562-9018).

Extending over 152 sq miles (394 sq km), Ko Lanta Marine National Park includes the southern tip of Ko Lanta Yai, parts of Ko Lanta Noi, and 15 smaller islands and reefs. Other islands in the park include **Ko Rok Nai** and **Ko Rok Nok**, 31 miles (50 km) south of Ko Lanta Yai; Ko Talabaeng to the east of Ko Lanta Noi with its limestone caves which are ideal for sea-kayaking; and tiny Ko Ha.

Ko Rok Nok, or Outer Rok Island, and Ko Rok Nai, or Inner Rok Island, are well offshore and best visited as a day trip from Ko Lanta Yai by speedboat. They can also be visited from Trang's Pak Meng pier. The islands are blessed with tropical forest and fine beaches. Visitors can explore the forested interiors and waterfalls, and snorkel in the coral reefs. The fauna and flora include a variety of birds, reptiles, and fish. The coral reefs off the island are home to beautiful staghorns and starflower.

Diving enthusiasts can also head to **Hin Daeng** and **Hin Muang**, two excellent dive sites, just 16 miles (26 km) southwest of Ko Rok, known for their colorful soft corals.

Ferries and boats lined up at the jetty to take visitors to nearby islands, Hat Pak Meng

Trang ⓱

ตรัง

Road Map C5. 82 miles (132 km) SE of Krabi. *150,000.* *3 miles (5 km) S of Trang.* *TAT, Trang (0-7521-5867).* *daily.* *Vegetarian Festival (Oct).*

A trading center since the 1st century AD, Trang grew to prosperity between the 7th and 15th centuries under the Srivijaya rulers. Capital of Trang province, today, it is still an important commercial town with rubber, palm oil, and fishing as the mainstays of its economy. Tourism is also becoming an important industry as the beaches, islands, and mountains of this area are becoming popular. Trang has a strong ethnic character due to the influx of migrant labor from China in the latter half of the 19th century. There are some very good Chinese cafés here – a testament to the ancestry of the locals. The architecture in the town is a combination of Western and Sino-Thai designs and includes shophouses as well as Chinese temples. A number of food markets add to the local color. There is a statue dedicated to Khaw Sim Bee Na-Ranong – the much-revered governor of Trang who adopted the title of Phraya Ratsadanupradit. The area is also famous for its Vegetarian Festival.

Chinese architectural motif

TRANG'S VEGETARIAN FESTIVAL

People thronging the streets during Vegetarian Festival

Trang's long association with southern China, and the Chinese heritage of many of its inhabitants manifests itself in the annual Vegetarian Festival, held on a full moon night in the beginning of October. On this occasion, Sino-Thai locals dress in white, and turn vegetarian for nine days to make merit and earn good fortune. Ascetics parade through the town with their followers, accepting offerings from devotees to the accompaniment of drums, cymbals, and firecrackers. They demonstrate extraordinary scenes of self-mortification including body-piercing, self-flagellation, walking on fire, and other such feats while possessed by religious fervor. The resulting injuries from these acts are surprisingly minimal.

Environs

Located 14 miles (22 km) southwest of Trang, **Kantang** is the historical site indicating the site of the first rubber tree that was ever planted in Thailand. Visitors can also stop by to see the historical mansion of governer Khaw Sim Bee Na-Ranong.

Hat Pak Meng ⓲

หาดปากเม็ง

Road Map C5. Along Hwy 4162, 25 miles (40 km) W of Trang. *TAT, Trang (0-7521-5867).*

A curved stretch of sand, Hat Pak Meng is a peaceful beach with decent accommodations and restaurants that are famous for spicy seafood. Hat Pak Meng is best known as the embarkation point for nearby **Ko Hai**, a beautiful and deserted island about 30 minutes by longtail boat. The jetty at the northern end of the beach has several travel agencies that organize both snorkeling and boat tours.

Hat Chang Lang ⓳

หาดฉางหลาง

Road Map C5. 28 miles (45 km) SW of Trang town. *TAT, Trang (0-7521-5867).*

Casuarina-lined Hat Chang Lang is a long and beautiful stretch of white sand. The southern end of the beach houses the headquarters for

For hotels and restaurants in this region see pp308–11 and pp331–3

the Hat Chao Mai National Park. The accommodations on this beach are mostly upscale. The Anantara Si Kao Resort *(see p310)* located near the northern end of the beach is the finest hotel in Trang province. However, there are cheaper accommodation options further down the beach. Hat Chang Lang also offers a range of watersports which include sea-kayaking, deep-sea fishing, and wind-surfing. Hat Chang Lang is also famous for its oysters and visitors should try the local seafood restaurants scattered along the beach.

A group of sea kayakers in the waters off Hat Yao

Hat Chao Mai National Park ⓴

พิพิธภัณฑสถานแห่งชาติหาดเจ้าไหม

Road Map C5. Park HQ Hat Chang Lang, 29 miles (47 km) SW of Trang town. *Park HQ (0-7521-3260).* *6am–6pm daily.* **www**.dnp.go.th

Established in 1982, the Hat Chao Mai National Park covers an area of 89 sq miles (231 sq km). Located to the west of Trang, the coastal landscape of the park includes mangrove creeks, coastal karsts, and hidden coves. The main beach, Hat Chao Mai, is backed by limestone outcrops with a series of historical caves. These caves have been found to house various prehistoric remains. The most notable among these caves is **Tham Chao Mai**, a large marine cave filled with stalagmites. These can be easily reached by longtail boat. Nine offshore islands are also protected under this park and include Ko Kradan and Ko Muk *(see p266)*.

Dugongs can sometimes be spotted in the surrounding waters; the park is also home to otters, dolphins, langurs, and wild boars. The best time to visit Hat Chao Mai National Park is during the cool season from November to February.

Hat Yong Ling ㉑

หาดหยงหลิง

Road Map C5. Hat Chao Mai National Park. *TAT, Trang (0-7521-5867).*

Located immediately south of Hat Chang Lang on the Trang coast is Hat Yong Ling. The two beaches are separated by a jetty that serves nearby Ko Muk in the Hat Chao Mai National Park. Hat Yong Ling is a curved white sand beach backed by a pine forest, with rocky outcrops at either end. The larger of these outcrops is pierced with numerous caves and entrances that can be explored on foot at low tide, or by boat, or by swimming during high tide. Some caves lead to small, hidden, and often very beautiful beaches, with low sand dunes forming private nooks. There is nothing much by way of accommodations at this unfrequented spot, and other facilities or places to eat and drink are similarly minimal. Visitors can use the services provided by the Hat Chao Mai National Park head-quarters at Hat Chang Lang.

Thin strip of beach bordered by casuarinas at Hat Chao Mai National Park

Hat Yao ㉒

หาดยาว

Road Map C5. Hat Chao Mai National Park. *TAT, Trang (0-7521-5867).*

Continuing south from Hat Yong Ling, the 3-mile (5-km) long Hat Yao, or Long Beach, is a perfect camping spot. The beach, lined with casuarinas and pines, is mostly deserted on weekdays. However, this long and pristine strip of white sand is gradually undergoing development and some bungalow accommodations, as well as a few restaurants and bars, have begun to appear. The warm waters here are ideal for swimming.

Beautiful resort with a private beach on the island of Ko Hai

Ko Hai ㉓

เกาะไหง

Road Map C5. 36 miles (58 km) SW of Trang. *from Pak Meng pier.* *TAT, Trang-Satun (0-7521-5867).*

A tiny, beautiful island off the southwest coast of Trang, Ko Hai, also known as Ko Ngai, is a verdant, tropical island with just about all the right elements – a shady, green interior, lovely white powdery sand, warm, shallow waters, and excellent coral reefs, close to the shore, swarming with fish. It is both possible and pleasant to stay on Ko Hai, but there are no budget range accommodations available. Visitors must be prepared for mid-range prices, but good quality bungalows and restaurants make this little island an ideal place for families with children. Apart from sunbathing, swimming, or just relaxing in a hammock, visitors can go sea-kayaking and snorkeling. It is also possible to arrange snorkeling and diving tours to isolated Ko Rok Nok *(see p263)*, about 19 miles (31 km) southwest of Ko Hai, through tour agents on the island.

Ko Muk ㉔

เกาะมุกด์

Road Map C5. Hat Chao Mai National Park. *from Pak Meng pier.* *TAT, Trang-Satun (0-7521-5867).*

Once a remote backpackers' retreat, Ko Muk, or Pearl Island, can also be accessed from the Kuan Tunku pier farther south. Inhabited by a handful of *chao lae* (sea gypsies), stunning Ko Muk, part of the Hat Chao Mai National Park, is fast developing into an upscale destination. The main beach on the island, **Hat Sai Yao**, is the principal visitors' attraction with white sands and warm waters, which are safe for swimming. There are some good mid-range resorts and restaurants here. Nearby, **Tham Morakot**, or Emerald Cave, is another major local attraction. Visitors have to swim a short distance, at high tide, through a water-filled cavern – part of which lies in virtual darkness – to reach a *hong* or underwater cave. This cave is otherwise shut off from the outside world. The only other access to the tunnel is over the top of the collapsed dome which allows sunlight into the depths below. Boats can also enter the lagoon, which has a small beach, at low tide. The east coast, however, is undeveloped and remains the domain of local fisherfolk.

Visitors starting the swim through the dark tunnel of Tham Morakot

Ko Kradan ㉕

เกาะกระดาน

Road Map C5. Hat Chao Mai National Park. *from Pak Meng pier.* *TAT, Trang-Satun (0-7521-5867).*

A gorgeous island easily accessible by boat from the Pak Meng pier, Ko Kradan is indeed one of the pearls of the Andaman Sea. A part of the Hat Chao Mai National Park, the interior of the island is a mix of dense tropical jungle and rubber plantations, there are fine coral reefs just offshore, offering excellent snorkeling opportunities. A couple of sunken Japanese ships from the World War II era offer another exciting diving site in the waters off the island. Ko Kradan is less developed than Ko Muk, but this may change given the increasing popularity of these offshore islands. At present, however, there are no upscale resorts here, only a couple of bungalow establishments, although camping is permitted. Visitors can also use the Kuan Tunku pier to get here.

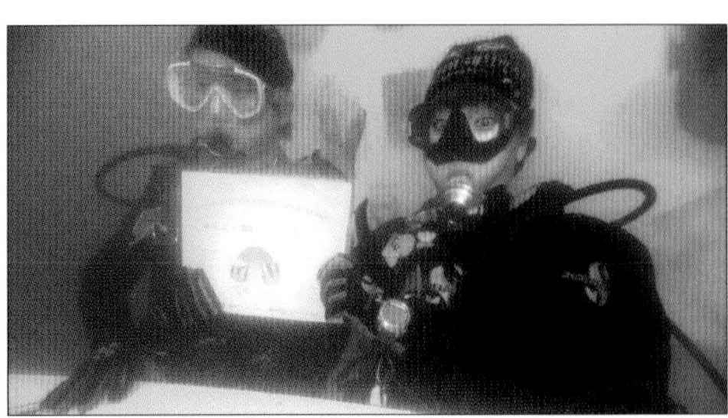

Couple showing their marriage license during an underwater wedding

KO KRADAN'S UNDERWATER WEDDINGS

Underwater weddings have been taking place in Trang on Valentine's Day each year since 1996. Although begun in a small way, by 2000 it had become a mass event, with groups of Thais and foreigners marrying underwater. The main venue for this event is Ko Kradan. The island entered the *Guinness Book of Records* in 2000 for hosting the largest underwater wedding in the world. Groups of around 40 couples in diving gear swim a short distance to an underwater altar where they are married by a local official also in dive gear. This event is now part of the Trang Season of Love. Before the ceremony, the brides and grooms sail along the coast in a flotilla of boats. Couples must have PADI diving licenses, or allow some time for the organizers on Ko Kradan to teach them the basics of diving.

Ko Libong ㉖

เกาะลิบง

Road Map B5. 8 miles (13 km) SW of Ko Kradan. ***Tel*** *0-7525-1932 (Libong Archipelago Wildlife Reserve).* *from Pak Meng pier.* *TAT, Trang-Satun (0-7521-5867).*

Lying further to the east than Ko Muk and Ko Kradan, Ko Libong is larger than both and can also be accessed from the nearby Chao Mai pier. Ko Libong so far remains untouched by the hectic commercial activity which seems to have swept across most of the country, and is home to several small Thai-Muslim fishing communities. The main beach on the island is at Ban Maphrao on the island's east coast. There are several mid-range resorts here, along with a handful of restaurants, small cafés, and bars. While activities such as swimming and snorkeling keep visitors busy, another attraction is the rich and varied wildlife of the island, under the aegis of the **Libong Archipelago Wildlife Reserve**. Here, explorers will find mangrove swamps as well as get a chance to see the endangered dugong, also known as the sea cow. Conservationists estimate that there may be as many as 20 pairs of dugongs breeding in the vicinity. Sea kayaks with guides are available for those who wish to see them in their natural habitat.

Longtail boats of local fishermen anchored at the pier in Ko Sukorn

Ko Sukorn ㉗

เกาะสุกร

Road Map C5. 14 miles (22 km) SE of Ko Libong. *from Tasae pier.* *TAT, Trang-Satun (0-7521-5867).*

To the east of Ko Libong, just off Laem Tasae and easily accessible by boat from Tasae pier, Ko Sukorn is another gem of the Trang Coast. Smaller than Ko Libong, and more densely populated, the island is home to a community of about 2,500 Thai-Muslims, mainly fishing families, and farmers growing coconuts, rice, and rubber. The island has simple bungalow accommodations, as well as shops, restaurants, and cafés, but no upscale resorts. The electricity supply is erratic, and usually limited at night. The locals on the island are friendly but conservative Muslims, whose main income comes from fish and lobster farming. Visitors can go swimming or snorkeling, or even explore the island on hired bicycles. Ko Sukorn can also be accessed from the Pak Meng pier.

Ko Phetra Marine National Park 28

อุทยานแห่งชาติเกาะเภตรา

Road Map C6. Park HQ off Hwy 416, 48 miles (77 kms) S of Trang. *Park HQ (0-7478-3074).* *from Pak Bara.*
www.dnp.go.th

Extending across the maritime territory of both Trang and Satun provinces, Ko Phetra Marine National Park comprises more than 30 islands including the main island of Ko Phetra which is also the largest in the group. Established in 1984, the park covers nearly 193 sq miles (500 sq km) of marine territory. Almost all the islands are made up of interesting limestone formations. Several of them are frequented by sea turtles during the egg-laying season. The cliffs are home to great colonies of bats and swiftlets. Rich coral reefs surround the islands and are ideal diving sites. The clear waters around the park also support numerous marine species, including the dugong, numerous colorful fish, and starfish. Although it is a national park, this is also an economically viable fishing zone with plenty of crabs, lobsters, and squid. On the islands, the vegetation is generally dense; there are mangroves as well as lush rain forests. Overnight visitors can stay at the park's lodges at Ko Li Di, or at the park headquarters on the mainland. Camping is also allowed in some places.

Idyllic stretch of sand bordered by turquoise waters, Ko Bulon Leh

Pak Bara 29

ปากบารา

Road Map C6. 34 miles (55 km) S of Trang. *TAT, Trang-Satun (0-7521-5867). Ko Tarutao Park HQ (0-7478-3485).*

A small seaside town and fishing village, Pak Bara is less a tourist destination and more a jumping-off point for Ko Phetra Marine National Park and Ko Tarutao Marine National Park *(see pp270–75)*. The park headquarters for Ko Phetra Marine National Park is located 3 km (2 miles) from Pak Bara. A visitors' center for Ko Tarutao is also located in this town. However, the town is a pleasant stopover with reasonable accommodation options, good seafood restaurants, and bars. A number of dive shops and travel agencies have been established to serve visitors. They can also arrange sea-kayaking tours in the surrounding waters.

Common starfish

Ko Bulon Leh 30

เกาะบุโหลนเล

Road Map C6. 24 miles (38 km) W of Pak Bara. *from Pak Bara.* *TAT, Trang-Satun (0-7521-5867).*

A tiny yet lovely island, Ko Bulon Leh is becoming popular as an offbeat holiday destination with beautiful white sand beaches and crystal-clear waters. Once a backpackers' hangout, the facilities on the island are turning increasingly upscale as commercial development is already under way. The main beach lies along **Ao Mamuang** or Mango Bay. A small *chao lae* community *(see p204)* lives in the northern part of the island. The local economy depends on fishing, coconut and rubber farming. Visitors can enjoy swimming and snorkeling among the offshore coral reefs. Ko Bulon Leh is best reached by boats that run daily from Pak Bara.

Satun 31

สตูล

Road Map C6. 71 miles (115 km) SE of Pak Bara. *22,000.* *TAT, Trang-Satun (0-7521-5867).* *daily.*

A quiet town lying close to the Malaysian border, Satun is the capital of the Satun province. The town has the highest Muslim population in Thailand; Thai and Malay-Muslims make up about 80 percent of the population.

Passengers at Pak Bara waiting to take ferries to nearby national parks

Yet, Satun is different from the other Muslim majority towns of Pattani *(see p284)*, Yala, and Narathiwat *(see p285)*. While these latter follow traditional orthodox Islamic practices, Satun is far more culturally and socially liberal; fundamentalist Islam or separatism does not enjoy any support here. This makes Satun the most laid-back of the Muslim-dominated provinces.

The town has quite a few attractions including the **Satung Friday Mosque**, also known as Masayit Mambang, built in Malay-Muslim style with a minaret and dome, and decorated with glazed tiles, glass, and marble. It also has a library in its basement. Housed in a fine Sino-Portuguese-style mansion, the **Satun National Museum** was the residence of the former governor of Satun. This two-story building has a collection of artifacts showcasing the local history and culture. Another important monument is **Wat Chanathipchaloem**, the town's first Buddhist temple that dates back 200 years. The entrance is guarded by two *yakshas* (nature spirits). The *wat* has a distinctive two-story *ubosot* – the first story is a preaching hall and the second is used for religious practices. The Po Je Kang Chinese Temple and the bustling fresh food market are other worthwhile sights. Visitors can also try the local cuisine which is an interesting blend of Malaysian, Thai, Chinese, and Muslim styles.

The colorful facade of Po Je Kang Chinese Temple, Satun

Satun National Museum
Soi 5, Satun Thani Rd. ***Tel*** *0-7472-2140.* *9am–4pm Wed–Sun.*

Wat Chanathipchaloem
Sulakanukoon Rd, Tambon Phiman. ***Tel*** *0-7471-1996.* *8am–4pm*

Thale Ban National Park ㉜

อุทยานแห่งชาติทะเลบัน

Road Map C6. Park HQ off Hwy 4184, 23 miles (37 km) E of Satun. *Park HQ (0-7475-0390).* **www**.dnp.go.th

A lush expanse of tropical rain forest, Thale Ban National Park was established in 1980. The park extends over the Banthat Mountains near the Malaysian border covering an area of 76 sq miles (196 sq km). Located around a valley, Thale Ban has several waterfalls and its limestone hills are dotted with caves. It is home to a variety of wildlife such as tapir, serow, barking deer, fishing cats, and sun bears. Visitors can see rare birds such as bat hawks, which feed on bats and other small prey, consuming them whole in midair. The park's marked trails lead to several pools and two waterfalls – the nine-level **Nam Tok Ya Roy**, 3 miles (5 km) north of the park headquarters, and **Nam Tok Ton Piew**, 6 miles (10 km) north of the park headquarters. There are bungalow accommodations, a campsite, and a restaurant. Satun acts as a gateway to the park.

Walkway leading to the quaint viewing platform near headquarters of Thale Ban National Park

Ko Tarutao Marine National Park ㉝

อุทยานแห่งชาติตะรุเตา

A nemo with white coral

Designated as Thailand's second marine national park in 1974, Ko Tarutao comprises 51 islands. Named after the largest island in the group, which is also the site of the park headquarters, Ko Tarutao is part of an ecologically rich area also comprising Malaysia's Langkawi islands, located 5 miles (3 km) to the south. World famous for its pristine diving sites, rich marine life, and outstanding beauty, this 575 sq mile (1,489 sq km) area is home to an incredible variety of flora and fauna. With olive ridley and hawksbill turtles, langurs, several species of squirrels, 25 percent of the world's tropical fish species, and over 100 varieties of birds, Ko Tarutao is a haven for wildlife enthusiasts.

KEY

☐ Area illustrated

★ Ko Rawi
An ideal spot for snorkeling, beautiful Ko Rawi remains relatively uninhabited. It is blessed with fine beaches, rich coral reefs, and a densely jungled interior.

Lovers' Gate at Ko Khai
The work of wind and waves over millennia, Lovers' Gate is a naturally carved limestone arch, now a famous symbol representing the marine national park.

Ko Adang, a picturesque isle covered with verdant rain forest, is surrounded by rich coral reefs.

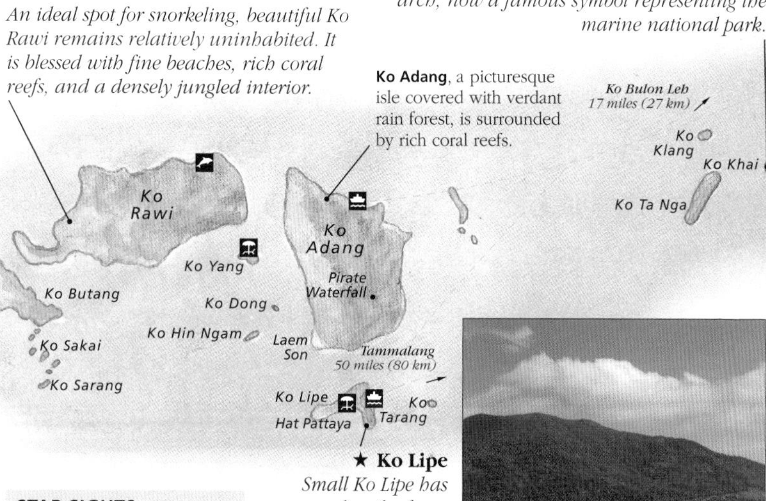

★ Ko Lipe
Small Ko Lipe has emerged as the focus of development in Ko Tarutao. Ko Lipe has a great selection of resorts and restaurants, and offers a variety of activities.

STAR SIGHTS

★ Ko Rawi

★ Ko Lipe

★ Dugong Sightings

Sea Turtles
Four different species of sea turtle – green, hawksbill, olive ridley, and leatherback, – find protection in the park. Ao Son, on Ko Tarutao, is a favored breeding and nesting ground for turtles.

VISITORS' CHECKLIST

Road Map C6. Park HQ 51 miles (82 km) W of Satun. *Park HQ (0-7478-3485 or 0-7478-3597). from Pak Bara; regular crossings mid-Nov to mid-Apr only.*

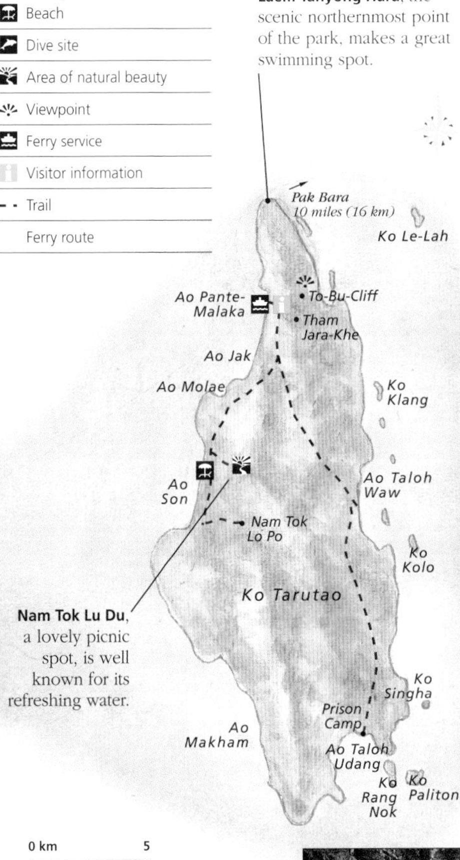

Laem Tanyong Hara, the scenic northernmost point of the park, makes a great swimming spot.

Nam Tok Lu Du, a lovely picnic spot, is well known for its refreshing water.

Jungle Treks
Trekking along nature trails makes for an interesting and rewarding alternative to a day at the beach. Trekkers will see an amazing variety of birds and animals.

★ Dugong Sightings
The waters off Ko Tarutao are famous for sightings of the gentle dugong. These rare mammals graze on verdant sea-grass beds and avoid contact with humans.

Prison Camp
Also notorious as Prison Island, Ko Tarutao housed several prison camps during World War II. The prisoners, forced to live in inhuman conditions without food or medicine, later took to piracy.

Exploring Ko Tarutao Marine National Park

The largest island of the marine park archipelago is the 16-mile (26-km) long Ko Tarutao, which offers great scenic variety. Tropical rain forests cover most of its surface, which reaches a maximum altitude of 2,300 ft (701 m). Ferries from Pak Bara dock at Ao Pante Malaka, the location of the park headquarters, bungalows, a restaurant, and the island's only store. Just east of Ao Pante Malaka lie the natural attractions of Tham Jara-Khe and To-Bu Cliff. Offshore islands such as Ko Adang, Ko Lipe, and Ko Rawi are popular beach destinations, while there is excellent diving at nearby Ko Kra and Ko Yang.

Bungalow housing the Ko Tarutao park headquarters, Ao Pante Malaka

Ao Pante Malaka

อ่าวพันเตมะละกา

51 miles (82 km) W of Satun.

from Pak Bara. *single park fee.* **www**.dnp.go.th

The site of the Ko Tarutao Marine National Park headquarters, Ao Pante Malaka is a lovely bay on the northwestern shore of Ko Tarutao. The long beach, lined with casuarinas, is great for swimming. Ao Pante Malaka offers more activities for visitors than any other spot on the main island. These include a biking trail and opportunities for sea-kayaking. The bay also serves as the harbor for boats from Pak Bara, 10 miles (16 km) away. A choice of bungalows, long houses, and cabins provide simple accommodations for visitors to the park. Camping is possible here, especially along the beach, but visitors must acquire prior approval of the park authorities.

A good park-run restaurant offers treats and refreshing cooling drinks. Visitors should also see the exhibition on the park's historical and natural background at the tourist service center. Longtail boats from Ao Pante Malaka also make the trip to Tham Jara-Khe, Ao Son, and Ao Taloh Udang nearby.

To-Bu Cliff

ผาโต๊ะบู

1 mile (2 km) E of Ao Pante Malaka.

A 20-minute walk inland from Ao Pante Malaka, through dense evergreen forest, leads visitors to the popular To-Bu Cliff. This 364-ft (111-m) high cliff is clearly visible from the Ko Tarutao park headquarters and offers spectacular views across the archipelago. The trek leading to this site begins close to the headquarters and visitors can stop to read about the large variety of flora and fauna in the forest described on plaques along the way.

To-Bu Cliff is considered to be an exceptionally beautiful and romantic spot from which to watch the sun setting over the Andaman Sea. Visitors, however, must be careful while making the trek to the cliff and head back before it gets dark. There is no electricity in the area and the descent of this rocky outcrop can get quite treacherous once the sun has set.

Tham Jara-Khe

ถ้ำจระเข้

2 miles (3 km) NE of Ao Pante Malaka.

Located near Laem Tanyong Hara, the northern cape of Ko Tarutao, Tham Jara-Khe is a 984-ft (300-m) deep cavern filled with beautiful stalactites and stalagmites. The cave is also notorious as Crocodile Cave because of the dangerous saltwater crocodiles that once inhabited it. Just 20 minutes away from Khlong Pante Malaka in Ao Pante Malaka, Tham Jara-Khe is accessible by longtail boat along the beautiful mangrove-lined canal. Explorers must use rafts to navigate their way within the cave, which is best visited at low tide when navigation is easier; the exploration takes about an hour. Visitors are advised to carry their own supplies, especially flashlights, while visiting the cave, as facilities here are minimal.

Kayakers rowing under the precipitous To-Bu Cliff

For hotels and restaurants in this region see pp308–11 and pp331–3

Secluded beach at Ao Son, housing a lone ranger station

Ao Jak and Ao Molae

อ่าวจากและอ่าวมอะและ

3 miles (5 km) S of Ao Pante Malaka.

Located to the south of Ao Pante Malaka, Ao Jak and contiguous Ao Molae are two beautiful bays with pristine white sand beaches, great for walks and picnics. Backed by dense coconut plantations, Ao Jak has no accommodations or other facilities.

Ao Molae, clearly the more developed of the two beaches, lies a little further south of Ao Jak. It can be reached by passing through a small mangrove swamp at low tide. At high tide, however, it is necessary to wade through the incoming seawater for a short distance. There are a few simple bamboo houses belonging to local fishermen here, along with some basic bungalow accommodations and a restaurant. A small ranger camp is also located here and visitors are allowed to camp on the beach.

Ao Son

อ่าวสน

8 miles (13 km) S of Ao Pante Malaka.

Situated further down the west coast of Ko Tarutao, Ao Son is a sizable bay with a long, white sandy beach. It offers good swimming and snorkeling opportunities and is best reached by longtail boat from Ao Pante Malaka. However, Ao Son can also be accessed on foot from Ao Molae, 5 miles (8 km) to the north. There is no road here, but a rough track leads south through clumps of wild banana and tall dipterocarp trees and the trek takes about two hours. Ao Son is visited by nesting turtles each year between September and April. The best time to see these gentle creatures is at night. There are no facilities of any kind on the beach, except for a small ranger station. Camping is possible here with the approval of the park authorities.

Treks from Ao Son to the interior of Ko Tarutao lead to two beautiful waterfalls – **Nam Tok Lu Du**, or Lu Du Falls which is a 1-hour hike away, and **Nam Tok Lo Po**, or Lo Po Falls, which is 2 hours away. Both the waterfalls offer freshwater pools which are good for bathing. Further south is Ao Makham, or Tamarind Bay, which is reached by a long and difficult trek through dense jungle; hiring a longtail boat from Ao Pante Malaka is usually advisable.

Ao Taloh Udang

อ่าวตะโละ อุดัง

15 miles (24 km) S of Ao Pante Malaka.

Situated at the southern tip of Ko Tarutao, Ao Taloh Udang is a deep, sheltered bay facing the tiny offshore island of Ko Rang Nok, home to thousands of swiflets. Undoubtedly associated with Ko Tarutao's intriguing past, this bay was the site of a prison camp for political captives. Several well-known prisoners, including the author of the first English-Thai dictionary and a grandson of Rama VII (r.1925–35), were incarcerated here. The inhuman prison conditions forced inmates to take to piracy, looting passing ships. This activity was curtailed by the British in 1946. Visitors can go to see the ruins of the prison. However, there are no facilities at Ao Taloh Udang, apart from a ranger station.

Statue at prison camp

Path leading to the remains of the prison camp at Ao Taloh Udang

Enthusiastic snorkelers making the most of the clear waters off Ko Adang

Ko Adang

เกาะอาดัง

26 miles (42 km) SW of Ao Pante Malaka. *from Ao Pante Malaka.*

About 12 sq miles (31 sq km) in area Ko Adang is almost completely covered in tropical rain forest. On the island's southwestern side lies Laem Son, passing the much smaller islets of Ko Klang and Ko Khai en route. Ko Adang is famous for its clear waters, fine quartz beaches, and well-preserved coral reefs, which provide a habitat for shoals of brightly colored fish and a host of other exotic marine flora and fauna.

The leafy interiors of Ko Adang are dotted with several beautiful waterfalls cascading from lofty heights of up to 2,300 ft (701 m); perhaps the highest is **Nam Tok Chon Salat**, which has water all year round. Another picturesque spot, **Pirate Waterfall** is reached by a 3-mile (2-km) walkway from near Laem Son. It is said to have been a source of freshwater for pirates living on the island. **Pha Chado**, a cliff located a 30-minute walk from the ranger station at Laem Son to the south of the island, offers fine views across the white sandy cape of Ko Adang.

Other smaller offshore islands such as Ko Lipe, Ko Dong, Ko Hin Ngam, and Ko Yang, are also great for swimming, diving, sea-kayaking, and sailing, and are easily approached from Ko Adang. **Ko Khai**, or Egg Island, located 11 miles (18 km) from Ko Adang, is too small to stay on, but makes a good diving or snorkeling stopover. The island has a lovely white sand beach, and a beautiful natural rock arch, and is favored by sea turtles for nesting.

Visitors can stay overnight at Ko Adang, although booking in advance is advisable. There is a restaurant serving fine local and Western dishes.

Ko Rawi

เกาะราวี

29 miles (47 km) SW of Ao Pante Malaka. *from Ko Lipe.*

The second largest island in the Adang-Rawi group, Ko Rawi covers an area of about 11 sq miles (28 sq km). It lies just 6 miles (10 km) to the west of Ko Adang, and is similarly blessed with fine beaches, crystal-clear seas, dense, jungled interior, and rich offshore coral reefs. Like Ko Adang, Ko Rawi has a marine park ranger station at Hat Sai Khao, but there are no accommodations on the island; nor are there any shops, restaurants, or other facilities. Camping, however, is a good option for those who want to get away from it all, but requires permission from the park authorities.

Best visited as a day trip from nearby Ko Adang or Ko Lipe, Ko Rawi offers fantastic swimming, snorkeling, and diving opportunities. The island is also easily accessible by chartered longtail boat from Ko Lipe.

Readying for a splash in the blue waters off Ko Rawi

For hotels and restaurants in this region see pp308–11 and pp331–3

Ko Lipe

เกาะหลีเป๊ะ

29 miles (47 km) SW of Ao Pante Malaka. *from Ao Pante Malaka.*

Located 2 miles (1 km) south of Ko Adang, the much smaller island of Ko Lipe, sometimes called Ko Sipe by locals, has become the most developed and popular destination of the Ko Tarutao Marine National Park. Originally inhabited only by a small community of *chao lae*, or sea gypsies, the island has been seeing rapid development, with a number of resorts and hotels being established on its beautiful beaches. Ko Lipe has just about everything going for it – fine, clear blue waters, good coral reefs, powdery white beaches, and a mountainous, thickly forested interior.

The main focus of development has been at **Hat Pattaya** on Ko Lipe's southern coast, where there are several bungalow-style resorts and a number of laid-back bars and restaurants. The main activities here are sunbathing, swimming, and snorkeling. In fact, the coral reefs, easily visible a short distance from the beach, are home to almost 25 percent of the tropical fish varieties found in the area.

A number of simple tracks, including one leading across the island's narrow center to Sunset Beach on its western coast, can be used to explore the interior of the island. Sunlight Beach, on the eastern side of the island, has bungalow-style accommodations and good views overlooking tiny Ko Kra offshore, yet another popular location. The main *chao lae* settlement is located just south of the beach. The area also houses several shops, a few restaurants, and utility stores such as a medical dispensary. Visitors can take longtail boats, manned by *chao lae*, to other offshore islands nearby.

The harmless hermit crab

Ko Yang

เกาะยาง

27 miles (43 km) SW of Ao Pante Malaka. *from Ko Lipe.*

A tiny but beautiful island equidistant from Ko Adang and Ko Rawi, Ko Yang remains uninhabited, even today. It has a small, perfect white sand beach, ideal for sunbathing. Ko Yang is surrounded by rich coral reefs, mainly comprising hard corals such as staghorn, leaf, and brain, making the island a popular snorkeling spot. Fortunately, its distance from the mainland and nearby Ko Lipe ensures that it is never crowded.

Ko Yang is best visited as a day trip from nearby Ko Lipe or Ko Adang, by hiring longtail boats.

Ko Hin Ngam

เกาะหินงาม

27 miles (43 km) SW of Ao Pante Malaka. *from Ko Lipe.*

Like Ko Yang nearby, Ko Hin Ngam, or Island of Beautiful Stones, is a tiny outcrop set in the immensity of the Andaman Sea. Located about 4 miles (6 km) northwest of Ko Lipe and about 3 miles (5 km) west of Ko Adang, beautiful Ko Hin Ngam is uninhabited and isolated making it the perfect snorkeling spot. The most striking feature of the island is its small beach which is covered with smooth black pebbles in various shapes and distinctive patterns. According to a local legend, Chaopho Tarutao, the guardian spirit of the marine park, curses anyone who dares to take away anything belonging to the park. True or not, visitors should avoid picking up these pebbles as souvenirs.

Ko Hin Ngam is best visited as a day trip from Ko Lipe in a hired longtail boat. It is advisable to combine a trip to Ko Hin Ngam with a visit to nearby Ko Yang before returning to the much more crowded Ko Lipe.

Visitors on the pebbly beach of Ko Hin Ngam

The narrow, jutting strip of the popular Sunset Beach at Ko Lipe

DEEP SOUTH

Among the loveliest and least visited regions of the country, the Deep South has more in common with neighboring Malaysia than with the rest of coastal Thailand. The region's distinct culture, food, history, and religion are a novel experience for travelers, yet, political strife keeps many away. The beautiful forested mountains, palm-fringed coastline, and relative isolation make this southern region an alluring and unusual holiday destination.

Despite being a part of Thailand for centuries, the Deep South is culturally different from the rest of the country. The influence of Indian, Chinese, and Malaysian cultures can be seen in the region's architecture and ethnic diversity. Skin tones are noticeably darker than in the rest of the country. The people speak an unusual intonated dialect of Thai and Malay (closely related to the language spoken in Malaysian Kelantan), and even the food is spicier, characterized by bitter curries laced liberally with turmeric. The diverse traditions of this region are especially evident in the town of Songkhla, a cosmopolitan cultural center with *wats*, museums, and an ancient Thai, Muslim, and Portuguese heritage. The area north of Songkhla has a Buddhist majority, while south of Songkhla, near the coast, most people are Muslim and the minarets of mosques replace the gilded spires of Buddhist temples. Pattani, an important semi-independent Malay kingdom in the 17th century, is now a Thai center of Islamic scholarship. Hat Yai, the commercial capital, has grown from an agricultural and railroad town to a destination for shopping and entertainment, while the fishing villages of the south have a distinct Muslim identity.

However, this complex ethnic mix has also led to violence perpetrated by separatists seeking autonomy. Guerilla warfare and bombings have disturbed the peace in this area. As a result, tourism has declined although none of the attacks have been directed toward foreign visitors.

A group of Muslim schoolgirls making their way across a bridge over the Songkhla Lakes

◁ **A combination of Islamic and Portuguese architectural styles in the Kru Se Mosque, Pattani**

Exploring the Deep South

Due to its proximity to Malaysia, the Deep South has more in common with its neighbor than the rest of Thailand. Extending over the provinces of Yala, Narathiwat, Songkhla, and Pattani, this southernmost belt of the country covers a huge area. Hat Yai is the commercial capital of the region and is also the main transport hub. The towns of Pattani, Saiburi, and Narathiwat with their large Muslim populations are an ethnic melting pot of Malay-Muslim culture. Songkhla is a charming town with a rich heritage and is regarded as the region's cultural capital. The sprawling Songkhla Lakes form the most significant geographical feature of the Deep South, and are home to a variety of wildlife especially birds. Although there are fewer natural attractions, this region's historical towns, mosques, and villages give it a unique flavor.

Aquatic plants covering the lake at Thale Noi Waterfowl Park

SIGHTS AT A GLANCE

Towns and Cities

Narathiwat 7
Pattani 5
Saiburi 6
Songkhla pp280–81 2
Tak Bai 8

Beaches and Islands

Hat Yai 1
Ko Yo 4

Areas of Natural Beauty

Songkhla Lakes p282 3

Painted *korlae* fishing boats at Khao Seng, Songkhla

For additional map symbols *see back flap*

Thailand's longest concrete bridge connecting the mainland to Ko Yo

GETTING AROUND

Hat Yai is the main base with direct and frequent road, rail, and air links to Bangkok and the rest of the region. Other ways to get to the Deep South are by road from Nakhon Si Thammarat to Phattalung. All the larger towns are well served by local and long-distance bus services, while Phatthalung, Hat Yai, and Yala have railway stations with services to either Bangkok or Malaysia. Cars can be easily hired and driving is the best way to explore this region.

KEY

- Expressway
- Major road
- Minor road
- Railway
- International border

SEE ALSO

- ***Where to Stay*** p311
- ***Where to Eat*** p333

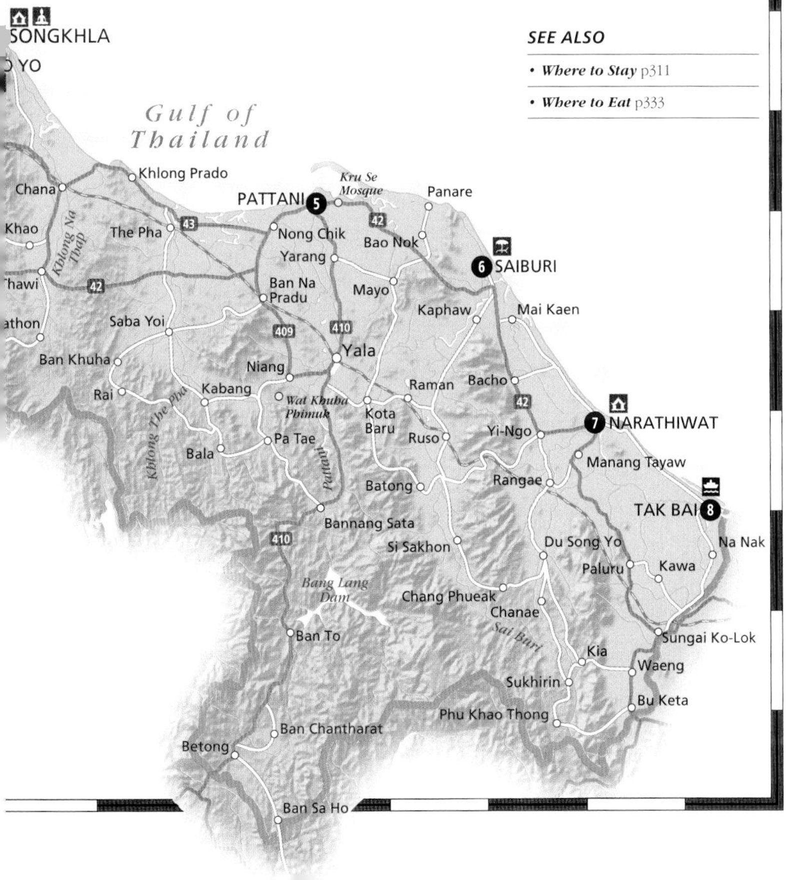

SONGKHLA
YO
Gulf of Thailand
Khlong Prado
Chana
Kru Se Mosque
Panare
PATTANI 5
Khao
Khlong Na Thap
The Pha
43
42
Nong Chik
Bao Nok
Yarang
6 SAIBURI
hawi
42
Ban Na Pradu
Mayo
Kaphaw
Mai Kaen
athon
Saba Yoi
409
410
Yala
Ban Khuha
Niang
Raman
Bacho
Rai
Kabang
Wat Khuha Phimuk
Kota Baru
42
7 NARATHIWAT
Khlong The Pha
Pa Tae
Ruso
Yi-Ngo
Bala
Pattani
Manang Tayaw
Batong
Rangae
Bannang Sata
TAK BAI 8
410
Si Sakhon
Du Song Yo
Na Nak
Paluru
Kawa
Bang Lang Dam
Chang Phueak
Chanae
Sai Buri
Ban To
Sungai Ko-Lok
Kia
Waeng
Sukhirin
Bu Keta
Phu Khao Thong
Ban Chantharat
Betong
Ban Sa Ho

Three young devotees praying at a Buddhist shrine, Hat Yai

Hat Yai ❶

หาดใหญ่

Road Map C5. 522 miles (840 km) S of Bangkok. *70,000.* *7 miles (11 km) W of Hat Yai.* *TAT, Hat Yai (0-7424-3747).* *daily.* *Chinese Lunar Festival (Sep/Oct).*

The commercial and transport capital of southern Thailand, Hat Yai has grown affluent due to its strategic railroad junction, its discounted products, and the constant flow of travelers from Malaysia on weekends. Various languages and dialects can be heard around the cosmopolitan downtown area.

Hat Yai is Thailand's third largest city, yet, it has few cultural attractions. Most visitors to the city spend their time shopping for bargains. Electrical goods at the Kim Yong market, fruits from street vendors, imported leather goods, and fashionable department stores are some of the popular options. Visitors can also take in a bullfighting bout. This sport, particular to the south, is different from its Spanish counterpart; here bulls fight other bulls and bets are placed on the outcome of the matches.

Wat Hat Yai Nai, near the city center, has the third largest Reclining Buddha image in the world – 115 ft (35 m) long and 49 ft (15 m) high.

Environs

Ton Nga Chang, 15 miles (24 km) west of Hat Yai comprises two streams cascading over seven tiers, which is best visited in the cool season from November to February.

Songkhla ❷

สงขลา

Once known as Singora, or Lion City, Songkhla grew to prominence as an important trade center in the 18th century. Located between the Gulf of Thailand and Thale Sap Songkhla, part of the country's largest lake system, it is an important fishing port, administrative, and educational center. A sense of history permeates the city and is evident in its architecture, cuisine, and language. Fringed by beaches, Songkhla is home to museums, bustling night markets, and *wats*. It is a melting pot of Thai and Muslim cultures where trendy bars coexist with fishing villages and old Portuguese-style houses, reflecting the city's multicultural heritage.

Bronze mermaid statue dedicated to Mae Thorani at Hat Samila

Hat Samila

หาดสมิหลา

Songkhla's main beach, Hat Samila is dominated by a bronze mermaid statue of Mae Thorani, the Hindu-Buddhist earth goddess. This revered statue is an icon for the whole province. Songkhla derives its name from the two lion-shaped islands, which are now called Ko Nu, or Rat Island, and Ko Maeo, or Cat Island. These are among Hat Samila's main attractions.

Khao Noi

เขาน้อย

One of two hills in Songhkhla, Khao Noi is located just a short distance south of Hat Samila. It offers great views of the city. There is an old *chedi* and a topiary garden on the hilltop as well as a park with tennis courts and food stalls at the bottom.

Songkhla National Museum

พิพิธภัณฑสถานแห่งชาติสงขลา

1 mile (2 km) S of Hat Samila, Wichianchon Rd. ***Tel*** *0-7431-1728.* *9am–4pm Wed–Sun.*

The museum is housed in a beautiful building that is in itself a major attraction for visitors. It was built in 1878, in the southern Thai-Chinese style as the residence for the then deputy governor of Songkhla – Phraya Suntharanuraksa. This old mansion was renovated and converted into a museum in 1977. A hidden grass courtyard flanks the two spiral staircases which lead to the wood-paneled second story where most exhibits are kept.

Former governor's residence presently housing Songkhla National Museum

For hotels and restaurants in this region see p311 and p333

Ornate entrance of Wat Chai Mongkhon, Songkhla

The fairly comprehensive collection covers most periods of Thai art and includes Benjarong pottery, 7th- to 9th-century Dvaravati plinths, Buddha images, and remnants of Ban Chiang pottery dating back to 3000 BC.

Wat Chai Mongkhon

วัดไชยมงคล

2 miles (3 km) S of Hat Samila, Chai-Phet Mongkhon Rd. *8am–4pm daily.*

A revered temple in Songkhla, Wat Chai Mongkhon has a *chedi* built to house a Buddha relic brought from Sri Lanka in 1892 by a monk called Na Issaro. The *wat* also houses a Reclining Buddha image.

Patrsee Museum

พิพิธภัณฑ์พัทศรี

2 miles (3km) S of Hat Samila, Wat Matchimawat, Saiburi Rd.

Wed–Sun.

Housed inside the Wat Matchimawat, which dates back 400 years, the Patrsee Museum has a wide range of artifacts indicating the importance of Songkhla's former trade links. Exhibits include a 14-in (35-cm) stone image of Ganesha, the Hindu elephant god, dating back to the late 6th century; enamelware from the Chinese Qing dynasty; 15th-century U Thong ware, and 18th-century European plates. However, the arrangement is slightly haphazard.

VISITORS' CHECKLIST

Road Map D5. 16 miles (26 km) NE of Hat Yai. *86,000.* *26 miles (42 km) SW of Songkhla.* *TAT, Hat Yai (0-7424-3747).* *daily.* *Chinese Lunar Festival (Sep/Oct).*

Khao Seng

เขาเส้ง

2 miles (3 km) S of Hat Samila.

A traditional Muslim fishing village, Khao Seng is located on a headland near Hat Samila. Famous for its colorful *korlae* boats *(see p285)*, the village also has an information center for the coastal fisheries and is a good place to learn about fishing – the mainstay of coastal Thailand.

Colorful *korlae* fishing boats anchored on the beach, Khao Seng

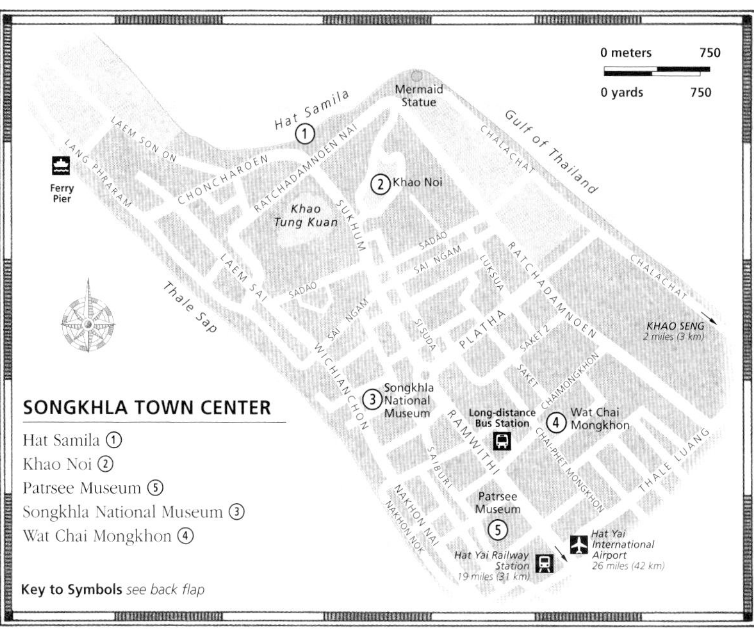

Songkhla Lakes ❸

ทะเลสาบสงขลา

Road Map C5. 6 miles (10 km) NW of Songkhla. *TAT, Hat Yai (0-7424-3747).*

The largest natural lake system in Thailand is formed by the Songkhla Lakes. A coastal lagoon, it consists of three interconnected water bodies – Thale Sap, Thale Luang, and Thale Noi. The lakes are separated from the sea by sandy ridges and are fed by water from the forested inland hills as well as seawater. They support an extraordinary biodiversity as the lakes are a feeding ground for thousands of birds migrating from as far as China. They are also home to a small population of the rare Irawaddy dolphin.

Longtail boats navigating through lotuses and other vegetation, Thale Noi

Thale Sap Songkhla

ทะเลสาบสงขลา

A brackish water lake, Thale Sap Songkhla is the southernmost of the three lakes lying between Phatthalung province to the west and Songkhla province to the east. This lake covers an area of 146 sq miles (378 sq km) and is a haven for bird-watchers. Because it is the closest to the sea, Thale Sap Songkhla is the most salty, and attracts more seabirds than its two northern neighbors.

Thale Luang

ทะเลหลวง

Located north of Thale Sap, Thale Luang is connected to the former by a narrow channel. This shallow lake covers an area of 190 sq miles (492 sq km). Although the water has high levels of salinity, it attains freshwater conditions during the rainy season. This lake is part of the protected wetlands area and is dotted with many small islands and surrounded by paddy fields. The **Khu Khut Waterbird Park** is the star attraction of the area. Established in 1976, this little-visited waterfowl park is home to over 200 species of birds, including a number of bitterns, egrets, and herons. The best time to visit is during early morning or late afternoon, between December and March. The park headquarters can be reached by bus or taxi from Songkhla. Visitors can hire boats from the fisheries department for special bird-watching tours.

A wattled jacana

Khu Khut Waterbird Park

Park HQ (0-7430-4552). dawn to dusk daily.

Restaurant on stilts at the Khu Khut Waterbird Park, Thale Luang

Thale Noi

ทะเลน้อย

The northernmost and smallest of the three lakes, Thale Noi is very shallow and almost entirely covered with aquatic plants with a few scattered islets. Although it is predominantly a freshwater lake, it becomes brackish between May and October. Thale Noi is home to the largest wetland bird sanctuary in Thailand – the **Thale Noi Waterfowl Park** – a resting ground for thousands of exotic migratory birds. The best way to explore the park, which covers 12 sq miles (30 sq km), is by longtail boat.

The best season for bird-watching is between January and April, when over 150 species of birds arrive at the park, swelling its population to about 100,000. There is a viewing platform on the lake and dawn is the best time for visitors to get a glimpse of Thale Noi's birds. Notable inhabitants include the purple swamp hen, and the long-legged *nok i-kong*.

Apart from lotuses and lilies, the most common vegetation covering the lake is *don kok*, a reed which the *nok i-kong* use to build nesting platforms. There are about 100 families who live in raised wooden houses along the lake and make a living from fishing and weaving reeds into mats.

Thale Noi Waterfowl Park

Park HQ (0-7468-5230). 8:30am–4:30pm daily. **www.**thailandbirdwatching.com

For hotels and restaurants in this region see p311 and p333

Muay Thai

Ancient *muay Thai* manuscript

Muay thai (Thai kickboxing) is the country's national passion. The origins of this unique sport remain uncertain; it is believed to have evolved from *krabi-krabong*, a related technique of self defence. The traditional form of *muay thai* is further divided – *muay korat* from the northeast, *muay lopburi* from the central region, *muay tasao* from the north, and *muay chaiya* in the south. Although enjoyed throughout Thailand, this sport is immensely popular in the south where the Khon Tai, people of the southern Thai peninsula, are believed to have a fiery nature. The sport's appeal extends from Nakhon Si Thammarat and Hat Yai to Phuket and Ko Samui. Once limited to Thailand and its neighboring countries, such as Cambodia, *muay thai* now attracts an immense following internationally – both as a martial art and a sport.

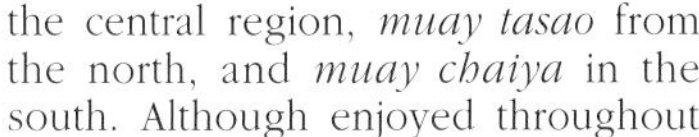

THAI BOXING

Thai kickboxing uses parts of the body not used in Western boxing, such as the feet and elbows. Thai boxing matches are also faster paced, and are thus limited to five rounds of three minutes each, separated by a short break. Professional boxers, who may start rigorous training as young as six years of age, often retire by 25.

Feet are kept bare in training sessions, although ankle covers may be worn during a match.

Amulets *(see p55)*, worn around the boxer's biceps during the match, are said to offer protection.

Kicks are common in Thai boxing.

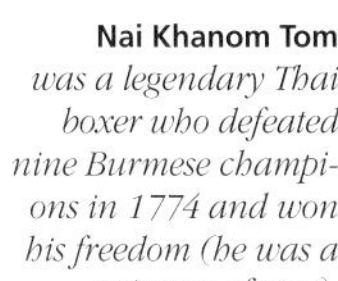

Nai Khanom Tom *was a legendary Thai boxer who defeated nine Burmese champions in 1774 and won his freedom (he was a prisoner of war).*

Before the match, *the boxer performs a dance* (wai khru ram muay) *to honor the teacher. The movements involve sweeping arm motions, which are said to draw the power of earth, air, fire, and water into the body.*

A ringside *piphat* band *is an essential element of* muay thai. *At the opening ceremony, the music is soft, but slowly increases in tempo, adding to the thrill of the match.*

In the stadium, *the audience becomes excited, shouting encouragement to the boxers. Thais bet furiously, often staking large sums on their favorite fighter. Bouts between famous boxers may be sold out well in advance.*

Ko Yo ❹

เกาะยอ

Road Map C5. 9 miles (14 km) SW of Songkhla.

A small and secluded island lying near the eastern end of Thale Sap, Ko Yo is best visited on a day trip from Hat Yai or Songkhla. The island is connected to the mainland by the 3-mile (2-km) long Prem Tinsulanond bridge. Built in 1986, this bridge directly links this secluded island with the other southern provinces. It can also be reached by longtail boats.

Ko Yo is covered with lush greenery and its chief attractions include orchards, two ancient *wats* – Wat Khao Bo and Wat Tai Yo – and the local handwoven cotton fabric available throughout the island. It is also famous for its fisheries and boasts a number of good seafood restaurants on its northern end. Visitors can hire a motorcycle to explore Ko Yo's bylanes. The excellent **Ko Yo Folklore Museum** established by the Institute for Southern Thai Studies in 1991, was built to preserve and showcase the folk traditions of this region. The museum is set in an attractive series of Thai *sala*-type buildings. It also houses a small café, a souvenir shop, a library of books on the culture of the Deep South, and a well-documented series of exhibits that includes *nang talung* puppets (*see p191*), musical instruments, textiles, basketry, household artifacts, fishing equipment, jewelry, and weapons. There is also a *suan yaa samunprai*, or a natural herb garden, within the museum's grounds.

Aerial view of the floating fish farms around Ko Yo.

Ko Yo Folklore Museum
Tel 07459-1611.
8.30am–5pm daily.

Pattani ❺

ปัตตานี

Road Map D6. 81 miles (130 km) SE of Songkhla. *74,000.* *TAT, Narathiwat (0-7352-2411).* *daily.* *Lim Ko Niaw Festival (Mar).*

Founded as early as the 15th century, Pattani was once the capital of an independent Malay-speaking sultanate. Capital of the Pattani province, today, it is a spiritual center of the Malay-Muslim region of the Deep South. About 75 percent of the population are Malay-speaking Muslims. This region has seen rising violence by Islamic extremists against the minority Buddhist population. Apart from the **Matsayit Klang** mosque, there are few buildings of much interest. However, Pattani is lively, especially around the harbor with its brightly colored *korlae* boats.

Environs

The **Kru Se** mosque, 4 miles (6 km) east of town was built by a Chinese merchant, Lim To Khieng who married a local woman and converted to Islam. As a display of his devotion he started building a mosque. His sister sailed from China to protest about his conversion. Although he promised her that he would return to his homeland upon its completion, he never did and she cursed the building and anyone who attempted to complete it. Her shrine **Chao Mae Lim Ko Niao** and the still incomplete mosque draw a number of devotees.

The partially built structure of the 16th-century Kru Se mosque, Pattani

For hotels and restaurants in this region see p311 and p333

Saiburi 6

ไทรบุรี

Road Map D6. 29 miles (47 km) SE of Pattani. *TAT, Narathiwat (0-7352-2411).*

Also called Selindung Bayu, meaning Wind Shelter, by the local fishing population, the small center of Saiburi is the capital of Saiburi district. This is the second-largest fishing harbor in Pattani province. The highlight of this place is the long stretch of beach which is more suited for fishing than lounging around on the beach. The nearby **Hat Wa Sukri** is famous for the annual Saiburi Fishing Competition in April which draws a number of both local and international anglers

Boats jostling for space at the busy fishing harbor in Saiburi

KORLAE FISHING BOATS

Colorful artwork on a *korlae* fishing boat, Saiburi

Colorful, painted fishing boats have been built and decorated by Muslim fishermen for hundreds of years all along the east coast of peninsular Thailand. The finest examples of this now declining industry originate in the boatyards of Saiburi district and Pattani province. Originally used as sailboats, *korlae* are now run with engines by local fishermen. Painted with Buddhist and Hindu characters by predominantly Muslim fishermen, the traditional *korlae* designs represent the cultural crossover between Thai Buddhism and Malay Islam.

Narathiwat 7

นราธิวาส

Road Map D6. 40 miles (65 km) SE of Saiburi. 68,000. *TAT, Narathiwat (0-7352-2411).* *daily.* *Chao Mae Toe Moe Festival (Apr); Narathiwat Fair (Sep).*

Capital of the Narathiwat province and a useful base for exploring the surrounding region, Narathiwat is a laid-back town. However, this province experiences frequent acts of violence carried out by Islamic extremists and Malay-Muslim separatists. Such acts of terrorism are aimed at the Thai-Buddhist administration rather than at Westerners or other visitors. The nearby port is another good spot to see traditional *korlae* boats. There are also a number of small and secluded beaches near Narathiwat, the best of which is Hat Manao. Small beachside shacks sell iced drinks and grilled fish, but alcohol is rarely found in these areas.

Environs

Taksin Palace, to the south of town, is the summer residence of the King and Queen of Thailand. Open to public when the royal family is not in residence, the palace gardens include an aviary. Khao Kong hill located 4 miles (6 km) southwest of town, has a monastery perched on its top with the tallest seated Buddha image in Thailand. The 79-ft (24-m) high statue is decorated with gilded mosaic tiles in the South Indian style.

Taksin Palace
Off Hwy 4084, 5 miles (8 km) S of Narathiwat. *daily.* *usually Aug & Sep.*

Tak Bai 8

ตากใบ

Road Map E6. 21 miles (34 km) SE of Narathiwat. *TAT, Narathiwat (0-7352-2411).*

The last point on the southern coast of Thailand, Tak Bai is located right at the border with Malaysia. The main attraction of the town is **Wat Chonthara Sing He**, erected in 1873, by Rama V (r.1868–1910) to stake his claim to a region that the British might have considered incorporating into their Malay colonies. This is an outpost of Thai Buddhism in a predominantly Muslim area. Interestingly, even today, Thai-Buddhist communities called Orang Syam in Malaysia live peacefully among their Muslim neighbors across the border, as they have for many centuries.

Mural depicting a busy rural scene, Wat Chonthara Sing He, Tak Bai

PHI PHI ISLAND
PHI PHI
PHI PHI ISLAND
PHI PHI
ISLAND
PHI PHI ISLAND
PHI ISLAND
PHI PHI ISLAND
PHI PHI
PHI PHI ISLAND
PHI PHI
PHI PHI
PHI PHI ISLAND
PHI PHI ISLAND
PHI PHI ISLAND
PHI PHI

TRAVELERS' NEEDS

WHERE TO STAY

Accommodations in Thailand come in all price ranges, although the distribution of hotels is very uneven. A lot of development in the beach resorts contrasts with the basic bungalows in rural areas. All the major cities have at least one hotel matching international standards, while Bangkok boasts some of the best hotels in the world. Mid-range accommodations are easily available in most towns and although these hotels have little character, they generally provide clean, efficient, and friendly service. A number of luxurious spas, resorts, and villas with contemporary and stylish decor are appearing at a rapid pace all over coastal Thailand. Guesthouses provide cheap accommodation options for travelers on a tight budget. Other alternatives are designated campsites, bungalows inside national parks, or spartan dormitories in monasteries.

Sign for a hotel

The lavishly decorated Conrad Room at Mandarin Oriental, Bangkok

HOTEL GRADING AND FACILITIES

Hotels in Thailand are not officially graded, although some are registered with the **Thai Hotels Association**. Price is thus the only indication of what to expect. Options range from basic to luxury. Often the best value is found in the once-luxury establishments that have been downgraded since the arrival of international chains. These hotels offer first-class facilities at a fraction of the cost.

LUXURY HOTELS

Thailand's luxury hotels are on a par with some of the best in the world. Rooms come with every conceivable comfort, from king-sized beds and massive televisions, to well stocked mini-bars, and private terrace Jacuzzis.

These upscale hotels offer a range of facilities, including business centers, conference rooms, shopping malls, coffee shops, fitness centers, pools, as well as a number of restaurants serving a wide range of cuisines. However, these hotels are now facing stiff competition from the smaller and super luxurious boutique hotels that emphasize attention to detail and offer a more personalized service.

RESORT HOTELS

Like the urban luxury hotels, the resort hotels of Thailand are also unsurpassed in style, comfort, and elegance by the majority of their international counterparts. Resorts such as the Banyan Tree Resort in Phuket *(see p307)*, and the Dusit Thani Hua Hin in Cha-am *(see p298)* are designer spaces and oases of opulence. Most resorts offer their guests a wide range of facilities including Jacuzzis, spas, saunas, tennis courts, watersports, and even horseback riding, or polo.

GUESTHOUSES

Guesthouses offer good value for money. In Bangkok, low-cost accommodations are often disappointing. Outside the capital, however, guesthouses are clean, friendly, and a cheap option for the budget traveler. Some of these have air-conditioning or fans, and may offer swimming pools and restaurants. In the cheapest guesthouses expect basic facilities, although the service is still quite good.

BUDGET OR THAI HOTELS

These budget hotels, also known as Thai hotels, are cheap, functional, and offer basic facilities. Most have fan-cooled or air-conditioned rooms and only a few have restaurants. Although few foreigners choose to stay in Thai hotels, they may be the only option for travelers in some remote areas.

Swimming pools at a smaller beachside resort, Ko Phi Phi

◁ An array of colorful refrigerator magnets for sale in Ko Phi Phi

Tents pitched for campers at Khao Sam Roi Yot National Park

STAYING IN MONASTERIES

In small towns, travelers can stay in a *wat* in return for a small donation. Facilities are basic and men and women have to live separately. In Bangkok it is expected that guests in a monastery would either wish to study meditation or ordain as a monk.

RENTALS

Rented accommodations are widely available throughout Thailand at reasonable rates. Serviced apartments are a popular choice for longstay visitors. Properties usually occupy prime locations and cover quite a range, offering guests privacy as well as the luxuries of an upscale hotel, at significantly lower prices.

NATIONAL PARKS

Most of the national parks allow camping on designated campsites, although visitors should be prepared for the minimal facilities. Mosquito nets and insect repellent are essential. Most parks have a limited number of bungalows and these should be booked in advance at the **Forestry Department** in Bangkok.

PRICES

Tourist accommodations can cost from 1,000 to 10,000 baht a night in Bangkok, Ko Samui, Pattaya, and Phuket. A comfortable room in a standard hotel goes between 700 and 1,500 baht, based on the season. Prices everywhere are at their peak in the cool season from November to February. In the other seasons, rates fall everywhere, except in Bangkok. A room in a Thai hotel in the capital costs 1,000 baht, falling to 400–750 baht in the provinces. The best deals are at guesthouses and beach bungalows that cost between 200 and 1,000 baht.

BOOKING

Advance booking is advisable for luxury hotels and resorts, especially during festivals. Thai hotels and guesthouses are unlikely to take bookings. In bigger towns, the staff speaks English. **TAT Offices** also make bookings.

TAXES

All hotels charge about seven percent VAT (Value Added Tax), and some luxury hotels will also add a 10 percent service charge on top of their basic rates. Some of the top hotels include taxes in the room rates. Less expensive hotels simply add the taxes to the final bill. Thus, it is important to check whether the price is inclusive of taxes while booking or before checking in.

BARGAINING

It is a good idea to ask about the possibility of a discount. It is not considered impolite to ask, but it is in bad taste to press the point. Many hotels offer special off-season prices and Thai proprietors will certainly inform their guests.

TIPPING

Tipping is not ingrained in Thai culture, but in hotels, bellmen should be given around 50 baht for delivering luggage to the room.

DIRECTORY

HOTEL GRADING AND FACILITIES

Thai Hotels Association
203-209/3 Ratchadamnoen Klang Avenue. ***Tel*** *0-2281-9496.*

NATIONAL PARKS

Forestry Department
Phahon Yothin Rd, Bangkok.
Tel *0-2562-0760.*

BOOKING

TAT Offices

Bangkok
Tel *1672.*
www.tourismthailand.org

Ko Samui
Tel *0-7728-8818.*

Krabi
Tel *0-7562-2163.*

Pattaya
Tel *0-3842-8750.*

Phuket
Tel *0-7621-1036.*

FACILITIES FOR CHILDREN

Very few mid-range hotels have facilities for children or nursing mothers. However, luxury hotels and resorts may offer babysitting services, and free stay for children as well as special paddle pools.

DISABLED TRAVELERS

Even luxury hotels have few facilities for disabled visitors. Wheelchair ramps are making an appearance, and nearly every luxury establishment has an elevator. That, however, is the limit of facilities in most hotels and they should be carefully chosen by visitors with special needs.

Pretty bungalows lining the beach at Ko Chang

Choosing a Hotel

Bangkok and coastal Thailand are home to some of the most spectacular resorts in the world. The hotels in this guide have been selected across a wide price range for their facilities, value, ambience, and location. The hotels are listed by region. For Bangkok map references, see pp88–95 and the road map on the inside back cover.

PRICE CATEGORIES
The following price ranges are for a standard double room per night, including taxes and service charges during high season.

Ⓑ Under 600 baht
ⒷⒷ 600–1,500 baht
ⒷⒷⒷ 1,500–3,000 baht
ⒷⒷⒷⒷ 3,000–5,000 baht
ⒷⒷⒷⒷⒷ Above 5,000 baht

BANGKOK

CHINATOWN New Empire Hotel ⒷⒷ

572 Yaowarat Rd 10100 ***Tel*** *0-2234-6990* ***Fax*** *0-2234-6997* ***Rooms*** *100* **City Map** *6 F2*

Just a short walk from the Hua Lampong railway station and the MRT underground, the New Empire Hotel offers standard accommodations in the heart of Bangkok's Chinatown. The sparse, clean, and comfortable rooms are housed in a basic eight-story building. The friendly staff is an added bonus. **www.newempirehotel.com**

CHINATOWN The Riverview Guesthouse ⒷⒷ

768 Soi Panurangsi, Songwat Rd, behind San Jao Tosuekong 10100 ***Tel*** *0-2234-5429* ***Rooms*** *45* **City Map** *6 F3*

Tucked away in the heart of Chinatown, but just five minutes from Hua Lampong Station, this is a great place to stay to experience the vibrancy of the area. Basic rooms are offset by excellent river views from its rooftop restaurant. Hard to find down the maze of alleyways, but this hotel is worth the effort. **www.riverviewbkk.com**

CHINATOWN Woodlands Inn ⒷⒷ

1158/5–7 Charoen Krung 32 Bangrak 10500 ***Tel*** *0-2235-3894* ***Fax*** *0-2237-5493* ***Rooms*** *75* **City Map** *6 F4*

Guests will find clean but basic accommodations at this renovated budget hotel located close to the river and within walking distance of a night market. The restaurant serves excellent Indian food as well as Thai and Western dishes. The staff is fluent in English, Hindi, Tamil, and Thai. **www.woodlandsinn.org**

CHINATOWN Grand China Princess Hotel ⒷⒷⒷ

215 Yaowarat Rd, Samphantawong 10100 ***Tel*** *0-2224-9977* ***Fax*** *0-2224-7999* ***Rooms*** *160* **City Map** *6 E1*

In the heart of Chinatown, surrounded by a maze of streets and shops, this hotel is housed in the Grand China Trade Tower, and has comfortable rooms and suites with full amenities. A revolving restaurant on the 25th floor offers panoramic views of the city and has a selection of international cuisine. **www.grandchina.com**

CHINATOWN Shanghai Mansion Bangkok ⒷⒷⒷⒷ

479–81 Yaowarat Rd, Samphantawong 10100 ***Tel*** *0-2221-2121* ***Fax*** *0-2221-2124* ***Rooms*** *75* **City Map** *6 F2*

Once the home of a wealthy Chinese merchant, this charming hotel celebrates the colors and romance of Chinatown. The decor is outstanding and showcases traditional Chinese designs. Guests can enjoy the lavish accommodations, indulge in the Yin Yang Spa or enjoy a drink in the Tea Room. **www.shanghaimansion.com**

DOWNTOWN A-One Inn Ⓑ

25/13–15 Soi Kasamsunt 1, Rama I Rd 10330 ***Tel*** *0-2215-3029* ***Fax*** *0-2216-4771* ***Rooms*** *25* **City Map** *8 B1*

Tucked away down a quiet side street, the A-One Inn is one of the few cheap guesthouses in the city center. It may be a little plain, but it is hard to beat its price and convenience. Rooms have TV, Internet, hot showers, and air-conditioning. Weekly and monthly rates are available. **www.aoneinn.com**

DOWNTOWN Soi 1 Guesthouse Ⓑ

220/7 Soi 1, Sukhumvit Rd 10110 ***Tel*** *0-2655-0604* ***Rooms*** *24* **City Map** *8 F1*

This popular hostel on a quiet, well-lit side street has air-conditioned dormitories, a 24-hour access lounge and games room, Wi-Fi, DVDs, and cable TV. However, the rooms are somewhat cramped, the ensuite bathrooms have showers only, and toilets are shared. The staff is friendly and knowledgeable. **www.soi1guesthouse.com**

DOWNTOWN Lub-d ⒷⒷ

4 Decho Rd, Bangrak 10500 ***Tel*** *0-2634-7999* ***Fax*** *0-2634 7510* ***Rooms*** *36* **City Map** *7 B4*

This youth hostel proves that cheap is not equivalent to grubby. A variety of accommodations are available ranging from double rooms to a ladies-only dormitory. Free Internet, helpful multilingual staff, and the bright and clean surroundings ensure a loyal clientele. **www.lubd.com**

DOWNTOWN Bossotel ⒷⒷⒷ

55/8–14 Soi Charoen Krung 42/1, Bangrak 10500 ***Tel*** *0-2630-6120* ***Fax*** *0-2630-6129* ***Rooms*** *81* **City Map** *6 F5*

This hotel boasts an excellent location with only the Shangri-la Hotel standing between it and the river. There is easy access to the Skytrain and river taxis. Facilities include both Continental and Thai restaurants as well as a small swimming pool. **www.bossotelinn.com**

Key to Symbols *see back cover flap*

DOWNTOWN City Lodge ฿฿฿

137/1–3 Sukhumvit Soi 9 10110 **Tel** *0-2253-7710* **Fax** *0-2253-7340* **Rooms** *28*

The hotel chain Amari is now catering to budget travelers with this hotel and a similar property on Sukhumvit Soi 19. Clean and well-managed, the hotel has a good restaurant serving Italian and Thai food. Guests can use the swimming pool and fitness center at the more upscale Amari Boulevard Hotel nearby. **www.oamhotels.com**

DOWNTOWN Narai Hotel ฿฿฿

222 Silom Rd, Bangrak 10500 **Tel** *0-2237-0100* **Fax** *0-2236-7161* **Rooms** *470* **City Map** *7 B4*

Once a top-level venue, this hotel is now overshadowed in ambience and price by its more modern neighbors. Yet this downtown venue offers good value for money and the location is perfect with easy access to the Skytrain and river taxis. It is clean, quiet, and unpretentious with a great breakfast buffet. **www.naraihotel.co.th**

DOWNTOWN Rose Hotel ฿฿฿

118 Surawong Rd, Bangrak 10500 **Tel** *0-2266-8268-72* **Fax** *0-2266-8096* **Rooms** *72* **City Map** *7 C3*

This modern hotel in downtown Bangkok is situated off the main Surawong Road, and is relatively quiet. There is a swimming pool with a poolside bar. Proximity to the Patpong nightlife might make the conservative traveler a little uncomfortable, however the low tariff is a major incentive. **www.rosehotelbkk.com**

DOWNTOWN S2S Boutique Resort ฿฿฿

21/1 Soi Ratchathapan, Ratchapararop Rd 10400 **Tel** *0-2642-4646* **Fax** *0-2245-4386* **Rooms** *38* **City Map** *4 E4*

This contemporary hotel has Thai-style interiors and rooms looking out on a well-tended garden. It is located in the central but non-touristic Pratunam district famous for its markets. It is also right next to a large public park, ideal for a morning walk or a jog. Monthly rates are also available. **www.moeleng-bangkok-resort.com**

DOWNTOWN Siam Heritage ฿฿฿

115/1 Surawong Rd, Bangrak 10500 **Tel** *0-2353-6101* **Rooms** *73* **City Map** *7 C3*

Right around the corner from the raucous streets of Patpong, the serene and traditional Siam Heritage provides an interesting contrast. The rooms are decorated in Thai style with hardwood floors and silk furnishings. Luxurious suites, a pool, Jacuzzi, spa, and a terrace restaurant are other facilities on offer. **www.thesiamheritage.com**

DOWNTOWN Silom Convent Garden ฿฿฿

35/1 Soi Piphat 2, Sathorn, Soi Convent 10500 **Tel** *0-2667-0130* **Fax** *0-2667-0144* **Rooms** *44* **City Map** *7 C4*

This centrally located facility is for those who do not like the impersonal nature of hotel rooms. There are serviced apartments with kitchen facilities along with regular rooms. A vibrant decor, two coffee shops, a roof garden, and a decidedly residential atmosphere make this place an attractive option. **www.silomconventgarden.com**

DOWNTOWN Swiss Lodge ฿฿฿

3 Convent Rd, Silom, Bangrak 10500 **Tel** *0-2233-5345* **Fax** *0-2236-9425* **Rooms** *46* **City Map** *7 C4*

In a quiet enclave of Bangkok's entertainment district, this hotel offers comfortable rooms fitted with the latest technology. The hotel's bijou restaurant, Three-On-Convent, serves Californian cuisine and excellent wines. Guests can relax at the pool terrace, library, or business lounge. **www.swisslodge.com**

DOWNTOWN Arnoma Hotel ฿฿฿฿

99 Ratchadamari Rd, Pathumwan 10330 **Tel** *0-2655-5555* **Rooms** *369* **City Map** *8 D1*

Located in the center of downtown Bangkok, this is a good mid-range choice for those interested in shopping. The CentralWorld, Zen, and Paragon malls are adjacent and the local Pratunam market is also nearby. Although not strong on ambience, the food is good, with Chinese, Thai, and Continental options. **www.arnoma.com**

DOWNTOWN Luxx Hotel ฿฿฿฿

6/11 Decho Rd, Bangrak 10050 **Tel** *0-2635-8800* **Fax** *0-2635-8088* **Rooms** *13* **City Map** *7 B4*

The Luxx, one of Bangkok's smallest hotels, is a converted Chinese shophouse. The original structure has been transformed into a stylish space using plenty of chrome and wood. Suites feature a wooden bathtub, LCD TV, DVD player, iPod dock, and a view of the courtyard. The whole place is Wi-Fi enabled. **www.staywithluxx.com**

DOWNTOWN Silom Serene ฿฿฿฿

7 Soi Piphat, Silom Rd Soi 3, Bangrak 10500 **Tel** *0-2636-6599* **Fax** *0-2636-6590* **Rooms** *86* **City Map** *7 C4*

The strategically located boutique-style hotel has spacious rooms, a large and attractive pool, and a quiet and shaded garden perfect for escaping the din of downtown Bangkok. Popular with businessmen, it has a well-equipped business center and meeting rooms. **www.silom-serene.com**

DOWNTOWN Siri Sathorn ฿฿฿฿

27 Soi Sala Daeng 1 Silom Rd, Bangrak10500 **Tel** *0-2266-2345* **Fax** *0-2267-5555* **Rooms** *111* **City Map** *8 D4*

The Siri Sathorn calls itself a "serviced residence". Aside from the central location near two Skytrain stops, attentive service, and elegant atmosphere, it offers suites that have up to two bedrooms with kitchens and laundry facilities, making it great for families. It also has a spa and a fitness center. **www.sirisathorn.com**

DOWNTOWN Banyan Tree ฿฿฿฿฿

21/100 South Sathorn Rd, Pathumwan 10120 **Tel** *02-679-1200* **Fax** *02-679-1199* **Rooms** *216* **City Map** *8 D4*

Located near the Silom business district, the Banyan Tree bills itself as an urban spa. Most units are suites tastefully appointed with elegant Asian motifs. Chic bars and restaurants abound, each with its own specialty. The stylish rooftop bar and restaurant on the 61st floor is a star attraction. **www.banyantree.com**

DOWNTOWN Dusit Thani ฿฿฿฿฿

946 Rama IV Rd 10500 **Tel** *0-2200-9000* **Fax** *0-2236-6400* **Rooms** *517* **City Map** *8 D4*

A flagship hotel of Thailand's most respected hotel brand, the Dusit Thani offers elegant rooms with Thai decor ranging from superior to the luxurious Thai Heritage Suites. Facilities include a spa, a golf range, and eight restaurants. It is also home to the Cordon Bleu, Dusit Academy of World Cuisine. **www.dusit.com**

DOWNTOWN The Four Seasons ฿฿฿฿฿

155 Ratchadamari Rd 10330 **Tel** *0-2250-1000* **Fax** *0-2253-9195* **Rooms** *353* **City Map** *8 D2*

The Four Seasons exudes restrained elegance. The rooms are adorned with hand-painted murals and guests can enjoy the spa and boutique plaza. The hotel has long been a favorite with well-off residents for its superb dining that includes Thai, Italian, and Japanese food, as well as an American steakhouse. **www.fourseasons.com**

DOWNTOWN Le Meridien Plaza Athénée ฿฿฿฿฿

10 Wireless Rd 10330 **Tel** *0-2650-8800* **Fax** *0-2650-8500* **Rooms** *378* **City Map** *8 E2*

Located in Bangkok's central business and diplomatic district, the Meridien Plaza Athénée is a short walk from the Skytrain station. The hotel is an iconic building with luxurious accommodations and award-winning restaurants. The finest traditional Thai hospitality awaits discerning guests. **www.starwoodhotels.com**

DOWNTOWN lebua at State Tower ฿฿฿฿฿

1055 Silom Rd, Bangrak 10500 **Tel** *0-2624-9555* **Fax** *0-2624-9998* **Rooms** *350* **City Map** *7 A5*

This "all-suite" hotel is probably best known for its vertiginous outdoor restaurant and bar on the 52nd floor. Guests can also revel in the super chic modern decor, great views, and superior service; or they can just retire to their own kitchenette for a simple meal or snack. **www.lebua.com**

DOWNTOWN The Mandarin Oriental ฿฿฿฿฿

48 Oriental Ave, Charoen Krung Soi 41 10500 **Tel** *0-2659-9000* **Fax** *0-2236-1937* **Rooms** *393* **City Map** *6 F4*

Built in 1867, and a favorite of authors Somerset Maugham and Joseph Conrad, the Mandarin Oriental combines a rich past with luxury. The restored Authors' Wing houses suites and the splendid location, service, and cuisine ensure that guests return. A cooking school and spa round off the package. **www.mandarinoriental.com**

DOWNTOWN Shangri-la Hotel ฿฿฿฿฿

89 Soi Wat Suan Plu, Charoen Krung Rd 10500 **Tel** *0-2236-7777* **Fax** *0-2236-8579* **Rooms** *799* **City Map** *6 F5*

The hotel has two wings – the Shangri-la Wing and the Krungthep Wing. The latter has rooms with a view of the river and a garden balcony overlooking a private pool. Butler service is included. All rooms are tastefully decorated in Thai style with teak and silk furnishings. There is also an excellent in-house spa. **www.shangri-la.com**

DOWNTOWN Sheraton Grande Sukhumvit ฿฿฿฿฿

250 Sukhumvit Rd 10110 **Tel** *0-2649-8888* **Fax** *0-2649-8000* **Rooms** *440*

Regarded as one of the finest business hotels in Asia, the Sheraton Grande Sukhumvit is located in the heart of Bangkok's business district. It includes award-winning restaurants, a jazz lounge, and a chic nightclub. As expected, it has all the usual facilities. **www.sheratongrandesukhumvit.com**

DOWNTOWN The Sukhothai ฿฿฿฿฿

13/3 South Sathorn Rd 10120 **Tel** *0-2344-8888* **Fax** *0-2344-8822* **Rooms** *210* **City Map** *8 D4*

Named after a city in northern Thailand that was the home to Thailand's first recorded dynasty, the Sukhothai tries to recapture that glorious past in the middle of modern Bangkok with a profusion of teak, silk, and Buddhist stupas in its magnificent gardens. Good food and a spa further recommend the place. **www.sukhothai.com**

DOWNTOWN Swissôtel Nai Lert Park ฿฿฿฿฿

2 Witthayu Rd, Pathumwan 10330 **Tel** *0-2253-0123* **Fax** *0-2253-6509* **Rooms** *338* **City Map** *8 E1*

Bangkok's Swissôtel Nai Lert Park is a five-story, low-rise hotel set in over eight-and-a-half acres of tropical plants, a garden, and a Thai-style canal. Guests are spoilt for choice at the eight restaurants including an alfresco dining terrace, a bar, and café. All rooms have private balconies. **www.swissotel.com**

DUSIT Bangkok International Youth Hostel ฿฿

25/2 Phitsanulok Rd 10200 **Tel** *0-2282-0950* **Fax** *0-2628-7416* **Rooms** *67* **City Map** *2 F3*

This is a youth hostel of the old school, mainly for those who are interested in staying in a safe and clean dormitory, although double rooms are also available. A library, café, Internet, and laundry service are available, as is a travel agency. It boasts a good location near the river and the Grand Palace. **www.hihostels.com**

DUSIT Swana Bangkok Hotel ฿฿

332 Wisut Kasat Rd, Phra Nakhon 10200 **Tel** *0-2282-8899* **Fax** *0-2281-7816* **Rooms** *55* **City Map** *2 E3*

This Bangkok property is situated in a relatively quiet area with interesting sites but without the tourist clutter. The restaurant serves both Thai and Western food. Good for families on a budget trip. All rooms have satellite TV and a mini-bar, and there is 24-hour room service. **www.swanabangkok.com**

DUSIT Hotel De' Moc ฿฿฿

78 Prajatipatai Rd, Phra Nakhon 10200 **Tel** *0-2282-2831* **Fax** *0-2280-1299* **Rooms** *92* **City Map** *2 E3*

The Hotel De' Moc offers surprisingly spacious rooms, a pleasant atmosphere, Wi-Fi, and bicycles for hire. Guests at this hotel can use the well-equipped fitness center at the nearby Buddy Lodge on Khao San Road. The De' Moc hotel also boasts a pretty pool surrounded by trees. **www.hoteldemoc.com**

Key to Price Guide *see p290* **Key to Symbols** *see back cover flap*

DUSIT New World Lodge Hotel ®®®

2 Samsen Rd, Banglampoo, Phra Nakhon 10200 ***Tel*** *0-2281-5596* ***Fax*** *0-2282-5614* ***Rooms*** *172* ***City Map*** *2 D3*

Geared toward both business and leisure travelers, this hotel provides good facilities and tidy rooms in a quiet but convenient location. There is a restaurant and outdoor café serving special *halal* food. Visitors can also choose from the many restaurants and bars in the vicinity. **www.newworldlodge.com**

OLD CITY Diamond House ®®

4 Samsen Rd, Banglampoo 10200 ***Tel*** *0-2629-4008* ***Fax*** *0-2629-4009* ***Rooms*** *22* ***City Map*** *2 D3*

Around the corner from Khao San Road, this hotel attracts families. Well located for sightseeing, it is neat and stylish, with good food and service. There is a rooftop pool with great views. It is located on a busy street so it is advisable to get a room at the back. **www.thaidiamondhouse.com**

OLD CITY Lamphu Tree House ®®

Prajatipatai Rd, 155 Wanchat Bridge 10200 ***Tel*** *0-2282-0991-2* ***Fax*** *0-2282-0993* ***Rooms*** *40* ***City Map*** *2 D4*

This hotel is located on a canal in the old city, and entered via a footbridge. All the rooms have balconies and are paneled in old teakwood. The atmosphere is quiet and friendly and the pool is clean. The restaurant serves a focused choice of Thai and international dishes. **www.lamphutreehotel.com**

OLD CITY Buddy Lodge ®®®

265 Khao San Rd, Banglampoo 10200 ***Tel*** *0-2629-4477* ***Fax*** *0-2629-4744* ***Rooms*** *76* ***City Map*** *2 D4*

Right in the middle of Bangkok's famous Khao San Road and originally a backpackers' haven, this hotel is rapidly becoming upscale but still retains its youthful and vibrant feel. Buddy Lodge offers clean and secure rooms, some with balconies, and a swimming pool on the roof that is great for catching the breeze. **www.buddylodge.com**

OLD CITY New Siam Riverside ®®®

21 Phra Athit Rd, Banglampoo 10200 ***Tel*** *0-2629-3535* ***Fax*** *0-2629-3443* ***Rooms*** *100* ***City Map*** *1 C3*

Located right on the riverfront, close to the Khao San backpacker ghetto and entertainment area, but much less crowded, this hotel features a small pool. It is just a short walk away from the Grand Palace, the National Museum, and Bangkok's most famous *wats*. **www.newsiam.net**

OLD CITY Phranakorn Nornlen ®®®

46 Thewet Soi 1, Phra Nakhon, Bang Khunprom ***Tel*** *0-2628-8188* ***Fax*** *0-2628-8600* ***Rooms*** *12* ***City Map*** *3 A4*

This hotel advocates the slow life. The food is vegetarian and purely organic and the place is small, but pays attention to details. The hotel is designed with the idea of making guests feel at home. The staff is from the neighborhood. The rooms are clean, comfortable, and without many frills. **www.phranakorn-nornlen.com**

OLD CITY Royal Hotel ®®®

2 Ratchadamnoen Ave, Banglampoo 10200 ***Tel*** *0-2222-9111* ***Rooms*** *300* ***City Map*** *2 D4*

Adjacent to Sanam Luang and very close to the Grand Palace, this hotel is located in the heart of old Bangkok. Designed in the 1950s style, the hotel has helpful staff and the spacious restaurant serves Chinese, Thai, and Continental food. The best part about the hotel is its proximity to neighborhoods rich in color and history.

OLD CITY Arun Residence ®®®®

36–38 Soi Pratu Nok Yung, Tha Maharat 10200 ***Tel*** *0-2221-9158* ***Fax*** *0-2221-9159* ***Rooms*** *6* ***City Map*** *5 B1*

This boutique hotel built in Sino-Portuguese style is a converted residence with split-level rooms and a suite with a private balcony. Located in the heart of historic Bangkok with easy access to other parts of town, this tiny, yet elegant lodging with a beautiful garden is personalized and provides quality service. **www.arunresidence.com**

OLD CITY Chakrabongse Villas ®®®®®

396 Maharat Road, Phra Nakhon, Tha Tien 10200 ***Tel*** *0-2224-6686* ***Fax*** *0-2225-3861* ***Rooms*** *4* ***City Map*** *5 B1*

Built in 1908 as the residence of Prince Chulachakrabongse, these incredibly luxurious villas lie on the Chao Phraya River between Chinatown and the Royal Palace. Apart from great views of the river and the nearby temples, the riverside restaurant serves delicious Thai food customized to individual taste. **www.thaivillas.com**

THONBURI Ibrik Resort on the River ®®®®

256 Soi Wat Rakang, Arunamarin Rd 10700 ***Tel*** *0-2848-9220* ***Fax*** *0-2866-2978* ***Rooms*** *3* ***City Map*** *1 B5*

No one will dispute Ibrik's claim of being the smallest resort in the world with three lovely well-equipped suites that provide views on the river in a quiet Thonburi residential neighborhood. This is a perfect romantic getaway for honeymooners. It is essential to book in advance. **www.ibrikresortcom**

THONBURI Anantara Bangkok Riverside Resort and Spa ®®®®®

257 Charoen Nakhon Rd, Thonburi 10600 ***Tel*** *0-2476-0022* ***Fax*** *0-2476-1120* ***Rooms*** *413*

A true resort in more than name, with great tropical gardens perfect for relaxing after a day spent sightseeing. The in-house spa is world class, and the food is also excellent, especially the Sunday brunch at the Trader Vic's bar and the Japanese spread at the Benihana restaurant. **www.bangkok-riverside.anantara.com**

THONBURI The Peninsula ®®®®®

333 Charoen Nakhon Rd, Klong San 10600 ***Tel*** *0-2861-2888* ***Fax*** *0-2861-1112* ***Rooms*** *370* ***City Map*** *6 F5*

Located across the river from Bangkok on the Thonburi side, this oasis of luxury offers a river view from every room and suite, and the hotel's private boats take guests into the city at their leisure. Restaurants offer Thai, Cantonese, and Mediterranean food, considered among the best in town. **www.peninsula.com**

FARTHER AFIELD Convenient Resort ⒷⒷ

9–11 Soi 38 Lat Krabang 10520 ***Tel*** *0-2327-4118* ***Fax*** *0-2327-4004* ***Rooms*** *67* ***Road Map*** *C1*

This aptly named non-smoking hotel, just five minutes from Suvarnabhumi International Airport, provides comfortable accommodations and is great for quick stopovers. Thai massage is offered for weary travelers. The restaurant is a perfect place to unwind with good views of the countryside. **www.convenientresort.com**

FARTHER AFIELD Amari Don Muang Airport Hotel ⒷⒷⒷⒷ

333 Chertwudthakas Rd 10210 ***Tel*** *0-2566-1020* ***Fax*** *0-2566-1941* ***Rooms*** *423* ***Road Map*** *C1*

Don Muang Airport remains open for the majority of domestic flights, so this deluxe hotel is still a good choice if there is time to kill between transfers to Suvarnabhumi International Airport. Amari Don Muang offers a high standard of accommodations at an affordable price, along with good restaurants and bars. **www.amari.com**

FARTHER AFIELD Novotel Suvarnabhumi Airport Hotel ⒷⒷⒷⒷⒷ

Moo 1, Nongprue Bang Phli, Samut Prakarn 10540 ***Tel*** *0-2131-1111* ***Fax*** *0-2131-1188* ***Rooms*** *612* ***Road Map*** *C1*

A 10-minute walk away from the main terminal, the Novotel Suvarnabhumi Airport Hotel is the perfect place to recharge your batteries. Guests can relax in the luxurious spa, restaurants, and bars, or sleep in comfort in the plush rooms. **www.novotel.com**

EASTERN SEABOARD

CHANTHABURI River Guest House Ⓑ

3/5–8 Sri Chan Rd 22000 ***Tel*** *0-3932-8211* ***Rooms*** *29* ***Road Map*** *E2*

This friendly guesthouse is conveniently located next to the Chanthaburi River and the gem district. There is a choice of fan-cooled or air-conditioned rooms and the former are situated at the back of the building which is more quiet. There is Internet and the owner is a good source of local information.

CHANTHABURI Kasemsarn Hotel ⒷⒷ

98/1 Benchamarachutit Rd 22000 ***Tel*** *0-3931-1100* ***Fax*** *0-393-4456* ***Rooms*** *60* ***Road Map*** *E2*

The two-story Kasemsarn Hotel presents itself as a chic but affordable boutique hotel. Located just north of the city center, it represents the best mid-range option in town. A decent restaurant serves Thai and Western food. Guests can also make use of the massage facilities. **www.kasemsarnhotel.com**

CHANTHABURI KP Grand Hotel ⒷⒷ

35/200–201 Trirat Rd 22000 ***Tel*** *0-3932-3201* ***Fax*** *0-3932-3214* ***Rooms*** *202* ***Road Map*** *E2*

This spacious and swanky hotel is located to the south of town. Rooms are carpeted and well-equipped, with satellite TV and mini-bars. Facilities include a big pool, fitness center, sauna, and massage service. The 18th floor has a restaurant serving creative European cuisine, and a karaoke bar. **www.kpgrandhotel.com**

KO CHANG Amber Sands Beach Resort ⒷⒷⒷ

Ao Dan Khao 23170 ***Tel*** *0-3958-6177* ***Rooms*** *7* ***Road Map*** *E2*

Located on the east coast of Ao Dan Khao, this family-run place is great for those who want a quieter holiday than that offered on the booming west coast. Other plus points include a freshwater pool and a thatched rooftop restaurant serving food that is famous throughout the island. **www.ambersandsbeachresort.com**

KO CHANG Ko Chang Lagoon Resort ⒷⒷⒷ

Hat Sai Khao 23170 ***Tel*** *0-3955-1201* ***Fax*** *0-3955-1203* ***Rooms*** *165* ***Road Map*** *E2*

Located in the middle of Hat Sai Khao, this two-story mid-range resort has attractive landscaped gardens and a range of well-equipped rooms. Some are in the main building, while others are in detached bungalows on the seafront. There are barbecues on the beach every evening. **www.kochanglagoonresort.com**

KO CHANG Noren Resort ⒷⒷⒷ

31/1/1 Moo 4, Klong Prao 23170 ***Tel*** *0-3955-7010* ***Rooms*** *15* ***Road Map*** *E2*

This European-managed resort offers great value for money. The rooms are basic cement bungalows but very clean and with nice finishing touches. The owner will assist with organizing tours and activities around the island, and the quiet location is perfect for families. **www.kochanglagoonresort.com**

KO CHANG Orchid Resort Bailan ⒷⒷⒷ

Ao Bai Lan 23170 ***Tel*** *0-3955-8137* ***Rooms*** *45* ***Road Map*** *E2*

This resort is reminiscent of Ko Chang from bygone days. Bungalows made of natural materials are set in a garden with a pool. As the name implies, the grounds have been planted with an incredible variety of orchids. There is one restaurant serving quality Thai and Continental fare. **www.orchidresortkohchang.com**

KO CHANG Siam Beach Resort ⒷⒷⒷ

Hat Tha Nam 23170 ***Tel*** *0-8702-65515* ***Fax*** *0-2417-1948* ***Rooms*** *72* ***Road Map*** *E2*

Located at the northern end of Hat Tha Nam, the southernmost beach on the west coast, this place has comfortable air-conditioned bungalows scattered over a hillside, plus some air-conditioned rooms with balconies on the beach. The resort is surrounded by nice trees providing shade. **www.siambeachresort.in.th**

Key to Price Guide *see p290* **Key to Symbols** *see back cover flap*

KO CHANG White Sand Beach Resort ⓑⓑⓑ

Hat Sai Khao 23170 ***Tel*** *08-1863-7737* ***Rooms*** *99* ***Road Map*** *E2*

Hat Sai Khao is the island's longest and most beautiful sandy stretch, but it gets rather crowded near the southern end. This resort, located further north on the beach, offers a quiet getaway. It has a range of rooms, some with air-conditioning and others with fan – most have sea views. **www.whitesandbeachresort.info**

KO CHANG Mercure Koh Chang Hideaway ⓑⓑⓑⓑ

111/1 Moo 1 Tambol, Ao Bai Lan 23170 ***Tel*** *0-3961-9111* ***Fax*** *0-3955-8059* ***Rooms*** *96* ***Road Map*** *E2*

This is a modern and stylish beach resort, with accommodations ranging from standard rooms in a low-rise block to villas with private pools and terraces. The decor throughout is strikingly contemporary, and even the standard rooms have up-to-the-minute amenities. There's a beautiful panorama of Bai Lan Bay.

KO CHANG Sea View Resort and Spa ⓑⓑⓑⓑ

Hat Kai Bae 23170 ***Tel*** *0-3955-2888* ***Rooms*** *126* ***Road Map*** *E2*

Set in a shaded garden, all the rooms at this resort, from standard cottages to suite spas, are beautifully designed and luxuriously furnished. Facilities include a spa, pool, fitness center, terrace restaurant, and a number of bars by the pool and on the beach. Some of the rooms have their own Jacuzzi. **www.seaviewkochang.com**

KO CHANG Aana Resort and Spa ⓑⓑⓑⓑⓑ

Hat Khlong Phrao 23170 ***Tel*** *0-3955-1539* ***Fax*** *0-3955-1540* ***Rooms*** *71* ***Road Map*** *E2*

Aana Resort and Spa is not directly located on the beach, rather guests have to kayak along the Khlong Phrao River to the coast. Less beach-oriented than other places, the Aana's emphasis is on spa treatments, a riverside pool, and a natural ambience. Many rooms have their own Jacuzzis. **www.aanaresort.com**

KO CHANG Aiyapura Resort ⓑⓑⓑⓑⓑ

Ban Khlong Son 23170 ***Tel*** *0-3955-5111* ***Fax*** *0-3955-5118* ***Rooms*** *88* ***Road Map*** *E2*

With its huge leaf-shaped pool, luxurious spa, and a variety of free-standing deluxe bungalows, the Aiyapura Resort is an excellent choice for an extravagant holiday. Located on a hill overlooking Hat Khong Son, this boutique-style resort is run by a friendly staff. There are excellent restaurants and a bar inside the pool. **www.aiyapura.com**

KO CHANG Amari Emerald Cove ⓑⓑⓑⓑⓑ

88/8 Moo 4, Hat Khlong Phrao 23170 ***Tel*** *0-3955-2000* ***Fax*** *0-3955-2001* ***Rooms*** *165* ***Road Map*** *E2*

Very well-managed by the Thai Amari hotel chain, this place is architecturally impressive and located right on the beach at Ao Khlong Phrao. There is a 165-ft (50-m) lap pool, an Italian restaurant, a spa, oversized guest rooms with bathtubs to match, and a game room for the kids. **www.amari.com**

KO CHANG Nirvana ⓑⓑⓑⓑⓑ

Ao Bang Bao 23170 ***Tel*** *0-3955-8061* ***Rooms*** *15* ***Road Map*** *E2*

The Nirvana is laid out over a strikingly scenic, semi-forested cape with a private sandy beach and views of the bay on one side and the Gulf of Thailand on the other. There is a freshwater plunge pool and a seawater pool with its own bar. Accommodations are in beautiful Balinese-style villas. **www.nirvanakohchang.com**

KO KUT Ngamkho Resort ⓑ

Ao Ngam Kho 23170 ***Tel*** *08-4653-4644* ***Rooms*** *9* ***Road Map*** *E2*

These classic thatched bungalows are without pretension and have basic amentites. Most of the guests are long stayers and Uncle Jo, the host, has a boat that can be rented (with him at the helm) for fishing or snorkeling. Seafood figures predominantly on the menu. Tents can be pitched at a campsite on the beach.

KO KUT Ko Kood Beach Resort ⓑⓑⓑⓑ

Ko Kut 23170 ***Tel*** *0-2630-9371* ***Rooms*** *18* ***Road Map*** *E2*

Ko Kut (or Kood) is one of the smaller islands to the south of Ko Chang. Seclusion still prevails and the beach bungalows are renowned for their good service, food, and activities such as kayaking to offshore islets, and treks exploring the inland areas of the island. There is also a pool. **www.kokoodbeachbungalows.com**

KO MAK Island Hut Resort ⓑ

Ao Kratung 23120 ***Tel*** *0-87139-5537* ***Rooms*** *20* ***Road Map*** *E2*

This simple resort run by a local family is a great place for relaxing. The decor is in bamboo and guests can just spend the whole day lazing in hammocks. The whole place is set in natural surroundings and the lack of other amenities are meant to contribute to the overall rustic experience.

KO MAK Good Time Resort ⓑⓑⓑⓑ

Ko Mak 23170 ***Tel*** *0-3950-1000* ***Rooms*** *17* ***Road Map*** *E2*

All the villas have either two or three bedrooms making it ideal for families or groups. There is a pool and a basic spa. The management retains the homely atmosphere of the place by offering authentic Thai cuisine. There is also a DVD library for visitors wishing to entertain themselves. **www.goodtime-resort.com**

KO SAMET Naga ⓑ

Ao Hin Khok 21160 ***Tel*** *0-3864-4935* ***Rooms*** *35* ***Road Map*** *D2*

Perched on a hillside, the Naga is something of a legend among budget travelers. It offers simple and clean bungalows at reasonable rates. Guests can enjoy the library, gym, a Thai boxing ring, and a good restaurant that serves home-made bread and cakes.

KO SAMET Jep's Bungalow Ⓑ Ⓑ

Ao Hin Khok 21160 ***Tel*** *0-3864-4112* ***Rooms*** *40* ***Road Map*** *D2*

One of Ko Samet's best value for money options, Jep's Bungalow offers a choice of fan-cooled or air-conditioned rooms in concrete or wooden bungalows spread across a hill. The rooms also have cable TV. The nearby beach is one of the best on the island for swimming and is popular among budget travelers. **www.jepbungalow.com**

KO SAMET Sai Kaew Villa Ⓑ Ⓑ

Hat Sai Kaew 21160 ***Tel*** *0-3864-4144* ***Rooms*** *100* ***Road Map*** *D2*

This place occupies a large compound on Ko Samet's most popular beach and offers good deals for budget travelers. From basic fan-cooled rooms to larger air-conditioned bungalows, this resort has several accommodation options. Discounts are available for guests staying several nights. **www.saikaew.com**

KO SAMET Tub Tim Resort Ⓑ Ⓑ

Ao Tubtim 21160 ***Tel*** *0-3864-4025* ***Fax*** *0-3864-4028* ***Rooms*** *100* ***Road Map*** *D2*

This is one of Ko Samet's longest running establishments, having opened in the early 1980s. The Tub Tim Resort is set at the southern end of a pretty bay on the east coast and offers comfortable facilities in its concrete and wooden rooms. It also has one of the island's best restaurants. **www.tubtimresort.com**

KO SAMET Samed Villa Ⓑ Ⓑ Ⓑ

Ao Phai 21160 ***Tel*** *0-3864-4094* ***Fax*** *0-3864-4093* ***Rooms*** *45* ***Road Map*** *D2*

Located on the headland at the southern end of Ao Phai, these Swiss-Thai bungalows are run by a family. They offer superb views of the ocean from the waterfront units and a tranquil forest garden ambience throughout. Competent and friendly staff can arrange snorkeling, kayaking, and beach barbecues. **www.samedvilla.com**

KO SAMET Sang Thian Beach Resort Ⓑ Ⓑ Ⓑ

Ao Thian 21160 ***Tel*** *0-3864-4255* ***Rooms*** *32* ***Road Map*** *D2*

The days when Ao Thian, or Candlelight Beach, had no electricity are long gone, and now this resort provides comfortable lodgings in small wooden bungalows on a hill and some large ones for big groups. Although the beach has developed, it is still quieter than those farther north on the east coast. **www.sangthianbeachresort.com**

KO SAMET Vongdeuan Resort Ⓑ Ⓑ Ⓑ

Ao Wong Deuan 21160 ***Tel*** *0-3864-4171* ***Rooms*** *49* ***Road Map*** *D2*

Ao Wong Deuan was one of the first of Ko Samet's beaches to be developed, and it is certainly one of the prettiest, with a lovely crescent-shaped bay. This resort has a variety of attractive cottages and Thai houses that are comfortably equipped. There is also a good restaurant serving local specialties. **www.vongdeuan.com**

KO SAMET Le Vimarn Cottages and Spa Ⓑ Ⓑ Ⓑ Ⓑ Ⓑ

Ao Phrao 21160 ***Tel*** *0-3864-4104* ***Fax*** *0-3864-4109* ***Rooms*** *31* ***Road Map*** *D2*

A tastefully opulent resort on the beach at Ao Phrao on Ko Samet's quiet west coast, these villas are furnished in bamboo, teak, and Thai woven fabrics and many have their own private Jacuzzis on the balcony. Also included are a spa, fitness center, a pool, and fine alfresco Italian dining at the water's edge. **www.samedresorts.com**

KO SAMET Moo Ban Talay Ⓑ Ⓑ Ⓑ Ⓑ Ⓑ

Ao Noi Na 21160 ***Tel*** *08-1838-8682* ***Fax*** *0-3864-4251* ***Rooms*** *21* ***Road Map*** *D2*

Spacious bungalows in a gorgeous setting make Moo Ban Talay one of the best of Ko Samet's many stylish resorts. Located on a private beach at the northern end of the island, the place radiates exclusivity. All rooms have platform beds and garden bathrooms, and some also have huge decks. **www.moobantalay.com**

KO SAMET Paradee Ⓑ Ⓑ Ⓑ Ⓑ Ⓑ

Ao Kiu Na Nok 21160 ***Tel*** *0-2438-9771* ***Rooms*** *45* ***Road Map*** *D2*

This expensive and luxurious resort may be the shape of things to come on Ko Samet even although the island is part of a marine national park. Paradee has spectacular villas with private Jacuzzis, spa, a butler, plus two private beaches. The resort also arranges diving or deep sea fishing trips for its guests. **www.kohsametparadee.com**

KO SAMET Sai Kaew Beach Resort Ⓑ Ⓑ Ⓑ Ⓑ Ⓑ

Hat Sai Kaew 21160 ***Tel*** *0-3864-4195* ***Fax*** *0-3864-4194* ***Rooms*** *87* ***Road Map*** *D2*

Located at the northern end of Hat Sai Kaew, this is one of the island's fanciest resorts, with a choice of expensive, deluxe bungalows located on a quiet stretch, or slightly cheaper superior cottages on a busier part of the beach. The decor is very stylish, plus there is a pool and a restaurant. **www.samedresorts.com**

KO SI CHANG Sichang Palace Ⓑ Ⓑ

81 Atsabang Rd 20210 ***Tel*** *0-3821-6276* ***Fax*** *0-382106939* ***Rooms*** *56* ***Road Map*** *D1*

This is the smartest place to stay on Ko Si Chang which has some interesting historic sights but no great beaches. The price of the rooms varies according to the view, but all of them are equipped with air-conditioning and cable TV. The hotel also has a standard restaurant, coffee shop, and a pool. **www.sichangpalace.com**

PATTAYA Ice Inn Ⓑ

528/2–3 Second Rd 20260 ***Tel*** *0-3872-0671* ***Rooms*** *32* ***Road Map*** *D1*

With its central location and well-maintained rooms, this place is one of Pattaya's best budget options. Rooms come with air-conditioning or fans, and some also have a TV and fridge. There is a handy Internet café on the ground floor, and the beach is only a few steps away. **www.pattayacity.com/iceinn**

Key to Price Guide *see p290* **Key to Symbols** *see back cover flap*

PATTAYA Diana Inn ⓑⓑ

216/6–20 between Soi 11–12 Second Rd 20260 ***Tel*** *0-3842-9675* ***Fax*** *0-3842-9870* ***Rooms*** *111* ***Road Map*** *D1*

This place has plain and comfortable rooms, and a large pool with its own bar. Room rates include an all-you-can-eat buffet breakfast. The evening buffet serves Thai and European food as well as beer at good rates. The central location makes this hotel popular with long-staying visitors. **www.dianapattaya.co.th**

PATTAYA Garden Lodge Pattaya Beach Resort ⓑⓑ

170 Moo 5, Naklua Rd, between Soi 18 and Soi 20 20260 ***Tel*** *0-3842-9109* ***Rooms*** *78* ***Road Map*** *D1*

Located to the north of town, this mid-range option is for those looking for a quiet spot in the middle of the bustling city. The Garden Lodge, true to its name, features a gorgeous outdoor area, a delightful pool, a welcoming restaurant, and well-furnished rooms. **www.gardenlodgepattaya.net**

PATTAYA Jomtien Boathouse ⓑⓑ

389/5–6 Jomtien Beach Rd 20260 ***Tel*** *0-3875-6143* ***Fax*** *0-3875-6144* ***Rooms*** *24* ***Road Map*** *D1*

This low-rise establishment has elegantly furnished rooms that contain all amenities. There is no pool, but the beach is good for swimming. The hotel is famous for its good food at the theme-based open-air restaurant and Elvis impersonator shows on Friday nights. **www.jomtien-boathouse.com**

PATTAYA Lek Hotel ⓑⓑ

284/5 Soi 13, Second Rd 20260 ***Tel*** *0-3842-5552* ***Fax*** *0-3842-6629* ***Rooms*** *158* ***Road Map*** *D1*

Affordable with a few classy touches, the Lek Hotel is comfortable, spacious, and clean. The rooms themselves are rather small and basic, but there is a swimming pool, a snooker room, and a roof terrace to make up for it. The hotel is only a few steps from Hat Pattaya and its shops. **http://lekhotel.tripod.com**

PATTAYA Woodlands Resort ⓑⓑⓑ

164/1 Moo 5, Pattaya-Naklua Rd 20260 ***Tel*** *0-3842-1707* ***Fax*** *0-3842-5663* ***Rooms*** *133* ***Road Map*** *D1*

This attractive Colonial resort is set in a quiet area to the north of Pattaya and is ideal for families. The bright and spacious rooms are comfortably furnished and the stylish restaurant serves good Thai and international cuisine. Cookery classes are available here. There is also a spa and a pretty garden. **www.woodland-resort.com**

PATTAYA Birds and Bees Resort ⓑⓑⓑⓑ

366/11 Moo 12, Phra Tam Nak 4 20150 ***Tel*** *0-3825-05567* ***Fax*** *0-3825-0557* ***Rooms*** *60* ***Road Map*** *D1*

A great place with a good cause, this resort is owned by a Thai NGO which specializes in community health, and has even received an award from the Bill Gates Foundation. Good work aside, it is a lovely family-oriented place with lovely gardens, a secluded beach, and a romantic seaside restaurant. **www.cabbagesandcondoms.co.th**

PATTAYA Hard Rock Hotel ⓑⓑⓑⓑ

429 Moo 9, Beach Rd 20260 ***Tel*** *0-3842-8755-9* ***Fax*** *0-3842-1673* ***Rooms*** *320* ***Road Map*** *D1*

There is something about Pattaya and the Hard Rock Hotel that go together perfectly. It has the biggest lagoon-style pool in Thailand, a manmade beach, theme parties, and the usual Hard Rock brand of fun. In addition to a relaxing spa, there is a great Lil' Rock program which keeps kids amused. **www.hardrockhotels.net**

PATTAYA Siam Bayview ⓑⓑⓑⓑ

310–12 Moo 10, Beach Rd 20260 ***Tel*** *0-3842-3871* ***Fax*** *0-3842-3879* ***Rooms*** *260* ***Road Map*** *D1*

One of Pattaya's most conveniently located hotels, the Siam Bayview sits right in the center of Ao Pattaya, and the rooms near the top of the nine-story main building enjoy excellent sea views. Facilities include tennis courts, swimming pools, restaurants, a business center, and a massage pavilion. **www.siamhotels.com**

PATTAYA Pattaya Marriott ⓑⓑⓑⓑⓑ

218 Moo 10, Beach Rd 20260 ***Tel*** *0-3841-2120* ***Fax*** *0-3842-9926* ***Rooms*** *295* ***Road Map*** *D1*

Located in the center of Ao Pattaya, this beautiful resort has elegantly furnished rooms, most of them with beach views, and a whole range of activities for guests. These include golf, horseback riding, scuba diving, and flying. There is also a huge pool, and a choice of several restaurants and bars. **www.marriotthotels.com**

PATTAYA Royal Cliff Beach Resort Hotel ⓑⓑⓑⓑⓑ

353 Moo 12, Pratumnak Rd 20260 ***Tel*** *0-3825-0421* ***Fax*** *0-3825-0511* ***Rooms*** *544* ***Road Map*** *D1*

Something of a legend among Pattaya hotels, this award-winning, super luxurious facility, set in 64 acres of sprawling grounds satisfies every wish. With several restaurants and bars, a spa, five swimming pools, tennis courts, a jogging trail, and a putting green, guests never need to leave the premises. **www.royalcliff.com**

PATTAYA Sheraton Pattaya Resort ⓑⓑⓑⓑⓑ

437 Pratumnak Rd 20260 ***Tel*** *0-3825-9888* ***Rooms*** *156* ***Road Map*** *D1*

Nestled in a picturesque headland south of Pattaya, this luxurious resort has a private beach and three swimming pools set in lush gardens, with sweeping views from the hillside rooms. Facilities are as one would expect from this respected chain, and the staff knows how to pamper guests. **www.starwoodhotels.com**

PATTAYA Sugar Hut ⓑⓑⓑⓑⓑ

391/18 Moo 10, Thabpraya Rd 20260 ***Tel*** *0-3825-1686* ***Fax*** *0-3825-1689* ***Rooms*** *28* ***Road Map*** *D1*

This gem of a hotel scores high for ambience and privacy. Although it is not close to the beach, the traditional Thai villas with curving roofs are set in a huge, rambling garden. Rooms are tastefully furnished, with two beds and mosquito nets, and the restaurant serves top-notch cuisine. **www.sugar-hut.com**

RAYONG Hin Suay Nam Sai Resort ฿฿฿

250 Moo 2, Charkpong, Klaeng 21190 **Tel** *0-3863-82605* **Fax** *0-3863-8034* **Rooms** *174* **Road Map** *D1*

This smart resort has excellent facilities, and its own private beach. All of the air-conditioned rooms with cable TV have sea views, and the health club offers several sports including tennis, squash, and badminton. There is also a multicuisine restaurant and karaoke bar. **www.travelthailand.com**

RAYONG Wang Gaew ฿฿฿

214 Pae-Klaeng Rd, Charkpong 21190 **Tel** *0-3863-8067* **Fax** *0-3863-8068* **Rooms** *30* **Road Map** *D1*

Probably only worthwhile for long stays, this eclectic collection of beach houses with their own kitchens on a private bay is favored by Thai families. This resort offers a more local experience than other places and is a good place to discover authentic Thai cuisine. **www.wangkaew.co.th**

RAYONG Purimas Beach Hotel ฿฿฿฿

4/5 Moo 3, Pae Klang Kam Rd **Tel** *0-3863-0382* **Rooms** *79* **Road Map** *D1*

A stylish resort with its own private beach, superb facilities, and attentive service. All the spacious and airy suites have private balconies as well as mini-bars, TVs, and comfortable furnishings. Guests can enjoy themselves at the beach, get pampered at the spa, and indulge themselves at the two excellent restaurants. **www.purimas.com**

TRAT Baan Jai Dee ฿

67 Chaimongkhon Rd **Tel** *0-3952-0678* **Rooms** *8* **Road Map** *E2*

This is a good option during a stopover in Trat. A handful of simple but clean rooms are split between an old building and a newer extension; the bathrooms are shared. The Baan Jai Dee has comfortable areas where the owners' artworks are displayed. The English and French breakfasts served during peak season are quite good.

UPPER WESTERN GULF COAST

CHA-AM Nana House ฿฿

208/3 Ruamchit Rd 76120 **Tel** *0-3243-3632* **Rooms** *25* **Road Map** *C1*

This cluster of bright purple buildings at the northern end of town are simple and affordable. The owner speaks good English and keeps the place spotless. The top-floor suite has a private balcony with great sea views. The beach is within splashing distance. **www.nanahouse.net**

CHA-AM Regent Chalet Regent Beach Cha Am ฿฿฿

849/21 Phet Kasem Rd 76120 **Tel** *0-3245-1240* **Fax** *0-3247-1492* **Rooms** *142* **Road Map** *C1*

An eco-friendly and less expensive alternative to the sister property, Regent Cha-am Beach resort, these garden chalets are suited for those who can forsake a more luxurious option. There is a spa and guests can also use all the facilities in the adjacent resort. **www.regent-chaam.com**

CHA-AM Dusit Thani Hua Hin ฿฿฿฿฿

1349 Phet Kasem Rd **Tel** *0-3252-0009* **Fax** *0-3252-0296* **Rooms** *300* **Road Map** *C1*

The upscale Dusit Thani Hua Hin is actually at Cha-am, not Hua Hin, but the latter's attractions are only ten minutes away. This stunning resort features plush rooms and balconies with sea views. There are two sublime swimming pools, a spa, and superb recreation facilities. **www.dusit.com**

CHA-AM The Hotel Cha Am ฿฿฿฿฿

115 Moo 7, Tambol Bangkao 76120 **Tel** *0-3270-9555* **Fax** *0-3247-3190* **Rooms** *72* **Road Map** *C1*

The Hotel Cha Am has a contemporary and very sophisticated atmosphere. Designed by a leading Thai architect Duangrit Bunnag, with two floors of rooms overlooking an enormous reflecting pool, the unique design elements are also reflected in the resort's rooftop restaurant. **http://hotel-cha-am.com**

CHUMPHON Chumphon Cabana Resort & Diving Center ฿฿฿

69 Moo 8, Hat Thung Wua Laen 86000 **Tel** *0-7756-0245* **Fax** *0-7756-0247* **Rooms** *139* **Road Map** *C3*

Located on a beautiful stretch of pristine white sand with crystal clear waters, this modern resort has bright standard rooms, private bungalows, and a breezy restaurant right on the beach. A specialized diving and snorkeling center offers PADI-approved diving courses and trips to the best sites. **www.cabana.co.th**

CHUMPHON Novotel Chumphon Beach Resort and Golf ฿฿฿

110 Moo 4 Hat Paradonpab 86000 **Tel** *0-7752-9529* **Fax** *0-7752-9500* **Rooms** *86* **Road Map** *C3*

The Novotel has a modern ambience and clean rooms, all with satellite TV and Wi-Fi, as well as a balcony. The nine-hole golf course adjacent to the property balances the recreation opportunities for those not keen on watersports. Good service and fine dining. **www.novotel.com**

CHUMPHON Tusita Haven Resort ฿฿฿฿

259/9 Moo 1 Paktako, Tung Tako 86220 **Tel** *0-7757-9151* **Fax** *0-7757-9050* **Rooms** *23* **Road Map** *C3*

Now under management of Away Resorts, Away Tusita Resort is located just outside Chumphon town and comprises rooms and free-standing villas, some of which have Jacuzzis. In addition to an elegant decor, the management offers a plethora of activities such as cycling, kayaking, and fishing. **www.tusitaresort.com**

Key to Price Guide *see p290* **Key to Symbols** *see back cover flap*

HUA HIN Araya Residence ®®

15/1 Chomsin Rd 77100 ***Tel*** *0-3253-1130* ***Rooms*** *12* ***Road Map*** *C2*

Centrally located, this intimate boutique hotel has an Asian Zen minimalist style about it, with teak furniture and contemporary Thai decor. The attractive rooms are comfortable with cable TV, mini-bar, and complimentary wireless Internet. The rooftop rooms have sun beds and sea views. **www.araya-residence.com**

HUA HIN K Place ®®

116 Naresdamri Rd 77100 ***Tel*** *0-3251-1396* ***Fax*** *0-3251-4506* ***Rooms*** *12* ***Road Map*** *C2*

In a resort town not known for its budget hotels, K Place is a surprising bargain with big rooms that are simple, yet spotlessly clean, all equipped with fridge and TV. It is close to the action and only a short stroll away from the beach and night bazaar.

HUA HIN Leng Hotel ®®®

113/14 Phet Kasem Rd, Soi Hua Hin 67 ***Tel*** *0-3251-3546* ***Fax*** *0-3253-2095* ***Rooms*** *12* ***Road Map*** *C2*

This popular guesthouse is close to Hat Hua Hin and the lively night bazaar. Its simple homely rooms are clean and come with fridge, cable TV, and Internet. There is a good swimming pool, a decent café, and friendly staff to help with transfers and excursions. Visitors need to book ahead. **www.lenghotel.com**

HUA HIN Sirin Hotel ®®®

6/3 Damnoenkasem Rd 77100 ***Tel*** *0-3251-1150* ***Fax*** *0-3251-3571* ***Rooms*** *25* ***Road Map*** *C2*

Centrally located in the thick of Hua Hin's shopping and entertainment area, this is a great mid-range option. While it might not win any design awards, the pleasant and well-maintained rooms have cable TV, a mini-bar, and a balcony. There is a small, shaded swimming pool and a casual restaurant. **www.surinhuahin.com**

HUA HIN Thipurai Beach Hotel ®®®

113/27 Phet Kasem Rd 77100 ***Tel*** *0-3253-2731* ***Fax*** *0-3251-2210* ***Rooms*** *59* ***Road Map*** *C2*

A short walk from Hat Hua Hin, this hotel has clean, bright rooms with mini-bars, and cable TV. The rooms in the main building are smart, while the cheaper rooms at the annex are homely with floral bedspreads and curtains. There is a small swimming pool and a casual eatery serving local Thai dishes. **www.thipurai.com**

HUA HIN Anantara Resort & Spa ®®®®®

45/1 Phet Kasem Rd 77100 ***Tel*** *0-3252-0250* ***Fax*** *0-3252-0259* ***Rooms*** *187* ***Road Map*** *C2*

This lovely resort with expansive fragrant gardens, exotic architecture, and excellent restaurants, is a perfect tropical destination. The rooms with sea views are hard to resist and the plush lagoon rooms with waterside balconies have access to a private swimming pool. The spa is one of Thailand's best. **www.anantara.com**

HUA HIN Anantasila By The Sea ®®®®®

35/15 Phet Kasem Rd, Nongkae 77110 ***Tel*** *0-3252-76389* ***Fax*** *0-3251-5914* ***Rooms*** *73* ***Road Map*** *C2*

Located on the coast just south of Hua Hin town, with a working fishing village further down the beach, this resort is small and intimate with a variety of accommodations and a fairly large swimming pool. It also organizes activities for young kids. **www.anantasila.com**

HUA HIN Chiva-Som International Health Resort ®®®®®

73/4 Phet Kasem Rd 77100 ***Tel*** *0-3253-6536* ***Fax*** *0-3251-1154* ***Rooms*** *57* ***Road Map*** *C2*

This seaside destination spa and health resort is set in tranquil gardens with lily ponds and Buddha statues. Guests receive a consultation on arrival. All meals, a wide array of spa treatments, fitness classes, and activities are included in the package. A minimum three-night stay is required. **www.chivasom.com**

HUA HIN Putahracsa ®®®®®

22/65 Naep Kaehat Rd 77100 ***Tel*** *0-3253-1470* ***Fax*** *0-3253-1488* ***Rooms*** *58* ***Road Map*** *C2*

Minimalist and uncluttered design in a residential area of Hua Hin, but within walking distance of the action, the stylish Putahracsa has a variety of rooms and villa suites, all tastefully designed and appointed. There are two properties astride a road, so not all rooms are on the beach. **www.putahracsa.com**

HUA HIN Sofitel Centara Grand Resort and Villas ®®®®®

1 Damnoenkasem Rd 77100 ***Tel*** *0-3251-2021* ***Fax*** *0-3251-1014* ***Rooms*** *249* ***Road Map*** *C2*

Originally opened in 1923, at the terminus of the new railway to Hua Hin, this classic hotel has been consistently voted as one of the top ten in Asia. The grand Colonial style building's expansive manicured grounds and beachfront location are simply fabulous. The private-pool villas are truly luxurious. **www.sofitel.com**

PHETCHABURI Royal Diamond Hotel ®®

555 Moo 1 Phet Kasem Rd 76000 ***Tel*** *0-3241-1061* ***Fax*** *0-3242-4310* ***Rooms*** *58* ***Road Map*** *C1*

A modern and respectable mid-range place on the outskirts of town with views of the city and the mountains, this hotel is frequented by Thai business people and families. A good restaurant serves Thai and European cuisine, and the outdoor beer garden has a pleasant, tropical atmosphere. **www.royaldiamondhotel.com**

PHETCHABURI Fisherman's Village Resort ®®®®®

170 Moo 1, Hat Chao Samrin 76100 ***Tel*** *0-3244-1370* ***Fax*** *0-3244-1380* ***Rooms*** *35* ***Road Map*** *C1*

This stylish boutique resort of luxury villas on the beautiful beachfront of Hat Chao Samrin, a traditional fishing village in rural Phetchaburi, has an inviting swimming pool, a lovely spa, and an array of activities including fishing, watersports, hiking, cycling, and bird-watching. **www.thefishermansresort.com**

PRACHUAP KHIRI KHAN Banito Beach Resort ฿฿฿

283 Klang Ao Road, Ban Krut ***Tel*** *0-3269-5282-3* ***Fax*** *0-3269-5282* ***Rooms*** *60* ***Road Map*** *C2*

The Banito has a variety of bungalows running inland from the beach to a nice swimming pool. Located on Ban Krut, which is the favorite beach for Thais who wish to escape the bustle of Hua Hin, this resort combines the best of both worlds. Good seafood is available at the seaside pavilions. **www.banitobeach.com**

PRACHUAP KHIRI KHAN Sailom Resort ฿฿฿

299 Moo 5, Mae Rumpeung, Bang Saphan 77140 ***Tel*** *0-3269-1003* ***Fax*** *0-3269-1439* ***Rooms*** *12* ***Road Map*** *C2*

Sailom Resort is clean and popular with Thai families for its suites and villas. There is a nice big pool and the adjacent beach is nearly deserted. The restaurant serves good quality Thai cuisine, and the resort offers car rental if you wish to explore the surrounding area. **www.sailombangsaphan.com**

PRANBURI Aleenta Resort & Spa ฿฿฿฿฿

183 Moo 4, Pak Nam Pran 77220 ***Tel*** *0-3261-8333* ***Rooms*** *21* ***Road Map*** *C2*

This sleek minimalist property on a pretty beach makes for an ideal seaside escape. With just 21 luxury suites, bungalows, and a beachhouse – all with sea views – guests are assured peace and privacy. Thoughtful touches include iPod docks, complimentary wireless Internet, and daily gourmet treats. **www.aleenta.com**

PRANBURI Brassiere Beach Resort ฿฿฿฿฿

210 Moo 5, Thambon Sam Roi Yot ***Tel*** *0-3263-0555* ***Fax*** *0-3263-0554* ***Rooms*** *12* ***Road Map*** *C2*

The two oddly shaped islands just off the coast are a local legend and are responsible for this hotel's name. Each of the 12 separate cottages has an overall Mediterranean theme, but with different touches. The place has quirky elements, as well as leisurely dining options. **www.brassierebeach.com**

PRANBURI Evason Hua Hin Resort - Hideaway and Six Sense Spa ฿฿฿฿฿

9 Moo 3, Hat Naresuan 77220 ***Tel*** *0-3263-2111* ***Fax*** *0-3263-2112* ***Rooms*** *185* ***Road Map*** *C2*

These adjacent eco-friendly resorts located on a beautiful palm-lined beach are ideal retreats. The Hideaway, with its luxurious villas is more exclusive but both share superb facilities, excellent restaurants, bars, a gorgeous swimming pool, and several spas, including the extraordinary Earth Spa. **www.evasonresorts.com**

LOWER WESTERN GULF COAST

KO PHANGAN Beam Bungalows ฿

Hat Thian 82480 ***Tel*** *08-9647-4245* ***Rooms*** *12* ***Road Map*** *C4*

A coconut grove lies between thatched bungalows and the beach, but there is still a clear sea view from the rooms, and the beach is a short walk away. The atmosphere is laid-back with many long-staying guests. The food is simple but tasty. This resort is a youthful and vibrant place attracting the backpacker crowd.

KO PHANGAN Dolphin ฿฿

Ao Thong Nai Phan Yai 84280 ***Rooms*** *16* ***Road Map*** *C4*

Regular guests swear that the Dolphin, beautifully set in a large tropical beachside garden, is paradise and that its wooden huts, simply furnished with beds and mosquito nets, are just perfect. Comprising several Thai pavilions strewn with cushions, the garden restaurant has a reputation as the best in the area.

KO PHANGAN B52 Beach Resort ฿฿฿

Ao Tong Sala, Ban Tai ***Rooms*** *18* ***Road Map*** *C4*

This hip resort features funky cement bungalows with conical grass roofs set around a central garden area. Inside, mod cons and attractive decor make them good value. The beachfront rooms are huge and ultra-luxurious. There's also an infinity pool and sunken pool bar. **www.b52resortphangan.com**

KO PHANGAN Cocohut Village ฿฿฿

Hat Seekantang 84280 ***Tel*** *0-7737-5368* ***Rooms*** *16* ***Road Map*** *C4*

Just over the hill from busy Hat Rin, Hat Seekantang, also called Leela Beach, is a better beach than the former. Cocohut Village offers a variety of accommodations ranging from basic to luxurious beachfront villas with outdoor Jacuzzis. The food is good and the atmosphere laid-back, but so is the service. **www.cocohut.com**

KO PHANGAN Milky Bay Resort ฿฿฿

102 Moo 1, Hat Ban Tai 84280 ***Tel*** *0-7723-8566* ***Fax*** *0-7737-7726* ***Rooms*** *34* ***Road Map*** *C4*

A good mid-range choice at Hat Ban Tai. Rooms and rates vary considerably, but most units are free-standing bungalows. Facilities are many and include massages, a herbal steam room, and a fitness center. Guests can spend time lounging on the lovely beach and enjoying the Thai and Italian cuisine. **www.milkybaythailand.com**

KO PHANGAN Sanctuary & Wellness Center ฿฿฿

Hat Thian 84280 ***Tel*** *08-1271-3614* ***Rooms*** *30* ***Road Map*** *C4*

Yoga, massage, meditation, fasting, and colonic irrigation are all offered here, although some guests come here just to escape from the parties and bustle that Ko Phangan is renowned for. A wide variety of rooms are available, some with their own kitchens. **www.thesanctuarythailand.com**

Key to Price Guide *see p290* **Key to Symbols** *see back cover flap*

KO PHANGAN Best Western Phanganburi Resort

ⒷⒷⒷⒷ

120/1 Hat Rin Nai 84280 **Tel** *0-7737-5481* **Fax** *0-7737-5482* **Rooms** *105* **Road Map** *C4*

Close to the nighttime activities of Ko Phangan, this attractive mid-range resort has two swimming pools, one right on the beach, and also offers a variety of watersports including kitesurfing. Not strong on style but clean and efficient. **www.phanganburiresort.net**

KO PHANGAN Mandalai

ⒷⒷⒷⒷ

Ao Chalok Lam 84280 **Tel** *0-7737-4316-9* **Fax** *0-7737-4320* **Rooms** *12* **Road Map** *C4*

Cool, modern, clean, and right on the beach outside a small fishing village, this boutique hotel offers a wide variety of activities including elephant trekking and fishing trips. The rooms are very well-appointed and the food is excellent. A good place for those who want to escape the backpacker scene. **www.mymandalai.com**

KO PHANGAN Salad Beach Resort

ⒷⒷⒷⒷ

Hat Salad 84280 **Tel** *0-7734-9274* **Rooms** *48* **Road Map** *C4*

Hat Salad is an idyllic beach at the northwestern end of the island and the Salad Beach Resort is stylish and very comfortable. The massage service, restaurant, and pool are mentioned favorably by many guests. The waterfall Jacuzzi and open-air restaurant are other attractions. **www.phangan-saladbeachresort.com**

KO PHANGAN Sunset Cove Resort

ⒷⒷⒷⒷ

78/11 Moo 8, Hat Chao Phrao 84280 **Tel** *0-7734-9211* **Fax** *0-7734-9215* **Rooms** *18* **Road Map** *C4*

This boutique hotel might be a bit too small to be called a resort, but it is nonetheless the nicest place on Hat Chao Phrao. The resort's attractions include a pool on the beach with great sunset views, excellent food, value for money, and friendly service, all of which ensure a loyal clientele. **www.thaisunsetcove.com**

KO PHANGAN Green Papaya

ⒷⒷⒷⒷⒷ

64/8 Moo 8, Hat Salad 84280 **Tel** *0-7734-9278* **Fax** *0-7737-4230* **Rooms** *18* **Road Map** *C4*

Set amid a fragrant garden filled with coconut palms and a curved swimming pool, these beautiful bungalows by the beach have polished wooden floors. The artwork on the walls is probably the most stylish on the island. The boat-shaped restaurant and beach bar offer spectacular sunset views. **www.greenpapayaresort.com**

KO PHANGAN Panviman Resort

ⒷⒷⒷⒷⒷ

22/1 Moo 5, Ao Thong Nai Phan Noi 84280 **Tel** *0-7744-5101* **Fax** *0-7744-5100* **Rooms** *72* **Road Map** *C4*

Panviman Resort is the most exclusive address on Ko Phangnan, set high on a hill above the beach which affords excellent sea views. The frequent hotel shuttles take guests to the beach. Its lovely beachside barbecue restaurant and in-house spa complete the package. **www.panviman.com**

KO SAMUI The Boardroom

ⒷⒷ

21/1 Moo 4 Bangrak 84280 **Tel** *0-7724-5135* **Rooms** *5* **Road Map** *C4*

The Boardroom beach bungalows are set in lovely tropical gardens and have direct access to the beachfront. Cheap, clean, and well kept, each has a fridge, hot shower, air con, and a private balcony. There is 24-hour security. An excellent and cheap beach bar run by the owners completes the experience.

KO SAMUI Shambala

ⒷⒷ

23/2 Moo 4, Hat Bangrak 84280 **Tel** *0-7742-5330* **Rooms** *15* **Road Map** *C4*

Run by an English couple, the Shambala offers a rustic and relaxed set of rooms close to the beach. Facilities are few, but the staff is friendly and helpful. Shambala supports responsible tourism and promotes local culture, making this a different kind of experience. **www.samui-shambala.com**

KO SAMUI Sunrise Bungalow

ⒷⒷ

Hat Lamai 84310 **Tel** *0-7742-4433* **Rooms** *16* **Road Map** *C4*

Near the Hin Ta Hin Yai rock at the southern end of Hat Lamai, Sunrise Bungalow is the longest-running place in Lamai. Rooms run the gamut from very basic fan-cooled huts to modern air-conditioned bungalows, some right on the beach and some in a garden at the back of the property. **www.sunrisebungalow.com**

KO SAMUI Am Samui Resort

ⒷⒷⒷ

227 Moo 3, Hat Taling Ngam 84140 **Tel** *0-7723-5165* **Rooms** *47* **Road Map** *C4*

Located on the quieter west coast of the island, this unpretentious set of bungalows is renowned for cleanliness and value. Casual and comfortable, it is a good place for families. The open-air restaurant serves good Thai and Western food. **www.amsamuiresort.com**

KO SAMUI Coral Cove Chalet

ⒷⒷⒷ

210 Moo 4, Hat Tong Takian 84320 **Tel** *0-7742-2260* **Fax** *0-7742-2496* **Rooms** *81* **Road Map** *C4*

These attractive chalets are nestled on a palm-covered hillside overlooking a cove. Coral Cove Chalet has its own private beach and the spacious rooms are painted in pastel colors with big beds covered with mosquito nets. It is possible to snorkel and scuba dive in the coral reefs offshore. **www.coralcovechalet.com**

KO SAMUI Jungle Club

ⒷⒷⒷ

Soi Panyadee School, Hat Chaweng 84280 **Tel** *08-1894-2327* **Rooms** *11* **Road Map** *C4*

This is an excellent respite from the frenetic beach scene, since it is built high on a hill above Hat Chaweng. The emphasis is on relaxation rather than crazy parties. There are a variety of accommodations from simple huts to lavish villas. The management is French and the food is quite good. **www.jungleclubsamui.com**

KO SAMUI Juzz'a Pizza ⒷⒷⒷ

6/3 Moo 1, Bophut 84320 **Tel** *0-7724-5662-3* **Rooms** *8* **Road Map** *C4*

A long-time favorite of those in the know, Juzz'a Pizza is one of Samui's hidden gems. Rooms are decorated with beautiful teak furnishings and antiques, and have extremely comfortable mattresses. The standout feature is the ground-floor restaurant, which serves Italian classics and Thai fusion dishes. **http://juzzapizza.com**

KO SAMUI Lamai Wanta ⒷⒷⒷ

124/264 Moo 3, Hat Lamai 84310 **Tel** *0-7742-4550* **Fax** *0-7742-4218* **Rooms** *74* **Road Map** *C4*

Close to all the action in Lamai, but far enough to be quiet and still directly on the beach, this hotel is quite clean and comfortable. Lamai Wanta is not super stylish or full of facilities, but it does have a nice infinity pool which is right next to the beach, as is the hotel's restaurant. **www.lamaiwanta.com**

KO SAMUI L'Hacienda ⒷⒷⒷ

98/2 Moo 1, Hat Bophut 84320 **Tel** *0-7724-5943* **Rooms** *12* **Road Map** *C4*

This place owned by a French couple is an odd mixture of Asian, Mediterranean, and South American styles, but the agreeable atmosphere, excellent food and service, and the rooftop swimming pool make it worth the while. Close to the beach and the village of Bophut, L'Hacienda offers value for money. **www.samui-hacienda.com**

KO SAMUI Ocean's 11 ⒷⒷⒷ

23 Moo 4, Bangrak, Bophut 84310 **Tel** *0-7724-5134* **Rooms** *6* **Road Map** *C4*

Ocean's 11 is the perfect choice for those looking for simple, elegant comfort on Samui. The hotel has a quiet strip of beachfront and well-priced rooms with contemporary Thai decor, flatscreen TVs, and good linens. The hotel restaurant is renowned on the island.

KO SAMUI Coconut Villa Resort and Spa ⒷⒷⒷⒷ

Laem Hin Khom, Ao Taling Ngam 84140 **Tel** *0-7733-4069* **Fax** *0-7733-4071* **Rooms** *53* **Road Map** *C4*

The main point of interest here is the seclusion – the resort is located on its own private beach. There are six villas, plush suites, two swimming pools, and good spa facilities. Kayaking trips complete the package. Visitors should hire a car to be able to travel around the area. **www.coconutvillaresort.com**

KO SAMUI Pinnacle Samui Coco Palm ⒷⒷⒷⒷ

26/19 Moo 4, Hat Mae Nam 84330 **Tel** *0-7742-7308* **Fax** *0-7743-7309* **Rooms** *70* **Road Map** *C4*

The Coco Palm, a long-time favorite at Mae Nam has been taken over by a Thai chain called Pinnacle. Except for the name change, much is the same. It is friendly and unpretentious, with the emphasis on cleanliness and value rather than style. Standard rooms and cottages are available. **www.pinnaclehotels.com**

KO SAMUI Anantara ⒷⒷⒷⒷⒷ

99/9 Moo 1, Ao Bophut 84320 **Tel** *0-7742-8300* **Fax** *0-7742-8310* **Rooms** *106* **Road Map** *C4*

With its exotic Thai architecture, Zen minimalist rooms, and tranquil tropical gardens replete with palms, lily ponds, lotus flowers, and pretty Thai pavilions, the Anantara is simply sublime. If these are not reasons enough to stay, there is also an infinity pool, an exotic spa, and superb restaurants and bars. **www.anantara.com**

KO SAMUI Blue Lagoon Hotel ⒷⒷⒷⒷⒷ

99 Moo 2, Hat Chaweng 84320 **Tel** *0-7742-2037* **Fax** *0-7742-2401* **Rooms** *74* **Road Map** *C4*

Beautiful Thai architecture and the location on an attractive stretch of Hat Chaweng make this resort a popular choice. Families love the swimming pools and the wide range of watersports including kayaking, snorkeling, sailing, and water-skiing. The hotel's Kantara restaurant is excellent. **www.bluelagoonhotel.com**

KO SAMUI Centara Villas Samui ⒷⒷⒷⒷⒷ

38/2 Moo 3, Hat Na Thian **Tel** *0-7742-4020* **Fax** *0-7742-4022* **Rooms** *1000* **Road Map** *C4*

Situated on the pretty, palm-lined Hat Na Thian in southern Samui, this property offers extremely luxurious free-standing villas. The bright and airy Thai-style villas feature colorful, contemporary decor, and some have private Jacuzzis or plunge pools. The beachside Reef Café is popular. **www.centarahotelresorts.com**

KO SAMUI Four Seasons ⒷⒷⒷⒷⒷ

219 Moo 5 Ang Thong, Laem Yai 84140 **Tel** *0-7724-3000* **Fax** *0-7724-3002* **Rooms** *74* **Road Map** *C4*

Sprawled across palm-covered hills overlooking a cove, these luxurious villas on stilts have private infinity pools with sea views. There are two superb restaurants serving Thai, Italian, and seafood dishes, a beachside lounge bar, and a sublime spa set amid the jungle. This is Samui's best resort. **www.fourseasons.com**

KO SAMUI The Library ⒷⒷⒷⒷⒷ

14/1 Moo 2, Hat Chaweng 84320 **Tel** *0-7742-2767* **Fax** *0-7742-2344* **Rooms** *26* **Road Map** *C4*

This chic designer hotel was developed around the idea of books and reading. The Library has a floor-to-ceiling glass room crammed with books, magazines, and CDs for guests to use, right beside the red-tiled swimming pool. The minimalist white rooms are striking and the restaurant called The Page is excellent. **www.thelibrary.co.th**

KO SAMUI Melati Beach Resort ⒷⒷⒷⒷⒷ

9/99 Moo 5, Bophut, Thongson Bay 84280 **Tel** *0-7791-3400-20* **Rooms** *77* **Road Map** *C4*

This stunning resort is designed to reflect elements of a traditional Thai village, while offering ultra-luxurious contemporary furnishings. Most rooms have private pools. The resort is not within walking distance of other amenities but there's a shuttle bus twice a day. **www.melatiresort.com**

Key to Price Guide *see p290* **Key to Symbols** *see back cover flap*

KO SAMUI Muang Kulaypan Hotel ⒷⒷⒷⒷⒷ

100 Moo 2, Hat Chaweng 84320 ***Tel*** *0-7723-0850* ***Fax*** *0-7723-0031* ***Rooms*** *42* ***Road Map*** *C4*

This hip hotel attracts a funky crowd. Its boho-chic rooms have tie-and-dye bed covers, big black bathrooms, and art on the walls. The sculptures around the property and a stunning black-tiled swimming pool add to the appeal of the place. Top it off with cocktails at the bar on the beach. **www.kulaypan.com**

KO SAMUI Napasai by Orient Express ⒷⒷⒷⒷⒷ

65/10 Moo 5, Mae Nam 84330 ***Tel*** *0-7742-9200* ***Fax*** *0-7742-9201* ***Rooms*** *45* ***Road Map*** *C4*

The Thai-style villas here are luxurious but not over the top. There is an infinity pool on the beach, but each villa has its own private plunge pool. There is an on-site spa, tennis courts, and a golf course which is a five-minute drive away. Deep-sea fishing and jungle trekking can be arranged by the resort. **www.napasai.com**

KO SAMUI Pavilion Samui Boutique Resort ⒷⒷⒷⒷⒷ

124/24 Moo 3, Hat Lamai 84310 ***Tel*** *0-7742-4030* ***Fax*** *0-7724-2029* ***Rooms*** *73* ***Road Map*** *C4*

Opulence and style pervade these villas, all with their own Jacuzzis or private pools. The atmosphere is romantic and in fact the resort specializes in honeymoon packages. The food is excellent but is confined to seafood specialties and fine wines. There is an on-site spa and a fully equipped fitness center. **www.pavillionsamui.com**

KO SAMUI Six Senses Hideaway ⒷⒷⒷⒷⒷ

9/10 Moo 5, Baan Plai Laem, Bophut 84320 ***Tel*** *0-7724-5678* ***Fax*** *0-7724-5671* ***Rooms*** *66* ***Road Map*** *C4*

This destination spa offers a collection of plush villas differing in size but not in luxury. All have either Jacuzzis or private infinity pools and are superbly appointed. The staff is extremely attentive and the food is excellent. This is probably one of the top three places for a luxurious stay on Ko Samui. **www.sixsenses.com**

KO SAMUI Weekender Resort ⒷⒷⒷⒷⒷ

124/19 Moo 3, Hat Lamai 84310 ***Tel*** *0-7742-4429* ***Fax*** *0-7742-4011* ***Rooms*** *122* ***Road Map*** *C4*

Weekender Resort is on the southern end of Hat Lamai and offers a wide range of accommodations, including luxurious suites. The style is contemporary and elegant. The restaurant – Sunday's Brasserie – offers an interesting beachside dining experience. An in-house spa completes the package. **www.weekender-samui.com**

KO SAMUI Zazen ⒷⒷⒷⒷⒷ

177 Moo 1, Bophut 84320 ***Tel*** *0-7742-5085* ***Fax*** *0-7742-5177* ***Rooms*** *22* ***Road Map*** *C4*

There is a lot of originality in style and design here – it is not just another boutique resort. The rooms and villas of this activity-oriented place have an orange sun-washed color scheme and tiled roofs. They are justifiably proud of their master chef and the restaurant is renowned for its interesting fusion food. **www.samuizazen.com**

KO TAO Ban's Diving Resort ⒷⒷ

Hat Sai Ri 84280 ***Tel*** *0-7745-6061* ***Fax*** *0-7745-6466* ***Rooms*** *12* ***Road Map*** *C3*

This is one of the most popular PADI centers in southeast Asia, and so tends to be busy and crowded. With the focus of the resort on diving, rooms and customer service tend to take a back seat. Top rooms are comfortable and stylish, but the cheaper, older rooms can be a bit poky and damp. **http://bansdivingresort.com**

KO TAO JP Resort ⒷⒷ

Ao Chalok Ban Kao 84280 ***Tel*** *0-7745-6099* ***Rooms*** *44* ***Road Map*** *C3*

This beach, located in the extreme south of Ko Tao, is much quieter than Hat Sai Ri, and the water is shallow so it is preferable for families. The JP Resort has a variety of pleasant and economically priced bungalows located on the hillside above their beachside restaurant. Everything is clean and solid without any frills. **www.jpresort.asia**

KO TAO Mango Bay Grand Resort ⒷⒷⒷ

Ao Mamuang 84280 ***Tel*** *0-7745-6097* ***Rooms*** *15* ***Road Map*** *C3*

This is an excellent mid-range choice on an isolated cove on the north shore of the island. It is not as spectacularly designed as some of the other places, but is still tasteful and the snorkeling in front of the resort is superb. It offers both Thai and Italian food and a wide variety of activities. **www.kotaomangobay.com**

KO TAO Nangyuan Island Dive Resort ⒷⒷⒷ

Ko Nangyuan 84280 ***Tel*** *0-7745-6088* ***Rooms*** *55* ***Road Map*** *C3*

This private island in a small three-island archipelago offers beautiful bungalows set among big boulders around a gorgeous azure-colored cove. Guests come for the excellent diving among superb marine life on the coral reef encircling the island. Depending on the tide, guests can walk or swim to the resort café. **www.nangyuan.com**

KO TAO Charm Churee Villa ⒷⒷⒷⒷ

30/1 Moo 2, Ao Jansom 82480 ***Tel*** *0-7745-6393* ***Fax*** *0-7745-6475* ***Rooms*** *73* ***Road Map*** *C3*

Located just south of Hat Sai Ri, this spectacular resort and spa has design elements right out of a movie set. There are quirky elements everywhere and guests can enjoy lunch at the beachside Elvis Café. Most of the bungalows are more like villas, and the views are spectacular. **www.charmchureevilla.com**

KO TAO Dusit Buncha Resort ⒷⒷⒷⒷ

31/3 Moo 1 Tambol Ko Tao 84280 ***Tel*** *0-7745-6730* ***Rooms*** *40* ***Road Map*** *C3*

Not affiliated with the Dusit group, this unique spot on the northwestern corner of the island overlooks Ko Nangyuan and is not too far from the bustling Hat Sai Ri. It is popular with Thais who enjoy the local version of eco-friendly resorts – the bungalows here blend with the natural environment. **www.dusitbuncharesort.com**

KO TAO Bamboo Huts ⒷⒷⒷⒷⒷ

30/2 Jax Trek, Koh Tao 84360 ***Tel*** *0-7745-6394* ***Rooms*** *20* ***Road Map*** *C3*

With a range of simple, bamboo-built huts clustered on a rocky hillside and linked by rustic walkways, the sunset views from this resort are spectacular. Rooms are furnished in charming, island-style decor, and top rooms feature private plunge pools. The staff is friendly. **http://kohtaobamboohuts.com**

KO TAO Jamahkiri Resort & Spa ⒷⒷⒷⒷⒷ

Ao Thian Ok 84360 ***Tel*** *0-7745-6400* ***Rooms*** *12* ***Road Map*** *C3*

The Resort and Spa's 12 bungalows are nestled among boulders on a hillside just above the shoreline thus merging into the natural surroundings. There is an on-site spa, excellent Western and Thai food, and well-managed diving tours. It is probably the most luxurious resort on Ko Tao. **www.jamakiri.com**

NAKHON SI THAMMARAT Grand Park Hotel ⒷⒷ

1204/79 Pak Nakhon Rd 80200 ***Tel*** *0-7531-7666-73* ***Fax*** *0-7531-7674* ***Rooms*** *82* ***Road Map*** *C4*

It does not have a park, nor is it particularly grand, but this hotel is clean, modern, fairly priced, and centrally located. This is the best choice for travelers on a stopover at Nakhon Si Thammarat while en route to a beach destination. Get a room with a view and try the southern curries on offer in the restaurant. **www.grandparknakhon.com**

NAKHON SI THAMMARAT Racha Kiri ⒷⒷⒷⒷ

Hat Nai Phlao 80210 ***Tel*** *0-7530-0245* ***Fax*** *0-7530-0295* ***Rooms*** *33* ***Road Map*** *C4*

If a trip to Ko Samui is not possible, this is a good second choice. Located on the mainland, a 15-minute drive from the ferry landing, the Racha Kiri replicates a tropical resort atmosphere in splendid isolation on the coast. However, the beach falls short compared to Ko Samui's lovely stretches. **www.rachakiri.com**

SURAT THANI Ban Don Hotel Ⓑ

268/2 Na Mueng Rd 84000 ***Tel*** *0-7726-2177* ***Rooms*** *16* ***Road Map*** *C4*

This is another good hotel for a stopover and the best budget choice in town. The ground floor has a decent Chinese restaurant, and upstairs there is a choice of fan-cooled or air-conditioned rooms with private baths, and at prices that are hard to find on Ko Samui. Look for a room off the street to escape the noise.

SURAT THANI 100 Islands Resort & Spa ⒷⒷ

19/6 Moo 3, Bypass Rd, Makhamtia 84000 ***Tel*** *0-7720-1151* ***Rooms*** *38* ***Road Map*** *C4*

If downtown Surat Thani does not appeal, this teakwood palace on the outskirts of town offers a lovely garden atmosphere and a swimming pool with a waterfall at very reasonable rates. Locals come here for meals at the excellent seafood restaurant. **www.roikoh.com**

UPPER ANDAMAN COAST

PHANG NGA BAY Pasai Cottage Bungalows Ⓑ

Ko Yao Noi 82160 ***Tel*** *0-8607-71257* ***Rooms*** *10* ***Road Map*** *B5*

Locally owned and managed, the basic nature of the place is offset by the friendly family atmosphere and excellent local food. The bungalows have a nice garden and face a lovely beach with a view of the offshore islands. There are queen-sized beds and 24-hour electricity, but the neighbor's chickens might annoy late risers.

PHANG NGA BAY Phang Nga Inn ⒷⒷ

2/2 Soi Lohakit, Phet Kasem Rd 82000 ***Tel*** *0-7641-1963* ***Rooms*** *12* ***Road Map*** *B5*

Once the stately home of a prosperous merchant, the inn is now divided into 12 teak-paneled units of varying shapes and sizes. The staff is friendly, helpful, and put together some great meals for the guests, including southern Thai curries. It is also off the main road so it is quiet.

PHANG NGA BAY Phang Nga Bay Resort Hotel ⒷⒷⒷ

20 Thadan Panyi 82000 ***Tel*** *0-7641-1067* ***Rooms*** *88* ***Road Map*** *B5*

This place offers something different from the regular beach-oriented hotels. Set on an estuary at a fair distance from the bay, the rooms offer incredible views of the surrounding jungle. The hotel's boat transports guests to some of the nearby beaches and islands. This place is slightly off the beaten track.

PHANG NGA BAY Yao Yai Resort ⒷⒷⒷ

Moo 7, Baan Lo Pareh, Pru Nai, Ko Yao Yai 82160 ***Tel*** *0-819684641* ***Fax*** *0-864714487* ***Rooms*** *21* ***Road Map*** *B5*

On the west coast of Ko Yao Yai, Hat Lo Pareh faces Phuket across Phang Nga Bay and has superb sunset views. This resort offers a choice of fan-cooled or air-conditioned bungalows, boat and diving trips, a lovely garden, helpful staff, and a good restaurant known for its fresh seafood. **www.yaoyairesort.com**

PHANG NGA BAY Lom Lae Beach Resort ⒷⒷⒷⒷ

Ko Yao Noi 82160 ***Tel*** *0-7659-7486* ***Rooms*** *7* ***Road Map*** *B5*

This small resort is set next to the beach in a spacious garden. Nice free-standing wooden bungalows are available at a mid-range price. There is an on-site dive shop. The resort is sometimes closed during the rains from May to September and visitors should call and check before making their way here. **www.lomlae.com**

Key to Price Guide *see p290* **Key to Symbols** *see back cover flap*

PHANG NGA BAY Six Senses Hideaway ⒷⒷⒷⒷⒷ

56 Moo 5, Ko Yao Noi 82160 **Tel** *0-7641-8500* **Fax** *0-7641-8518* **Rooms** *88* **Road Map** *B5*

Six Senses is synonymous with uncompromised standards of luxury. Each villa has a private infinity pool and a personal staff member to attend to every whim. There is a superb on-site spa. Winner of awards for luxury, style, and social responsibility, this is a truly lavish and exclusive resort. **www.sixsenses.com**

PHANG NGA COAST Khao Lak Banana Bungalows ⒷⒷ

4/147 Moo 7, Khuk Kak, Khao Lak 82190 **Tel** *0-7648-5889* **Rooms** *30* **Road Map** *B5*

A ten-minute walk from the beach, these clean and well-maintained bungalows get consistently good reviews and are a good budget option in Khao Lak. There is also a lush garden and large pool which is used for diving lessons. Choose between air-conditioned or fan-cooled rooms. **www.khaolakbanana.com**

PHANG NGA COAST Poseidon Bungalows ⒷⒷ

1/6 Khao Lak, Laem Kaen 82210 **Tel** *0-7644-3258* **Rooms** *15* **Road Map** *B5*

Located south of Hat Khao Lak, these bungalows offer a more relaxed choice for those who are looking for something quiet. Owned and managed by an environmentally conscious Swedish-Thai couple, they also offer trekking and diving tours of the Similan Islands. **www.similantour.nu**

PHANG NGA COAST Nangthong Bay Resort ⒷⒷⒷ

Ao Nang Thong, Khao Lak 82210 **Tel** *0-7648-5088* **Rooms** *79* **Road Map** *B5*

Right next to Hat Khao Lak and close to the restaurants and shopping area, this mid-range resort is a good choice for families since some of the rooms are huge and accommodate extra beds easily. The food is quite good and the staff aim to please but their English is shaky at times. **www.nangthongbeachresort.de**

PHANG NGA COAST Golden Buddha Beach Resort ⒷⒷⒷⒷ

Ko Phra Thong 82150 **Tel** *08-1892-2208* **Rooms** *27* **Road Map** *B5*

Located just off the coast in the north of Phang Nga province, Ko Phra Thong is an excellent respite from commercial beaches. This eco-resort has a homely atmosphere and specializes in new-age activities such as yoga, although more traditional pursuits also abound. **www.goldenbuddharesort.com**

PHANG NGA COAST Aleenta ⒷⒷⒷⒷⒷ

33 Moo 2, Khok Kloy 82140 **Tel** *0-7658-0333* **Fax** *0-7658-0350* **Rooms** *50* **Road Map** *B5*

This chic resort set on a deserted stretch of beach makes for an accessible and secluded escape. The sleek and minimalist suites have stunning sea views, iPods, yoga mats, and plunge pools. There is a cool beach bar and an excellent restaurant. **www.aleenta.com**

PHANG NGA COAST Khao Lak Wanaburee Resort ⒷⒷⒷⒷⒷ

26/11 Moo 7, Khuk Khak, Takua Pa 82190 **Tel** *0-7648-5333–5* **Fax** *0-7648-5750* **Rooms** *24* **Road Map** *B5*

Located on Hat Nang Thong, Wanaburee Resort offers first-class accommodations right on the beach. The free-standing villas are interspersed among lagoons and set in a forest-like garden. The rooms are comfortable and sturdy structures. The resort offers a variety of outdoor activities. **www.wanaburee.com**

PHANG NGA COAST Le Meridien Khao Lak ⒷⒷⒷⒷⒷ

9/9 Moo 1, Kuk Kak, Takua Pa, Khao Lak 82190 **Tel** *0-7642-7500* **Fax** *0-7642-7575* **Rooms** *120* **Road Map** *B5*

It is located south of Khao Lak town, but urban travelers will miss nothing since Le Meridien has everything. A truly sumptuous facility with three pools and lovely well-maintained gardens. The accommodations start with deluxe rooms right up to villas with private pools. **www.starwoodhotels.com**

PHANG NGA COAST Mukdara Beach Villa & Spa Resort ⒷⒷⒷⒷⒷ

26/14 Moo 7, Khuk Khak, Takua Pa 82190 **Tel** *0-7642-9999* **Fax** *0-7648-6199* **Rooms** *40* **Road Map** *B5*

With two pools – one beachside, one in the garden – visitors are spoiled for choice. The location is close to other restaurants but quiet. The villas come in a variety of shapes and sizes and are good for families despite not being as chic as some of the more design-oriented properties. **www.mukdarabeach.com**

PHANG NGA COAST Ranyatavi Resort and Spa ⒷⒷⒷⒷⒷ

32/7 Moo 5, Hat Pilai, Kok Kloy, Takuatung **Tel** *0-7658-0800* **Fax** *0-7658-0888* **Rooms** *53* **Road Map** *B5*

Located in the Hat Pilai area, it is close to Phuket town and visitors can easily travel there for entertainment options. The resort is renowned for its reliable management and excellent Thai food. Accommodations range from standard rooms to free-standing villas. Good for families. **www.ranyatavi.com**

PHANG NGA COAST Sarojin ⒷⒷⒷⒷⒷ

60 Moo 2, Khu Kak, Hat Bang Sak 82190 **Tel** *0-7642-7900–4* **Rooms** *56* **Road Map** *B5*

Located north of Khao Lak, Sarojin is a luxurious boutique resort which gets regular accolades from the travel press, as well as many returning guests. The grounds are spacious and the villas are beautifully designed. This is an intimate and expensive resort. **www.sarojin.com**

PHUKET Casa Brazil ⒷⒷ

9 Soi Luang Por Chuan 1, Hat Karon 83100 **Tel** *0-7639-6317* **Rooms** *21* **Road Map** *B5*

Brazilian motifs prevail throughout the hotel and the ambience is homely as well as ethno-chic. The decor is a celebration of South American arts and life with a Thai flair. The rooms are air-conditioned and clean, with vibrant furnishings. There is a nice garden and restaurant in the central courtyard. **www.phukethomestay.com**

PHUKET Fantasy Hill Bungalow ⒷⒷ

8/1 Patak Rd, Hat Karon 83100 ***Tel*** *0-7633-0106* ***Rooms*** *35* ***Road Map*** *B5*

Located on a hill between Hat Kata and Hat Karon, these clean budget bungalows offer excellent value and have an understated atmosphere. All units have a balcony and the bigger ones come with a porch around the veranda. There is a choice of fan-cooled or air-conditioned rooms, and a nice shaded garden.

PHUKET Laemka Beach Inn ⒷⒷ

159 Viset Rd, Chalong, Rawai 83100 ***Tel*** *0-7638-1305* ***Rooms*** *20* ***Road Map*** *B5*

On the southeastern coast of Phuket, the atmosphere is less frenetic than on the west coast beaches. This area is more the domain of yachtsmen, but Hat Laemka is calm and relaxed. The thatched-roof bungalows are close to the beach, and while some are air-conditioned, all of them are pleasantly airy.

PHUKET Shanti Lodge ⒷⒷ

1/2 Soi Bangrae, Choafa Nok Rd, Ao Chalong ***Tel*** *0-7628-0233* ***Rooms*** *20* ***Road Map*** *B5*

Located in a village off the coast, Shanti Lodge offers an excellent alternative to the beach scene where travelers can actually meet the local people. The lodge puts an emphasis on yoga and vegetarian food, although there are other options as well. It is inexpensive and relaxing, but not run down. **www.shantilodge.com**

PHUKET Square One ⒷⒷ

241/34 Ratuthit Rd, Hat Patong 83150 ***Tel*** *0-7634-9909* ***Fax*** *0-7634-9908* ***Rooms*** *14* ***Road Map*** *B5*

This budget hotel has simply decorated rooms that are spotlessly clean, with cable TV and fridge. Long-stay guests should upgrade to a suite, which is considerably more comfortable. There is wireless Internet and a small swimming pool, but hardly any space for sunbathing. **www.square1.biz**

PHUKET Baan Krating Resort ⒷⒷⒷ

11/3 Moo 1, Wiset Rd, Ao Sane, Rawai, 83130 ***Tel*** *0-7628-8264* ***Fax*** *0-7638-8108* ***Rooms*** *65* ***Road Map*** *B5*

Managed by the reliable Thai Amari chain, this secluded boutique resort is located in a unique jungle setting in the steep hills above Ao Sane. The hotel has a nice bar and restaurant set on a peaceful private beach, a short walk away. Excellent food. **www.amari.com**

PHUKET Baipho ⒷⒷⒷ

205/12-13 Rat-U-Tit Rd, Hat Patong 83150 ***Tel*** *0-7629-2074* ***Fax*** *0-7629-2207* ***Rooms*** *20* ***Road Map*** *B5*

A very chic little boutique hotel in the center of the action, Baipho is under Swiss management and everything runs like clockwork. The decor is modern with local touches, and the clientele is mainly young. The hotel serves excellent European food and special Jacuzzi rooms offer a touch of luxury. **www.baipho.com**

PHUKET Benyada Lodge ⒷⒷⒷ

106/52 Moo 3, Cherng Talay, Hat Surin 83110 ***Tel*** *0-7627-1261–4* ***Fax*** *0-7627-1265* ***Rooms*** *29* ***Road Map*** *B5*

This is a nice beach that has long been a favorite with locals. The five-story Benyada Lodge is close to the beach, has helpful staff, nice but ordinary rooms, and is done up in contemporary Thai style. The neighborhood offers quite a few dining options. **www.benyadalodge-phuket.com**

PHUKET Kamala Dreams ⒷⒷⒷ

74/1 Moo 3, Ao Kamala, Katu 83120 ***Tel*** *0-7627-9131* ***Fax*** *0-7627-9132* ***Rooms*** *18* ***Road Map*** *B5*

Situated on lovely, low-key Hat Kamala, Kamala Dreams is set around a decent-sized pool and consists of comfortable studios with sea views. Rooms have kitchenettes with a fridge and microwave. There is a small garden and a footbridge leading to the beach. **www.kamaladreams.net**

PHUKET Nai Harn Garden Resort ⒷⒷⒷ

Hat Nai Harn 83110 ***Tel*** *0-7628-8319* ***Fax*** *0-7628-8320* ***Rooms*** *23* ***Road Map*** *B5*

Located in the village of Nai Harn, this mid-range resort of bungalows and villas is a good choice, especially if guests have their own transportation to explore the back roads in this part of the island. There is a spa, Internet café, swimming pool, and a piano bar. The restaurant serves good food. **www.naiharngardenresort.com**

PHUKET Sino House ⒷⒷⒷ

1 Montree Rd, Phuket town 83000 ***Tel*** *0-7623-2494–5* ***Fax*** *0-7622-1498* ***Rooms*** *57* ***Road Map*** *B5*

An excellent mid-range choice in Phuket town, this hotel has a modern building, but the decor and atmosphere are retro-Chinese, with antiques and traditional Chinese artworks throughout. It is stylish and comfortable with an on-site spa and attracts a long-staying clientele. The staff is helpful. **www.sinohousephuket.com**

PHUKET Summer Breeze Inn Hotel ⒷⒷⒷ

85/130 Iravadee Village, Phuket town 83000 ***Tel*** *0-8189-37651* ***Fax*** *0-7652-6686* ***Rooms*** *5* ***Road Map*** *B5*

This friendly, no-frills guesthouse is located on a quiet side street close to the bus station. Clean rooms with air-conditioning and TVs have been decorated with care by the enthusiastic owners. Personal service goes above and beyond and you'll have the opportunity to mix with Thai people in their own environment. **www.summerbreezeinn.com**

PHUKET Coral Island Resort ⒷⒷⒷⒷ

48/11 Chofa Rd, Ko Hai, Chalong 83130 ***Tel*** *0-7628-1060* ***Fax*** *0-7638-1957* ***Rooms*** *63* ***Road Map*** *B5*

An excellent alternative to the bustling beaches of Phuket, this resort is located on Ko Hai, a few miles from the town of Chalong. This resort offers great mid-priced bungalows, lovely beaches, and a large swimming pool which is also used for PADI-certified dive courses. It is a good place for families. **www.coralislandresort.com**

Key to Price Guide *see p290* **Key to Symbols** *see back cover flap*

PHUKET Naithon Beach Resort ®®®®

23/31 Moo 4, Nai Thon Beach Rd 83110 **Tel** *0-7620-5379-80* **Fax** *0-7620-5381* **Rooms** *15* **Road Map** *B5*

For those traveling to the west coast who do not want a party scene, Hat Nai Thon with its windy beaches and sunset views is perfect. This mid-range resort consists of free-standing bungalows of varying sizes and a quaint poolside bar and restaurant. There are many dive shops in the area. **www.phuket-naithon.com**

PHUKET Royal Phuket City Hotel ®®®®

154 Phang Nga Rd, Phuket town 83000 **Tel** *0-7623-3333* **Rooms** *251* **Road Map** *B5*

This is mainly a businessman's hotel, so it offers efficiency, practicality, and good value, rather than a laid-back holiday atmosphere. Still, it is a pleasant and comfortable place to recuperate from beach or island forays. Good spa, fitness center, and views of the city from the pool. **www.royalphuketcity.com**

PHUKET Amanpuri ®®®®®

118 Moo 3, Sri Santhorn Rd, Hat Pansea 83110 **Tel** *0-7632-4333* **Fax** *0-7632-4100* **Rooms** *70* **Road Map** *B5*

Amanpuri aptly reflects the tranquility and peace after which it is named. This luxurious pavilion and villa complex, nestled within coconut groves, overlooks a white sand beach. The infinity pools have spectacular sea views and the superb restaurants are very romantic at night. **www.amanresorts.com**

PHUKET Banyan Tree Resort ®®®®®

33/37 Moo 4, Sri Soonthorn Rd 83110 **Tel** *0-7632-4374* **Fax** *0-7632-4375* **Rooms** *168* **Road Map** *B5*

Overlooking a lagoon, with an open lobby surrounded by water courts, this luxurious resort exudes serenity. The water theme continues throughout, from the pools to the lavish villas with private plunge pools and the special Spa Pool Villa, where a glass-encased bedroom appears to float on water. **www.banyantree.com**

PHUKET Diamond Cliff Resort & Spa ®®®®®

284 Phra Barami Rd, Kalim, Patong 83150 **Tel** *0-7634-0501* **Fax** *0-7634-0507* **Rooms** *333* **Road Map** *B5*

While the architecture and the interiors look dated, this big resort keeps families and groups entertained with eight restaurants and cafés, themed nights, and myriad activities, including cooking classes, vegetable carving, batik painting, glass painting, and massages, as well as tennis and golf lessons. **www.diamondcliff.com**

PHUKET Evason Six Senses Spa Resort ®®®®®

100 Viset Rd, Moo 2, Hat Rawai 83100 **Tel** *0-7638-1010* **Fax** *0-7638-1018* **Rooms** *260* **Road Map** *B5*

Sprawled across a tropical garden, this eco-friendly resort has something for everyone, from pool suites for couples seeking privacy to family-sized villas, all of which are superbly appointed. There is a children's pool and kids' club if parents want to retreat to the sublime infinity pool for adults. **www.sixsenses.com**

PHUKET Honeymoon Island Phuket Resort ®®®®®

100 Moo 7, Thambol Vichit, Ko Maiton 83110 **Tel** *0-7621-4954* **Fax** *0-7619-1117* **Rooms** *45* **Road Map** *B5*

This comfortable resort is set on a picturesque island 6 miles (10 km) from Phuket, and true to its name is a perfect romantic retreat with special honeymoon packages including kayaking, sailing, snorkeling, diving, as well a lovely private beach. **www.honeymoonislandphuket.com**

PHUKET Indigo Pearl ®®®®®

Hat Nai Yang 83110 **Tel** *0-7632-7006* **Fax** *0-7632-7015* **Rooms** *277* **Road Map** *B5*

The striking design at this hotel evokes the area's tin-mining history while incorporating recycled objects, found after the tsunami, and the owners' family heirlooms into the decor. Although it is large, clever architecture and landscaping succeed in making it feel more intimate. The pools are stunning. **www.indigo-pearl.com**

PHUKET Laguna Beach Resort ®®®®®

323 Sri Sunthorn Rd, Cherng Thalae 83110 **Tel** *0-7632-4353* **Fax** *0-7632-4174* **Rooms** *252* **Road Map** *B5*

Set around a tropical lagoon, this large resort is very comfortable. Rooms are spacious, with contemporary Thai decor and lagoon views. There are several alfresco eating places and an array of sports activities for the whole family, including a water park and a supervised kids' club. **www.lagunabeach-resort.com**

PHUKET Le Meridien Phuket ®®®®®

29 Soi Karon Nui, Tambon Karon 83100 **Tel** *0-7637-0100* **Fax** *0-7634-0479* **Rooms** *470* **Road Map** *B5*

Located in a hidden cove between Hat Patong and Hat Karon, Le Meridien brings more than a touch of French panache to the party. Lots of physical activities including tennis, rock climbing, and swimming in the many pools. There is an exclusive spa and fine cuisine is served at its restaurants. **www.starwoodhotels.com**

PHUKET Manathai ®®®®®

121 Sri Sunthorn Rd, Hat Surin 83000 **Tel** *0-7627-0900* **Fax** *0-7627-0911* **Rooms** *52* **Road Map** *B5*

This chic boutique resort features spacious, stylish rooms with contemporary teak furniture, Thai furnishings, Oriental antiques, and other amenities. Public spaces include a pool that is enchantingly lit at night, a lounge area that is wonderful for cocktails, and the superb Weaves restaurant. **www.manathai.com**

PHUKET Mom Tri's Villa Royale ®®®®®

12 Kata Noi Rd, Hat Kata Noi 83100 **Tel** *0-7633-3569* **Fax** *0-7633-3001* **Rooms** *28* **Road Map** *B5*

Mom is a Thai title reserved for nobility, and this hotel is named after its *bon vivant* owner, Mom Tri. He has established an oasis of good taste and luxury on a headland between Hat Kata Noi and Hat Kata Yai. All units are suites or free-standing villas. The food is famous throughout Phuket. **www.villaroyalephuket.com**

PHUKET The Royal Phuket Yacht Club ฿฿฿฿฿

23/3 Moo 1, Viset Road Rawai 83100 **Tel** *0-7638-0200–19* **Fax** *0-7638-0280* **Rooms** *110* **Road Map** *B5*

This lovely property was Phuket's first luxury hotel and is now a part of the Puravarna group. No longer the most luxurious hotel, this nevertheless remains a fine place to stay. The nine-story building seems to float up the hillside at the northern end of Hat Nai Harn. Superb facilities and fine food. **www.puravarna.com**

PHUKET Sugar Palm Resort ฿฿฿฿฿

20/10 Kata Rd, Hat Kata 83100 **Tel** *0-7628-4404* **Fax** *0-7628-4438* **Rooms** *129* **Road Map** *B5*

This stylish resort with modern rooms in pastel shades and a black-tiled swimming pool in the central courtyard is replete with designer touches and a youthful vibe. A perfect spot for the young urbanite on holiday, it is close to other shops and restaurants and the beach is only ten minutes away. **www.sugarpalmphuket.com**

PHUKET Thara Patong Beach Resort ฿฿฿฿฿

81 Thaweewongse Rd, Patong 83150 **Tel** *0-7634-0135* **Fax** *0-7634-0446* **Rooms** *172* **Road Map** *B5*

The smart lobby and friendly staff gives way to an attractive resort with several restaurants, bars, and cafés, along with two swimming pools, Jacuzzis, tennis courts, and sauna facilities. There is a pool for kids and an excellent seafood restaurant. Special promotional packages offer good deals. **www.tharapatong.com**

RANONG AREA Ko Chang Resort ฿

Ao Yai, Ko Chang 85000 **Tel** *08-1896-1839* **Rooms** *20* **Road Map** *B3*

These bungalows suit this quiet place well. This Ko Chang is not to be confused with the one on the eastern coast and is a much quieter counterpart. The resort fits in beautifully with the natural environment and is clean with a friendly and efficient staff. Splurge and get the biggest bungalow. **www.kochangandaman.com**

RANONG AREA Suta House Bungalows ฿

Ruangrat Rd 85000 **Tel** *0-7783-2707–8* **Rooms** *20* **Road Map** *B3*

These free-standing bungalows are nothing fancy, but they are an excellent budget choice in Ranong. The bungalows are centrally located but set back from the road so it is quiet here. There is a good on-site restaurant, but even better ones are nearby at a walking distance. Not much English is spoken here.

RANONG AREA Vijit ฿

Ko Phayam 85000 **Tel** *0-7783-4082* **Rooms** *30* **Road Map** *B3*

A long-standing locally owned bungalow operation on Ko Phayam, this place gets consistently good reviews for its cleanliness, efficiency, and good food. The mid-range accommodations are spacious and they have two-bedroom units ideal for families. Fishing and snorkeling tours are available. **www.kohpayam-vijit.com**

RANONG AREA Tinidee Hotel ฿฿฿

41/144 Tamuang Rd, Tambol Kao Nives 85000 **Tel** *0-7783-5240* **Fax** *0-7783-5238* **Rooms** *138* **Road Map** *B3*

This modern six-story building qualifies as Ranong's most comfortable hotel. It is in the city center, near the market. Mainly a business hotel, it is also good for a bit of recuperation after roughing it out on the islands. Several restaurants include a poolside barbecue. **www.tinidee-ranong.com**

LOWER ANDAMAN COAST

KO LANTA Sanctuary ฿฿

186 Moo 2, Ao Phra-Ae 81150 **Tel** *08-1891-3055* **Fax** *0-7568-4508* **Rooms** *18* **Road Map** *B5*

Located at the southern end of Ao Phra-Ae, also known as Long Beach, these thatched bungalows are a good budget choice. There is a definite hippy vibe here. Vegetarian food with an emphasis on Indian cooking, and yoga classes are part of the scene. The nearby clubs can get a bit noisy for early sleepers. **www.sanctuarykohlanta.com**

KO LANTA Narima Bungalow Resort ฿฿฿

98 Moo 5, Khlong Nin 81150 **Tel** *0-7566-2668* **Fax** *0-7566-2669* **Rooms** *32* **Road Map** *B5*

This designer bungalow resort and dive school is beautiful and sensitive to the environment. Its verandas and hammocks are positioned to take full advantage of the tropical garden and sea view. There is a good restaurant and jazz bar, but what really makes the resort special is the warmth of its owners. **www.narima-lanta.com**

KO LANTA Costa Lanta Resort ฿฿฿฿

212 Moo 1, Saladan 81150 **Tel** *0-7566-8186* **Rooms** *22* **Road Map** *B5*

This sleek beach resort is rather unique with its contemporary and minimalist architecture and it attracts a hip young crowd. The open-sided polished concrete rooms are not for those who value privacy, but style-seekers love them. The large restaurant and bar has a relaxed ambience. **www.costalantaresort.com**

KO LANTA Kaw Kwang Beach Resort ฿฿฿฿

16 Moo 1, Saladan, Ko Lanta Yai 81150 **Tel** *0-7568-4462* **Fax** *0-7568-4167* **Rooms** *43* **Road Map** *B5*

These little wooden cottages may not win any design awards, but there is a wide choice from standard rooms without a view to deluxe options with a sea vista. All are spacious, comfortable, and set in lush grounds, but highlights are the big, round swimming pool and lovely beachside location. **www.lanta-kawkwangresort.com**

Key to Price Guide *see p290* **Key to Symbols** *see back cover flap*

KO LANTA Pimalai Resort & Spa ⒷⒷⒷⒷⒷ

99 Moo 5, Hat Ba Kan Tiang 81150 ***Tel*** *0-7560-7999* ***Fax*** *0-7560-7998* ***Rooms*** *121* ***Road Map*** *B5*

This award-winning resort, with luxurious pavilion suites and villas, has superb cafés, bars, and restaurants, including the beachside Rak Talay, where guests can dine with their toes in the sand. There are two infinity pools, complimentary bicycles, watersports, island excursions, and sunset cruises. **www.pimalai.com**

KO LANTA Sri Lanta Resort ⒷⒷⒷⒷⒷ

111 Moo 6, Hat Khlong Nin 81150 ***Tel*** *0-7566-2688* ***Fax*** *0-7566-2687* ***Rooms*** *49* ***Road Map*** *B5*

This stunning boutique resort set in a large swathe of tropical hillside combines a chic sense of style with a rustic warmth rarely found in modern hotels. The black-tiled beachside swimming pool is enticing, the Sri Spa is sublime, and the beach bar and café are wonderfully relaxing. Service is excellent. **www.srilanta.com**

KO PHI PHI Ao Ton Ko Bungalows ⒷⒷ

Ao Ton Ko 81000 ***Tel*** *0-8153-7052-8* ***Rooms*** *32* ***Road Map*** *B5*

The beautiful, deserted beach with white sands and great snorkeling are the attractions here, and while these bungalows are basic, they do have decent-sized balconies with stunning beach and sea views. The friendly owner and staff, the good little restaurant, and the hillside bar with spectacular views add to its charm.

KO PHI PHI Phi Phi Natural Resort ⒷⒷⒷ

Mu 8, Laem Thong 81000 ***Tel*** *0-7581-9030* ***Rooms*** *48* ***Road Map*** *B5*

This was the first set of bungalows on Hat Laem Thong and they have a pleasant and slightly rustic charm. Somehow a Thai elementary school operates amid the bungalows which are built at a distance from each other among large trees. The food and management are more than satisfactory. **www.phiphinatural.com**

KO PHI PHI Phi Phi Island Village Beach Resort & Spa ⒷⒷⒷⒷⒷ

49 Moo 8, Ao Nang 81000 ***Tel*** *0-7562-8900–09* ***Fax*** *0-7562-8955* ***Rooms*** *112* ***Road Map*** *B5*

Located on one of Thailand's best beaches among lush vegetation and thick with coconut palms, this is as perfect as tropical resorts can get. There are plenty of accommodations from hillside pool villas to beachfront bungalows as well as restaurants, bars, swimming pools, watersports, and a PADI dive center. **www.ppisland.com**

KO PHI PHI Zeavola ⒷⒷⒷⒷⒷ

11 Moo 8, Laem Tong 81000 ***Tel*** *0-7562-7000* ***Fax*** *0-7562-7023* ***Rooms*** *48* ***Road Map*** *B5*

These charming teak villas with a rural Thai decor featuring tribal textiles are more suited to the Thai countryside than a plush beach resort, but the owner's aim was to recreate a luxurious Thai village right on the beach. The place is an experience in itself. **www.zeavola.com**

KRABI Chan Cha Lay Ⓑ

55 Uttarakit Rd 81000 ***Tel*** *0-7562-0952* ***Rooms*** *12* ***Road Map*** *B5*

This is an excellent budget choice in the middle of Krabi town. Cheerful, bright, and clean rooms with a touch of Mediterranean decor and helpful staff make it a good place from which to organize further forays into Krabi. There is a clean café serving simple food and a little garden. **www.chanchalay.com**

KRABI Ao Nang Village ⒷⒷⒷ

49/3 Mu 2, Ao Nang 81000 ***Tel*** *0-7563-7544* ***Rooms*** *28* ***Road Map*** *B5*

A locally owned and managed place with a nice green garden very close to the beach, these are a mixture of free-standing bungalows and rooms in a row, united by their extreme cleanliness and utter lack of stylishness. The idyllic quiet and family-run atmosphere is their biggest draw. **www.aonangvillage.com**

KRABI Sunrise Tropical Resort ⒷⒷⒷ

39 Moo 2, Ao Nang, Hat Rai Leh East 81000 ***Tel*** *0-7562-2599* ***Fax*** *0-7562-2597* ***Rooms*** *40* ***Road Map*** *B5*

An attractive resort set in a sumptuous garden on the less upscale Hat Rai Leh East, this place is a better deal than its neighbors. It is a quick walk to Rai Leh West and the even nicer Hat Tham Phra Nang. The teakwood villas are quite sumptuous, some with open-air showers and other nice touches. **www.sunrisetropical.com**

KRABI Krabi Resort ⒷⒷⒷⒷ

232 Moo 2, Ao Nang 81000 ***Tel*** *0-7563-7030* ***Fax*** *0-7563-7051* ***Rooms*** *170* ***Road Map*** *B5*

This picturesque resort is better known for its range of activities that include excursions, canoeing, fishing, rock climbing, sailing, scuba diving, snorkeling, cycling, horseback riding, and elephant trekking, rather than its uninspiring if comfortable rooms and bungalows scattered throughout a lush garden. **www.krabiresort.net**

KRABI Peace Laguna Resort ⒷⒷⒷⒷ

193 Moo 2, Ao Nang 81000 ***Tel*** *0-7563-7344-7* ***Fax*** *0-7563-7347* ***Rooms*** *149* ***Road Map*** *B5*

About a five-minute walk to the beach and set against a backdrop of a limestone karst, Peace Laguna Resort, as its name suggests, comprises cottages constructed around a lagoon. There are three pools and the atmosphere is quieter and more family-oriented than the beachside resorts. **www.peacelagunaresort.com**

KRABI Phra Nang Inn ⒷⒷⒷⒷ

119 Moo 2, Ao Nang 81000 ***Tel*** *0-7563-7139* ***Fax*** *0-7563-7134* ***Rooms*** *38* ***Road Map*** *B5*

This resort is constructed from pine and coconut palm wood and has a charming rustic air with tropical gardens, whimsical decor, and mismatched furniture. The Phra Nang Inn oozes character and is also centrally located with great views over Ao Nang. It has a terrific restaurant and a decent pool. **www.vacationvillage.co.th**

KRABI Krabi Sheraton ⒷⒷⒷⒷⒷ

Hat Khlong Muang 81000 ***Tel*** *0-7562-8000* ***Fax*** *0-7562-8028* ***Rooms*** *246* ***Road Map*** *B5*

The Krabi Sheraton is located on the upscale Hat Khlong Muang. Two swimming pools overlook the beach and the low-rise accommodations are set amid tropical gardens. Private speedboats take guests to the tiny offshore islands, and a resident elephant makes it a good family destination. **www.starwoodhotels.com**

KRABI Railei Beach Cub ⒷⒷⒷⒷⒷ

Hat Rai Leh West 81000 ***Tel*** *0-7562-2582* ***Fax*** *0-7581-9445* ***Rooms*** *24* ***Road Map*** *B5*

Ideal for families and groups, these traditional Thai teak houses are situated in a large private estate on a beautiful beach that is accessible only by boat. There are big verandas, gardens, and great views, and a clubhouse with rooms. Activities include diving, snorkeling, fishing, and bird-watching. **www.raileibeachclub.com**

KRABI Rayavadee ⒷⒷⒷⒷⒷ

214 Moo 2, Tambon Ao Nang 81000 ***Tel*** *0-7562-0740* ***Fax*** *0-7562-0630* ***Rooms*** *103* ***Road Map*** *B5*

This hotel spells indulgence right from the luxurious speedboat shuttle to its location on one of Thailand's most stunning beaches. Its two-story villas decorated with antiques, an excellent spa, two fine restaurants, an Asian crafts boutique, and exquisite attention to detail, make Rayavadee an exclusive retreat. **www.rayavadee.com**

SATUN Ang Yee's Guest House & Art Café Ⓑ

21/23 Tirasatit ***Tel*** *0-8053-4005-7* ***Rooms*** *5* ***Road Map*** *C6*

This delightful guesthouse is a rarity in Satun. Well-run, clean, and with friendly and obliging staff who can't do enough for their guests, it's an excellent budget choice when visiting the city. There are three air-conditioned rooms and two rooms with fans. There's also a bar and a shady, cool garden. **www.angyeesguesthouse.com**

SATUN National Park Bungalows ⒷⒷ

Ko Tarutao National Marine Park ***Tel*** *0-7478-1285* ***Rooms*** *16* ***Road Map*** *C6*

While these bungalows are quite basic, the beach setting is incredibly beautiful and it is a true delight for nature lovers. The resort facilities include toilets and showers, an information center, a mini-supermarket, and even a restaurant serving quality food and beer all day.

SATUN Sinkiat Thani Hotel ⒷⒷ

50 Burivanich Road 91000 ***Tel*** *0-7472-1056* ***Rooms*** *50* ***Road Map*** *C6*

This hotel is the best choice in Satun, right in the center of town, next door to On's excellent restaurant and provision stores. A good place to prepare for a trip to the islands, or to wash the salt and sand off in a nice big bathtub after an active day. Some of the rooms offer great views over the town and surrounding countryside.

SATUN Castaway Resort ⒷⒷⒷ

Sunrise Beach, Ko Lipe 91110 ***Tel*** *08-1170-7605* ***Rooms*** *20* ***Road Map*** *C6*

The resort lives up to its name with solid wooden bungalows in a rustic atmosphere on a remote island which is a three-hour boat trip from the mainland. Guests are rewarded with splendid isolation and a healthy environment. There is a dive shop with PADI instructors on-site, and the food is great. **www.castaway-resorts.com**

SATUN Pansand Resort ⒷⒷⒷ

Ko Bulon Leh 91110 ***Tel*** *0-7521-8035* ***Fax*** *0-7521-1010* ***Rooms*** *26* ***Road Map*** *C6*

This place is reminiscent of Phuket of a bygone era. All free-standing units, these nice cottages are well maintained and clean. The staff is extremely helpful and the restaurant serves excellent food. Since Bulon Leh is the closest island to the coast, it is the most visited, so book ahead. **www.pansand-resort.com**

TRANG Ko Mook Charlie Beach Resort ⒷⒷ

164 Ko Muk, Moo 2, Kantang 92000 ***Rooms*** *80* ***Road Map*** *C5*

This long-running resort used to be the only place to stay overnight at Ko Muk or Mook for all the visitors who came to see the famous Emerald Cave on the island. It has now morphed into a larger setup, with basic to mid-range choices. Good food and local information is available. **www.kohmookcharlieresort.com**

TRANG Le Dugong Resort ⒷⒷ

15 Moo 5, Ko Libong 92110 ***Tel*** *08-7972-7228* ***Rooms*** *10* ***Road Map*** *C5*

These rustic but utterly charming bungalows built of coconut, bamboo, and wood are a refreshing change from the luxurious resorts. The main activity here is scuba diving, but it is also ideal for lazing around. The resort derives its name from the dugong, an enormous marine mammal that lives in the nearby waters. **www.libongresort.com**

TRANG Coco Cottage ⒷⒷⒷ

109/77 Moo 9, Thambol Koke-Lor 92000 ***Tel*** *0-7522-4387* ***Rooms*** *26* ***Road Map*** *C5*

This low-key eco-friendly resort on the lovely island of Ko Ngai makes for an ideal beach getaway. Travel around the tranquil car-free island by foot or boat. The thatched-roof log cottages are simply decorated, and there are "longhouses" for families. The Thai owners are very hospitable. **www.coco-cottage.com**

TRANG Sukorn Beach Bungalows ⒷⒷⒷ

174 Moo 1, Ko Sukorn 92120 ***Tel*** *0-7520-7707* ***Rooms*** *20* ***Road Map*** *C5*

A very pleasant mid-range choice on one of Trang's undeveloped islands where the traditional way of life is still more important than tourists. The bungalows are decent and the management can organize kayaking, mountain biking, or fishing trips for guests. **www.sukorn-island-trang.com**

Key to Price Guide *see p290* **Key to Symbols** *see back cover flap*

TRANG Thumrin Thana Hotel ฿฿฿

69/8 Huayyod Rd 92000 **Tel** *0-7521-1211* **Fax** *0-7522-3288* **Rooms** *289* **Road Map** *C5*

This upscale hotel in central Trang town has plush, comfortable rooms with good views of the city and thoughtful extras that include complimentary soft drinks, daily newspapers, and free airport transfers. There is a good Japanese restaurant, bakery, and a popular pub and karaoke bar with VIP rooms. **www.thumrin.co.th**

TRANG Anantara Si Kao Resort ฿฿฿฿฿

Pak Meng Chang Lang Rd, Hat Chang Lang 92150 **Tel** *0-7520-5888* **Fax** *0-7520-5899* **Rooms** *144* **Road Map** *C5*

Trang's limestone peaks, pristine sandy beaches, tropical forests, waterfalls, and caves see less foreign tourists and, for many, that is the main attraction. The elegant design of the luxurious Anantara takes advantage of the spectacular surroundings, with sea-facing rooms and alfresco dining. **www.sikao.anantara.com**

TRANG Koh Mook Sivalai Beach Resort ฿฿฿฿฿

211/1 Moo 2, Ko Muk, Trang, 92110 **Tel** *0-8765-0999* **Rooms** *21* **Road Map** *C5*

These beautiful thatched-roof bungalows, nestled under coconut palms, are within splashing distance of the sea. The glass doors of the rooms open on to the beach, with the water just a few steps away. Also available are a good restaurant, a big swimming pool, and a range of watersports. **www.komooksivalai.com**

DEEP SOUTH

HAT YAI Louise Guesthouse ฿

21–23 Thamnoonvitti Rd 90110 **Tel** *0-7422-0966* **Rooms** *22* **Road Map** *C5*

Backpackers love this simple guesthouse, definitely the best deal in town. The staff is warm and friendly and can give reliable travel advice that is essential in this region. The hotel is close to transport connections and the bustling eating and shopping scene. While rooms may be spartan, they are well maintained and clean.

HAT YAI Regency Hotel ฿฿

23 Prachatipat Rd 90220 **Tel** *0-7435-3333–47* **Fax** *0-7423-4102* **Rooms** *436* **Road Map** *C5*

A decent mid-range choice in downtown Hat Yai. There are two wings – the Regent and the fancier Royal with 28 floors and over 400 rooms. The great location and right pricing make up for the slightly laid-back attitude of the staff. Skip the over-priced restaurants. **www.theregencyhatyai.com**

HAT YAI Novotel Centara ฿฿฿

3 Sanehanusorn Rd 90110 **Tel** *0-7435-2222* **Fax** *0-7435-2223* **Rooms** *245* **Road Map** *C5*

Aimed at business travelers, Novotel Centara in the center of Hat Yai is very comfortable, with well-appointed rooms with Internet. Guests can also rent DVDs from the hotel's collection. It is a rather stylish establishment with good restaurants, bars, and a fantastic rooftop swimming pool. **www.centralhotelsresorts.com**

NARATHIWAT Ao Manao Resort ฿

171/2 Tambon Kalong Nuea, Ao Manao 96000 **Tel** *0 7351 3640* **Rooms** *28* **Road Map** *D6*

Ao Manao or Lime Bay has a nice beach a few miles outside of Narathiwat. Earlier, this collection of decent bungalows within a walled compound used to be lively, but today there are few visitors. Still, it is fun to wander around the largely deserted beach and mix with the fisherfolk.

NARATHIWAT Imperial Narathiwat ฿฿฿

228 Pichitbumrung Rd 96000 **Tel** *0-7351 5041–50* **Fax** *0-7351 5040* **Rooms** *117* **Road Map** *D6*

Part of the upscale Thai Imperial Hotels group, this property caters mainly to visiting businessmen and politicians. It is located in the city center and, although it is quite cheap because of strained political conditions in the area which have reduced tourist footfall, the facilities are as per international standards. **www.imperialhotels.com**

PATTANI My Gardens Hotel ฿

8/28 Charoenpradit Rd 94000 **Tel** *0-7333-1055–8* **Rooms** *135* **Road Map** *D6*

Located near the clock tower with several good restaurants in the vicinity and close to the long-distance bus station, this hotel has clean rooms, safe premises, and is quite reasonably priced. The restaurant serves quality food. However, this establishment lacks the gardens after which it is named.

PATTANI CS Pattani ฿฿฿

299 Moo 4, Nong Jik Rd 94000 **Tel** *0-7333-5093* **Fax** *0-7333-1620* **Rooms** *125* **Road Map** *D6*

Pattani's prestigious address for visiting dignitaries is located a little outside of town. There are eight floors of modern convenience and comfort along with two pools, good restaurants, and friendly, well-trained staff who love to practice their English. The culinary specialty is birds' nest soup. **www.cspattanihotel.com**

SONGKHLA Rajamangala Pavilion Beach Resort ฿฿

1 Ratchadamnoen Nok Rd 90000 **Tel** *0-7448-7222* **Fax** *0-7448-7353* **Rooms** *34* **Road Map** *D5*

Located on Ao Samila, a short drive outside downtown Songkhla, this tastefully appointed two-story resort hotel is not to be confused with the Pavilion Hotel, which is not as nice. All the rooms have views of the Gulf of Thailand from their private balconies. **www.pavilionhotels.com/rajaman**

WHERE TO EAT

Thailand is fortunate in being a land of plenty. Much of the land is fertile and since the population has always been small relative to the size of the country, famine has been all but unknown. In the 13th century, King Ramkhamhaeng of Sukhothai, the first Thai kingdom, recorded: "This land is thriving … in the water are fish, in the fields there is rice". He might also have mentioned the wide range of tropical fruits, vegetables, and spices, to which have been added, since his day, a wealth of imports from South America, thriving in their new Oriental setting. The range of dishes, as well as the variety and freshness of the ingredients, make for one of the world's great cuisines. Thais love to eat – six or seven times a day is common. Apart from flavor and freshness, Thais also appreciate the harmonious presentation of food. The dishes of even a modest meal will often be garnished with flowers and rosettes carved out of colorful vegetables and fruit.

Sign for good quality restaurants

Staff preparing an elaborate buffet at an upscale hotel in Bangkok

RESTAURANTS

Bangkok's dining scene is one of the most cosmopolitan in Southeast Asia. Italian and French cuisines have been part of the culinary landscape for long, but now diners can also enjoy Japanese restaurants, Mexican and Tex-Mex bars and grills, and Sunday brunches at upscale hotels, in addition to traditional Thai food. Most urban restaurants, especially, those serving Western food, open at about 11am and close between 10pm and midnight. This can mean that finding a Western-style breakfast is difficult, in which case a regular Thai omelette may have to serve as a substitute.

Virtually every major city and resort in Thailand has at least one free tourist listings magazine. They can be picked up in hotel reception lobbies, at banks, money changers, and restaurants. These list restaurants by cuisine and specialty, often giving details of how to get there, along with telephone numbers. Away from the major tourist destinations, the main hotels in every town will have air-conditioned restaurants offering a mixture of Thai and Chinese cuisine.

Thais have taken to Italian and Japanese food with enthusiasm; the most popular imports are pasta and sushi, found in some of the larger towns. Pizzas are another favorite, but McDonalds's or Burger King outlets are relatively few and they have had to introduce local dishes, aimed at pleasing Thai palates, to attract Thai customers.

COFFEE SHOPS

A coffee culture has increasingly been taking hold in Thailand, with excellent, reasonably priced, and locally run coffee shops opening on every other street. Popular with Thais and foreigners alike, they do not include expensive Western franchises except in some larger cities. Local coffee shops are still favored by older citizens, who prefer a strong, sweet coffee, filtered through a cotton bag. Served with condensed milk, the coffee is excellent for dunking *paton go*, a traditional deep-fried Chinese breakfast doughnut.

ROADSIDE AND MARKET FOOD STANDS

Some of the best and most reasonably priced food in Thailand can be found at any of the numerous roadside food stalls. Such establishments are usually clean and unpretentious and are often mobile, allowing the proprietors to push them home and clean them every night. The ingredients are openly displayed behind glass panels. Fast cooking processes, such as flash-frying, grilling over

A beach bar and restaurant at Hat Tha Nam, Ko Chang

Bright neon signs announcing various eateries in Pattaya

charcoal, or boiling are often used. So the fare, invariably fresh, should also be well cooked and safe to eat.

A sure way of measuring a stall's popularity, as anywhere in the world, is by its patrons. If there are plenty of locals sitting at the simple tables most stalls provide, chances are that the food is good. Visitors should not be surprised to find a businessman with a Mercedes parked nearby sitting at the same stall as a tuk-tuk driver. Thais from all sections of society know how to appreciate good, cheap food.

Menus are rarely in English, so it is a good idea to memorize the names of some of the tastier dishes from the food glossary *(see pp316–17)*. Alternatively, it is possible for visitors to point at a dish and ask to taste before ordering.

PRICES

Buying meals is one of the cheapest aspects of a visit to Thailand. Prices are usually displayed – menus invariably list them next to each dish. The prices for shellfish are often given by weight. The cost of alcohol, however, can often be more than the meal itself. In larger establishments and hotels of international-class, a service charge and tax will usually be levied. These extra costs will be clearly detailed on the check.

Even at establishments which are small, prices are usually fixed and marked on a board. Bargaining is limited to bulk purchases in local markets selling fresh food.

SEAFOOD

Thailand offers some of the best seafood and it does not come any fresher than in the kingdom's coastal regions. Visitors can choose from an excellent range, absolutely fresh and generally on display. Everything from swordfish steak to lobster and giant crabs is available, but for conservation reasons, turtle and turtle's eggs are no longer on the menu. Visitors should also avoid eating shark's fin soup.

TIPPING

Tipping was once unknown, but its popularity is increasing as Thais grow accustomed to tips from tourists. Visitors should avoid applying a percentage: 10 percent of 50 baht may be appropriate, but 10 percent of an expensive meal would be far too much.

EATING HABITS IN THAILAND

The Thai philosophy of nutrition is simple – eat if hungry. Nothing should stand in the way. Most Thais, moreover, eat little but often, sometimes snacking six or seven times a day. The concept of three meals simply does not apply in Thailand. Although people do indeed eat breakfast, lunch, and dinner, they may also stop for a bowl of noodles, a fried snack, or a sweet at any time during the day.

Eating is a simple pleasure and does not involve complex rituals of etiquette, although

Fruits, popular with Thais and a favorite snack

visitors should note a few rules. Thais eat with a fork held in the left hand and a spoon held in the right hand. The fork is usually used only to push food onto the spoon; eating straight from a fork is considered crude. Since food, especially meat, is cut into pieces before it is cooked, knives are not needed.

Thai noodle dishes are often strongly influenced by Chinese culinary traditions, and they are eaten using chopsticks and a spoon. Another exception to the general rule is *khao niaw* (sticky rice), which is eaten delicately using the fingers.

Food in Thailand is usually served communally in a series of large bowls. Only small rice bowls are reserved for individual use. Rice is traditionally served first, and then a spoon is used to ladle two or three spoonfuls from the communal bowls on top of the rice. Feel free to ask for more if necessary. However, overloading the plate is regarded as uncouth since there is no need to hurry, and always plenty more in the kitchen.

Visitors enjoying a meal at one of the many street food stalls in Thailand

The Flavors of Thailand

Thai food is famous for its aromatic and spicy qualities. Chili peppers were first imported to Thailand from the New World in the 16th century by European traders and were adopted into Thai cuisine with great enthusiasm. However, mildly spiced dishes are also easily available. Although influences from China and India can be noticed in stir-fries and curries, Thai creativity has yielded a wide range of dishes unique to the country. The cuisine is full of distinctive flavors and complementary textures, nutritionally balanced and delightfully presented.

Phrik nam pla

A wide variety of fresh seafood for sale at Chinatown in Bangkok

RICE AND NOODLES

In common with all its Southeast Asian neighbors, the Thai diet is based on the staples of rice and noodles. The most popular type of rice is the long-grained *khao hom mali* (fragrant jasmine rice), which is usually steamed. However, in the north and northeast, locals prefer *khao niaw* (sticky rice), which is eaten with the fingers, rolled into little balls, and dipped in sauces. *Jok* (rice porridge) is a typical breakfast dish, with egg, chilies, and rice vinegar.

Kuaytiaw (rice noodles), *bami* (wheat and egg) or *wun sen* (mung beans), are usually served fried or in a soup. The most well-known Thai noodle dish among foreigners is *phad thai* (which literally means Thai fry). This delicious mix of noodles fried with fresh or dried shrimp, egg, beancurd (tofu), and bean sprouts, competes with *tom yam kung* for the title of Thailand's national dish.

THE FOUR FLAVORS

All Thai dishes strike a balance between the four flavors – sweet, sour, salty, and hot – although the balance varies from dish to

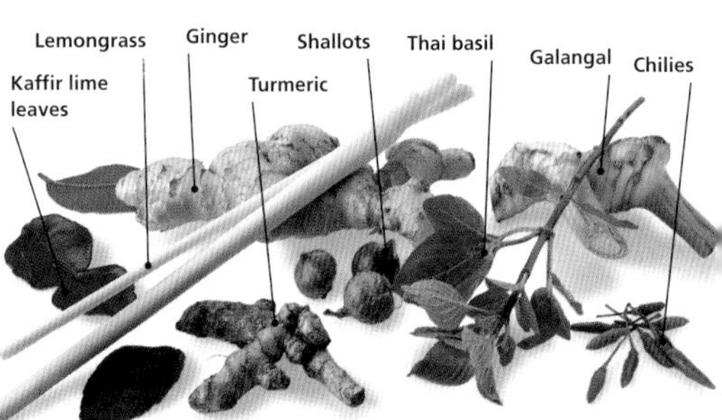

Selection of typical Thai herbs, spices, and flavorings

REGIONAL DISHES AND SPECIALITIES

Food in central Thailand has been strongly influenced by Chinese cuisine and these dishes feature on menus nationwide, including the country's signature dish *tom yam kung*. Northern Thai cuisine takes much of its inspiration from Burma and the Yunnan province in China. Examples include *khao soi*, a delicious dish of boiled and crispy noodles in a mild curry broth, and *kaeng hang le*. Northeastern Thais like their food with a kick, and one of their best-known imports from nearby Laos is the tangy, crunchy *som tam* salad. Southern food is the most fiery of the lot, where creamy coconut, turmeric, and sharp tamarind feature in typical dishes as the spicy and sour *kaeng leung pla*.

Pea eggplants (aubergines)

Tom Yam Kung *uses chili, lemongrass, galangal, and kaffir lime to flavor this hot and sour shrimp broth.*

Traders selling their fresh produce at one of Bangkok's floating markets

dish. While Thai cuisine is liberal with its use of chilies, it also features a variety of subtly flavored dishes that make use of different aromatic herbs and spices such as galangal, lemongrass, kaffir lime leaves, basil, and coriander (cilantro) to enhance aroma and taste. Pastes using these ingredients are pounded in a mortar to ensure the freshest flavor. However, the real key to Thai cuisine is *nam pla* (fish sauce), which adds its typical piquancy to most dishes. Mixed with chilies, garlic, and lemon it becomes the popular condiment *phrik nam pla*.

THE THAI MEAL

A typical Thai meal consists of a soup, a curry, a stir-fry and a spicy Thai salad, as well as side dishes of raw or steamed vegetables, served with a big bowl of rice. The meal is rarely divided into formal courses. Westerners who do not realize this often order a soup or a salad as a starter although they are supposed to complement the main dish. The spiciness of these dishes is intended to be toned down by eating them with rice. However, Thai restaurant staff are likely to serve all dishes ordered at the same time anyway. The only concession that Thais make to courses is with dessert, which is usually a plate of mixed fruit intended to clear the palate after the savory dishes. Many foreign visitors also like to indulge in the national favorite – *khao niaw mamuang* (mango with sticky coconut rice).

Expertly carved melons in Thai style for use as table decoration

WHAT TO DRINK

Fruit juices Thailand's wealth of luscious fruits, such as watermelon, mango, lychee, and papaya, are blended into refreshing juices, shakes, and smoothies. Coconut water, drunk through a straw straight from the nut, is a perfect drink for a hot day on the beach.

Beers There is a good range of beers available. Popular choices are the full-bodied local Singha and Chang.

Wines and spirits As well as locally made rice wine, wines from Europe and the New World are widely available. Thai vineyards are also starting to produce acceptable varieties. The local spirits, Mekong and Sang Som, are very palatable when mixed with ice and soda.

Coffee and tea While not traditional Thai drinks, excellent varieties of both are now grown in the northern hills.

Kaeng Hang Le, *a dry, mild curry of pork with ginger, peanuts, and garlic, served with rice and Chinese greens.*

Som Tam *is shredded unripe papaya and other vegetables, with lime juice, chili, fish sauce, and dried shrimps.*

Kaeng Leung Pla *is a spicy fish soup with bamboo shoots, flavored with tamarind, chili, garlic, and palm sugar.*

A Glossary of Typical Thai Dishes

Khanom krok (coconut pudding)

Thai cuisine is famously innovative and varied. Even street vendors delight in their culinary skills, and it is not uncommon to see food being encased in a banana leaf as delicately as if it were being gift wrapped. Such artful presentations and the sheer range of dishes can be bewildering for first timers as it may not even be obvious what is savory or sweet. This glossary covers typical dishes; phonetic guidance for food words is on page 382.

Visitors enjoying a meal in an open-air beach shack in Ko Chang

CHOOSING DISHES

Restaurant menus in tourist areas may include descriptions in English, and sometimes other languages. The Thai names of dishes are often derived from the main elements – for instance, the dish *khao mu daeng* translates literally as "rice", "pork" and "red". Thus, the basic components of any dish can often be worked out with only a little knowledge of Thai.

If there is no menu, the dishes of the day will be on display. If one does not recognize the dish, pointing and saying *ni arai mai* (what is this?) should elicit a list of ingredients.

Vegetarians should find it easy to order *mai ao nua* (food without meat), but ought to be aware that fish sauce is used in many dishes. Dairy products feature rarely in Thai cuisine, so vegans should not fare worse than vegetarians. Foreigners often ask *phed mai?* (is the dish spicy), or requesting *mai ao phet na* (a non-spicy meal). To enliven any dish, diners can use the ubiquitous condiments of chilies in vinegar, chili flakes, sugar (for savory dishes), and fish sauce usually placed on most tables.

SNACKS

Thais love to eat. Almost every street corner has a selection of food stalls selling raw and freshly cooked snacks.

Chicken satay

Bami mu daeng
บะหมี่หมูแดง
Egg noodles with red pork.

Khai ping
ไข่ปิ้ง
Charcoal-roasted eggs.

Kai yang
ไก่ย่าง
Charcoal-grilled chicken.

Khanom beuang
ขนมเบื้อง
Stuffed sweet pancakes.

Khanom krok
ขนมครก
Coconut pudding.

Khao tom mat
ข้าวต้มมัด
Sticky rice served in banana leaves.

Kluay ping
กล้วยปิ้ง
Charcoal-grilled bananas.

Look chin ping
ลูกชิ้นปิ้ง
Meatballs with a chili sauce.

Po pia tod
ปอเปี๊ยะ
Deep-fried spring rolls.

Sai krok
ไส้กรอก
Thai beef or pork sausages.

Satay
สะเต๊ะ
Slivers of beef, pork, or chicken grilled on a stick; served with peanut sauce and cucumber.

Tua thod
ถั่วทอด
Roasted cashews or peanuts.

Vendor selling an array of snacks from his boat-cum-restaurant in Krabi

NOODLES

Rice noodles come as *sen yai* (broad), *sen lek* (medium), and *sen mi* (thin). *Bami* are egg noodles. *Wun sen* are thin, transparent soy noodles.

Bami nam
บะหมี่น้ำ
Egg noodles in a broth with vegetables, meat, or fish.

Kuaytiaw haeng
ก๋วยเตี๋ยวแห้ง
Rice noodles served dry with vegetables, meat, or fish.

Kuaytiaw nam
ก๋วยเตี๋ยวน้ำ
Rice noodles in a broth with vegetables, meat, or fish.

Kuaytiaw look chin pla
ลูกชิ้นปลา
Fishballs with noodles.

Phad thai
ผัดไทย
Rice noodles fried with egg, beancurd, dried shrimp, bean sprouts, peanuts, and chili.

RICE DISHES

Rice is the staple food. A familiar Thai greeting *kin khao mai?*, (how are you?) literally translates into "have you eaten rice?"

Khao man kai
ข้าวมันไก่
Chinese-style chicken with rice cooked in chicken stock.

Khao mok kai
ข้าวหมกไก่
Thai-style chicken biryani.

Khao mu daeng
ข้าวหมูแดง
Chinese-style red pork served on a bed of fragrant rice.

Khao na ped
ข้าวหน้าเป็ด
Roast duck served on a bed of fragrant rice.

Khao phad mu/kung
ข้าวผัดหมูหรือกุ้ง
Fried rice with pork or shrimp.

SOUPS

Thai soups are very inventive. Some, such as *jok*, are eaten for breakfast. The word *"sup"* is widely recognized.

Jok
โจ๊ก
Ground rice porridge with minced pork and ginger.

Khao tom
ข้าวต้ม
Rice soup with a selection of meat and vegetable side dishes.

Tom jeud tao hu
ต้มจืดเต้าหู้
Mild broth with beancurd and minced pork.

Tom kha kai
ต้มข่าไก่
Chicken soup with galangal, coconut milk, and lemongrass.

Tom yam kung
ต้มยำกุ้ง
Shrimp, mushrooms, lemon-grass, galangal, and coriander.

CURRIES

Curries are served either *rat khao* (on a plate of rice) or in a bowl as an accompaniment to a central bowl of rice.

Kaeng kari kai
แกงกะหรี่ไก่
Indian-style chicken and potato.

Kaeng khiaw wan
แกงเขียวหวาน
Slightly sweet green curry.

An extensive selection of wines at the Shades restaurant in Ko Samui

Kaeng matsaman
แกงมัสมั่น
A mild curry from the Deep South with chicken, peanuts, potatoes, and coconut milk.

Kaeng phanaeng
แกงแพนง
Southern-style creamy curry with coconut milk and basil.

Kaeng phed
แกงเผ็ด
A hot curry with red chilies, lemongrass, and coriander.

Kaeng som
แกงส้ม
A hot and sour curry, usually with fish.

SEAFOOD

A wide variety of seafood is available at reasonable prices, particularly in the Deep South.

Hoi malaeng pu op
หอยแมลงภู่อบ
Steamed green mussels.

Hoi thod
หอยทอด
Oysters fried in an egg batter, served on a bed of bean sprouts.

Southern style seafood platter

Kung mangkon phao
กุ้งมังกรเผา
Grilled lobster.

Pla meuk yang
ปลาหมึกย่าง
Roasted sliced squid.

Pla nung khing
ปลานึ่งขิง
Steamed fish with ginger, chili, and mushrooms.

Pla thod
ปลาทอด
Crispy deep-fried fish which is combined and served with various sauces.

Pu neung
ปูนึ่ง
Steamed crab which is served with a pungent and spicy sauce.

REGIONAL DISHES

Kaeng hang le
แกงฮังเล
A northern delicacy, pork curry with peanut, and ginger.

Khao soi
ข้าวซอย
Chicken or beef curry served with wheat noodles, fresh lime, and pickled cabbage. A Northern specialty.

Larb ped
ลาบเป็ด
northern spicy minced duck.

Som tam
ส้มตำ
Green papaya salad with peanuts, from the northeast.

Yam thalay
ยำทะเล
Southern spicy seafood salad.

DESSERTS

Known as *khong wan* or sweet things, these are mostly coconut or fruit based.

Foy thong
ฝอยทอง
Sweet, shredded egg yolk.

Khao niaw mamuang
ข้าวเหนียวมะม่วง
Fresh mango served with sticky rice and coconut milk.

Kluay buat chi
กล้วยบวดชี
Bananas in coconut milk.

Mo kaeng
หม้อแกง
Thai-style egg custard.

DRINKS

Bia
เบียร์
Beer. Usually served in bottles.

Cha ron
ชาร้อน
Tea with condensed milk.

Kafae
กาแฟ
Coffee, often instant.

Nam cha
น้ำชา
Chinese-style tea without milk.

Nam kuad
น้ำขวด
Bottled water.

A coconut seller at the floating market

Choosing a Restaurant

These restaurants have been selected for their excellent food, ambience, and location. On remote beaches and islands, places offering good value have been suggested. They are listed by region and then by price. Map references refer either to the Bangkok Street Finder on *pp88–95*, or to the road map on the inside back cover.

PRICE CATEGORIES

The following price ranges are the equivalent of an evening meal for one, made up of a range of dishes, including service, but not alcohol.

Ⓑ Under 150 baht
ⒷⒷ 150–300 baht
ⒷⒷⒷ 300–600 baht
ⒷⒷⒷⒷ 600–1,000 baht
ⒷⒷⒷⒷⒷ Above 1,000 baht

BANGKOK

CHINATOWN Punjab Sweets Ⓑ

436/5 Chak Phet Rd, Phahurat 10200 ***Tel*** *08-1869-3815* **City Map** *6 D1*

Vegetarian restaurants are few in Bangkok, but there are some tucked away in the Indian district of Phahurat, on the border of Chinatown. This small and basic restaurant serves authentic Indian cuisine, including *dosa*, *puri*, *samosa*, and Indian sweets. This is one of two Punjab Sweets outlets in the Chak Phet area.

CHINATOWN Roti Mataba Ⓑ

136 Pha Athit Rd, Chansasongkram 10220 ***Tel*** *0-2282-2119* **City Map** *1 C3*

A small Thai-Muslim eatery, Roti Mataba is a favorite with travelers. An inexpensive place to enjoy a classic Indian/Malay *roti* (a delicious fried flatbread) served with a small bowl of *dal* (lentil curry) or curry sauce as dip. This satisfying dish is traditionally served as a breakfast meal. The restaurant is open all day.

CHINATOWN Chote Chitr ⒷⒷ

146 Prang Pu Thorn, Tanao Rd 10200 ***Tel*** *0-2221-4082* **City Map** *2 D5*

A five-table clean, hole-in-the-wall restaurant, Chote Chitr prides itself for serving Thai food cooked as per ancient royal recipes using rare ingredients. The restaurant is a local favorite for its crispy noodle dishes but the *gaeng som* curry is equally famous. Those preferring something more exotic can ask for the chef's recommendations.

CHINATOWN Fisherman's Seafood Restaurant ⒷⒷ

1/12 Soi Mahathat, Maharaj Rd 10200 ***Tel*** *0-2222-8082* **City Map** *1 C5*

Located on the banks of the Chao Phraya River with views of the Royal Palace, this well-known restaurant has been given a modern makeover and is one of the most enjoyable places to eat Thai and Western seafood. Try the grilled seafood *satay* and the steamed blue swimming crab with ginger sauce.

CHINATOWN Hemlock ⒷⒷ

56 Phra Athit Rd 10200 ***Tel*** *0-2282-7507* **City Map** *2 D3*

A stylishly small, air-conditioned place, Hemlock is popular with Thai elite and artists who often host art and photography exhibitions here. The menu is extensive and includes some exotic delicacies. Try the *miang kham* – fresh piper leaves with pieces of lime, ginger, and shallot.

CHINATOWN Oh My Cod! ⒷⒷ

Rambuttri Village Inn, Soi Ram Buttri 10200 ***Tel*** *0-2282-6553* **City Map** *2 D3*

A great place to try some of the best fish and chips east of London, as well as other British favorites such as sausages, beans, and fried bread. Located just a quick walk from Khao San Road, visitors can enjoy a meal indoors or in a pleasant quiet courtyard.

CHINATOWN Raan Jay Fai ⒷⒷ

327 Maha Chai Rd 10200 ***Tel*** *0-2223-9384* **City Map** *2 E5*

Located near Wat Saket in the Democracy Monument area, this is probably Bangkok's most famous place for fried noodles, especially *phad khii mao* (drunkard's noodles) – spicy rice noodles with chicken and basil. The ambience leaves something to be desired, but locals drive for miles to eat here.

CHINATOWN Deck by the River ⒷⒷⒷ

Arun Residence, 36–38 Soi Pratu Nok Yoong, Maharaj Rd 10200 ***Tel*** *0-2221-9158* **City Map** *6 B1*

A neat little boutique hotel with great views of the famous Wat Arun across the river, this is an ideal place to visit, especially at sunset. The food is mainly traditional Thai, but prepared with great skill and using only the highest quality ingredients. The restaurant also serves a few Western dishes.

CHINATOWN Hua Seng Hong ⒷⒷⒷ

371–373 Yaowarat Rd 10200 ***Tel*** *0-2222-0635* **City Map** *6 F2*

This is a classic Cantonese-style restaurant offering popular Chinese dishes. The quality of the food distinguishes it from similar places in the neighborhood – the cacophonous epicenter of Chinatown. Duck dishes and *dim sum* are sure winners. Service is efficient, not gracious.

Key to Symbols *see back cover flap*

CHINATOWN Kai Yang Boran ®®®

474–476 Tanao Rd, Banglamphu 10200 **Tel** *0-2622-2349* **City Map** *2 D3*

Albeit a little expensive, this is an excellent place to try delicacies from Thailand's northeastern Issan region. The place takes its name from the region's signature dish, *kai yang* (marinated roast chicken, served with a variety of side dishes). Food is cooked in a hygienic environment.

DOWNTOWN Hai Somtam ®®

2/4–5 Convent Rd, Silom 10500 **Tel** *0-2631-0216* **City Map** *7 C4*

An excellent place to try authentic *aharn issan* from northeastern Thailand. This unassuming, open-fronted restaurant is packed at lunchtime and early evenings with locals eating spicy *somtam* (green papaya salad), grilled chicken, sun-dried pork, sticky rice, and other Issan favorites.

DOWNTOWN Suda ®®

6–6/1 Sukhumvit Soi 14 10110 **Tel** *0-2229-4664*

A favorite evening haunt of the expatriate community in the Sukhumvit area, Suda is an inexpensive restaurant serving delicious Thai cuisine. The open-sided dining room is conveniently located close to the Asoke Skytrain station. Popular menu choices include tuna with chilies and cashews, and green curry.

DOWNTOWN Taling Pling ®®

60 Pun Rd, Silom, Bangrak 10500 **Tel** *0-2234-4872* **City Map** *7 B4*

A two-story restaurant in a converted family home, Taling Pling is located between Silom and Sathorn roads. Bright contemporary design and excellent Thai food. Many of the dishes are uncommon, the accompanying picture menu with lucid descriptions is useful. Also noted for an extensive dessert menu and superior wine list.

DOWNTOWN Bua ®®®

1/4 Convent Rd, Silom 10500 **Tel** *0-2237-6640* **City Map** *7 C4*

The popular Bua is frequented by both locals and foreigners, drawn to its elaborate menu of delicious Thai dishes at reasonable prices. The food includes appetizers, salads, soups, and seafood from four of Thailand's main regions. Dishes such as *pla neung mannao* (steamed seabass in lime juice) have made the restaurant popular.

DOWNTOWN Cabbages & Condoms ®®®

6 Sukhumvit Soi 12 10110 **Tel** *0-2229-4611*

Run by Thailand's Population & Community Development Association (PDA), Cabbages & Condoms' menu includes Thai classics, seafood, and other regional dishes. The profits from the restaurant support family planning and AIDS-prevention projects in Thailand.

DOWNTOWN Indus ®®®

71 Soi 26, Sukhumvit Rd 10110 **Tel** *0-2258-4900*

This flagship restaurant of Kashmiri chef and food writer Sonya Sapru brings modern Indian cuisine to Bangkok. Light, simple dishes place emphasis on health, without sacrificing flavor. The dining room decor draws on northern India's cultural heritage, with stunning results. A bar and café add to the restaurant's ambience.

DOWNTOWN Mrs Balbir's ®®®

155/18 Sukhumvit Soi 11/1 10110 **Tel** *0-2651-0498*

Located in an obscure corner next to the Swiss Park hotel, this unpretentious Punjabi restaurant serves good north Indian favorites. The owner, after whom the restaurant is named, is a local TV personality who takes Indian cooking classes and has worked with Thai Airways International, providing Indian food on flights.

DOWNTOWN Pandanus Bar and Bistro ®®®

50 Soi Nantha, Sathorn Soi 1 10120 **Tel** *0-2286-5646* **City Map** *8 E4*

The decor of this cheerful bar bistro is as appealing as the food. The interior would not be out of place in downtown Manhattan. The emphasis is on Thai and Italian fusion cuisine. Sweet treats include banoffee chocolate ice cream and mud pie with peanut butter. For cool drinks, head upstairs to the stylish cocktail bar.

DOWNTOWN Silver Palace ®®®

5 Soi Phiphat, (Soi 3) Silom Rd 10500 **Tel** *0-2235 5118-9* **City Map** *7 C4*

Located next door to the huge Bangkok Bank tower, the Silver Palace is famous for its Peking duck, which is carved tableside. The restaurant is an excellent choice for lunch, with quality *dim sum* at reasonable prices. The dining room is large and with modern decor.

DOWNTOWN Somboon Seafood ®®®

169 Suriwong Rd, Bangrak 10500 **Tel** *0-2233-3104* **City Map** *7 B4*

One of the best places to delve into an exotic array of squid, fish, clam, shrimp, crab, and lobster dishes, Somboon Seafood also serves classic dishes such as crab with curry powder, and stir-fried clams with roast chili paste. The restaurant is usually fully booked; dinner reservations are advised.

DOWNTOWN Tamarind Café ®®®

27/1 Sukumvit Soi 20, Klong Toey 10110 **Tel** *0-2663-7421* **City Map** *3 A5*

A vegetarian restaurant-cum-art gallery, Tamarind Café is also popular with non-vegetarians. The converted chic townhouse, complete with a rooftop garden is perfect for enjoying an eclectic vegetarian menu that features creative sushi, *burritos*, and cocktails. The on-site gallery, F-stop, hosts regular photography exhibitions.

DOWNTOWN Biscotti ⒷⒷⒷⒷ

Four Seasons Hotel, Ratchadamri Rd 10100 **Tel** *0-2251-6127* **City Map** *8 E1*

Located in the upscale hotel, The Four Seasons *(see p292)*, Biscotti is a stylish, but warm and friendly, Italian bistro with an open kitchen and well-polished wooden tables and floors. Instead of Italian haute cuisine, it serves a variety of pizzas and other favorites. Top quality ingredients, good service, and value.

DOWNTOWN Coyote Bar & Grill ⒷⒷⒷⒷ

575–579 Sukhumvit Rd, Klong Toey Nua, Wattana 10110 **Tel** *0-2662-3838* **City Map** *7 C4*

Voted as one of Bangkok's best Mexican restaurants, Coyote Bar & Grill is a bright, cheerful restaurant and bar. It also has a sister outlet on Convent Road. Diners can enjoy *quesadillas, burritos, enchiladas*, and racks of pork ribs. Diners are spoilt for choice with more than 75 different types of margaritas.

DOWNTOWN Cy'an ⒷⒷⒷⒷ

Metropolitan Bangkok Hotel, 27 South Sathorn Rd 10120 **Tel** *0-2625-3388* **City Map** *8 D4*

Offering a nice view of the pool at the Metropolitan Hotel in a chic minimalist atmosphere, Cy'an offers creative Mediterranean cuisine. Try the seared tuna slices with tender celery hearts and roast shallots and red wine sauce on a bed of mashed celery. Excellent dessert menu.

DOWNTOWN Eat Me ⒷⒷⒷⒷ

1/6 Soi Phiphat 2, off Convent Rd, Silom 10500 **Tel** *0-2238-0931* **City Map** *8 F1*

With a loft-style look appropriate for a venue that bills itself as a restaurant as well as an art gallery, Eat Me's main attraction is its excellent food. Try the house specialty, yellow-fin tuna tartare with soba noodles, or asparagus lasagne with New Zealand goat Camembert and Champagne bechamel.

DOWNTOWN Face Bar & Restaurant ⒷⒷⒷⒷ

29 Soi, 38 Sukhumvit Rd 10110 **Tel** *0-2713-6048*

Thai, Indian, and Japanese cuisine are served in a trendy bar and restaurant within a converted traditional Thai house. This restaurant is a bit off the beaten track, but worth finding. Service is excellent and although it is on the expensive side, the food is very good. Try the mojitos.

DOWNTOWN Le Dalat Indochine ⒷⒷⒷⒷ

57 Soi Prasarnmitr Sukhumvit 23, Sukhumvit Rd 10110 **Tel** *0-2664-0670*

Run by Madame Doan-Hoa-Ly, the head of a respectable French-Vietnamese family, Le Dalat Indochine is renowned for the culinary blend of the owner's two cultures. The restaurant's signature dish, *cua raeng mee* (pan-fried crab with tamarind sauce, spring onion, and garlic), is a favorite.

DOWNTOWN Basil ⒷⒷⒷⒷⒷ

Sheraton Grande Sukhumvit Hotel, 250 Sukumvit Rd 10110 **Tel** *0-2649-8366*

An excellent place for a contemporary Thai dining experience, this restaurant is located in the Sheraton Grande Sukhumvit Hotel *(see p292)*. With a repertoire of more than 100 dishes, Basil has a well-deserved reputation for serving high-quality cuisine, in a sophisticated environment. À la carte and set menus available.

DOWNTOWN Bed Supper Club ⒷⒷⒷⒷⒷ

26 Sukhumvit Rd, Soi 11 10110 **Tel** *0-2651-3537*

An upscale restaurant, Bed Supper Club is also a music club and art gallery. The decor resembles the interior of a spaceship and diners can enjoy the food while reclining on a divan suspended from the walls. The staff is dressed in sci-fi garb and the DJ plays foot-tapping numbers. The food is a good fusion of Thai dishes.

DOWNTOWN China House ⒷⒷⒷⒷⒷ

48 Oriental Avenue 10050 **Tel** *0-2659-9000* **City Map** *6 F5*

Inspired by the Art Deco period of 1930s Shanghai, China House, at Mandarin Oriental *(see p292)*, is an avant-garde restaurant serving classic cuisine with a contemporary twist. Guests can enjoy exquisite dishes such as roast Peking duck with traditional condiments, and hand-pulled noodles with shredded abalone.

DOWNTOWN Koi ⒷⒷⒷⒷⒷ

26 Sukhumvit Soi 20 10110 **Tel** *0-2258-1590*

This upscale Japanese restaurant is a stunning addition to Bangkok's increasingly eclectic dining scene. With branches in Los Angeles and New York and a contemporary interior, it attracts Bangkok's glitterati, who come here for the sushi and sashimi presented with great flair.

DOWNTOWN Le Normandie ⒷⒷⒷⒷⒷ

48 Oriental Avenue 10500 **Tel** *0-2237-0041* **City Map** *6 F4*

Said to be the finest French restaurant in Asia, Le Normandie offers an elegant setting in Mandarin Oriental's Garden Wing. Impeccable service, an exceptional wine list, and à la carte seafood and meat dishes. Thai celebrities, politicos, and royalty often dine here. Try the breast of Bresse pigeon with *foie gras*.

DOWNTOWN Oam Thong ⒷⒷⒷⒷⒷ

7/4–5 Soi 33, Sukhumvit Rd 10110 **Tel** *0-2279-5958*

Exquisite food and contemporary decor define Oam Thong. The ambience and traditional music make this restaurant an ideal choice for a romantic dinner or a special evening with friends. Try the coconut milk soup with chicken and galangal, wing bean salad with minced pork and shrimps, and sizzling seafood hot plate.

Key to Price Guide *see p318* **Key to Symbols** *see back cover flap*

DOWNTOWN Reflexions ฿฿฿฿฿

Le Meridien Plaza Athénée, 10 Wireless Rd 10030 ***Tel*** *0-2650-8800* **City Map** 8 E2

Located on the third floor of Le Meridien Plaza Athénée *(see p292)*, Reflexions is a sophisticated restaurant offering delectable French fare. Chef Thibault Chiumenti's cuisine has won many awards over the years. Dishes are made using the finest seasonal ingredients and served with style and creativity.

DOWNTOWN Sala Rim Naam ฿฿฿฿฿

48 Oriental Avenue 10500 ***Tel*** *0-2659-9000* **City Map** 6 F5

The signature Thai restaurant of Mandarin Oriental, Sala Rim Naam's lunch consists of a lavish buffet, while evening diners are treated to a set gourmet dinner menu and a performance of traditional Thai dance. The cuisine is complemented by a selection of Thai wines. An open-air pavilion overlooks the Chao Phraya River.

DOWNTOWN Vertigo Grill & Moon Bar ฿฿฿฿฿

The Banyan Tree, 21/100 South Sathorn Rd 10120 ***Tel*** *0-2679-1200* **City Map** 8 D4

Voted one of the best bars in the world, Vertigo Grill & Moon Bar is a fabulous open-air restaurant on the 60th floor of the Banyan Tree *(see p291)*. The view is breathtaking and a meal or cocktail here is almost obligatory. Dishes include red mullet *en papillote* with thyme, and grilled scallops with coriander butter.

DUSIT Kaloang Home Kitchen ฿฿

2 Soi Wat Tevarakunchorn 10300 ***Tel*** *0-2281-9228* **City Map** 2 E2

Although a little hard to find, Kaloang Home Kitchen is worth a visit. Tucked away behind the National Library, this alfresco, riverside venue serves excellent and inexpensive Thai cuisine. Must-try dishes include the fried cotton fish with a green mango salad, seafood *tom yam* (spicy soup), and stir-fried crab with chili powder.

DUSIT May Kaidee's Vegetarian Restaurant II ฿฿

33 Soi 1, Sam Sen Rd 10300 ***Tel*** *08-9137-3173* **City Map** 2 D3

With a considerable reputation among vegetarians, May Kaidee's original branch is on Tanao Road. The eateries are quite prominent on the meat-free diner's map. Spring rolls, green curry with tofu, and *phad thai* feature on the extensive menu. The chef gives cooking lessons and also runs a guesthouse.

DUSIT Tara Tara Thai ฿฿฿

131/4 Kao Rd, Sam Sen Dusit 10300 ***Tel*** *0-2241-7900* **City Map** 2 E1

A riverside restaurant with an expansive terrace, diners can watch food being prepared over an open grill. The menu includes salads, curries, and stir-fries. Try the *goong ob wuen sen* (baked noodles with river prawns). A dining boat leaves every evening at 7:30pm for a 2-hour cruise on the Chao Phraya River. Excellent lunch buffet.

THONBURI Prime ฿฿฿฿฿

Millennium Hilton, 123 Charoen Nakhon Rd 10600 ***Tel*** *0-2442-2000* **City Map** 6 F5

Regarded as one of the best steakhouses in Bangkok, Prime serves the finest imported beef, fresh lobster, and oysters. Diners can watch salads being skillfully prepared at their tables. Fine wines accompany an excellent shellfish platter. A chic decor and sweeping river views add to the ambience of this upscale restaurant.

THONBURI Supatra River House ฿฿฿฿฿

266 Soi Wat Rakhang, Arun Amarin Rd 10700 ***Tel*** *0-2411-0305* **City Map** 5 D1

With an enchanting view of Wat Arun lit up against the night sky, Supatra River House is perfect for a memorable Thai seafood dinner by the Chao Phraya River. Try the fried soft-shelled crab with garlic and pepper sauce, or charcoal-grilled mixed seafood. Set menus are also available.

THONBURI Trader Vic's ฿฿฿฿฿

Anantara Bangkok Riverside, 257 Charoen Nakhon Rd 10600 ***Tel*** *0-2476-0022*

A Polynesian ambience, fine food, and cocktails on the riverside deck make Trader Vic's a unique dining experience. The spectacular Sunday Mai Tai jazz brunch is a weekly highlight. The fabulous spread of international gourmet cuisine is one of the best in the city and provides excellent value at reasonable prices.

FARTHER AFIELD Hsien Jong Vegetarian Restaurant ฿

1146/4–5 Thanon Chan 10120 **Road Map** C1

This inexpensive but cheerful Chinese vegetarian restaurant, with an open-fronted dining area, serves a wide variety of dishes. The menu is displayed on stainless-steel trays, and diners can simply point to what they want. It is easily accessible by taxi from the Skytrain station at Surasak.

FARTHER AFIELD Thip Samai ฿฿

313 Mahachai Rd, Samramrat, Phra Nakhon 10200 ***Tel*** *0-2221-6280* **Road Map** C1

Popular with locals as the best place in the city for *phad thai*, Thip Samai has been in business for 40 years. The restaurant serves seven different variations of the dish. *Phad thai* with egg and dry shrimp and *phad thai song-krueng* made with glass noodles, shrimp roe, prawn, egg, crab, cuttlefish, and mango are recommended.

FARTHER AFIELD Pola Pola ฿฿฿

150/7 Soi 55, Sukhumvit Rd 10110 ***Tel*** *0-2381-3237* **Road Map** C1

A popular restaurant, Pola Pola serves authentic Thai and Italian dishes. The traditional thin-crust pizzas, baked in a brick oven, are a favorite with diners. Salads, pasta dishes, and special set menus are also available. Children can enjoy drawing with crayons on the white-paper tablecloths. Pola Pola has four branches in Bangkok.

FARTHER AFIELD Spring & Summer ฿฿฿

199 Soi Promsi 2, Soi 39, Sukhumvit Rd 10110 ***Tel*** *0-2392-2757* ***Road Map*** *C1*

A glamorous restaurant, Spring & Summer is owned by a Thai actor and housed in two buildings from the 1950s. The restaurant promotes a unique culinary concept – Spring serves classic Thai dishes in a contemporary setting, while neighboring Summer is the perfect place to try out home-made cakes and desserts.

FARTHER AFIELD L'Opera ฿฿฿฿

53 Soi 39, Sukhumvit Rd, Wattana 10110 ***Tel*** *0-2258-5606* ***Road Map*** *C1*

One of Bangkok's most highly regarded Italian restaurants, L'Opera has a warm, rustic atmosphere. The delicious cuisine makes it a favorite among the expatriate community. Try the thinly sliced Chianina veal from Tuscany served with grilled vegetables, and the classic tiramisu for dessert. There is also a good wine list.

FARTHER AFIELD Watermark Italian Restaurant ฿฿฿฿

131 Soi Sukhumvit 53 (Paidee-Madee), Sukumvit Rd, Wattana 10110 ***Tel*** *0-2712-9129* ***Road Map*** *C1*

With a reputation among discerning diners for beautifully executed classic Italian dishes, La Villa brings a touch of Italian chic to Bangkok. A bar, a family room, and two private rooms also feature in this delightful restaurant. Excellent selection of wines.

EASTERN SEABOARD

CHANTHABURI Chanthorn Pochana ฿฿

Srijan Rd 22000 ***Tel*** *0-3931-2339* ***Road Map*** *E2*

A centrally located restaurant, Chanthorn Pochana has a tempting variety of curries, spicy Thai salads, and delicious stir-fries on an extensive menu. Try the local specialty *sen mi phad pu* (egg noodles topped with delicious crab meat) – a sure winner.

CHANTHABURI Muen Baan ฿฿

Saritdet Rd 22000 ***Road Map*** *E2*

An excellent restaurant providing a delectable array of home-cooked food, Muen Baan, which means just like home, serves a variety of options for vegetarians. The restaurant is conveniently located next to the bus station, and the owners are warm and friendly.

KO CHANG The Bay ฿฿

Ban Bang Bao Pier 23170 ***Road Map*** *E2*

One of several seafood restaurants located on the pier, in the picturesque fishing village of Bang Bao at the southern end of Ko Chang. The Bay has a sophisticated atmosphere and a good range of cocktails. The restaurant is popular with the diving crowd.

KO CHANG Invito ฿฿

Hat Sai Khao 23170 ***Tel*** *0-8434-55035* ***Road Map*** *E2*

Ideal for a romantic Italian dinner by candlelight, Invito is an old northern Thai house transported from Chiang Mai and rebuilt in its current location. The food is excellent – from pizzas to fine dining choices covering all regional cuisines of Italy. The restaurant also has a pleasant outdoor terrace.

KO CHANG Oodie's Place ฿฿

Hat Sai Khao 23170 ***Tel*** *08-1853-1271* ***Road Map*** *E2*

A lively restaurant on pretty Hat Sai Khao, Oodie's Place is run by a local musician who entertains his guests by playing covers of rock classics most nights from around 10pm. Diners can choose from a reliable menu of Thai dishes as well as French specialties.

KO CHANG Paddy's Palms ฿฿

Hat Sai Khao 23170 ***Tel*** *0-3961-9085* ***Road Map*** *E2*

An Irish pub with bright green interiors, Paddy's Palms is incongruous with the rest of Hat Sai Khao. The food however is authentic – shepherd's pie and beer-marinated beef. Try the Sunday roast. The pub also has an attached guesthouse for visitors who would like to stay the night.

KO CHANG Sabay Bar ฿฿

Hat Sai Khao 23170 ***Tel*** *0-3955-1097* ***Road Map*** *E2*

For the past few years, this has been one of the most popular spots to spend an evening on Hat Sai Khao. Sabay Bar's successful formula involves the choice between a fancy air-conditioned interior where a live band plays nightly, and alfresco dining with mats and cushions on the sand.

KO CHANG Tonsai ฿฿

Klong Prao 23170 ***Tel*** *08-9895-7229* ***Road Map*** *E2*

A tree-house restaurant, Tonsai is set in and around a huge banyan tree. This is an ideal spot for an afternoon drink or evening dinner in Hat Sai Khao. The menu offers Thai as well as international cuisine and vegetarians can choose from a variety of options.

KO SAMET Jeb's Ⓑ

Ao Hin Khok 21160 ***Tel*** *0-3864-4112* ***Road Map*** *D2*

Offering a wide variety of Thai, Western, Indian, and Mexican dishes, Jeb's is an inviting place where diners can enjoy a perfect outdoor eating experience. As with most restaurants on Ko Samet, seafood is the most popular item on the menu. There is a wide a variety of cocktails to choose from.

KO SAMET Naga Ⓑ

Ao Hin Khok 21160 ***Road Map*** *D2*

Started by an astute English woman, Naga *(see p295)* – a guesthouse and restaurant – serves simple fare, using fresh vegetables and baked goods from its famous bakery. The chefs still cook the food according to the high standards set by its founder. Stroll down to the beach bar after dinner.

KO SAMET Ploy Talay ⒷⒷⒷ

Hat Sai Kaew 21160 ***Tel*** *0-3864-4212* ***Road Map*** *D2*

One of the most popular beach bar and restaurants on Hat Sai Kaew, Ploy Talay sets out mats and cushions on the beach each evening for diners. The food is good, albeit a little overpriced. Diners can enjoy fire spinning shows or visit the equally popular disco.

KO SAMET Tub Tim Resort ⒷⒷⒷ

Ao Tub Tim 21160 ***Tel*** *0-3864-4025* ***Road Map D2***

A beautiful resort with stunning views of the bay, Tub Tim Resort *(see p296)* has a beachside restaurant with tables and chairs placed right by the water. There is an extensive menu with excellent food. Try the *hor mok talae* (spicy soufflé with seafood steamed in banana leaf).

KO SAMET Breeze Restaurant ⒷⒷⒷⒷⒷ

Ao Prao Resort, Ao Phrao 21160 ***Tel*** *0-3864-4100* ***Road Map*** *D2*

Beautiful and stylish, Breeze Restaurant occupies a breezy balcony shaded by a canopy of trees, in the Ao Prao Resort on the west coast of the island. Diners can choose from a selection of elegantly served Thai or international dishes. Good selection of wines.

KO SI CHANG Pan and David ⒷⒷ

Mu 3, Makham Thaew Rd 20210 ***Tel*** *0-3821-6629* ***Road Map*** *D1*

Owned by an American-Thai couple, Pan and David is surprisingly sophisticated for Ko Si Chang, a relatively less-visited island. There is an impressive range of classic Thai specialties, pasta dishes, and steaks as well as a good spread of vegetarian dishes. Fine selection of wines and desserts.

PATTAYA Food Wave Ⓑ

Top Floor, Royal Garden Plaza, Beach Rd 20260 ***Road Map*** *D1*

A crowded food court, Food Wave offers a wide variety of cuisines including Thai, Vietnamese, Indian, Japanese, and Western dishes at reasonable prices. Diners can eat the delicious food while enjoying an excellent view of the bay. Try the salads and Chinese duck with noodles.

PATTAYA Lobster Pot Ⓑ

228 Beach Rd 20260 ***Tel*** *0-3842-6083* ***Road Map*** *D1*

An excellent place for seafood as well as authentic Thai cuisine and steaks, Lobster Pot is perched on the pier in South Pattaya. Diners are allowed to choose their own lobster, crab, or fish from an aquarium, which is then cooked to order. Try the lobster thermidor or grilled tiger prawns. Good selection of wines.

PATTAYA Sketch Book Art Café and Restaurant Ⓑ

478/938 Moo 12 Thappraya Rd, Dongtarn Beach 20260 ***Tel*** *0-3825-1625* ***Road Map*** *D1*

The menu here has a variety of Western and Thai classics, and dishes are very moderately priced. The standout feature of the restaurant, however, is the beautiful garden, where you can enjoy your meal in serene surroundings. Painting lessons are also on offer, as well as a playground for children.

PATTAYA Ali Baba ⒷⒷ

1/13–14 Central Pattaya Rd 20260 ***Tel*** *0-3836-1620* ***Road Map*** *D1*

Ideal for a taste of classic Indian food, Ali Baba serves typically North Indian fare, such as *tandoori* dishes and *nan* breads, in the indoor restaurant. The menu for the outdoor restaurant is from South India and focuses on specialties including spicy vegetable curries and *dal*.

PATTAYA The Grill House ⒷⒷ

Rabbit Resort, Hat Dongtan, Jomtien 20260 ***Tel*** *0-3825-1730* ***Road Map*** *D1*

One of the most romantic restaurants in Jomtien, The Grill House serves a wide variety of Thai and Western dishes – a generous buffet breakfast as well as steaks and seafood skewers – from the charcoal beach grill, in the evening. For maximum effect, arrive just before sunset.

PATTAYA PIC Kitchen ⒷⒷ

10 Soi 5, Second Rd 20260 ***Tel*** *0-3842-8387* ***Road Map*** *D1*

Authentic Thai food is served in a compound of traditional teak houses with low tables and floor cushions, making for a memorable dining experience. The restaurant also has a few private dining rooms, a jazz bar, and occasional performances of classical Thai dances.

PATTAYA Mantra ⒷⒷⒷⒷ

Amari Orchid Resort, 240 Mu 5, Beach Rd 20260 ***Tel*** *0-3842-9591* ***Road Map*** *D1*

Admirable architecture and elegant red and black decor, coupled with mouth-watering Asian and Mediterranean dishes, make Mantra an excellent restaurant. Try the piping-hot Sichuan seafood soup or the *tandoori* lamb chops and choose from an extensive list of 140 wines.

SRI RACHA Grand Seaside ⒷⒷ

Soi 18 Cherm Chop Hon 21500 ***Tel*** *0-3831-2537* ***Road Map*** *D1*

Located near the pier from where ferries leave for Ko Si Chang, Grand Seaside serves excellent seafood. Classy and elegant, diners can enjoy mesmerizing sea views and stylish decor while eating seafood rice clay pot or crab with chili. Wash it down with refreshing iced coffee.

SRI RACHA Chua Li ⒷⒷⒷ

46/22 Sukhumvit Rd 21500 ***Tel*** *0-3831-1244* ***Road Map*** *D1*

The small town of Sri Racha is famed for *nam prik si racha* (Sri Racha pepper sauce) and seafood restaurants. Those traveling between Bangkok and Pattaya should make a stop at this popular restaurant for a plate of lobster or grilled prawns, doused in the delicious local sauce.

TRAT Cool Corner Ⓑ

21–23 Thoncharoen Rd 24000 ***Road Map*** *E2*

Located in the middle of Trat town, Cool Corner is simply but tastefully furnished, and offers travelers' favorites such as home-made bread and pancakes, in addition to tasty Thai curries. Diners can peruse books with travelers' experiences and tips on places to visit in nearby Ko Chang.

UPPER WESTERN GULF COAST

CHA-AM Beachside Seafood Stands ⒷⒷ

Ruamchit Rd 76120 ***Road Map*** *C1*

A favorite among locals, Cha-am's simple beachside seafood stands sell some of the best fare from the surrounding sea. Freshly caught fish is sold raw and cooked to order. Unlike a night market, most stands consist of buckets of fish swimming in salt water and a wok to cook them in.

CHA-AM Rabiang-lay ⒷⒷ

Verandah Resort & Spa, 737/12 Mung Talay Rd 76120 ***Tel*** *0-3270-9000* ***Road Map*** *C1*

A trendy, white, open-air *sala* (pavilion) right on the beach at Cha-am is the setting for this relaxed Thai fusion restaurant. The menu has a strong emphasis on seafood. Try the excellent, although seasonal, oysters, a delicious *tom yam kung* (spicy and sour shrimp soup), and stir-fried soft-shell crab.

CHA-AM Da Vinci's ⒷⒷⒷ

274/5 Ruamjit Rd 76000 ***Tel*** *0-3247-1871* ***Road Map*** *C1*

An excellent place to try European food in Cha-am, Da Vinci's emphasis is on seafood. However, there are plenty of other choices. The chef is Swedish, as is much of the clientele, so the food may taste a bit different. Try the excellent Italian dishes.

CHA-AM Poom Restaurant ⒷⒷⒷ

274/1 Ruamchit Rd 76120 ***Tel*** *0-3247-1036* ***Road Map*** *C1*

In the same area as the seafood stands, Poom offers a relatively more refined alternative – comfortable chairs and tables and even air-conditioning. It has a considerably wider menu compared to the beachside stands, including various shellfish. A favorite with locals.

CHUMPHON Khrua Pagsod Ⓑ

10/32 Paradorn Rd 86000 ***Tel*** *0-7757-1731* ***Road Map*** *C3*

An ideal place for vegetarians, Khrua Pagsod (fresh vegetable kitchen), offers a wide variety of vegetarian choices including Western and Asian cuisines, made with farm-fresh vegetables. The food is excellent, and the ambience is chic and contemporary.

CHUMPHON Papa Seafood ⒷⒷⒷ

188/181 Krom Luang Chumporn Rd 86000 ***Tel*** *0-7751-1972* ***Road Map*** *C3*

A standard indoor/outdoor seafood emporium, with the "choose from tank" option available. It is distinguished by the good service, attention to cleanliness, and vibrant atmosphere, including live music. Only open in the evenings. The adjacent disco, however, is not very alluring.

HUA HIN Chatchai Market Ⓑ

Soi 72, between Phetkasem and Sa Song Roads 77100 ***Road Map*** *C2*

A vibrant, crowded market with dozens of fresh food stalls, Chatchai Market is ideal for a taste of inexpensive, yet delicious, Thai street food. The standard of cleanliness is high. Try the classic *phad thai* with fresh shrimps, *hoi thot* (fried oyster omelette), a variety of noodle soups, and generous portions of fresh fish.

Key to Price Guide *see p318* **Key to Symbols** *see back cover flap*

HUA HIN Coustiero ฿฿

AKA Resort, 152 Mu 7, Ban Nong Hiang 77100 **Tel** *0-3261-8900* **Road Map** *C2*

With a delightful setting, Coustiero is a charming restaurant with a refined, French-influenced menu. The china patterns are as pretty as the locale, and the flavors are fabulous. The menu is seasonal, but dishes involving *foie gras*, scallops, and seafood are excellent.

HUA HIN Let's Sea ฿฿

83/155 Soi Talay 12, Khao Takiab 77100 **Tel** *0-3253-6888* **Road Map** *C2*

An alfresco restaurant, Let's Sea places emphasis on delectable seafood and great sea views. The dishes are Thai, albeit with an international twist, and work well with the setting. Try the fish cakes wrapped in mini-croutons and the lobster carpaccio.

HUA HIN Moon Smile & Platoo ฿฿

Poon Suk Rd 77110 **Tel** *0-3251-1664* **Road Map** *C2*

This charming little local restaurant offers inexpensive, good quality Thai food along with friendly service. It's not the place for a quiet, romantic dinner, as it gets very busy and tables are not widely spaced, but for good portions and prices it can't be beaten. Show up early to avoid the queues.

HUA HIN Baan Itsara ฿฿฿

7 Napkehad Rd 77100 **Tel** *0-3251-4517* **Road Map** *C2*

Operating from a seaside bungalow a few miles north of Hua Hin, Baan Itsara, meaning "House of Freedom", was once the home of a Thai artist. The atmosphere is quite casual and relaxed and although the food is standard Thai seafood, it is prepared with exceptional skill.

HUA HIN Som Moo Joom ฿฿฿

51/6 Dechanuchit Rd 77100 **Road Map** *C2*

There might not be any English signs directing visitors to this unassuming seafood eatery with indoor and outdoor seating, but the hunt is worth the effort. The seafood soup with noodles is a favorite, besides a wide variety of other seafood dishes. Overall, the food is inexpensive and fresh.

HUA HIN Hagi ฿฿฿฿

Sofitel Centara Grand Resort and Villas, 1 Damnoernkasem Rd 77100 **Tel** *0-3251-2021* **Road Map** *C2*

A stylish restaurant serving a varied and excellent selection of contemporary and traditional Japanese dishes, Hagi in the Sofitel Centara Grand Resort and Villas *(see p299)*, presents food with an artistic flair. A 16-seater teppanyaki kitchen turns cooking into a memorable experience. Diners can watch their meal being cooked.

HUA HIN La Villa ฿฿฿฿

12/2 Poonsuk Rd 77110 **Tel** *0-3251-3435* **Road Map** *C2*

Voted the best Italian restaurant in Hua Hin by locals, La Villa's chef Marco has been serving Italian classics at this restaurant since 1987. The restaurant makes its own pasta, and the house specialty is green lasagne. An extensive wine list and a good selection of home-made desserts.

HUA HIN McFarland House ฿฿฿฿

Hyatt Regency Hua Hin, 91 Hua Hin Takiab Rd 77100 **Tel** *0-3252-1234* **Road Map** *C2*

Set within the secluded compound of the Barai Spa Villas at the Hyatt Regency, McFarland House is among the best casual restaurants in Hua Hin. Try the blue crab and corn cakes with chili and coriander salsa, shredded duck and cucumber rolls, succulent grilled Angus beef, and mushroom and zucchini skewers. Excellent Sunday lunches.

HUA HIN Museum Tea Corner ฿฿฿฿

Sofitel Centara Grand Resort & Villas, 1 Damnoenkasem Rd 77100 **Tel** *0-3251-2036* **Road Map** *C2*

With a classic setting, reminiscent of a bygone Colonial era, the Museum Tea Corner is one of the restaurants in the upscale Sofitel Centara Grand Resort and Villas. It offers an excellent selection of coffee and tea. Also on offer are tempting chocolate cakes and a delectable afternoon tea medley of sweet and savory delights.

HUA HIN Tapas ฿฿฿฿

62 Naresdamri Rd 77100 **Tel** *0-8008-06811* **Road Map** *C2*

A wide range of authentic and delicious tapas prepared by a Spanish chef are served in this beautiful old wooden house with elegant Vietnamese furnishings. Perfect for those craving a change from Asian food. There's outdoor seating at the front of the restaurant and a small garden patio at the back.

HUA HIN White Lotus ฿฿฿฿

Hilton Hua Hin Resort & Spa, 33 Naresdamri Rd 77100 **Tel** *0-3253-8999* **Road Map** *C2*

The seating at this stylish restaurant at the top of the Hilton Resort is positioned to take advantage of the stunning views of the town and coastline. The menu focuses on contemporary Chinese dishes from the Sichuan and Guangdong provinces, with a couple of degustation menus. Excellent service and a decent wine list.

HUA HIN Chao Lay Seafood ฿฿฿฿฿

15 Naresdamri Rd 77100 **Tel** *0-3251-3436* **Road Map** *C2*

A large outdoor restaurant on a wooden pier, Chao Lay Seafood is a favorite with both visitors and locals. The proximity to the ocean is key to the focus of the menu – seafood. With ample seating and fresh food, it is a great place to enjoy some Thai specialties. Service can be a little disappointing.

HUA HIN Supatra By The Sea ⒷⒷⒷⒷⒷ

122/63 Soi Muu Baan Takiab, Nong Gae 77100 **Tel** *0-3253-6561* **Road Map** *C2*

With one of the best settings in Hua Hin, Supatra By The Sea boasts pavilions offering panoramic sea views in front of a terraced tropical garden. The menu is a mix of contemporary and traditional Thai dishes, with emphasis on fresh seafood. Try the crab and minced pork and deep-fried fish.

PHETCHABURI Rabiang Rim Nam Ⓑ

1 Shesrain Rd 76100 **Road Map** *C1*

Located in a guesthouse, Rabiang Rim Nam serves excellent food in a picturesque riverside garden. Although the guesthouse is not worth a visit and the restaurant is quite run-of-the-mill, it is a good place to have some excellent Thai food or a Western breakfast.

PHETCHABURI Ban Khanom Thai ⒷⒷ

130 Petchkasem Rd 76100 **Tel** *0-3242-8911* **Road Map** *C1*

Located in a town justifiably famous for its delicious Thai sweets, Ban Khanom Thai (House of Thai sweets) is an ideal place for those with a sweet tooth. Try the *khanom mo kaeng* (firm custard of mung bean, egg, coconut, and sugar). It is a market staple and goes wonderfully with the local coffee.

PRACHUAP KHIRI KHAN Pan Pochana ⒷⒷⒷ

84/2–3 Salachep Rd 77000 **Road Map** *C2*

An exciting addition to sleepy Prachuap town, Pan Pochana is located south of the fishing pier. There is a nice, shady terrace, perfect for admiring the sea. Food is unpretentious, but excellent. A great place to try shellfish, which is much cheaper here than in other areas frequented by tourists, and probably fresher.

PRACHUAP KHIRI KHAN Phloen Samut ⒷⒷⒷⒷ

44 Beach Rd 77000 **Tel** *0-3260-1866* **Road Map** *C2*

Perennially popular with both locals and visitors to Prachuap Khiri Khan, Phloen Samut is a good place to try the local specialty *pla samli daet diaw* (flash-fried, sun-dried cotton fish), served with a green mango salad. Other Thai dishes featuring seafood come highly recommended as well.

LOWER WESTERN GULF COAST

KO PHANGAN Om Ganesh Ⓑ

Hat Rin 84280 **Tel** *0-7737-5123* **Road Map** *C4*

An excellent antidote to the hectic pace of partying on Hat Rin, Om Ganesh serves delicious, authentic Indian cuisine for those who can stomach the spices. Try the *lassi* (refreshing drink made with yogurt in water, salt, pepper, and ice), Indian vegetarian dishes, and chicken *tandoori*. Also a great breakfast venue.

KO PHANGAN Cucina Italiana ⒷⒷ

Chalok Lam 84280 **Road Map** *C4*

An ideal setting for a mug of beer and a pizza, Cucina Italiana is located on the northern coast of Ko Phangan. Although the name overstates the variety of food on offer, the restaurant serves excellent pizza. Try the Italian chef's home-made pasta dishes and fresh, grilled seafood.

KO PHANGAN Beach Club Bar & Grill ⒷⒷⒷ

Ban Pranburi, Thong Nai Pan Yai 84280 **Tel** *0-7744-5075* **Road Map** *C4*

One of Ko Phangan's most popular spots, Beach Club Bar & Grill is an excellent place for seafood grilled at live cooking stations. Diners can watch the skillful chef work the flames, as they sit at bamboo tables and chairs placed on the sand, within splashing distance of the sea. An ideal setting for a romantic dinner.

KO PHANGNAN Luna Lounge ⒷⒷⒷⒷ

8/25 M5 Thong Nai Pan Noi 84280 **Tel** *0-7744-5035* **Road Map** *C4*

A favorite on the island since it opened in 2006, Luna Lounge serves a varied menu of specialties from around the world, as well as Thai classics and a fish grill. It's located two minutes from the beach, in a rustic traditional Thai building with modern touches.

KO SAMUI Black Diamond Ⓑ

Hat Lamai 84310 **Tel** *0-7742-4392* **Road Map** *C4*

Popular with the locals for serving authentic Thai food at reasonable prices, Black Diamond keeps diners entertained with a pool table. Otherwise a no-frills restaurant. The chef is from Bangkok, and makes standard central Thai dishes such as *kaeng khiaw wan gai* (green chicken curry).

KO SAMUI The Islander Restaurant Ⓑ

Chawang Beach Road, Hat Chaweng 84320 **Tel** *0-7723-0836* **Road Map** *C4*

Both Thai and Western dishes are on offer at this budget eatery famous for its generous breakfasts and fish burgers. There is a kids' menu, a few pool tables, and a TV which can be used to view the latest movies. Worth a visit for its reasonable prices and good Thai food, toned down for foreign palates.

Key to Price Guide *see p318* **Key to Symbols** *see back cover flap*

KO SAMUI Billabong Surf Club ⒷⒷ

Fisherman's Village, Bo Phut 84320 ***Tel*** *0-7743-0144* ***Road Map*** *C4*

A friendly and inviting place with plenty of beer and generous portions of food. Famous for doorstop sandwiches, chip butties, *chimichangas*, and nachos as beer snacks, as well as main courses such as BBQ ribs, lamb chops, Down Under Aussie burgers, 21 oz (600g) steaks, and authentic Indian curries.

KO SAMUI Elephant & Castle ⒷⒷ

Big Buddha Beach 84320 ***Road Map*** *C4*

An authentic London pub in Ko Samui, Elephant & Castle is popular with British expatriates. An ideal place for an afternoon or evening pint. On offer is sausage and mash, fish and chips, steak and kidney pies, and baked spuds among others. Famous throughout the island for its Sunday roasts. Good selection of vegetarian dishes.

KO SAMUI Shabash ⒷⒷ

Chalee Bungalows, Big Buddha Beach 84320 ***Tel*** *0-7724-5035* ***Road Map*** *C4*

A Singaporean couple with Indian, Jewish, and Chinese roots and former residents of Indonesia, bring the most diverse culinary background on the island. A wide variety of Indian curries as well as plenty of Middle Eastern (even *kosher*) specialties made with fresh condiments and spices from the kitchen garden. Good vegetarian fare.

KO SAMUI Will Wait ⒷⒷ

Hat Lamai 84310 ***Tel*** *0-7742-4263* ***Road Map*** *C4*

One of the original "we cook everything" venues in Ko Samui, Will Wait has branches across the island. Serves Thai, Chinese, Western, and Japanese fare, but neither the food nor the decor is inspired. The place is clean and the price right and they offer good home-made bread and pastries.

KO SAMUI La Brasserie ⒷⒷⒷ

Beachcomber Hotel, 3/5 Mu 2, Hat Chaweng 84320 ***Tel*** *0-7742-20413* ***Road Map*** *C4*

Offering a satisfying beachfront dining experience, La Brasserie is an excellent place to dine. The lapping waves are accompanied by separate Italian and Thai menus, as well as a wide variety of seafood such as king prawns and rock lobster. An ideal setting for a romantic dinner. Dinner reservations advised.

KO SAMUI Rimbang Seafood ⒷⒷⒷ

Baan Bang Makham, Na Thon 84140 ***Tel*** *0-7723-6047* ***Road Map*** *C4*

With great views of Ang Thong Marine National Park *(see pp180–81)*, Rimbang Seafood is located off the beaten track in the northern part of the island. The local owner prides himself in cooking all dishes according to traditional recipes from Ko Samui.

KO SAMUI Rocky's ⒷⒷⒷ

Rocky's Resort, Hat Lamai 84310 ***Tel*** *0-7723-3020* ***Road Map*** *C4*

Located on the grounds of a boutique resort on Hat Lamai, Rocky's is worth visiting for the excellent yet reasonably priced food. Delicious array of home-made pizzas, seafood, and authentic Thai food. There are several events such as cocktail evenings, beach barbecues, and Thai festivals.

KO SAMUI Tamarind ⒷⒷⒷ

91/2–3 Mu 3, Hat Chaweng Noi 84320 ***Tel*** *0-7742-2011* ***Road Map*** *C4*

A harmonious confluence of East meets West, Tamarind is an elegant restaurant. The most popular item on the menu is the seafood basket for two, consisting of everything from rock lobster to snapper *satay*. Try the crispy-skinned snapper fillet with plantains and coconut curry sauce for the main course.

KO SAMUI The Three Monkeys ⒷⒷⒷ

Chawang Beach Road, Hat Chaweng 84320 ***Tel*** *0-8182-19388* ***Road Map*** *C4*

A bar-restaurant, with a classic Thai pub atmosphere, The Three Monkeys is ideal for a meal with the whole family. Children should try Mrs Crab (a crab burger) and Panda fried rice, while adults will enjoy the Mango Monkeys (marinated king prawns topped with mango sauce).

KO SAMUI The Cliff Bar & Grill ⒷⒷⒷⒷ

On cliff between Hat Chaweng and Hat Lamai 84320 ***Tel*** *0-7741-4266* ***Road Map*** *C4*

Stylish but relaxed, this great bar and grill would be a standout even without the stunning views of the bay. The menu is Mediterranean, with dishes made with fresh produce and presented in an uncomplicated style. The seafood platter and steaks are outstanding. Great for a sundowner. Dinner reservations advised.

KO SAMUI The Five Islands Restaurant ⒷⒷⒷⒷ

Ban Taling Ngam 84120 ***Tel*** *0-7741-5359* ***Road Map*** *C4*

Located on the idyllic southwestern coast of the island, diners can arrive early and enjoy a boat cruise to some of the offshore islands before a cocktail. The food is Thai fusion, prepared to a high standard. Also good for lunch, which is followed by a Thai dance show.

KO SAMUI Budsaba ⒷⒷⒷⒷⒷ

Muang Kulaypan Hotel, 100 Mu 2, Hat Chaweng 84320 ***Tel*** *0-7723-0850* ***Road Map*** *C4*

The most intimate restaurant along busy Hat Chaweng, Budsaba consists of a contemporary dining room and 14 private *salas*, generously spaced for privacy. The royal Thai cuisine on offer is fittingly indulgent, and the traditional music and dancing on most nights add another dimension to the enchanting atmosphere.

KO SAMUI Chef Chom's ฿฿฿฿฿

84 Mu 5, Hat Bophut 84320 ***Tel*** *0-7724-5480* ***Road Map*** *C4*

With breathtaking sea views, this spacious and airy restaurant is the perfect venue to try some spicy royal Thai cuisine. Dishes from central Thailand and delicate curries are exemplary. Try the *tong sai thai* salad with seafood. Live Thai music and dance on Fridays.

KO TAO La Matta ฿฿

Pier Road, Mae Had 84280 ***Tel*** *0-7745-6517* ***Road Map*** *C3*

La Matta is the first and continues to be the best restaurant on an island which has an impressive range of Italian eateries. The chef is Italian and makes the pasta onsite. The gnocchi as well as the pizza are especially good. A new branch on Hat Sai Ri offers an excellent buffet.

KO TAO Ko Tao Cottage ฿฿฿

19/1 Chalok, Ao Khao 84280 ***Tel*** *0-7745-6133* ***Road Map*** *C3*

A favorite with repeat visitors to Ko Tao, Ko Tao Cottage is pleasantly isolated from the main center of activity at Ban Hat Sai Ri. The menu includes freshly caught seafood as well as Thai staples and a sprinkling of Western dishes – all served in a low-key setting.

NAKHON SI THAMMARAT Khrua Nakhon ฿฿

Bovorn Bazaar, Ratchadamnoen Rd 80200 ***Road Map*** *C4*

Set in the middle of a central courtyard, this restaurant is a great place to sample southern Thai curries. Try the curries from steaming pots or the stir-fried dishes cooked to order. Sampling platters are offered with a little of everything for those who cannot decide from the main menu.

SURAT THANI Ban Don Hotel Restaurant ฿

Thanon Namuang 84000 ***Tel*** *0-7727-2167* ***Road Map*** *C4*

An ideal place for visitors passing through Surat Thani on their way to the beaches of Ko Samui and Ko Tao, Ban Don Hotel Restaurant offers appetizing, clean, and inexpensive comfort food. A step up from bus or train station eateries and excellent for those who have a few hours to while away.

SURAT THANI Suan Issan ฿฿฿

Off Donnok Road, 1 Damnern Kasem Rd 84000 ***Road Map*** *C4*

Set in an atmospheric, traditional Thai house, Suan Issan is a good choice for visitors to Surat Thani. The menu features delicious northeastern specialties. Favorites include *kai yang* (spicy grilled chicken), which is a perfect accompaniment to *som tam* (tangy green papaya salad with peanuts).

UPPER ANDAMAN COAST

PHANG NGA BAY Cha-Leang ฿

Phetkasem Rd 82140 ***Tel*** *0-7641-3831* ***Road Map*** *B5*

A favorite with locals and passing businessmen who come to the restaurant during breaktimes, Cha-Leang is a simple place without frills, but the seafood dishes are well prepared, although usually spicy. Try the *hor mok thalay* (spiced chunks of seafood mixed in a savory custard and steamed). Nice balcony seating.

PHANG NGA BAY Duang ฿฿

122 Phetkasem Rd 82140 ***Tel*** *0-7641-2216* ***Road Map*** *B5*

Both Chinese and southern Thai cuisine feature on this restaurant's menu. The seafood is particularly good. Try the delicious, spicy dishes such as *tom yam talay* (spicy seafood soup), *kung phao* (grilled shrimp), the excellent dried shrimp and papaya salad, or a mouthwatering glass-noodle salad.

PHANG NGA COAST Stempfer Café ฿

Phetkasem Rd, Baan La On, Khao Lak 82190 ***Road Map*** *B5*

This long-standing favorite serves an excellent German breakfast. It is also well known as a great place to buy mouthwatering cakes and other pastries. Good for sandwich lunches and beer. However, the Thai food is not as good as in some of the other restaurants.

PHANG NGA COAST Viking Steak House ฿฿฿

Phetkasem Rd, Baan La On, Khao Lak 82190 ***Tel*** *0-7642-0815* ***Road Map*** *B5*

A no-frills restaurant which offers great European and Thai food including pizzas at reasonable prices. Everything is clean and proper, with quick service, but without any pretensions. A good salad bar and daily specials. It gets busy, even rowdy, late in the evening.

PHUKET Pan Yaah Thai Restaurant ฿

249 Prabaramee Rd, Patong 83150 ***Tel*** *0-7629-04501* ***Road Map*** *B5*

Situated 1 mile (2 km) north of Patong, Pan Yaah Thai Restaurant combines excellent food with breathtaking sea views. The food is simple, nourishing fare of classic Thai seafood and noodle dishes, carefully prepared with fresh and fragrant local ingredients.

Key to Price Guide *see p318* **Key to Symbols** *see back cover flap*

PHUKET Somjit Noodles ฿

214/6 Phuket Rd, Phuket town 83000 ***Tel*** *0-7625-6701* ***Road Map*** *B5*

A small, clean, and unassuming daytime noodle shop, Somjit Noodles has been around for over half a century. It offers an excellent range of Thai and Hokkien noodle dishes. This is a great place to try the island's best-known dish, *khanom chin nam ya Phuket* (Chinese noodles in a curried fish sauce).

PHUKET Angus O'Tool's ฿฿

516/20 Patak Rd, Soi Islandia, Karon 83100 ***Tel*** *0-7639-8262* ***Road Map*** *B5*

A lively atmosphere, reasonable prices, and a choice of specials makes Angus O'Tool's a favorite stopover for visitors to Phuket. It is best to call ahead and book for dinner during high season. Great Sunday roast. Known for the most generous breakfast spreads in Phuket.

PHUKET China Inn Café ฿฿

20 Thalang Rd, Phuket town 83000 ***Tel*** *0-7635-8239* ***Road Map*** *B5*

Set up in a restored Sino-Portuguese building, China Inn Café resembles a tasteful, eclectic antique shop. The outdoor seating offers diners a relaxed ambience in which to peruse the exhaustive Thai and Western menus. The spring rolls and duck curry are particularly good. Good breakfast on offer.

PHUKET Ka Jok See ฿฿

26 Takua Pa Rd, Phuket town 83000 ***Tel*** *0-7621-7903* ***Road Map*** *B5*

Hidden down a small *soi* in the center of Phuket town, Ka Jok See is a lively Thai restaurant, popular throughout Thailand. Besides a selection of Thai dishes prepared with a special flair, there is live music and dancing – an ideal place for a fun evening. Dinner reservations advised.

PHUKET Kampong Kata Hill Restaurant ฿฿

West Patak Rd, Kata 83100 ***Tel*** *0-7633-0103* ***Road Map*** *B5*

Built in a traditional Thai-style house, on top of a hill above Hat Kata, this restaurant offers great value. Consistently fine standard Thai dishes. The attached art gallery offers works by local artists and some reproductions of antique pieces are worth a look.

PHUKET Lair Lay Tong ฿฿

Soi Dr Wattana, Patong 83100 ***Tel*** *0-7634-1140* ***Road Map*** *B5*

Located at the end of a small *soi*, off Beach Road in Patong, this lively restaurant offers both Thai and international fare at reasonable prices. Seafood courses abound. Try the *pae sa* – a whole, steamed fish in a tangy broth with cabbage and other vegetables, served on a brazier.

PHUKET Lotus Restaurant ฿฿

31/13 Banyan Tree Beachfront, Bang Tao, Cherng Talay 83110 ***Tel*** *0-7636-2625-6* ***Road Map*** *B5*

A long-running beachside purveyor of fresh seafood, Lotus Restaurant predates the upscale hotels that now surround Phuket. Consider trying the Penang chicken, besides the fresh seafood. Tour groups visit the restaurant; dinner reservations are advised.

PHUKET Natural Restaurant ฿฿

66/5 Soi Phuthon, Bangkok Rd, Phuket town 83000 ***Tel*** *0-7622-4287* ***Road Map*** *B5*

Situated in the heart of Phuket town, this garden/treehouse restaurant is full of hidden nooks and even little waterfalls – an ideal place to relax. The food, however, is quite straightforward with a selection of most world cuisines, including Japanese, German, and Thai. All are reasonably priced and served with a smile.

PHUKET Red Onion ฿฿

Patak East Rd, Karon 83100 ***Road Map*** *B5*

Although the exterior and decor of Red Onion leave a lot to be desired, the standard Western food – chicken steak with fries, Wiener schnitzel – is clean and tasty. Thai food is also good, albeit simple fare. It has a local expatriate following, so arrive early during peak periods.

PHUKET Savoey ฿฿

Patong 83100 ***Tel*** *0-7634-1171-4* ***Road Map*** *B5*

A reliable seafood emporium at the foot of Soi Bangla in Patong, Savoey offers a wide variety of fresh seafood. Despite a seating capacity of 400 and three operating kitchens, the service is quick and the prices quite reasonable. Diners sit in a casual, covered outdoor pavilion. Gets busy as the day progresses.

PHUKET Sawasdee Thai Cuisine ฿฿

38 Katekwan Rd, Karon 83100 ***Tel*** *0-7633-0979* ***Road Map*** *B5*

One of the few places on Phuket's beaches offering good Thai food at reasonable prices, Sawasdee has an agreeable atmosphere. Seafood dishes are more expensive, but the *tom kha gai* (spicy chicken soup) is a bargain. Located across the street from the guesthouse of the same name.

PHUKET Baluchi ฿฿฿

Horizon Beach Resort, Soi Kepsap, Patong 83100 ***Tel*** *0-7629-2526* ***Road Map*** *B5*

Often referred to as the best Indian restaurant in Phuket, there is no denying that the north Indian fare is excellent at Baluchi. The chefs are from the subcontinent, as is a good deal of the clientele. Located within the grounds of a nice boutique resort. Famous for the *dal* as well as the fixed menus.

PHUKET Kan Eang II

9/3 Chofa Road, Ao Chalong 83130 **Tel** *0-7638-1323* — ⓑⓑⓑ — **Road Map** *B5*

Set in beautiful gardens with an adjacent sandy beach, Kan Eang II is a great place for children. Although the chain has been around for more than 30 years, Kan Eang II is better than its namesake at the pier in Chalong. The restaurant offers great food. The Vietnamese restaurant next door, belonging to the same chain, is also good.

PHUKET Kantok Restaurant at Burasari Resort

Burasari Resort, 18/110 Ruamjai Rd, Patong 83100 **Tel** *0-7629-2929* — ⓑⓑⓑ — **Road Map** *B5*

Serving a wide range of Thai dishes, with the duck red curry and fish cakes proving firm favorites, Kantok Restaurant is set in romantic lush, tropical gardens. There is live entertainment every night with traditional Thai dancing. Worth a visit, even if you are not staying in the resort.

PHUKET L'Orfeo

Ban Sai Yuan Rd, Rawai 83110 **Tel** *0-7628-8935* — ⓑⓑⓑ — **Road Map** *B5*

A relaxed, casual restaurant and bar, L'Orfeo has an almost Arabian setting. The soundtrack spans several genres, as does the international menu. The standouts are the home-made gnocchi with pine nuts and parsley butter sauce, and the Angus beef tartare with tomato chutney. Dinner reservations advised.

PHUKET Salvatore's

15 Rasada Rd, Phuket town 83000 **Tel** *0-7622-5958* — ⓑⓑⓑ — **Road Map** *B5*

Chef and owner Salvatore, originally from Sardinia, gave the restaurant his name. A popular place, Salvatore's has relocated to a more sedate area downtown. Trattoria-style decor and cuisine done to perfection and competently served in a tasteful and laid-back atmosphere. Separate pizzeria next door.

PHUKET Taste

Surin Beach Road 83110 **Tel** *0-7627-0090* — ⓑⓑⓑ — **Road Map** *B5*

A chic beachfront venue south of Bang Tao, Taste is frequented by visitors staying in the upscale hotels and resorts nearby. Good value with Mediterranean fare and a pleasant ambience. Try the five-spice snapper, served with plenty of fresh vegetables. A wide selection of Thai desserts round off a good meal.

PHUKET Tatonka

Sri Suthorn Rd, Bang Thao 83110 **Tel** *0-7632-4349* — ⓑⓑⓑ — **Road Map** *B5*

Located just outside the grounds of the Laguna Beach Resort *(see p307)*, Tatonka offers a "globetrotters' cuisine" influenced by various countries from across the world. It offers several unique and mouthwatering creations, such as the sashimi spring rolls. Pleasant outdoor atmosphere.

PHUKET The Whispering Cock

Outside Laguna Resort, Bang Thao 83110 **Tel** *0-7625-6560* — ⓑⓑⓑ — **Road Map** *B5*

Among the best English pubs on the island, The Whispering Cock offers authentic interiors, good steak and kidney pies, a wide choice of beers, and a pleasant beer garden, great for whiling away an afternoon. Darts and a regular showing of English sporting events complete the package.

PHUKET Baba Dining Lounge

Sri Panwa Resort, Laem Panwa 83130 **Tel** *0-7637-1006* — ⓑⓑⓑⓑ — **Road Map** *B5*

Located on the grounds of the Sri Panwa resort on the southern tip of the island, Baba Dining Lounge is the dining area of a larger entertainment venue which also offers a chic nightclub. The name and decor come from the Chinese-Malay hybrid culture of the area, but the food is largely Western.

PHUKET La Gaetana

352 Phuket Rd, Phuket town 83000 **Tel** *0-7625-0523* — ⓑⓑⓑⓑ — **Road Map** *B5*

An intimate Italian eatery in the downtown area, La Gaetana is known for its Italian version of haute cuisine, such as a starter of mixed carpaccio of salmon, tuna, beef, and an especially tasty smoked duck breast. Try baked portobello mushroom in gorgonzola sauce for the main course. It also has a great wine list.

PHUKET Ratri Jazztaurant

Patak Rd, Kata 83100 **Tel** *0-7633-3638* — ⓑⓑⓑⓑ — **Road Map** *B5*

A hip, two-story restaurant famous for its sunset views. In addition to an oyster bar, it features Thai and other Asian delights in the dining pavilion and cool jazz from the live band. Menu highlights are the sirloin salad and salmon sashimi for starters and *gaeng masaman nuah* or *gai* (beef or chicken Muslim curry).

PHUKET Sala Bua

Impiana Phuket Cabana Resort & Spa, 41 Taweewong Rd, Hat Patong 83110 **Tel** *0-7634-0138* — ⓑⓑⓑⓑ — **Road Map** *B5*

A romantic and discreet beachfront pavilion is the setting for this award-winning restaurant. Filipino chef Ronnie Macuja is one of the best-known on the island, and his East-meets-West creations are inventive. Try the celebrated pan-seared New Zealand beef tenderloin, which comes with a surprising kiwi-fruit relish.

PHUKET Watermark

Phuket Boat Lagoon, Ao Sapam 83500 **Tel** *0-7623-9730* — ⓑⓑⓑⓑ — **Road Map** *B5*

Located on the grounds of the classy Phuket Boat Lagoon on the sedate east coast of the island, this award-winning contemporary and chic restaurant offers only classic dishes. The menu is international, with plenty of Thai food as well as pizzas and pastas.

Key to Price Guide *see p318* **Key to Symbols** *see back cover flap*

PHUKET Baan Yin Dee ⒷⒷⒷⒷⒷ

7 Muean Ngen Rd, Patong 83110 ***Tel*** *0-7629-4104-6* ***Road Map*** *B5*

Located just south of Patong on a hill overlooking the bay, Baan Yin Dee is on the grounds of a boutique resort. The atmosphere is elegant and opulent, as is the food – mainly high-end gourmet treats such as lobster and scallops cooked by a French chef. Book in advance to get a table with a good view.

PHUKET Black Ginger ⒷⒷⒷⒷⒷ

Indigo Pearl, Hat Nai Yang 83110 ***Tel*** *0-7623-6550* ***Road Map*** *B5*

A good reason to visit the unique Indigo Pearl resort *(see p307)*, which draws its design elements from Phuket's tin-mining past, Black Ginger has a traditional Thai pavilion painted in black and built on stilts over a lake. Offers an elegant dining experience, with superb renditions of classic Thai dishes.

PHUKET The Boathouse Wine & Grill ⒷⒷⒷⒷⒷ

West Patak Rd, Kata 83100 ***Tel*** *0-7633-0015* ***Road Map*** *B5*

The first Phuket project of Thailand's aristocratic hotelier and restaurateur Mom Tri, located on the grounds of his boutique resort. The food is Mediterranean and Thai with good service and an excellent selection of wines. There are other great Mom Tri restaurants in Phuket as well. Events taking place at the restaurant include cooking classes.

PHUKET Da Maurizio Bar Ristorante ⒷⒷⒷⒷⒷ

223/2 Pravaramee Rd, Ao Kalim 83100 ***Tel*** *0-7634-4079-276* ***Road Map*** *B5*

With a mainly organic menu, Da Maurizio leads the way in Phuket, with fresh, delicious Italian cuisine and an impressive wine list. Located right on the beach, on a clifftop setting, it has a relaxed ambience and fabulous views. Book ahead, especially in high season.

PHUKET La Trattoria ⒷⒷⒷⒷⒷ

Dusit Thani Laguna Resort, Bang Tao 83110 ***Tel*** *0-7632-4320* ***Road Map*** *B5*

Classic and elegant in its decor, La Trattoria offers several specialties prepared by Italian chefs. Try a fillet of sole and sea scallops with saffron sauce and green peppercorns. The Italian coffee cocktail Gennaro with Sambuca, rum bianco, coffee, and whipped cream is especially divine.

PHUKET Siam Indigo ⒷⒷⒷⒷⒷ

8 Phang Nga Rd, Phuket town 83000 ***Tel*** *0-7625-6697* ***Road Map*** *B5*

Housed in a historic building and decorated with original artworks, Siam Indigo offers an elegant yet relaxed atmosphere. The restaurant specializes in Thai-Chinese fusion dishes. Try the New Zealand lamb, green mussels, and marinated pork *satay*. The massaman curry is also rather tasty. The interior courtyard is ideal for dining.

PHUKET Siam Supper Club ⒷⒷⒷⒷⒷ

Tinlay Place, Bang Tao 83110 ***Tel*** *0-7627-0936* ***Road Map*** *B5*

Just outside the gates of the Laguna Beach Resort, the Siam Supper Club offers a mainly Western menu of steaks and pastas as well as some Thai dishes. The atmosphere is informal but classy and the bar is quite popular with youngsters. A good family place. Kids will love the cheesecake.

RANONG Thanon Ruangrat Market Ⓑ

Ruangrat Rd, Ranong 85000 ***Road Map*** *B3*

At first glance, Thanon Ruangrat Market looks more like a produce market, but visitors will find some great food here. Food stalls with a few tables fight for space with some real restaurants. Good, fresh seafood. In the evening, another market appears on Kamlangsap Road.

RANONG Chaong Thong ⒷⒷ

8–10 Ruangrat Rd, Ranong 85000 ***Road Map*** *B3*

A good choice of both Thai and Chinese dishes, served promptly and in a clean environment. Caters to travelers with a varied selection of vegetarian dishes and herbal teas. Breakfast is quite delectable. Some of the staff members speak English and can help with travel tips.

RANONG Sophon's Hideaway ⒷⒷ

Ruangrat Rd, Ranong 85000 ***Tel*** *0-7783-2730* ***Road Map*** *B3*

The primary *farang* (European) hangout in Ranong, Sophon's Hideaway is a good place to gather travel tips, including visa renewal trips to Burma. The food is good although not exceptional and includes a wide choice of both Western and Thai dishes. A beautiful garden and pool table complete the picture.

LOWER ANDAMAN COAST

KO LANTA Funky Fish ⒷⒷ

Ao Phra-Ae 81150 ***Tel*** *08-1275-9501* ***Road Map*** *B5*

Probably the first restaurant/bungalow operation to spring up on Ao Phra-Ae, Funky Fish is famous for its great pizzas and good music. The Thai food is toned down to suit Western palates. Can get quite noisy and crowded especially in the evening.

KO LANTA Red Snapper ⒷⒷ

Ao Phra-Ae 81150 ***Tel*** *0-7585-6965* ***Road Map*** *B5*

One of the better restaurants on Ao Phra-Ae, Red Snapper has a unique atmosphere. Set in a garden, the Dutch owners have done a good job on the menu and the decor. A great place for a pleasant afternoon or evening meal. Start with the *tapas*, then try the catch of the day. The restaurant also has an impressive wine list.

KO LANTA Time for Lime Cooking School ⒷⒷ

Hat Klong Dao 81150 ***Tel*** *0-7568-4590* ***Road Map*** *B5*

Started as a cooking school which later evolved into a restaurant, Time for Lime Cooking School also offers bungalow accommodations. The Norwegian owner still trains Thais in the finer points of European cooking while her Thai staff teaches Thai cooking to visitors. Wide choice of culinary delights prepared by trained cooks.

KO LANTA Mango Bistro ⒷⒷⒷ

Ko Lanta Old Town 81150 ***Tel*** *0-7569-7181* ***Road Map*** *B5*

This Chinese-style house on stilts along the coastline was once an opium den, but today has been renovated into the Mango Bistro. An excellent restaurant with a small library, Mango Bistro offers a wide variety of Thai and European dishes. The owner also rents the charming fisherman's houses nearby.

KO LANTA Sayang Beach Resort ⒷⒷⒷ

Ao Phra-Ae 81150 ***Tel*** *0-7568-4156* ***Road Map*** *B5*

Even visitors not staying at Sayang Beach Resort are regulars for lunch and dinner at its restaurant. Located on a headland at the north end of Ao Phra-Ae, the restaurant is noted for its chic ambience and wide choice of Thai and Indian food, prepared by a chef from the subcontinent.

KO PHI PHI Ciao Bella ⒷⒷ

Ao Lo Dalam 81000 ***Tel*** *08-1894-1246* ***Road Map*** *B5*

A romantic beachside Italian restaurant on Ao Lo Dalam, Ciao Bella is very popular with Italian visitors. Pizzas and pastas are excellent, as is the grilled seafood. Some Thai dishes, including the fresh seafood, are also worth trying. Includes a nice selection of cocktails and pleasant music.

KO PHI PHI Madame Restaurant ⒷⒷ

Ton Sai 81000 ***Road Map*** *B5*

A popular hangout in central Ton Sai, the main village in Ko Phi Phi, Madame Restaurant offers great Thai curries and good pizzas – all for a reasonable price and served with a smile. Try the *tom yam*, which is very good. There is also an excellent spread for the vegetarians to dig into. The evening movie always attracts a crowd.

KO PHI PHI HC Anderson ⒷⒷⒷ

Ao Ton Sai 81000 ***Tel*** *08-6267-6628* ***Road Map*** *B5*

A Danish owned steakhouse, HC Anderson specializes in expensive, but delicious imported New Zealand beef and lamb. Mid-priced European food is also on offer, largely of the roasted meat variety. The restaurant offers good wines and has a lively atmosphere in the evenings.

KO PHI PHI Tacada ⒷⒷⒷ

Zeavola Resort 81000 ***Tel*** *0-7562-7000* ***Road Map*** *B5*

Located on the grounds of the very luxurious Zeavola resort *(see p309)* at the northeast end of the island, Tacada is the place to head after a long, tiring day of sightseeing. An open-air venue on the beachside that offers both Thai and Western food, this is definitely one of the best places for a meal on Ko Phi Phi.

KRABI Ruan Pae Ⓑ

Utarakit Rd 81000 ***Tel*** *0-7561-1956* ***Road Map*** *B5*

A well-known floating restaurant on the Krabi River, Ruan Pae is a good place for soaking up the beautiful surroundings over a chilled beer and good Thai food, especially around sunset. Visitors must beware of the mosquitoes. Try the house specialty – *tom yam thalay* (spicy seafood soup).

KRABI Baie Toey ⒷⒷ

Khong Kha Rd 81000 ***Road Map*** *B5*

Located close to a nice park along the river in the center of town, this Thai restaurant is a favorite among locals who come here after work. A fine menu allows diners to experiment with their orders. Look for the booth seating downstairs by the river. Closes early.

KRABI Lavinia ⒷⒷ

Beach Rd, Ao Nang 81000 ***Road Map*** *B5*

The nicest place in Ao Nang for Italian food beyond pizza. There are also good sandwiches, made with dark grain bread, perfect for a mid-day snack. The restaurant makes its own ice cream and has a good selection of imported beers and wines. Picturesque location just across the beach.

KRABI May and Mark ⒷⒷ

Maharat Rd, Soi 2 81000 ***Road Map*** *B5*

The best place in Krabi town for Western food, catering mainly to backpackers. Good food at reasonable prices. Great vegetarian selection including burgers and some Mexican dishes. Opens early and serves breakfast. Try the delicious fruit shakes.

Key to Price Guide *see p318* **Key to Symbols** *see back cover flap*

KRABI Rock Restaurant ⒷⒷ

East Hat Rai Leh, Rai Leh 81000 **Road Map** *B5*

Perched on a steep hill, Rock Restaurant can only be reached by climbing up the hill, but the view is worth it. Located above Highland Resort, it serves good Thai as well as Western dishes at very reasonable prices. Visit during the day to enjoy the beautiful jungle-like setting.

KRABI Lae Lay Grill ⒷⒷⒷⒷⒷ

89 Moo 3, Ao Nang 81000 ***Tel*** *0-7566-1588* **Road Map** *B5*

This restaurant offers complimentary transport to and from any hotel on the Ao Nang stretch. It's expensive, so well suited for a romantic meal or special occasion. Try to be there for the sunset views from the lovely outside deck. Another nice touch is the open kitchen. The seafood grill is excellent.

KRABI Ruen Mai ⒷⒷⒷⒷⒷ

Maharat Rd 81000 ***Tel*** *0-7563-1797* **Road Map** *B5*

Considered the best restaurant in Krabi town, Ruen Mai is set in a beautiful garden. The menu, which mainly offers seafood, also has a wide selection of Thai curries which are reputed for their careful and authentic preparation. Although more expensive than market food stalls, it is still cheaper than other places in Ao Nang.

SATUN On's – The Living Room Ⓑ

48 Burivanich Rd 91000 **Road Map** *C6*

A popular place with visitors to Satun, On's offers Western food such as fish and chips, pizzas, and sandwiches. A good place to sit and read or gather local travel information. While the Thai food is pretty good, the Night Market two blocks north of the restaurant offers even better delights.

SATUN Time ⒷⒷ

43 Satun Thani Rd 91000 ***Tel*** *0-7471-2286* **Road Map** *C6*

A step up in comfort from On's, Time is air-conditioned, with an appealing decor and an efficient staff. Popular with Thai families for its cleanliness. The picture menu is extensive, covering everything from roast duck to banana blossom salad as well as some delightful desserts. A good place to experiment.

TRANG German Beer Bar ⒷⒷ

Thanon Huay Yod 92000 ***Tel*** *08-7283-0454* **Road Map** *C5*

Despite its name, Beer Bar offers much more than beer. The German sausages and *sauerkraut* (finely chopped cabbage fermented in brine), although not elaborately presented, are excellent, as are the steaks and burgers. True to its name, the bar also has a wide choice of imported beers. Good place to gather useful travel tips.

TRANG Namui ⒷⒷ

Rama VI Rd 92000 **Road Map** *C5*

An extensive menu and reasonable prices make this a local favorite. Namui focuses on Thai and Chinese seafood, but also offers great vegetarian fare. Try the *pla krapong nueng manao* (steamed sea bass in lemon broth). A great place for outdoor dining in a veranda located behind the main dining room.

DEEP SOUTH

HAT YAI Hua Lee ⒷⒷ

Nipat Uthit 3 Rd 90110 **Road Map** *C5*

Very popular with Hat Yai's Chinese community, who head here for exotic delicacies such as bird's nest soup and *hu chalam* (shark fin soup), which do not usually appeal to Western palates or cultural sensibilities. However, there are many other choices, including an inexpensive but delicious vegetarian fare. Open late into the night.

HAT YAI Sumatra ⒷⒷ

55/1 Ratthakan Rd 90110 ***Tel*** *0-7424-6459* **Road Map** *C5*

This modest eatery specializes in Malaysian cuisine with a distinctly Indonesian flavor. Try typical dishes such as the *mee goreng* (fried yellow noodles mixed with eggs and shrimp), *nasi goreng* (fried rice with eggs and flavored with shrimp), and *rojak* (a filling spicy salad with a peanut sauce).

NARATHIWAT Rim Nam ⒷⒷ

Narathiwat Tak Bai Rd 96000 ***Tel*** *0-7351-1559* **Road Map** *D6*

A garden restaurant a few miles south of town, Rim Nam offers both central and southern Thai food. Seafood predominates, but there is a variety of other choices. Good food with friendly service, ideal for a fun evening with the family. It also offers free transport from a visitor's hotel to the restaurant.

SONGKHLA Khao Noi Thai Ⓑ

14/22 Vichianchom Rd 90000 ***Tel*** *0-7431-1805* **Road Map** *D5*

Only open until mid-afternoon, Khao Noi Thai is an unassuming place, very popular with locals for the curries which are of central and southern varieties. The rest of the menu includes Thai stir-fries. Very clean, the staff is efficient and serve with a smile, although their English skills are limited.

SHOPPING IN THAILAND'S BEACHES AND ISLANDS

Thailand is well known as a country that offers good shopping. The high quality, wide variety, and low prices of many Thai goods are a major attraction. Arts and crafts are probably the most tempting buys. These range from inexpensive wicker rice steamers to valuable antiques, and include many typically Thai items such as triangular cushions, colorful hill-tribe artifacts, and finely crafted silver jewelry. Thai silk has an international reputation and comes in a variety of designs. The country is renowned for its rich supply of gems, and towns such as Chanthaburi are major gem trading centers. With shopping malls sharing space alongside vibrant markets, Thailand offers shoppers a mix of the traditional and contemporary.

Bronze carved Buddha head

OPENING HOURS

Most small stores open from about 8am to 8pm or 9pm, while department stores, shopping malls, and tourist shops open from 10:30am until 9pm or 10pm. Business days are normally Monday to Saturday, but most shops in Bangkok, tourist areas, and resorts also open on Sundays and public holidays. During the Thai New Year *(see p34)* and the Chinese New Year *(see p37)*, many shops shut for several days. Market hours are usually dawn to mid-afternoon for fresh produce, and late afternoon to midnight, or even later, for tourist souvenirs.

HOW TO PAY

The Thai baht, linked to the US dollar, is relatively stable. The baht will always be accepted throughout the country. Credit cards can be used in many stores in Bangkok as well as in island resorts, and increasingly so in provincial towns such as Songkhla. VISA and MasterCard are the most widely accepted credit cards followed by American Express. Upscale places usually take all major cards. Many shops will add a surcharge of up to 5 percent on payment by credit card.

RIGHTS AND REFUNDS

Visitors should ask for a *bai set* (receipt) with the shop's address and tax number when buying costly items. Shops usually fill out a form for visitors who wish to reclaim the 7 percent sales tax. This form must be presented to customs at the airport. If arranging to have goods shipped home, visitors must ensure that they confirm all the costs involved with the supplier in advance.

Refunds are almost unheard of, but exchange of faulty or poorly fitting non-sale goods from reputable stores should be possible.

BARGAINING

The trend in cities, especially Bangkok, is toward chain stores with fixed prices and endless discount sales. However, the Thai love of bargaining means visitors can often negotiate at small shops, specialty retailers, and market stands. Visitors should be aware of the going rate for items so as not to offer embarrassingly low sums. Learning the Thai for numbers may restrain the vendor's initial bid. Faking disinterest if the seller's bids remain high also works and is better than enthusiastically bargaining and then deciding not to buy once the vendor agrees.

Swanky interiors of the popular Siam Paragon in Bangkok

Stalls selling a variety of items at a busy street market in Bangkok

DEPARTMENT STORES AND MALLS

International-style department stores are the mainstay of shopping in Bangkok and larger resorts such as Pattaya and Phuket. However, many stores fill their aisles with bargain stands. The main Thai chains are **Robinson's**, with a branch – **Robinson's Ocean Department Store** – in Phuket, and the more upscale **Central Department Store**. Residents

Asia Books, one of the most popular bookstores in Thailand

of Bangkok already have countless downtown malls, such as **Peninsula Plaza**, to choose from, as well as luxury shopping complexes such as **Emporium**, **CentralWorld Plaza**, and **Siam Paragon**. But the trend is for big malls out of the center of the city – such as **Fashion Island**.

Two of the world's five biggest shopping malls are in outer Bangkok. **Seacon Square** on Srinakharin Road, southeast of the city, extends for over 1 mile (2 km). A few modern malls are also situated in other large towns and resorts. These include the **Jungceylon Shopping Complex** in Phuket and **Mike Shopping Mall** in Pattaya.

ENGLISH LANGUAGE BOOKSTORES

Thailand has three English language book and magazine chains: **Asia Books**, which has several branches in Bangkok, **Kinokuniya**, and **Bookazine** also with several branches in the country. **DK Book House** in Seacon Square is Southeast Asia's largest bookstore. Second-hand books are widely available in Pattaya, Ko Samui, and Phuket.

MARKETS AND STREET VENDORS

There is a market at the heart of every Thai town and even the smallest will offer a good range of fresh produce. Larger markets sell everything – local crafts, fruits, vegetables, and household items.

Mobile roadside stands are also found across the country. Some sell items such as jasmine rings, while others are good for souvenirs. Pattaya and Patong in Phuket have many such stands. They are also seen on Silom and Sukhumvit roads in Bangkok.

THAI SILK

The ancient art of Thai silk-weaving was revived by an American, Jim Thompson *(see p77)* after World War II and is now a booming export business. Silk can be patterned, plain, or in the subtle *mut mee* style made from dyed thread. This heavy, bright, and slightly rough cloth is now used for ties, dresses, shirts, skirts, and other Western outfits. It also makes excellent cushion covers, hangings, as well as sundry ornaments.

Most silk comes from the north and northeast, but some is woven in and around Bangkok. Surawong Road in Bangkok is a reliable place from where such items can be bought. **Jim Thompson**, and **Shinawatra** on Sukhumvit Road, however, are among the best. Jim Thompson also has outlets in Hua Hin, Ko Samui, Pattaya, and Phuket.

CLOTHES

Thai tailors can make suits and dresses to order for low prices. It is advisable to assess the designs, fabric, and cut beforehand and insist on a couple of intermediate fittings. In Bangkok, Chinese and Indian tailors advertise in tourist magazines and outside their shops along Sukhumvit, Charoen Krung, and Khao San roads. Designs are usually copied, often with great skill, from magazines or catalogues of famous brands such as Armani and Hugo Boss. The quality of workmanship can vary considerably; so make sure to ask around for recommendations.

An array of wooden and bronze carved items at a local shop

A dazzling selection of swatches of colorful Thai silk

Other popular items of Thai clothing include baggy fisherman's pants, batik sarongs, (especially in the Deep South) and vests and trousers made from hill-tribe silk, and other northeastern fabrics.

ARTS AND CRAFTS

Although most Thai handicrafts are produced in the north and northeast, these are available in Bangkok and throughout the coastal regions, albeit at slightly higher prices.

High-quality ethnic crafts at fixed prices are available from boutiques in upscale hotels – **Silom Village**, **River City Complex**, and the less expensive **Narayana Phand** in Bangkok. In the south, **Phuket Orchid Garden and Thai Village** in Phuket town is a good bet.

HILL-TRIBE ARTIFACTS

The costumes and artifacts of the hill tribes make fascinating souvenirs. Items might include Akha coin headdresses, Lahu geometric blankets and cushion covers, Hmong red-ruffled black jackets, and brightly colored Lisu tunics.

A wide range of hill-tribe souvenirs and clothing is on sale at markets and in arcades throughout the south, especially in the markets of Bangkok and Phuket.

CERAMICS

Delicate Benjarong pottery used to be made in China and sent to Thailand to be decorated with intricate floral patterns using five colors. Today, the work is done entirely in Thailand. Visitors can buy dinner services in Benjarong in myriad designs, including the more typical spherical pots. In Bangkok, Chatuchak Market is cheaper and offers a wider choice than the downtown shops.

The heavier celadon pottery style is distinguished by its etched designs under a thick, translucent green, brown, or blue glaze with a cracked patina. It is available in Bangkok at **Thai Celadon House** as well as in many other craft shops such as those on Silom and Charoen Krung roads.

LACQUERWARE

Lacquerware usually has floral, flame, or portrait designs in black and gold on bamboo and wood. More common is the Burmese style of red ocher on bamboo and rattan with pictorial scenes or floral patterns. Traditional items include boxes for food and jewelry and are available in Bangkok as well as in Phuket.

NIELLOWARE AND PEWTERWARE

Nielloware, the intricate process of silver (or at times gold) inlay in a black metal amalgam, makes for beautiful items such as cufflinks, pill boxes, and jewelry. Some of the finest items are from Nakhon. Southern Thailand has significant tin deposits, so pewterware is a major craft there. Typical items include vases, tankards, plates, and jewelry boxes.

MASKS, PUPPETS, AND MUSICAL INSTRUMENTS

Musical instruments including *khaens* (northeastern pan pipes), *piphat* ensemble gongs, and drums make impressive souvenirs. They are available at Silom Village, Narayana Phand, Chatuchak, and Nakorn Kasem markets in Bangkok as well as in the local markets of Ko Samui and Phuket. These places are also good sources of classic *khon* masks, *hun krabok* puppets, *nang talung*, and *nang yai* shadow puppets.

Colorful puppets, inspired by the Ramakien, for sale in Bangkok

In the south, these can be bought from the **Shadow Puppet Theater**. Guided tours also show visitors how these intricate puppets are made.

ANTIQUES

The delicacy and charm of Thai antiques are so appealing to shoppers that the few remaining antiques in the country are either very expensive, fake, or illegally obtained. Thailand is, in fact, one of the principal outlets for antiques from all over Southeast Asia. Some shops resemble museums, with tapestries, statues, cabinets, puppets, lacquerware, and temple artifacts. The main sources in Bangkok are Charoen Krung Road, River City Complex, Chatuchak Market, and Nakorn Kasem. Antique auctions are held at River City Complex on the first Saturday of each month.

Recommended shops include **The Fine Arts** and **NeOld** in Bangkok. **Chan's Antique House** in Phuket has an excellent reputation.

Export permits are required for antiques and all Buddha images from the Fine Arts Department, via the **National Museum**, and take at least a week to obtain.

Attractive display of fine ceramic products

JEWELRY

Thai jewelry tends to be large and expressive, often with superb detailing. Necklaces, bracelets, earrings, and Lao-style belts are typical in employing silver thread and filigree detail, often incorporating silver beads and large, plate-like pendants. More affordable modern costume jewelry sells well in Siam Square and Chatuchak Market. Some of Thailand's best jewelry is found in Peninsula Plaza as well as hotels such as the Dusit Thani. Some shops, notably **Uthai's Gems**, will also custom design jewelry. **Astral Gemstone Talisman** also sells pendants and rings customized according to the buyer's zodiac sign.

GEMS

Bangkok is possibly the world's biggest gem-trading center. Local stones include rubies, red and blue spinels, orange and white zircons, and yellow and blue sapphires. Markets also operate around Chanthaburi where gems are cheaper than in Bangkok. Phuket is Thailand's only good source of high quality pearls; **Mook Phuket** sells very good examples.

The **Asian Institute of Gemological Sciences** is a specialized institute that helps in the grading and identification of gems. It also runs short-term courses on gem recognition and grading. These can help in preventing buyers from buying fake products.

DIRECTORY

DEPARTMENT STORES AND MALLS

Central Department Store
Silom Complex, 191 Silom Rd, Bangkok. **City Map** 7 A4. ***Tel*** *0-2231-3333.* **www**.central.co.th

CentralWorld Plaza
Ratchadamri Rd, Bangkok. **City Map** 8 D1. ***Tel*** *0-2635-1111.* **www**.centralworld.co.th

Emporium
Sukhumvit Rd, Prompong, Bangkok. **City Map** 8 F1. ***Tel*** *0-2664-8000.* **www**. emporium-thailand.com

Fashion Island
5/5 Ramindra Rd, Bangkok. ***Tel*** *0-2947-5000.* **www**.fashionisland.co.th

Jungceylon Shopping Complex
181 Rat-U-Thit 200 Pee Rd, Patong, Phuket. ***Tel*** *0-7660-0111.*

Mike Shopping Mall
262 Moo 10, Pattaya Beach Rd, Pattaya. ***Tel*** *0-3841-2000.*

Peninsula Plaza
Ratchadamri Rd, Bangkok. **City Map** 8 D1. ***Tel*** *0-2253-9762.*

Robinson's
259 Sukhumvit Rd, Between Soi 17 and 19, Bangkok. **City Map** 8 D3. ***Tel*** *0-2252-5121.*

Robinson's Ocean Department Store
Jungceylon Shopping Complex, 181 Rat-U-Thit 200 Pee Rd, Patong, Phuket. ***Tel*** *0-7625-6500-12.*

Seacon Square
904 Srinakharin Rd, Bangkok. ***Tel*** *0-2721-8888.* **www**.seaconsquare.com

Siam Paragon
Rama I Rd, Bangkok. **City Map** 7 C1. ***Tel*** *0-2658-1000.* **www**.siamparagon.co.th

ENGLISH LANGUAGE BOOKSTORES

Asia Books
221 Sukhumvit Rd, Bangkok. ***Tel*** *0-2651-0428.* **www**.asiabooks.com

Bookazine
Floor 1, CP Tower, 313 Silom Rd, Bangkok. **City Map** 7 C4. ***Tel*** *0-2231-0016.*
Hat Chaweng, Opposite McDonald's, Ko Samui. ***Tel*** *0-7741-3616.*
Royal Garden Plaza, 218/2-4 Moo 10 Beach Rd, Pattaya. ***Tel*** *0-3871-0472.*
18 Bangla Rd, Hat Patong, Kathu, Phuket. ***Tel*** *0-7634-5883.*

DK Book House
3rd Fl, Seacon Square, 904 Srinakharin Rd, Nongbon, Praves, Bangkok. ***Tel*** *0-2721-9190.*

Kinokuniya
3rd Fl, Room 301-3 Emporium Shopping Complex, 622 Sukhumvit 24 Rd, Klong Toey, Bangkok. ***Tel*** *0-2664-8554.*

THAI SILK

Jim Thompson
9 Surawong Rd, Bangkok. **City Map** 3 C5. ***Tel*** *0-2632-8100.* **www**.jimthompson house.org
Hilton Hua Hin Resort and Spa, 33 Naresdamri Rd, Hua Hin. ***Tel*** *0-3253-3486.*
Centara Grand Samui Beach Resort, 38/2 Moo 3 Borpud, Hat Chaweng, Ko Samui. ***Tel*** *0-7723-0521.*
Royal Cliff Beach Resort, 353 Moo 12, Phra Tamnuk Rd, Pattaya. ***Tel*** *0-3825-2292.*
Kata Thani Beach Resort and Spa, 14 Kata Noi Rd, Hat Kata Noi, Phuket. ***Tel*** *0-7633-0010.*

Shinawatra
94 Sukhumvit Rd, Soi 23, Bangkok. ***Tel*** *0-2258-0295.*

ARTS AND CRAFTS

Narayana Phand
Ratchadamri Rd, Bangkok. **City Map** 8 D1. ***Tel*** *0-2252-4670.*

Phuket Orchid Garden and Thai Village
52/11 Thepkasattri Rd, Muang Phuket. ***Tel*** *0-7621-4860.*

River City Complex
23 Trok Rongnamkaeng, Yotha Rd, Bangkok. **City Map** 6 F3. ***Tel*** *0-2237-0077.*

Silom Village
Silom Rd, Bangkok. **City Map** 7 A4. ***Tel*** *0-2234-4448.* **www**.silomvillage.co.th

CERAMICS

Thai Celadon House
8/3–8/5 Ratchadapisek Rd, Sukhumvit, Bangkok. ***Tel*** *0-2229-4383.*

MASKS, PUPPETS, AND MUSICAL INSTRUMENTS

Shadow Puppet Theater
110/18 Si Thammasok Soi 3, Nakhon Si Thammarat. ***Tel*** *0-7534-6394.*

ANTIQUES

Chan's Antique House
99/42 Moo 5, Chalermkiat R9 Rd, Tambon Rasada, Phuket. ***Tel*** *0-7626-1416.* **www**.chans-antique.com

The Fine Arts
3/F Room 354 River City, Bangkok. **City Map** 6 F3. ***Tel*** *0-2237-0077* ext *354.*

National Museum
Fine Arts Department, 1 Na Phra That Rd, Bangkok. **City Map** 1 C4. ***Tel*** *0-2224-1370.*

NeOld
149/2–3 Surawong Rd, Bangkok. **City Map** 7 B4. ***Tel*** *0-2235-8352.*

JEWELRY

Astral Gemstone Talisman
1st Fl, 123-C All Season Place, 87/208 Wireless Rd, Bangkok. ***Tel*** *0-2252-1230.* **www**.astralgemstone-talismans.com

Uthai's Gems
28/7 Soi Ruam Rudi, Phloen Chit Rd, Bangkok. **City Map** 8 F2. ***Tel*** *0-2253-8582.*

GEMS

Asian Institute of Gemological Sciences
33rd Floor, Jewellery Trade Center, 919/1 Silom Rd, Bangkok. **City Map** 7 A4. ***Tel*** *0-2267-4315.* **www**.aigsthailand.com

Mook Phuket
65/1 Moo1, Chao Fa Rd, Phuket town. ***Tel*** *0-7621-3766.* **www**.mookphuket.com

ENTERTAINMENT IN THAILAND'S BEACHES AND ISLANDS

Modern Thailand is a melting pot of cultures and while it may have adopted many foreign pursuits, ranging from Hollywood movies to karaoke bars, traditional forms of entertainment still flourish. Classical *khon* dance dramas still survive and are showcased through cultural programs for visitors. A large number of Thai people still nurture a passion for the popular *muay thai*. A sense of *sanuk* (fun) pervades most activities on the beaches and islands of Thailand, even during solemn religious festivals. Indulging in local passions is essential to understanding and enjoying life here, whether it be live music at a bar, a colorful temple fair, the acrobatic *takraw* game, or watching the latest Thai blockbuster film.

Colorful bar sign

INFORMATION SOURCES

Details of major events and festivals taking place throughout the country are provided in booklets available at TAT offices. Thailand's leading English-language listings and features magazine, *Big Chilli*, is a useful source for events in the capital as well as in the rest of the country. Other Bangkok-based magazines such as *BK Magazine* and *Bangkok Recorder* are also useful guides to the city. The major resort areas, Hua Hin, Ko Samui, Krabi, Pattaya, and Phuket, also produce a number of free monthly listings magazines. Free maps, marked with entertainment venues, are available at airports and at big resorts. Even lesser developed islands such as Ko Phangan and Ko Tao produce a few useful maps.

BOOKING TICKETS

Big hotels and travel agents can book tickets for cultural shows and sports events. Alternatively, visitors can buy tickets directly from venues or through websites offering ticketing services for concerts and other performances.

Big Chilli, Thailand's leading listings and features magazine

TRADITIONAL THEATER AND DANCE

Watching the stylized masked *khon* performance by graceful male dancers is akin to watching the murals of Wat Phra Kaeo *(see pp56–61)* in motion. Sadly, interest in these dance dramas based on the Ramakien *(see p59)* is waning, and performances of *khon*, and the elaborate if less formal *lakhon*, are becoming increasingly rare. In even greater danger of extinction are the *Hun krabok* marionette shows *(see pp26–7)*.

The most atmospheric place to watch traditional dance is at Sanam Luang during royal ceremonies such as the king's birthday or a funeral when dozens of stages are built to provide nightlong entertainment. Complete performances can go on for days, so abridged scenes are chosen for shows at the **National Theater** on the last Friday and Saturday of every month, and at the **Sala Chalermkrung Theater** in Bangkok.

Countless dinner shows in major cities and resorts offer dance performances from all over the country. Reliable venues in Bangkok include the **Rose Garden** and **Silom Village**, while the Mandarin Oriental's Sala Rim Nam restaurant *(see p321)* presents authentic *khon*. In Hua Hin, the **Sasi Restaurant** offers a fine variety show of traditional dance and martial arts. *Lakhon* can also be witnessed in Bangkok, at the Lak Muang shrine near Sanam Luang, and the Erawan Shrine. Traditional puppetry can be seen at the **Joe Louis Thai Restaurant** in Phuket.

The most widespread dance drama is *likay*, commonly featuring in temple fairs, festivals, and television. Its bawdy, slapstick, and satirical elements ensure a strong following. *Manora* is the ancient equivalent from southern Thailand. While *nang talung*,

A traditional *khon* performance at the National Theater, Bangkok

or shadow puppet, shows are still widespread in Malaysia and Indonesia, they have almost disappeared from Thailand and survive only in the provinces of Phatthalung and Nakhon Si Thammarat. Performances of *nang talung* at local festivals can continue through the night, but are shortened for visitors. Even rarer are performances of *nang yai*, in which enormous, flat leather puppets are manipulated by a team of expert puppeteers.

Scene from the famous musical *Phra Lor* at Patravadi Theater, Bangkok

CONCERTS, EXHIBITIONS, AND MODERN THEATER

Thailand's major concert and exhibition halls are located in Bangkok. The state-of-the-art **Thailand Cultural Center** has excellent facilities and attracts big international names. The German **Goethe-Institut** and the **Alliance Française** host good exhibitions and concerts, and top stars frequently perform in the ballrooms of upscale hotels.

The **Patravadi Theater** is usually the venue for dramatic musicals based on classical tales – these are easily understood by non-Thais.

The **Phuket FantaSea** has an elaborate nightly performance entitled Fantasy of a Kingdom which takes visitors through different eras of Thai history through a stunning audio-visual show.

MOVIES

Thais are avid moviegoers and Bangkok now has a number of multiplexes. These modern theaters coexist with about 2,000 mobile units in the country that offer impromptu open-air screenings in villages. The film industry in Thailand has a long and somewhat erratic history. Despite the production of serious art cinema such as *Luk Isan* (1978), the majority of the films are formulaic melodramas, violent action films, or comedies. Action films from Hong Kong have always been popular, and have been supplemented by Hollywood movies since the early 1990s. In recent years, however, Thai cinema is enjoying a revival and is now regarded as one of the most creative in Southeast Asia. The capital also hosts the increasingly prestigious annual Bangkok International Film Festival.

Many theaters such as **The Century Movie Plaza** and **EGV Siam Square** in Bangkok, **Major Cineplex** and **Royal Garden Plaza** in Pattaya and **SF Cinema City Jungceylon** in Phuket, show movies with their original soundtracks.

DISCOS, BARS, LIVE MUSIC, AND FOLK CLUBS

Despite being challenged by international rock, Thai pop and folk music has retained its popularity and can be heard throughout the country.

The main styles include the exuberant, rhythmic *ram wong*, a folk dance with drums; *look thung* folk music combining big band music, costumed dance troupes, and singing; and the sentimental *look krung*. *Molam* music from the northeast has an upbeat sound and uses *khaen* pipes and rap-like vocals. The radical *phleng phua chiwit*, or songs for life, have a protest-based theme and are a mix of traditional Thai folk music with Western rock.

The **Raintree** in Bangkok showcases folk music, while new rock bands often play at **O'Reilly's Irish Pub**. The hotels are home to classier venues such as Grand Hyatt Erawan's **Spasso**, Shangri-La's **Angelini**, and Mandarin Oriental's **Lord Jim's** and **Bamboo Bar**. These live music haunts are supplemented by karaoke, theme bars, and discos in Bangkok's fashionable districts. There are many large nightclubs in Bangkok including the popular **Narcissus**. Sarasin Road is a popular strip with restaurants and bars. The gay scene is centered on Silom Soi 2.

Dancer in Calypso Cabaret

Clubs are found in all major resorts in Thailand. In Pattaya, **Tony's** is the most famous entertainment option. Phuket's Soi Bangla on Hat Patong is the epicenter of the island's nightlife. Ko Samui's burgeoning nightlife is split between Hat Chaweng and Hat Lamai.

Notorious red-light districts such as Patpong, Nana Plaza (Sukhumvit Soi 3), and Soi Cowboy in Bangkok, plus Pattaya and Patong in Phuket are infamous for their bizarre entertainment. Travelers should be wary of getting cheated. It is better to stick to the King's group of bars which are slightly better than the others. These areas are also home to the famous *kathoeys*, or flamboyant transvestites, who are a part of this industry and put up colorful shows. Cabarets are also popular and the best of these are at **Calypso Cabaret**, Bangkok; **Simon Cabaret**, Phuket; and **Alcazar**, Pattaya.

Visitors enjoying drinks at a colorful theme bar, Bangkok

Thais preparing *krathongs* for the Loy Krathong festival

TEMPLE FAIRS AND FESTIVALS

The Thai calendar is packed with national holidays and local festivals *(see pp34–7)*. These may be religious festivals or those that honor a local hero, celebrate seasonal changes and harvests, or are dedicated to activities such as boat racing and kite flying.

Apart from hosting other events, most *wats* stage temple fairs. Along with scheduled fairs such as the Golden Mount Temple Fair in Bangkok and Loy Krathong *(see p37)*, there are a number of smaller regional festivals and celebrations. The smaller ceremonies are often as entertaining as the main event itself, with vendors selling food and trinkets, and flamboyantly dressed *kathoeys* adding color. Folk music such as *likay* and *ram wong*, beauty contests, and games add to the general festivities. These also include cockfighting and Siamese fighting fish contests.

MUAY THAI AND KRABI-KRABONG

Muay thai *(see p283)* is a national passion. Most provinces have a boxing arena, but the top venues are in Bangkok. **Lumphini Stadium** has bouts every Tuesday, Friday, and Saturday, and there are boxing matches at the **Ratchadamnoen Boxing Stadium** on Mondays, Wednesdays, Thursdays, and Sundays. Krabi's **Ao Nang Krabi Stadium** is the south's largest arena with bouts every Friday. Visitors interested in actually learning the skills of this sport should contact the **International Amateur Muay Thai Federation**, who should be able to recommend suitable gyms and instructors.

Another revered, long-established Thai martial art is *krabi-krabong*, meaning sword-staff, after some of the hand weaponry used in this sport. The techniques are taught according to ancient rules and standards, although skill and stamina, rather than injuries inflicted, are now the measure of an accomplished fighter. *Krabi-krabong* is often demonstrated at cultural performances for tourists.

Muay thai fighters enact a bout

TAKRAW

This acrobatic sport, which is similar to volleyball, is popular all over Southeast Asia and played by young males on any clear patch of ground. The idea is to keep a woven rattan ball in the air using any part of the body apart from hands. The players' extraordinary agility and speed are a treat for visitors reared on more ponderous sports. There are elaborate versions of this game, but the classic style has a team trying to get the ball into a basketball-like net during a set time frame more times than their rivals. Despite *sepak takraw* (a competitive version of the original *takraw*), being incorporated into the Asian Games and Olympics, professional games of this sport are surprisingly rare.

SOCCER, RUGBY, AND SNOOKER

Thais have always been enthusiatic about football or soccer and the game was introduced to the country as early as 1897 and came under the king's royal patronage a few years later. In 1996, a professional soccer league – the Thai Premier League with 18 clubs – was introduced. Rugby has also sparked remarkable interest, with its own league and participation in the Hong Kong Sevens. Matches are held in Bangkok at **National Stadium**, **Hua Mark Indoor and Outdoor Stadiums**, **Army Stadium**, and **Royal Bangkok Sports Club**.

Thailand is one of the most successful non-Anglophone countries to adopt snooker. Revived by an Englishman, Maurice Kerr, Managing Director of the Royal Bangkok Sports Club, it was thereafter popularized throughout the country by the world seeded, James Wattana. Since then snooker has become professional and both domestic and world ranking events are held in Bangkok.

An acrobatic bout of the the game of *takraw*

DIRECTORY

TRADITIONAL THEATER AND DANCE

Joe Louis Thai Restaurant
181 Fl 2 Zone A, Jungceylon, Patong, Kathu, Phuket.
Tel *0-7636-6740.*
www.joelouisthairestaurant.com

National Theater
Rachinee Rd, Bangkok.
City Map 1 C4.
Tel *0-2224-1342.*

Rose Garden
Off Hwy 4, 20 miles (32 km) W of Bangkok.
Tel *0-2295-3261.*
www.rosegardenriverside.com

Sala Chalermkrung Theater
66 Charoen Krung Rd, Bangkok.
City Map 6 D1.
Tel *0-2222-0434.*
www.salachalermkrung.com

Sasi Restaurant
83/159 Nhongkae, Hua Hin.
Tel *0-3251-2488.*
www.sasi-restaurant.com

Silom Village
286 Silom Rd, Bangkok.
Map 7 A4.
Tel *0-2234-4448.*
www.silomvillage.co.th

CONCERTS, EXHIBITIONS, AND MODERN THEATER

Alliance Française
29 Sathorn Tai Rd, Yannawa, Bangkok.
City Map 8 D4. ***Tel*** *0-2670-4200.* **www**.alliance-francaise.or.th

Goethe-Institut
18/1 Soi AtthakanPrasit, Sathorn Tai Rd, Bangkok.
City Map 8 E4.
Tel *0-2287-0942.* **www**.goethe.de/bangkok

Patravadi Theater
69/1 Soi Wat Rakhang, Arun Amarin Rd, Thonburi, Bangkok.
City Map 1 B5.
Tel *0-2412-7287.* **www**.patravaditheatre.com

Phuket FantaSea
99 Moo 3, Hat Kamala, Kathu, Phuket.
Tel *0-7638-5000.* **www**.phuket-fantasea.com

Thailand Cultural Center
Ratchadaphisek Rd, Bangkok.
Tel *0-2247-0028.*

MOVIES

EGV Siam Square
6th Fl, Siam Discovery Center, Rama I Rd, Bangkok. **City Map** 8 C1.
Tel *0-2812-9999.*
www.egv.com

Major Cineplex
The Avenue, Soi 13, 2nd Rd, Pattaya.
Tel *0-3805-2227.*
www.majorcineplex.com

Royal Garden Plaza
Royal Garden Center, South Pattaya, Pattaya.
Tel *0-3842-8057.* **www**.royalgardenplaza.co.th

SF Cinema City Jungceylon
3rd Fl, Jungceylon Patong, Hat Patong, Phuket town.
Tel *0-7660-0555*
www.sfcinemacity.co.th

The Century Movie Plaza
15 Phaya Thai Rd, Ratchathewi, Bangkok.
City Map 4 E3.
Tel *0-2247-1111.* **www**.centurythemovieplaza.com

DISCOS, BARS, LIVE MUSIC, AND FOLK CLUBS

Alcazar
Pattaya 2nd Rd, Pattaya.
Tel *0-3841-0224–5.*
www.alcazarpattaya.com

Angelini
Shangri-La Hotel, 89 Soi Wat Suan Phu, Bangkok.
City Map 6 F5.
Tel *0-2236-7777.*
www.shangri-la.com

Bamboo Bar
Mandarin Oriental, 48 Oriental Ave, Bangkok.
City Map 6 F4. ***Tel*** *0-2659-9000.* **www**.mandarinoriental.com

Calypso Cabaret
Asia Hotel, 296 Phaya Thai Rd, Bangkok.
Tel *0-2216-8973*
www.calypsocabaret.com

Lord Jim's
Mandarin Oriental, 48 Oriental Ave, Bangkok.
City Map 6 F4. ***Tel*** *0-2659-9000.* **www**.mandarinoriental.com

Narcissus
112 Sukhumvit Soi 23, Bangkok. ***Tel*** 0-2258-4805. **www**.narzbangkok.com

O'Reilly's Irish Pub
62 Silom Rd, Bangkok.
City Map 8 C4. ***Tel*** *0-2632-7515.* **www**.oreillyspubbangkok.com

Raintree
116/64 Soi Rang Nam, off Phaya Thai Rd, Bangkok.
City Map 4 E4.
Tel *0-2245-7230.*

Simon Cabaret
100/6–8 Moo 4, Karon Rd, Patong, Phuket.
Tel *0-7634-2011.* **www**.phuket-simoncabaret.com

Spasso
Grand Hyatt Erawan Hotel, 494 Ratchadamri Rd, Bangkok. **City Map** 8 D1.
Tel *0-2254-1234.* **www**.bangkok.grand.hyatt.com

Tony's
200/3 Soi 16, Walking Street, South Pattaya.
Tel *08-1862-0083.*
www.tonydisco.com

MUAY THAI AND KRABI-KRABONG

Ao Nang Krabi Stadium
Hat Noppharat Thara, Krabi.
Tel *0-7562-1042.*

International Amateur Muay Thai Federation
Pathumwan Stadium, 154 Rama I Rd, Bangkok.
City Map 7 B1.
Tel *0-2215-6212–4.*

Lumphini Stadium
Rama IV Rd, Bangkok.
City Map 8 E4.
Tel *0-2251-4303.*
www.muaythailumphini.com

Ratchadamnoen Boxing Stadium
1 Ratchadamnoen Nok Rd, Bangkok.
City Map 2 F4.
Tel *0-2281-4205.*

SOCCER, RUGBY, AND SNOOKER

Army Stadium
Wiphawadirangsit Rd, Bangkok.
Tel *0-2278-5095.*

Hua Mark Indoor and Outdoor Stadiums
2088 Ramkhamhaeng Rd, Bangkok.
Tel *0-2318-0946.*

National Stadium
154 Rama I Rd, Bangkok.
City Map 7 B1.
Tel *0-2214-0120.*

Royal Bangkok Sports Club
1 Henri Dunant Rd, Pathumwan, Bangkok.
City Map 8 D2.
Tel *0-2652-5000.*
www.rbsc.org

OUTDOOR ACTIVITIES AND SPECIAL INTERESTS

Thailand offers an impressive range of outdoor activities and special interests. The coastal regions are ideal for all kinds of aquatic pursuits from sailing, water-skiing, jet-skiing, and windsurfing to big game fishing, snorkeling, and diving. Trekking in this spectacular region is also a popular pastime, especially in the forested hills and mountains of southern peninsular Thailand. Coastal Thailand also has an extensive network of national parks. Exciting ways to explore the country's natural wilderness include white-water rafting and kayaking, canoeing, sailing, elephant riding, wildlife watching, and rock climbing. Visitors can also take advantage of the growing number of excellent golf courses in various resorts such as Phuket and Hua Hin, or learn a variety of cultural skills such as Buddhist meditation forms, traditional Thai massage, and the delicious secrets of Thai food and culinary techniques.

Adventurous windsurfing

DIVING AND SNORKELING

Abundant, gorgeous coral reefs thronging with aquatic life, and serviced by countless diving operations, make Thailand one of the world's most accessible and rewarding destinations for underwater exploration. The Andaman coast and islands in particular, have some stunning reefs, ocean drop-offs, and sub-merged pinnacles, as well as visibility that often exceeds 100 ft (30 m). A rich variety of marine life – such as huge whale sharks off the exotic Burma Banks *(see p205)* – can be spotted in these waters.

Much of the best diving is to be found in national marine parks, such as the Surin, Similan, and Ko Tarutao archipelagos; Ko Tao; and Ko Chang. The once magnificent Ko Phi Phi has not been protected by this reserve status, and has been damaged by anchoring and snorkelers breaking the coral. Reckless fishing with dragnets, harpoons, and explosives has also killed some reefs, while siltation and pollution pose growing threats. Although the tsunami of 2004 caused a tragic loss of life, its effect on the coral reefs of the Andaman Sea was minimal.

Because of rough weather brought on by monsoons, the Andaman sites are accessible only from November to April; the waters of the Western Gulf are best visited between January and October. The Eastern Seaboard, however, is accessible all-year round.

Diving trips vary in length from one to several days, and many tours accommodate snorkelers also. The *Asian Diver Scuba Guide: Thailand* (Asian Diver) and *Diving in Thailand* (Asia Books) have comprehensive listings and details of dive sites. Additional information is available online

Divers swimming with a leopard shark off the Andaman coast

Beachside dive shop at Hat Khlong Phrao, Ko Chang

at **Dive Info**, a good source of diving information. PADI-approved diving courses are widely available in Thailand. The main centers offering courses are **Dive Asia**, **Santana Diving and Canoeing**, and **Sunrise Divers** in Phuket; **Sea Dragon Dive Center** in Khao Lak; **Blue Diamond Dive Resort** and **Phoenix Divers** in Ko Tao; **Samui International Diving School** in Ko Samui; **Haad Yao Divers** in Ko Phangan; **Phi Phi Scuba** and **Viking Divers** in Ko Phi Phi, Krabi; and Pattaya. Basic diving rules include: inspecting equipment properly, making sure it fits well; only diving after adequate training; diving with a buddy system; making sure the group is not too large; being confident in the abilities of the instructor; and never touching the coral.

Snorkeling is an alternative to diving, since all one needs is the ability to swim. **Medsye** offers great snorkeling trips to the Similan Islands. Most hotels and guesthouses located near the reefs rent out equipment, but to make the most of the experience, it is best to buy one's own. It is also important to be constantly aware of one's position and not venture too far.

SAILING

Thailand's dramatic coastline is popular with the yachting fraternity who come to Phuket every December for the King's Cup Regatta *(see p228)*. Chartering a yacht – with or without a skipper – is possible, although rates for this exclusive activity are not cheap.

Sailing companies such as **Gulf Charters Thailand** operate on the Eastern Seaboard, where sea breezes are often ideal, but the widest choice of sailing companies is in Phuket. Some of the best known are **Phuket Sailing**, **Yachtpro**, and **South East Asia Liveaboards**.

WATERSPORTS

Watersports are popular at many Thai resorts, but the disturbance they cause to the environment has resulted in them being banned in places such as Krabi. However, at most other seaside towns it is possible to rent windsurfing boards and jet skis. Banana boat rides are common, even in places such as Ko Samet.

For the best range of such sports, vacationers should head to Hat Jomtien in Pattaya, or try resorts in Hua Hin, Cha-am, and Hat Patong or Hat Karon in Phuket.

Anglers can make use of the excellent big-game fishing opportunities with **Pattaya Fishing** in Chonburi and **Dorado Game Fishing** or **Aloha Tours** in Phuket, but they must pay in excess of 10,000 baht for boat rental. The **Barracuda Bar** in Pattaya also arranges for freshwater lake fishing.

CANOEING

Sea-canoeing is not just the most peaceful way to enjoy the unusual karst islets of Phang Nga Bay and the Ang Thong archipelago, but also the only way to explore their collapsed sea caves. Ringed by forest and often containing tiny beaches, many of these spectacular *hongs*, or underwater caves, were discovered by **John Gray's Sea Canoe Thailand**, which, along with **Sea Canoe Thailand**, runs the most responsible tours to these fragile "lost worlds". Another reliable outfit that operates tours around Phang Nga Bay, Ko Tarutao Marine National Park, and the huge reservoir in Khao Sok National Park is **Paddle Asia**.

Kayaking, an adventurous way to explore the mangroves and caves

WHITE-WATER RAFTING AND KAYAKING

Sedate bamboo rafting is a popular tourist pastime, particularly in the Phang Nga area where **Adventure Camp** is the acknowledged leader. More exciting, although, is white-water rafting on hardy inflatables. No experience is necessary apart from the ability to swim, since instruction is given to paddlers before setting out, and each raft has a crew capable of dealing with any emergency. **The Wild Planet** provides good information on the best times and places. The season for white-water rafting and kayaking lasts from July to December.

Enjoying a game of golf in one of the many courses in Hua Hin

GOLF

With green and caddie fees cheaper than in the West, it is easy to see why many visitors to Thailand include a round of golf on their itinerary.

Many clubs are open to non-members, and golfing vacation packages are particularly popular at places such as **Laem Chabang International Country Club** in Pattaya, **Blue Canyon Country Club**, **Mission Hills Golf Resort**, and **Phuket Country Club** in Phuket, **Palm Hills Golf Club** in Cha-am, and the **Black Mountain Golf Club** in Hua Hin. Ko Samui has recently improved its golfing facilities with the addition of the **Santiburi Samui Country Club**. Visit the **GolfThailand.Net** website to see what is on offer. The best printed guides to courses are the *Thailand Golf Map* and *Thailand Golf Guide*. TAT also publishes a free directory of the country's top 75 courses. The David Leadbetter Academy of Golf at the **Thana City Golf and Country Club** is a great place to remove handicaps.

ELEPHANT RIDING

After the mechanization of logging and its supposed ban in 1989, elephants were no longer used for logging work, and their mahouts were reduced to begging on city streets for a living. Offering elephant rides is a positive move toward ensuring the survival of this magnificent national symbol, since their lowland forest habitat has been largely destroyed.

Visitors will find the best opportunities for elephant riding in the south and east, especially at **Nong Nooch Village** to the south of Pattaya and **Pattaya Elephant Village**, where there are daily elephant shows and elephant rides into the nearby countryside. Similarly, Ko Chang's **Ban Kwan Chang Elephant Camp** and Samui's **Namuang Safari Park** offer rides, as do Bangkok's Dusit Zoo and Safari World.

TREKKING

Thailand offers some ideal terrain for trekking. The precipitous karst forests of Krabi and Khao Sok, in particular, have outstanding hiking trails.

Useful tips include lining backpacks with plastic bags to keep damp out; sleeping in dry clothes (even if it means wearing wet clothes by day); wearing a sun hat and cream for protection against sunburn, and long trousers to protect against leeches; using insect repellent; and wearing worn-in hiking boots or at least supportive athletic shoes. The best time to trek is from November to February and early in the wet season, in June and July. Eco-friendly visitors can try **Evolution Tour**, **Khao Sok Trekking Club**, **Siam Safari**, and **Phuket Trekking Club**; **Friends of Nature** also organizes ecological treks.

Elephant rides, an exotic way of exploring regions in Thailand

WILDLIFE WATCHING

Unfortunately, much of Thailand's wildlife has been hunted almost to extinction, so there is little point in spending a few days in a hide in the hope of seeing a wild tiger or a bear. However, the country has a wide network of national parks, where some effort has been made to protect pockets of natural beauty. Here, visitors might well see rare and colorful birds, huge butterflies, and foot-long centipedes. The entrance fee to national parks for foreigners has been doubled to 400 baht. Some parks have campsites, and most have log cabin-style accommodations that can be reserved through the **National Park, Wildlife, and Plant Conservation Department**. The more popular parks, such as Khao Sok, Khao Sam Roi Yot *(see pp144–5)*, and Khao Phanom Bencha *(see p245)*, have well-marked nature trails, but in less popular parks, visitors should ask park rangers to lead them to interesting features.

Trekking through Thailand's beautiful and varied rain forests

BOAT TRIPS

Before the arrival of motor cars, boats were the only form of transportation in Thailand, apart from walking. Low-lying areas of the country were criss-crossed by canals that enabled locals to visit friends and do their daily shopping. These days, however, floating markets are strictly for vacationers who can enjoy the colorful spectacle of it all.

Apart from these floating markets, there are several other locations where visitors can go sightseeing by boat. In Bangkok, **Chao Phraya Express Boats** offers short tours with commentary on the main riverside sights. In the south, companies such as **Sayan Tour** organize half- and full-day trips on longtail boats around the limestone stacks in Phang Nga Bay; visitors also have the option of canoeing for an hour.

CYCLING

With cycling growing in popularity worldwide, it is no surprise that more and more people consider touring Thailand on a cycle. Not only is it healthy and environmentally sound, it also guarantees meaningful encounters with local people along the way – just put a bike on a bus or train and head for quieter rural areas. The terrain is mostly cyclist-friendly, and several companies organize guided rides along country lanes.

Visitors considering a cycling holiday are advised to consult the websites of the **Thai Cycling Club** and **Biking Southeast Asia**. The best time to cycle in Thailand is from November to February; the worst is in the hot season

Thailand's best rock climbing at Hat Rai Leh near Krabi

between March and May. Cycling in the rainy season is also worth considering. **Bike and Travel** and **Spice Roads** are two recommended cycling tour operators with offices in Bangkok and Pathum Thani near Bangkok.

ROCK CLIMBING

Those looking for an activity that gets the adrenalin flowing will find rock climbing hard to beat. Thailand is one of the most popular destinations for this sport.

Krabi is the epicenter of rock climbing, especially at Hat Rai Leh, where several companies offer half- to three-day courses for beginners and rent out equipment to experienced climbers; the more reliable operators include **Tex Rock Climbing**, **King Climbers**, and **Hot Rock**. More than 700 bolted routes in the region offer climbs which are graded according to the French system. Ko Phi Phi has a similar limestone terrain, and a few local companies, such as **Spidermonkey Climbing**, offer instructions for beginners at Ton Sai Tower and Hin Taek.

Well-geared cyclist

BUNGEE JUMPING

Visitors who want to go bungee jumping should head to **Jungle Bungy Jump**, a successful company operating in popular tourist locations such as Phuket and Pattaya. A certificate is issued on completion of the jump.

HORSE RACING AND RIDING

As one of the few forms of gambling allowed in Thailand, horse racing attracts a strong local following, and the atmosphere is always vibrant. Races are held on weekends in Bangkok at the **Royal Bangkok Sports Club** and the **Royal Turf Club**. For a more hands-on equine experience, check out the activities on offer at the **International Riding School** near Pattaya and the **Phuket Riding Club**.

CULTURAL STUDY

Courses in meditation can give a valuable insight into Thai culture and also provide invaluable skills to help cope with stress. Participants are required to dress in white and adhere to the fundamental vows of Buddhism – refraining from killing, stealing, lying, and eating after midday. Practitioners are expected to be up before dawn and to plan their day around sessions of walking and sitting meditation, as well as abstaining from entertainment (no TV or music) and idle chat (no mobile phones). Since the Dharma, which means Way of the Higher Truths, or code of conduct, is given for free, most places suggest that students make a donation to cover their lodging and food. For meditation sessions in English and longer, disciplined retreats, contact the **World Fellowship of Buddhists**. Visitors are welcome to join the 10-day course run by the **International Dharma Heritage** near Chaiya, at the beginning of each month at Wat Suan Mokkh *(see p161)*. Other options include the famous **Wat Mahathat** *(see p62)* in Bangkok, **Wat Khao Tham** *(see p177)* on Ko Phangan, as well as the **Dhammakaya Foundation**'s retreats and Sunday sessions. Some locations have facilities for women, while others are only for men.

Visitors can also study Thai massage, a vigorous combination of yoga, reflexology, and acupressure. Courses typically last between one and two weeks, and consist of theory, demonstration, and practice, leading to a certification of competence. Popular training in English is conducted at Wat Pho *(see pp64–5)*.

The technique of preparing Thai food – including fruit and vegetable carving – can be learned at cooking schools in hotels such as Dusit Thani *(see p291)* and Mandarin Oriental *(see p74)* in Bangkok, the **Blue Elephant** restaurant and cooking school and **Baipai Thai Cooking School** also in Bangkok, **Happy Home Thai Cooking** in Pattaya, **Pat's Home Thai Cooking School**, in Phuket and the **Samui Institute of Thai Culinary Arts** in Ko Samui.

Visitors learning to cook Thai food in the Baipai Thai Cooking School

DIRECTORY

DIVING AND SNORKELING

Blue Diamond Dive Resort
24/21 Moo 2, Mae Hat, Ko Tao.
Tel 0-7745-6880.
www.bluediamonddiving.com

Dive Asia
24 Karon Rd, Hat Kata, Phuket.
Tel 0-7633-0598.
www.diveasia.com

Dive Info
Ban Chuancheun, Pattanakarn 57, Bangkok.
Tel 08-1825-9607.
www.diveinfo.net

Haad Yao Divers
Sandy Bay Bungalows, Hat Yao, Ko Phangan.
Tel 08-6279-3085.
www.haadyaodivers.com

Medsye
78/46 Moo 5, Thap Lamu, Thai Muang Ko Similan.
Tel 0-7648-6796.
www.similanthailand.com

Phi Phi Scuba
Ao Ton Sai, Ko Phi Phi.
Tel 0-7561-2665.
www.ppscuba.com

Phoenix Divers
1 Moo 1, Hat Sai Ri, Ko Tao.
Tel 0-7745-6033.
www.phoenix-divers.com

Samui International Diving School
30/1 Moo 4, Bophut, Ban Bangrak, Ko Samui.
Tel 0-7724-2386.
www.samui-diving.com

Santana Diving and Canoeing
49 Thaweewong Rd, Hat Patong, Phuket.
Tel 0-7629-4220.
www.santanaphuket.com

Sea Dragon Dive Center
5/51 Moo 7, T Khuk Khak, Khao Lak.
Tel 0-7648-5418.
www.seadragondivecenter.com

Sunrise Divers
269/24 Patak Rd, Karon Plaza, Hat Karon, Phuket.
Tel 0-7639-8040.
www.sunrise-divers.com

Viking Divers
Moo 7, Ko Phi Phi.
Tel 08-1719-3375.
www.vikingdiversthailand.com

SAILING

Gulf Charters Thailand
Ocean Marina, 167/5 Sukhumvit Rd, Sattahip.
Tel 0-3823-7752.
www.gulfchartersthailand.com

Phuket Sailing
20/28 Soi Suksan, Moo 4, Tambon Rawai, Phuket.
Tel 0-7628-9656.
www.phuket-sailing.com

South East Asia Liveaboards
PO Box 381, Phuket town, Phuket.
Tel 0-7652-2807.
www.seal-asia.com

Yachtpro
Adjacent to Yacht Haven Marina, Phuket.
Tel 0-7634-8117.
www.sailing-thailand.com

WATERSPORTS

Aloha Tours
44/1 Viset Rd, Ao Chalong, Phuket.
Tel 0-7638-1215.
www.phuket.com/aloha

Barracuda Bar
157/132–133 Moo 5, Pattaya-Naklua Rd, Chonburi province.
Tel 08-4778-8125.
www.barracudabar-pattaya.com

Dorado Game Fishing
101/172 Moo 5, Chalermprakiet Ror 9 Rd, Rasada, Phuket.
Tel 0-7629-3167.
www.phuket-fishing.com

Pattaya Fishing
SEAduction Dive Centre, Bali Hai Pier, 551/2 Moo 10, Tambon Nongprue, Banglamung, Chonburi.
Tel 0-3871-0029.
www.pattayafishing.com

CANOEING

John Gray's Sea Canoe
124 Soi 1 Yaowarat Rd, Phuket town.
Tel 0-7625-4505.
www.johngray-seacanoe.com

Paddle Asia
9/71 Rasdanusorn Rd, Phuket.
Tel 0-7624-0952.
www.paddleasia.com

Sea Canoe Thailand
125/461 Moo 5, Baan Tung Ka – Baan Sapam Rd, Phuket.
Tel 0-7652-8839.
www.seacanoe.net

WHITE-WATER RAFTING AND KAYAKING

Adventure Camp
125/1 Phang Nga Rd, Phuket town.
Tel 0-7622-2900.
www.sealandcamp.com

The Wild Planet
666 Sukhumvit 24, Bangkok.
Tel 0-2261-4412.
www.thewildplanet.com

GOLF

Black Mountain Golf Club
12/16 Phet Kasem Rd, Hua Hin. *Tel 0-3261-8666.*
www.bmghuahin.com

Blue Canyon Country Club
165 Moo 1, Thepkasattri Rd, Thalang, Phuket.
Tel 0-7632-8088.
www.bluecanyonclub.com

GolfThailand.Net
www.golfthailand.net

Laem Chabang International Country Club
106/8 Moo 4, Beung, Sri Racha, near Pattaya.
Tel 0-3837-2273.
www.laemchabanggolf.com

Mission Hills Golf Resort
195 Moo 4 Pla Khlok, Thalang, Phuket.
Tel 0-7631-0888.
www.missionhillsphuket.com

Palm Hills Golf Club
1444 Phet Kasem Rd, Cha-am.
Tel 0-3252-0801.
www.palmhills-golf.com

Phuket Country Club
80/1 Vichitsongkram Rd, Moo 7, Kathu, Phuket.
Tel 0-7631 9200.
www.phuketcountryclub.com

Santiburi Samui Country Club
12/15 Moo 4, Baan Don Sai, Ko Samui.
Tel 0-7742-1700.
www.santiburi.com

Thana City Golf and Country Club
100-100/1 Moo 4, Bang Na Trat Rd, off Hwy 34, near Bangkok.
Tel 0-2336-1968.

DIRECTORY

ELEPHANT RIDING

Ban Kwan Chang Elephant Camp
Jungle Way,14 Moo 3, Khlong Son, Ko Chang. ***Tel*** *08-9223-4795.* **www**.jungleway.com

Namuang Safari Park
25/11 Moo 2, Namuang, Ko Samui. ***Tel*** *0-7742-4663.* **www**. samuinamuangsafari.net

Nong Nooch Village
163 Sukhumvit Road, Pattaya. ***Tel*** *0-3870-9358.*

Pattaya Elephant Village
48/120 Moo 7, Nong Pue, Pattaya. ***Tel*** *0-3824-9818.* **www**.elephant-village-pattaya.com

TREKKING

Evolution Tour
30/1/7 Moo 4, Baan Khlong Phrao, Ko Chang. ***Tel*** *0-3955-7078.* **www**.evolutiontour.com

Friends of Nature
133/21 Ratchaprarop Rd, Bangkok. **City Map** 4 E5. ***Tel*** *0-2642-4426.* **www**. friendsofnature93.com

Khao Sok Trekking Club
58 Moo 6, Klong Sok, Phanom, Surat Thani. ***Tel*** *08-9287-3217.* **www**.khaosoktrekking. com

Phuket Trekking Club
55/779–780 Villa Daowroong Village, East Chao Fa Rd, Tambon Vichit, Phuket. ***Tel*** *0-7637-7344.* **www**. phukettrekking club.com

Siam Safari
45 Chao Fa Rd, Chalong, Phuket. ***Tel*** *0-7628-0116.* **www**.siamsafari.com

WILDLIFE WATCHING

National Park, Wildlife, and Plant Conservation Department
61 Phaholyothin Rd, Chatuchak, Bangkok. ***Tel*** *0-2561-0777.* **www**.dnp.go.th

BOAT TRIPS

Chao Phraya Express Boats
78/24–29 Maharaj Rd, Phra Nakhorn, Bangkok. **City Map** 2 C4. ***Tel*** *0-2623-6001.* **www**. chaophrayaboat.co.th

Sayan Tour
209 Phang Nga Bus Terminal, Phang Nga. ***Tel*** *0-7643-0348.* **www**.sayantour.com

CYCLING

Bike and Travel
802/756 River Park, Moo 12, Prathum Thani, near Bangkok. ***Tel*** *0-2990-0274.* **www**.cyclingthailand.com

Biking Southeast Asia
www.mrpumpy.net

Spice Roads
14/1-B Soi Promsri 2, Sukhumvit Soi 39, Bangkok. ***Tel*** *0-2712-5305.* **www**.spiceroads.com

Thai Cycling Club
www.thaicycling.com

ROCK CLIMBING

Hot Rock
Hat Rai Leh, near Krabi. ***Tel*** *0-7562-1771.* **www**. railayadventure.com

King Climber
Hat Rai Leh, near Krabi. ***Tel*** *0-7563-7125.* **www**.railay.com

Spidermonkey Climbing
Ton Sai Village, Ko Phi Phi. ***Tel*** *0-7581-9384.* **www**.spidermonkey climbing.com

Tex Rock Climbing
Hat Rai Leh, near Krabi. ***Tel*** *0-7563-1509.*

BUNGEE JUMPING

Jungle Bungy Jump
Pattaya
Tel *08-6378-3880.* **www**.junglebungy.com
Phuket
Tel *0-7632-1351.* **www**.junglebungy.com

HORSE RACING AND RIDING

International Riding School
100 Moo 9, Tambon Pong, Amphur Banglamung, Chonburi. ***Tel*** *0-3824-8026.* **www**.riding schoolasia.com

Phuket Riding Club
95 Viset Rd, Rawai, Phuket. ***Tel*** *0-7628-8213.* **www**.phuketridingclub. com

Royal Bangkok Sports Club
1 Henri Dunant Rd, Bangkok. **City Map** 7 C3. ***Tel*** 0-2652-5000. **www**.rbsc.org

Royal Turf Club
Phitsanulok Rd, Dusit, Bangkok. ***Tel*** *0-2628-1810.* **www**.royalturfclub.com

CULTURAL STUDY

Baipai Thai Cooking School
150/12 Soi Naksuwan, Nonsi Rd, Chong Nonsi, Yannawa, Bangkok. **City Map** 6 F3. ***Tel*** *0-2294-9029.* **www**.baipai.com

Blue Elephant
233 South Sathorn Rd, Bangkok. ***Tel*** *0-2673-9353.* **www**. blueelephant.com/school

Dhammakaya Foundation
40 Moo 8, Khlong Song, Khlong Luang, Prathum Thani. ***Tel*** *0-2831-1000.* **www**.dhammakaya.org

Happy Home Thai Cooking School
81/65 Central Pattaya, Soi 14 (Soi Thidawan), Pattaya. ***Tel*** *08-4417-5258.* **www**.happyhome-thaicookingschool.com

International Dharma Hermitage
Wat Suan Mokkh, Chaiya, Surat Thani. ***Tel*** *0-7743-1552.* **www**.suanmokkh.org

Pat's Home Thai Cooking School
26/4 Moo 3, Chao Fa Rd, Phuket town. ***Tel*** *08-1538-8272.* **www**.phuketindex.com/ pathomethai cookingschool

Samui Institute of Thai Culinary Arts
46/6 Moo 3, Hat Chaweng, Ko Samui. ***Tel*** *0-7741-3172.* **www**.sitca.net

Wat Khao Tham
Near Ban Tai, Ko Phangan. **www**.watkowtahm.org

Wat Mahathat (Section Five)
Maharat Rd, Bangkok. **City Map** 1 C5. ***Tel*** *0-2222-6011.*

World Fellowship of Buddhists
616 Benjasiri Park, Soi Medhinivet, off Sukhumvit 24, Bangkok. ***Tel*** *0-2661-1284.* **www**.wfb-hq.org

Spa Breaks

Typical aroma oil burners

Coastal Thailand has numerous spas offering every kind of treatment possible. Its sultry weather, idyllic landscapes, and sense of tranquility make it an ideal destination for a spa break. Traditional Thai architecture, serene Zen-minimalist decor, and enchanting gardens blend with the Thai people's gentle and giving nature to make it a memorable experience. Massage has been practiced in Thailand for some 2,500 years, and while it is possible to have a cheap shoulder rub in a backstreet shop, nothing beats the pampering at a luxury resort or an afternoon at a day spa.

Relaxing in the peaceful garden of the Anantara Resort and Spa

HOTEL AND RESORT SPAS

Travelers tend to visit a hotel or resort spa as part of a wider holiday, with the main focus being a beach or a cultural experience. However, the luxurious, upscale hotels and resorts in Thailand are home to some of the world's very best spas, offering an enormous range of professional, unique, and blissful treatments.

The greatest concentration of spas is on the islands of Phuket and Ko Samui and in the beach resort towns of Hua Hin and Cha-am. The country's foremost spa resorts include the exotic **Four Seasons Resort, Ko Samui**, the popular **Banyan Tree Spa, Phuket**, the **Evason Phuket Resort and Six Senses Spa**, and the **Anantara Resort and Spa** in Hua Hin as well as Ko Samui.

Spa treatments are generally an added extra, but many resorts are increasingly offering all-inclusive packages. The Anantara resorts offer three- and seven-day programs that include between 4 and 10 treatments.

SPA RETREATS

Thailand has a number of luxury resorts situated in truly breathtaking settings. Visitors looking for an intimate getaway on a deserted white-sand beach skirted by palm trees should head to the **Six Senses Hideaway, Hua Hin**, south of Hua Hin, or the **Aleenta Resort and Spa, Phang Nga**. Those who like the idea of retreating into the tropical forests to rejuvenate the body and spirit should visit the **Tamarind Retreat** in Ko Samui. This spa offers two different kinds of treatments – classic and forest spas – with an exotic treat in the form of a herbal steam cave and dipping pool. The aim of staying here is to experience the local culture and lush environment as much as it is to have a spa experience. The fact that these resorts are often set in remote locations and may be accessible only by speedboat such as the **Rayavadee Spa** near Krabi, adds to the allure. The **Pimalai Resort and Spa** on Ko Lanta provides treatment rooms named after local flowers and massages with aromatic herbs. The spas at these resorts offer daily treatment programs for those who really want to unwind.

DESTINATION SPAS

Revitalizing the mind, body, and spirit is the central purpose of destination spas, with guests rarely leaving the resort once they have checked in. Thailand's first and best, the **Chiva-Som International Health Resort**, in Hua Hin, offers more than 150 treatments focused on relaxation and rejuvenation, stress relief, detoxification, and weight loss. Guests undergo an extensive health consultation upon arrival, and a program is specifically created to match their goals. There is a three-night minimum stay, although most guests stay a week or more, and nutritious spa cuisine, activities, and treatments are included in the rate. Another famous destination spa is the **Kamalaya Wellness Sanctuary and Holistic Spa** in Ko Samui.

Because spa resorts tend to provide an array of non-spa activities too – from elephant and water-buffalo riding to mountain climbing – signature treatments at destination spas

A rejuvenating massage at Banyan Tree Spa, Phuket

also cater to travelers who may be suffering from some painful aftereffects.

DAY SPAS

Travelers can easily find day spas – stand-alone operations not attached to resorts or hotels. Many hotels also offer treatments to non-guests on a per-session basis. Most day spas are in Bangkok and include the stylish **Being Spa**, **Pirom Spa**, the **Harnn Heritage Spa**, and **Spa of Qinera**.

SPA TREATMENTS

Working out stress through yoga at Chiva-Som International Health Resort

Despite Thailand's long history of therapeutic massage and natural healing – including *nuad paen boran* (traditional Thai massage), medicinal herbs, and natural springs – the country offers unique, cutting edge treatments. Thai spa treatments are meant to be both relaxing and rejuvenating, and offer holistic healing which invigorates not just the body, but also the soul. Expect to see anything and everything on a spa menu, from Tropical Sprinkles and Tranquility Mists at the Banyan Tree Spa, Phuket, to their famous four-hand Harmony Banyan treatment, where two therapists work on the client at once. Other frequently visited spas, such as the Six Senses Spa and Anantara Spas offer versions of this indulgent treatment. While some treatments are indigenous to Thailand – the traditional Thai massage, for example – others such as hydrotherapy, thalassotherapy, aromatherapy, and Ayurvedic treatments, can be found all over the world. Thai masseurs do not make use of any oils or lotions for their massages and a traditional massage is given to the client who is asked to lie on a mat or mattress. Many spas have also developed their own signature treatments. The Four Seasons Spas, for example, have an array of sensual offerings connected to the cycles of the moon, with exotic treatments that should be experienced only during certain lunar phases.

DIRECTORY

HOTEL AND RESORT SPAS

Anantara Resort and Spa
Phet Kasem Beach Rd, Hua Hin.
Tel 0-3252-0250.
www.anantara.com

99/9 Moo 1, Bophut Bay, Ko Samui.
Tel 0-7742-8300.

Banyan Tree Spa, Phuket
33 Moo 4, Srisunthorn Rd, Cherngtalay, Phuket.
Tel 0-7632-4374.
www.banyantreespa.com

Evason Phuket Resort and Six Senses Spa
100 Vised Rd, Moo 2 Tambol Rawai, Phuket.
Tel 0-7638-1010.
www.sixsenses.com

Four Seasons Resort, Ko Samui
219 Moo 5, Ang Thong, Ko Samui.
Tel 0-7724-3000, 0-7724-3002.
www.fourseasons.com

SPA RETREATS

Aleenta Resort and Spa, Phang Nga
33 Moo 5, T Khokkloy, Phang Nga.
Tel 0-7658-0333.
www.aleenta.com

Pimalai Resort and Spa
99 Moo 5, Ba Kantiang Beach, Ko Lanta.
Tel 0-7560-7999.
www.pimalai.com

Rayavadee Spa
214 Moo 2, Tambol Ao-Nang, Amphur Muang, Krabi. *Tel 0-7562-0740-3.*
www.rayavadee.com

Six Senses Hideaway, Hua Hin
9/22 Moo 5, Hat Naresuan, Pranburi, Prachuap Khiri Khan.
Tel 0-3261-8200, 0-3263-2111.
www.sixsenses.com

Tamarind Retreat
205/3 Thong Takian, Ko Samui.
Tel 0-7742-4221, 0-7742-4311.
www.tamarind retreat.com

DESTINATION SPAS

Chiva-Som International Health Resort
Phet Kasem Rd, Hua Hin.
Tel 0-3253-6536, 0-2711-6900.
www.chivasom.com

Kamalaya Wellness Sanctuary and Holistic Spa
102/9 Moo 3, Laem Set Rd, Na-Muang, Ko Samui.
Tel 0-7742-9800.
www.kamalaya.com

DAY SPAS

Being Spa
88 Soi Sukhumvit, 53 Klongton Nua, Bangkok.
Tel 0-2662-6171.

Harnn Heritage Spa
Siam Paragon, 4th Floor, Bangkok. **City Map** 7 C1.
Tel 0-2610-9715.

Pirom Spa
87 Nai Lert Building, Sukhumvit Rd, Bangkok.
Tel 0-2655-4177.
www.piromspa.com

Spa of Qinera
172/1 Soi Phiphat 2, Chong Nonsi, Bangkok.
Tel 0-2638-8306.

SURVIVAL GUIDE

PRACTICAL INFORMATION

Thailand is well equipped to cater to its growing number of tourists. The millions of people who visit the country each year find one of the biggest and best organized tourism industries in Asia. The headquarters of the helpful, government-run Tourism Authority of Thailand (TAT) is in Bangkok, and there are offices across the country and several overseas branches. The relevant TAT address and telephone number is given for each town and sight throughout this guide. The industry is developing rapidly, and the adventurous traveler need no longer be restricted to organized tours or only major tourist destinations such as Bangkok, Pattaya, and Phuket. There are many reputable travel agencies all over Thailand. These agencies offer valuable advice, book flights and accommodations, and also organize sightseeing tours. Some pre-travel planning is necessary to avoid the worst of the rainy season and holiday periods such as the Chinese New Year *(see p37)*.

Changing of the Royal Guard, Bangkok

WHEN TO GO

Thailand's weather can be tempestuous, with year-round humidity, high temperatures, and heavy rainfall. However, the optimum time to visit is during the cooler months from November to February. This is the peak tourist season, and sights may get crowded. The hot season, from May to June, can be unbearable, while the rainy season, which generally lasts from June to September, is the least predictable of the three periods. Climate and rainfall charts can be found on pages 36–7.

WHAT TO TAKE

As the climate in Thailand is generally hot and humid, it is advisable to dress in cool clothes made from natural fibers. Throughout Thailand, the rainy season brings sudden downpours, so a light raincoat is handy. If visiting temples, appropriate dress is required *(see p355)*, as is easily removable footwear. Visitors should also carry a basic first-aid kit.

VISA AND PASSPORTS

Many nationalities, including citizens of most European countries, Australia, and the US, can enter Thailand for up to 30 days without a pre-arranged visa. However, proof of a confirmed return flight or other ongoing travel arrangements must be presented upon arrival. For those wishing to stay longer, a 60-day tourist visa can be arranged from a Thai embassy or consulate prior to arrival in Thailand.

A 90-day non-immigrant visa must be applied for in the visitor's home country and requires a letter of verification from a Thai source giving a valid reason, such as business or study, for spending three months in Thailand. This visa is slightly more expensive than the 60-day tourist visa.

With all visas, entry into Thailand must occur within 90 days of issue. Visa extensions are at the discretion of the **Immigration Department** in Bangkok or any other immigration office in Thailand. Over-staying a visa carries a fine of 500 baht per day and can result in serious penalties. Travelers to Thailand should have at least six months validity left on their passport.

Relaxing under shady beach umbrellas at Hat Kata Noi, Phuket

IMMUNIZATION

There are no immunization requirements unless a visitor is from a country known to be infected with yellow fever. It is recommended that visitors be immunized against polio, tetanus, typhoid, and hepatitis A. In addition, those traveling to remote areas, or who are staying more than three weeks should get BCG (tuberculosis), hepatitis B, rabies, diphtheria, and Japanese encephalitis vaccinations. For the latest information, contact a doctor, who can advise on the current guidelines for the prevention of diseases such as malaria.

CUSTOMS INFORMATION

Customs regulations in Thailand are standard. During an inbound flight, travelers

◁ **Picturesque beach at Ko Phi Phi Don, lined with longtail fishing boats** will be given a customs form that must be filled and handed over at the customs desk after claiming baggage. Thai customs restrictions for goods carried into the country include 200 cigarettes and one liter of wine or spirits. For complete details about export declarations, duty payments, and VAT refunds visit **The Customs Department** website. Carrying of drugs, firearms, or pornography is prohibited.

Antiques and images of the Buddha are not allowed out of Thailand without authorization. If visitors wish to export such items, they must first contact the **Fine Arts Department** of the National Museum in Bangkok at least five days before the date of shipment to fill in a form accompanied by two frontal photographs of the object being purchased. However, contemporary works of art, such as paintings, do not fall under this category. It is also illegal to leave Thailand with more than 50,000 baht without authorization.

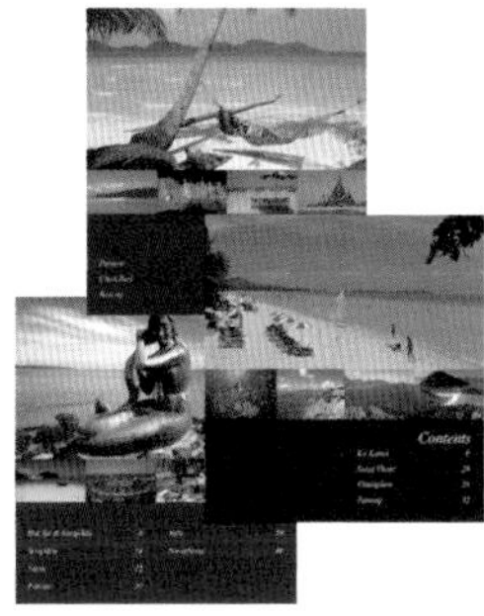

Content pages of some popular destinations from TAT's e-brochures

TOURIST INFORMATION

The many branches of the **Tourism Authority of Thailand** (TAT) are very helpful, offering plenty of information on sights and festivals, as well as maps, brochures, guides, and posters. They also have a useful list of reputable travel agents and hotels.

ADMISSION CHARGES

Admission charges to sights in Thailand generally range from 10–50 baht. National parks, however, charge either 200 or 400 baht as admission fee. Some museums in Thailand have free entry, but others may charge up to 200 baht. Occasionally, foreigners may be charged a higher admission fee than locals.

Buddha images wrapped and ready for sale in Bangkok

OPENING HOURS

Most destinations and sights in Thailand can be visited throughout the year, although accommodations on, and ferry services to, some of the southern islands are limited in the rainy season. In general, major tourist attractions open at 8am or 9am and close between 3:30pm and 6pm. A few places also shut for lunch between noon and 1pm. Most major sights open daily, but a few museums close for public holidays as well as on Mondays and Tuesdays.

Large department stores are usually open 10am–9pm, and smaller shops are open 8am–9pm. In smaller towns, there are daily markets.

Commercial offices are open 8am to noon and 1–5pm Monday to Friday. Government offices are open 8:30am to noon and 1–4:30pm Monday to Friday. During the Chinese New Year, many businesses may close. For details of banking hours see page 358.

FACILITIES FOR THE DISABLED

There are few facilities for disabled travelers in Thailand. Sidewalks can be uneven and pedestrian bridges are often accessed only by steep steps. Wheelchair access is limited to luxury hotels in major cities. Public transport, including buses and Skytrains is inaccessible for the disabled and even the Suvarnabhumi International Airport has few elevators or disabled access toilet facilities. The easiest way to travel is to book an organized tour *(see p365)* or contact the **Association of Physically Handicapped People** for information.

FACILITIES FOR CHILDREN

The larger hotels in Thailand have babysitting services, and TAT offers advice on attractions that have special appeal to kids, such as zoos and amusement parks. Hats and sunblock are a must for children (as well as adults) out in the tropical sun.

LANGUAGE

It is useful to learn a few Thai phrases *(see pp382–5)*, and Thais will be delighted with the effort. Many local people in popular tourist towns speak some English, as do most hotel receptionists. Sight and road names in these areas are transliterated, and menus are often in English as well as Thai. Prices and road numbers are generally in Arabic numerals.

Tourist information center, Than Bok Koranee

THAI TIME SYSTEM AND CALENDAR

Bangkok time is seven hours ahead of Greenwich Mean Time (GMT), 12 hours ahead of Eastern Standard Time, and 15 hours ahead of Pacific Standard Time.

Two calendars are used in Thailand – the Gregorian (Western) and the Buddhist calendars. The Buddhist Era (BE) starts 543 years before the Gregorian era, thus AD 1957 is the equivalent of 2,500 BE.

ELECTRICITY

The electric current for the whole of Thailand is 220 volts AC. Dual-prong rounded pin plugs as well as flat-pin plugs can be used in sockets. Major hotels in Bangkok also have 110-volt outlets for electric razors. Adaptors can be bought from any department store or electrical store. These outlets also sell power-surge cables, which are vital if one is traveling with a laptop. It is advisable for visitors traveling to smaller towns or villages to keep a flashlight handy.

CONVERSIONS

US to Metric
1 inch = 2.54 centimeters
1 foot = 30 centimeters
1 mile = 2 kilometers
1 ounce = 28 grams
1 pound = 454 grams
1 gallon = 3.79 liters

Metric to US
1 millimeter = 0.04 inch
1 centimeter = 0.4 inch
1 meter = 3 feet 3 inches
1 kilometer = 1 mile
1 gram = 0.04 ounces
1 kilogram = 2.2 pounds
1 liter = 2.1 pints

PHOTOGRAPHY

Digital photography is popular in Thailand. Photography shops are quite easy to find, and they make prints or load digital images on to a disk at very reasonable rates. Those using film may find it slightly harder to obtain, although there are several professional photography stores in the capital Bangkok.

ETIQUETTE

It is not without reason that Thailand is often referred to as "the land of smiles". Thais are exceptionally friendly and helpful people, and getting along with them is easy. A few taboos do exist, however, mostly with regard to the monarchy and Buddhism. Visitors should be particularly careful to behave respectfully at *wats* and in front of any image of the Buddha. Confrontation is considered extremely rude. Losing one's temper or shouting is seen as an embarrassing loss of face.

Bargaining is quite common throughout the country, but it is best to avoid getting too loud or aggressive.

Tipping on the other hand is not as common a practice in Thailand, as it is in the West.

GREETING PEOPLE

The Thai greeting is known as the *wai* and consists of the palms being pressed together and lifted toward the chin. Traditionally, the inferior party initiates the *wai* and holds it higher and for longer than the superior, who returns it according to his or her social standing. Thais use first names to address people, even in formal situations. The polite form of address is the gender-neutral title Khun, followed by the first name or nickname. Every Thai person has a nickname, usually a one- or two-syllable name with a simple meaning, such as Moo, which means pig, or Koong, which means shrimp.

Two Thais addressing each other with a *wai*, the traditional greeting

BODY LANGUAGE

The head is considered a sacred part of the body by Thais, so touching someone's head, even that of a child, should be avoided. The feet are seen as the lowliest part of the body and to point the feet toward someone or rest them on a table is considered rude. When sitting on the floor, especially inside a temple, it is best to tuck one's legs behind or to the side and avoid stepping over others.

SMOKING

Smoking is prohibited in all public areas and on all public transport in Bangkok. It is also banned in restaurants as well as in pubs.

ROYALTY

The royal family is the most revered institution in Thailand. Criticizing or defaming it in any way can be considered as an affront to the monarchy. Not only could this mean a jail sentence, but Thai people will nearly always be deeply offended. Coins, bills, and stamps bear the images of Thai kings and should be treated respectfully by visitors.

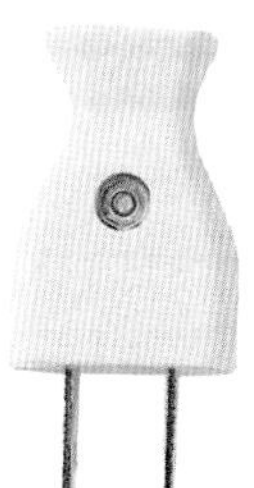

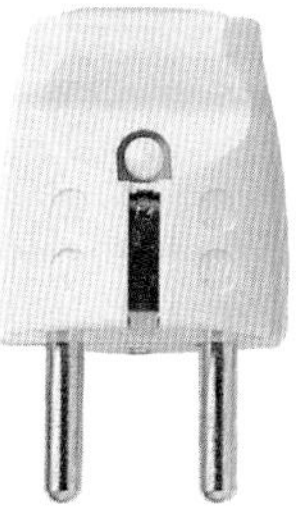

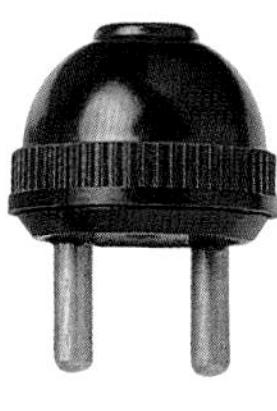

A range of plugs and adaptors that can be used in Thailand

THE NATIONAL ANTHEM

The national anthem is played twice daily, at 8am and 6pm, on radio and through tannoys in smaller towns and some public spaces. It is polite to stop whatever one is doing and stand still. In theaters, the national anthem is played before all performances. The audience stands in silent respect to a portrait of the king.

MONKS

The *sangha* (monkhood) is a respected institution, second only to the monarchy. Most taboos in dealing with monks concern women. It is prohibited for a monk to touch a woman or to receive anything directly from her. When traveling by public transportation, women should avoid sitting next to a monk.

ETIQUETTE AT WATS

Decorum should be observed when entering any *wat*. Temples are quiet places, so visitors should try to avoid disturbing the peace. The clothes one wears must be clean and respectable. Shoes must be removed before entering any *wat*. All Buddha images are sacred, even small, ruined, or neglected ones. Visitors must never sit with their feet pointing toward them.

Devotees kneeling before a shrine with their feet facing away

Surin Islands National Park regulations

SUITABLE DRESS

Thais are a modest people, so visitors, especially women, must remember to wear clothes that are not too revealing. Topless sunbathing is frowned upon everywhere.

RESPONSIBLE TRAVEL

Thai authorities are now actively promoting eco-tourism by creating awareness of the need for conservation through various means. They are prohibiting locals from fishing with dynamite, and drag-netting coral reefs, and encouraging tourists to "leave nothing but your footprints."

"No shoes" sign

Ecologically aware dive companies visiting marine parks such as Similan and Surin, forbid visitors from taking away even a seashell, and in extreme cases will "name and shame" those who violate this basic rule. Similarly, visitors are increasingly discouraged from taking plastic bags and water bottles into national parks. With increasing awareness, the kingdom is already more engaged than its Southeast Asian neighbors in promoting responsible travel.

However, the government's efforts have been thwarted by environmentally destructive shrimp farms, expensive, water-intensive golf courses, the clearing of natural forests for palm oil plantations, and even the breeding of tigers in captivity for their body parts.

Visitors can set an example by carefully disposing off garbage, choosing to boycott noisy and polluting water-sports such as jet scooters, and refusing to eat food derived from endangered species such as shark's fin soup and sea turtle eggs or meat. Most Thais are sensitive, so setting an example will certainly help kick-start Thailand's nascent eco-tourism industry.

DIRECTORY

VISAS AND PASSPORTS

Immigration Department
Soi Suanphlu, Sathorn Tai Rd, Bangkok. **City Map** 8 D5. ***Tel*** *0-2287-3101*. **www**.immigration.go.th

CUSTOMS INFORMATION

The Customs Department
1 Sunthornkhosa Rd, Khlong Toey, Bangkok. ***Tel*** *0-2667-7100*. **www**.customs.go.th

Fine Arts Department
National Museum, 1 Na Phra That Rd, Phra Nakhon, Bangkok. **City Map** 1 C4. ***Tel*** *0-2628-5033*. **www**.finearts.go.th

TOURIST INFORMATION

Tourism Authority of Thailand
1,600 New Phetchaburi Rd, Bangkok. **City Map** 7 A3. ***Tel*** *1672*. **www**.tourismthailand.org

FACILITIES FOR THE DISABLED

Association of Physically Handicapped People
73/7–8 Tivanond Rd, Talad Kwan, Nonthaburi. ***Tel*** *0-2951-0567*.

EMBASSIES

Canada
15th Floor, Abdulrahim Place, 990 Rama 4 Rd, Bangkok. ***Tel*** *0-2636-0540*.

Malaysia
33–35 South Sathorn Rd, Bangkok. ***Tel*** *0-2629-6800*.

Myanmar (Burma)
132 Sathorn Nua Rd, Bangkok. ***Tel*** *0-2234-4698*.

United Kingdom
1031 Witthayu (Wireless) Rd, Bangkok. ***Tel*** *0-2305-8333*.

United States
95 Witthayu (Wireless) Rd, Bangkok. ***Tel*** *0-2205-4000*.

Personal Health and Security

Thailand is a fairly safe country, and simple health and safety precautions keep the vast majority of travelers out of trouble. The infrastructure of emergency services for both health and crime is efficient throughout Bangkok and other larger towns. As a rule of thumb, the more remote the area, the higher the health risk and less support available in the event of any mishap. The main hospitals in Bangkok, the main islands, as well as other large cities have modern equipment and well-trained doctors, many of whom speak good English. Even on smaller beaches and islands, medical facilities have improved dramatically.

Tourist policeman wearing a beret, and an ordinary officer

A well stocked pharmacy in Ban Bophut, Ko Samui

IN AN EMERGENCY

For English-speaking help, call the **Tourist Assistance Center**, which will contact the appropriate service. Lines are open from 8am to midnight, after which visitors will have to rely on English-speaking hotel staff. During office hours, TAT *(see p355)* may also be able to help. The **Metropolitan Mobile Police** covers general emergencies in Bangkok. All Bangkok hospitals have 24-hour trauma and emergency departments.

GENERAL PRECAUTIONS

Bangkok and the coastal areas are relatively safe. Usually discretion and sobriety are the best means of avoiding problems. Be on guard at tourist locations (scam artists can direct tourists to pricier, less impressive sights), and at bus and train stations. It is advisable not to flash large amounts of cash or leave luggage unattended. If leaving valuables in a hotel safe, make sure to get a receipt, and do not let credit cards out of sight. Drugging and robbing tourists on long-distance trains and buses has occurred, so politely decline food or drink from strangers.

DRUGS

Thai law prohibits the sale or purchase of opium, heroin, or marijuana. Charges for possession, smuggling, or dealing can lead to a 2–15 year jail sentence or, in extreme cases, the death sentence.

DANGER SPOTS

In some parts of the Deep South, the militant Malay-Muslim group, PULO (Pattani United Liberation Organization) can be dangerous. It is wise to stay away from the remote border areas.

WOMEN TRAVELERS

Female travelers are unlikely to be harassed in Thailand. The coastal areas are quite safe for women, as are hotels. Taxis are readily available.

TOURIST POLICE

There are tourist police stations in Bangkok, Ko Samui, Pattaya, and Phuket. Tourist police officers all speak some English and are attached to TAT offices. They help with anything from credit card scams to excessive surcharges. They are also helpful in emergencies, and can act as an English-speaking liaison. The Bangkok branch of the tourist police is located close to Lumphini Park *(see p74)*.

Patrol car used by the tourist police, seen mainly in cities

MEDICAL FACILITIES

Medical insurance is advisable when traveling in Thailand. Private hospitals such as **Phuket International Hospital** in Phuket, **Bangkok General Hospital** and **Bumrungrad Hospital** in Bangkok, as well as other public hospitals, are modern, clean, and efficient. Waiting times are longer in public hospitals, but their doctors are trained abroad.

Outside the capital, the best facilities are in the large towns. For dental or eye care, however, it is best to seek treatment in Bangkok.

PHARMACIES

There are plenty of pharmacies in Bangkok and the coastal areas. They can all dispense antibiotics over the counter, without a prescription. Most pharmacies are open from 8am–9pm. In small towns, however, pharmacies are less prolific.

COPING WITH THE HEAT

It is not advisable to exert oneself for the first few days. Drink lots of fluids, take plenty of rest in the shade, and avoid being out in the midday sun. Once acclimatized, continue a high intake of fluids, especially bottled water, or special electrolyte drinks.

The tropical sun is very powerful; a good sunscreen and a wide-brimmed hat are therefore indispensable.

FIRST-AID KIT

A basic first-aid kit should include any personal medication; aspirin or pain killers for fevers and minor aches and pains; an antiseptic for cuts and bites; a digestive pill or syrup to soothe an upset stomach; insect repellent; bandages; scissors, tweezers, as well as a thermometer.

MINOR STOMACH UPSETS

Should diarrhea occur, eat plain food for a few days and drink plenty of fluids. It is not wise to drink tap water – bottled water is readily available across the country. Ice should be fine in main hotels and restaurants, but crushed iced drinks from street vendors are best avoided.

Drugs such as Lomotil and Imodium can bring relief from diarrhea, but rehydrating solutions, available at pharmacies, are usually the best remedy. For immediate relief, a single 500 mg dose of Ciprofloxacin is safe and effective.

Mosquito repellents

INSECT-BORNE DISEASES

Seven of Thailand's 410 mosquito species carry malaria. Symptoms of the disease include headache, fever, and violent chills. Visitors experiencing such symptoms, should seek medical advice.

The main towns and islands are largely free of malarial mosquitoes. For latest information, call a travel clinic or,

Spicy street food, best avoided by those with a delicate stomach

in the US, the Tourist Assistance Center, for information on health matters.

Malarial mosquitoes are active from sundown till sunrise, so use plenty of repellent, wear long-sleeved clothing and use mosquito nets and coils. Another mosquito-borne disease, dengue fever, is a risk during the daytime. However, few mosquitoes are infected with the virus, and the symptoms, although intense and unpleasant, are rarely fatal. These include fever, headache, severe joint and muscle pains, and a rash. No preventive treatment or vaccination is available.

PEOPLE- AND ANIMAL-BORNE DISEASES

Acquired Immune Deficiency Syndrome (AIDS) is passed through bodily fluids. The high turnover of Thailand's sex industry means that unprotected sex carries a serious risk.

Blood transfusion methods in Thailand are not always reliable and it is safest to seek treatment only in the main hospitals. The same goes for inoculations – make sure needles are new or bring a personal supply.

Hepatitis B is also transmitted through bodily fluids. Symptoms include fever, nausea, fatigue, and jaundice, and it can severely damage the liver. A prophylactic vaccine is available. Vaccines are also available for rabies and tetanus.

DIRECTORY

IN AN EMERGENCY

Ambulance
Tel *1669 or 1554 (across Thailand).*

Metropolitan Mobile Police
Tel *191 (Bangkok).*

Tourist Assistance Center
Tel *1155 (Bangkok).*

Tourist Police
Bangkok ***Tel*** *0-2356-0582 or 1155.*
Ko Samui ***Tel*** *0-7743-016 or 1155.*
Pattaya ***Tel*** *0-3829-371 or 1155.*
Phuket ***Tel*** *0-7622 3891 or 1155.*
Trat ***Tel*** *0-3955-7382 or 1155.*

MEDICAL FACILITIES

Bangkok General Hospital
Soi Soonvijai, New Phetchaburi Rd. **City Map** 6 E1. ***Tel*** *0-2310-3000.* **www**.bangkokhospital.com

Bumrungrad Hospital
Sukhumvit, Soi 3. **City Map** 8 F1. ***Tel*** *0-2667-1000 or 1155.* **www**. bumrungrad.com

Phuket International Hospital
44 Chalermprakiat Ror 9 Rd. ***Tel*** *0-7624-9400.* **www**. phuketinternationalhospital.com

FOOD- AND WATER-BORNE DISEASES

Dysentery is a severe form of food or water poisoning. Bacillary dysentery, characterized by stomach pain, vomiting, and fever, is highly contagious but rarely lasts longer than a week. Amebic dysentery has similar symptoms but takes longer to develop. Medical help should be sought without delay.

Hepatitis A is passed on in conditions of poor sanitation, contaminated water or food, and can now be prevented with a vaccine. Typhoid is also transmitted through contaminated water or food. Medical attention is essential as complications such as pneumonia can occur. The available vaccine is not always reliable.

Banking and Local Currency

Commercial Bank credit card logo

Throughout Bangkok and the main provincial towns such as Krabi and Surat Thani, banking facilities and exchange services are plentiful, well run, and easy to access. In the major centers, tellers often speak some English. Exchange booths are usually located in the central parts of towns, and mobile exchange units are stationed near larger tourist attractions. Automatic Teller Machines (ATMs) can be found in all cities. Smaller towns are less likely to have exchange facilities, but most have banks or ATMs. Rural villages, unless they are tourist spots, might not have banking or currency exchange services.

HSBC, an international bank operating in Bangkok

BANKS AND BANKING HOURS

The three main banks in Thailand are the **Bangkok Bank**, the **Kasikorn Bank**, and the **Siam Commercial Bank**. The **Bank of Ayudhya** and **CIMB Thai**, along with several smaller but reliable banks, have branches throughout the country. Foreign banks such as **Bank of America**, **Citibank**, **Deutsche Bank**, **HSBC**, and **Standard Chartered Bank** offer full commercial banking services in Bangkok and operate major branches.

Banking hours are generally 8:30am–3:30pm, Monday to Friday. Some banks have branches in department stores which are open 8am–8pm. Exchange booths are open daily through the day. Apart from providing banking services, the major banks can also organize international money transfers. Most banks in cities have an associated ATM.

Automatic Teller Machines, found in Bangkok and many Thai towns

ATM SERVICES

Most ATMs provide instructions in both Thai and English. Any ATM displaying the VISA or MasterCard sign will accept these cards and dispense cash in baht using the regular PIN. There are surcharges for such transactions. For visitors planning to stay in Thailand for several months or more, it might be a good idea to open an account at a Thai bank. This would allow access to any ATM or bank without having to worry about exchange rates or inter-provincial charges on Thai ATM cards.

CHANGING MONEY

Banks usually offer the best exchange rates, and rates differ little between banks. Hotels usually offer the worst rates, while those at exchange booths can vary greatly. US dollars are the most widely accepted foreign currency when buying baht, although sterling is also accepted. In Bangkok, small exchange booths can be found in most major department stores, shopping malls, and on big roads. Mobile exchange units can often be found near tourist attractions and around market areas. These are generally open every day 7am–9pm. Exchange rates are published in the *Bangkok Post* and the *Nation*.

DIRECTORY

BANKS

Bangkok Bank
333 Silom Rd, Bangkok.
City Map 7 C4.
Tel *0-2231-4333.*

Bank of America
CRC Tower, 33rd Floor
Wireless Rd, Bangkok.
City Map 7 A1.
Tel *0-2305-2800.*

Bank of Ayudhya
1222 Rama 3, Bangkok.
Tel *0-2296-2000.*

CIMB Thai Bank
44 Luangsuan Rd, Bangkok. **City Map** 7 B5.
Tel *0-2626-7000.*
www.cimbthai.com

Citibank
399 Sukhumvit Rd, Bangkok.
Tel *0-2788-2000.*
www.citibank.co.th

Deutsche Bank
208 Wireless Rd, Bangkok.
City Map 7 A1.
Tel *0-2651-5000.*

HSBC
Rama IV Rd, Bangkok.
City Map 7 A1.
Tel *0-2614-4000.*

Kasikorn Bank
1 Thai Farmers Lane, Ratburana Rd, Bangkok.
Tel *0-2222-0000.*

Siam Commercial Bank
9 Ratchadaphisak Rd, Bangkok. **City Map** 4 E3.
Tel *0-2544-1111.*
www.scb.co.th

Standard Chartered Bank
990 Rama IV Rd, Bangkok.
City Map 7 B4.
Tel *0-2724-4000.*

CREDIT CARDS

American Express
Tel *0-2273-5544.*

MasterCard
Tel *001-800-11-887-0663.*

VISA
Tel *001-800-441-3485.*

CREDIT CARDS

Credit cards are accepted in major hotels, department stores, and upscale shops and restaurants. They can also be used at major banks (and some exchange kiosks) for cash advances. A surcharge will be applied. **VISA** and **MasterCard** are the most widely accepted cards; the use of **American Express** cards are more limited.

All Thai commercial banks accept cash withdrawals from both MasterCard and Visa credit or debit cards. Visitors may need to show their passports at these transactions. Credit and debit cards can also be used at local ATMs, but a surcharge will be levied.

As the popularity of plastic money increases, so too does the incidence of credit-card fraud and travelers should always carefully check bills before they sign.

CURRENCY

The Thai unit of currency is the baht, usually seen abbreviated to "B". There are 100 satang in a baht, but the satang represents such a small sum today that it is scarcely used. 25 satang is sometimes known as a saleung. However, inflation is rendering this colloquial term redundant.

Banknotes come in different sizes and colors. They are available in denominations of 20 baht (green), 50 baht (blue), 100 baht (red), 500 baht (purple), and 1,000 baht (brown). Finding change for large denomination notes in rural areas can be difficult. The coin denominations are 25 satang or 1 (saleung), 50 satang, 1 baht, 2 baht, 5 baht, and 10 baht. Possible confusion over different sized coins of the same denomination is becoming less likely as the older and larger 1 and 5 baht coins are gradually being phased out in favor of smaller versions. Old coins have Thai numerals only, while newer coins have both Thai and Arabic numerals.

Bangkok Bank
The Asian International Bank

Logo for one of Thailand's long-established banks

TRAVELERS' CHECKS

Travelers' checks are the safest way to carry money and can be encashed at banks, hotels, and exchange booths. Banks provide the lowest surcharge and charge a fee per check, so cashing large amounts works out the cheapest.

VAT

Thailand imposes a 7 percent Value Added Tax (VAT) on goods and services. Tourists can redeem purchases above 5,000 baht at the customs counter at airports against bonafide receipts.

20 baht

50 baht

100 baht

500 baht

1,000 baht

Coins come in the following denominations:

25 satang

50 satang

1 baht

2 baht

5 baht

10 baht

Communications and Media

Wireless Internet sign

Thailand's communication network is becoming increasingly sophisticated. The telephone system is run by the Telephone Organization of Thailand (TOT) under the umbrella of the Communications Authority of Thailand (CAT). It is possible to make international calls and send faxes from all business centers and hotels. Public phones are found on most roads while cell phone networks have penetrated the whole country. The postal system, however, can be erratic and it is advisable to use a courier service for valuables. Major international, as well as local English language newspapers and magazines are found in hotels, bookstores, and newsstands. Internet and Wi-Fi facilities are available even in the smaller towns.

INTERNATIONAL CALLS

All major hotels and most guesthouses offer international dialing services, although there is a surcharge levied well above the call charges. Business centers and Internet cafés in small towns usually offer e-mail and phone services. Bangkok's Central Post Office on Charoen Krung New Road and some major post offices around the country have a CAT center that can arrange, collect, and credit card calls. In Bangkok, these are open from 7am to midnight, with reduced hours in the provinces. To dial from a hotel room, contact the desk, or dial 001 (for an international line) followed by the country code and telephone number. It is also possible to use 007, 008, or 009 to prefix your number, to get cheaper rates. Alternatively, dial the international operator at 100. Blue and yellow international pay phones are found on streets, shopping malls, and airports. The blue phones take credit cards while the yellow phones can be used with stored value cards, sold in post offices and by authorized agents.

Phone card for international calls

LOCAL CALLS

Local calls can be made from any public pay phone other than the blue and yellow international pay phones. Domestic calls can be made from blue and silver coin phones or green card-phones. Coin-operated phones accept 1, 5, and 10-baht coins whereas cards for card-phones can be bought at post offices, bookstores, and hotels and come in denominations of 25 baht, 50 baht, 100 baht, and 250 baht. The long-distance domestic service covers calls within different regions of Thailand, as well as to Malaysia and Laos.

Cell phone networks enabling communication on offshore islands

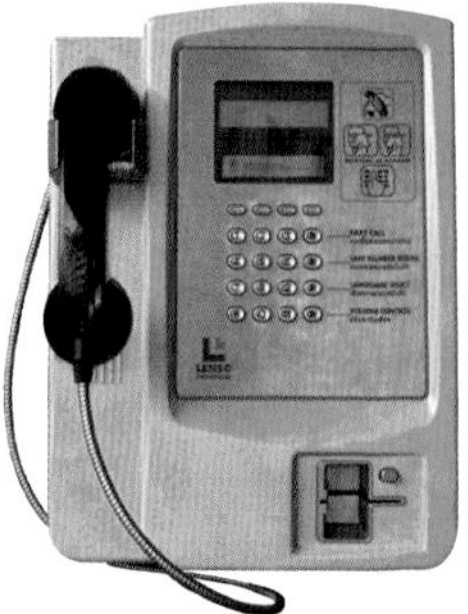
A card-phone for local and long-distance domestic calls

CELL PHONES

Cell phones are extremely cheap in Thailand. SIM cards can be bought from mobile phone shops, but visitors must present a form of identification, such as a passport. Customers can pay through scratch cards with a dial-in code to top up their credits. Cards range from 50–500 baht in value and are sold in minimarts throughout the country.

In most of Thailand's coastal areas, cell phone coverage is good. Of the several service providers, AIS has the best coverage but is expensive. Any island with an indigenous population now also has good coverage. Weak signals might cause problems within the larger national parks.

TELEVISION AND RADIO

Thailand has many television channels and programs are mostly in Thai, although in Bangkok, some are broadcast with an English simulcast on FM radio. Satellite and cable networks are fast expanding all over Asia, and most international English language networks such as BBC, CNN, Al Jazeera, and CNBC are readily available. Many hotels provide satellite and cable television as well as an in-house video channel. Visitors should check the *Bangkok Post* and *The Nation* for details.

There are more than 400 radio stations operating on a nationwide scale. English language stations manned by local DJs are listed in the *Outlook* section of the *Bangkok Post*. The national public radio station, Radio Thailand, broadcasts English-language programs on 107 and 105 FM 24 hours a day, and listings for shortwave frequencies that receive BBC, VOA, Radio Australia, Radio Canada, RFI (French), and Deutsche Welle are found in the *Focus* section of *The Nation*.

NEWSPAPERS AND MAGAZINES

The best English-language newspapers in Thailand are the *Bangkok Post* and *The Nation*. Both these publications provide reliable local, regional, and international coverage. The daily supplements, *Outlook* (Bangkok Post) and *Focus* (The Nation), include features on lifestyle, travel, human interest, as well as listings for restaurants, films, concerts, and exhibitions in Bangkok. Both are widely sold in news kiosks and shops throughout Bangkok. The *International Herald Tribune* and the *Asian Wall Street Journal* are sold in hotels and English-language bookstores such as Asia Books and Bookazine, which also stock a good selection of international magazines. News weeklies including *The Economist*, *Time*, and *Newsweek* are also widely available. Among the local English language monthly publications are the useful listings guide *Bangkok 101* with information on city-based events and reviews and the society rag *Thailand Tatler*. In addition to these, helpful free guides are available in restaurants, bars, and bookstores and include *BK Magazine*, *Absolute Lifestyle Magazine* and *Thaiways*.

***The Nation*, one of Bangkok's leading business newspapers**

MAIL

Thailand has a reliable postal service. Letters and postcards usually take at least one week to reach Europe and North America from Thailand. Stamps are available at all post offices and can also be bought at many hotels. Packages and valuable items should be sent by registered mail or via International Express Mail (EMS), which can be a cheaper alternative to international shipping companies. General delivery facilities are available at all main post offices in the country. Letters will normally be held for up to three months. To claim mail from general delivery, visitors must show their passport and sometimes pay a small fee. Letters should be addressed to the visitor (with the last name written in capitals and underlined), GPO, address, town, and Thailand. Thus for Bangkok's main GPO, correspondents should send mail written as care of GPO, Charoen Krung Road, Bangkok. Post offices are usually open 8:30am–4:30pm, Monday to Friday and 9am to noon on Saturdays.

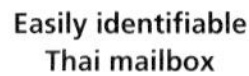
Easily identifiable Thai mailbox

INTERNET ACCESS

Internet access is available all over Thailand. Charges range from 20 baht an hour in a local Internet café to 250 baht an hour in an upscale hotel. Wireless connection hotspots are becoming very common, even in the provinces. Once a monopoly, Internet services are now provided by a number of companies.

COURIER SERVICES

Main international courier companies, such as **DHL**, **FedEx**, and **UPS** operate at multiple locations in Thailand, so it is easy to send goods by air freight. However, for very large items, such as furniture, shipping is usually more affordable. Many shops or courier companies can arrange this as well as provide the necessary paperwork.

USEFUL DIALING CODES

- For international calls, dial 001, 007, 008, or 009 followed by country code. To put a call through the international operator, or to report technical problems, dial 100.
- Country codes are: UK 44; Ireland 353; France 33; US and Canada 1; Australia 61; New Zealand 64. It may be neccessary to omit the first digit of the destination area code.
- For directory assistance dial 1133 from anywhere in the country.
- For domestic calls dial a 9-digit number for Bangkok beginning with (02) and a 10-digit number for other provinces. Callers need to dial 08 before calling a mobile phone.
- To speak to the domestic operator, dial 101.
- To make a domestic reverse charge call dial 101.

DIRECTORY

COURIER SERVICES

DHL
209 K Tower A 12th Floor, Sukhumvit 21 Rd, Bangkok.
Tel *0-2345-5000.* **www**.dhl.co.th

FedEx
Green Tower, 3656/22 Rama IV, Bangkok. **City Map** 8 E4.
Tel *1782.* **www**.fedex.com.th

UPS
16/1 Soi 44/1 Sukhumvit Rd, Bangkok. ***Tel*** *0-2762-3300.*
www.ups.com

TRAVEL INFORMATION

Logo of a popular airline

For most visitors, flying is the most convenient way of getting to Thailand's beaches and islands – other routes are by ferry, road, or rail from Malaysia and Cambodia. Domestic flights within Thailand are easy and reduce the traveling time considerably, with several provincial airports located around the country. Flights to neighboring countries are often cheaper if they are booked within Thailand. Rail services run on a regular basis between Bangkok and Singapore, via Kuala Lumpur, Butterworth, and some southern Thai towns. Rail travel is both comfortable and efficient. Long-distance and provincial buses run to all towns and most villages. For local transportation, visitors can choose between a variety of taxis, *songthaews*, and tuk-tuks.

ARRIVING BY AIR

Thailand is served by many different airlines. Direct flights are available from North America, Europe, Australasia, Africa, and Asia. A flight from the US may entail an overnight stay in Japan or Taiwan. **Thai Airways International** operates direct flights from Los Angeles to Bangkok. **British Airways**, **United Airlines**, and **Delta Airlines** have a connecting service from New York. Some flights from Asia land at Phuket, Hat Yai, Krabi, and Ko Samui. Other international airlines operating in Thailand are **Qantas Airlines** and **Singapore Airlines**. Low-cost carriers operating in the domestic circuit and within Asia include **Bangkok Airways**, **Air Asia**, and **Nok Air**.

AIR FARES

The cost of air tickets to and from Thailand vary according to the destination, the airline, and the time of year. In countries in the northern hemisphere, low fares to Thailand are available from September to April, while in the southern hemisphere, cheap tickets can usually be booked between March and November.

SUVARNABHUMI INTERNATIONAL AIRPORT

After years of planning and numerous delays, Bangkok's Suvarnabhumi International Airport opened in September 2006. Located 18 miles (29 km) east of the capital, this is one of the busiest airports in Asia. Suvarnabhumi is used for all international flights as well as many domestic ones.

Arriving passengers enter the terminal on the second floor of the concourse buildings. After passing through the passport checkpoints and customs, they can proceed to the arrivals hall, where they will find transportation and accommodation counters, as well as a tourist information center. A meeting point on the third floor allows passengers to get to their next destination as well as get any required information.

GETTING TO AND FROM SUVARNABHUMI INTERNATIONAL AIRPORT

Metered taxis are available outside the first floor. A trip into the city will cost roughly 400 baht, including expressway charges, and would take around 45 minutes, depending on traffic. Passengers may also make use of the shuttle bus.

A rail link connecting the airport to the city center has two services: the SA City Link, which makes local stops into Bangkok and takes 30 minutes, or the SA Express Line which takes 15 minutes and goes to Makkasan City Air Terminal or Phayathai station.

Keep in mind that check-ins, particularly at the Thai Airways International counter, are often subject to delays, and the walk from the passport checkpoint to the flight lounge is also long.

License plates of a taxi with yellow and black registration numbers

Pale green registration plates of an airport limousine

DOMESTIC FLIGHTS

A number of domestic flights from Bangkok leave from the Don Muang Airport which serves the domestic flights of all local budget carriers.

Thai Airways International and Bangkok Airways fly to all major domestic destinations such as Hat Yai, Ko Samui, Krabi, and Phuket. Air tickets can be bought through travel agents and hotels, or booked directly

An aircraft displaying the colors and logo of Thai Airways International

Beautiful interiors created out of natural products at Ko Samui Airport

through the airlines. On public holidays *(see p37)* and on weekends, when there are more people traveling, it can be difficult to get a flight; visitors are advised to book tickets in advance or travel on weekdays.

GREEN TRAVEL

Travel around Thailand's beaches and islands is easy, convenient, and cheaply priced, but not very eco-friendly. Most visitors travel by train and long-distance buses, these being less polluting. Hired cars are also preferred by many, but they are not very eco-friendly. Thailand's roads are well maintained although driving may be hazardous at times, especially in remote areas. The rising price of gas and the prevalent pollution in large cities has caused the introduction of the less polluting and environment-friendly Liquid Petroleum Gas (LPG). However, this is still work in progress and few self-driven vehicles use LPG yet. There are hardly any LPG stations outside the major cities. Another alternative is to use Gasohol, a gas which combines fuel derived from sugar cane with ordinary benzene. Both LPG and Gasohol are to some extent subsidized by the government to encourage their use. Leaded gas has almost been phased out. Other ways to minimize an individual traveler's carbon footprint is by using shared taxis, buses, and ferries rather than flying or hiring longtail boats. Although motorcycles remain the most common way of getting around on the smaller islands, it is best to avoid the environmentally unfriendly and noisy two stroke motorcycles. The most green and healthy way to travel and explore the local sights of any area is by foot or on a bicycle.

DIRECTORY

ARRIVING BY AIR

Air Asia
Tel *0-2515-9999.*
www.airasia.com

Bangkok Airways
Tel *1771.*
www.bangkokair.com

British Airways
Tel *0-2627-1701; (0845) 773- 3377 (UK).*
www.britishairways.com

Delta Airlines
Tel *0-2660-6900; (800) 221-1212 (US).* **www**.delta.com

Nok Air
Tel *1318.*
www.nokair.com

Qantas Airlines
Tel *0-2236-2800; (0845) 774-7767 (UK).* **www**.qantas.com

Singapore Airlines
Tel *0-2353-6000; (800) 742-3333 (US).*
www.singaporeair.com

Thai Airways International
Tel *0-2356-1111; (800) 426-5204 (US).* **www**.thaiairways.com

United Airlines
Tel *0-2253-0558; (800) 825-9035 (US).* **www**.united.com

Visitors traveling between various offshore islands on public ferries

AIRPORT	TEL INFORMATION	DISTANCE TO TOWN OR RESORT	AVERAGE TAXI FARE	AVERAGE JOURNEY TIME
Bangkok: Don Muang	0-2535-1111 0-2535-1253	City center 12 miles (19 km)	300 baht	Rail: 50 minutes Road: 1–2 hours
Bangkok: Suvarnabhumi	0-2132-1888	City center 16 miles (26 km)	400 baht	Road: 45 minutes
Hat Yai	0-7422-7231	City center 7 miles (12 km)	200 baht	Road: 25 minutes
Phuket	0-7632-7230-7	City center 18 miles (29 km)	550 baht	Road: 45 minutes
Ko Samui	0-7742-8500	Chaweng 14 miles (22 km)	150 baht	Road: 30 minutes

Local Transportation

Sign for taxis and tuk-tuks

After years of traffic congestion, Bangkok finally launched the BTS (Bangkok Mass Transit System) Skytrain in 1999, and an underground network in 2004. This well-maintained service, along with the Chao Phraya Express Pier, has revolutionized travel in the capital. Transportation in the provinces is less frenetic with a choice of *samlors* (bicycle rickshaws), tuk-tuks (auto rickshaws), and *songthaews* (converted pickup trucks). Bargaining over fares is also a part of the Thai experience.

Samlors, a common mode of transportation for short journeys

GETTING AROUND BANGKOK

In downtown Bangkok, the efficient Skytrain has two lines – the Sukhumvit route from Morchit Station in the north to Bearing Station in the east, and the Silom route from National Stadium to Wongwian Yai in Thonburi, with an interchange between the two at the Siam Center. The airport rail link is a direct route to Suvarnabhumi Airport, offering both express and local services. The express service takes 15 minutes and the local service 30 minutes.

The MRT (Mass Rapid Transit) underground runs for 12 miles (19 km) from Hua Lampong Station to Bang Sue. Other forms of city transport include riverboats, buses, limousines, and tour buses, along with taxis, and tuk-tuks.

Express riverboats serve popular piers on the Chao Phraya River. Ferries link the east and west banks, and it is possible to rent a longtail boat at some piers.

One-way bus lanes make for speedy road transport. The *Tourist Map Bangkok City* and *Tour 'n' Guide Map to Bangkok* show the routes. Blue air-conditioned buses, and white Metrobuses are comfortable and cover the popular routes. Non air-conditioned buses are cheap, cover all of Bangkok, and run into the night. Buses outside Bangkok are not easy to use for non-Thai speakers, but tuk-tuks, *songthaews*, and taxis are readily available.

Brightly colored tuk-tuk

TAXIS

Meter taxis operate all over Bangkok and Hat Yai, distinguishable by the Taxi-Meter sign on the roof. Drivers tend to know the names and locations of only the major hotels and sights. In non-meter taxis (in Bangkok these are now quite rare and not recommended at all), visitors will have to bargain for the fare before getting in.

Motorcycle taxis operate in some towns. Drivers tend to congregate near markets and long *sois* and can be identified by their colorful numbered vests. Prices are usually negotiable.

SONGTHAEWS, SAMLORS AND TUK-TUKS

Songthaews, literally, two rows, are vans or converted pickup trucks with two rows of seats in the back. They are more common than city buses outside Bangkok and run popular routes for set fares, typically between 20 and 40 baht. There are no fixed schedules for departure or arrival as drivers wait until they are at least half occupied before starting out. Routes are sometimes written in English on the sides of the vans. A *songthaew* can also be rented like a taxi, but they are generally less comfortable.

Samlors are three-wheeled non-motorized vehicles or rickshaws that can transport one or two people up to a few kilometers. Motorized *samlors* are also known as tuk-tuks. Their two-stroke engines, introduced by the Japanese during World War II, are very noisy. In heavy traffic or during the rainy season, tuk-tuks can be uncomfortable and unstable, but are always popular with tourists. 30–60 baht is reasonable for short trips. Visitors should do some prior research and negotiate a price before climbing into either of the two.

A Skytrain pulling into a station in Bangkok

Organized Tours

Hundreds of tour companies are based in Bangkok and major resorts such as Phuket and Pattaya. Most hotels throughout the country also offer a variety of tours. Typical excursions range from daylong city tours to more comprehensive itineraries taking in different towns and sights over several days. Costs are generally higher, but using public transport within the city can be time consuming, especially in congested areas such as Greater Bangkok. The drawback of most organized tours is that there is no freedom of choice and there is rarely any time to linger.

Booking counter for local transportation in the Eastern Seaboard

BOOKING A TOUR

It is often possible to book a tour of Thailand from a prospective traveler's home country and the package usually includes all travel and accommodation arrangements. Such all-inclusive tours typically last between one and two weeks and include a few nights in Bangkok followed by excursions to Hua Hin, Ko Samui, Krabi, or Phuket. Other packages are more specialized, concentrating, say, on visiting Khao Lak or Phuket and trekking in Khao Sok National Park *(see pp206–7)*, and may vary from a few days to several weeks in duration. Bangkok-based **Diethelm Travel**, **Thai Overlander Travel & Tour**, **Arlymear Travel**, **NS Travel & Tours**, **Regale International Travel**, **STA Travel**, and **World Travel Service Ltd** are major operators offering packages.

Most regional hotels and many guesthouses also offer tours, or are in contact with local tour companies. The local TAT office will also be able to recommend reputable tour companies. Day trips to the most popular sights can be booked just a day in advance. Tours to more distant sights should include arrangements for accommodations, and have at least one departure day each week. Tour companies often pick up visitors from their respective hotels or guesthouses.

TOUR BUSES AND BOATS

Many tour operators use VIP or luxury coaches, with reclining seats, refreshments, air-conditioning, and a toilet. Air-conditioned minibuses are also common, as well as jeeps for the remote areas. Most vehicles are well maintained and quite safe. Boat tours are popular. Day trips to islands often include watersports. Hotel transfers are also part of the deal. Boat trips to remote islands also usually come with onboard accommodations and diving facilities.

Speedboats ready to take tourists to the Similan Islands

GUIDED TOURS

Bilingual guides accompany many tours, especially to cultural sights such as Nakhon Si Thammarat or Phetchaburi. For diving and snorkeling trips, a qualified guide is essential for safety reasons. The quality of guides and tours vary and listings of reputable guided tours along with good maps are published by the provincial TAT offices.

DIRECTORY

BOOKING A TOUR

Arlymear Travel
6th Floor, CCT Building, 109 Surawong Rd, Bangkok.
City Map 7 C3. ***Tel*** *0-2236-9317.* **www**.arlymear.com

Diethelm Travel
12th Floor, Kian Gwan Building II, 140/1 Witthayu Rd, Bangkok.
City Map 7 B1. ***Tel*** *0-2660-7000.*
www.diethelmtravel.com

NS Travel & Tours
133/48 Ratchaprarop Rd, Bangkok. **City Map** 4 E4.
Tel *0-2640-1440.*
www.nstravel.com

Regale International Travel
191/1-2 Soi Suksaviddhaya, Sathorn Nua Rd, Bangkok.
City Map 7 B5. ***Tel*** *0-2635-2450.* **www**.regaleintl.com

STA Travel
14th Floor, Wall Street Tower Building, Suriwong Rd, Bangkok.
City Map 2 E5. ***Tel*** *0-2236-0262.*
www.statravel.co.th

Thai Overlander Travel & Tour
407 Sukhumvit Rd (between Sukhumvit Soi 21 and 23), Bangkok. ***Tel*** *0-2258-4779.*

World Travel Service Ltd
1053 Charoen Krung Rd, Bangkok.
City Map 7 A4. ***Tel*** *0-2233-5900.* **www**.wts-thailand.com

Traveling by Train, Bus, and Boat

Railway crossing sign

The State Railway of Thailand (SRT) has four major lines connecting Bangkok with other parts of the country. Although trains are safe and comfortable, they are slow and the number of towns on the network is limited. Phuket, Krabi, and Trang, for instance, do not have train stations. By contrast, long-distance buses connect all major cities to Bangkok, while provincial buses serve smaller towns and villages. Ferry services serve the main islands.

RAILROAD NETWORK

Bangkok's main station, **Hua Lampong Station**, which opened in 1916, serves all four major lines and over 130 trains to different parts of Thailand. The first line runs to Chiang Mai via the central plains. A second, which later divides in two, runs to Nong Khai and Ubon Ratchathani in northeast Thailand. A third connects Bangkok to the Eastern Seaboard and Cambodia, and a fourth runs down the peninsula to Malaysia. This station is the principal departure point for trains to the coastal areas.

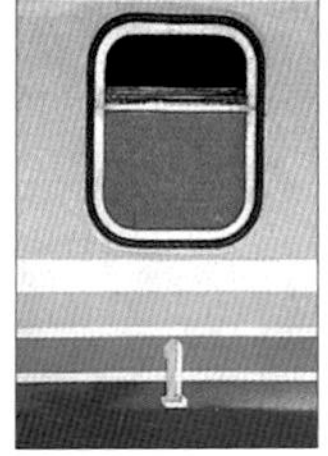

Window of a first-class coach in a train

TRAINS

Train services are labeled Special Express (the fastest), Express, Rapid, and Ordinary. Travel times, even on Express trains, can be longer than by road. The trip from Bangkok to **Surat Thani Station**, for instance, takes 11–12 hours.

First-class coaches (available on Express and Special Express trains) consist of individual cabins with air-conditioning. Second-class coaches have reclining seats and a choice of fan-cooled or air-conditioned coaches. Sleepers in this class have individual seats that are converted into curtained-off beds at night. Toilets (there should be at least one Western toilet) and washing facilities are usually located at the end of the coaches.

Most tourists find that a second-class train compartment is comfortable enough for long distances and it is far more relaxing than a bus journey.

Third-class coaches have wooden benches, each seating two or three passengers: they are cheap but not recommended for long distances. Most trains are clean and well maintained. Uniformed vendors move along the aisles with refreshments, and buffet cars are attached to trains on long-distance routes.

TRAIN TICKETS AND FARES

A train timetable in English is available from Hua Lamphong Station in Bangkok. Visitors should remember that tickets in peak periods (weekends and holidays) can be sold out days in advance. Hua Lampong has an advance booking office with English-speaking staff. Some travel agents also book train tickets.

Fares depend on the speed of the train and the class of the carriage. A second-class ticket between Bangkok and Surat Thani is about 438 baht, with supplements included in the price. Second-class sleeper tickets cost about 848 baht. Shorter trips, such as from Bangkok to Pattaya, cost between 15–120 baht.

Tourists can also buy 20-day rail passes. These cost 1,000–2,000 baht. Information about these passes are available at the Hua Lampong Station.

Fountain at the entrance to Hua Lampong Station, Bangkok

LONG-DISTANCE BUSES

Long-distance buses run from the **Eastern (Ekamai)**, **Northern (Morchit)**, and **Southern (Boromratchonnee Rd)** bus terminals in Bangkok. Provincial capitals can be reached directly from Bangkok. **Surat Thani Station** is an important point in southern Thailand with both long-distance and local connections. Buses can be faster than trains and are very comfortable as the vehicles are air-conditioned, with a toilet, reclining seats, and plenty of leg room. "VIP" buses have the best facilities, including free refreshments served by a stewardess. Overnight buses are especially popular. The air-conditioned buses can get

Double-decker luxury buses for traveling on long-distance routes

EASTERN AND ORIENTAL EXPRESS

The world-renowned Eastern & Oriental Express operates between Bangkok and Singapore. This journey is in style taking three days and two nights, including stops at Butterworth and Kuala Lumpur in Malaysia. Its 22 carriages have fabrics and fittings evocative of 1930s luxury rail travel. Double and single cabins come in private and presidential classes, and there are two restaurants, a saloon car, a bar, and an observation deck. Such luxuries are also reflected in the price.

Dining car on the Eastern and Oriental Express

quite cold and travelers should dress suitably in long-sleeved shirts and long pants, although blankets are usually provided.

BUS TICKETS AND FARES

Fares for long-distance bus journeys are similarly priced as second-class train tickets. VIP buses cost about 20 to 50 percent more. Book well in advance through a travel agent or at the bus station if traveling on a weekend or public holiday. Otherwise, just turn up at the coach station at least half an hour before departure. Bus tickets are always bought on a one-way basis.

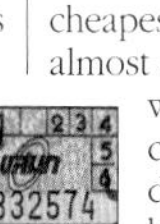

Stub of a bus ticket

PROVINCIAL BUSES

The government bus company is called *Bor Kor Sor* (BKS). The BKS buses are frequent, relatively reliable, and the cheapest form of travel around Thailand. Booking is rarely necessary. On many buses, travelers just need to pay the driver or conductor. Almost every town will have a BKS terminal. *Rot thamadaa* (non-air-conditioned) buses are the cheapest and slowest, and stop almost everywhere along the way. The *rot aer* (air-conditioned) local buses do not always provide blankets, so visitors are advised to take a jacket or sweater, especially for the night.

Traveling on provincial buses is a good way to meet local people and reach the more obscure villages and sights en route. Travelers should beware that refreshment and toilet stops may be infrequent, and buses may be crowded and in poor shape. Local services are nearly always slow and the skills of drivers will vary. Back seats are reserved for monks, so be prepared to move or stand. Women should especially avoid sitting next to monks.

Ticket counter at Krabi for boats to the nearby islands

BOATS TO THE ISLANDS

Scheduled ferries are erratic, since their service is heavily dependent on the weather conditions. Regular services are available to Ko Samui, Ko Phangan, and Ko Tao from Surat Thani. Smaller islands have less regular services that depend on the number of seats filled. These makeshift ferries or longtail boats are run by local fishermen and services often stop in the rainy season.

DIRECTORY

TRAINS

Hua Lampong Station
Krung Kasem Rd, Bangkok.
Tel *1690. Advance booking office open 7am–4pm daily.*
www.railway.co.th

Surat Thani Station
9 miles (14 km) W of Surat Thani, Tha Kham Town.
Tel *0-7731-1213.*

Eastern and Oriental Express
Tel *(020) 7921 4010 (UK).*
Tel *(866) 674-3689 (US).*
Tel *0-2255-9150 (Bangkok).*
Tel *(65) 392 3500 (Singapore).*
www.orient-express.com

LONG-DISTANCE BUSES

Eastern (Ekamai)
Sukhumvit Rd, Bangkok.
Tel *0-2391-8097.*

Northern (Morchit)
Kampheng Phet Rd, Morchit, Bangkok.
Tel *0-2793-8111.*

Southern
Boromratchonnee Rd, Phra Pin Klao, Bangkok. ***Tel*** *0-2793-8111.*

Surat Thani Station
Talat Kaset Bus Terminal, Tha Thong Rd, Surat Thani.
Tel *0-7731-1963; 0-7731-1213.*

Renting a Car, Moped, or Bicycle

Kilometer marker

Driving in Thailand is definitely not for the faint hearted. Hazards come in the form of potholed roads, confusing intersections, badly maintained vehicles, and dangerous driving. For many visitors wanting to explore the country off the beaten track, hiring a car and a driver familiar with the roads is by far the best option. International and local car rental firms of varying standards operate all over Thailand. In the resorts, mopeds and jeeps are popular options.

RENTING A CAR

A valid international driver's license is a necessity for most visitors, while those from ASEAN countries (Association of Southeast Asian Nations) need only have a license from their home countries. International rental agencies offer safe cars and extensive insurance and backup services. **Avis** and **Budget** have desks at some airports and in major cities. Charges range from about 1,800 baht for a day to 35,000 baht for a month. **Siam Express** is another prominent rental agency

With other car rental companies, visitors should check the small print on the contract for liabilities. Obtain a copy of the vehicle registration carry it around.

HIRING A CHAUFFEUR-DRIVEN CAR

Hiring an experienced driver with a car is becoming a popular option for visitors to Thailand. The cost is often less than 50 percent extra on top of the normal price of the car rental. Some drivers know about local sights and suggest interesting spots. Most car rental firms can arrange drivers. Siam Express offers packages including a chauffeur, car, and accommodations in a range of hotels.

Typical traffic congestion in Thailand's notoriously busy capital

RENTING A MOPED

Mopeds and motorcycles are widely available for rent in resorts, big cities, and other towns as well as beaches.

In areas with a lot of guesthouses, visitors can rent anything from a moped to a heavy-duty dirt bike. Driver's licenses are rarely requested, and few firms bother with insurance. Costs are as low as 200–300 baht for a day's rental. Safety precautions are essential. Check tires, oil, and brakes before setting out. Wear a helmet (compulsory in Thailand) and proper shoes. Long sleeves and trousers will minimize cuts and grazes in a minor accident. Take great care on dirt roads and avoid driving alone in rural areas. Visitors should remember that medical help is not always easily available.

Mopeds for rent at Hat Sai Khao, Ko Chang

GASOLINE AND SERVICING

Gas stations in Thailand are well manned and are located on main roads in towns and along highways. They are modern and most provide unleaded fuel. Attendants will fill the tank, wash the windows, and pump air into the tires. Some garages have a resident mechanic for major jobs, or will at least recommend one. Most of them have a small general store, and all have squat toilet facilities. Many garages are open 24 hours, while others close at about 8pm. Gas itself is often cheaper in Thailand than it is in the West.

PARKING

Multistoried parking lots in Bangkok are usually attached to major hotels and departmental stores. Parking is generally free for hotel guests and visitors for up to a few hours. For general parking, issued entry tickets should be stamped and paid for while exiting. Yet, parking can be difficult in the congested streets of the capital.

Pavements painted with red and white stripes indicate a no-parking zone. In smaller towns, many hotels and guesthouses provide free parking. In quieter towns, visitors can park anywhere that is obviously not going to obstruct passing traffic.

Traffic policeman managing the rush at a Bangkok intersection

ROADS AND ROAD SIGNS

Multi-lane national highways exist mostly in and around Bangkok. A toll is charged on the expressways, including the one leading to Bangkok airport. The fee is indicated above the booth and exact change is required at most manually operated booths. Expressways are less congested than other roads, but they are still prone to traffic jams. Many roads in Bangkok are one way, although there are special lanes reserved for buses traveling in the opposite direction.

National highways (also known as routes), such as Highway 1 through the central plains, are fast and efficient, despite being congested in places. Provincial highways are paved and vary in quality. Smaller roads linking villages are sometimes no more than dirt tracks. Main roads in towns are called *thanons* and numbered lanes leading off these are called *sois* and *troks*. Most roads can get quite flooded in the rains.

Destinations are marked in both Roman and Thai script. Arabic numerals are used for distances, and kilometer markers are placed along all main roads. Road markings and traffic symbols are quite clear and easy to understand.

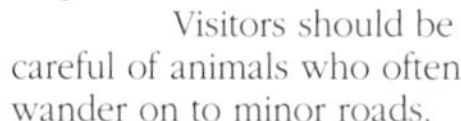

Ornately decorated Thai street sign

RULES OF THE ROAD

Driving is on the left hand side of the road. The speed limit is 35 mph (60 kph) within city limits, unless signed otherwise, and 50 mph (80 kph) on open roads. The standard international road rules apply, but are hardly followed by Thai drivers. The only consistent rule is determined by the size of the vehicle one is driving.

The rather eccentric use of indicators and headlights can be unnerving. A left signal can indicate to another driver that it is alright to pass, while a right signal can indicate hazardous oncoming traffic. A flash of the headlights means a vehicle is coming through.

For what it is worth, horns are hardly used, except in emergencies as it is thought to be impolite. Drivers think nothing of rash driving and it is wise to yield to larger vehicles at unmarked intersections. It is legal to turn left at red lights if there is a blue sign with a white left arrow, or if one happens to be in the left lane. Visitors should be careful of animals who often wander on to minor roads.

Traffic fines are commonly imposed for illegal turns. If a visitor gets a ticket and the license is taken, he should go to the local police station, the address of which will be on the ticket, and pay the fine. Visitors should drive slowly through army checkpoints in border areas, and be prepared to stop if necessary.

Visitors cycling through rough terrain on mountain bikes

ROAD MAPS

Most Thais rely on memory and see no need for maps. Tourist maps are widely available but cover major roads only. Some, foldout maps produced by the Prannok Witthaya Map Center are excellent, showing all roads and reliefs, but are sold at few outlets. The *Thailand Highways Map* by the Auto Guide Company and the *Thailand Highway Map* by the Roads Association are the best atlases, written in both Thai and Roman scripts.

RENTING A BICYCLE

In the cool season, cycling in the quieter areas is a pleasant way to explore the place. Guesthouses and small rentals have bicycles for hire for 20–100 baht a day, although the bikes may be rickety. New mountain bikes may be available, but costs could exceed those of mopeds. Taking plenty of water is essential and, of course, great care must be taken while riding on busy roads.

DIRECTORY

RENTING A CAR

Avis
2/12 Witthayu (Wireless) Rd, Bangkok.
Tel *0-2251-1131.*
www.avisthailand.com
Phuket Airport.
Tel *0-7635-1243.*

Budget
19/23 Royal City Avenue, Bangkok.
Tel *1-800-283-438.*
www.budget.co.th

Siam Express
90/34-35 Sathorn Nua Road, Bangrak, Bangkok.
Tel *0-662-236 5970.*
www.siamexpressonline.com

RULES OF THE ROAD

Highway Police
Tel *1193.*

General Index

Page numbers in **bold** refer to main entries

N

O

P

Q

R

S

T

Acknowledgments

Dorling Kindersley would like to thank the many people whose help and assistance contributed to the preparation of this book.

Main Contributor
Andrew Forbes has a Ph.D. in Central Asian History. He lives in Chiang Mai and is an editor with CPA Media. He has authored many books on Thailand and Eastern Asia.

David Henley is a widely published photographer whose work has appeared in *National Geographic*, *The Washington Post* and numerous international publications and travel guides.

Peter Holmshaw has lived in Chiang Mai for more than 20 years, and has contributed to several travel guides on Southeast Asia.

Fact Checker Peter Holmshaw

Indexer Cyber Media Services Ltd

Thai Translator Sulaganya Punyayodhin

Design and Editorial
Publisher Douglas Amrine
List Manager Vivien Antwi
Project Editor Michelle Crane
Editorial Consultants Hugh Thompson, Scarlett O Hara
Project Designer Shahid Mahmood
Senior Cartographic Editor Casper Morris
Managing Art Editor (jackets) Karen Constanti
Jacket Design Kate Leonard
Senior DTP Designer Jason Little
Senior Picture Researcher Ellen Root
Production Controller Vicky Baldwin
Revisions Claire Baranowski, Emer FitzGerald, Maite Lantaron, James Marshall, Catherine Palmi, Natalie Revie, Rose Teare

Additional Photography
Rob Ashby, Philip Blenkinsop, Gerard Brown, Jane Burton, Peter Chadwick, Andy Crawford, Philip Gatward, Steve Gorton, Frank Greenaway, Will Heap, Stuart Isett, Hugh Johnson, Dave King, Mathew Kurien, Cyril Laubscher, James Marshall, Alan Newham, David Peart, Roger Phillips, Tim Ridley, Alex Robinson, Rough Guides/ Ian Aitken, /Simon Racken, Steve Shott, Michael Spencer, Kim Taylor and Jane Burton, Karen Trist, Richard Watson, James Young.

Special Assistance
Ruengsiri Sathirakul at Anantara Hua Hin Resort & Spa, Suwan Chakchit at Baipai Thai Cooking School, Fann Kulchada and Joyce Ong at Banyan Tree Phuket, Adam Purcell at The BigChilli Magazine, Puritad Jongkamonvivat at Nation Multimedia Group, Sirin Yuanyaidee at The National Museum Bangkok, Toby To at Patravadi Theater, Somchai Bussarawit at Phuket Aquarium, Nam and Prompeth L at Tourism Authority of Thailand.

Photography Permissions
Dorling Kindersley would like to thank the following for their assistance and kind permission to photograph at their establishments:
Abhisek Dusit Throne Hall, Jim Thompson's House, Joe Louis Theater, King Mongkut Memorial Park of Science and Technology, Marine Research Center, Marukhathaiyawan Palace, The National Museum Bangkok, Royal Carriage Museum, Thai Ramakien Gallery, Than Bok Koranee National Park, Than Bok Koranee National Park, Under Water World Pattaya.
Also all the other temples, museums, hotels, restaurants, shops, galleries and other sights too numerous to thank individually.

Picture Credits
Placement Key- a = above; b = below/bottom; c = center; f = far; l = left; r = right; t = top.

The publisher would like to thank the following individuals, companies, and picture libraries for their kind permission to reproduce their photographs:

4CORNERS IMAGES: SIME/Giovanni Simeone 46-47, /Schmid Reinhard 2-3. MATTHIAS AKOLCK: 181cr. ALAMY IMAGES: AA World Travel Library 259br; Ace Stock Limited 4br, 15b; Victor Paul Borg 32bl; Pavlos Christoforou 14, 101tr, 204crb; Thomas Cockrem 79tr; Ray Evans 35br; F1online digitale Bildagentur GmbH 21bl; David Fleetham 20cl; Mike Goldwater 34bl; Ingolf Pompe17 163cr; Norma Joseph 80cr; Paul Kingsley 36c; John Lander 55bl; Chris McLennan 177br; Robert Harding Picture Library Ltd 215tr; Leonid Serebrennikov 220cl; Neil Setchfield 17tr; Martin Strmiska 204bl; Peter Titmuss 146-147; Peter Treanor 24br, 97b, 109bl; WaterFrame 21tr; Terry Whittaker 206c; Andrew Woodley 23br. ANANTARA HOTELS, RESORTS & SPAS: 348cl. ARDEA.COM: Jean Paul Ferrero 153br. BAIPAI THAI COOKING SCHOOL: 345br. BANGKOK AIRWAYS CO., LTD: 363tl. BANYAN TREE SPA PHUKET: 348br. THE BIGCHILLI MAGAZINE: 338c. BLACK MOUNTAIN RESORT AND COUNTRY CLUB CO., LTD.: 343bc. THE BRIDGEMAN ART LIBRARY: The King of Siam on his Elephant, from an account of the Jesuits in Siam, 1688 (w/c on paper), French School, (17th century) /Bibliotheque Nationale, Paris, France /Archives Charmet /109cl. CHIVA-SOM: 349tr. CORBIS: Bettmann 42tr, 44tl, 44bc; Christophe

Boisvieux 24clb; John Van Hasselt 26-27c, 338bl; Ingo Jezierski 256-257; Brooks Kraft 45br; Franklin McMahon 8-9; Narong Sangnak 35c; Scott Stulberg 48br; Sunset Boulevard 213br; Sygma /Jean Leo Dugast 25cr; Staffan Widstrand 145cra. CPA MEDIA: Oliver Hargreave 209bl; David Henley 24tr, 41tr, 43tl, 43cr, 44c, 77br, 151cl, 151tc, 340br; Daniel Kestenholz 70clb; Pictures from Asia/David Henley 70tr. GERALD CUBITT: 18cl, 18cr, 18crb, 18bc, 19tc, 19cl, 19cb, 19bc, 19br, 20tr, 247crb. DK IMAGES: Courtesy of the Buddha Padipa Temple, Wimbledon/ Andy Crawford 24tl; Courtesy of The National Birds of Prey Centre, Gloucestershire/ Frank Greenaway 247tc; David Peart 21br, Courtesy of Whipsnade Zoo, Bedfordshire/ Dave King 201. FLPA: Terry Whittaker 18cb. GETTY IMAGES: AFP /Saeed Khan 45t, /Pornchai Kittiwongsakul 45crb, /Saeed Khan 45t, /Peter Parks 239clb; Iconica /Angelo Cavalli 163tl; Photographer's Choice /Georgette Douwma 21tl, /Gavin Hellier 50; Stone /David Hanson 191c; Taxi /Hummer 369bc. THE GRANGER COLLECTION, NEW YORK: 151cr. ISTOCKPHOTO.COM: Kevin Miller Photography 13tr; Rontography 271tl; ShyMan 315c. THE KOBAL COLLECTION: 20th Century Fox / Mountain Peter 253tl. LONELY PLANET IMAGES: Anders Blomqvist 243tr; Austin Bush 171clb, 180br; Felix Hug 31tr; Noboru Komine 37bl; Bernard Napthine 268tr; Bill Wassman 171bc; Carol Wiley 191br. MARY EVANS PICTURE LIBRARY: 9c, 41bc, 42cl, 47c, 154clb, 287c, 351c. MASTERFILE: Brad Wrobleski 360bl. NATIONAL AERONAUTICS AND SPACE ADMINISTRATION: 12bl. THE NATIONAL MUSEUM BANGKOK: 39ca, 39cb, 41cb, 62c. NATION MULTIMEDIA GROUP: 361tc. NATUREPL.COM: Geogette Douwma 20bl, 21cr. RAYMOND ONG: 195tl. ORIENT-EXPRESS HOTELS TRAINS & CRUISES: 367ca. PATRAVADI THEATRE: 339cl. PHOTOBANK (BANGKOK): 25tl, 25cra, 26tl, 26tr, 26cla, 26clb, 26bl, 26br, 27tl, 27tr, 27cr, 27crb, 27bl, 27bc, 27br, 29cr, 30tr, 30bl, 30-31c, 31cr, 37c, 40tl, 40cb, 42c, 42-43c, 43tr, 43clb, 69cb, 73cl, 73bl, 109ca, 109cr, 138cl, 149br, 151crb, 155b, 161bl, 161br, 171cl, 187b, 227tr, 239crb, 239br, 263tr, 278cl, 283tc. PHOTOLIBRARY: age fotostock/ Chua Wee Boo 150c, /Alan Copson 260br, /Alvaro Leiva 255tr, /P Narayan 33cr, 350-351; All Canada Photos/ Kurt Werby 169tr; Brand X Pictures 11tr; Alexander Blackburn Clayton 51b; CPA Media 183tl; Digital Vision/ Nicholas Pitt 178-179; Hemis/ Safra Sylvain 34tc; Imagebroker.net/ Norbert Eisele-Hein 345tl; Imagestate/ Art Media 43c, /Mark Henley 49tr, / Steve Vidler 16bl, 212br, /The British Library 24-25c; Index Stock Imagery/ Jacob Halaska 1c; Jon Arnold Travel/ Alan Copson 119tl; Lonely Planet Images/ Claver Carroll 340tl, /James Marshall 171tc; LOOK-foto/Ingolf Pompe 11bc; Mauritius/ Birgit Gierth 32cl; Oxford Scientific (OSF)/ Splashdown Direct 186bl; Robert Harding Travel/ Gavin Hellier 283cl; Tips Italia/ Luca Invernizzi Tettoni 130, 218-219; WaterFrame - Underwater Images/ Reinhard Dirscherl 20br, 22br, 196. PRIVATE COLLECTION: 151bc, 283cr. REFLEXSTOCK: Alamy/ sdbphoto.com 59br. BRIAN NG TIAN SOON: 195br. SUPERSTOCK: Ben Mangor 239cl; Westend61 22-23c. THAI AIRWAYS INTERNATIONAL PUBLIC COMPANY LIMITED: 362tc, 362bl. TOURISM AUTHORITY OF THAILAND: 138br, 264bl, 267tr, 342bl, 344bl, 353cl. Front Endpaper: GETTY: Photographer's Choice/Gavin Hellier tl; PHOTOLIBRARY: WaterFrame - Underwater Images/ Reinhard Dirscherl cl; Tips Italia/ Luca Invernizzi Tettoni cr

Cover Picture Credits

FRONT – AXIOM PHOTOGRAPHIC AGENCY: Ellen Rooney.

BACK – AWL IMAGES: Katja Kreder clb; DORLING KINDERSLEY: David Henley cla; bl; GETTY IMAGES: Georgette Douwama tl.

SPINE– AXIOM PHOTOGRAPHIC AGENCY: Ellen Rooney t.

Phrase Book

Thai is a tonal language and regarded by most linguists as head of a distinct language group, although it incorporates many Sanskrit words from ancient India, and some modern English ones, too. There are five tones: mid, high, low, rising, and falling. The particular tone, or pitch, at which each syllable is pronounced determines its meaning. For instance "mâi" (falling tone) means "not," but "maˇi" (rising tone) is "silk." The Thai script uses one of the most elaborate alphabets in the world, running left to right and using over 80 letters. In the third column of this phrase book is a phonetic transliteration for English speakers, including guidance for tones in the form of accents. This differs from the system used elsewhere in the guide, which follows the Thai Royal Institute's recommended romanization of common names.

GUIDELINES FOR PRONUNCIATION

When reading the phonetics, pronounce syllables as if they form English words. For instance:

a	as in "**a**go"
e	as in "h**e**n"
i	as in "th**i**n"
o	as in "**o**n"
u	as in "g**u**n"
ah	as in "r**a**ther"
ai	as in "Th**ai**"
air	as in "p**air**"
ao	as in "M**ao** Zedong"
ay	as in "d**ay**"
er	as in "ent**er**"
ew	as in "f**ew**"
oh	as in "g**o**"
oo	as in "b**oo**t"
OO	as in "b**oo**k"
oy	as in "t**oy**"
g	as in "**g**ive"
ng	as in "si**ng**"

These sounds have no close equivalents in English:

eu	can be likened to a sound of disgust – the sound could be written as "**errgh**"
bp	a single sound between a "b" and a "p"
dt	a single sound between a "d" and a "t"

Note that when "p," "t," and "k" occur at the end of Thai words, the sound is "swallowed." Also note that many Thais use an "l" instead of an "r" sound.

THE FIVE TONES

Accents indicate the tone of each syllable.

no mark	The **mid tone** is voiced at the speaker's normal, even pitch.
á é í ó ú	The **high tone** is pitched slightly higher than the mid tone.
à è ì ò ù	The **low tone** is pitched slightly lower than the mid tone.
ǎ ě ǐ ǒ ǔ	The **rising tone** sounds like a questioning pitch, starting low and rising.
â ê î ô û	The **falling tone** sounds similar to an English speaker stressing a one-syllable word for emphasis.

MALE AND FEMALE POLITE FORMS

In polite speech, Thai men add the particle "**krúp**" at the end of each sentence; women add "**ká**" at the end of questions and "**kâ**" at the end of statements. These particles have been omitted from all but the most essential polite terms in this phrase book, but they should be used as much as possible. The polite forms of the word "I" are, for men, "**pǒm**" and, for women, "**dee-chún**."

In an Emergency

Help!	ช่วยด้วย	*chôo-ay dôo-ay!*
Fire!	ไฟไหม้	*fai mâi!*
Where is the nearest hospital?	แถวนี้มีโรงพยาบาลอยู่ที่ไหน	*taˇir-o née mee rohng pa-yah-bahn yòo têe-naˇi?*
Call an ambulance!	เรียกรถพยาบาลให้หน่อย	*rêe-uk rót pa-yah-bahn hâi nòy!*
Call the police!	เรียกตำรวจให้หน่อย	*rêe-uk dtum ròo-ut hâi nòy!*
Call a doctor!	เรียกหมอให้หน่อย	*rêe-uk moˇr hâi nòy!*

Communication Essentials

Yes	ใช่ *or* ครับ/ค่ะ	*châi or krúp/kâ*
No	ไม่ใช่ *or* ไม่ครับ/ไม่ค่ะ	*mâi châi or mâi krúp/ mâi kâ*
Please can you …?	ช่วย …	*chôo-ay …*
Thank you	ขอบคุณ	*kòrp-kOOn*
No, thank you	ไม่เอา ขอบคุณ	*mâi ao kòrp-kOOn*
Excuse me/sorry	ขอโทษ (ครับ/ค่ะ)	*koˇr-tôht (krúp/kâ)*
Hello	สวัสดี (ครับ/ค่ะ)	*sa-wùt dee (krúp/kâ)*
Goodbye	ลาก่อนนะ	*lah gòrn ná*
What?	อะไร	*a-rai?*
Why?	ทำไม	*tum-mai?*
Where?	ที่ไหน	*têe naˇi?*
How?	ยังไง	*yung ngai?*

Useful Phrases

How are you?	คุณสบายดีหรือ (ครับ/คะ)	*kOOn sa-bai dee reu (krúp/kâ)?*
Very well, thank you – and you?	สบายดี (ครับ/ค่ะ) แล้วคุณล่ะ	*sa-bai dee (krúp/kâ) – láir-o kOOn lâ?*
How do I get to …?	… ไปยังไง	*… bpai yung- ngai?*
Do you speak English?	คุณพูดภาษาอังกฤษเป็นไหม	*kOOn pôot pah-saˇh ung-grìt bpen mái?*
Could you speak slowly?	ช่วยพูดช้าๆหน่อยได้ไหม	*chôo-ay pôot cháh cháh nòy dâi mái?*
I can't speak Thai.	พูดภาษาไทยไม่เป็น	*pôot pah-saˇh tai mâi bpen*

Useful Words

woman/women	ผู้หญิง	*pôo-yiˇng*
man/men	ผู้ชาย	*pôo-chai*
child/children	เด็ก	*dèk*
hot	ร้อน	*rórn*
cold	เย็น *or* หนาว	*yen or naˇo*
good	ดี	*dee*
bad	ไม่ดี	*mâi dee*
open	เปิด	*bpèrt*
closed	ปิด	*bpìt*

left	ซ้าย	*sái*
right	ขวา	*kwaˇh*
straight ahead	อยู่ตรงหน้า	*yòo dtrong nâh*
on the corner of	ตรงหัวมุม	*dtrong boˇo-a mOOm*
near	ใกล้	*glâi*
far	ไกล	*glai*
entrance	ทางเข้า	*tahng kâo*
exit	ทางออก	*tahng òrk*
toilet	ห้องน้ำ	*hôrng náhm*

Telephoning

Where is the nearest public telephone?	แถวนี้มีโทรศัพท์อยู่ที่ไหน ที่นี่ได้ไหม	*taˇir-o née mee toh-ra-sùp yòo têe-naˇi? nêe dâi mái?*
Hello, this is … speaking.	ฮันโล (ผม/ดิฉัน) … พูด (ครับ/ค่ะ)	*hello (poˇm/dee-chún) … pôot (krúp/kâ)*
I would like to speak to …	ขอพูดกับคุณ … หน่อย (ครับ/ค่ะ)	*koˇr pôot gùp kun … nòy (krúp/kâ)*
Could you speak up a little, please?	ช่วยพูดดังๆหน่อยได้ไหม	*chôo-ay pôot dung dung nòy dâi mái?*
local call	โทรศัพท์ภายในท้องถิ่น	*toh-ra-sùp pai nai tórng tìn*
phone booth/kiosk	ตู้โทรศัพท์	*dtôo toh-ra-sùp*
phone card	บัตรโทรศัพท์	*but toh-ra-sùp*

Shopping

How much does this cost?	นี่ราคาเท่าไร	*nêe rah-kah tâo-rài?*
I would like …	ต้องการ …	*dtôrng-gahn …*
Do you have …?	มี … ไหม	*mee … mái?*
I am just looking.	ชมดูเท่านั้น	*chom doo tâo-nún*
Do you take credit cards/travelers' checks?	รับบัตรเครดิต/เช็คเดินทางไหม	*rub but cray-dit/chék dern tang mái?*
What time do you open/close?	เปิด/ปิดกี่โมง	*bpèrt/bpìt gèe mohng?*
Can you ship this overseas?	ส่งของนี้ไปต่างประเทศได้ไหม	*sòng koˇng nee bpai dtàhng bpra-tâyt dâi mái?*
cheap	ถูก	*tòok*
expensive	แพง	*pairng*
gold	ทอง	*torng*
hill-tribe handicrafts	หัตถกรรมชาวเขา	*hùt-ta-gum chao kaˇo*
silver	เงิน	*ngern*
Thai silk	ผ้าไหมไทย	*pâh-maˇi tai*
department store	ห้าง	*hâhng*
market	ตลาด	*dta-làht*
newsstand	ร้านขายหนังสือพิมพ์	*ráhn kaˇi núng-sěu pim*
pharmacy	ร้านขายยา	*ráhn kaˇi yah*
tailor	ร้านตัดเสื้อ	*ráhn dtùt sêu-a*

Sightseeing

travel agent	บริษัทนำเที่ยว	*bor-ri-sùt num têe-o*
tourist office	สำนักงานการท่องเที่ยว	*suˇm-núk ngahn gahn tôrng têe-o*
tourist police	ตำรวจท่องเที่ยว	*dtum-ròo-ut tôrng têe-o*
beach	หาด *or* ชายหาด	*hàht or chai-hàht*
coral	หินปะการัง	*hiˇn bpa-gah-rung*
festival	งานออกร้าน	*ngahn òrk ráhn*
hill/mountain	เขา	*kaˇo*
historical park	อุทยานประวัติศาสตร์	*ÒO-ta-yahn bpra wùt sàht*
island *(ko)*	เกาะ	*gòr*
temple *(wat)*	วัด	*wút*
museum	พิพิธภัณฑ์	*pí-pít-ta-pun*
national park	อุทยานแห่งชาติ	*ÒO-ta yahn hàirng châht*
park/garden	สวน	*soˇo-un*
river	แม่น้ำ	*mâir náhm*
Thai boxing	มวยไทย	*moo-ay tai*
Thai massage	นวด	*nôo-ut*
trekking	การเดินทางเท้า	*gahn dern tahng táo*
waterfall	น้ำตก	*náhm dtòk*

Transportation

When does the train for … leave?	รถไฟไป … ออกเมื่อไร	*rót fai bpai … òrk meu-rài?*
How long does it take to get to …?	ใช้เวลานานเท่าไรไปถึงที่ …	*chái way-lah nahn tâo-rài bpai těung têe …?*
A ticket to … please.	ขอตั๋วไป … หน่อย (ครับ/ค่ะ)	*koˇr dtoˇo-a bpai … nòy (krúp/kâ)*
I'd like to reserve a seat, please.	ขอจองที่นั่ง	*koˇr jorng têe nûng*
Which platform for the … train?	รถไฟไป … อยู่ชานชาลาไหน	*rót fai bpai … yòo chahn cha-lah naˇi?*
What station is this?	ที่นี่สถานีอะไร	*têe nêe sa-taˇhn-nee a-rai?*
Where is the bus stop?	ป้ายรถเมล์อยู่ที่ไหน	*bpâi rót may yòo têe-naˇi?*
Where is the bus station?	สถานีรถเมล์อยู่ที่ไหน	*sa-taˇhn-nee rót may yòo têe-naˇi?*
Which buses go to …?	รถเมล์สายไหนไป …	*rót may saˇi naˇi bpai …?*
What time does the bus for … leave?	รถเมล์ไป … ออกกี่โมง	*rót may bpai … òrk gèe mohng?*
Would you tell me when we get to …?	ถึง … แล้วช่วยบอกด้วย	*těung … láir-o chôo-ay bòrk dôo-ay?*
arrivals	ถึง	*těung*
booking office	ที่จองตั๋ว	*têe jorng dtoˇo-a*
bus station	สถานีรถเมล์	*sa-taˇhn-nee rót may*
departures	ออก	*òrk*
baggage room	ที่ฝากของ	*têe fàhk koˇrng*
ordinary bus	รถธรรมดา	*rót tum-ma-dah*
tour bus	รถทัวร์	*rót too-a*
ticket	ตั๋ว	*dtoˇo-a*
ferry	เรือข้ามฟาก	*reu-a kâhm fâhk*
train	รถไฟ	*rót fai*
railroad station	สถานีรถไฟ	*sa-taˇhn-nee rót fai*
moped	รถมอเตอร์ไซค์	*rót mor-dter-sai*
bicycle	รถจักรยานต์	*rót jùk-gra-yahn*
taxi	แท็กซี่	*táirk-sêe*

Staying in a Hotel

Do you have a vacant room?	มีห้องว่างไหม	*mee hôrng wâhng mái?*
double/twin room	ห้องคู่	*hôrng kôo*
single room	ห้องเดี่ยว	*hôrng dèe-o*
I have a reservation.	จองห้องไว้แล้ว	*jorng hôrng wái láir-o*
Will you spray some mosquito repellent, please?	ช่วยฉีดยากันยุงให้หน่อยได้ไหม	*chôo-ay chèet yah gun yOOng hâi nòy dâi mâi?*
air conditioner	เครื่องปรับอากาศ	*krêu-ung bprùp ah-gàht*
fan	พัดลม	*pùt lom*
key	กุญแจ	*gOOn-jair*
toilet/bathroom	ห้องน้ำ	*hôrng náhm*

Eating Out

A table for two please.	ขอโต๊ะสำหรับสองคน	*ko˘r dtó su˘m-rùp so˘rng kon*
May I see the menu?	ขอดูเมนูหน่อย	*ko˘r doo may-noo nòy*
Do you have …?	มี … ไหม	*mee … mái?*
I'd like …	ขอ	*ko˘r …*
Not too spicy, ok?	ไม่เอาเผ็ดมากนะ	*mâi ao pèt mâhk na*
Is it spicy?	เผ็ดไหม	*pèt mái?*
I can eat Thai food.	ทานอาหารไทยเป็น	*tahn ah-ha˘hn tai bpen*
May I have a glass of water, please.	ขอน้ำแข็งเปล่าแก้วหนึ่ง	*ko˘r núm ka˘irng bplào gâir-o nèung*
I didn't order this.	นี้ไม่ได้สั่ง (ครับ/คะ)	*nêe mâi dâi sùng (krûp/kâ)*
Waiter/waitress!	คุณ (ครับ/คะ)	*kOOn (krúp/kâ)*
The check, please.	ขอบิลหน่อย (ครับ/ค่ะ)	*ko˘r bin nòy (krúp/kâ)*
bottle	ขวด	*kòo-ut*
chopsticks	ตะเกียบ	*dta-gèe-up*
fork	ส้อม	*sôrm*
menu	เมนู	*may-noo*
spoon	ช้อน	*chórn*
water	น้ำ	*náhm*

Health

I do not feel well.	รู้สึกไม่สบาย	*róo-sèuk mâi sa-bai*
It hurts here.	เจ็บตรงนี้	*jèp dtrong née*
I have a fever.	ตัวร้อนเป็นไข้	*dtoo-a rórn bpen kâi*
I'm allergic to …	(ผม/ดิฉัน) แพ้ …	*(po˘m/dee-chún) páir …*
asthma	โรคหืด	*rôhk hèut*
dentist	ทันตแพทย์ *or* หมอฟัน	*tun-dta-pâirt or mŏr fun*
diabetes	โรคเบาหวาน	*rôhk bao wăhn*
diarrhea	ท้องเสีย	*tórng sěe-a*
dizzy	เวียนหัว	*wee-un hŏo-a*
doctor	หมอ	*mo˘r*
dysentery	โรคบิด	*rôhk bìt*
fever	ไข้	*kâi*
heart attack	หัวใจวาย	*ho˘o-a jai wai*
hospital	โรงพยาบาล	*rohng pa-yah-bahn*
injection	ฉีดยา	*chèet yah*
medicine	ยา	*yah*
penicillin	ยาเพนนิซีลลิน	*yah pen-ní-seen-lin*
prescription	ใบสั่งยา	*bai sùng yah*
prickly heat	ผด	*pòt*
sore throat	เจ็บคอ	*jèp kor*
stomach ache	ปวดท้อง	*bpòo-ut tórng*
temperature	ตัวร้อน	*dtoo-ah rórn*
traditional medicine	ยาแผนโบราณ	*yah pa˘irn boh-rahn*
vomit	อาเจียน	*ah-jee-un*

Numbers

0	๐ *or* ศูนย์	*sŏon*
1	๑ *or* หนึ่ง	*nèung*
2	๒ *or* สอง	*so˘rng*
3	๓ *or* สาม	*sa˘hm*
4	๔ *or* สี่	*sèe*
5	๕ *or* ห้า	*hâh*
6	๖ *or* หก	*hòk*
7	๗ *or* เจ็ด	*jèt*
8	๘ *or* แปด	*bpàirt*
9	๙ *or* เก้า	*gâo*
10	๑๐ *or* สิบ	*sìp*
15	๑๕ อๆ สิบห้า	*sìp-hâh*
20	๒๐ *or* ยี่สิบ	*yêe-sìp*
30	๓๐ *or* สามสิบ	*sa˘hm-sìp*
40	๔๐ *or* สี่สิบ	*sèe-sìp*
50	๕๐ *or* ห้าสิบ	*hâh-sìp*
60	๖๐ *or* หกสิบ	*hòk-sìp*
70	๗๐ *or* เจ็ดสิบ	*jèt-sìp*
80	๘๐ *or* แปดสิบ	*bpàirt-sìp*
90	๙๐ *or* เก้าสิบ	*gâo-sìp*
100	๑๐๐ *or* หนึ่งร้อย	*nèung róy*
200	๒๐๐ *or* สองร้อย	*so˘rng róy*
1,000	๑๐๐๐ *or* หนึ่งพัน	*nèung pun*
10,000	๑๐,๐๐๐ *or* หนึ่งหมื่น	*nèung mèun*
100,000	๑๐๐,๐๐๐ *or* หนึ่งแสน	*nèung sa˘irn*

Time and Seasons

one minute	หนึ่งนาที	*nèung nah-tee*
one hour	หนึ่งชั่วโมง	*nèung chôo-a mohng*
half an hour	ครึ่งชั่วโมง	*krêung chôo-a mohng*
quarter of an hour	สิบห้านาที	*sìp-hâh nah-tee*
midnight	เที่ยงคืน	*têe-ung keun*
noon	เที่ยงวัน	*têe-ung wun*
a day	หนึ่งวัน	*neung wun*
a weekend	สุดสัปดาห์	*sÒOt sùp-pah-dah*
a week	หนึ่งอาทิตย์	*nèung ah-tìt*
a month	หนึ่งเดือน	*nèung deu-un*
a year	หนึ่งปี	*nèung bpee*
cool season	หน้าหนาว	*nâh na˘o*
hot season	หน้าร้อน	*nâh rórn*
rainy season	หน้าฝน	*nâh fo˘n*
vacation	วันหยุด	*wun yÒOt*